ROBERT W. DANIEL   GLENN LEGGETT
University of Tennessee   *University of Washington*

The Written Word

Forms of Writing

PRENTICE-HALL, INC.   *Englewood Cliffs, N.J.*

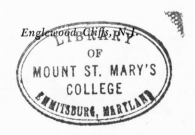

PRENTICE-HALL ENGLISH LITERATURE SERIES

Maynard Mack, Editor

© 1960

PRENTICE-HALL, INC.

Englewood Cliffs, N. J.

Library of Congress Catalog Card No.: 60-9176

First printing ....*March, 1960*
Second printing ....*September, 1961*
Third printing ....*July, 1962*

PRINTED IN THE UNITED STATES OF AMERICA

97150—C

Preface

When a new anthology designed for the college student of English is published, an account of the principles on which it was assembled is owed to the instructor who may be considering it for his class. This collection has grown out of its editors' generalizations about the first year's work in English, which is normally a course in elementary composition that is also expected to prepare students for the subsequent study of literature. Such courses aspire to produce better writers and better readers, in the knowledge that these capacities are but the two faces of one coin. The materials required for the enterprise include a handbook of English usage, a dictionary, and an anthology of writings, new and old, by professionals. Once the ground rules have been established, the first two books become reference works, to which the student turns for answers to specific questions, particularly when he is correcting his papers. The anthology, on the other hand, becomes increasingly responsible for the fulfilment of the twin aspirations of the course. Freshman writers need professional works as models and as sources of facts and ideas; but they also need to find in their anthology—so our experience as teachers suggests—a concise account of how these works may be read with understanding, and how the principles adduced from them may be transferred to their own unpractised compositions. Many teachers realize, moreover, that introducing their students to the nature of the language, the principles of systematic logic, and the meaning of the word *style* fully justifies the effort entailed. And students, who tend to identify all prose works as "stories," improve their grasp of non-discursive or imaginative literature by apprehending the differences among literary forms and acquiring the basic vocabulary needed in analyzing them.

These suppositions have led us to divide our anthology into four parts. Part 1, an essay by the editors, sets forth in some detail our understanding of the relationship between good reading and good writing, at a level that we trust will be found neither too depressed nor too elevated. Part 2, consisting of essays by latter-day writers, is designed to suggest topics for writing by acquainting the student with some of the topics that have recently been written about. We have been at pains to include here many pieces not much longer than a freshman's weekly paper, as well as a few examples of documentation. Part 3 combines essays on thought, language, and style with others on writers and writing. Part 4, an introduction to the forms of literature, begins with representatives of the classic essay, from Montaigne to Thomas Henry Huxley, and includes four recent stories, a play, and about forty short poems. Some principles of reading and subjects for writing will be found in the *Suggestions* appended to nearly all the works reprinted.

If an instructor chooses to organize his course around the three main parts of the book, he may treat Part 1 as collateral reading for the first several assignments and ask his students to base each of their early papers on one of the ten groups of essays in Part 2. He may devote the middle of the year to discussing matters of thought, language, and composition that will arise from assignments in Part 3. We have placed the last part where it is because we believe that most instructors wish students to improve their own writing, which is mainly discursive, before their intensive study of non-discursive literature. Besides, the introduction to literature is normally transitional to their courses in sophomore English.

Our policy in editing the works reprinted in these pages has been to explain, by either bracketed words or footnotes, the allusions, foreign words, and other puzzles that most freshmen could probably not solve without research beyond the limits of their dictionaries. In the *Suggestions,* we call their attention to expressions that we think they will find unfamiliar and that their dictionaries will elucidate. If the reader comes upon others that he wishes we had explained or else designated in that manner, he must blame either our ignorance or our optimism, as his mood directs.

Although to edit an anthology is perhaps a less arduous undertaking than to compose an original work, we doubt that *The Written Word* would have been completed without the generous help of many friends and acquaintances. Our particular gratitude has been earned by Mr. James Justus, of the University of Washington; Mrs. Maurine Lewis, Mr. Paul O'Connell, and Mr. William Worcester, of Prentice-Hall, Inc.; Professor Maynard Mack, our series editor; Mr. Donald R. Hammonds; Professor Monroe C. Beardsley, of Swarthmore College; Professor John Hansen, Professor Albert Rapp, and Mr. Ronald G. Mahan, of the University of Tennessee; and Miss Eleanor Goehring and the rest of the staff of the University of Tennessee Library.

R.W.D.
G.L.

Contents

v

x *Contents*

A dagger (†) before a title indicates that the work is reprinted in this book.

1

Reading—and Writing

"Write a paper of two or three pages," your English instructor will probably say, perhaps as early as the first meeting of the class. More specific instructions may follow: write on your summer vacation, on an opinion that you strongly uphold, or on the first chapter of your textbook after you have read it carefully. But whether he permits you to choose your own topic or specifies one as definite as your summer vacation, he quite possibly leaves you wondering why his instructions are so vague. Or you may have understood his reason already. Most writing, if it is to be readable, must be to some extent personal; much of it will be entirely so, and the more exactly the instructor outlines the topic, the less personal your paper will be. Probably he would like you to make your own decision from the outset, so that you would first choose a subject and then define that small part of it which will be as much as you can cover in a short paper. But for any of several reasons he may limit the assignment in some such way as those mentioned: perhaps to give you practice at different kinds of writing, or to provide the slower students with a push that will get them started.

Suppose, anyway, that you have survived the first decision, with or without your instructor's help, and know what you are going to write about. There is no need to tell you that your problems are just beginning. Do you really understand what sort of paper you are expected to produce? Of course students are sometimes invited to turn in short stories or poems, but most of the papers they have to write are of the kind known as *themes* or *comps* or just *papers*. These terms suggest writings in the neighborhood of five hundred words, for which the writer's own experience provides the material. By that we do not mean imaginary experience; themes are not in the main supposed to be fictions. But we do mean both kinds of real experience: not only the direct kind, such as a summer vacation or a preference for brunettes over blondes, but also the experience that results from reading. A theme may explain how the writer feels about life in Russia, though he has never been there, or it may be about some aspect of a novel that he has read. Certainly an encounter with the substance of a piece of writing is just as much an experience as a visit to one's grandmother or a date.

This definition of a theme, however, leaves us without the answer to a larger question. How does anyone master the art of writing effectively even after he knows what he wants to say? Plenty of evidence exists, fortunately, that writing is learned much as other complicated activities are: by grasping the ways in which the thing has been done before.[1] After that, one may start introducing one's own improvements. The real basis of good writing, in other words, is good reading. The amateur writer has to learn to read the work of professionals in such a way as to discover what elements have been combined in it—and by what methods—so as to fill it with interest and point. But reading to find out *why* a successful piece of writing has interest and point means reading more analytically than we usually do when only passing the time.

What, then, do we look for when not merely reading but reading in order to analyze? The most general dissection of a piece of writing distinguishes three main elements in it. First, its *substance*—which may be a series of facts, the steps in an argument, the emotions aroused by real and imagined experiences, or any combination of these. Second, its *structure*—which results from the writer's decisions about the best way to arrange his substance. And third, an element for which we have no precise name—a unifying factor of some sort, which may be an opinion or a belief (the conclusion of an argument, perhaps), or an abstract condition-of-things. For the time being let

---

[1] For instance, see the recollections of Franklin and Edmund Wilson: † "Writing Self-Taught," and † "The Problem of English." *A dagger* (†) *before a title means that the work is reprinted in this book.*

us use the word *point* to describe this element, as when we speak of the point of a joke. As often as not, the writer's point will be implied rather than expressed, just as the point of a joke is—and for much the same reason.

These three elements must be clearly in the reader's mind if he is to say that he has read anything thoroughly. Getting them clear is not always easy, even though one may think one has "learned to read" a dozen years before. But if the process presents difficulties, it also offers great rewards. Leaving aside what may be learned in this way about general human experience, consider what analytical reading can contribute to your own abilities as a writer. The substance of what we read often consists of usable material: facts and figures, perhaps, or new arguments that support our own beliefs. Beyond that, however, we learn the methods by which previous writers have presented their substance and made their points—methods discovered long ago, many of them, yet still quite up to date. Does the most important matter go at the beginning, in the middle, or at the end? This is a structural question, whose answer no one really understands until he has seen it work in practice. And finally, the analytical reader improves his grasp of style, the choice and arrangement of words, which is the aspect of structure that seems to have mainly interested such writers as Franklin and Stevenson in their efforts to learn to write by reading.

Thus far we have considered "professional writing" as though it were a single thing. Actually, of course, there are as many substances and as many styles as there are professional writers. The methods, too, by which writing has been structured are beyond counting; and we may even distinguish one kind of point from another. Hence, when you read a particular piece of writing it is essential to have in mind some general knowledge of these differences. The more you know what you may expect, the better able you will be to read any writing with the greatest possible profit. And in particular you will know which of the different kinds of writing most nearly resembles the papers that are expected by your English instructor.

Various kinds of writing

A century or so ago the essay was probably the kind of writing—or at least the kind of prose—most widely read. In the eighteenth century the short story as a literary form was almost unknown. Although the novel was emerging, it was the essay that largely made the reputations of a majority of the great writers. Swift, Addison, Steele, Johnson, Goldsmith, and Franklin—the "classic essayists"—are examples; some of their works are printed in Part 4 of this book. In the nineteenth century the essay remained a dominant form despite competition from both novels and short stories, which developed rapidly after such writers as Scott, Dickens, Poe, and Hawthorne brought them into favor. Some people think that nowadays the essay is dead, but it would be nearer the truth to say that it has only changed its name. We usually speak of students' *themes* or *papers* rather than students' essays, of the *articles* rather than the essays in magazines, and of the *columns* by such newspaper writers as Ruark, Childs, and Lippmann. But all of these bear a resemblance—in form, if not necessarily in quality—to the writings of Addison or Goldsmith.

Perhaps the modern essay-form that reaches the most people is the *commentary,* spoken over radio or television by such commentators as Paul Harvey, Edward P. Morgan, and Edward R. Murrow. Commentaries have become so popular that some of them have been collected and made into books, and the preface to one of these offers a neat description of what is supposed to be their value:

> These are radio broadcasts, printed for the eye of the mind as they were originally written for the outer and inner ear.
> They are news "commentaries," or what CBS prefers to call news "analyses." I'm not sure what the difference is, but if there is one, it is a difference of intent. I think CBS shies away from the word "commentary" because it is too much identified with the Pooh-Bahs of an earlier radio, the gentry who generally had to hear what they said before they knew what they thought. The CBS idea is that people should be persuaded to listen and think because the broadcaster says what he says, not because he is who he is.[2]

To persuade people to listen and think: that is the intent of the commentary, as it should be of a student's theme—the success of which, to speak more exactly, depends upon its ability to persuade the instructor and the other students to read and respond, if not with admiration, at least with respect.

The development of this ability, as we have seen, comes with knowing how to read and analyze the writings of professionals. And it is only plain sense, when we are seeking a place to start, to choose a piece of work as nearly as possible like the kind that we ourselves are learning to write. Commentaries or news analyses, like those that Eric Sevareid describes in the paragraphs just quoted, are very

---

[2] Sevareid, *In One Ear.*

useful for this purpose. They are not, to be sure, great works of literature; but that is only one of their likenesses to most student writing. First of all, they are short—not much longer than the average student essay. Second, they are concerned with ordinary topics of general interest to the commentator and his listeners; they at least try to be both interesting and pointed. And third, most of them are written in informal language. As an example let us consider one from Sevareid's own book:

DECLINE AND FALL OF THE ADJECTIVE

ERIC SEVAREID

Reprinted from IN ONE EAR *by Eric Sevareid, by permission of Alfred A. Knopf, Inc.* © *1952 by Eric Sevareid.*

Historians looking back on this particular age will have to have some handy label for it. They may, of course, call it the age that destroyed civilization; but we have a suspicion they might call it the age that destroyed the adjective. Since the adjective is of ancient lineage and is a basic tool in our trade, its decline fills us with a certain sense of sadness. We understand how an old-fashioned woodworker must feel these days, with all the machine-made plastic stuff around. You know how it is with many of these glamorous-looking plastic things—they get busted and nobody can repair them. That is what is happening with adjectives today—they're getting busted all over the place. The only difference is that people go on using them, not realizing that they are busted.

If civilization busts in our time, the Russian Communists get our personal blame for it; but it's a different story with the adjectives. We Americans think we are totally unlike the Russian Communists in every respect, but the unhappy truth is that we and the Politburo are just alike in respect to adjectives. Both have arrested, tortured, imprisoned, poisoned, and thereby destroyed more adjectives than any other people in any other time. Of course, we bust different kinds of adjectives. We are a private-enterprise system, so we bust private-enterprise adjectives. What the advertising business, especially in the movies, has done to such noble adjectives as *colossal, stupendous,* and *earth-shaking* hardly bears thinking about. Those adjectives have simply been used up, they have lost their meaning; and an adjective without meaning is a dead adjective. They give forth an odor now because nobody has thought to bury them.

The Russians have a political system, so of course they kill political adjectives. During the Lenin anniversary meeting in the Bolshoi Theater last night (which is what started us on this obituary in the first place), the leading theoretical thinker of the Communist party, Mr. Peter Pospelov, reversed the usual order of things and hurled all manner of dead fruit—decayed adjectives—at the audience. Speaking of the United States, he said we are *bloody-handed, insane, stench-filled, shark-like,* and *a rampant beast,* and when he began to run down he lamely called us *imperialist warmongers.*

Some foreign-affairs experts think the Russian state will collapse when it has killed off all its original minds. Personally, we think it will collapse when it has run out of adjectives to beat up. Lenin was wrong in saying that religion is the opiate of the people—adjectives are the opiate of the people, and think what will happen when the Russians are deprived of their adjectives.

Suppose that Vishinsky were suddenly to run out of his daily dosage and substitute words like *Americans are nice.* Well, have you ever seen a group of opium-smokers deprived of their dope? The Russian people would go mad, the Kremlin would be stormed, and the world would be saved. We can illustrate this if we turn it around and suppose that Metro-Goldwyn-Mayer were to put out a picture with Clark Gable, Frank Sinatra, *and* Hopalong Cassidy, and merely advertised it with the words, *Quite Entertaining.* After the initial shock, the movie houses couldn't hold the mobs that would storm the box-office.

One thing that bothers us is that Americans show signs of destroying political adjectives too, and we shouldn't—it's not our line. Look what we are doing to that once sound and splendid word, *freedom-loving.* It has appeared in so many of the President's speeches it is beginning to sound like an official slogan, a sign of approaching death for any adjective. The only time in years that we have seen the word produce an effect was during the '48 campaign. A Massachusetts Congressman, orating from Mr. Truman's train platform, slipped a syllable and shouted: "All you free-loving people."

The effect . . . well, we were going to say the effect was electrifying, but MGM has killed that one, too.

If we were inventing study questions about this essay, we should make them lead you to analyze it with the help of the three terms discussed on page 2: substance, structure, and point. Something like this:

1. Can you justify including the anecdote of the Massachusetts Congressman in the structure of this essay?

2. What is its point? If that is a hard question, remember that the point, instead of being expressed, may be implied by the interaction of the structure and substance.

Until the next-to-last paragraph the structure of the essay is clear enough: it begins with a general statement echoing the title, supported by examples of how the meanings of certain words are being exhausted by unscrupulous use in both the United States and Russia, the two dominant countries of the world. Then, after a couple of jokes indicating that the power of the Russian rulers depends upon their abuse of language, the next-to-last paragraph adds that in the U.S. this practice is not confined to movie advertising (everybody makes harmless jokes about the methods used by Hollywood press-agents), but is beginning to show up in the speeches of government officials. The relations between these subordinate parts and the contention that overworked words become meaningless seems plain enough; and in thus tracing the very straightforward structure of the essay we have at the same time been able to summarize its substance.

We now come to the question about the point. Here the answer is not easy. Any of several groups of words in the essay might be thought to make a concise summary of it, if that is what we mean by its point. Shall we select "the unhappy truth is that we and the Politburo are just alike in respect to adjectives"? or "adjectives are the opiates of the people"? or perhaps "Americans show signs of destroying political adjectives too, and we shouldn't"? Surely the essay means something more momentous than any of these—a feeling that is supported by at least two facts: the essay begins with a reference to the destruction of civilization, and its title parodies the title of Gibbon's *Decline and Fall of the Roman Empire*. In the era that Gibbon's work describes, the Roman Empire and civilization were the same.

Putting the meaning of all these parts together, it seems safe to say that the point should be worded something like this: It is sad to see that we Americans permit language to be abused just as the Russians do; for this surrender of our minds may cost us our freedom, and the end of American freedom would mean the end of civilization. A momentous meaning indeed!

It is essential to notice that while this point is only suggested, it is nevertheless there, a constituent or function of the meaning, not "read into it" by ingenious interpretation. In no other way can we account for the feeling that "Decline and Fall of the Adjective" is about something more than just adjectives, the topic mentioned in the title.

Are you inclined to doubt that meanings can be present without being stated? Then grant that the Congressman's error would not have made the audience laugh had it not suggested the word *freedom-loving,* the word that he failed to say. This is what justifies Sevareid's statement that he saw the word produce an effect on that occasion. The word was not spoken, yet it was a part of the occasion just the same. The anecdote not only made us laugh but also remained subtly related to the main point of the essay in a variety of ways. Did you notice, for example, how the incident proves the deadness of *freedom-loving* by showing what happened when it was unexpectedly brought back to life? And even more important, how the audience's joyful laughter (this is suggested too) exemplifies the freedom that we now have and that the essay wished us to keep? Would a Russian audience have dared to laugh? Surely the answer to our second question—What is the point of the essay?—is now clear.

Thesis and theme

To draw the full meaning out of one short, simple-looking essay has been a complicated process, not made easier by our having to use the word *point* in more than one sense. When we first introduced it we indicated that it is rather a makeshift term for the unifying factor in a piece of writing, the principle that controls and is implied by the substance and structure. Do we actually know what we are doing when we use it this way? *Point* is not at all a simple word. One desk dictionary gives thirty-three definitions of it as a noun—of which the nineteenth, *the exact or essential fact or idea under consideration,* seems nearest to our usage. But this definition does not entirely correspond to what we have found to be the meaning of "Decline and Fall of the Adjective." That Americans and Russians permit language to be abused is a *fact* (that is, it purports to be); that abuse of language brings loss of freedom and, in turn, the end of civilization is an *idea.* We have seen, though, that the feeling of sadness about these happenings is a very important element in the essay. This feeling is introduced by name in the third sentence, and carries over into the parallels between Russians and Americans that are later established.

It appears that we are dealing with two different elements which for the sake of clear analysis should be separated, and that we had better let the word *point* go. One element is that civilization will be wrecked if Americans become too much like Russians in regard to language, together with the supporting facts. Notice that this is a contention, a belief that someone is trying to get accepted. (Of course not every reader is going to accept it; it will in the nature of things provoke disagreement from some—and perhaps many—thoughtful persons. That is partly what makes it interesting.) Let us use the word *thesis* for an element of this kind. A thesis is a belief or opinion; it can generally be formulated in a *that*-clause. Being an opinion, a thesis may be expected to encounter resistance; it will be disputable. In "Decline and Fall of the Adjective" the thesis is the unifying factor, showing what material should be included and what should be left out. Therefore it is that part of the meaning which is of ultimate importance.

The feeling of sadness, on the other hand, arises from the relation between the facts presented in the essay and a large, general process, the process of decline or—as the opening sentences suggest—of destruction. Undeniably things change, and in the process of change good things as well as bad are swept away. This part of the essay, then, expressing sadness over the decline of language and the menace to freedom, will presumably not encounter resistance from anybody. It is just there. Let us use the word *theme* for the general condition-of-things that a piece of writing suggests, and to identify a theme let us use an abstract noun or noun-phrase (such as *the decline of freedom*) rather than a *that*-clause. Although the terms *thesis* and *theme* are not always sharply distinguished, in this book *thesis* will always mean a disputable opinion, whereas *theme* will mean a state or process which the substance of a piece of writing brings to mind. A theme is regularly implied, not stated, and often has a markedly emotional coloring. It is the particular abstraction towards which, as it is embodied in the work, the reader's feelings are directed. Thus Sevareid invites the reader to feel sadness over the corruption of language. But in "Decline and Fall of the Adjective" the matter of dominant interest is the thesis, to which the theme plays only a supporting role. As we shall see in a few moments, however, it is not by any means true of all writings that themes are merely subordinate.

Our analysis of "Decline and Fall of the Adjective" has touched upon several principles that will prove valuable in all our reading and writing. So as to have them clearly in mind, let us summarize them in the most general way possible:

1. In any piece of writing some of the most important meanings may be implied rather than stated.

2. A piece of writing may derive its value from advancing a disputable opinion, not one that can be proved.

3. The substance of a piece of writing should all be related to a unifying factor, a thesis or a theme or both.

To explore the differences between *thesis* and *theme* further, we must now consider another kind of writing. The following work differs basically from Sevareid's, in spite of the fact that it came out in a book called *Essays of Elia*.

DREAM CHILDREN

A Reverie

Children love to listen to stories about their elders, when *they* were children; to stretch their imagination to the conception of a traditionary great-uncle, or grandame, whom they never saw. It was in this spirit that my little ones crept about me the other evening to hear about their great-grandmother Field, who lived in a great house in Norfolk (a hundred times bigger than that in which they and papa lived) which had been the scene—so at least it was generally believed in that part of the country—of the tragic incidents which they had lately become familiar with from the ballad of "The Children in the Wood." Certain it is that the whole story of the children and their cruel uncle was to be seen fairly carved out in wood upon the chimney-piece of the great hall, the whole story down to the Robin Redbreasts, till a foolish rich person pulled it down to set up a marble one of modern invention in its stead, with no story upon it. Here Alice put out one of her dear mother's looks, too tender to be called upbraiding.

Then I went on to say, how religious and how good their great-grandmother Field was, how beloved and respected by everybody, though she was not indeed the mistress of this great house, but had only the charge of it (and yet in some respects she might be said to be the mistress of it too) committed to her by the owner, who preferred living in a newer and more fashionable mansion which he had purchased somewhere in the adjoining county; but still she lived in it in a manner as if it had been her own, and kept up the dignity of the great house in a sort while she lived, which afterwards came to decay, and was nearly pulled down, and all its old ornaments stripped and carried away to the owner's other house, where they were set up, and looked as awkward as if someone were to carry away the old tombs they had seen lately at the Abbey, and stick them up in Lady C.'s tawdry gilt drawing-room. Here John smiled, as much as to say, "That would be foolish, indeed."

And then I told how, when she came to die, her funeral was attended by a concourse of all the poor, and some of the gentry too, of the neighborhood for many miles round, to show their respect for her memory, because she had been such a good and religious woman; so good indeed that she knew all the Psaltery by heart, ay, and a great part of the Testament besides. Here little Alice spread her hands.

Then I told what a tall, upright, graceful person their great-grandmother Field once was; and how in her youth she was esteemed the best dancer—here Alice's little right foot played an involuntary movement, till upon my looking grave, it desisted—the best dancer, I was saying, in the county, till a cruel disease, called a cancer, came, and bowed her down with pain; but it could never bend her good spirits, or make them stoop, but they were still upright, because she was so good and religious. Then I told how she was used to sleep by herself in a lone chamber of the great lone house; and how she believed that an apparition of two infants was to be seen at midnight gliding up and down the great staircase near where she slept, but she said "those innocents would do her no harm"; and how frightened I used to be, though in those days I had my maid to sleep with me, because I was never half so good or religious as she—and yet I never saw the infants. Here John expanded all his eyebrows and tried to look courageous.

Then I told how good she was to all her grandchildren, having us to the great house in the holidays, where I in particular used to spend many hours by myself, in gazing upon the old busts of the twelve Caesars, that had been emperors of Rome, till the old marble heads would seem to live again, or I to be turned into marble with them; how I never could be tired with roaming about that huge mansion, with its vast empty rooms, with their worn-out hangings, fluttering tapestry, and carved oaken panels, with the gilding almost rubbed out—sometimes in the spacious old-fashioned gardens, which I had almost to myself, unless when now and then a solitary gardening man would cross me—and how the nectarines and peaches hung upon the walls without my ever offering to pluck them, because they were forbidden fruit, unless now and then—and because I had more pleasure in strolling about among the old melancholy-looking yew-trees, or the firs, and picking up the red berries, and the fir apples, which were good for nothing but to look at— or in lying about upon the fresh grass, with all the fine garden smells around me—or basking in the orangery, till I could almost fancy myself ripening too along with the oranges and the limes in that grateful warmth—or in watching the dace that darted to and fro in the fishpond, at the bottom of the garden, with here and there a great sulky pike hanging midway down the water in silent state, as if it mocked at their impertinent friskings—I had more pleasure in these busy-idle diversions than in all the sweet flavors of peaches, nectarines, oranges, and such like common baits of children. Here John slyly deposited back upon the plate a bunch of grapes which, not unobserved by Alice, he had meditated dividing with her, and both seemed willing to relinquish them for the present as irrelevant.

Then in somewhat a more heightened tone, I told how, though their great-grandmother Field loved all her grandchildren, yet in an especial manner she might be said to love their uncle, John L——, because he was so handsome and spirited a youth, and a king to the rest of us; and, instead of moping about in solitary corners, like some of us, he would mount the most mettlesome horse he could get, when but an imp no bigger than themselves, and make it carry him half over the county in a morning, and join the hunters when there were any out—and yet he loved the old great house and gardens too, but had too much spirit to be always pent up within their boundaries—and how their uncle grew up to man's estate as brave as he was handsome, to the admiration of everybody, but of their great-grandmother Field most especially; and how he used to carry me upon his back when I was a lame-footed boy— for he was a good bit older than me—many a mile when I could not walk for pain; and how in after-life he became lame-footed too, and I did not always (I fear) make allowances enough for him when he was impatient and in pain, nor remember sufficiently how considerate he had been to me when I was lame-footed; and how when he died, though he had not been dead an hour, it seemed as if he had died a great while ago, such a distance there is betwixt life and death; and how I bore his death as I thought pretty well at first, but afterwards it haunted and haunted me; and though I did not cry or take it to heart as some do, and as I think he would have done if I had died, yet I missed him all day long, and knew not till then how much I had loved him. I missed his kindness, and I missed his crossness, and wished him to be alive again, to be quarreling with him (for we quarreled sometimes) rather than not have him again, and was as uneasy without him as he, their poor uncle, must have been when the doctor took off his limb. Here the children fell a-crying, and asked if their little mourning which they had on was not for uncle John, and they looked up, and prayed me not to go on about their uncle, but to tell them some stories about their pretty dead mother.

Then I told how for seven long years, in hope sometimes, sometimes in despair, yet persisting ever, I courted the fair Alice W——n; and, as much as children could undersand, I explained to them what coyness, and difficulty, and denial meant in maidens—when suddenly, turning to Alice, the soul of the first Alice looked out at her eyes with such a reality of representment that I became in doubt which of them stood there before me, or whose that bright hair was; and while I stood gazing, both the children gradually grew fainter to my view, receding and still receding till nothing at last but two mournful features were seen in the uttermost distance, which without speech, strangely impressed upon me the effects of speech: "We are not of Alice, nor of thee, nor are we children at all. The children of Alice call Bartrum father. We are nothing, less than nothing, and dreams. We are only what might have been, and must wait upon the tedious shores of Lethe millions of ages before we have existence and a name"—and immediately awaking, I found myself quietly seated in my bachelor arm-chair where I had fallen asleep, with the faithful Bridget unchanged by my side—but John L. (or James Elia) was gone for ever.

The first proposition in "Dream Children," that children love to listen to stories about their elders, looks like a thesis, for certainly it can be disputed. But in the end the reader sees that this statement is only a part of the trap, the sad joke on which "Dream Children" is founded, and its truth or falsity does not concern him. He accepts it as though it merely meant that Alice and John loved to listen to such stories: a proposition that of course encounters no resistance. "Dream Children," indeed, is not ultimately about children at all, though it keeps us aware of the children's existence by periodically mentioning their small actions. Its theme is adult loneliness, and the reader's attention is soon switched from the children to the speaker's relations with Mrs. Field, his brother John, Alice W——n, and, at the very end, the faithful Bridget. There is no thesis; instead, every word is related to the feeling of sympathy for those whose loneliness leads them into compensating reveries, the feeling engendered by the theme.

Here we must notice that "Dream Children" implies no such general proposition as that all lonely people indulge in reveries, or that they need to do so, or that they ought not to. It limits itself to a depiction of one lonely man's reverie. But this limitation does not detract from its value. Quite the opposite: the poignant insight that it gives into the meaning of loneliness is made possible by its limitation. And poignancy is its enduring quality—for it was first published in the year 1822.

Besides being organized around a theme rather than a thesis, "Dream Children" differs from "Decline and Fall of the Adjective" in a second important way. It is wholly self-contained and self-sufficient. True, a biography of its author, Charles Lamb, will show us how closely Lamb followed reality in composing this work. He himself had a brother named John and a grandmother, Mrs. Field, who was the housekeeper of a country estate. But these external facts do not concern us when we are reading and responding to "Dream Children." The biography will tell us also that he had a sister, Mary, to whom "the faithful Bridget" does not correspond very accurately. But that does not matter either. The name of the dreamer is not Lamb but Elia—though Lamb was whimsical enough to call Elia's brother John L. and then correct himself in the last line, without changing the others. The narrative creates the character Elia, who misses the joys of his childhood, who courted but failed to win the fair Alice W——n, and who now has only the faithful Bridget for a companion. In short, it tells us all that we can know about him on the present occasion. Bridget is not Elia's sister. In other of his essays she is called his cousin; but since "Dream Children" does not mention a relationship, we are not forced to imagine that there is any at all.

This distinction between "Dream Children" and "Decline and Fall of the Adjective" is a fundamental one, and we need a pair of terms that will identify the two kinds of writing represented by these works.

Discursive and non-discursive

Unlike "Dream Children" the essay "Decline and Fall of the Adjective" is not self-contained. Its subject is what we call real life, the world that would exist whether or not it had been written. Some of its sentences state facts, or what should be facts; the others state conclusions that ought to follow logically from these facts. Consequently our answer to the question "Is it any good?" depends to a large extent on testing its factual statements and the correctness of its reasoning. To do this we must, so to speak, step outside it and compare it with the real world, which it is talking about. A work of this kind is called *discursive.*

"Dream Children," on the other hand, is *non-discursive.* If it had not been written, the world of Elia, Bridget, and the others would not exist, for it has called that world into being. It makes statements only about itself. (The opening statement about children is, as we have seen, of trifling importance.) We evaluate it not so much by referring it to reality as by asking whether it obeys the laws of its own being. That Mary Lamb was a sore trial to her brother Charles, for example, is beside the point. But to have represented Bridget as glamorous would have been a fatal mistake. To call her *faithful,* a somewhat patronizing word, is just right. The quality of "Dream Children" is determined by the vividness with which it creates a world of its own.

The fact that Alice and John exist only in Elia's dreams emphasizes the non-discursive character of this work, but is not what makes it so. The children exist in precisely the same way as the bachelor dozing in his armchair: that is, only in the author's and the reader's imagination. The final words are just as non-discursive as the rest.

The difference between discursive and non-discursive writing involves important differences of both substance and structure. It does not, however, make a difference in value. "Dream Children" may be just as much worth reading as an essay, a history, a work of science, or any other example of discursive writing. All fictions— short stories, novels, poems, and plays—are characteristically non-discursive, and any good fiction is truthful: by implication, that is to say, it gives insight into the nature of things as they are. But it does so by the creation of an imagined world, not by making statements about the real one.[3]

Notice the statement that fiction is *characteristically* non-discursive. Any fiction—particularly a novel, which is a most flexible kind of writing—may contain passages similar to the first sentence of "Dream Children." The novel *War and Peace,* for instance, contains a number of passages discussing the causes of historical events (one of them, † "History," is printed in this book). But these are really inserted essays. *War and Peace* is a novel in spite of them. Moreover, it includes scenes based on real events of French and Russian history. But these do not make it a discursive work either, for it must actualize or recreate whatever history it includes. If it makes a mistake of history it loses little of its value as a novel. "Dream

[3] See the interview with Georges Simenon, † "The Art of Fiction," particularly the paragraph in which Simenon describes how "little by little a small world will come into my mind, with a few characters."

Children," of course, can make no mistakes of history, for it contains none.

Again, it is characteristic of non-discursive writing to be organized around a theme. But this does not rule out the possibility of its also containing a thesis. † *The Man of Destiny*, which is a play, implies that Napoleon was a great man, and that his greatness resulted from his ability to surmount flimsy conventions which hamstring almost everybody else. These are beliefs about the real world that provoke plenty of disagreement. *War and Peace*, in fact, flatly contradicts them both.

We cannot say, on the other hand, that any discursive work will have a thesis. Far from it. A great many such works are written to illuminate the real world for us, not to persuade us to accept opinions about it. A highway sign reading SLIPPERY WHEN WET, a recipe in a cookbook—these are bits of discursive writing. So is the following essay, to take a more complicated example. When you have read it, can you distinguish its *theme* from the facts that it presents?

SEA MONSTERS

RACHEL L. CARSON   ⸺⸱⸲

From THE SEA AROUND US. © *1950, 1951 by Rachel L. Carson. Reprinted by permission of Oxford University Press, Inc.*

The existence of an abundant deep-sea fauna was discovered, probably millions of years ago, by certain whales and also, it now appears, by seals. The ancestors of all whales, we know by fossil remains, were land mammals. They must have been predatory beasts, if we are to judge by their powerful jaws and teeth. Perhaps in their foragings about the deltas of great rivers or around the edges of shallow seas, they discovered the abundance of fish and other marine life and over the centuries formed the habit of following them farther and farther into the sea. Little by little their bodies took on a form more suitable for aquatic life; their hind limbs were reduced to rudiments, which may be discovered in a modern whale by dissection, and the forelimbs were modified into organs for steering and balancing.

Eventually the whales, as though to divide the sea's food resources among them, became separated into three groups: the plankton-eaters, the fish-eaters, and the squid-eaters. The plankton-eating whales can exist only where there are dense masses of small shrimp or copepods to supply their enormous food requirements. This limits them, except for scattered areas, to arctic and antarctic waters and the high temperate latitudes. Fish-eating whales may find food over a somewhat wider range of ocean, but they are restricted to places where there are enormous populations of schooling fish. The blue water of the tropics and of the open ocean basins offers little to either of these groups. But that immense, square-headed, formidably toothed whale known as the cachalot or sperm whale discovered long ago what men have known for only a short time—that hundreds of fathoms below the almost untenanted surface waters of these regions there is an abundant animal life. The sperm whale has taken these deep waters for his hunting grounds; his quarry is the deep-water population of squids, including the giant squid Architeuthis, which lives pelagically at depths of 1500 feet or more. The head of the sperm whale is often marked with long stripes, which consist of a great number of circular scars made by the suckers of the squid. From this evidence we can imagine the battles that go on, in the darkness of the deep water, between these two huge creatures—the sperm whale with its 70-ton bulk, the squid with a body as long as 30 feet, and writhing, grasping arms extending the total length of the animal to perhaps 50 feet.

The greatest depth at which the giant squid lives is not definitely known, but there is one instructive piece of evidence about the depth to which sperm whales descend, presumably in search of the squids. In April 1932, the cable repair ship *All America* was investigating an apparent break in the submarine cable between Balboa in the Canal Zone and Esmeraldas, Ecuador. The cable was brought to the surface off the coast of Colombia. Entangled in it was a dead 45-foot male sperm whale. The submarine cable was twisted around the lower jaw and was wrapped around one flipper, the body, and the caudal flukes. The cable was raised from a depth of 540 fathoms, or 3240 feet.

"Sea Monsters" is a short essay having many characteristics of a work of science: that is, a work which is valuable if it simply gives trustworthy information about the world of nature. The precise specification of places, times, and dimensions; the division of whales into three groups; the technical terms—*fauna, pelagically, Architeuthis, caudal;* the assignment of evidence for each statement, with careful distinction between what is certain and what merely probable—all these suggest the cold, impersonal approach of a marine biologist. And no doubt a part of its value is that the information in it is entirely trustworthy. Nevertheless, "Sea Monsters" is also a work of literature, and one of considerable interest.

There are two ways of explaining this matter. One is to say that, as you may have already discovered, this essay is organized around a theme. Every word in it contributes to a sense of the wonder and mystery of the external world. Even where the style is seemingly most impersonal, the reader is aware of an implied exclamation—"How incredible!" or something of that sort.

If this is so, however, if responses to the facts about whales and squids permeate the essay, then the facts are being given not directly but as they appear to an individual observer. Hence the literary or non-scientific quality of "Sea Monsters" is established by the presence of an implied speaker: a speaker who reports the substance, who is characterized by the attitudes displayed towards that substance, and who, to the extent that the essay is successful, controls the attitudes of the reader. We have seen how much of the effect of "Decline and Fall of the Adjective" derives from its speaker's humor and irony, as well as his concern for freedom. The same applies to the pathos and whimsicality of Elia, the speaker in "Dream Children." Because a speaker is more prominent in these works than in "Sea Monsters," they belong more obviously to the domain of literature. Yet a close reading of "Sea Monsters" shows that in it too a speaker is everywhere present, making judgments and responding emotionally to the wondrousness of the presented facts.

Let us look at a few examples. The first sentence is so written as to suggest that whales are smarter than men, for they penetrated the ocean's depths millions of years sooner; and this suggestion, repeated in the middle of the second paragraph, is reinforced by the personification of the whales in the next sentence: "The sperm whale has taken these deep waters for his hunting grounds. . . ." A quite imaginary competition between whales and men is thus suggested, lending dramatic warmth to the cold facts. What these devices add to the essay is not information but interest; they are related to its theme, rather than to its substance. The implied presence of the speaker is also felt in the sprinkling of emotive words —*powerful,* which implies at least respect; the repeated *enormous,* suggesting astonishment at whales' capacity for food; *immense, formidably toothed,* and *writhing,* with their overtones of awe, not unmixed with terror. As a final example, consider what the last paragraph leaves unsaid. If there was an *apparent* break in the cable, then the cable was not broken. But it is up to the reader to understand the total meaning: "What was the amazement of the crew to discover that the trouble had not been caused by a break in the cable but by a sperm whale, caught in it at a depth of 3240 feet! ! !"

Is "Sea Monsters" then a scientific essay? Certainly it is not unscientific, in the sense of being unreliable. But a pure work of science should be written as impersonally as possible. In that way it can best do its proper job: to marshal and classify facts, distinguishing certainties from probabilities, and so inform us about the external world. A work of literature may do these things too, but its paramount concern is to present the impact of some situation upon a sensitive observer. All literary works, discursive and non-discursive alike, have this in common. The British writer John Macmurray, noting the "profound impersonality" of science, defines the difference clearly:

> Knowledge is always personal, always somebody's; but information is just anybody's. Science wants facts, atoms of information, which must all be indifferent to their being known; all equally valid for anybody at all. Science is not the personal knowledge of this scientist or that; it is information, the raw material out of which you and I can pick and choose what we want for our purpose, to build up our own knowledge, which is real knowledge just because it is ours and nobody else's.[4]

Whether one would wish to speak of science in such slighting terms or not, Macmurray's statement sharply defines the distinction that separates all discursive works into two groups. Reality from the scientific standpoint is impersonal; from the literary standpoint, it is personal.

Our examination of "Dream Children" and "Sea Monsters" has added four more principles of reading and writing to the three already given.

4. The immediate question to be asked about a non-discursive work is whether it is internally consistent rather than whether it has any relation to real life.

5. A non-discursive work must include within itself everything necessary for its understanding.

6. A non-discursive work characteristically has a theme; a discursive work may or may not have a thesis.

7. An essential element in any literary work, discursive or non-discursive, is the implied attitude of a speaker toward the presented substance.

[4] From *Reason and Emotion,* by John Macmurray. Reprinted by permission of Appleton-Century-Crofts, Inc.

What students write

You may find these seven principles hard to keep in mind until you have practised analyzing a number of literary works with their help. The effort will seem worth making as you find that they give you a better understanding of what you read. Now let us see how they can help to answer the question of what you are to write when the instructor asks for a paper.

Possibly he wants a short story, a poem, or even a play—in which case, of course, you will have to try your hand at some non-discursive writing. But it is more probable that he expects a discursive work, one that is founded on your experience of external reality. This may be only the impersonal presentation of the facts about a given topic: a piece of scientific writing, in the broad sense we have assigned to that term. A description of a helicopter, an explanation of a process (how to bake a cake or change a tire), a summary of the plot of a novel—these are examples of this kind of paper. They are usually called *reports,* and hardly anyone endures a college composition course without writing two or three of them.

In all likelihood, though, your instructor would welcome something more personal, and his reason is simple. Learning to write well is essential to your education not alone because it has "practical value." True, writing well may one day help you to a promotion and is very handy whenever you have a letter to get off. But it offers richer rewards than these. By writing better essays students develop their ability to respond to experience: to see things more vividly, to form clearer opinions, to understand their own feelings. Writing has an important part to play in the process of maturing. And so your instructor probably expects you also to write essays—works of literature rather than science.

Now to say that your papers should be literary does not mean that you must rival Shakespeare, or even reveal the expertness of such professionals as Eric Sevareid and Rachel L. Carson. It means only that you must treat your subject in such a way as to give your writing interest and point. If an essay is to be personal, and at the same time unified, it must have either a thesis or a theme, expressed or implied. Almost any subject can be treated either way, but it is essential that the writer know what he is doing.

For a convenient example let us return to our old friend the summer vacation. Suppose you are asked to write about yours. If your essay suggests that the beach is a better place for a vacation than the mountains, or the other way round, then you have written to a thesis. But you may turn out just as good an essay by describing your two weeks at the beach or your trip to the mountains, provided you have made it clear that you responded to the experience in some definite way. The exhilaration of getting close to nature, the speed with which those two glorious weeks slipped by, the frustrations of successive rainy days in a beach cottage—any of these makes a perfectly respectable theme. But however you write the essay, when it is finished you will have experienced that vacation far more deeply than at the beginning. Writing about an experience makes it mean more.

In explaining the difference between these two kinds of essays we have had to deal in generalities, and necessarily so—the experience was yours, not ours, and you alone possess the meaningful details that can make it a bit of *knowledge,* as John Macmurray uses the word. In the true sense, nobody can write an essay for you. If it is your thesis that the mountains are preferable to the seashore, nobody else knows why you think so. If you were frustrated by a series of rainy days at the beach, nobody else has the means of bringing this theme to life. Either way, the quality of your essay will largely depend on the particulars of the experience that you decide to include.

Let us put the same idea in other words. If you are writing to a thesis, remember that a thesis is a disputable opinion. Because it is bound to provoke disagreement from somebody, it must be carefully supported with reasons, illustrations, evidence. The more specific these are, the sturdier will be the support that they lend. You may not succeed in converting the reader to your opinion, but you will at least have made him respect it. Any writing which can do that is successful writing. If, on the other hand, your essay is to be organized around a theme, then specific details are essential to make it vivid. Only details can give a definite impression of a speaker and a situation to which he is responding. Short essays cannot stand many generalities; most of their space must be devoted to supporting detail. Often, in fact, it is good strategy to suppress the general statements and let the details do the work. This is the method that the next example follows. Its particulars only suggest the theme, which is the destruction of the natural world by the progress of society.

ILLINOIS BUS RIDE

ALDO LEOPOLD

From A SAND COUNTY ALMANAC: AND SKETCHES HERE AND THERE. © *1949 by Oxford University Press. Reprinted by permission.*

A farmer and his son are out in the yard, pulling a crosscut saw through the innards of an ancient cottonwood. The tree is so large and so old that only a foot of blade is left to pull on.

Time was when that tree was a buoy in the prairie sea. George Rogers Clark may have camped under it; buffalo may have nooned in its shade, switching flies. Every spring it roosted fluttering pigeons. It is the best historical library short of the State College, but once a year it sheds cotton on the farmer's window screens. Of these two facts, only the second is important.

The State College tells farmers that Chinese elms do not clog screens, and hence are preferable to cottonwoods. It likewise pontificates on cherry preserves, Bang's disease, hybrid corn, and beautifying the farm home. The only thing it does not know about farms is where they came from. Its job is to make Illinois safe for soybeans.

I am sitting in a 60-mile-an-hour bus sailing over a highway originally laid out for horse and buggy. The ribbon of concrete has been widened and widened until the field fences threaten to topple into the road cuts. In the narrow thread of sod between the shaved banks and the toppling fences grow the relics of what once was Illinois: the prairie.

No one in the bus sees these relics. A worried farmer, his fertilizer bill projecting from his shirt pocket, looks blankly at the lupines, lespedezas, or Baptisias that originally pumped nitrogen out of the prairie air and into his black loamy acres. He does not distinguish them from the parvenu quack-grass in which they grow. Were I to ask him why his corn makes a hundred bushels, while that of non-prairie states does well to make thirty, he would probably answer that Illinois soil is better. Were I to ask him the name of that white spike of pea-like flowers hugging the fence, he would shake his head. A weed, likely.

A cemetery flashes by, its borders alight with prairie puccoons. There are no puccoons elsewhere; dog-fennels and sow-thistles supply the yellow *motif* for the modern landscape. Puccoons converse only with the dead.

Through the open window I hear the heart-stirring whistle of an upland plover; time was when his forebears followed the buffalo as they trudged shoulder-deep through an illimitable garden of forgotten blooms. A boy spies the bird and remarks to his father: there goes a snipe.

22

The sign says, "You are entering the Green River Soil Conservation District." In smaller type is a list of who is co-operating; the letters are too small to be read from a moving bus. It must be a roster of who's who in conservation.

The sign is neatly painted. It stands in a creek-bottom pasture so short you could play golf on it. Near by is the graceful loop of an old dry creek bed. The new creek bed is ditched straight as a ruler; it has been "uncurled" by the county engineer to hurry the run-off. On the hill in the background are contoured strip-crops; they have been "curled" by the erosion engineer to retard the run-off. The water must be confused by so much advice.

Everything on this farm spells money in the bank. The farm-stead abounds in fresh paint, steel, and concrete. A date on the barn commemorates the founding fathers. The roof bristles with lightning-rods, the weathercock is proud with new gilt. Even the pigs look solvent.

The old oaks in the woodlot are without issue. There are no hedges, brush patches, fencerows, or other signs of shiftless husbandry. The cornfield has fat steers, but probably no quail. The fences stand on narrow ribbons of sod; whoever plowed that close to barbed wires must have been saying, "Waste not, want not."

In the creek-bottom pasture, flood trash is lodged high in the bushes. The creek banks are raw; chunks of Illinois have sloughed off and moved seaward. Patches of giant ragweed mark where freshets have thrown down the silt they could not carry. Just who is solvent? For how long?

The highway stretches like a taut tape across the corn, oats, and clover fields; the bus ticks off the opulent miles; the passengers talk and talk and talk. About what? About baseball, taxes, sons-in-law, movies, motors, and funerals, but never about the heaving ground-swell of Illinois that washes the windows of the speeding bus. Illinois has no genesis, no history, no shoals or deeps, no tides of life and death. To them Illinois is only the sea on which they sail to ports unknown.

The lesson afforded by "Illinois Bus Ride" is that explicit comments are not so necessary as we often imagine. Some parts of it, such as the question "For how long?" and the last sentence, come close to being generalizations; but even these play only an indirect part in presenting the theme. This method runs no risk of insulting the reader's intelligence; it makes him feel instead that he is co-operating with the speaker in the creation of the substance. He feels as if he were being invited to draw his own conclusions—though his choice of conclusions is quite restricted—from the abundance of concrete details offered to him. Some writers on writing, indeed, go so far as to state that the basic principle of all good writing is contained in the two words *BE CONCRETE.*

This is probably being too condensed; such a rule would tend to disqualify some pre-eminent examples of good writing, the Declaration of Independence and the Gettysburg Address among them. As great writings go, however, these are exceptional. *Be concrete* is nearly always an excellent slogan, and the dictionary tells us why. One meaning of the adjective *concrete* is *characterized by things or events that can be perceived by the senses; real; actual.* Things and events that the senses can perceive make writing seem actual—that is, alive. They bring it as near to reality as it can get; they give it the *illusion of reality.*

Does this description of good writing appear to ask the impossible? If so, a specimen of student writing, one representing the great average, should prove reassuring. We include one that you will probably agree is in some ways very good—though you may also like to see it made better, or at least we hope so. But before coming to it we had better correct two mistaken impressions that you may have received from what we have said about details drawn from experience.

Since even the slightest experience consists of details infinite in number, no piece of writing can include them all. The writer necessarily selects a few that best support his thesis or his theme—that are *relevant* to it, in a word. It might be supposed further that he must leave out any detail which has an opposing effect. As everyone knows, though, experience is never so simple as that. Oversimplifying it merely tends to destroy the illusion of reality—the effect, as we have seen, for which writing must strive. To include a few opposing details, in spite of which the thesis or theme is maintained, gives an air of mature consideration to the writer's views. The relevance of these details will be their suggestion that a complicated experience has been encompassed without distortion.

So much talk of experience may also have led you to suppose that essays must sternly confine themselves to the literal truth, there being no place for invention in discursive writing. But what is invention, anyway? Usually, what we do when we invent is to remember and combine—perhaps events from a similar experience, or ones that somebody has told us about, or even ones that we have met in reading. Not all experience, as we have seen, is direct. When an event that we hear or read about really impresses us, it becomes a part of our experience too. The chances are that your instructor will not object if your essay borrows an incident from another occasion, or even includes some indirect experiences, so long as you make this material relevant to what you are writing about. If you do that, he is not likely to complain.

Read the following essay with these points in mind. Could it have been written by someone who was not actually present at the testing of the bomb?

MY IMPRESSION OF THE HYDROGEN BOMB

A student essay.

In May, 1956, I had the privilege of being an observer in the Marshall Islands for the first hydrogen bomb test. I was serving on board the aircraft carrier USS *Badoeng Strait* (CVE-116), which was one of the ships in Task Group 7.3, assembled for the tests to be held in the immediate area of the Marshall Islands. We were at sea thirty miles from the target area.

Everyone not on watch on board the carrier was assembled on the flight deck before daylight in order that as many as possible could see the blast. Sixty seconds before the blast was to go off, we were told to put our arms over our faces and turn aft on the carrier. At 5.07 a.m. the bomb was exploded. The light was so brilliant we were able to see through our arms with our eyes closed. We could see the bones in our arms as though we were looking into an X-ray machine. The heat was terrific. The cold morning air warmed up about thirty-five degrees and felt as if someone had turned a heater on us. When we were allowed to turn around, a huge, grotesque, cone-shaped fireball began to rise. The fireball was first a brilliant red, then turned rose, pink, orange, lavender, purple, and proceeded to blend into many other beautiful colors. Around the fireball emerged a huge, circular, snow-white vapor-cloud. The cone and vapor-cloud rose about one hundred miles in the air and slowly faded away.

The hydrogen bomb test was one of the most beautiful and awesome things I have ever seen. I believe the power of the hydrogen bomb can be used for peaceful means and will contribute greatly to the improvement of living conditions in the world. Heat from the bomb was great enough to warm thousands of homes many years.

My hopes are that the hydrogen bomb is never used for war. It would probably destroy the world if dropped in great numbers.

"My Impression of the Hydrogen Bomb" consists of only 335 words. It is a pretty average student essay, in some ways better than most, and in other ways worse. Richer in material than one can hope to find ordinarily, it is sadly disunified and marred by crudities of style that make it sound like a rough draft. Had the student revised it better, he would have kept all his vivid details, while cutting out the repetitious words and phrases. Above all, a good revision would have brought together the various implied meanings.

Suppose we had to show the writer how to improve this work. First we should urge him to retain every one of the details in the first two paragraphs, for the precise figures and proper names in Paragraph 1 establish the speaker's authority as a reliable witness, and the vivid particulars of Paragraph 2 give life to the theme, the beauty and awesomeness of the explosion. If the writer did not seem to understand this very well, which detail would you single out as best justifying the speaker's sense of awe? Which ones best support the word *beautiful*?

We should next try to improve the roughness of the style. Repetition, it would be well to explain, can be an excellent device, but it must always appear to be deliberate. It is distressing to find a word repeated in a different sense, for then the repetition appears to have been unconscious. In Paragraph 2 the verb *turn* is used three times. Does it seem to you that this was done on purpose?

Tightening up the style, especially in Paragraph 2, would make room for a more gradual approach to the moment of the explosion. For a day at least before the bomb was tested, tension must have run pretty high aboard the carrier. This feeling could have been exploited to make the climax of the essay more dramatic.

The hardest part of the revision would be the unifying process. As we should first have to make sure that the writer understood our objections, the distinction between *thesis* and *theme* would here prove invaluable. Of course we could say that the last two paragraphs appear to have been merely tacked on—but what if the writer then asked why we thought so? He would need to be convinced that the awesome-beauty theme, which is the main one, is distinct from the thesis of Paragraph 3 (that the bomb can become an instrument of progress), and that Paragraph 4 is not now related to either one of these. How would you describe the theme or thesis of Paragraph 4?

Let us try revising the essay ourselves. Notice that the ideas in the last two paragraphs do not have to be dropped out. They can be kept, provided a sensible way is found of relating them to the main theme.

CONE-SHAPED FIREBALL

Revised essay. The new title is a striking phrase taken from Paragraph 2 of the original. Essays must have titles, and this is a good trick when you are at a loss for one.

A few hydrogen bombs would probably destroy the earth if they were dropped in a war. On the other hand, the discovery of the H-bomb may be a great step in human progress, for one hydrogen explosion generates enough heat to warm thousands of homes for many years. The testing of the first hydrogen bomb was thus one of the most important events in history, for good or evil, and I was privileged to be an observer of it.

In May, 1956, I was a seaman on board the USS *Badoeng Strait* (CVE-116), an aircraft carrier. It was one of the ships in Task Group 7.3, assembled near the Marshall Islands for the bomb test. When our ship was anchored on the evening before, we were all brought on deck and given instructions. We were told that the center of the target area was thirty miles away, that we were "probably" out of danger, but that this was an assumption to be proved, not to be taken for granted. The captain then said he would be happy to put a launch at the disposal of any of us who wanted to move farther away. There were a number of trembling grins and half-steps forward at this announcement, but no one took up the offer. Then a kind of momentous quiet settled over the ship. The officers and men went about their tasks calmly; there was none of the usual horseplay—in fact, there was little conversation at all. Everyone seemed preoccupied with his own thoughts.

Before daylight the next morning, every man not on watch was assembled on the flight deck so that as many as possible could witness the blast. Sixty seconds before the time set for it, we were told to turn aft, away from the target area, and put our arms over our faces. The bomb was exploded at 5.07. The light was so brilliant that, with our eyes closed, we could see the bones in our arms as though we were looking into an X-ray machine. The heat was terrific. The temperature of the cool morning air rose about thirty-five degrees. When we were allowed to turn around, we saw a huge, grotesque fireball in the shape of a cone beginning to rise. The cone was first brilliant red; then it changed to rose, pink, orange, lavender, and purple in succession. A snow-white cloud of vapor was forming around it. The cone-shaped fireball and its surrounding vapor-cloud rose about one hundred miles in the air and then slowly faded away.

The hydrogen bomb test is the most beautiful and awesome thing that I have ever seen. Being an observer of it has made me realize that the bomb must never be exploded in a war. Instead, I sincerely hope its tremendous power will be used for the betterment of human life.

Getting started

The essay that we have just analyzed and rewritten is included in this book to show you an example of what your instructor probably expects from you. It is not supposed to suggest that writing can be made easy. That would be very misleading advice, for all the evidence points to the fact that even professional writers find their trade a hard one, no matter how many years they may have been writing. But the piece about the H-bomb does show what a college student can learn to produce after a comparatively short training period, and most of us find it consoling to learn that the task before us is within the realm of the possible.

Having made your way through this specimen of another student's writing, you are probably waiting for some principles that will prove helpful to you in your own. Since this is not a grammar book, we are assuming that you are already on friendly terms with the ground-rules: that you can define a paragraph, know what punctuation is, make your verbs agree with their subjects, and so on. But many students who get high scores on objective tests covering these matters nevertheless find themselves tied in knots when it comes to creating an essay of their own. It is this mental hazard, as golfers call it, that we hope to undermine by some commonsense advice.

Often the first obstacle to be removed is the mistaken notion that a good writer is one who can write an essay straight out, beginning with the title and working right through to the final sentence. If you imagine your success depends upon developing that degree of facility, no wonder your heart sinks when the instructor assigns a paper! Let us assume on the contrary that all writers, no matter how skilful, have to write their first drafts over before they obtain one that they wish to keep. (We are glad you can't know how often we rewrote these pages.) Faced with the job of producing an essay, what you first put down on paper may be the title that will eventually head your final draft. Or it may not. It is just as likely to be a concrete detail that will find its way into the third paragraph. So consider the first words committed to paper as merely raw material, later to be fitted into their proper places in the finished masterpiece. You didn't really hope to avoid making a fair copy of your rough draft, did you?

Getting started is the hard part—so you think. Well then, start by finding paper and a pencil, pen, or typewriter. Shut the door, turn off the TV, write your signature thirty times, do anything else necessary to turn your thoughts to that summer vacation, or whatever the assigned or chosen topic is. The poet Schiller kept apples in his desk drawer because, for some unknown reason, their rotting odors helped him to concentrate. Writing comes out of a sort of self-hypnosis, by which the writer puts himself to sleep to the outside world the better to be awake to the world of his subject-matter. The light concentrated on a sheet of paper, the details of his own handwriting, the row of words filing out of his typewriter, these act upon him in much the same way as the hypnotist's staring eyes or the watch that he oscillates before his victim. Pretty soon you will find that some thought or some detail relating to your topic will float into your mind. Write it down.

In short, don't worry much about where to begin. Seize upon any raw material that the gods send you; it can be put into shape later. Once you have started, the very act of writing will deepen that state of concentration we have just described, and thus induce more material out of your subconscious. Some authorities advise you to begin by making a list of phrases that will become the specific details of the finished essay. Thus:

        ripe blackberries
        six-pound largemouth bass
        altitude 3,600 feet

and so on. But if it occurs to you instead to write out a full paragraph, complete with subjects and verbs, then do that. Later you can decide where it belongs in your general plan. Others think it is best to begin by making an outline, so as to decide at once on the order of your ideas. Excellent—if at this point you have any ideas to organize. Some of your best ones, as we have seen, will arrive while you are writing.

Sooner or later, of course, you will probably need an outline. Otherwise you risk falling into the disunity that spoils "My Impression of the Hydrogen Bomb." But an outline can be made at any stage of the process. An outline is an abstract; what you need in the beginning is a grasp of the concrete realities of your topic. It is better to begin by fishing the memory for details, the more specific the better. You will thus be making certain that your essay has substance. Its structure, which the outline will control, had better proceed from its substance, rather than the other way around. But by all means experiment with any method that you happen to hear about. Every writer's methods differ from every other's, and one reason for your being required to write a fairly large number of papers is that continual practice will help you to discover the method that suits you personally. Writing is a personal matter, as we have been saying all along.

Whichever method you follow, it is advisable to conclude the preliminaries by making a revised, final note-sheet. This should consist of three parts, corresponding to the three elements that were defined on pp. 2 and 9: *substance, structure,* and *thesis* or *theme.*

The substance of your essay will be represented by a collection of details, perhaps resembling the list beginning "ripe blackberries." There may not be enough of these for your final purposes, but the ones you have will provide a working basis.

The structure will be shown by a brief outline (and notice that the word modifying *outline* is *brief*). An outline should not include details: they would hamper its purpose, which is to remind you of the order of your general ideas. And a short essay, as we know, has room for only three or four of these.

The third part of your note-sheet will be a sentence labeled either *Thesis* or *Theme*. You are the one to decide which kind of unifying principle will control what you put into your essay and what you leave out. If there is to be a subordinate thesis or theme, let that matter wait. The function of this sentence is to make the essay unified.

What kind of beginning?

With a final note-sheet you are well started on the labor of writing, but you must still decide how to begin the essay itself. All good beginnings achieve the same general effect: they raise a question in the reader's mind, a question to which the rest of the essay must supply the answer. There are innumerable ways of doing this; we shall mention only three.

1. Begin by defining the thesis or theme. With this method, exemplified by "Cone-Shaped Fireball," you explain at once what the reader is to think and feel about the topic. If the substance falls logically into three or four parts, the first paragraph indicates what these divisions are. Such a beginning leaves the reader in no doubt as to what question you are going to answer, and he may admire you for being plain-spoken. He may, on the other hand, wish you were a little more subtle; and after several uses you may get bored with this method yourself. Often the thesis or theme is better implied than stated, as we know.

2. Begin by telling of a relevant event. "Sea-Monsters" begins with a generalized account of how whales and seals discovered their prey at great depths. For your essay a better beginning might be a concrete anecdote, especially a personal one, as in † "On Not Being a Philosopher." "Illinois Bus Ride" simply begins by stating that two men are sawing an old tree. (You might also reread page 1, of this chapter.) This kind of beginning has an interest of its own—or it should. Its structural use is to set the reader wondering how the meaning of the event is related to the topic of the essay. Be sure to convince him that a relation exists, even if you have to follow the event with a paragraph of the kind described in *1*.

3. Begin by contradicting another's thesis, or mentioning an irrelevant one. Remember "Historians . . . may call it the age that destroyed civilization; but. . . ." on page 5? And "Children love to listen to stories about their elders" on page 10? Such beginnings are sometimes known as *bait,* and most readers enjoy being led into a trap if they see you have done it on purpose. Like *2*, this method has the advantage of engaging the reader's attention to a much greater extent than the first method, which does all the work for him. Beginnings *2* and *3*, because they are oblique rather than plain-spoken, enjoy the charm of subtlety. But beware of falling into the trap yourself, or becoming so interested in your false beginning that you fail to put the reader on the right track soon enough. You have few words to waste.

Giving it body

The beginning of an essay resembles a head. Its structure, or order of meanings, is the skeleton, and the details are its flesh and blood. These familiar metaphors suggest that if your essay is to have a sound body it must be strengthened by concrete details and its parts must be well articulated. Good articulation involves two things: finding an arrangement that appeals to the reader's sense of order, and connecting the parts firmly together. The joints must be muscular.

The outline, of course, guides you in creating the structure. The arrangement of the parts depends so much upon what the parts are— that is, upon the substance being presented—that few specific rules for it can be laid down. Perhaps the best advice would be that you should so order the parts that the finished essay will resemble Cleopatra, of whom Shakespeare wrote:

> Other women cloy
> The appetites they feed, but she makes hungry
> Where most she satisfies.

Each part, in other words, should not only do its own job but also suggest that the next part will be even more interesting. And the next one must satisfy this expectation. It might seem natural to place your most exciting material first, but that could only result in the reader's interest growing weaker instead of stronger. "Dream Children" affords a fine example of the right arrangement. If you follow the order of climax you can hardly go wrong. The bother of writing an outline would be justified if it accomplished nothing but the placing of the best material at the end. What the reader reads last he remembers longest.

With the beginning out of the way, you proceed to finish a rough draft of the whole essay. Your note-sheet supplies you with an outline as a guide, and with a collection of details to be absorbed into the structure. If other details occur to you while you are writing, don't hesitate to include them. The importance of concrete details cannot be overstated—but the question of how detailed an essay ought to be cannot be exactly answered either. A useful test is to ask: *Does it contain a good sprinkling of (a) proper names, (b) color-*

words, (c) measurements or other numbers, and (d) quotations (both dialogue and borrowings like the one from *Antony and Cleopatra* in the preceding paragraph)? If so, it is concretely written. A good essay will as a rule be characterized by at least one of these kinds of detail. "My Impression of the Hydrogen Bomb," even in its original form, scores high on the first three parts of this test; it has plenty of flesh and blood. Examine the concreteness of the following paragraph, written by a poet about a pretty abstract topic: the obscurity of poetry.

> The University of Michigan recently made a survey of the reading habits of the American public; it decided that forty-eight per cent of all Americans read, during a year, no book at all. I picture to myself that reader—non-reader, rather; one man out of every two—and I reflect, with shame: "Our poems are too hard for him." But so, too, are *Treasure Island, Peter Rabbit*, pornographic novels—any book whatsoever. The authors of the world have been engaged in a sort of conspiracy to drive this American away from books; have, in 77 million out of 160 million cases, succeeded. A sort of dream-situation often occurs to me in which I call to this imaginary figure, "Why don't you read books?"—and he always answers, after looking at me steadily for a long time: "Huh?" [5]

In making sure that your writing is concrete you will also find this rule valuable: *Never make a general statement without illustrating it*. Like most other good rules, it may be broken. But only occasionally.

Even though the body of an essay is filled with concrete details and its parts arranged in a satisfactory order, the essay may nevertheless be incoherent. If it is perfectly coherent, it is bound to be unified. *Coherence* refers to the connections between the parts; taken literally, it means what glue does. There are two principal kinds of connections you have to worry about: between the sentences of each paragraph, and between the paragraphs. In the first of these coherence is less of a problem, because if the sentences really belong together in one paragraph their relations are likely to be plain. It would be rather hard, even if you tried, to avoid linking each sentence to the one before it. A writer almost automatically introduces the standard devices, which are mainly these: (1) echoing a word (see *incoherent, coherent, Coherence* in the first three sentences of this paragraph) ; (2) using a pronoun that refers to a meaning in the foregoing sentence (see *it* in the second sentence, *these* in the fifth);

[5] From *Poetry and the Age* by Randall Jarrell, by permission of Alfred A. Knopf, Inc. © 1953 by Randall Jarrell.

and (3) introducing a connective *(but, furthermore, on the contrary)*.

Coherence between paragraphs, on the contrary, is not always obvious and must usually be made explicit. You have already detected the way this was just done, and often the same devices that are used to link sentences will serve to link paragraphs. Other times a whole sentence is needed, at either the end of the old paragraph or the beginning of the new one, a sentence that adds little to the substance but is included to tighten the structure. Such sentences are called *transitional sentences*. They cause the reader's mind to move backward and forward by reminding him of what previous paragraphs have said and hinting at what is to come. Thus a strong joint is created. Sevareid's second paragraph begins with a transitional sentence, and we can illustrate further by beginning this next paragraph with one.

A solidly written essay is characterized, then, by concrete details, by orderly arrangement of its parts, and by coherence between its parts. Highly skilled writers probably have all these necessities in mind the whole time that they are writing, but a beginner need not do so. He must expect that a great deal of energy will go into revising his rough draft. But it is generally best to finish a rough draft before worrying about revision.

Winding it up

What the reader reads last, as we have said before, he remembers longest. Therefore the final paragraph will reward all the effort you put on it. As it is your last chance to assert the uniqueness of your essay, you would not wish to be bound by very specific rules in writing it. Yet a few general principles do apply.

First, the conclusion should bear some resemblance to the beginning, for by this time the reader probably needs to be reminded of your principal meaning. However important the material just before the conclusion, it is not all that you have to say, but only part of it. If you have sharply divided your substance ("There are three reasons why I prefer the mountains to the beach," for instance), you had better reiterate that each of these is only a part of the whole. Otherwise the reader may confuse the smaller with the larger. But his mind may need to be directed back to the main topic even though there have been no sharp divisions. The essays by Sevareid and Rachel Carson both conclude with such tactics. Sevareid's last sentence reminds us that we are reading about exhausted adjectives, a fact that the story of the Congressman, whose adjective was all too lively, may have obscured. Rachel Carson finishes with a specific event proving the ability of a whale to dive deeply. Without it we might chiefly remember the horror of the imagined battles between whales and squids.

Second, the conclusion is not the place to introduce new ideas, except for a very special effect. By "special effect" we mean, for instance, the disclosure at the end of "Dream Children." In discursive writing, though, if an idea is important enough to appear at the point of greatest emphasis, then surely it also deserves to be developed earlier. The reason "My Impression of the Hydrogen Bomb" falls apart is that its most important meanings are not even suggested till the last two paragraphs. Its author, if we could question him, would probably admit that they were afterthoughts.

Finally, a conclusion that has an air of finality is satisfying to the reader's sense of form. It makes him feel that you have your material well in hand, and know when to stop, having said enough. Such expressions as "Finally" and "In conclusion" enhance this effect, but careful analysis of the concluding paragraphs of essays that you think possess it is the way to master the art of winding up.

Revising

When you have put the period at the end of the last sentence, your next act had better be to give the rough draft a title, or at least to take another look at the tentative title and see if it can't be improved. You may have an embarrassment of riches: so many striking phrases in your manuscript that you find it hard to decide which one to choose. Of course the title does not have to come from the essay; that is only one possibility. But it is strange how often students complain that titles are hard to find, when this simple solution of the problem is lying right under their noses.

The next step is to decide when to revise the rough draft before making a fair copy of it. Let us hope that you have time to put it away and forget it for a while, since at this moment you are too close to it—your relationship to it is still too personal—to be able to revise it as well as you could if you waited a day or so. It may seem odd, but successful revision necessitates a change in the writer's personality, or let us say a change of roles. Until now you have been the creator, presumably delighting in every word you put down. Before you can improve those words you must become a critic, trying to find as many faults in them as you can. It takes time for most people to change from one mental state to the other. But forcing oneself to write the rough draft at least a day before the deadline is of course a test of character.

When you do read over the rough draft, imagine that you are not yourself but your instructor. The question to be asked of every word—and every comma too—is, "How will it strike HIM?" You are fortunate, when you stop to think about it, in having a captive audience. The instructor's judgment may not always be perfect, but when he has returned the paper to you, graded and commented on, you at least know how your writing affects one representative reader. If he has whims, such as forbidding you to use *get* more than once to a page, so probably will your reader in some future practical situation. We once knew a college president who condemned all sentences long enough to require semicolons.

Becoming a critic is much easier for some writers than others. If you find the question "How will it strike him?" not helpful enough, then you had better make your own list of more specific ones. The following words, discussed previously in this chapter, might serve as the basis of your list. Print *SUBSTANCE* at the top of one sheet of note-paper, *STRUCTURE* at the top of another, and *THESIS/THEME* at the top of a third. Under *SUBSTANCE* you could write questions based on the four rules-of-thumb for concreteness that have already been given. One obvious question under *THESIS/THEME* would be, "Have I made it clear to him?" A less obvious but equally necessary one is, "Have I made it *too* clear?" That is, to have suggested the thesis or theme might have been more effective than stating it in so many words.

The power of suggestion is also to be kept in mind when you are reviewing the style of your sentences. The more you write and revise, the more you will find yourself fighting the temptation to include unnecessary words. But to improve the economy of your style does not mean to make it say less. The question is, "Can I use fewer words to present the same number of details, ideas, etc.?" If you have determined to cut out some of the words in your rough draft, begin by scrutinizing the adverbs—particularly *very, too, quite,* and *rather,* as well as those in *-ly.* For instance, if your instructor frowns on split infinitives, you may find that at least half of yours can be cured by discarding the adverb, instead of moving it somewhere else in the sentence. Then, after screening the adverbs, proceed to the adjectives.

Criticizing the rough draft in the light of all these questions may require several rereadings. That takes time. But once you have concocted the questions you have them—ready for use on all future essays. The more often you use them, the more familiar they will become, and the less time revisions will require.

When you have brought the rough draft as near perfection as possible and made a fair copy of it, remember that the fair copy needs to be proofread. Typists especially should take warning at this point. Slips of the pen are rare; typographical errors, especially on the part of student typists, are legion. Since no typist enjoys marring a beautifully typed page with pencilled corrections, his subconscious keeps telling him while he is proofreading that the page contains no errors. The subconscious can be a shocking liar. A nation-wide survey shows that typed essays have lost more points by errors of typing than they have gained by soothing instructors' eyes.

The fair copy finished, it is advisable to count the words—unless your instructor tells you not to. This is the most accurate way of finding out how much you have written. All words are included, even words quoted from another writer, and, as the law of averages is here quite dependable, *a, I,* and *O* count the same as *antidisestablishmentarianism.* Count every word if you wish, but a surprisingly close estimate can be made if you are not frightened by a little arithmetic. Count the words in ten consecutive lines, divide by ten, and multiply the result by the number of lines on that page. (You might preserve this number, for, unless your handwriting and your taste in paper vary markedly, you can apply it to your subsequent writing.) You now know the number of words on a page, and have probably divined that this must be multiplied by the number of pages. Write "437 words," or whatever the answer is, at the end of your essay. That will assure your instructor, and yourself, that its length satisfies his requirements.

And finally

It seems a long while ago that we imagined your English instructor uttering the words, "Write a paper of two or three pages," and you struggling with the question of what sort of paper you were expected to produce. We confessed then that the subject has difficulties, and suggested that it can only be mastered by analytical reading of other people's writing, particularly the works of professionals. A few of these have been analyzed for you, and some general principles of writing essays formulated. All this has required a good many pages, and the worst of it is that no specific rules apply to all situations. Writing, being an art, is a personal matter, and someone else's rules are not much more than the clues in a treasure-hunt. Every writer who has mastered the art has to some extent made his own rules. But our rules, so we hope, will prove helpful to you as you begin the process. Your own rules will come into being as you study the successes of the professionals—and it is to their writings that the remaining pages of this book are devoted.

2

The Contemporary Essay

Writers develop, as we have seen, by studying the work of other writers as well as by their own practice. In the pages following you will meet some fifty examples of discursive writing, mainly contemporary, illustrating a variety of subjects and methods. These essays are divided into ten groups: the first half of them illustrating a kind of subject—*characters* and *places,* for instance; and the second half illustrating a method of presentation, such as *arguments.* Within each group you will find that, roughly, the essays range from relatively simple to more complex. The divisions are matters of convenience, not in the least unchangeable. A literary work is like a friend, and we seldom regard a friend simply as "a friend." On one occasion we may think of him as a football player, on another as a student of English composition. If he gets sick, we visualize him as a sufferer; if the car breaks down, as—possibly—a mechanic. And so with an essay: sometimes it may be convenient to consider its subject and call it a character-sketch; at another time we may think of its tone and call it an exercise in irony, an *indirection.* There is, accordingly, nothing hard and fast about the classification found here, and many of these essays might just as reasonably have been placed in a different group. Nonetheless, this classification is a useful one, for each group will not only suggest an idea for an essay of your own but also a method of presentation. All in all, the groupings make the possibilities of composition clearer, so that this week you will think of aiming your talents at the portrayal of a person or an animal; on another occasion, at the presentation of your attitude obliquely; and so on.

This section of the book will also remind you that your college essays are to be, not heaps of inert facts, but literary works, in the rather elementary sense of the term explained in Part 1. All the works in this part, that is, imply not only a subject but a speaker who expresses an attitude toward that subject. You will be reminded of this important fact in the list of *Suggestions* that follows almost every essay. Thus it would not be wise to suppose that any of these essays is as simple as it may look at first glance. Like any other literary work, it is complicated to the extent that it consists of three elements: speaker, subject, and the speaker's attitude toward the subject. Some important part of its meaning, moreover, is nearly always implied, and therefore somewhat elusive and subtle.

You must also expect to find that some of these writers, though nearly all are professionals, have met their problems more successfully than others. The importance of the subject, the length of the essay, the reputation of the writer are by no means the best criteria for making such comparative judgments. You will have to read critically, with a great deal of attention to such things as direction, arrangement, and focus of detail. And in time you will be able to see where one writer has triumphed over his problems of composition, where another merely evades them or finds himself being pushed around by them. Indeed, the study of a near-success may be even more rewarding to a student of writing than the study of a complete success.

Another way in which the *Suggestions* will lead to better reading is by sending you to the dictionary, both to clear up doubts about the meanings of words in the essays and to make you familiar with some critical terms that are useful in the analysis of literary works. In the end, though, the best way to appreciate an essay is to try to emulate it. In this way, you have something real and concrete against which to measure your own powers, and you will shortly discover that skill in writing comes with continued practice.

C H A R A C T E R S

VALENTINO

H. L. MENCKEN

Reprinted from A MENCKEN CHRESTOM-
ATHY *by H. L. Mencken, by permission of Alfred A. Knopf, Inc.* © *1927,
1949 by Alfred A. Knopf, Inc.*

By one of the chances that relieve the dullness of life and make it instructive, I had the honor of dining with this celebrated gentleman in New York, a week or so before his fatal illness. I had never met him before, nor seen him on the screen; the meeting was at his instance, and, when it was proposed, vaguely puzzled me. But soon its purpose became clear enough. Valentino was in trouble and wanted advice. More, he wanted advice from an elder and disinterested man, wholly removed from the movies and all their works. Something that I had written, falling under his eye, had given him the notion that I was a judicious fellow. So he requested one of his colleagues, a lady of the films, to ask me to dinner at her hotel.

The night being infernally warm, we stripped off our coats, and came to terms at once. I recall that he wore suspenders of extraordinary width and thickness. On so slim a young man they seemed somehow absurd, especially on a hot summer night. We perspired horribly for an hour, mopping our faces with our handkerchiefs, the table napkins, the corners of the tablecloth, and a couple of towels brought in by the humane waiter. Then there came a thunderstorm, and we began to breathe. The hostess, a woman as tactful as she is charming, disappeared mysteriously and left us to commune.

The trouble that was agitating Valentino turned out to be very simple. The ribald New York papers were full of it, and that was what was agitating him. Some time before, out in Chicago, a wandering reporter had discovered, in the men's wash-room of a gaudy hotel, a slot-machine selling talcum-powder. That, of course, was not unusual, but the color of the talcum-powder was. It was pink. The news made the town giggle for a day, and inspired an editorial writer on the Chicago *Tribune* to

41

compose a hot-weather editorial. In it he protested humorously against the effeminization of the American man, and laid it lightheartedly to the influence of Valentino and his sheik movies. Well, it so happened that Valentino, passing through Chicago that day on his way east from the Coast, ran full tilt into the editorial, and into a gang of reporters who wanted to know what he had to say about it. What he had to say was full of fire. Throwing off his 100% Americanism and reverting to the *mores* of his fatherland, he challenged the editorial writer to a duel, and, when no answer came, to a fist fight. His masculine honor, it appeared, had been outraged. To the hint that he was less than he, even to the extent of one half of one per cent, there could be no answer save a bath of blood.

Unluckily, all this took place in the United States, where the word honor, save when it is applied to the structural integrity of women, has only a comic significance. When one hears of the honor of politicians, of bankers, of lawyers, of the United States itself, everyone naturally laughs. So New York laughed at Valentino. More, it ascribed his high dudgeon to mere publicity-seeking: he seemed a vulgar movie ham seeking space. The poor fellow, thus doubly beset, rose to dudgeons higher still. His Italian mind was simply unequal to the situation. So he sought counsel from the neutral, aloof and seasoned. Unluckily, I could only name the disease, and confess frankly that there was no remedy—none, that is, known to any therapeutics within my ken. He should have passed over the gibe of the Chicago journalist, I suggested, with a lofty snort—perhaps, better still, with a counter gibe. He should have kept away from the reporters in New York. But now, alas, the mischief was done. He was both insulted and ridiculous, but there was nothing to do about it. I advised him to let the dreadful farce roll along to exhaustion. He protested that it was infamous. Infamous? Nothing, I argued, is infamous that is not true. A man still has his inner integrity. Can he still look into the shaving-glass of a morning? Then he is still on his two legs in this world, and ready even for the Devil. We sweated a great deal, discussing these lofty matters. We seemed to get nowhere.

Suddenly it dawned upon me—I was too dull or it was too hot for me to see it sooner—that what we were talking about was really not what we were talking about at all. I began to observe Valentino more closely. A curiously naïve and boyish young fellow, certainly not much beyond thirty, and with a disarming air of inexperience. To my eye, at least, not handsome, but nevertheless rather attractive. There was some obvious fineness in him; even his clothes were not precisely those of his horrible trade. He began talking of his home, his people, his early youth. His words were simple and yet somehow very eloquent. I could still see the mime before me, but now and then, briefly and darkly, there was a flash of something else. That something else, I concluded, was what is commonly called, for want of a better name, a gentleman. In brief, Valentino's agony was the agony of a man of relatively civilized feelings thrown into a situation of intolerable vulgarity, destructive alike to his peace and to his dignity—nay, into a whole series of such situations.

It was not that trifling Chicago episode that was riding him; it was the whole grotesque futility of his life. Had he achieved, out of nothing, a vast and dizzy success? Then that success was hollow as well as vast—a colossal and preposterous nothing. Was he acclaimed by yelling multitudes? Then every time the multitudes yelled he felt himself blushing inside. The old story of Diego Valdez once more, but with a new poignancy in it. Valdez, at all events, was High Admiral of Spain. But Valentino, with his touch of fineness in him—he had his commonness, too, but there was that touch of fineness—Valentino was only the hero of the rabble. Imbeciles surrounded him in a dense herd. He was pursued by women—but what women! (Consider the sordid comedy of his two marriages—the brummagem, star-spangled passion that invaded his very death-bed!) The thing, at the start, must have only bewildered him. But in those last days, unless I am a worse psychologist than even the professors of psychology, it was revolting him. Worse, it was making him afraid.

I incline to think that the inscrutable gods, in taking him off so soon and at a moment of fiery revolt, were very kind to him. Living, he would have tried inevitably to change his fame—if such it is to be called—into something closer to his heart's desire. That is to say, he would have gone the way of many another actor—the way of increasing pretension, of solemn artiness, of hollow hocus-pocus, deceptive only to himself. I believe he would have failed, for there was little sign of the genuine artist in him. He was essentially a highly respectable young man, which is the sort that never metamorphoses into an artist. But suppose he had succeeded? Then his tragedy, I believe, would have only become the more acrid and intolerable. For he would have discovered, after vast heavings and yearnings, that what he had come to was indistinguishable from what he had left. Was the fame of Beethoven any more caressing and splendid than the fame of Valentino? To you and me, of course, the question seems to answer itself. But what of Beethoven? He was heard upon the subject, *viva voce,* while he lived, and his answer survives, in all the freshness of its profane eloquence, in his music. Beethoven, too, knew what it meant to be applauded. Walking with Goethe, he heard something that was not unlike the murmur that reached Valentino through his hospital window. Beethoven walked away briskly. Valentino turned his face to the wall.

Here was a young man who was living daily the dream of millions of other young men. Here was one who was catnip to women. Here was one who had wealth and fame. And here was one who was very unhappy.

Suggestions

1. "Valentino" manages to give a vivid impression of its main character by concentrating on just one of his traits: his sense of honor. It thus affords a striking example of *selectivity*.[1] But the characterization is not all; the essay also expresses the speaker's attitude toward Valentino's profession and toward the society that elevated him, an actor of limited ability, to a "vast and dizzy success." Clearly a thesis is present concerning the lack of taste and integrity in the United States—but this is subordinate to the speaker's sympathetic interest in Valentino and to the theme that emerges near the end. The theme is one of the most familiar in literature: the discrepancy between what we expect from life and what we receive. In following these changes of subject we are helped by the shifts of *tone*: from the straightforward estimate of Valentino, to the sarcastic humor of the attack on actors and American standards, to the serious, even melancholy tone of the last paragraph.

2. Notice that "Valentino" is complicated but not disunified, since the central character provides a sort of launching-platform for the thesis, as well as being a sad example of the young man who is made unhappy by the realization of his dreams of happiness.

3. Study the concrete details that establish the temperature of the hotel room, and point out the *hyperbole,* the humorous exaggeration, in this paragraph. Besides contributing to the humor of the essay, this passage lends support to both the thesis and the theme. The discomfort of the luxurious hotel parallels Valentino's disappointment in his career and in American life.

4. The thesis and theme are further supported by the *allusions* to Diego Valdez and to Beethoven. In order to feel the force of the second one we must understand the *rhetorical question,* "Was the fame of Beethoven any more caressing and splendid than the fame of Valentino?" This evidently implies, "A thousand times more so"—yet Beethoven looked upon the public with scorn, just as Valentino finally would.

5. Structurally "Valentino" follows the second method of beginning described on page 31. Analyze the way in which this narrative beginning catches the reader's interest and prepares him for the reception of the thesis.

6. The most important transitional expression is the *paradox* at the beginning of ¶5. It means that Mencken had misunderstood Valentino because he had taken Valentino's words at face value instead of making inferences about their deeper meaning. Relate this explanation both to your definition of *paradox* and to the structural importance of this sentence in the essay.

---

[1] In studying these and other *Suggestions* be particularly sure that you understand the italicized terms, even if that should mean using your dictionary.

7. Point out other transitions between paragraphs: e.g., show how the second word in ¶3 links it to ¶1.

8. Explain: *instance, disinterested, hot-weather editorial, dudgeon, mime, viva voce.*

9. Discuss the truth of Mencken's contention about the significance of the word *honor* in the United States.

10. By recalling acquaintances and historical figures, decide whether Valentino's disappointment with fame and fortune is a common experience.

A TIGRESS

JACK LAWSON ---✠   *From* A MAN'S LIFE *by kind permission of Hodder & Stoughton.*

I have spoken at length of my father so that you might understand what a contrast he was to my mother. He was broad-minded, strict in discipline, yet gentle. She was powerful in body, passionate, with a lava-heated, ungovernable temper, narrow-minded, never forgiving an injury or fancied wrong—and they were often fancied. She was absolutely illiterate, and a very dominant woman. The temper of the two often clashed, yet they were a devoted couple—devoted in a very moving way, as I shall show later. If I draw a picture of her which may seem doubtfully dutiful in a son, it is not only because I want to give a faithful portrait, but also because I think it is necessary to a proper understanding of the wild, rugged, forceful personality which alone enabled her to conquer conditions which would have overwhelmed the average mother. For she was a great mother. Her punishments were sometimes unmerited because they were the result of the temper which swept her before it. She was a tigress who punished at times almost to the point of cruelty; but if she struck her cubs with her claws now and then, she stood on duty at the lair with bared teeth and snarling lips ready to fight to the death for her own. She faced the world in her primitive way. She never fondled or kissed any of us that I remember, for she clearly regarded these things as weakness. Sometimes a gentle mood would come over her, and those rare moments of distant affection remain with me. She had her rigid code of conduct, which she enforced on herself and others: fight your battles and no whining, tell the truth, pay your debts, and so conduct yourself

that you need never be ashamed. We received the blow, and often had
to find out for ourselves what it was for. Perhaps it was from the hand
and perhaps it was from the handiest thing she could lay hold of. But let
anyone else dare to hurt us, man or woman, and there was trouble. No
neighbor who crossed her once ever repeated the mistake. Once, when
we had gone to Durham, I was well thrashed by a boy in the same street,
and my face bore testimony to it. Stern enquiry by my mother brought
out the story, and I was further thrashed and chased out to redeem the
family honor. Driven to desperation, I rushed upon the boy in the street
and engaged him in such a way that the tables were being turned when I
was seized from behind by his father. Kicking and raging, I was suddenly
dropped, and rushed into battle again. But in a little while my opponent
seemed more interested in something else than me. And on looking
round, there was my mother standing toe to toe fighting the boy's father
in man style. I can see her now, her dark brown hair rather loose in the
coil, with gleaming eyes, and grim, granite-like face, slogging like a
regular fighter. The street was out of doors to see the battle; the man
was furious at being so exposed, but my mother's strength and angry
attacks engaged him seriously. Never for a moment was I concerned for
mother, for to me the fight could only have one end—mother would
win, for she had always won. And I was proud of her all-conquering
powers. It was a great fight until neighbors interfered and ended it. My
mother was Savage by name and she was savage by nature. She came of
a race of giants on her mother's side—the Grahams of Cockermouth—
famed in Border history as a race of wrestlers. And she was worthy of
them, for she wrestled with poverty and hunger that her children might
be fed and clothed. When I remember that she brought up ten of us
children in days of scanty wages and scanty work, when there was no
help in sickness or unemployment, when few cared whether you lived
or died; when I remember her almost fierce independence of spirit, and
that we all survived strong in body, I am proud of that mother who
said to me in her old age:

"I punished you, I was rough, I was ignorant, but I brought you all
through safely, and I never did a thing of which any of you might be
ashamed."

And I replied: "Mother, there is much education today and what
men call culture. But there were not many who can show such a record
as you; few mothers as good, and none better."

I can see her yet, in the Kells days, coming up the steep road from
the beach below, where she had been to gather coals to keep our fire going. There she came, body bent, waddling like some strange animal, with
a great bag of coal on her back which she had carried more than a mile
up a terrific incline. Then I see her when she has reached the allotted
span of three score years and ten, gentled by time, humble, proud of

her own, outside the fierce arena of life, a real Joan with her Darby in a little miner's home where tender affection and dear delight in each other charmed and held all who beheld them.

And, looking now on the results in the light of long experience, if I had to choose between the mother who is indulgent to the point of softness and my mother's stern discipline and unbridled temper, I would a thousand times over plump for my own mother. For, as I used to tell her in later years when, with a twinkle in her eyes, she used to boast she had "walloped" me: "Yes, Mother, and I sometimes think that was the best part of my education." And I think there is more than a grain of truth in that, for discipline is good—and, anyhow, it is often the things we don't like that are best for us.

Suggestions

1. Although much of Lawson's portrait of his mother consists of general statements about her, it is enlivened mainly by two scenes depicting her at different periods of her life. The details of these scenes should be carefully examined and contrasted. They may then be related to the question of *sentimentality,* a danger that is peculiarly acute when a writer is describing his mother.

2. Explain the speaker's admission (in the sixth sentence) that his frankness "may seem doubtfully dutiful." Do you blame him for it? What two reasons for it does he give?

3. Evaluate the allusion to Darby and Joan (an elderly, devoted couple in an eighteenth-century song) as a means of (a) being brief, and (b) avoiding sentimentality.

4. Formulate the speaker's thesis about the discipline of children. Is it dwelt on at too great length?

5. List the qualities of his mother's character with which the speaker finds fault.

6. In writing an essay about one or both of your parents, consider using Lawson's first sentence as a launching-pad. That is, confine yourself to the ways in which your father's character contrasts with that of your mother.

7. Before writing your essay, make notes on the methods by which you will avoid being overly sentimental.

SNAPSHOT OF A DOG

JAMES THURBER ⸺ *Permission the author; © 1935, The New Yorker Magazine, Inc.*

I ran across a dim photograph of him the other day, going through some old things. He's been dead twenty-five years. His name was Rex (my two brothers and I named him when we were in our early teens) and he was a bull terrier. "An American bull terrier," we used to say, proudly; none of your English bulls. He had one brindle eye that sometimes made him look like a clown and sometimes reminded you of a politician with derby hat and cigar. The rest of him was white except for a brindle saddle that always seemed to be slipping off and a brindle stocking on a hind leg. Nevertheless, there was a nobility about him. He was big and muscular and beautifully made. He never lost his dignity even when trying to accomplish the extravagant tasks my brothers and myself used to set for him. One of these was the bringing of a ten-foot wooden rail into the yard through the back gate. We would throw it out into the alley and tell him to go get it. Rex was as powerful as a wrestler, and there were not many things that he couldn't manage somehow to get hold of with his great jaws and lift or drag to wherever he wanted to put them, or wherever we wanted them put. He could catch the rail at the balance and lift it clear of the ground and trot with great confidence toward the gate. Of course, since the gate was only four feet wide or so, he couldn't bring the rail in broadside. He found that out when he got a few terrific jolts, but he wouldn't give up. He finally figured out how to do it, by dragging the rail, holding onto one end, growling. He got a great, wagging satisfaction out of his work. We used to bet kids who had never seen Rex in action that he could catch a baseball thrown as high as they could throw it. He almost never let us down. Rex could hold a baseball with ease in his mouth, in one cheek, as if it were a chew of tobacco.

He was a tremendous fighter, but he never started fights. I don't believe he liked to get into them, despite the fact that he came from a line of fighters. He never went for another dog's throat but for one of its ears (that teaches a dog a lesson), and he would get his grip, close his eyes, and hold on. He could hold on for hours. His longest fight lasted from dusk until almost pitch-dark, one Sunday. It was fought in East Main Street in Columbus with a large, snarly nondescript that belonged to a big colored man. When Rex finally got his ear grip, the brief whirlwind of snarling turned to screeching. It was frightening to listen to and to watch. The Negro boldly picked the dogs up somehow and began swinging them around his head, and finally let them fly like a hammer in a hammer throw, but although they landed ten feet away with a great plump, Rex still held on.

The two dogs eventually worked their way to the middle of the car tracks, and after a while two or three streetcars were held up by the fight. A motorman tried to pry Rex's jaws open with a switch rod; somebody lighted a fire and made a torch of a stick and held that to Rex's tail, but he paid no attention. In the end, all the residents and storekeepers in the neighborhood were on hand, shouting this, suggesting that. Rex's joy of battle, when battle was joined, was almost tranquil. He had a kind of pleasant expression during fights, not a vicious one, his eyes closed in what would have seemed to be sleep had it not been for the turmoil of the struggle. The Oak Street Fire Department finally had to be sent for—I don't know why nobody thought of it sooner. Five or six pieces of apparatus arrived, followed by a battalion chief. A hose was attached and a powerful stream of water was turned on the dogs. Rex held on for several moments more while the torrent buffeted him about like a log in a freshet. He was a hundred yards away from where the fight started when he finally let go.

The story of that Homeric fight got all around town, and some of our relatives looked upon the incident as a blot on the family name. They insisted that we get rid of Rex, but we were very happy with him, and nobody could have made us give him up. We would have left town with him first, along any road there was to go. It would have been different, perhaps, if he'd ever started fights, or looked for trouble. But he had a gentle disposition. He never bit a person in the ten strenuous years that he lived, nor ever growled at anyone except prowlers. He killed cats, that is true, but quickly and neatly and without especial malice, the way men kill certain animals. It was the only thing he did that we could never cure him of doing. He never killed, or even chased, a squirrel. I don't know why. He had his own philosophy about such things. He never ran barking after wagons or automobiles. He didn't seem to see the idea in pursuing something you couldn't catch, or something you couldn't do anything with, even if you did catch it. A wagon was one of the things he couldn't tug along with his mighty jaws, and he knew it. Wagons, therefore, were not a part of his world.

Swimming was his favorite recreation. The first time he ever saw a body of water (Alum Creek), he trotted nervously along the steep bank for a while, fell to barking wildly, and finally plunged in from a height of eight feet or more. I shall always remember that shining, virgin dive. Then he swam upstream and back just for the pleasure of it, like a man. It was fun to see him battle upstream against a stiff current, struggling and growling every foot of the way. He had as much fun in the water as any person I have known. You didn't have to throw a stick in the water to get him to go in. Of course, he would bring back a stick to you if you did throw one in. He would even have brought back a piano if you had thrown one in.

That reminds me of the night, way after midnight, when he went a-roving in the light of the moon and brought back a small chest of drawers that he found somewhere—how far from the house nobody ever knew; since it was Rex, it could easily have been half a mile. There were no drawers in the chest when he got it home, and it wasn't a good one—he hadn't taken it out of anybody's house; it was just an old cheap piece that somebody had abandoned on a trash heap. Still, it was something he wanted, probably because it presented a nice problem in transportation. It tested his mettle. We first knew about his achievement when, deep in the night, we heard him trying to get the chest up onto the porch. It sounded as if two or three people were trying to tear the house down. We came downstairs and turned on the porch light. Rex was on the top step trying to pull the thing up, but it had caught somehow and he was just holding his own. I suppose he would have held his own till dawn if we hadn't helped him. The next day we carted the chest miles away and threw it out. If we had thrown it out in a nearby alley, he would have brought it home again, as a small token of his integrity in such matters. After all, he had been taught to carry heavy wooden objects about, and he was proud of his prowess.

I am glad Rex never saw a trained police dog jump. He was just an amateur jumper himself, but the most daring and tenacious I have ever seen. He would take on any fence we pointed out to him. Six feet was easy for him, and he could do eight by making a tremendous leap and hauling himself over finally by his paws, grunting and straining; but he lived and died without knowing that twelve- and sixteen-foot walls were too much for him. Frequently, after letting him try to go over one for a while, we would have to carry him home. He would never have given up trying.

There was in his world no such thing as the impossible. Even death couldn't beat him down. He died, it is true, but only, as one of his admirers said, after "straight-arming the death angel" for more than an hour. Late one afternoon he wandered home, too slowly and too uncertainly to be the Rex that had trotted briskly homeward up our avenue for ten years. I think we all knew when he came through the gate that he was dying. He had apparently taken a terrible beating, probably from the owner of some dog that he had got into a fight with. His head and body were scarred. His heavy collar with the teeth marks of many a battle on it was awry; some of the big brass studs in it were sprung loose from the leather. He licked at our hands and, staggering, fell, but got up again. We could see that he was looking for someone. One of his three masters was not home. He did not get home for an hour. During that hour the bull terrier fought against death as he had fought against the cold, strong current of Alum Creek, as he had fought to climb twelve-foot walls. When the person he was waiting for did come through the gate, whistling, ceasing to whistle, Rex walked a few wabbly paces toward him, touched his hand with his muzzle, and fell down again. This time he didn't get up.

Suggestions

1. Most successful writing about animals as individuals involves *personification*. In "Snapshot of a Dog," for instance, the proper names at the beginning of the passage about the dogfight suggest an account of a professional boxing-match. Later the fight is called "Homeric." (Can you explain the *allusion?*) Such expressions may be regarded as a kind of *hyperbole*. What do you consider the most extreme example of hyperbole in the essay? Show by examples the importance of these and other figures of speech in creating the humorous tone.

2. Hyperboles, which are not to be taken literally, must be distinguished from exaggerations that are meant to be believed. Do you at any time suspect the speaker of exaggerating Rex's prowess? Discuss in detail.

3. Does the speaker's affection for Rex seem excessive? If he concedes that Rex had any faults, point them out.

4. Decide whether the title suits the essay—and notice that "Snapshot" is a *metaphor*. Does this title necessitate a description of Rex's physical appearance? Single out the details that make Rex vivid as a bull terrier.

5. Identify the master whom Rex is waiting for in the last paragraph. Does this paragraph make a suitable conclusion for a humorous essay?

6. Write a "snapshot" of a pet animal, treating him as though he were a person. (Guard against sentimentality.)

7. Or else, disclaiming any intention to personify, write about the pet purely as an animal.

"PRROU"

COLETTE

From CREATURES GREAT AND SMALL, trans. by Enid McLeod. © 1957. Used by permission of the publishers, Farrar, Straus and Cudahy, Inc.

When I made her acquaintance she was living in a dingy old garden, long and narrow as a drawer, that had been forgotten between two new buildings. Being afraid of dogs and men, she only went out at night, when she would rummage in trash-cans. When it rained she used to squeeze herself between the iron grating of a cellar and the dusty panes of its ventilator; but the rain would quickly reach her refuge and then she would patiently tuck her paws in under her, the thin paws of the homeless cat, slender and hard as those of a hare.

She would stay there for hours at a time, now and again lifting her eyes to the sky or toward my raised curtain. Since her misery was not accidental, she did not look scared or wretched. She knew my face but she never begged, and all I could read in her expression was the weariness of being hungry and cold and wet, and a patient waiting for the sun which momentarily lulls and heals stray creatures.

I made my way three or four times into the old garden, catching my skirt on the slats of the fence. The cat did not run away at my approach, but she always slithered away like an eel at the very moment when I thought she was under my hand. After I had gone, she bravely managed to wait until what breeze there was in the old garden had wafted away my scent and the echo of my footsteps. Then she would eat the meat I had left near the ventilator, betraying her haste only by the gulping movement of her neck and the twitching of her spine.

She did not give in right away to the sleep that overcomes animals when they have eaten their fill; she would first try to make herself a little cleaner, smoothing her gray coat with its black stripes, a poor, dull, scruffy coat, for cats who do not eat do not wash either, having little saliva.

When February came, the old garden behind its iron railings looked like a cage full of small, wild animals. There were tomcats from cellars and garrets, from the fortifications and vacant lots, their spines like strings of beads and the fur of their necks rubbed as though they had escaped from the hangman's rope; hunting tomcats without ears or tail, the dread enemies of rats; tomcats from the grocer's and the dairy, randy and fat, heavy and soon out of breath; black tomcats with cherry-colored ribbons round their necks and white tomcats with collars of blue beads.

I used to listen at night to their songs of love and battle. First a faint, musical lament, sweet, long-drawn-out, and distant. Then, to provoke the rival, an ironic call, answered immediately in the same tone. This is the prelude to an interminable dialogue, with no other action than the play of ears now flattened and now pricked up, eyes alternately closed and opened, the baring of teeth in an expressive threatening smile, and an occasional snorting through the nostrils between two insulting replies. Then suddenly hoarse voices rise in an unexpected and terrifying crescendo, infuriated caterwauls and screechings mingling in the air like the voices of two frightful demons borne along in an approaching thunder-cloud. Then silence, the night wind in the little garden, claws combing the bark of a tree, and the gentle song of the she-cat, the indifferent she-cat for whose sake the males have just been tearing each other to pieces, the voice of my poor little skinny she-cat, quite worn out from love and malnutrition.

This tragic and voluptuous hurricane died down at last, and when I saw the drab and emaciated gray cat again she was more timid than ever, and trembled at every sound. In the ray of sunlight which at noon penetrated the depths of the dark garden, she dragged her swollen flanks along, heavier every day, until the wet morning when I found her, feverish, conquered at last, suckling five tough little kittens, born, as she had been, on the bare ground.

I had been looking forward to that moment, and so had she. All I had to do was to gather up the little ones in my skirt, and the mother followed me.

Her name is "Prrou," and roll the r's, if you please. It was she who told us her name. She coos it all day long over the black kitten we let her keep: "Prrou, prrou. . . ."

She lives in Brittany, on a warm terrace bordering a field which slopes down to the shore. She has herself fixed the limits of her domain, which extends from the steps to the hedge of flowering privet hiding the brick wall. She never goes farther than the big lime-trees which cast their shadow over my house of russet stone. Does she know that below the terrace there tosses unceasingly an ever-changing sea, blue and green in the sunlight, purplish under a storm and mauve at daybreak? I doubt it.

Although we ask nothing of her, Prrou in her modest coat is determined to set us an example of the dreariest virtues. She is clean and gentle and humble, and she brings up her only son most creditably. She does better than that: she *fools* us all. With exquisite tact and a cunning that you never suspect, she manages always to remain "the poor thing who used to be so unhappy." Fat and sleek as she now is, she still has the timid glance of the half-starved cat, and the cook calls her "poor creature."

She sleeps on a downy cushion, but in the huddled position of those who sleep outdoors. She shrinks aside to let us pass, and we immediately draw back ourselves, our hearts torn with pity, beseeching her not to disturb herself. If we happen to step on the extremity of her paw or the tip of her tail, she gives a quick, hoarse cry and then purrs stoically, with a look of martyrdom in her eyes, while we murmur: "Poor creature! To think we should have done that to her, *who used to be so unhappy!*"

Under the low branch of the lime-tree, a cork hangs at the end of a piece of string and swings in the breeze. Prrou keeps an eye on it and sometimes, in a fit of mad playfulness, she springs at it; but if she catches sight of us, her triangular face at once assumes an expression of renunciation and sadness, as if to say: "Whatever am I doing? To think I was nearly guilty of such frivolous conduct, I *who used to be so unhappy!* Games of that kind a're not for such as me. Alas, I nearly forgot it."

She broods passionately over her unkempt and diabolical black son, caressing him with her gestures and with the only word she knows: "Prrou, prrou. . . ." But she has only to catch sight of us to turn on him and scare the life out of him with a dozen smart cuffs of her whip-like paw, a grim look on her face, as if to say: "That's the way we bring up foundlings where I come from!"

You must admit the crafty Prrou deserves admiration. See how her close-fitting, short-haired coat imitates the colors of the gray slug and the markings of the twilight moth. Across her chest lies a triple necklace of jet, like the sober ornament of a lady-bountiful. The bracelets round her slender paws are black too, and so is the row of regular spots, which look as though they are buttoning her tight-fitting coat down the stomach. Prrou is more than clothed; she is disguised.

Her deportment is so modest and her fur of so discreet a shade that you might fail to notice the cruel hardness of her wide skull, her formidable, nervous paws set with curved claws in perfect fighting trim, her well developed chest and supple loins—in a word, all the hidden beauty of this solid beast, who is made for love and slaughter.

Suggestions

1. Like Rex, Prrou is personified, but only in the second half of the essay. Partly for this reason, she appears to be presented more objectively than Rex is. Identify the point at which *personification* begins. Do you find other kinds of *hyperbole* in "Prrou," or suspect the speaker at any time of exaggeration?

2. Decide whether "Snapshot of a Cat" would make a suitable title for "Prrou." What part do figures of speech play in the cat's physical description?

3. The speaker's matter-of-fact tone may seem inappropriate to an essay on a pet. Nevertheless, what evidence of her fondness for Prrou can you point out?

4. If "Prrou" is a humorous essay, the main reason is the satiric touches in its second half, which make fun of the speaker and her cook as much as they make fun of the cat. In which essay, "Snapshot of a Dog" or "Prrou," is the speaker more sharply characterized? Write a character-sketch of Prrou's owner.

5. To what extent does Prrou typify all felines? to a greater extent than Rex typifies bulldogs? Write an essay comparing Colette's attitude toward cats with your own. Include in it a comment on the concluding words, showing how earlier passages prepare for them.

HARDING

HERBERT AGAR ---◄{

From THE PEOPLE'S CHOICE *by Herbert Agar.* © *1933 by Houghton Mifflin Company.*

Warren Gamaliel Harding was born in Ohio in 1865. His father was a farmer, and later became a physician. Harding attended the local school and the Ohio Central College—which was an advanced secondary school, not an institute of higher learning. After trying, and abandoning, the study of law, Harding got a job on one of the weekly newspapers in Marion, a town of about four thousand inhabitants. A little later he and a friend bought a moribund weekly paper for three hundred dollars, and within a few years Harding had made this a paying venture.

In 1891, Harding married Mrs. Florence Kling De Wolfe, a widow. Her father was a banker, and apparently a man of some discernment, for he opposed the match. Harding, by this time, was a strikingly handsome man—tall and strong-looking, good-natured, affectionate, and weak. He had a reputation for dissipation, but that is probably too strong a word to use for his activities. Shortly after his marriage, Harding transformed the *Star* from a weekly into a daily paper. It continued to prosper, and Harding became a man of some importance in the little town, and also in the local Republican Party. He was soon a director of the Marion County Bank, a trustee of the Baptist Church, a Mason, and an Elk.

In addition to good looks, Harding had a strong, effective voice. As a result of these physical assets, and of the political position that his editorship gained him, he began to take part in local campaigns. At the close of the century, he was sent to the State Senate, and at about the same time he met Harry Daugherty—the man who was to make him President and then to ruin him. In 1902, Harding was elected Lieutenant-Governor of Ohio. In 1910, he was the Republican candidate for Governor, but was defeated. In 1914, with the help of Daugherty and his political "gang," he was elected to the United States Senate.

In the Senate, Harding was "regular" and safe. He never said or did anything that attracted attention, but he was a friend of Big Business and a partisan anti-Wilson man. Also, he was a good friend of the Anti-Saloon League, supporting the Eighteenth Amendment (which was passed on the wave of moral uplift that accompanied the War) and the Volstead Act, and making useful suggestions for overcoming opposition to these measures. Aside from his official record, Harding was soon known to be an enthusiastic drinker and gambler, and a man of genuine good-nature who made friends quickly among the unexacting. What was not so well

55

known was that in 1917 a woman named Nan Britton became his mistress, and that in 1919 Harding and Nan Britton had a daughter. This, however, is probably the reason why he was elected President a year later.

It was in 1919 that Harry Daugherty, political organizer, spoils-man, and head of the "Ohio Gang," began to push Harding for the Presidency. He had no popular support in the primaries, not even winning the entire delegation from his own state. Yet Daugherty insolently predicted that after a long deadlock in the Nominating Convention, at two o'clock some morning, a little group of the real Republican leaders would meet in a smoke-filled hotel room and would decide to make Harding the party's nominee. And this is exactly what happened. In the early ballots at the Convention, Harding was nowhere; but after a long struggle there was an early-morning meeting in the hotel room of Colonel George Harvey, and it was decided to give Harding the nomination. His qualifications were that he was good-looking, that he sounded significant, that he meant nothing, and that he came from Ohio. The last point was important. Grant, Hayes, Garfield, Harrison, McKinley, Taft—most of the Republican Presidents had come from Ohio. It is not, unhappily, that only Ohio can produce the typical President; it is simply that Ohio, since the Civil War, has been a crucial state. Farther east, the Republicans felt safe; farther south, the Democrats were invincible; the West voted chiefly on the price of wheat, which could not easily be changed for the sake of the election; but Ohio was fairly divided between the two parties, so the Republicans usually chose a man who had shown that he could carry that state.

Before committing themselves to Harding, Harvey and his fellow-oligarchs showed their knowledge of Washington gossip by calling their prospective candidate before them and asking if there were any reason in his past life why he should not be nominated. Rightly considering that Nan Britton and her daughter belonged to his present rather than his past life, Harding answered no. He was nominated the same day. Harvey's comment was, "He was nominated because there was nothing against him, and because the delegates wanted to go home." In judging that there was nothing against Harding, Colonel Harvey showed the same acumen that had led him to pick Wilson as an easy man to use.

The League of Nations was the ostensible campaign issue. In fact, the League was a symbol for the high purpose, the whole atmosphere of effort and uplift, for which the Progressives had stood, and of which the nation was tired. The return to national isolation, which the repudiation of the League involved, was felt to mean a return to the old days of slackness and *laissez-faire* which had preceded Roosevelt. Senator Brandegee remarked that the time did not require "first-raters." Harding, with his one creative effort in the realm of the spirit, coined the word "normalcy" to express the general desire. "Back to normalcy" was the phrase that summed up the American temper. Harding was elected by a huge majority.

The new Cabinet contained some respected men, like Hughes, Mr. Hoover, and Mr. Mellon, and some cheap politicians like Daugherty and Fall. Below the Cabinet officers there were evil, disquieting figures, such as Charles R. Forbes, the head of the Veterans' Bureau, and Colonel Miller, the Alien Property Custodian. And below them there was a worse group still: hangers-on and go-betweens of whom the public as yet knew nothing. Within a month of Harding's inauguration, the whole atmosphere of Washington had changed. Both officially and socially, the tone became relaxed, care-free, abandoned.

The chief Administration policies were dictated by the Senatorial clique and by the three leading men in the Cabinet. The adoption of a National Budget—a reform which had been brought almost to completion under Wilson—and the Washington Conference are the achievements of which the Administration could be most proud. Meanwhile, behind the scenes, there was taking place a series of steals more wild, quick, brazen, and bizarre than anything that had yet happened in America. Harding, being a man without courage or character, was powerless. The "Ohio Gang" owned him. With Daugherty as Attorney-General and Fall as Secretary of the Interior, and with Nan Britton and the baby to use in blackmailing Harding if, having learned too much of what was going on, he tried to interfere, they seemed safe. It is a sign of the grade of character these men possessed that they soon overplayed their hands so grossly that suicide, murder, or jail was the end of many of them.

Two months after his inauguration, Harding signed an order transferring the naval oil reserves from the control of the Navy Department to that of the Department of the Interior, over which Fall ruled. The game was under way. A little later, when leases of great value were made to the Doheny and Sinclair oil interests, and the Senate threatened an investigation into why this had been done, Harding announced that he entirely approved of the acts of the Department of the Interior. Meanwhile, the Department of Justice was blackmailing violators of the Prohibition law, making them pay bribes as an alternative to prosecution; and the Director of the Veterans' Bureau and the Alien Property Custodian were looting on a scale and with an openness that suggested insanity. The quality of what was going on may be suggested by the subsequent history of the chief actors: Attorney-General Daugherty was twice tried upon criminal charges but the juries failed to agree on a verdict; Secretary Fall was sent to prison; Forbes and Miller were sent to prison; Jess Smith, chief collector of blackmail for the Department of Justice, committed suicide (or possibly was murdered); C. F. Cramer, the attorney for the Veterans' Bureau, committed suicide; Thurston, an attorney who helped expedite the Alien Property Custodian cases, died suddenly; John T. King, indicted with Miller and Daugherty in an Alien Property Custodian case, died suddenly; C. F. Hateley, undercover agent for the Department of Justice and special emissary for Daugherty, died suddenly.

The strangest of these sudden deaths, however, was that of President Harding. In June, 1923, he and his wife and a large party left Washington for a trip to Alaska.[1] Newspapermen accompanying the party noticed that the President was worried and anxious. In Kansas City he had an interview with the wife of Secretary Fall, after which his anxiety was noticeably greater. While in Alaska he received a long code message from Washington, and for the next two days he appeared to be on the verge of a collapse. Shortly after this, he asked some of his friends among the reporters what a President could do when he had been betrayed. On returning to the United States, he was said to be suffering from ptomaine poisoning. Five days later, in San Francisco, he died suddenly. The cause was said to be an embolism, but the newspaper accounts at the time were confused and contradictory—even on the question as to whether General Sawyer, Harding's personal physician, was with him at the time of his death, or whether Harding was alone with his wife.[2]

Had Harding lived a few months longer, he would have been impeached, and the scandal would, for the time at least, have destroyed the Republican Party, and would have dragged down several of the important men who sat in the Harding Cabinet and who spoke no word, although all Washington suspected what was happening. Harding undoubtedly knew what lay before him. It has been alleged that he told his wife he intended to escape with Nan Britton and the child, and that she, to save his reputation and the party, and to serve her own jealousy, murdered him. It has also been suggested, with more likelihood, that Harding had the courage to kill himself. Or he may have died of a timely embolism.

The important point about the Harding régime is the indifference of the American public to the scandals that resulted. Vice-President Coolidge, who sat mum while the evil work was done, was elected President in 1924. And the man who succeeded him, in 1928, had been a member of Harding's Cabinet, and had not felt called upon either to draw attention to what was going on about him, or to resign from the little group of thieves to which he had been appointed.

---

[1] Shortly before starting on this trip, he is alleged to have told his sister that he did not expect to return.

[2] It is an interesting fact that about a year later, when Mrs. Harding was visiting General Sawyer at his home in Ohio, he, too, died suddenly—*The New York Times* commenting that "General Sawyer's death was almost identical with the manner of death of the late Warren G. Harding."

Suggestions

1. "Harding" differs from the essays before it in that its author did not know his subject personally; it is an essay in contemporary history. Yet it is not a mere presentation of facts—facts are introduced only as needed to justify the speaker's emotion. (Notice how swiftly and in what general terms the scandals of the administration are summarized.) The speaker's contempt for Harding is as marked as Lawson's devotion to his mother or Thurber's fondness for Rex, and its expression involves the usual weapons of the satirist: *sarcasm, innuendo,* and *irony.* Can you point out the sentence in which the attitude is first manifested?

2. Explain: "This, however, is probably the reason why he was elected President a year later" (¶ 4).

3. Explain the irony in the reference to Colonel Harvey's acumen.

4. List the personal qualities of Harding that made him a popular candidate, and the qualities that made him an unsuitable one.

5. Analyze the sarcasm that prefaces the introduction of Harding's phrase "Back to normalcy." Has the coinage any advantage over the established word *normal?*

6. Count the number of persons who are said to have "died suddenly." What is the effect of this repetition?

7. Relating "Harding" to the title of the book from which it is taken, show that its satire has a greater target than simply the character of the President.

8. Describe the speaker's tone, assuming that it is typified by "a series of steals . . . wild, quick, brazen, and bizarre."

9. Write an account of the death of Harding, agreeing or disagreeing with the explanation of it that the essay considers most probable.

10. Before writing an essay on a historical figure or contemporary celebrity, state the attitude toward him that you will express. Include only facts that support your attitude.

THE GENERAL WHO WALKED
ON THE GRASS

DAVID WAGONER —◄{

Jacob Sechler Coxey was a general who never wore a uniform (he preferred a swallowtail coat, a foulard tie, a wing collar, and a black homburg), but he was called "General" so often by serious friends and amused newspapermen that he finally accepted the title. And when he walked through the mud and melting snow and climbed into his carriage on Easter morning, 1894, and headed up Main Street of Massillon, Ohio, he rode in the midst of a ragged group of unemployed workingmen, already known throughout the country as "Coxey's Army." Their destination was Washington; their slogan, on banners and placards, was "Good Roads, Fiat Money, and Work for the Unemployed."

This man, who in later years was to befriend the official King of the Hoboes, was anything but a tramp himself. He was a rich man, an owner of extensive property including a stone quarry and an arsenic mine, a breeder of thoroughbred horses, a respected if puzzling member of Ohio society. He frequently demonstrated his liking for good cigars and vintage wines; he spoke in educated accents and wore his silver-rimmed spectacles with the set precision of a banker. When he tipped his hat to the ladies and gentlemen of Massillon, the air around him crackled with money, dignity, and social position.

Yet from that morning on, and for years afterward, Coxey did his best to throw away all three. He became the outspoken foe of what he called "confidence money" and urged the government to issue legal tender by fiat directly to the people; he slated the "boodlers and bankers" responsible for interest-bearing bonds (the main source of economic misery, according to Coxey); and he surrounded himself, to the dismay and glee of editors, politicians, and policemen, with what were surely some of the more notable eccentrics of any era: Carl Browne, a cartoonist and agitator for Populist causes who wore a Buffalo Bill costume and was known as "Old Greasey"; Cyclone Kirtland, an extremely loud astrologer; Douglas McCallum, author of a treatise called *Dogs and Fleas by One of the Dogs,* who wore a coat lined with unidentifiable fur; Honore Jackson, an apparently genuine half-breed Indian chief; Oklahoma Sam Pfrimmer, a trick rider; and "The Great Unknown" Smith whom the newspapers labeled at various times as an ex-ringmaster of a circus, a Secret Service man, the drillmaster of the Colorado National Guard, and a captain in the British Army—and who turned out to be a patent-medicineman from Chicago named Bozarro.

Led by these lieutenants, some of whom rode on Coxey's blooded horses, the Army marched through Pennsylvania and Maryland, much of the time in bitter weather. The now-famous "Petition in Boots" wore out its boots, suffered for lack of overcoats and gloves, lived chiefly on the charity of towns it passed through, and finally arrived in Washington with some four hundred members, many having joined it along the way. Coxey had tried hard to keep out what he called "Thieves, anarchists, drunks, and tramps" and succeeded to a remarkable degree. Referring to reports of alleged looting during the journey, he was able to say, "You cannot find so much as a chicken feather among my men," and he added that by cleaning the cigar butts out of the gutters of a hundred towns, his men had performed an act of notable civic service free of charge.

But the reform bills he had drawn up for passage by Congress were ignored. Those who opposed his ideas were able to smother them with the ridicule his aggregation of bums had produced. When, after a parade through Washington on the first of May, Coxey tried to give a speech on the steps of the Capitol, he and two of his lieutenants, the latter having been beaten by police billyclubs, were arrested for walking on the grass. The movement withered and died while the three spent twenty days in jail.

Much of what Coxey advocated, when he began the march with his infant son named Legal Tender in his arms, has since come to pass— public works, controlled inflation, municipal bond-issues with very low interest—but he was never acknowledged as the source. Although he led a similar army to Washington in 1914, appeared about to do so again in 1928, ran unsuccessfully for the Senate, became mayor of Massillon briefly in the Thirties, and kept turning out pamphlets and handbills on monetary reform, his single mark on the public imagination was the phrase to which he lent his name—"Coxey's Army"—used to describe any disorganized, disreputable group. And the man who led it and died fifty-seven years later in 1951 at the age of ninety-seven remained stuck in the 19th Century: a paradoxical figure, a wealthy man who argued for the poor, who spent the money he detested in order to publicize a new kind, who sought attention for his ideas through the laughter of others, only to be drowned out when the laughter became too loud.

Suggestions

1. Much shorter and apparently simpler than "Harding," "The General Who Walked on the Grass" is actually more complex. Whereas the speaker's attitude toward Harding is easily identified, this speaker's attitude toward Coxey is summarized in the phrase "a paradoxical figure" (last sentence). And *paradoxes* cause complications. Furthermore, the theme of "The General Who Walked on the Grass," though it may be readily found (at the beginning of the last paragraph), is hard to formulate. It is what comes to mind when we read that the steamboat

was at first known as "Fulton's Folly" and the purchase of Alaska as "Seward's Folly."

2. Defining *paradox* in your own words, enumerate the principal paradoxes in Coxey's career. Can you connect the title of the essay with this element in it?

3. Write a character-sketch of Coxey; e.g. what evidence is there that he had a sense of humor?

4. Write an essay entitled "If Coxey's Army Had Accomplished Its Mission."

5. Write an essay on the public's attitude toward Fulton, Seward, and Coxey.

6. Write an essay on some other paradoxical figure. (It is commonly believed that all human beings are paradoxical.)

THE BRAIN-CHILD OF SIR ARTHUR CONAN DOYLE

SYLVIA CAMPBELL ⸺ⓒ *1960 by Sylvia Campbell; reprinted by her permission.*

Sherlock Holmes is one of the most famous fictional characters ever to be created, and in the manner of Frankenstein and Don Quixote, he ran away with his creator, Sir Arthur Conan Doyle. Already a published author when he took his M.D. degree, Doyle later found it necessary to turn to writing for a good part of his income when his practice failed to materialize.[1]

For one of his novels Doyle chose a detective story. It was to be about "a man who had reduced the pursuit of criminals to an exact science." [2] This man was patterned after Joseph Bell, M.D., of Edinburgh, who used deductive reasoning to help in his diagnoses and to astound his students, and named after Oliver Wendell Holmes and a bowler whose name was Sherlock. But his personality was that of Doyle, who later played detective himself.[3] *A Study in Scarlet* was finished in April, 1886, and published at Christmas-time 1887.

[1] John Dickson Carr, *The Life of Sir Arthur Conan Doyle* (New York, 1949), p. 63.
[2] *Ibid.*, p. 45.
[3] Vincent Starrett, "Enter Mr. Sherlock Holmes," *Atlantic Monthly*, CL (July, 1932), 82. See also Vincent Starrett, "The Real Sherlock Holmes," *Golden Book Magazine*, XII (December, 1930), 81.

Two years later, *Lippincott's Magazine* asked for another Sherlock Holmes novel, and in 1890, *The Sign of Four* again brought Holmes into the public eye.[4] From then on, Doyle was never at peace with his creation. Fans and publishers demanded more stories of Holmes. Doyle set the price of a new series of short stories at 1000 pounds, hoping to discourage the *Strand Magazine,*[5] but the editors snapped up the offer, and in 1893 the *Memoirs of Sherlock Holmes* followed the very popular *Adventures of Sherlock Holmes* (1890).

Doyle was sick and tired of this detective who had gotten entirely out of hand,[6] and "The Final Problem," the last of the *Memoirs,* was devoted to the demise of Sherlock Holmes. In December 1893, the public learned of the untimely death of Holmes and protested loud and long.[7] Doyle was in Switzerland at the time, however, and missed the brunt of the clamor.

But the ghost of Sherlock Holmes would give Doyle no peace. Although he refused to revive Holmes, in 1897 he wrote the play *Sherlock Holmes,* which was produced in 1889 starring a perfect Holmes, William Gillette. In 1902, Doyle published the novel *The Hound of the Baskervilles,* and finally in 1905, he brought Holmes back to life in "The Adventure of the Empty House" by spinning a tale of escape up a sheer cliff and exile in Tibet. After 1907, Doyle wrote two more short stories and *The Valley of Fear,* and in 1926, he wrote *The Case Book of Sherlock Holmes,* the last stories of his dear enemy. Doyle died July 7, 1930.

Still Holmes lives on in the minds of his avid fans. Even when Doyle was alive, Holmes was a controversial character, and some people even believed he was really alive.[8] Now that Doyle is no longer on hand to defend himself, some people are trying to make Holmes more than just a fictional character.[9] But all are working to make him last forever.

Rufus Tucker treated Doyle as merely a literary agent for Watson in his "Genealogical Notes on Holmes," and even went to the trouble of writing out a family tree for the detective in order to prove his point that Holmes was a real live person. He forgot, though, that Micah Clarke, one of Holmes' "ancestors," was also a character from the pen of Dr. Doyle.[10]

Marvin Grasse stated and proved after a fashion that Watson and Mycroft, Sherlock's brother, not Moriarty, actually killed Holmes, and then primed another man to take his place at the critical moment. The

---

[4] Carr, p. 58.
[5] *Ibid.,* p. 69.
[6] *Ibid.,* p. 80.
[7] *Ibid.*
[8] Arthur Bartlett Maunce, "Forty Years of Sherlock Holmes," *Bookman,* LXVI (October, 1927), 160:
"Ten years or so ago Sir Arthur Conan Doyle was in the Argonne, a dinner guest of a number of French general officers. It was General Humbert who fixed the Englishman with his hard eyes and demanded: 'Sherlock Holmes, est-ce qu'il est un soldat dans l'armée anglaise?' There was an embarrassed moment. 'Mais, mon general,' stammered Doyle, 'il est trop vieux pour service.' "
[9] Edgar W. Smith, "Foreword," in ed. Edgar W. Smith, *Profile By Gaslight* (New York, 1944).
[10] Rufus S. Tucker, "Genealogical Notes on Holmes," in *Profile By Gaslight,* pp. 125–136.

"second irregularity [between the first and second Holmes] occurred in *The Adventures of the Bruce-Partington Plans,* a case Sherlock undertook *after* his spectacular return. In that adventure he professed ignorance of the three famous agents, Oberstein, La Rothière, and Eduardo Lucas, although in *The Adventure of the Second Stain,* a case Sherlock solved *before* he vanished, he mentioned them by name!" [11]

Just recently, Doyle's son, Adrian Conan Doyle, and John Dickson Carr made a study of Doyle's style and wrote some Sherlock Holmes stories on their own—*The Exploits of Sherlock Holmes*—and are planning to do more in future years, using those many cases that Dr. Watson alluded to but never related.[12]

The Baker Street Irregulars are also serving to keep the memory of Sherlock Holmes alive. The name is taken from "the sharp-eyed, wide-eared newsboys and street Arabs who went everywhere, heard everything, and picked up oddments of information in Victorian London for their idol, Sherlock Holmes." [13] This is mostly a social group devoted to drinking and quizzing each other on the Sacred Writings—all those stories about Sherlock written by Doyle. With the help of the Marylebone Town Councilors, they created a home for Holmes at what would be 221B Baker Street, and it was furnished and decorated with his trophies through the courtesy of those people who were willing to part with their treasures. A Boy Scout troop even furnished the plaster cast of the foot of the hound of the Baskervilles.[14]

Excuse me, I must end now. Someone has just come in. . . . Now what can I do for you, sir? . . . Sherlock who? !

Suggestions

1. Decide whether Doyle or Holmes is the main subject of this essay.

2. The theme is stated in ¶1. Does it successfully unify the rest of the essay? Are there other unifying devices?

3. What pieces of factual information seem irrelevant to the theme?

4. What general statements appear to need more supporting facts?

5. Is there a clear indication of the speaker's attitude toward the subject?

6. Analyze the *documentation* of the essay. Is there a footnote wherever one is needed? Are there unnecessary footnotes?

---

[11] Marvin Grasse, "Who Killed Holmes?" *Atlantic Monthly,* CXCV (June, 1955), 89.
[12] John Dickson Carr and Adrian Conan Doyle, *Exploits of Sherlock Holmes* (New York, 1954), *passim.*
[13] Louis Untermeyer, "Introduction," in *Profile By Gaslight.*
[14] E. Borneman, "Diggings in Baker Street," *Harper's Magazine,* CCIII (September, 1951), 81–83.

P L A C E S

PLAZA DE MERCADO

JEAN HERTEL — *Reprinted by permission of the author.*

It is six o'clock in the morning. The market, or *plaza de mercado*, throbs with the activity of the South American peasants who come to buy and sell their wares. Huge cuts of meat hang from hooks in the ceiling of the butcher shed. Live chickens squawk indignantly as their owners hand them ungently from the same hooks. The vegetable stalls are almost lifted from the ground by the jostling crowds that press their way inside. The vendors yell hoarsely, praising the quality and freshness of their products, while equally loud customers stubbornly protest the prices "imposed" upon them.

Outside the stalls groups of somberly clad women talk animatedly about the weather, Padre Garcia's sermon, the price of yucca, and the idiocy of American tourists. Most of these women, and all of the older ones, wear black because of the long mourning periods that they observe. The men, standing in separate groups, discuss the more serious side of life with equal liveliness: whitewashing used on their adobe huts, the maximum weight of coal that a burro can carry, the price of tobacco, and the idiocy of American tourists. The everyday scene would not be complete without the children, who race in and out of the throngs of people with rare agility.

By ten o'clock in the morning, the sun's rays have pierced the enthusiasm of the assemblage and scattered the people to the shade of their mud abodes. The vendors no longer argue over prices, for the meat that is left is discolored by the heat and covered with flies. All the chickens have been sold; the only sound heard is the occasional yelp of a scavenging dog as it is kicked away from the rotting meat. A dank odor surrounds the vegetable stalls, where wilted leftover produce awaits the vendor's stewpot. The narrow cobblestone pathways are no longer filled with effusive gatherers, but with the litter peculiar to

65

deserted meeting places. At noon there is no move or sound in the market except for the click of a camera shutter belonging to an American tourist.

Suggestions

1. The effect of this descriptive piece is achieved through highly selective details that convey the impression of the market (cuts of meat, chickens, vegetable stalls). These details are further used to advantage by the principle of contrast: the market at six and at ten o'clock. A concentration of effect is assured by repetition of the same specific details in both the first and last paragraphs. What would have been the effect if different details had not been introduced into the final paragraph?

2. Where do you see signs of personal feeling in what seems to be an objective picture of a market? How would you describe the *tone* of "Plaza De Mercado"?

3. What is the function of the gentle *irony* in the phrase, "the more serious side of life," as applied to the topics for the men's discussion?

4. Does the detail about mourning clothes contribute to the picture of the market? Does it detract from it?

5. Where does the speaker stand on the issue of the "the idiocy of American tourists"? Is it dominant enough to be called a *thesis?*

6. Write a three-paragraph description of a place that changes its character within a brief time. You might choose (a) a department store counter before, during, and after a sale; (b) a popular beach or mountain resort by day and by night; or (c) a hotel lobby at various times during the night.

NORTH FAYER HALL

EVAN S. CONNELL, JR.

From THE ANATOMY LESSON AND OTHER STORIES *by Evan S. Connell, Jr.* © *1953 by Evan S. Connell, Jr. Reprinted by permission of The Viking Press, Inc.*

North Fayer Hall stood on the final and lowest hill of the university, a little askew from the other buildings as if it were ashamed of its shabbiness and had turned partly away. Its windowsills were pocked by cigarette burns and the doors of its green tin lockers had been pried open for so many years that few of them would lock any more; the creaking floors were streaked and spattered with drops of paint, dust lay upon the skylights, and because the ventilating system could not carry off so many fumes it seemed forever drenched in turpentine. Mercifully the little building was hidden each afternoon by the shadows of its huge, ivy-jacketed companions.

Just inside the front door was the office and studio of Professor A. B. Gidney, head of the art department, who taught ceramics, bookbinding, fashion design, and lettering. Professor Gidney's door was always open even when he was teaching class somewhere else in the building, and in his studio were teacups and cookies and a hot plate which the students were free to use whenever they pleased. There was also a record player and a soft maple cabinet containing albums of operettas and waltzes: every afternoon punctually at five the music started.

Behind his office were the student ateliers, each with twenty or thirty short-legged chairs placed in a semicircle around the model's platform, and at the extreme rear of the building next to the fire escape, and reached by a dim corridor which multiplied every footstep, stood the studio of the other instructor.

This final studio was shaped like an up-ended coffin. In the rafters which surrounded its skylight spiders were forever weaving, and because the window had not been opened in years the air was as stale as that of an attic, always cold in December and always close in July. The window as a matter of fact could not even be seen because of the magazines and newspapers heaped atop a huge, iron-bound trunk with a gibbous lid. In one corner of the room a board rack held rows of somber oil paintings, each nearly the same: marshes in the center of which one hooded figure was standing with head bowed. The first few strokes of another such painting rested on an easel in the center of the room, and around this easel a space had been cleared, but the material that was banked against the walls and rose all the way to the ceiling threatened to engulf it at any moment. There were gilt picture frames, some as large as a door, there were crocks and pails half filled with coagulated liquids, cartons, milk bottles, splintered crates covered with layers of dust and tobacco crumbs, rolls of linen canvas with rectangles ripped out, jugs of varnish and turpentine lined up on an army cot with a broken leg, brushes, rags, tubes, apple cores, wrappers of chocolate bars, Brazil nuts, toothpicks, and pictures everywhere—glued on the walls or on boxes or, it seemed, on whatever was closest: pictures of madonnas, airplanes, zebras, rapiers, gargoyles, schooners, adobe pueblos, and a host of others. There seemed to be no plan or preference: a solarized print of a turkey feather had been stuck to the trunk so that it half obliterated a sepia print of the Bosporus. The glue pot itself could be traced by its smell to a cobwebbed corner where, because it had cracked and was leaking, it sat on a piece of wrapping paper. On this paper was an inscription, printed at one time in red conté but now almost invisible. Beneath the glue and ashes the letters read:

> *I am here,*
> *I have traversed the Tomb,*
> *I behold thee,*
> *Thou who art strong!*

Here and there on the floor lay bits of what looked like chalk but which were the remains of a little plaster cast of Michelangelo's *Bound Slave.* The fragments suggested that the statuette had not fallen but had been thrown to the floor. Also scattered about were phonograph records; most of them looked as if someone had bitten them. Several rested on the collar of a shaggy overcoat which in turn was draped over a stepladder. The phonograph itself lay on its side, the crank jutting up like the skeleton of a bird's wing and the splintered megaphone protruding from beneath one corner of a mattress like some great ear. In the middle of the night when the university campus was totally deserted there would occasionally come from the rear of North Fayer Hall the muffled sound of plain-song or Gregorian chant, to which was sometimes added for a few bars a resonant bass voice in absolute harmony, that of the instructor whose name was printed in gold on the studio door, a door that was always locked: ANDREV ANDRAUKOV, DRAWING & PAINTING.

Suggestions

1. The arrangement of this extract is simple: it moves from a rapid description of the art building (¶ 1) into more detailed treatment of two office-studios. The movement is a narrowing of focus, from the general to the particular. Notice, however, that the description of the building is specific rather than general: its physical appearance of shabbiness suggested by concrete images, its smell precisely accounted for, its individual "character" differentiated from the other buildings on campus. As in † "Snapshot of a Dog" and † " 'Prrou' " the technique involves *personification.*

2. The two office-studios are described by *implicit contrast.* Summarize the character of each professor, neither of whom makes an appearance, as it is implied by their surroundings.

3. How does each professor's choice of music help characterize him?

4. Examine instances of *parallelism* that help to make the essay more unified.

5. Do you think that too many objects are catalogued in the last two paragraphs? How are these descriptions related to the users of the studios? Why are there fewer specific items listed for Professor Gidney?

6. Explain: *ateliers, gibbous, adobe pueblos, plain-song, Gregorian chant.*

7. Write an essay describing a single room used by two people, keeping in mind that personalities can be implied by objects used by those two people.

8. Write a description of (a) a house familiar to you, (b) a curio or souvenir shop, or (c) a movie theatre. Use the pattern of moving from the general to the particular.

UNDER GROUND

GEORGE ORWELL ⟶

From THE ORWELL READER, "Fiction, Essays, and Reportage" *by George Orwell,* © *1956, by Harcourt, Brace and Company, Inc. and Secker & Warburg, Ltd. and reprinted with their permission.*

Our civilization, *pace* Chesterton, is founded on coal,[1] more completely than one realizes until one stops to think about it. The machines that keep us alive, and the machines that make the machines, are all directly or indirectly dependent upon coal. In the metabolism of the Western world the coal miner is second in importance only to the man who ploughs the soil. He is a sort of grimy caryatid upon whose shoulders nearly everything that is not grimy is supported. For this reason the actual process by which coal is extracted is well worth watching, if you get the chance and are willing to take the trouble.

When you go down a coal mine it is important to try and get to the coal face when the "fillers" are at work. This is not easy, because when the mine is working, visitors are a nuisance and are not encouraged, but if you go at any other time, it is possible to come away with a totally wrong impression. On a Sunday, for instance, a mine seems almost peaceful. The time to go there is when the machines are roaring and the air is black with coal dust, and when you can actually see what the miners

[1] According to the English essayist G. K. Chesterton (1874–1936), it was founded on Christianity.

have to do. At those times the place is like hell, or at any rate like my own mental picture of hell. Most of the things one imagines in hell are there—heat, noise, confusion, darkness, foul air, and, above all, unbearably cramped space. Everything except the fire, for there is no fire down there except the feeble beams of Davy lamps and electric torches which scarcely penetrate the clouds of coal dust.

When you have finally got there—and getting there is a job in itself: I will explain that in a moment—you crawl through the last line of pit props and see opposite you a shiny black wall three or four feet high. This is the coal face. Overhead is the smooth ceiling made by the rock from which the coal has been cut; underneath is the rock again, so that the gallery you are in is only as high as the ledge of coal itself, probably not much more than a yard. The first impression of all, overmastering everything else for a while, is the frightful, deafening din from the conveyor belt which carries the coal away. You cannot see very far, because the fog of coal dust throws back the beam of your lamp, but you can see on either side of you the line of half-naked kneeling men, one to every four or five yards, driving their shovels under the fallen coal and flinging it swiftly over their left shoulders. They are feeding it on to the conveyor belt, a moving rubber belt a couple of feet wide which runs a yard or two behind them. Down this belt a glittering river of coal races constantly. In a big mine it is carrying away several tons of coal every minute. It bears it off to some place in the main roads where it is shot into tubs holding half a ton, and thence dragged to the cages and hoisted to the outer air.

It is impossible to watch the "fillers" at work without feeling a pang of envy for their toughness. It is a dreadful job that they do, an almost superhuman job by the standards of an ordinary person. For they are not only shifting monstrous quantities of coal, they are also doing it in a position that doubles or trebles the work. They have got to remain kneeling all the while—they could hardly rise from their knees without hitting the ceiling—and you can easily see by trying it what a tremendous effort this means. Shoveling is comparatively easy when you are standing up, because you can use your knee and thigh to drive the shovel along; kneeling down, the whole of the strain is thrown upon your arm and belly muscles. And the other conditions do not exactly make things easier. There is the heat—it varies, but in some mines it is suffocating—and the coal dust that stuffs up your throat and nostrils and collects along your eyelids, and the unending rattle of the conveyor belt, which in that confined space is rather like the rattle of a machine gun. But the fillers look and work as though they were made of iron. They really do look like iron—hammered iron statues—under the smooth coat of coal dust which clings to them from head to foot. It is only when you see miners down the mine and naked that you realize what splendid men they are. Most of them are small (big men are at a disadvantage in that job) but nearly all of them have the most noble bodies: wide shoulders tapering to slender supple waists, and small pronounced buttocks and sinewy thighs, with not an ounce of waste flesh anywhere. In the hotter mines they wear only a pair of thin drawers, clogs, and knee-pads; in the hottest mines of all, only the clogs and knee-pads. You can hardly tell by the look of them whether they are young or old. They may be any age up to sixty or even sixty-five, but when they are black and naked they all look alike. No one could do their work who had not a young man's body, and a figure fit for a guardsman at that; just a few pounds of extra flesh on the waistline, and the constant bending would be impossible. You can never forget that spectacle once you have seen it—the line of bowed, kneeling figures, sooty black all over, driving their huge shovels under the coal with stupendous force and speed. They are on the job for seven and a half hours, theoretically without a break, for there is no time "off." Actually they snatch a quarter of an hour or so at some time during the shift to eat the food they have brought with them, usually a hunk of bread and dripping and a bottle of cold tea. The first time I was watching the "fillers" at work I put my hand upon some dreadful slimy thing among the coal dust. It was a chewed quid of tobacco. Nearly all the miners chew tobacco, which is said to be good against thirst.

Probably you have to go down several coal mines before you can get much grasp of the processes that are going on round you. This is chiefly because the mere effort of getting from place to place makes it difficult to notice anything else. In some ways it is even disappointing, or at least is unlike what you have expected. You get into the cage, which is a steel box about as wide as a telephone box and two or three times as long. It holds ten men, but they pack it like pilchards in a tin, and a tall man cannot stand upright in it. The steel door shuts upon you, and somebody working the winding gear above drops you into the void. You have the usual momentary qualm in your belly and a bursting sensation in the ears, but not much sensation of movement till you get near the bottom, when the cage slows down so abruptly that you could swear it is going upward again. In the middle of the run the cage probably touches sixty miles an hour; in some of the deeper mines it touches even more. When you crawl out at the bottom you are perhaps four hundred yards under ground. That is to say you have a tolerable-sized mountain on top of you; hundreds of yards of solid rock, bones of extinct beasts, subsoil, flints, roots of growing things, green grass, and cows grazing on it—all this suspended over your head and held back only by wooden props as thick as the calf of your leg. But because of the speed at which the cage has brought you down and the complete blackness through which you have traveled, you hardly feel yourself deeper down than you would at the bottom of the Piccadilly tube.[2]

[2] I.e. the London subway.

What *is* surprising, on the other hand, is the immense horizontal distances that have to be traveled under ground. Before I had been down a mine I had vaguely imagined the miner stepping out of the cage and getting to work on a ledge of coal a few yards away. I had not realized that before he even gets to his work he may have to creep through passages as long as from London Bridge to Oxford Circus.[3] In the beginning, of course, a mine shaft is sunk somewhere near a seam of coal. But as that seam is worked out and fresh seams are followed up, the workings get farther and farther from the pit bottom. If it is a mile from the pit bottom to the coal face, that is probably an average distance; three miles is a fairly normal one; there are even said to be a few mines where it is as much as five miles. But these distances bear no relation to distances above ground. For in all that mile or three miles as it may be, there is hardly anywhere outside the main road, and not many places even there, where a man can stand upright.

You do not notice the effect of this till you have gone a few hundred yards. You start off, stooping slightly, down the dim-lit gallery, eight or ten feet wide and about five high, with the walls built up with slabs of shale, like the stone walls in Derbyshire. Every yard or two there are wooden props holding up the beams and girders; some of the girders have buckled into fantastic curves under which you have to duck. Usually it is bad going underfoot—thick dust or jagged chunks of shale, and in some mines where there is water it is as mucky as a farmyard. Also there is the track for the coal tubs, like a miniature railway track with sleepers a foot or two apart, which is tiresome to walk on. Everything is gray with shale dust; there is a dusty fiery smell which seems to be the same in all mines. You see mysterious machines of which you never learn the purpose, and bundles of tools slung together on wires, and sometimes mice darting away from the beam of the lamps. They are surprisingly common, especially in mines where there are or have been horses. It would be interesting to know how they got there in the first place; possibly by falling down the shaft—for they say a mouse can fall any distance uninjured, owing to its surface area being so large relative to its weight. You press yourself against the wall to make way for lines of tubs jolting slowly toward the shaft, drawn by an endless steel cable operated from the surface. You creep through sacking curtains and thick wooden doors which, when they are opened, let out fierce blasts of air. These doors are an important part of the ventilation system. The exhausted air is sucked out of one shaft by means of fans, and the fresh air enters the other of its own accord. But if left to itself the air will take the shortest way round, leaving the deeper workings unventilated; so all short-cuts have to be partitioned off.

At the start to walk stooping is rather a joke, but it is a joke that soon

[3] About three miles.

wears off. I am handicapped by being exceptionally tall, but when the roof falls to four feet or less it is a tough job for anybody except a dwarf or a child. You have not only got to bend double, you have also got to keep your head up all the while so as to see the beams and girders and dodge them when they come. You have, therefore, a constant crick in the neck, but this is nothing to the pain in your knees and thighs. After half a mile it becomes (I am not exaggerating) an unbearable agony. You begin to wonder whether you will ever get to the end—still more, how on earth you are going to get back. Your pace grows slower and slower. You come to a stretch of a couple of hundred yards where it is all exceptionally low and you have to work yourself along in a squatting position. Then suddenly the roof opens out to a mysterious height—scene of an old fall of rock, probably—and for twenty whole yards you can stand upright. The relief is overwhelming. But after this there is another low stretch of a hundred yards and then a succession of beams which you have to crawl under. You go down on all fours; even this is a relief after the squatting business. But when you come to the end of the beams and try to get up again, you find that your knees have temporarily struck work and refuse to lift you. You call a halt, ignominiously, and say that you would like to rest for a minute or two. Your guide (a miner) is sympathetic. He knows that your muscles are not the same as his. "Only another four hundred yards," he says encouragingly; you feel that he might as well say another four hundred miles. But finally you do somehow creep as far as the coal face. You have gone a mile and taken the best part of an hour; a miner would do it in not much more than twenty minutes. Having got there, you have to sprawl in the coal dust and get your strength back for several minutes before you can even watch the work in progress with any kind of intelligence.

Coming back is worse than going, not only because you are already tired out but because the journey back to the shaft is probably slightly uphill. You get through the low places at the speed of a tortoise, and you have no shame now about calling a halt when your knees give way. Even the lamp you are carrying becomes a nuisance and probably when you stumble you drop it; whereupon, if it is a Davy lamp, it goes out. Ducking the beams becomes more and more of an effort, and sometimes you forget to duck. You try walking head down as the miners do, and then you bang your backbone. Even the miners bang their backbones fairly often. This is the reason why in very hot mines, where it is necessary to go about half naked, most of the miners have what they call "buttons down the back" —that is, a permanent scab on each vertebra. When the track is downhill the miners sometimes fit their clogs, which are hollow underneath, on the trolley rails and slide down. In mines where the "traveling" is very bad all the miners carry sticks about two and a half feet long, hollowed out below the handle. In normal places you keep your hand on top of the stick and in the low places you slide your hand down into the hollow. These sticks are a great help, and the wooden crash-helmets—a comparatively recent invention—are a godsend. They look like a French or Italian steel helmet, but they are made of some kind of pith and very light, and so strong that you can take a violent blow on the head without feeling it. When finally you get back to the surface you have been perhaps three hours underground and traveled two miles, and you are more exhausted than you would be by a twenty-five-mile walk above ground. For a week afterward your thighs are so stiff that coming downstairs is quite a difficult feat; you have to work your way down in a peculiar sidelong manner, without bending the knees. Your miner friends notice the stiffness of your walk and chaff you about it. ("How'd ta like to work down pit, eh?" etc.) Yet even a miner who has been long away from work—from illness, for instance—when he comes back to the pit, suffers badly for the first few days.

It may seem that I am exaggerating, though no one who has been down an old-fashioned pit (most of the pits in England are old-fashioned) and actually gone as far as the coal face, is likely to say so. But what I want to emphasize is this. Here is this frightful business of crawling to and fro, which to any normal person is a hard day's work in itself; and it is not part of the miner's work at all, it is merely an extra, like the City man's daily ride in the tube. The miner does that journey to and fro, and sandwiched in between there are seven and a half hours of savage work. I have never traveled much more than a mile to the coal face; but often it is three miles, in which case I and most people other than coal miners would never get there at all. This is the kind of point that one is always liable to miss. When you think of a coal mine you think of depth, heat, darkness, blackened figures hacking at walls of coal; you don't think, necessarily, of those miles of creeping to and fro. There is the question of time, also. A miner's working shift of seven and a half hours does not sound very long, but one has got to add on to it at least an hour a day for "traveling," more often two hours and sometimes three. Of course, the "traveling" is not technically work and the miner is not paid for it; but it is work as makes no difference. It is easy to say that miners don't mind all this. Certainly, it is not the same for them as it would be for you or me. They have done it since childhood, they have the right muscles hardened, and they can move to and fro underground with a startling and rather horrible agility. A miner puts his head down and *runs,* with a long swinging stride, through places where I can only stagger. At the workings you see them on all fours, skipping round the pit props almost like dogs. But it is quite a mistake to think that they enjoy it. I have talked about this to scores of miners and they all admit that the "traveling" is hard work; in any case when you hear them discussing a pit among themselves the "traveling" is always one of the things they discuss. It is said that a shift always returns from work faster than it goes; nevertheless the miners all say that it is the coming away, after a hard day's work, that is especially irksome. It is part of their work and they are equal to it, but certainly it is an effort. It is comparable, perhaps, to climbing a smallish mountain before and after your day's work.

When you have been down two or three pits you begin to get some grasp of the processes that are going on underground. (I ought to say, by the way, that I know nothing whatever about the technical side of mining: I am merely describing what I have seen.) Coal lies in thin seams between enormous layers of rock, so that essentially the process of getting it out is like scooping the central layer from a Neapolitan ice. In the old days the miners used to cut straight into the coal with pick and crowbar—a very slow job because coal, when lying in its virgin state, is almost as hard as rock. Nowadays the preliminary work is done by an electrically driven coal-cutter, which in principle is an immensely tough and powerful band-saw, running horizontally instead of vertically, with teeth a couple of inches long and half an inch or an inch thick. It can move backward or forward on its own power, and the men operating it can rotate it this way and that. Incidentally it makes one of the most awful noises I have ever heard, and sends forth clouds of coal dust which make it impossible to see more than two or three feet and almost impossible to breathe. The machine travels along the coal face cutting into the base of the coal and undermining it to the depth of five feet or five feet and a half; after this it is comparatively easy to extract the coal to the depth to which it has been undermined. Where it is "difficult getting," however, it has also to be loosened with explosives. A man with an electric drill, like a rather smaller version of the drills used in street-mending, bores holes at intervals in the coal, inserts blasting powder, plugs it with clay, goes round the corner if there is one handy (he is supposed to retire to twenty-five yards distance) and touches off the charge with an electric current. This is not intended to bring the coal out, only to loosen it. Occasionally, of course, the charge is too powerful, and then it not only brings the coal out but brings the roof down as well.

After the blasting has been done the "fillers" can tumble the coal out, break it up, and shovel it on to the conveyor belt. It comes out at first in monstrous boulders which may weigh anything up to twenty tons. The conveyor belt shoots it on to tubs, and the tubs are shoved into the main road and hitched on to an endlessly revolving steel cable which drags them to the cage. Then they are hoisted, and at the surface the coal is sorted by being run over screens, and if necessary is washed as well. As far as possible the "dirt"—the shale, that is—is used for making the roads below. All that cannot be used is sent to the surface and dumped; hence the monstrous "dirt-heaps," like hideous gray mountains which are the characteristic scenery of the coal areas. When the coal has been extracted to the depth to which the machine has cut, the coal face has advanced by five feet. Fresh props are put in to hold up the newly exposed roof, and during the next shift the conveyor belt is taken to pieces, moved five feet forward, and re-assembled. As far as possible the three operations of cutting, blasting, and extraction are done in three separate shifts, the cutting in the afternoon, the blasting at night (there is a law, not always kept, that forbids its being done when there are other men working near by), and the "filling" in the morning shift, which lasts from six in the morning until half-past one.

Even when you watch the process of coal-extraction you probably only watch it for a short time, and it is not until you begin making a few calculations that you realize what a stupendous task the "fillers" are performing. Normally each man has to clear a space four or five yards wide. The cutter has undermined the coal to the depth of five feet, so that if the seam of coal is three or four feet high, each man has to cut out, break up and load on to the belt something between seven and twelve cubic yards of coal. This is to say, taking a cubic yard at weighing twenty-seven hundredweight, that each man is shifting coal at a speed approaching two tons an hour. I have just enough experience of pick-and-shovel work to be able to grasp what it means. When I am digging trenches in my garden, if I shift two tons of earth during the afternoon, I feel that I have earned my tea. But earth is tractable stuff compared with coal, and I don't have to work kneeling down, a thousand feet underground, in suffocating heat and swallowing coal dust with every breath I take; nor do I have to walk a mile bent double before I begin. The miner's job would be as much beyond my power as it would be to perform on the flying trapeze or to win the Grand National. I am not a manual laborer and please God I never shall be one, but there are some kinds of manual work that I could do if I had to. At a pitch I could be a tolerable road-sweeper or an inefficient gardener or even a tenth-rate farm hand. But by no conceivable amount of effort or training could I become a coal miner; the work would kill me in a few weeks.

Suggestions

1. "Under Ground" is much more than a description of a coal mine. Its concentration on the physical shape of the mine dramatizes the difficulty of the miner's work and expresses the speaker's feelings about a class of men whose labors are essential to the continuance of civilization.

2. A considerable portion of the essay is devoted to "the immense horizontal distances that have to be traveled under ground." Relate this section to the speaker's theme. Is the length of it out of proportion to the space devoted to other areas of the mine?

3. Summarize the attitude of the speaker toward his subject, commenting on such figures of speech as that of the *caryatid* in the third sentence.

4. Discuss the function of such passages as the descriptions of mice and of the miners' bodies. Are these *digressions?*

5. Point out examples of emotive language, such as *superhuman, stupendous task, splendid men.* Should this essay have been restricted to objective reporting?

6. Discuss the value of the final paragraph and its careful mathematical calculation of the work performed by a miner.

7. Explain: *pace, metabolism, Davy lamps, pilchards, sleepers, Neapolitan ice, Grand National.*

8. Write a comparable description of the activities in a printing plant, a textile mill, a ship's engine room, a hospital, or any industrial plant or mill.

WONDERFUL TOWN?

MORRIS FREEDMAN   *First published in* THE NEW REPUBLIC. © *1957 by Morris Freedman.*

"New York, New York, it's a helluva town,
The Bronx is up and the Battery's down,
The People ride in a hole in the ground. . . ."

The one thing even the most hardened New Yorker (Chicagoan, Philadelphian) cannot avoid is the sheer presence of the city, its physical bulk, its complexities of movement, its squashing crowds, its oppression and indifference. Where Sherwood Anderson was the chronicler of small town terrors, John Cheever today records metropolitan and suburban horrors. For cities exist by size, by forcing huge numbers of people through funnels into small areas, by neglecting utterly the eye's need and the body's need of nature, the mind's need for occasional separateness. Sooner or later, the plain difficulty of daily living—of getting from home to work and back again; of shopping; of going to the theatre, concert hall, or museum—makes anything the city may offer just not worth it. Only a whimsical, arch romanticist like E. B. White can after many years still address poems of adoration to the city, but then he has his Maine refuge.

Take New York. You can't get from any Long Island community into the city in much under an hour, and a quite uncomfortable one too, whether you drive through crowded traffic or bounce in a Long Island Railroad car or stand in the subway, lurching, elbows pinned, sweating, all the way to or from Jamaica or Flushing. I speak of Long Island, but it's the same for Westchester, Connecticut, New Jersey, Riverdale. That much publicized commuter's bus in Chicago with luxurious accommodations is just a desperate effort to do something about the problem; it would take a fleet of such buses, snarling traffic all the more, to take care of all Chicago commuters.

Return to the city? Before we left New York—never to return we hope—such a movement was growing. Defeated, frustrated suburbanites were giving up their daily two-to-three-hour battle of attrition. They sold their split-level and ranch homes, took apartments at huge rents in the city, enrolled their children in private schools, disposed of their cars (or else settled down with them to that peculiar game adults play in New York, like musical chairs, of periodic daily shifting of parked automobiles). They accepted the lack of space, of greenery, of views of sky; the presence of smoke, soot, dirt, and noise.

But the worst thing these returning exiles accepted, I feel now, was a kind of living with the ever-present sense of the imminence of disaster. I am aware now, away from the city for nearly two years, of how casually one accepts sudden death in New York—the killing of a woman crossing Herald Square, her skull crumpled by a truck (I saw that); a plane hitting the Empire State Building (I worked across the street); the forcing of someone off a crowded subway platform into the path of a train (I used to look at daily headlines describing that; they said the person jumped or fell, but how could anyone ever know?); the falling of a flower pot or a wooden beam from the heights of a building, to hit an old Negro man or kill a chauffeur in a Rolls-Royce (I read about these); and the countless daily acts of mayhem, so commonplace they never got into the newspapers. I remember two great winter strikes in New York in recent years that threatened disaster, one resulting in a shortage of milk, the other, of fuel. I remember, too, the shudder that swept the city when international politics seemed to be getting out of control and everyone became a private, momentary volunteer for Civil Defense, watching the skies for the plane that carried the little bomb. There was that occasional comic feeling, too, not unmixed with panic, of being jammed on Manhattan Island as in a Marx Brothers' stateroom.

One accepts the nightmares of the city for the sake of culture, sophisticated society, jobs. As for the culture, during our last year in New York, my wife and I went to the theatre just once. That night cost us, with modest tickets, close to $20 and several hours of nervous harassment.

Even the museums and art galleries get intolerably crowded. Perhaps one can work harried and exhausted; it is more difficult to respond to art in that condition. Metropolitan social life and metropolitan jobs, too, once the enchantment wears off, become thoughtlessly competitive. Social caste becomes determined by work caste, and that, in turn, all too often, by one-upmanship. Insiderism, snobbism, intrigue, become techniques of daily living. The most routine and essential services become marked by callousness; bus drivers ignore you in the rain; doctors and hospitals treat you as a moving cadaver on an assembly line. Anonymity is Everyman; as one must forget one's identity in the frantic motions at the beginning, middle, and end of the work day, so one forgets it in his office, at parties, with friends, even, at last, with his family and with himself.

Not everyone, of course, is lost, nor do all the lost lose themselves in the same way, but those that survive illustrate what it takes to stay alive and at what expense. I think of people I know who are not anonymous bodies in the big city. All are persons of the greatest self-understanding and independence of spirit and mind. But they, too, have clearly compromised with the demons; it is obvious that their work could be so much richer were they not required to spend so much of their resources countering the hazards of the city.

I know about the "cosmopolitanism" of New Yorkers. To me they are monstrous solipsists (as I was), with a built-in provincialism far narrower and more pernicious than anything found in the provinces. The urban area is their universe. In part, like any provincialism, this comes from innocence; in greater part, however, it is the result of the general competitive atmosphere: if one successfully bulls his way through the subway, through an office, through a cocktail shindig, through domestic difficulties, then the results *must* be worth it. If the game is worth the playing, it must be worth the winning. To some degree, every big city dweller must be afflicted with this notion, else why does he remain? Why else does he allow himself to live in tenements, in an outrageous climate (there isn't a big city in this country today with a decent climate), tied down to a job sometimes easily duplicated elsewhere?

The answer is that more and more he is breaking away. Sometimes reasons of health force him, against his will, to join the exodus; other times, retirement gives him an excuse for release; and sometimes, he flees in sudden awareness of the Kafka-esque bleakness. Relocation is becoming a national pastime, with more Americans living outside the state they were born in than ever before. It has become easier, even cheaper, to travel and to move one's household. The American family, as social workers and sociologists have been discovering with some surprise, has a built-in cohesiveness and stability it takes with it anywhere. The highways of the country are dotted with station wagons carrying families and pulling trailers. Cities and towns have become so much the same everywhere that one can pick up and leave home, school, church, shopping center, and a thousand miles away find everything duplicated. And if television has brought the glories of the big cities to the countryside at large, it has also brought that countryside into the big cities, one way or another. There is no longer a great unknown west of the Hudson or of the Mississippi.

The big-city exodus is not unrelated to the growing sense of responsibility toward one's family. *Life* magazine recently reported on businessmen who retired young and moved their families away from the city to live in vacation territory, where they might spend more time with wives and children. There's a growing feeling that one just isn't doing right by one's offspring if the child isn't exposed to the countryside, some time, some way. Witness the boom in children's summer camps surrounding big cities. What makes more sense than to move the whole kit and caboodle to that countryside for all four seasons?

Artists, writers, free-floating intellectuals, who once made their way in droves to the big cities, are now finding small centers in congenial countryside which satisfy their longings. A Joseph Wood Krutch moves to Arizona; a Stanley Walker to Texas; a Leslie Fiedler to Montana. And one suddenly realizes that writers have long functioned well removed from the big city: William Faulkner and Eudora Welty in Mississippi; Oliver La Farge, Ramon Sender in New Mexico; Walter van Tilburg Clark, until his recent move to California, in Nevada and Montana.

American cultural life which used to be centripetally focused on big cities is now becoming centrifugal. Advertising and business-administration college graduates may still head for New York or Chicago first, but scientists and engineers are spreading out. Young people interested in writing, painting, music, or just scholarship no longer find that they have to head for the metropolis. The state universities more and more are meeting local needs. One of the high-powered creative-writing college programs in the country is in Iowa, the heart of the corn belt that used to send so many young writers to Greenwich Village. The state universities of Ohio, Michigan, Wisconsin, Illinois are now foremost centers for study in the humanities. The University of New Mexico, in Albuquerque, is planning to sponsor a young artist for a summer of creative work at the D. H. Lawrence ranch in Taos, given by Frieda Lawrence Ravagli to the University before her death. Frank Lloyd Wright has a major center for architectural thought and production in Arizona, at Taliesin West. Colonies of creative workers—of varying degrees of seriousness, to be sure—are to be found in the Carmel area of California, in Santa Fe and Taos in New Mexico, clustered about the many universities one finds in the climatically and scenically pleasing Far West and Southwest. Even persons who for one reason or another cannot break away completely from the big city try to reduce their dependence on it. Television and publishing personages in New York, for example, get out to the Connecticut woods or the Virginia hills and come to Manhattan only on business.

There is no real possibility, I suppose, of the big city's disappearing, or of its growing significantly smaller. But there is also no question, it seems to me, that the attractions once thought to be exclusive to the big city are now available in some form in the remotest areas of the country. Mencken has gone, and with him the definition of the hinterland as a cultural "Sahara." Artur Rubinstein, returning from a recent tour through that Sahara, commented: "Small towns throughout America are more receptive to fine music than old cities in France. . . ." Not only do small cities offer musical recitals of various sorts (I have just attended a concert of the Modern Jazz Quartet), symphony concerts, art exhibitions (including traveling displays from the big Eastern museums), theatre productions (unfortunately all too often imitative of Broadway box-office hits although I have just seen a first-rate presentation of *The Devil's Disciple* in Albuquerque), opportunities for study and thought, but also all sorts of things big cities no longer, and in some cases, never did offer—a relaxed pace of living, attractive physical setting, usually an authentic and as yet uncorrupted atmosphere, companions of the same stimulating type to be found in big cities and also of a type never to be found there. And you can *choose* among these offerings.

The small city abominations Anderson, Lewis, and Mencken catalogued have all but disappeared as the result of the greatly changed technology and sociology in American life since the twenties. Books and television are as ubiquitous as the latest enlightened theories of psychology, sociology, literature, history, and politics, broadcast far and wide by *Life,* Murrow, and Anchor Books. Privacy, if one wants that, is as available as in New York or Chicago, in some ways more available, for small cities tend not to become fragmented like big ones into neighborhoods and tenement communities, or into social cliques centering around one's job, with everyone jostling one another. The campus of the University of New Mexico is a freer and more relaxed place, intellectually more curious and open, than many institutions of higher learning in the metropolitan centers of the Midwest and East. Rotarians, Kiwanians, and Lions are all now "enlightened," and kid themselves, not least, to be sure, because of what Anderson, Mencken, and Lewis wrote. What many would consider the minimum essentials of civilization have spread everywhere: name a city of 100,000 or so, and it will surely have a first-rate restaurant offering a continental cuisine, a hi-fi shop, and a haberdashery discreetly advertising Ivy League suits and accessories. The big city is no longer the exclusive showplace for the signs of wealth and urbanity.

Nor is the widespread enlightenment I speak of merely a matter of mass consumption of culture; creativity, I submit, is flourishing widely and significantly outside the city. It is true that writers, artists, musicians, thinkers cannot meet for lunch or drinks in the country at large as regularly and endlessly as in the cafés of Greenwich Village or Morningside Heights. But then the work turned out today in the metropolitan centers alone is often of a rather special character and comes from a different impulse from the work produced elsewhere. There was a time when artists had to borrow strength and assurance from one another, and the Chicago and New York salons were indispensable hothouses for cultivating talent, but today the soil is fertile almost anywhere but in the city, where it has become, at best, almost used up, at worst, poisoned. There is a nervous, frenetic quality about art exclusively manufactured in the city, in subject, tone, and achievement; it is focused narrowly inward; it springs as much from a badgering jealousy as from serious intention. (A friend, I learn, is to have a play produced on Broadway next year. I applaud him now and share unreservedly in his good fortune; two years ago, in New York, my feelings would have been less generous, instinctively competitive.)

Creation must always be, even ultimately in the city, entirely personal and lonesome, indifferent to society. A Saul Bellow, a Bernard Malamud, a Herbert Gold, a Leslie Fiedler, a Flannery O'Connor, a John Steinbeck, a Tennessee Williams, all move through the world at large, quite alone, and write. As for that catalytic contact with personalities and ideas, always so important anywhere for productivity, one gets that at writers' conferences, with students (always stimulating and fresh in their responses and challenges), or with genuinely responsive people anywhere. Young writers used to complain to me that the togetherness of artists in the city had somehow crippled and sabotaged them; either they spent their time in interminable talk, evading their tasks; or the sirens of advertising, television, and publishing lured them away from their most serious purpose; or they fell into the easy and ready patterns established for them by dominant figures. The important idioms of our time have come from the lone artists, those geographically self-exiled from metropolis—Hemingway and Faulkner—or spiritually alienated from it—Cheever and Salinger.

Let me concede that the city always beckons, always lurks as the arena where the artist must submit himself to judgment. The city will always remain a place for occasional sojourn, where the artist can measure the response to his work and find out what is going on everywhere in his discipline. He carries on his routine business in the city and may even get himself recharged there, like a salesman attending a convention. But he does his solid work in the field, in the setting which provides an opportunity for a more authentic engagement with people, with ideas, and with oneself than most cities today can—in Jackson, Mississippi, on a Cuban island, in Santa Fé, in Majorca.

Subject, of course, to all sorts of exceptions and modifications, it seems easier to be eccentric, or to put it more happily, to be yourself, in a small city today amidst normal surroundings than in a big one. The most important thing smaller cities now almost alone offer in the United States is the one great thing it was thought in the twenties only the big city could offer (benighted metropolitan captives still think this)—a genuine chance to become most fully oneself, to carry out thought to serious conclusions, to develop meaningful relationships with family and friends, to work productively with one's best talents.

I was born, raised, and earned my living in New York, but the finest hour for me was when I picked up my hat and said, Farewell, my unlovely.

Suggestions

1. Summarize the thesis of "Wonderful Town?" making clear that the essay has two main parts: The Nightmare and The Awakening. List several striking examples of each one.

2. Both the title and the *epigraph* are *allusions* to two musical plays by Leonard Bernstein which celebrate the unique and satisfying experiences to be found in New York City: *On the Town*, 1949, and *Wonderful Town*, 1953. What indicates that the attitude of the essay is the exact opposite of theirs?

3. Besides the main thesis, there is another one concerning American writers. What is it? Discuss.

4. For the sake of debate, attack the views expressed in ¶5–¶7.

5. Is Freedman's sociology (¶8) supported by any recent articles or books you have read or cases you have known?

6. Do you see any inconsistency between the exodus described in ¶8 and the "trend" of ¶4?

7. Relate the connotation of such terms as *whole kit and caboodle* and *cocktail shindig* to the style and tone of the essay.

8. Explain: *monstrous, solipsists, ubiquitous, frenetic.*

9. Write an essay similar in structure to "Wonderful Town?" on the Nightmare of the Small Town.

10. "Wonderful Town?" contends that the disparagement of small-town living in the writings of the 1920's is out-of-date. Read one of the following to decide for yourself: Sinclair Lewis, *Main Street;* H. L. Mencken, *Prejudices;* Sherwood Anderson, *Winesburg, Ohio.* Now write an essay based on this reading and the present relevance of its attitudes.

INSOUCIANCE

D. H. LAWRENCE

Reprinted from THE LATER D. H. LAWRENCE, *by D. H. Lawrence, by permission of Alfred A. Knopf, Inc.* © *1928, 1952 by Alfred A. Knopf, Inc.*

My balcony is on the east side of the hotel, and my neighbors on the right are a Frenchman, white-haired, and his white-haired wife; my neighbors on the left are two little white-haired English ladies. And we are all mortally shy of one another.

When I peep out of my room in the morning and see the matronly French lady in a purple silk wrapper, standing like the captain on the bridge surveying the morning, I pop in again before she can see me. And whenever I emerge during the day, I am aware of the two little white-haired ladies popping back like two white rabbits, so that literally I only see the whisk of their skirt-hems.

This afternoon being hot and thundery, I woke up suddenly and went out on the balcony barefoot. There I sat serenely contemplating the world and ignoring the two bundles of feet of the two little ladies which protruded from their open doorways, upon the end of the two *chaises longues*. A hot, still afternoon! the lake shining rather glassy away below, the mountains rather sulky, the greenness very green, all a little silent and lurid, and two mowers mowing with scythes, downhill just near: *slush! slush!* sound the scythe-strokes.

The two little ladies become aware of my presence. I become aware of a certain agitation in the two bundles of feet wrapped in two discreet steamer rugs and protruding on the end of two *chaises longues* from the pair of doorways upon the balcony next me. One bundle of feet suddenly disappears; so does the other. Silence!

Then lo! with odd sliding suddenness a little white-haired lady in grey silk, with round blue eyes, emerges and looks straight at me, and remarks that it is pleasant now. A little cooler, say I, with false amiability. She quite agrees, and we speak of the men mowing; how plainly one hears the long breaths of the scythes.

By now we are *tête-à-tête*. We speak of cherries, strawberries, and the promise of the vine crop. This somehow leads to Italy and to Signor Mussolini. Before I know where I am, the little white-haired lady has swept me off my balcony, away from the glassy lake, the veiled mountains, the two men mowing, and the cherry trees, away into the troubled ether of international politics.

84

I am not allowed to sit like a dandelion on my own stem. The little lady in a breath blows me abroad. And I was so pleasantly musing over the two men mowing: the young one, with long legs in bright blue cotton trousers, and with bare black head, swinging so lightly downhill, and the other, in black trousers, rather stout in front, and wearing a new straw hat of the boater variety, coming rather stiffly after, crunching the end of his stroke with a certain violent effort.

I was watching the curiously different motions of the two men, the young thin one in bright blue trousers, the elderly fat one in shabby black trousers that stick out in front, the different amount of effort in their mowing, the lack of grace in the elderly one, his jerky advance, the unpleasant effect of the new "boater" on his head—and I tried to interest the little lady.

But it meant nothing to her. The mowers, the mountains, the cherry trees, the lake, all the things that were *actually* there, she didn't care about. They even seemed to scare her off the balcony. But she held her ground, and instead of herself being scared away, she snatched me up like some ogress, and swept me off into the empty desert spaces of right and wrong, politics, Fascism, and the rest.

The worst ogress couldn't have treated me more villainously. I don't care about right and wrong, politics, Fascism, abstract liberty, or anything else of the sort. I want to look at the mowers, and wonder why fatness, elderliness, and black trousers should inevitably wear a new straw hat of the boater variety, move in stiff jerks, shove the end of the scythe-stroke with a certain violence, and win my hearty disapproval, as contrasted with young long thinness, bright blue cotton trousers, a bare black head, and a pretty lifting movement at the end of the scythe-stroke.

Why do modern people almost invariably ignore the things that are actually present to them? Why, having come out from England to find mountains, lakes, scythe-mowers, and cherry trees, does the little blue-eyed lady resolutely close her blue eyes to them all, now she's got them, and gaze away to Signor Mussolini, whom she hasn't got, and to Fascism, which is invisible anyhow? Why isn't she content to be where she is? Why can't she be happy with what she's got? Why must she *care*?

I see now why her round blue eyes are so round, so noticeably round. It is because she "cares." She is haunted by that mysterious bugbear of "caring." For everything on earth that doesn't concern her she "cares." She cares terribly because far-off, invisible, hypothetical Italians wear black shirts, but she doesn't care a rap that one elderly mower whose stroke she can hear, wears black trousers instead of bright blue cotton ones. Now if she would descend from the balcony and climb the glassy slope and say to the fat mower: *"Cher monsieur, pourquoi portez-vous les pantalons noirs?* Why, oh, why do you wear black trousers?"—then I should say: What an on-the-spot little lady!—But since she only torments me with international politics, I can only remark: What a tiresome off-the-spot old woman!

They care! They simply are eaten up with caring. They are so busy caring about Fascism or Leagues of Nations or whether France is right or whether Marriage is threatened, that they never know where they are. They certainly never live on the spot where they are. They inhabit abstract space, the desert void of politics, principles, right and wrong, and so forth. They are doomed to be abstract. Talking to them is like trying to have a human relationship with the letter x in algebra.

There simply is a deadly breach between actual living and this abstract caring. What is actual living? It is a question mostly of direct contact. There was a direct sensuous contact between me, the lake, mountains, cherry trees, mowers, and a certain invisible but noisy chaffinch in a clipped lime tree. All this was cut off by the fatal shears of that abstract word *Fascism,* and the little old lady next door was the Atropos who cut the thread of my actual life this afternoon. She beheaded me and flung my head into abstract space. Then we are supposed to love our neighbors!

When it comes to living, we live through our instincts and our intuitions. Instinct makes me run from little over-earnest ladies; instinct makes me sniff the lime blossom and reach for the darkest cherry. But it is intuition which makes me feel the uncanny glassiness of the lake this afternoon, the sulkiness of the mountains, the vividness of near green in thunder-sun, the young man in bright blue trousers lightly tossing the grass from the scythe, the elderly man in a boater stiffly shoving his scythe-strokes, both of them sweating in the silence of the intense light.

Suggestions

1. If "Insouciance" is about a place, it is about people, too. It is also about ideas. The view from a balcony is a point of departure for the thesis that intuition should guide man through day-to-day life, which is all too often cluttered by attempts to regulate the world at large. The white-haired English lady represents all who neglect the understanding of their immediate world and their relationship to it, while wasting their energies on a futile attempt to understand the world beyond their reach. Notice the easy transition from "she" to "they" (¶13).

2. The first three paragraphs and the last sentence create a sort of frame around the portrait of the speaker and his preferences. Contrast this arrangement with the arrangement of † "Under Ground."

3. Using the title, "Insouciance," as an indicator of the *thesis,* write an analysis of the essay. Relate specific details to the frame just mentioned.

4. Describe the function of contrast in "Insouciance." How does it differ from the way contrast functions in † "North Fayer Hall"?

5. Much of the vividness of "Insouciance" comes from a skilful use of *repetition*. Find examples of repetition (a) of words and phrases and (b) of ideas, both of which help to give *coherence* to the essay.

6. Explain: *chaises longues, tête-à-tête, boater, Fascism, sensuous, Atropos;* and by contrast, *instincts* and *intuitions*.

7. Write an essay from the standpoint of the "little white-haired lady in grey silk." Remember that the opposing views about "actual living" (¶13) are framed by a place.

8. Discuss in writing: "There simply is a deadly breach between actual living and this abstract caring." You may wish to consider recent developments in international politics to make your points.

E X P E R I E N C E S

CULTURE AFTER BREAKFAST

DEAN ACHESON ⟶ *First published in* THE REPORTER.

In the years when I had some connection with the United States Information Service and the Voice of America I heard a good deal about American culture—from those who contributed to it, from those who absorbed it, from those who dispensed it, and from the Congress, which took a very dark view of it in any form. Only recently I have a new view from a young colleague who has just toured South Asia, the Soviet Union, and the eastern European satellites. Whatever, he reported, might be said about American foreign policy—and much was said—American jazz reigned unchallenged from Bombay through Tashkent, from Moscow to Warsaw and Belgrade. "How," he asked a Pole, "can you listen to this stuff?" "Ah!" said the Pole. "You ought to hear what we have had to hear for ten years!" Well, I thought, what gurgles like water in a weary land is worth a taste.

But the example of the Poles alone would not have been enough to make me switch on the radio in the morning. An occasional concert in the evening, yes; but after breakfast, never. What finally turned the trick was boredom. For years the summer-morning drive from our Maryland farm to Washington was a joy of fresh, clean day before the sullen heat had spoiled it. But now only the first few miles are that—the red-winged blackbirds and meadow larks along the honeysuckled fences, the wood doves here and there on a telephone wire, the mockingbirds with their aristocratic drawling flight, and their wings left open for an instant after alighting, like an eighteenth-century Corinthian about to raise his quizzing glass, cattle still eager for the damp grass, and my friend the nurseryman cultivating between his rows of box rootings. This soon ends as our rolling and twisting country road drains into the eight-lane divided highway and one development merges into another, each announcing itself as such-and-such Gardens, Hills, Knolls, Valley, or Arcadia. That is when I push the first radio-station button and begin to learn again what has grown dim since last year.

A female voice greets me singing, with depressing vivacity, "The most beautiful thing in Silver Spring is a Loving Chevrolet." Surrounded by this sprawling young metropolis—the second city of Maryland—flowing over farms, woods, and streams like lava from an urban Vesuvius, one acknowledges that she may well be right. And then the mind drifts off to wonder whether a Chevrolet really could be loving. I once had an open blue Chrysler with wings on the radiator cap that definitely was. But the music cuts off reverie.

There is something unique and categoric about all orchestral selections played from, say, eight-thirty to ten o'clock in the morning. The aim of the performers is, apparently, to make every wind instrument sound like every other wind instrument, and to make all of them sound like Donald Duck. The result is as disintegrating to the nervous system as a ray gun. Sheer reflex makes one press the next button, and the next. But it's no use. *Plus ça change, plus c'est la même chose* [The more it changes, the more it's the same].

What a sheltered life one leads who reads books and listens to records chosen by himself! No preparation, this, for coping with the world around us. The radio listener is better conditioned. He takes what he is told he likes and likes it.

Then comes a respite—or rather it used to be a respite: the news. But this summer the news has been a depressant. Of course the facts have always been there, but my own experience has sheltered me from the kind of apprehension of them that has come from listening to the news this summer with our cook as I drive her into town on Thursdays. She is a woman of sense and sensibility, an old friend, from whom I have had many a shrewd, amused, and amusing observation on life as she sees it in and out of our house. Now a sense of shame comes over me, and a constraint comes between us as, together, we listen to reports of statesmen declaiming that to propose giving her simple rights of citizenship (she lives in Virginia) is a cunning scheme to rule the South with Federal bayonets; of race riots in Chicago over a picnic; of a minister beaten in Tennessee while protecting colored children on their way to school; of two colored youths kidnaped and beaten for trying to buy ice cream at a wayside stand serving white people only.

To turn the radio off would be worse than leaving it on. So we sit through it in silence. It is a relief—even when I am alone—to have the exposition of this side of our culture end.

For end it does, back comes the music, and with it what is becoming an absorbing interest, the song of matutinal appeal for the American disc jockey. What does it portend? Something significant I am sure, but just what I do not yet venture to say. Here are some tentative findings.

First of all, there is no doubt at all that between nine and ten A.M. the American radio is concerned almost exclusively with love. All the other great subjects of song from the earliest ballad and Icelandic saga down don't add up to two per cent of the time. War songs, marching songs, patriotic songs, drinking songs, songs of old times, songs of laughter and of lament, lullabies, mother-and-home songs—they can't hold a candle to love. It seems a little like ending breakfast with a stiff bourbon. But then, I once knew a Swedish entomologist who fortified himself for his morning with his net on beer, pickled raw herring, and goat's cheese. It's all in what one is used to.

But love songs, as sung over the morning radio, are quite a bit more varied in mood than one might imagine. In general they are keyed down, a sound concession to the hour so difficult for those whose zest for life gathers momentum slowly. Of this genre is the philosophical love song. The writer of one of these songs clearly was entrapped by the dilemma posed by Bishop Berkeley regarding the nature of reality. Can, for instance, a violet blush unseen when color is the effect produced on the retina of the eye by an object? This writer crashes right into the whole tangled mess. The issue about which he becomes lyrical is whether he loves his inamorata because she is beautiful or whether she seems to him to be beautiful because he loves her. Well, there you are. In my view, it's anyone's guess, though it might be a help to have a look at the girl before guessing. But my real puzzlement is over what difference it makes to him practically. Then, too, he ought to look at it from the girl's point of view.

Another type is the materialistic song, the one which believes that love can be bought. In one of these the troubadour promises to buy his lady a rainbow, and then in a burst of reckless extravagance throws in the moon, too. I am dead against this sort of idea being put in girls' heads.

Some woman probably wrote it. It can lead to no end of trouble and might undermine the home.

"A Teenager's Romance" looks at the matter from a new and somewhat arresting point of view. To them, so he sings, love is only another facet of an old problem—their elders. This time the old spoilsports, who appear under the incognito of "they," have apparently insisted that the young Romeo and Juliet are not to be relied upon, as it is euphemistically put, to tell black from white. At first glance, "they" would seem to have something of a point, as the old man is probably trying to get him at least through high school unencumbered. Then one wonders how good, on the record, "they" are at telling black from white themselves. Most arguments between adults end by each telling the other that he is unable to do just that.

In the world of song "they" is a sinister concept. They can't take away the sunset, they can't take away the moon. "They" is what makes a man sorry for himself and usually is himself.

The songs in which love poses an unusual, and often unique, problem have a special interest for me. One never knows how they are coming out. I have two in mind, one sung by a man, one by a woman. The man's song is called "It's Not for Me to Say." The title suggests a wide field, but what he picks out as not for him to say seems very odd indeed—it is that his girl loves him. This seems so reasonable a proposition that one wonders what bothers him. He goes on to explain. All he has to go on, he says, is hope, as he holds her in his arms and presses his lips to hers, that perhaps day by day this may blossom into love. But if this is not to be and if fate sends them on their separate ways never to meet again, it has all been worthwhile. This man takes whatever the future may bring without flinching.

The girl has a different problem. She warns us not to be misled by the cold gleam in her eye because down below the flames in her heart fairly roar—so much so, in fact, that she suggests alerting the fire department before the next meeting. A very fair girl, a little aghast at her own potential, greatly to be commended for giving a man a break by posting the notice "Road open. Proceed at your own risk."

This brings us to the last and proportionately much the largest category—the songs of unrequited love. The early-morning troubadours can't resist these. They begin with the revived and much-sung favorite entitled "I'm Going to Sit Right Down and Write Myself a Letter." Conduct otherwise incomprehensible is explained by a lady so indifferent that the postman doesn't even ring once. This pathetic case is followed by "Love Letters in the Sand," whose depressing message needs no elaboration, though of course "aches" and "breaks" furnish needed rhymes throughout. My son tells me of the acme of defeat in love that used to come over the radio to the men in the Pacific during the war, perhaps played by Tokyo Rose, containing the morale-building thought that the singer was born to lose and now was losing her. In "Dark Moon," unrequited love goes into an astronomical phase. Why, the moon is asked, is its splendor gone; and the anthropomorphic suggestion is advanced that perhaps it shares the sorrow of a lost love. The moon is too much of a lady to reply that she is at her darkest just before the new moon.

A final note of hope among the ruins is "Love in the Afternoon." Are its title and thought perhaps a little reminiscent of Hemingway? At any rate, it brings to those who see the shadows lengthening the hope that between them and the chill of the evening there may still be Something.

As I turn into the garage and switch off the radio, I ponder the observation of Andrew Fletcher of Saltoun that if a man could write the songs of a nation, he need not care who should make the laws. Is it possible that between legislators and minstrels the score at the top of the ninth is nothing to nothing, with two out and no hits?

Suggestions

1. Since nearly all essays derive their material from experience of one kind or another, it may seem arbitrary to single out a few as Essays of Experience. The distinguishing mark of such works, however, is that the speaker's own experience forms the center of attention—as it does in "Culture After Breakfast" and the four following. Whatever places, events, and other persons are mentioned derive their importance from his responses to them. No writing, then, is more personal than an essay of this kind; none shows more vividly the elements of *speaker, attitude,* and *situation* discussed in Part 1 of this book. And no writing is easier to emulate so far as finding the material goes.

2. Characterize the speaker of "Culture After Breakfast," mentioning his education, probable income, and tastes. How does ¶9 suggest his physical response to the experience? How is the experience framed and limited in a way that emphasizes its brevity? Comment on the phrase "tentative findings" (¶7) as contributing to the tone of light satire.

3. The tone arises mainly from the instances of *understatement* and wry *sarcasm.* (Which would you call the title?) Examples occur in the last sentences of ¶11 and ¶16. Point out other examples.

4. Relate ¶1 to what follows. Is it unnecessary? Does it detract from the effectiveness of the ride as a frame for the essay?

5. Discuss the *hyperbole* of ¶4 in relation to the understatement in most of the other paragraphs.

6. Discuss the seriousness of ¶6 in relation to the rest of the essay. What other kind of unity may it promote?

7. Comment on the observation of Andrew Fletcher of Saltoun (last ¶).

8. Explain: *Corinthian, Vesuvius, matutinal, anthropomorphic, respite.*

9. Write an essay on (a) uncomical comic strips or (b) themes of current movies. Organize it around a single experience, guarding against excessive sermonizing.

10. Write an essay defending a disc-jockey program. Be at least as specific as "Culture After Breakfast" is.

CLIMBING BY THE BOOK

WOODROW WILSON SAYRE ---⋇{ *First published in* SPORTS ILLUSTRATED.

Book learning, I have always believed, can make up for a lot of experience. The only question is—how much? Enough, for instance, to enable a man who had never even held an ice ax in his hand to climb Mount McKinley, the highest peak in North America?

I had a hunch that books could do it—and I wanted a crack at Mount McKinley. Norm Hansen, a good Boston friend of mine, had seen the mountain in Alaska a year or so before, and he got excited about it, talked a lot about it, and got me excited too. We had been armchair critics of all the big climbs for so long that we felt it was only fair to try our own hand at it, and McKinley, rearing four miles up into the sky, seemed a most worthy opponent. It has conditions of ice and snow and weather which approach and sometimes may exceed those of the Himalayas. Its approaches are long and taxing; it needs a real expedition to tackle it. Norm was willing, so we made our plans for the summer of 1954, set about reading everything we could lay our hands on, and tried to get what actual experience we could on eastern mountains.

We didn't get much. We did some rock climbing with the Appalachian Mountain Club, where we learned to tie the knots used in roping up. But when we tried to get some snow experience on the beginners' training trip to Mount Washington, we were refused because we had not yet gone on the continuous rock-climbing trip. In other words, we were not yet qualified to begin to learn the fundamental techniques of ice ax and crampons. Regretfully we murmured, "Well, McKinley, here come some real 18-carat amateurs!"

But Mount McKinley, we next discovered, doesn't like amateurs. There are rules for climbing it—and with good reason. There must be at least four in the party, your equipment must be inspected, you must inform the park rangers of the route you will climb, there must be a rescue party on call, and you must be experienced in all aspects of snow-ice technique.

Naturally, these rules worried us. It would be unthinkable to get all the way to Alaska and then be turned away. The rescue rule is a good one if only to spare our already overworked park rangers. And we felt the other rules were reasonable enough if you wanted to be safe, but if you wanted to be safe, you could stay home in bed. That we finally did get permission to tackle Mount McKinley was due to great good luck in finding three UCLA students who also wanted to climb in July. They had mountaineering experience and were able to provide the names of a rescue party. We met them, Jac Lasner, Norman Sanders, and Jon Gardi, on July 14 at the McKinley Park Station. There was the usual jockeying to impress each other with talk of equipment and mountains surmounted before we drove ninety miles to our jump-off point some twenty miles from the mountain.

For some obstacles the books I had read weren't much help. For instance, we had to cross the McKinley River. It turned out to be a mile-wide gravel bed laced with dozens of channels of racing ice water. Some were shallow, but others were not; and when the level rose to our hips, we could just barely stand. If it went higher, we were swept under. And with 105 pounds on our backs we did not get up again without some quick help.

Three channels went really deep and we had to hunt up- and downstream to find places where they might be split enough to cross. I remember being stuck in the middle of one. I could just barely hold myself in trembling balance with the current. I knew if I lifted a foot to go forward or backward I would be swept away. Yet I had to do something soon, for I could feel my legs getting numb and the current undermining my feet. I tried a gamble and just let go, half running and half stumbling downstream. It worked. The instant I started running, my feet, which weighed forty pounds apiece when I held them against the current, became weightless. I was able to angle over to the far bank.

The books hadn't mentioned this little trick. Of course, you run the risk of stumbling or going into a hole, but this is more than balanced by the increased mobility of your feet.

The books had also failed to convey to me the true evils of tundra, which we encountered after the McKinley River. Tundra is one of the most miserable mixtures in the world to walk on. It resembles balloons scattered loosely on top of caramel pudding. As long as our balance was good enough, we could stay upright. But sooner or later we were bound to go down. With such footing we had to break our packs into two fifty-pound loads. We could only average a mile an hour, and the nearly twenty miles to the mountain became three times the number.

As if this were not enough, we were constantly dive-bombed, in the rainy tundra country, by 451,000 mosquitoes. The rain soaked us and soaked the spongy ground and soaked the waist-high bushes we had to thrash through. Our gear got heavier and heavier as it, too, gradually soaked through. We slept in sodden bags and put on cold, wet clothes, and long before McKinley itself we wondered aloud what form of insanity had ever brought us to this torture chamber. And then the mists lifted without warning and the summit emerged in a stunning alpine glow against a mysterious purple sky, and we suddenly knew again why we had come.

After six days we gratefully left the tundra and the mosquitoes behind and moved out onto the Muldrow Glacier. Here, at last, our ignorance might show, so Norm and I watched our California friends closely. Do you walk with the blade of the ice ax forward or backward? What happens to the wrist strap when the ax is left standing in the snow? Ah, you slip it over the pick. What are the best ways of avoiding crevasses in actual practice? I had read that the Stuck party [1] (first to climb McKinley) had probed every step of the way. Looking at some of these hundred-foot troughs with their paper-thin snow coverings, this seemed very reasonable to me. So when Norm and I took the lead we probed more thoroughly than ever. We barely crawled, and the others got cold and impatient.

"Why waste time probing?" they asked. "So you find there *is* a hidden crevasse in front of you; you still have to cross it. Why not just walk ahead in the first place? One man isn't going to drag two more in!"

Very true, but I still feel that in an unexpected fall with fifty pounds on his back a man might well end the expedition by losing his pack or smashing an arm or a leg. I can also see that with my method we might be there yet. Anyway, when my turn came to step off in the lead again, I felt pretty much like one of the goats the troops used to drive ahead of them to clear a mine field. But as time passed I relaxed a bit. And then, on the way back from the second relay that night, I let go and turned my safekeeping over to God, and from then on the crevasses no longer bothered me.

We were a week hauling our supplies to the head of the Muldrow. We tried to travel at night when the snow was tight-frozen. I was surprised to discover what a thin covering would hold me then and, conversely, what a thick covering would not hold me when the snow became mushy during the day. I knew that I should *not* have been surprised, but this is one of the troubles of depending on books. Many obviously important facts just don't sink in.

Whenever the weather let up we would push until we dropped. This meant fourteen, sixteen, and once even twenty-two hours at a stretch. We couldn't stop to cook because it was too cold sitting around outside and,

[1] One led by the Rev. Hudson Stuck, Episcopal Archdeacon of Alaska.

anyway, it wasted too much fuel. So we went foodless and waterless. A little half-melted ice on our axes or boots became a prize.

The evening after the twenty-two-hour marathon, we packed ten days' supplies into a single forty-pound load and set out for the top via Karstens Ridge. This is a spectacular affair three-quarters of a mile high and one and a half miles long. It is a knife edge most of the way, dropping off to 3,000 feet on the Muldrow side and over 5,000 feet on the other. It is considered the toughest obstacle on the route. But for us, waist-deep powder made it comparatively safe, although exhausting when climbing at a forty-degree angle or more.

The ridge took us eighteen hours. The last four were spent battling a windstorm which gradually got pretty grim. Seventy-five-mile-per-hour gusts pelted us with ice, crusting our goggles and freezing our faces until it hurt to speak. The whirlwinds slapped at us first from one side and then the other so that we could barely hang on. When at last the slope eased enough to make an emergency camp, we weren't sure we could raise a tent. So we all lay like stranded sardines inside one collapsed tent until enough warmth had returned to try it. We succeeded, and there we stayed for two days while the snow piled up outside.

How does it feel to be on a big mountain without experience? Well, Karstens Ridge seemed like mountaineering at its best. The soul leaped to the sight and feel of it—to its variety, its beauty, and even its continuous exposure.

By contrast, our spirits were depressed by the monotony of the tundra and the glacier. Nothing diverted us from our discomforts. There is also a subtle, over-all depression which comes, I think, from getting so far from the "outside." A little voice says: It's a long way back and shouldn't we really be heading out tomorrow? Only for many tomorrows you know you will be heading in. And this can lead to a kind of weight carried inside, of which are only partly aware. It is bound up, too, with an uneasy sense of dependence—dependence on dozens of small things, like a boot or a stove or a crampon—and dependence on big things like weather and health and reasonable traveling conditions. Any big mountain makes you increasingly aware of the tremendous forces it could unleash at you. You walk on the back of a sleeping leviathan, but you know that only good fortune keeps him sleeping.

We moved onto the steep slopes above Harper Glacier in another snowstorm. After five hours and only four hundred yards we decided to camp on the lower lip of a small crevasse protected on the upper side by an ice pinnacle. We turned in and slept, but at about 1:30 a.m. there was a sudden whoosh and the tent collapsed on us. A bank of snow from the pinnacle above had dropped down. The tent was ripped and a pole broken. Jac predicted doom if we did not move, but it was snowing and dark and cold, and, after all, where would we move? Jac's tentmates, for all their edge in experience, showed no more enthusiasm than we. We stayed where we were. We were sewing up the rips in the tent—Norm outside, I in my sleeping bag inside, pushing the needle back and forth to each other when, an hour later, the avalanche came.

To me it was a steady humming vibration, which lasted perhaps fifteen seconds but which seemed much longer. The weight built up very fast. I pushed hard to hold the tent up above my head, but the weight of the snow pushed my arms steadily down. I remember thinking that it must stop in a very few seconds or all the air would be squeezed out. My head itself was being pushed down when, with thanksgiving, I heard it stop. There was a final fillip, and then everything was very dark and very quiet.

I could move my arms and I had a little space around my face which let me breathe. The rest of me was held in a vice. I had a few panicky moments when the tent flap wouldn't come open. When it did, the snow bulged in, but I punched it back. Digging upward with my hand, I could see a bluish light while the tent ventilator showed a whiter blue above me, so I thought I was not too far down. I called to Norm, for he had been unprotected outside. He had made it all right, half hopping and swimming to the front of the fall. I could hear his footsteps above me, but apparently he could not hear me.

We were lucky—very lucky. There were five feet of snow on top of the tent, and it took a half hour to dig me free. The others had come off better since they were a bit to one side. The next few hours were spent moving a few yards down the slope and probing for lost equipment and sewing up the several feet of rips in our tent without gloves in the cold wind. When at last we crawled into our new bivouac, we all knew that the expedition was over unless we got a sunny day to dry us out. The avalanche had sifted snow into everything, which later melted or iced.

The next day *was* sunny. We dried out and moved up against a strong headwind to 16,000 feet. The weather looked so good we decided to try for the summit in one push. It felt fine to be without packs but the altitude was troublesome. The morning's headache hung on and I had to take one to four breaths each step. Finally, at about 19,000, I felt that I had passed my limit, and Norm and I turned back. We returned to camp, and four hours later the others straggled in. They had made it but were so tired they couldn't eat until the next afternoon. Jon's returning words were: "Well, you couldn't ever pay me enough to do that again!"

Meanwhile, Norm and I were resigned to our "good try." But as we got rested, we were gradually able to think of another effort, if the weather held. And it did hold.

That night at Denali Pass the wind dropped and we grew excited, feeling that we might have a chance after all. The summit above us turned to deep gold against the obsidian-blue backdrop of a high-altitude sky. And the following day was calm and clear.

We made our try, and it was a sign of how worn we were that it took us ten hours to climb the 2,120 feet to the top that day. But at last we stood there. We were too tired to feel any great thrill. But there was gratitude for such a wonderful day and for being there at all. We photographed frantically in all directions. After fifteen minutes we started down.

The expedition's descent took four days. Tempers wore thin. We noticed that we were all barking at each other quite regularly. Still, I don't think we realized how long-term weary we were. At home, I found I had lost fifteen pounds. Food seemed rather tasteless and I seemed to notice far fewer sights and sounds. I felt as if I were underwater. I noticed that I rarely whistled or sang. Most of the symptoms left in a fortnight. But the dead spots on my fingers and toes and the glacier burns on my lips lasted over a month.

Was our lack of experience a real handicap? On this particular trip, thanks to great good fortune, I do not think it was. But if various emergencies had risen, needing a sure technique of ice ax or rope handling, the story might have been a different one.

Certainly, there is a lot of fetish in mountain climbing, as there is in any specialty, and a lot of sacred cows which could well be shot and eaten. But, if the nonexpert is planning to beard the expert in his den he should be always aware that the odds are against him. The most important piece of equipment I had with me on Mount McKinley, along with my book learning, was a genuine, guaranteed, pretested, and foolproof rabbit's foot.

Suggestions

1. If we regard "Climbing By the Book" as an extended answer to a question, its unity becomes clear. The conclusion answers the question that is framed in ¶1. We should look, then, for evidence throughout that (a) the question is not forgotten during the account of the experience and (b) the answer to the question is sufficiently prepared for. With these in mind, analyze the following episodes: the harassment of the rangers' rules, the swift river, the evils of the tundra, a troublesome avalanche, and the exhaustion that followed the climb. The image of the amateur performing a professional's job is the heart of the essay.

2. The overly careful probing, which might show the superiority of the amateurs over the seasoned climbers, is carefully detailed. What does it prove?

3. What incidents support the conclusion that "luck is the indispensable factor in success by the inexperienced"?

4. Sayre's style is generally straightforward with a minimum of *figurative* language. But the piece is not devoid of striking, dramatic uses of language—e.g., his description of the tundra. Point out other examples and analyze their appropriateness to the subject.

5. Comment on the ratio between the space given to the ascent and the space given to the time spent on the summit and the descent.

6. Explain: *Himalayas, crampons, tundra, obsidian, fetish.*

7. What devices give the paragraphs *coherence* within themselves and with each other?

8. Write an essay about a personal experience on a sporting expedition for which you were unprepared, making sure your attitude, focus, and theme are clear.

VOYAGE TO CEYLON

LEILA HADLEY ⸺

From GIVE ME THE WORLD *by Leila Hadley.* © *1958, by Leila Hadley. Reprinted by permission of Simon and Schuster, Inc.*

Early that night I was wakened by the discordant, clanging clatter of the sheet-blocks. The schooner was heeled so far over that my bunk felt as if it were at a ninety-degree angle with the sea, a notion which seemed only slightly exaggerated once I had turned on the light. The chart room was a shambles. Everything movable had shifted from starboard to port in a frightful jumble of papers and charts and books. "What's happening?" I shouted up through the binnacle hole.

Hal's voice returned, faint above the clanging and keening of the schooner. "We've just hit one hell of a squall, that's what's happening, lady!"

Amazingly, Kippy was still asleep. I pulled the poncho over him to keep off the water that was leaking through the overhead. And then, bundling myself into somebody's leather jacket that came down to my knees, I tugged the hatch open.

It was raining, and the wind was chill and harsh. The sea rushed past the hull in turbulent mounds glimmering with phosphorescence. There was a ghostly spurt of light as a freak wave dashed against the shrouds and broke over the deck in a gleaming track. Slipping and stumbling, I made my way along the deck and crawled into the wheelhouse. It was fuggy with the wet-dog smell of Scupper and the fumes of Hal's pipe. Hunched over the pale glow of the binnacle light, Hal looked tense and grim. Vic, Art, and Yvor were shouting to each other through the wind-shriek as they ran down the mainsail and the Genny. Through the patch

Hal kept rubbing on the misty window of the wheelhouse, I could see the undulating ranges of water racing alongside and swirling across the gunwales on my left. A mountain of water soared behind the stern, subsided and rose again, vanishing and re-forming with swift and ominous repetition. The sea hissed and roared and, strangely, above all the clamor, I could hear the shrill cheeping of sea birds—a mournful, lonely sound.

Art often said of me that I knew too little about the sea to be frightened by it, and it was quite true. The threat of danger intensified my sense of adventure, and for a few hours I felt elated, an adventurous stranger to myself, and then, shiveringly, I hugged the leather jacket about me and swore at the wind and the water which swept through the lacings of the wheelhouse's canvas sides and pooled on the cushion I was sitting on.

A little after three in the morning the worst of the squall blew over, and Vic crumpled wearily into the seat beside me. "Boy," he said. "I haven't felt such a wind since Christ was a cowboy. Must have been hitting fifty knots for a while back there. Must have been at least a Force Ten while it lasted."

For once Hal didn't question Vic's pronouncement. He had fallen into a preoccupied silence, his pipe dangling from his lips, and only by the way he kept both hands gripped on the wheel did he indicate that anything unusual had happened.

The squall ushered in a series of lesser squalls which approached with tedious regularity about two every afternoon for the next four days, broke with gusts of wind and an angry downpouring of rain, and then went away again just before suppertime. In the calm, candent mornings, mattresses, pillows, and clothes were spread on deck and knotted to the life lines to dry, but as they dried only to get wet again in the afternoon, the schooner was overhung with a strong odor of mold, distinctly noticeable for a day or two and then becoming less and less evident as we became accustomed to it.

Following a west-by-southwest course across the Bay of Bengal, we made some headway toward Ceylon, but not nearly enough to satisfy Vic, who was highly impatient with such a slow passage. Secretly, I was pleased that the passage was slow, since it was the final lap of the voyage, and I hoped that the nine hundred miles from the Nicobars to Colombo would last as long as possible. In spite of the dank discomfort of the afternoon squalls, the mornings and nights remained infinitely pleasurable.

In a world where there was nothing but the sea, the sky, and the schooner, the introduction of anything new took on significance, the appearance of anything unexpected became An Event. In these terms, the mornings were eventful, as almost every morning was accompanied by the manifestations of some new natural phenomenon. We were followed for a while by a trio of tropical birds with sweeping, three-plumed tails.

Splendid and white, the birds swooped about us in easy, dashing flight, vanishing as suddenly as they had appeared before any of us ever found out what they were.

Once a waterspout materialized on the horizon; it poked through the distant haze like the trunk of some celestial elephant. It was visible for some time before the inside part of it paled, and then the sharp outline on either side gradually became fuzzy and blurred into nothingness.

The day after the appearance of the waterspout, the trailing line fastened to an eye bolt on the stern tautened, and we pulled aboard a skip-jack tuna weighing about thirty pounds. It was silvery and plump, with flaring fins, its appearance as maudlin and cherubic as a Disney cartoon creation. Landed on deck, its colors shimmered and then waned, dimming like a rainbow in the sun. Yvor butchered it expertly, and Art supervised the cooking of it, all the way from choice fillets to the inevitable chowder.

The day of the tuna was also the day of the flying squid. I was in the wheelhouse when I heard a rustling behind me as though leaves were being twirled in an autumn wind. Looking aft, I saw a column of small oblong things rising straight out of the sea. Spurting upward to a height of perhaps ten feet, they described a perfect parabola and landed a few seconds later in soft thuds about my feet. The creatures were about six inches long, reddish, with feathery tentacles at one end and parachutelike membranes at the other. They were capable of exhaling a spurt of water with remarkable force. Kippy quickly recognized their possibilities as water pistols, and with his face heavy with concentration, he pressed the torso of one squid after another, shooting water at Scupper. Yvor showed Kippy how to dip the squid into a bucket of water so that they could obligingly recharge themselves, and this diversion kept Kippy wide-eyed and shrieking with pleasure until he happened to squeeze one poor creature too vigorously and a protesting jet of dark, viscous fluid was discharged over the wheelhouse tarpaulin. Art, surveying the mess, coldly put an end to any further experimenting, and the excitement died down as quickly as it had begun.

There was a day which was, as Hal said, hotter than a bandit's pistol, and none of us felt like doing much. Earlier in the morning Vic had dared me to climb up to the yardarm.

"How's it up there, kiddy?" Vic shouted.

"Fine," I replied glibly, and then looked below at the yawning deck, an easy two-story drop. I became a terrified idiot, and the crew howled and hooted with laughter.

But now the subject had palled, and Vic was sitting on the hatch, poring over Bertrand Russell and alternately soaking his feet in a solution of Lysol and daubing them with tincture of merthiolate in an attempted hurry-up cure of athlete's foot. Art was trying to get a good picture of Scupper "singing" while Hal played the harmonica. Yvor was lying on his stomach, his elbows resting on the gunwales, and was indolently trapping jellyfish with my string shopping bag, which he had attached to the gaff hook. Suddenly, some twenty yards away, the arching, glossy back of a blue whale slowly rose above the water. As a fine white mist appeared above its head, there was a huge sound, like the noise of steam siffling from a locomotive. Almost instantly we were enveloped with the heated, fetid odor of the whale's breath. In all the world there is nothing quite like the halitosis of a whale.

The whale was easily as long as the schooner. Set in its huge, vaulted bulk was an eye the size of a dinner plate. For a moment the eye stared at us. Then, with a low sucking sound, its flukes at right angles with the water, the whale submerged and swam directly beneath the hull of the *California*.

"Well, call me Ishmael," Yvor said. "Who does he think he is? Moby Dick?"

"If that brute gets the notion to breach, we're in one hell of a tight spot. I kid you not," Vic said.

We all regarded the whale with tense interest. It seemed an eternity before the whale glided away and broke water some distance beyond.

"I guess we're not going to be capsized this time," Vic said, and went back to soaking his feet in Lysol.

Apart from these appearances of natural phenomena and the cyclic occurrence of Cook Days, there was little to distinguish one day from another. In between boat-keeping chores, we talked, read, and drank quarts of coffee. The crew weren't much for writing letters, but I was obsessed with the delight of using the *California's* schooner-silhouetted stationery and preposterously worldly envelopes marked AIR MAIL in French, Arabic, Chinese, and English, and I wrote to everyone I knew. I also spent a good deal of time working on the magazine article that had been my original ticket to board the schooner. Every night after supper I would get out my typewriter and a folder of notes and diagrams and begin to question the crew, until one of them would yawn and stretch and say, "Time for beddy-by, Hadley. It's time the rest of us hit the sack."

I felt that I had hardly had any sleep at all when I heard Vic say, "Okay, you can't sleep forever." He shook my shoulder. "Come on, now. Up. You're on watch." Slow with drowsiness, I pushed myself out of the bunk and followed him up the ladder.

It was cooler on deck. The Bay of Bengal, phosphoric and flashing, as if imprisoning millions of sub-aquatic fireflies, showered the bowsprit with brilliance and enfolded the hull with sparkling froth. The schooner sailed smoothly forward, streaming radiance. There was a rhythmic creaking as the bowsprit rose and fell with majestic monotony. I lingered for a moment and then climbed into the wheelhouse and settled myself on the narrow seat ledge opposite Vic. We exchanged companionable grunts. I squinted sleepily at the binnacle. "Due southwest?"

"Due southwest. No strain. Easy steering," he said, and yawned noisily. "I'm going to catch me some shut-eye. She's all yours."

After he went below, I checked the compass once more and, bracing one of the wheel spokes against my left knee, I leaned back and looked at the sky, wondering which star I would choose to steer by. Arcturus, obviously, a veritable giant among stars, pendent now over the yardarm, the brightest of golden orange drops. I remembered how, when we had first started out, I had spent the watch sitting and staring at the dim glow of the binnacle, hardly taking my eyes off the compass card. Now I had learned how to steer by the stars, which was a different matter entirely. The schooner seemed to rest motionless, and I had the illusion that I was no longer her helmsman. Instead, I felt that I was controlling the course of the stars. A gentle pull of the wheel toward me, and Boötes the Herdsman marched off toward the north, taking Arcturus with him. Faint little Virgo sidled closer, hardly noticeable except for Spica, her only jewel. When I eased the wheel back and pushed it two spokes away from me, Virgo skittered off with the Herdsman in full chase, and Alcaid soared above the mast at the tip of the handle of the Big Dipper. Mizar followed, and even tiny Alcor was visible. Then the sails started flapping and the blocks rattled angrily on the travelers. I brought Arcturus quickly back into place.

The dawn watch. It was one of those chance rewards of travel, a magic moment, untranslatable from its time and place, a moment which lives on perpetually, with all its colors made fast. Just then there was no sign of dawn. The masts were still black against the luminous darkness of the sky, the sails gray in the starlight. There was a thrilling flush of wind against my skin. I listened to the chorus of rustlings and creakings and whisperings, the clicks and bangs of loose and swaying things below. Lazily, I stretched my right leg forward, keeping my other leg against the wheel, and with my foot I maneuvered the small alarm clock on the ledge of the flag locker around so that I could see what time it was. Six-ten. A little less than two hours to go. The sun should rise around six-thirty. It was rising later every day. We gained an hour because it did. If you were east of Greenwich, your time was later than Greenwich time. West of Greenwich, earlier. Something like that, anyway. Hal had explained it to me three times with diagrams and had thrown in a lot of miscellaneous information about parallels of latitude and longitude, but I still didn't understand it. "God, women are dumb goofs," Hal had said. If I did nothing else aboard, at least I served as a constant reaffirmation of male superiority.

Lighting a cigarette that was musty with mold and keeping an eye on

Arcturus, I contemplated on the wonder that I was aboard. It was a situation that called to mind all the clichés of the escapologist, all the fictive fancies about tropical islands, tropical nights, and languorous kisses in the moonlight. Life aboard the *California* transcended the stuff of all the movies I had sat through, all the books I had ever read. It was an experience filled with satisfaction and beauty, the memory of which I knew would serve me as a sanctuary for the rest of my life. Realizing this, it was hard not to think too much about the days as they happened. Like pulling a flower apart to examine its petals, it was a mistake to try to be aware of and to profit by every second. I had schooled myself to resist this temptation so that even now, with Ceylon only a few days away, I relaxed carelessly, as though there would never be an end to the voyage.

Although I was sure that in the minds of the crew, who really knew what they were about, much of my activity on board had the quality of a little girl playing house, I had the feeling that the boat was the one place in the world where I truly belonged, the one place where I had the least need of an exterior self to make conversation and put on a show for other people. There was another world, another way of living, and all sorts of urgent and important things which didn't matter. They existed somewhere past the horizon, hints of a past life, seen but shapeless, images and sensibilities which had ghosted away the day we had sailed from Singapore. The *California* was the only world I recognized.

On land there was such an infinite variety of people and things over which my consciousness could flow, but now all my consciousness and senses were suddenly confined and focused on the minute area of a schooner whose over-all length was sixty-three feet, and whose beam at her widest point was only fourteen feet—a universe that I could walk around in seconds. It was as if I had disconnected my emotions from a lawn sprinkler and had hooked them up to a fire hose. I looked at a ring bolt the way I used to look at a mountain. I anthropomorphized practically everything aboard, cherishing the sails as though they were babies and making tentative overtures of friendship to the stove. I felt about the schooner and the crew in a way I supposed I could never feel about anything or anyone else.

As for the crew, aboard the schooner each one could qualify as a great man. Perhaps in another environment which called for different facets of personality and character, they might lose the quality which made them great. But aboard the boat they were secure in their heroic roles and they kept me in a state of decent humility.

What a change, I thought, from New York. I looked down at my toes, and although I couldn't see them clearly, they felt dirty, and I thought about all the shoes, all those rows of polished discomfort I had left behind me in New York. All the clothes. That giant closetful, a small part of which was included in the trunk that was probably waiting for me now in Ceylon. It was odd to reflect on the turn events had taken. The closetful of demanding elegance had given way to a trunkful of practicality, and the trunkful had been replaced by a ridiculously small locker, a little less than a foot square, in which my entire collection of boat clothes was stuffed—things with legs and sleeves and a hole to put my head through. It seemed to me that there was a direct ratio between the size of my wardrobe and the quantity of my problems. Clothes and problems—I had so few now of either. There was a kind of poetic justice about the fact that the only girdle I had brought with me, a symbol of uncomfortable deception if ever there was one, was now wrapped around a leaking pipe in the engine room.

When Art came on deck to relieve me of the watch, the wind had died down, and he scowled as he took over the wheel. "We should've been in Colombo by now," he said sullenly. "Well, go down for breakfast. Beans and dog food are now being served."

Because of the calms and the alternate headwinds we had run into, the voyage was taking longer than the crew had anticipated. Our provisions were almost finished, and it was the fourth day that our diet had been restricted to corn meal, beans, and an Australian brand of corned-beef hash which originally had been bought for Scupper. Our main source of anxiety, though, was that the water supply might give out. Ever since we had left the Nicobars, the water had become increasingly orange with rust, a sure sign that the tanks were almost empty. Just how much water was left was anyone's guess, so we rationed the water on a don't-take-a-drink-unless-you-absolutely-have-to basis, and hoped for the best.

Water still trickled thinly out of the pump the day we sailed into the harbor of Colombo. It was a clear, bright day, and we sailed past the breakwater under full sail. We came into the wind, and as the sails began to flap, the schooner fell back on the wind, the sails were dropped and the anchor was set. Then we all went below to wait for the immigration and customs officials to come aboard.

As I glanced through the ship's papers which had been laid out in advance on the lounge table, I saw that I was listed in the crew manifest not as cook but as seaman.

"We figured you deserved a promotion, kiddy," Vic said, giving me a good-natured clout across my shoulder blades that made my head judder.

Suggestions

1. A key passage in "Voyage to Ceylon" begins with the first sentence in ¶10. The theme—adjustment to an unfamiliar world through a succession of experiences—is stated here and suggested by other passages: by the remark of the speaker's shipmate who told her she "knew too little

about the sea to be frightened by it," by her bravado on the yardarm, by her confession that to the crew her activity "had the quality of a little girl playing house." Point out passages that reinforce the theme less explicitly than these.

2. The account of the voyage is clear and lively, despite the sprinkling of nautical terms. Does the casual use of such terms in the description of the squall contradict the theme?

3. Summarize the experiences that you consider most important in creating "the feeling that the boat was the one place in the world where I truly belonged" (¶30). Does the occurrence of this statement just after the episode of the dawn watch mean that that episode is climactic? How does the contrast between life on land and at sea support this feeling? Explain the example of poetic justice mentioned in ¶33.

4. Analyze the *imagery* of ¶4. How many of the reader's senses does it address?

5. Comment: "Like pulling a flower apart to examine its petals, it was a mistake to try to be aware of and to profit by every second" (¶29).

6. Explain: *sheet-blocks, Genny, candent, Bay of Bengal, binnacle, anthropomorphized.*

7. Write an analysis of the other characters in "Voyage to Ceylon," showing how they are subordinate to the speaker's attitude toward the situation.

8. Write an account of an experience of your own that required an adjustment to a new situation, or an essay about the one place on earth where you feel you truly belong.

THE BOTTOM RAIL ON TOP

WILLIAM ALEXANDER PERCY

Reprinted from LANTERNS ON THE LEVEE *by W. A. Percy, by permission of Alfred A. Knopf, Inc.* © *1941 by Alfred A. Knopf, Inc.*

As a youngster I had not loved Father deeply, though I had admired him boundlessly. He was stern, though he never corrected me, and shy, and high-spirited at all the points where I was flat. During my religious period I resented his unchurchliness. I must have been a hard child to get close to. But now that I had learned a little sense, though not much, he was my chief delight. Of all my experiences our daily walks together to and from the office are those I would least want to forget, and they continued through the years, until I had to do my walking alone. He emitted sunshine and strength. We talked of everything—of the condition of the crops (it was always too wet or too dry), of the market, which, to my disapproval, he loved to play, of the Mississippi judiciary and its decline, of the parlous state of American politics, of friends and enemies, of everything. Once—this was in the early days—I asked him if he'd heard that one of our young married friends had brought on a miscarriage. He looked vague. I launched into a moral diatribe and averred that such conduct merited social ostracism. He still looked vague. It dawned on me that he knew all about it and was not aghast. I sensed we were diverging in judgment on a matter I considered important: I was confused and distressed. He knew I would learn in time and he knew that a narrow idealism at the start is bracing and formative. But he said nothing—advice was for those not strong enough to make their own decisions or to apply the decisions others make for them, advice was waste of time.

As summer approached we would always concoct delirious plans for trips to strange ports. Travel and the thought of travel fascinated him as much as they did me and he thoroughly approved my reckless determination to spend every cent I earned on going places. We barred Australia, Siberia, South Africa, and Iceland, but every other nook of the globe allured us, especially those full of the ghosts of countless generations, holy with their dust and tears.

When he would stop suddenly with his hands in his pockets and exclaim: "Consound Cam's kittycats!" I would know what had happened: Mother had filched more than her quota from his trousers pockets as he slept. It was a custom, one indulged in by her with skill and elaborate secrecy and consented to by him with considerable amusement. She could and did check unreservedly on his account, but the booty from these forays was her very own and she never reported the uses to which it was put. She would decide some poor girl needed a new evening gown, or the washerwoman needed a ton of coal and a gold tooth, or Mrs. X's roof was leaking, or Mrs. A should go to Memphis for the opera, and she supplied their needs by this violent brigandage. He never upbraided her, but only tried to resolve after some especially outrageous depredation to carry less cash on his person. He could never remember his resolution, and Mother never repented or reformed.

After a while I discovered to my amazement that Father did not like to work. He was a tireless worker and had a large demanding practice, but he worked only because he had a family to support and wanted the pleasant things of life for himself and them. He would have preferred to play golf with that extravagant high-betting foursome of his, or to hunt lions in Africa or tigers in India or moose in Alaska, or merely to lie on the deck of a sunny steamer with a hundred detective novels, *Ivanhoe,* and *The Light of Asia.*

He was hunting birds in Arkansas when Senator McLaurin of Mississippi died. It was a death that did not stir my pulse or suggest to me consequences that might have any personal bearing on me or mine. It was a turning-point in my life.

The most prominent politician in Mississippi at that time was James K. Vardaman, a kindly, vain demagogue unable to think, and given to emotions he considered noble. He was a handsome, flamboyant figure of a man, immaculately overdressed, wearing his black hair long to the shoulders, and crowned with a wide cowboy's hat. He looked like a topnotch medicine man. He had made a good governor of Mississippi and he craved public office because the spot-light was his passion and because, eternally in need of money, he abhorred work. At the slightest opportunity he would quote Bobby Burns fervently and with appreciation, but his oratory was bastard emotionalism and raven-tressed rant. For political platform he advertised his love of the common people and advocated the repeal of the Fifteenth and the modification of the Fourteenth Amendments to the Federal Constitution. He did love the common man after a fashion, as well he might, but although he hated the "nigger," as he called the Negro, he had never studied the effects of the abolition of the Fifteenth Amendment and he had never considered by what verbiage the Fourteenth Amendment could be modified. He stood for the poor white against the "nigger"—those were his qualifications as a statesman. He was very popular in Mississippi; they called him the Great White Chief.

Father rather liked Vardaman—he was such a splendid ham actor, his inability to reason was so contagious, it was so impossible to determine where his idealism ended and his demagoguery began. Besides he had charm and a gift for the vivid reckless phrase. A likable man, as a poolroom wit is likable, but surely not one to set in the councils of the nation. Father considered his Negro-baiting mischievous and his proposed changes in the Constitution impractical and undesirable. He was not a moral idiot of genius like Huey Long; he was merely an exhibitionist playing with fire. So Vardaman announced his candidacy for the United States Senate while Father was hunting quail in Arkansas.

Father wanted to be a force for good government, but he did not want to hold office. He did not want to be senator from Mississippi, but he wanted to keep Vardaman from being. Vardaman stood for all he considered vulgar and dangerous. Most people we knew felt the same way about him. The vacancy created by Senator McLaurin's death was to be filled, not by popular vote, but by the Mississippi legislature. Everyone conceded that on the first ballot of that body Vardaman would receive a plurality, but it was hoped that if several anti-Vardaman candidates ran, between them they could muster a majority and hold it until they could agree on the strongest of their number as the anti-Vardaman candidate for the final ballot. With this strategy in mind and confident that no Delta man and no gentleman could possibly be elected, Father consented to be one of five prominent citizens to enter the race against Vardaman. The strategy decided on succeeded, but only after an increasingly bitter battle in the legislature which lasted for fifty-seven interminable nerve-racking days. When the last ballot was cast, only five votes prevented Vardaman from representing Mississippi in the Senate. The anti-Vardaman forces won and the state was torn to shreds.

I don't suppose a state legislature is ever an impressive body of men. Mississippi's at that session was not: its members were not venal, but most of them were timid and third-rate. I moved to Jackson, the state capital, for the eight weeks of the fight in order to be with Father and to help as best I could, and Father's two brothers, Uncle Walker from Birmingham and Uncle Willie from Memphis, both brilliant and both popular, joined us. Father couldn't get chummy with people and, though his friends worshipped him and would have died for him, they did not call him LeRoy. As the struggle in the legislature progressed he became beyond question the dominant figure of the anti-Vardaman forces, although on the first ballot he had received only thirteen votes. His trouble was that he was a natural leader of men. Unwillingly the other four candidates conceded his pre-eminence and fitness and on the fifty-seventh ballot withdrew in his favor. So, at the last, it was Father against Vardaman. On the night of Washington's birthday 1910, a night of frenzied excitement, by a vote of eighty-seven to eighty-two, Father was elected United States Senator from Mississippi.

Nothing is so sad as defeat, except victory. There was the wildest enthusiasm among our people. Arriving home by train the next night, we were greeted by crying crowds, bands, and a torchlight procession. They had even found a little cannon for the levee, about like the one Fabre and his grandchildren used to test the hearing of cicadas. Our townsfolk were as deaf with joy as his cicadas. But Father was worn out and oppressed by the responsibilities ahead. Mother and I, though happy in a way, were dazed. And I was haunted by that desperate figure of Vardaman rushing up and down the rostrum after the last ballot screaming: "Black as the night that covers me."

The years Father served in the Senate were not dramatic or crucial years in the history of our country, but they were the end of a period in which great men represented our people. Father admired Mr. Root and Joe Bailey, disliked Lodge, loved John Sharp Williams, and was drawn to that Western group, so able and so feared by the Republicans, Dolliver, LaFollette, Borah, Cummings, and Norris. He fought the Civil War pensions racket, opposed our breach of faith with Great Britain in the Panama tolls case, helped with levee legislation, concerning which he knew more than any other man in Congress, and contributed materially to an excellent survey of our immigration laws. President Taft trusted and liked him in spite of Father's friendship with the ex-President; and Secretary of War Dickinson was his old and good friend. Had he been returned to the Senate he would have served our people helpfully and with distinction during the great period of the war.

But he was not returned by the people of Mississippi. Hardly had he taken his seat in Washington when he became engrossed in his race before the people for re-election, probably the most vicious and sordid campaign experienced by Mississippi since reconstruction days. While the overt issue in Father's race with Vardaman before the legislature had been Vardaman's stand on the Negro question, the undeclared issue had been the unanswerable charge against Father that he was a prosperous plantation-owner, a corporation lawyer, and unmistakably a gentleman. In his race before the people the Negro issue was to disappear with the emergence from under cover of the increasingly popular social issue and with the unexpected appearance of a new issue.

About two months after Father's election one of Vardaman's supporters in the legislature appeared before a grand jury and announced that one of Father's supporters had bribed him to vote for Father, that he had accepted the bribe money in bills, that he had taken them home and kept them in his safe, that he was now returning them intact to the grand jury. He added that he had broken his promise to vote for Father and instead had voted for Vardaman. We were stunned. Although we knew the shady reputation of the accuser we were not sure his story was false because the alleged bribe-giver was no intimate of ours but only an enemy of Vardaman. We were sick to the soul. But it occurred to the district attorney to examine the bills left with the grand jury. It was found to our own astonishment and relief that many of them had been issued after the date on which the self-accused bribe-taker said he had received them; indeed, after the date of the election. His story was a palpable and proved lie. But it was a lie with a thousand lives. The liar became the hero of the hour and his lie Vardaman's campaign ammunition. Vardaman's stand on the Negro question, Father's stand on current legislation in the Senate, simply held no interest for the sovereign voters of Mississippi. They were eager to learn if Father was a member of any church, if he hunted on Sunday, if his house was painted, if he had Negro servants, if Mother was a Catholic. They printed such questions and presented them to him when he spoke. He answered them truthfully, and unsatisfactorily. All over the state roved the self-accused bribe-taker vomiting his own infamy and cheered to the echo. The Hearst papers took up the hue and cry; George Creel published a foul attack in the *Cosmopolitan;* the professional lovers of carrion snickered and pointed.

A man of honor was hounded by men without honor—not unusual perhaps, but the man was my Father.

The man responsible for tearing Father's reputation to tatters and saddening three lives was a pert little monster, glib and shameless, with that sort of cunning common to criminals which passes for intelligence. The people loved him. They loved him not because they were deceived in him, but because they understood him thoroughly; they said of him proudly, "He's a slick little bastard." He was one of them and he had risen from obscurity to the fame of glittering infamy—it was as if they themselves had crashed the headlines. Vardaman's glamour waned and this man rode to power.

Such was the noisome situation in which Father found himself mired and out of which he must fight his way with only integrity, courage, and intelligence for his weapons. A different assortment was needed—those count only in a world of honor. But the world in which he used them was not a world of honor; it was a new-born, golden age of demagoguery, the age of rabble-rousers and fire-eaters, of Jeff Davis and Tillman and Bleese and Heflin, of proletarian representatives of the proletariat. Vardaman was not the first nor Huey Long the last. I accompanied Father and his dear friend and campaign manager, Will Crump, from one end of the state to the other, at the first to try my hand at being agreeable to the voters and at the last to guarantee that Father received sherry and raw eggs and a little rest every day, for he was fagged and weak and, though not a big man, he had lost thirty pounds.

I recall a speaking at Black Hawk in a clearing of the woods with a few hundred persons present in spite of the drizzle. I had learned that the crowd planned to rotten-egg Father. I had found the hampers of eggs and stood by them with a pistol in my pocket which I intended to use. I looked over the ill-dressed, surly audience, unintelligent and slinking, and heard him appeal to them for fair treatment of the Negro and explain to them the tariff and the Panama tolls situation. I studied them as they milled about. They were the sort of people that lynch Negroes, that mistake hoodlumism for wit and cunning for intelligence, that attend revivals and fight and fornicate in the bushes afterwards. They were undiluted Anglo-Saxons. They were the sovereign voter. It was so horrible it seemed unreal. But they didn't throw any eggs. They didn't refrain from fear of me, but Father was not the sort of person you threw eggs at—his eyes held a fearful warning. I have seen him cow better men than that gang of poor degenerates.

The worst day of all, as I remember it, was at Lauderdale Springs. A few of us had gone over from home to hear the speech, armed and sick at heart. Uncle Walker came to my room after midnight to say that one of our group would have to kill the bribe-taker in the morning as he was to attend our meeting and was scheduled to denounce Father. At six we met in the cold dreary dining-room for breakfast, Uncle Walker, his seventeen-year-old son, LeRoy, and I sitting at a table to ourselves. I had target-practiced most of the night in front of the mirror, so as not to forget to release the safety. A few yards from us at a table alone sat our intended victim. Uncle Walker had a voice like Polyphemus', but he couldn't hit a balloon. Suddenly he leaned across the table, pointed to the man, and boomed out the epithet which makes an American fight if he's a man. The object of his outburst did not fall for the ruse, he made no motion to his hip or elsewhere, he kept on eating oatmeal.

At last we arrived at Lauderdale Springs, where a thousand or more people were seething about in front of a vacant hotel from the porch of which Father was to speak. Father's few local supporters drew him aside and told him the situation was grave. They insisted that on no account should he mention Vardaman or his henchmen in his speech, but that he must confine his remarks to noncontroversial topics like the tariff. Otherwise there would be bloodshed. With that admonition they took the morning train back to Meridian. Father and Uncle Walker sat together an hour, painfully weighing this advice. They concluded it was too late in life to start being intimidated and this was not the occasion to talk tariff.

When Father rose to speak he was greeted with a roar of boos, catcalls, hisses, and cries of "Vardaman! Vardaman!" It was impossible to hear a word he might say. The din was insane and intolerable, and it showed no sign of diminishing. Obviously the crowd was determined to make it impossible for him to speak at all. The self-accused bribe-taker sat smiling on the porch at his immediate left. Father faced that obscene pandemonium, paused for the courtesy of silence, and, when he did not receive it, his eyes narrowed. Then burning-cold insults poured from his lips, he jeered them as cowards afraid to listen, and dared them to keep on. He cowed them by sheer will-power and lashed them into silence by leaping invective. At last the whole crowd was shamed into silence except one heavy man who sat in the middle toward the front and kept on howling insanely: "Vardaman! Vardaman!" I was glad to observe Billy Hardie immediately behind him with his pistol across his lap. Suddenly out of the crowd leapt a wiry stranger who jumped to the porch and, holding to a post, leaned out over the audience. He pointed into the face of the big man screaming "Vardaman" and called: "I know who you are and you know who I am. Shut up—or I'll come down after you." His eyes blazed like gray fire. The man shut up. He was wise. We found afterwards our unknown ally was Hunter Sharp, the best pistol-shot in Mississippi, noted for his daring and the number of his victims. Quiet restored, Father launched into the most scathing denunciation I have ever heard from human lips. It was the only speech of the kind he made during the campaign. He exposed Vardaman in all his weakness and the methods used by his henchmen with his consent. At the climax he turned to the man sitting next to him and, white with avenging anger, blasted him with his own infamy. The bear-baiting cowardly crowd, wild with excitement, cheered and cheered and cheered.

A few weeks before election day, coming back together from a hard week, Father asked me: "What do you think of it?" and I had to answer: "Not a chance." He smiled a little and said: "Right." The night the polls were closed and all Mississippi was counting ballots, Father, Mother, and I felt so relieved to be at last from under the long humiliating strain that we went to bed early and slept soundly. Father was not only defeated, but overwhelmingly. Thus at twenty-seven I became inured to defeat: I have never since expected victory.

Father did not like to lose at poker or golf or politics; in fact, he couldn't be called a good loser, if by that is meant one who loses without visible irascibility. But in this, the great defeat of his life, he was tranquil and found smiles and little spurts of merriment for his broken-hearted supporters. The only effect on him I could detect was an inner sadness, beyond reach, the kind of look I suppose Lazarus never outgrew after he had once died.

An old man wet with tobacco juice and furtive-eyed summed up the result: "Wal, the bottom rail's on top and it's gwiner stay thar." He wasn't much as a human being, but as a diagnostician and prophet he was first-rate. It was my first sight of the rise of the masses, but not my last. Now we have Russia and Germany, we have the insolence of organized labor and the insolence of capital, examples both of the insolence of the parvenu; we have the rise of the masses from Mississippi east, and back again west to Mississippi. The herd is on the march, and when it stampedes, there's blood galore and beauty is china under its hoofs. As for Mississippi, I don't mean to imply she has reached the nadir toward which she is heading. We still have Will Whittington in the lower and Pat Harrison in the upper house of Congress and that's creditable for any state. When Father was defeated good men all over the South were heart-broken, but today Mississippi is like the rest of the South, and the South is like the rest of the nation: the election of demagogues horrifies nobody. The intelligent are cynically amused, the hoi-polloi are so accustomed to victory they no longer swagger. The voters choose their representatives in public life, not for their wisdom or courage, but for the promises they make. Vardaman was a great forerunner of a breed of politicians not more able but less colorful than himself.

Perhaps it is a strengthening experience to see evil triumphant, valor and goodness in the dust. But whatever the value of the experience, it is one that comes sooner or later to anyone who dares face facts. Mine came sooner because of Father's defeat. Since then I haven't expected that what should be would be and I haven't believed that virtue guaranteed any reward except itself. The good die when they should live, the evil live when they should die; heroes perish and cowards escape; noble efforts do not succeed because they are noble, and wickedness is not consumed in its own nature. Looking at truth is not at first a heartening experience—it becomes so, if at all, only with time, with infinite patience, and with the luck of a little personal happiness. When I first saw defeat as the result of a man's best efforts, I didn't like the sight, and it struck me that someone had bungled and perhaps it wasn't man.

Suggestions

1. A lesson learned through a painful experience: notice the parallel between "The Bottom Rail on Top" and † "Climbing by the Book," different though the subjects are. Here a simple theme—the pain of learning to accept defeat—merges with a thesis: the pain is worse because inflicted by a group who should not have that kind of power. The issue is social, and the attack on the masses makes a moral point as well as a social one. The rise of the lowest class, the speaker implies, has debased the dream of progress by democratic action and contributed to the degeneration of moral character.

2. Test the thesis by specific events of state politics (in Mississippi or elsewhere) during the past twenty years.

3. Considering the structure of the essay, how do the first four paragraphs contribute to either the theme or the thesis?

4. Explain the statement that Vardaman was "a kindly, vain demagogue" by examples drawn from the essay.

5. Explain: *parlous, ostracism, venal, Polyphemus, irascibility, Lazarus, parvenu, nadir.*

6. Do you consider the cynicism of the last sentence out of proportion to the event described? How does it differ from the cynicism of the entire last paragraph?

7. Discuss: "Perhaps it is a strengthening experience to see evil triumphant, valor and goodness in the dust."

8. Write an essay on the popularity of a public figure who possesses "that sort of cunning which passes for intelligence." You may want to use a labor leader, a corporation executive, a senator, a governor, or anyone else who depends on the good will of the people.

9. Write an essay on the criticisms of American society in † "Wonderful Town?", † "Culture After Breakfast," and "The Bottom Rail on Top." Remember that their effect depends partly on the *tone* in which the criticisms are made.

STRANGER IN THE VILLAGE

JAMES BALDWIN --ᢙ{ *From* NOTES OF A NATIVE SON, *Beacon Press, Inc., 1955.*

From all available evidence no black man had ever set foot in this tiny Swiss village before I came. I was told before arriving that I would probably be a "sight" for the village; I took this to mean that people of my complexion were rarely seen in Switzerland, and also that city people are always something of a "sight" outside of the city. It did not occur to me—possibly because I am an American—that there could be people anywhere who had never seen a Negro.

It is a fact that cannot be explained on the basis of the inaccessibility of the village. The village is very high, but it is only four hours from Milan and three hours from Lausanne. It is true that it is virtually unknown. Few people making plans for a holiday would elect to come here. On the other hand, the villagers are able, presumably, to come and go as they please—which they do: to another town at the foot of the mountain, with a population of approximately five thousand, the nearest place to see a movie or go to the bank. In the village there is no movie house, no bank, no library, no theater; very few radios, one jeep, one station wagon; and, at the moment, one typewriter, mine, an invention which the woman next door to me here had never seen. There are about six hundred people living here, all Catholic—I conclude this from the fact that the Catholic church is open all year round, whereas the Protestant chapel, set off on a hill a little removed from the village, is open only in the summertime when the tourists arrive. There are four or five hotels, all closed now, and four or five *bistros,* of which, however, only two do any business during the winter. These two do not do a great deal, for life in the village seems to end around nine or ten o'clock. There are a few stores, butcher, baker, *épicerie,* a hardware store, and a money-changer—who cannot change travelers' checks but must send them down to the bank, an operation which takes two or three days. There is something called the *Ballet Haus,* closed in the winter and used for God knows what, certainly not ballet, during the summer. There seems to be only one schoolhouse in the village, and this for the quite young children; I suppose this to mean that their older brothers and sisters at some point descend from these mountains in order to complete their education—possibly, again, to the town just below. The landscape is absolutely forbidding, mountains towering on all four sides, ice and snow as far as the eye can reach. In this white wilderness, men and women and children move all day, carrying washing, wood, buckets of milk or water, sometimes skiing on

Sunday afternoons. All week long boys and young men are to be seen shoveling snow off the rooftops, or dragging wood down from the forest in sleds.

The village's only real attraction, which explains the tourist season, is the hot spring water. A disquietingly high proportion of these tourists are cripples, or semi-cripples, who come year after year—from other parts of Switzerland, usually—to take the waters. This lends the village, at the height of the season, a rather terrifying air of sanctity, as though it were a lesser Lourdes. There is often something beautiful, there is always something awful, in the spectacle of a person who has lost one of his faculties, a faculty he never questioned until it was gone, and who struggles to recover it. Yet people remain people, on crutches or indeed on deathbeds; and wherever I passed, the first summer I was here, among the native villagers or among the lame, a wind passed with me—of astonishment, curiosity, amusement, and outrage. That first summer I stayed two weeks and never intended to return. But I did return in the winter, to work; the village offers, obviously, no distractions whatever and has the further advantage of being extremely cheap. Now it is winter again, a year later, and I am here again. Everyone in the village knows my name, though they scarcely ever use it, knows that I come from America—though, this, apparently, they will never really believe: black men come from Africa—and everyone knows that I am the friend of the son of a woman who was born here, and that I am staying in their chalet. But I remain as much a stranger today as I was the first day I arrived, and the children shout *Neger! Neger!* as I walk along the streets.

It must be admitted that in the beginning I was far too shocked to have any real reaction. In so far as I reacted at all, I reacted by trying to be pleasant—it being a great part of the American Negro's education (long before he goes to school) that he must make people "like" him. This smile-and-the-world-smiles-with-you routine worked about as well in this situation as it had in the situation for which it was designed, which is to say that it did not work at all. No one, after all, can be liked whose human weight and complexity cannot be, or has not been, admitted. My smile was simply another unheard-of phenomenon which allowed them to see my teeth—they did not, really, see my smile and I began to think that, should I take to snarling, no one would notice any difference. All of the physical characteristics of the Negro which had caused me, in America, a very different and almost forgotten pain were nothing less than miraculous—or infernal—in the eyes of the village people. Some thought my hair was the color of tar, that it had the texture of wire, or the texture of cotton. It was jocularly suggested that I might let it all grow long and make myself a winter coat. If I sat in the sun for more than five minutes some daring creature was certain to come along and gingerly put his fingers on my hair, as though he were afraid of an electric shock, or put his hand on my hand, astonished that the color did not rub off. In all of this, in which it must be conceded there was the charm of genuine wonder and in which there was certainly no element of intentional unkindness, there was yet no suggestion that I was human: I was simply a living wonder.

I knew that they did not mean to be unkind, and I know it now; it is necessary, nevertheless, for me to repeat this to myself each time that I walk out of the chalet. The children who shout *Neger!* have no way of knowing the echoes this sound raises in me. They are brimming with good humor and the more daring swell with pride when I stop to speak with them. Just the same, there are days when I cannot pause and smile, when I have no heart to play with them; when, indeed, I mutter sourly to myself, exactly as I muttered on the streets of a city these children have never seen, when I was no bigger than these children are now: *Your mother was a nigger.* Joyce is right about history being a nightmare—but it may be the nightmare from which no one *can* awaken. People are trapped in history and history is trapped in them.

There is a custom in the village—I am told it is repeated in many villages—of "buying" African natives for the purpose of converting them to Christianity. There stands in the church all year round a small box with a slot for money, decorated with a black figurine, and into this box the villagers drop their francs. During the *carnaval* which precedes Lent, two village children have their faces blackened—out of which bloodless darkness their blue eyes shine like ice—and fantastic horsehair wigs are placed on their blond heads; thus disguised, they solicit among the villagers for money for the missionaries in Africa. Between the box in the church and the blackened children, the village "bought" last year six or eight African natives. This was reported to me with pride by the wife of one of the *bistro* owners and I was careful to express astonishment and pleasure at the solicitude shown by the village for the souls of black folk. The *bistro* owner's wife beamed with a pleasure far more genuine than my own and seemed to feel that I might now breathe more easily concerning the souls of at least six of my kinsmen.

I tried not to think of these so lately baptized kinsmen, of the price paid for them, or the peculiar price they themselves would pay, and said nothing about my father, who having taken his own conversion too literally never, at bottom, forgave the white world (which he described as heathen) for having saddled him with a Christ in whom, to judge at least from their treatment of him, they themselves no longer believed. I thought of white men arriving for the first time in an African village, strangers there, as I am a stranger here, and tried to imagine the astounded populace touching their hair and marveling at the color of their skin. But there is a great difference between being the first white man to be seen by Africans and being the first black man to be seen by whites. The white man takes the astonishment as tribute, for he arrives to conquer and to convert the natives, whose inferiority in relation to himself is not even to be questioned; whereas I, without a thought of conquest, find myself among a people whose culture controls me, has even, in a sense, created me, people who have cost me more in anguish and rage than they will ever know, who yet do not even know of my existence. The astonishment with which I might have greeted them, should they have stumbled into my African village a few hundred years ago, might have rejoiced their hearts. But the astonishment with which they greet me today can only poison mine.

And this is so despite everything I may do to feel differently, despite my friendly conversations with the *bistro* owner's wife, despite their three-year-old son who has at last become my friend, despite the *saluts* and *bonsoirs* which I exchange with people as I walk, despite the fact that I know that no individual can be taken to task for what history is doing or has done. I say that the culture of these people controls me—but they can scarcely be held responsible for European culture. America comes out of Europe, but these people have never seen America, nor have most of them seen more of Europe than the hamlet at the foot of their mountain. Yet they move with an authority which I shall never have; and they regard me, quite rightly, not only as a stranger in their village but as a suspect latecomer, bearing no credentials, to everything they have—however unconsciously—inherited.

For this village, even were it incomparably more remote and incredibly more primitive, is the West, the West onto which I have been so strangely grafted. These people cannot be, from the point of view of power, strangers anywhere in the world; they have made the modern world, in effect, even if they do not know it. The most illiterate among them is related, in a way that I am not, to Dante, Shakespeare, Michelangelo, Aeschylus, Da Vinci, Rembrandt, and Racine; the cathedral at Chartres says something to them which it cannot say to me, as indeed would New York's Empire State Building, should anyone here ever see it. Out of their hymns and dances come Beethoven and Bach. Go back a few centuries and they are in their full glory—but I am in Africa, watching the conquerors arrive.

The rage of the disesteemed is personally fruitless, but it is also absolutely inevitable; this rage, so generally discounted, so little understood even among the people whose daily bread it is, is one of the things that makes history. Rage can only with difficulty, and never entirely, be brought under the domination of the intelligence and is therefore not susceptible to any arguments whatever. This is a fact which ordinary representatives of the *Herrenvolk,* having never felt this rage and being unable to imagine it, quite fail to understand. Also, rage cannot be hidden, it can only be dissembled. This dissembling deludes the thoughtless, and strengthens rage and adds, to rage, contempt. There are, no doubt, as many ways of coping with the resulting complex of tensions as there are black men in the world, but no black man can hope ever to be entirely liberated from this internal warfare—rage, dissembling, and contempt having inevitably accompanied his first realization of the power of white men. What is crucial here is that, since white men represent in the black man's world so heavy a weight, white men have for black men a reality which is far from being reciprocal; and hence all black men have toward all white men an attitude which is designed, really, either to rob the white man of the jewel of his naïveté, or else to make it cost him dear.

The black man insists, by whatever means he finds at his disposal, that the white man cease to regard him as an exotic rarity and recognize him as a human being. This is a very charged and difficult moment, for there is a great deal of will power involved in the white man's naïveté. Most people are not naturally reflective any more than they are naturally malicious, and the white man prefers to keep the black man at a certain human remove because it is easier for him thus to preserve his simplicity and avoid being called to account for crimes committed by his forefathers, or his neighbors. He is inescapably aware, nevertheless, that he is in a better position in the world than black men are, nor can he quite put to death the suspicion that he is hated by black men therefore. He does not wish to be hated, neither does he wish to change places, and at this point in his uneasiness he can scarcely avoid having recourse to those legends which white men have created about black men, the most usual effect of which is that the white man finds himself enmeshed, so to speak, in his own language which describes hell, as well as the attributes which lead one to hell, as being as black as night.

Every legend, moreover, contains its residuum of truth, and the root function of language is to control the universe by describing it. It is of quite considerable significance that black men remain, in the imagination, and in overwhelming numbers in fact, beyond the disciplines of salvation; and this despite the fact that the West has been "buying" African natives for centuries. There is, I should hazard, an instantaneous necessity to be divorced from this so visibly unsaved stranger, in whose heart, moreover, one cannot guess what dreams of vengeance are being nourished; and, at the same time, there are few things on earth more attractive than the idea of the unspeakable liberty which is allowed the unredeemed. When, beneath the black mask, a human being begins to make himself felt one cannot escape a certain awful wonder as to what kind of human being it is. What one's imagination makes of other people is dictated, of course, by the laws of one's own personality, and it is one of the ironies of black-white relations that, by means of what the white man imagines the black man to be, the black man is enabled to know who the white man is.

I have said, for example, that I am as much a stranger in this village today as I was the first summer I arrived, but this is not quite true. The villagers wonder less about the texture of my hair than they did then, and wonder rather more about me. And the fact that their wonder now exists on another level is reflected in their attitudes and in their eyes. There are the children who make those delightful, hilarious, sometimes astonishingly grave overtures of friendship in the unpredictable fashion of children; other children, having been taught that the devil is a black man, scream in genuine anguish as I approach. Some of the older women never pass without a friendly greeting, never pass, indeed, if it seems that they will be able to engage me in conversation; other women look down or look away or rather contemptuously smirk. Some of the men drink with me and suggest that I learn how to ski—partly, I gather, because they cannot imagine what I would look like on skis—and want to know if I am married, and ask questions about my *métier*. But some of the men have accused *le sale nègre* [the dirty Negro]—behind my back— of stealing wood, and there is already in the eyes of some of them that peculiar, intent, paranoiac malevolence which one sometimes surprises in the eyes of American white men when, out walking with their Sunday girl, they see a Negro male approach.

There is a dreadful abyss between the streets of this village and the streets of the city in which I was born, between the children who shout *Neger!* today and those who shouted *Nigger!* yesterday—the abyss is experience, the American experience. The syllable hurled behind me today expresses, above all, wonder: I am a stranger here. But I am not a stranger in America and the same syllable riding on the American air expresses the war my presence has occasioned in the American soul.

For this village brings home to me this fact: that there was a day, and not really a very distant day, when Americans were scarcely Americans at all but discontented Europeans, facing a great unconquered continent and strolling, say, into a marketplace and seeing black men for the first time. The shock this spectacle afforded is suggested, surely, by the promptness with which they decided that these black men were not really men but cattle. It is true that the necessity on the part of the settlers of the New World of reconciling their moral assumptions with the fact—and the necessity—of slavery enhanced immensely the charm of this idea, and it is also true that this idea expresses, with a truly American bluntness, the attitude which to varying extents all masters have had toward all slaves.

But between all former slaves and slave-owners and the drama which begins for Americans over three hundred years ago at Jamestown, there are at least two differences to be observed. The American Negro slave could not suppose, for one thing, as slaves in past epochs had supposed and often done, that he would ever be able to wrest the power from his master's hands. This was a supposition which the modern era, which was to bring about such vast changes in the aims and dimensions of power, put to death; it only begins, in unprecedented fashion, and with dreadful implications, to be resurrected today. But even had this supposition persisted with undiminished force, the American Negro slave could not have used it to lend his condition dignity, for the reason that this supposition rests on another: that the slave in exile yet remains related to his past, has some means—if only in memory—of revering and sustaining the forms of his former life, is able, in short, to maintain his identity.

This was not the case with the American Negro slave. He is unique among the black men of the world in that his past was taken from him, almost literally, at one blow. One wonders what on earth the first slave found to say to the first dark child he bore. I am told that there are Haitians able to trace their ancestry back to African kings, but any American Negro wishing to go back so far will find his journey through time abruptly arrested by the signature on the bill of sale which served as the entrance paper for his ancestor. At the time—to say nothing of the circumstances—of the enslavement of the captive black man who was to become the American Negro, there was not the remotest possibility that he would ever take power from his master's hands. There was no reason to suppose that his situation would ever change, nor was there, shortly, anything to indicate that his situation had ever been different. It was his necessity, in the words of E. Franklin Frazier, to find a "motive for living under American culture or die." The identity of the American Negro comes out of this extreme situation, and the evolution of this identity was a source of the most intolerable anxiety in the minds and the lives of his masters.

For the history of the American Negro is unique also in this: that the question of his humanity, and of his rights therefore as a human being, became a burning one for several generations of Americans, so burning a question that it ultimately became one of those used to divide the nation. It is out of this argument that the venom of the epithet *Nigger!* is derived. It is an argument which Europe has never had, and hence Europe quite sincerely fails to understand how or why the argument arose in the first place, why its effects are so frequently disastrous and always so unpredictable, why it refuses until today to be entirely settled. Europe's black possessions remained—and do remain—in Europe's colonies, at which remove they represented no threat whatever to European identity. If they posed any problem at all for the European conscience, it was a problem which remained comfortingly abstract: in effect, the black man, *as a man,* did not exist for Europe. But in America, even as a slave, he was an inescapable part of the general social fabric and no American could escape having an attitude toward him. Americans attempt until today to make an abstraction of the Negro, but the very nature of these abstractions reveals the tremendous effects the presence of the Negro has had on the American character.

When one considers the history of the Negro in America it is of the greatest importance to recognize that the moral beliefs of a person, or a people, are never really as tenuous as life—which is not moral—very often causes them to appear; these create for them a frame of reference and a necessary hope, the hope being that when life has done its worst they will be enabled to rise above themselves and to triumph over life. Life would scarcely be bearable if this hope did not exist. Again, even when the worst has been said, to betray a belief is not by any means to have put oneself beyond its power; the betrayal of a belief is not the same thing as ceasing to believe. If this were not so there would be no moral standards in the world at all. Yet one must also recognize that morality is based on ideas and that all ideas are dangerous—dangerous because ideas can only lead to action and where the action leads no man can say. And dangerous in this respect: that confronted with the impossibility of remaining faithful to one's beliefs, and the equal impossibility of becoming free of them, one can be driven to the most inhuman excesses. The ideas on which American beliefs are based are not, though Americans often seem to think so, ideas which originated in America. They came out of Europe. And the establishment of democracy on the American continent was scarcely as radical a break with the past as was the necessity, which Americans faced, of broadening this concept to include black men.

This was, literally, a hard necessity. It was impossible, for one thing, for Americans to abandon their beliefs, not only because these beliefs alone seemed able to justify the sacrifices they had endured and the blood that they had spilled, but also because these beliefs afforded them their only bulwark against a moral chaos as absolute as the physical chaos of the continent it was their destiny to conquer. But in the situation in which Americans found themselves, these beliefs threatened an idea which, whether or not one likes to think so, is the very warp and woof of the heritage of the West, the idea of white supremacy.

Americans have made themselves notorious by the shrillness and the brutality with which they have insisted on this idea, but they did not invent it; and it has escaped the world's notice that those very excesses of which Americans have been guilty imply a certain unprecedented uneasiness over the idea's life and power, if not, indeed, the idea's validity. The idea of white supremacy rests simply on the fact that white men are the creators of civilization (the present civilization, which is the only one that matters; all previous civilizations are simply "contributions" to our own) and are therefore civilization's guardians and defenders. Thus it was impossible for Americans to accept the black man as one of themselves, for to do so was to jeopardize their status as white men. But not so to accept him was to deny his human reality, his human weight and complexity, and the strain of denying the overwhelmingly undeniable forced Americans into rationalizations so fantastic that they approached the pathological.

At the root of the American Negro problem is the necessity of the American white man to find a way of living with the Negro in order to be able to live with himself. And the history of this problem can be reduced to the means used by Americans—lynch law and law, segregation and legal acceptance, terrorization and concession—either to come to terms with this necessity, or to find a way around it, or (most usually) to find a way of doing both these things at once. The resulting spectacle, at once foolish and dreadful, led someone to make the quite accurate observation that "the Negro-in-America is a form of insanity which overtakes white men."

In this long battle, a battle by no means finished, the unforeseeable effects of which will be felt by many future generations, the white man's motive was the protection of his identity; the black man was motivated by the need to establish an identity. And despite the terrorization which the Negro in America endured and endures sporadically until today, despite the cruel and totally inescapable ambivalence of his status in his country, the battle for his identity has long ago been won. He is not a visitor to the West, but a citizen there, an American; as American as the Americans who despise him, the Americans who fear him, the Americans who love him—the Americans who became less than themselves, or rose to be greater than themselves by virtue of the fact that the challenge he represented was inescapable. He is perhaps the only black man in the world whose relationship to white men is more terrible, more subtle, and more meaningful than the relationship of bitter possessed to uncertain possessor. His survival depended, and his development depends, on his ability to turn his peculiar status in the Western world to his own advantage and, it may be, to the very great advantage of that world. It remains for him to fashion out of his experience that which will give him sustenance, and a voice.

The cathedral at Chartres, I have said, says something to the people of this village which it cannot say to me; but it is important to understand that this cathedral says something to me which it cannot say to them. Perhaps they are struck by the power of the spires, the glory of the windows; but they have known God, after all, longer than I have known him, and in a different way, and I am terrified by the slippery bottomless well to be found in the crypt, down which heretics were hurled to death, and by the obscene, inescapable gargoyles jutting out of the stone and seeming to say that God and the devil can never be divorced. I doubt that the villagers think of the devil when they face a cathedral because they have never been identified with the devil. But I must accept the status which myth, if nothing else, gives me in the West before I can hope to change the myth.

Yet, if the American Negro has arrived at his identity by virtue of the absoluteness of his estrangement from his past, American white men still nourish the illusion that there is some means of recovering the European innocence, of returning to a state in which black men do not exist. This is one of the greatest errors Americans can make. The identity they fought so hard to protect has, by virtue of that battle, undergone a change: Americans are as unlike any other white people in the world as it is possible to be. I do not think, for example, that it is too much to suggest that the American vision of the world—which allows so little reality, generally speaking, for any of the darker forces in human life, which tends until today to paint moral issues in glaring black and white—owes a great deal to the battle waged by Americans to maintain between themselves and black men a human separation which could not be bridged. It is only now beginning to be borne in on us—very faintly, it must be admitted, very slowly, and very much against our will—that this vision of the world is dangerously inaccurate, and perfectly useless. For it protects our moral high-mindedness at the terrible expense of weakening our grasp of reality. People who shut their eyes to reality simply invite their own destruction, and anyone who insists on remaining in a state of innocence long after that innocence is dead turns himself into a monster.

The time has come to realize that the interracial drama acted out on the American continent has not only created a new black man, it has created a new white man, too. No road whatever will lead Americans back to the simplicity of this European village where white men still have the luxury of looking on me as a stranger. I am not, really, a stranger any longer for any American alive. One of the things that distinguishes Americans from other people is that no other people has ever been so deeply involved in the lives of black men, and vice versa. This fact faced, with all its implications, it can be seen that the history of the American Negro problem is not merely shameful, it is also something of an achievement. For even when the worst has been said, it must also be added that the perpetual challenge posed by this problem was always, somehow, perpetually met. It is precisely this black-white experience which may prove of indispensable value to us in the world we face today. This world is white no longer, and it will never be white again.

Suggestions

1. The experience of an American Negro in a Swiss village gives rise to observations on history, morals, ethics, and happier human relations.

The thesis of "Stranger in the Village," that the presence of the Negro in America has made the American white wholly different from his European cousin, is developed through an ordered arrangement of ideas. Before the speaker makes the comparison between his reception by the Swiss and his position in America, we hear the Swiss children crying *"Neger! Neger!"*—and this cry becomes a structural device to unify the parts of the essay. The village custom of "buying" Africans introduces another important point, the inaccessibility to the Negro of a culture built by white men. What ideas in addition to these do you consider of special importance in the essay?

2. Though the thesis is clear-cut, the speaker's attitude toward the white man is not so firm. Point out passages in which it is *ambiguous,* and decide whether the essay gains or loses by this ambiguity.

3. Explain: *bistros, Lourdes, chalet, Herrenfolk, naïveté, métier, paranoiac, malevolence, tenuous, ambivalence.*

4. Discuss in writing:
The rage of the disesteemed is personally fruitless, but it is also absolutely inevitable. . . . (¶10)

. . . the same syllable riding on the American air expresses the war my presence has occasioned in the American soul (¶14).

The identity of the American Negro comes out of this extreme situation. . . . (¶17)

Americans are as unlike any other white people in the world as it is possible to be (¶24).

5. Write an essay comparing "Stranger in the Village" and † "The Bottom Rail on Top," deciding whether there are likenesses in the attitudes they present toward the Swiss village and Mississippi.

6. Write an essay on the last sentence of "Stranger in the Village," perhaps centering your discussion on (a) non-white immigration to the United States, or (b) nationalism among Asians and Africans.

E V E N T S

THE GREAT FIGHT THAT WASN'T

BERNARD SHAW *First published in the British journal* THE NATION, *1919. This abridgment is published by permission of* NEW STATES-MAN.

If you were not at the Great Fight, and are at all curious about it, imagine four thousand people packed by night into a roofed enclosure with a gallery round it. I had better not call it a building, because that word has architectural associations; and this enclosure has none. The four thousand people are all smoking as hard as they can; and the atmosphere, which will be described in the morrow's papers as electric, is in fact murky, stifling, and fumesome. In the midst is a scaffold, or place of execution, twenty-four feet square, fenced by ropes. On the scaffold is a mild man, apparently a churchwarden but really a referee, patiently watching two hard-working Britons earning a precarious livelihood by boxing for the amusement of the four thousand. They are tired, and have not the smallest animosity to give a bitter sweat to their exertions. It seems indelicate to stare at them; and I proceed to study the audience.

Like all sporting audiences it consists mostly of persons who manifestly cannot afford the price of admission. My seat has cost me more than ten times what I have paid to hear *Parsifal* at Bayreuth or Beethoven's Ninth Symphony at a very special performance at the Grand Opera in Paris. Certainly there are people here who can spare ten guineas or twenty-five easily enough: honorables and right honorables, explorers, sporting stockbrokers, eminent professional men, plutocrats of all sorts, men with an artistic interest in the display like Robert Loraine, Granville Barker, Maurice Baring, Arnold Bennett, and myself. Here and there is a lady. Not any particular sort of lady or no lady; just an ordinary lady. The one who happens to be sitting by me is one next whom I find myself in the stalls of any theatre, or in church. My lady neighbor watches the weary breadwinners on the scaffold and tries to feel excited, but I fancy she is trying to stifle a suspicion that she had better stayed at home and spent the price of her ticket on a new hat. As for me, nothing would have induced me to stay in the place four minutes had I not been waiting for the not very far off undivine event towards which the sporting section of creation had moved.

Everything comes to an end at last. The boxers retired and the scaffold was occupied by men unknown to me. One of these philanthropists earned my gratitude by adjuring the audience, if it loved the champions, to refrain from smoking; after which the atmosphere cleared until it was no thicker than an average fog.

Then the cheering began, rather localized, because from most of the seats little could be seen except the platform. Even the Prince of Wales had some difficulty in procuring silence for his brief speech when he entered. As it happened I was near the gangway by which the champions came in, and therefore saw at once that the cheering was for Mr. Joseph Beckett, who was approaching in an unpretentious dressing gown. Mr. Beckett can be described exactly as a very sensible-looking man. He mounted the scaffold and went to his corner. A burst of louder cheering made me look round again to the gangway; and this time I was startled by a most amazing apparition; nothing less than Charles XII, "the madman of the North," striding along the gangway in a Japanese silk dressing gown as gallantly as if he had not been killed almost exactly 201 years before. The effect of the audience on the two men was very noticeable. Beckett, too sensible to be nervous, put up with the crowd of people staring at him as a discomfort that was all in the day's work. Carpentier rose at the crowd, and would have had it forty thousand instead of four if he could. He was at home with it; he dominated it; he picked out his friends and kissed hands to them in his debonair way quite naturally, without swank or mock modesty, as one born to move assemblies.

The descriptive reporters began to scribble their tale of a frail French stripling and a massive British colossus. Utter nonsense. The physical omens were all against the Briton. Beckett, who was trained, if anything, a little too fine, has a compact figure, a boxlike chest, stout, stumpy arms useful only for punching, and a thickish neck too short to take his head far out of harm's way. Carpentier, long and lithe, has a terrible pair of arms, very long, with the forearms heavy just where the weight should be. He has a long chest, a long reach, a long flexible neck, and, last but not least, a long head. He is long all over.

The change in Carpentier's face when he sets to work is so startling that the spectators can see nothing else. The unmistakable Greek line digs a trench across his forehead at once; his color changes to a stony grey; he looks 10,000 years old; his eyes see through stone walls; and his expression of intensely concentrated will frightens everyone in the hall except his opponent, who is far too busy protecting himself to attend to such curiosities.

There was no fight. There was only a superb exhibition spar, with Beckett as what used to be called a chopping block. For a few moments he wisely stuck close to his man; but Mr. Angle, the referee, gave the order to break away; and Beckett then let the Frenchman get clear and faced him for out-fighting. From that moment he was lost. Carpentier simply did the classic thing: the long shot with the left—the lead-off and get-away. The measurement of distance—and such a distance!—was exact to an inch, the speed dazzling, the impact like the kick of a thoroughbred horse. Beckett, except for one amazed lionlike shake of his head, took it like a stone wall; but he was helpless: he had not time to move a finger before Carpentier was back out of his reach. He was utterly outspeeded. Three times Carpentier did this, each hit more brilliant, if possible, than the last.

Beckett was for a moment dazed by the astonishing success of the attack; and in that moment Carpentier sent in a splendidly clean and finished right to the jaw. It is not often that perfect luck attends perfect style in this world; but Carpentier seemed able to command even luck. The blow found that mysterious spot that is in all our jaws, and that is so seldom found by the fist. There was no mistaking the droop with which Beckett went prone to the boards. In an old-fashioned fight he would have been carried by his seconds to his corner and brought up to the scratch in half a minute quite well able to go on. Under modern rules he had to lie unhelped; and at the end of ten seconds Carpentier was declared the winner.

The usual orgy followed. Pugilists are a sentimental, feminine species, much given to kissing and crying. Carpentier was hoisted up to be chaired, dragged down to be kissed, hung out by the heels from the scaffold to be fondled by a lady, and in every possible way given reason to envy Beckett. Beckett's seconds, by the way, so far forgot themselves as to leave their man lying uncared for on the floor after he was counted out until Carpentier, indignant at their neglect, rushed across the ring and carried Beckett to his corner.

Now for the seamy side of the affair, the betting side. As I pushed my way through the crowd in Holborn, I could see by the way my news was received that every poor dupe of the sporting papers had put his shillings or pence or even his quid or two on Beckett. Never had a betting ramp been more thoroughly organized. When the war was over nobody knew whether military service had spoiled Carpentier for boxing purposes or left him as good as ever. If he were as good, or better, then clearly oceans of money could be made at a risk no greater than any gambler will take, by persuading the public that his sun had set and that the Carpentier who knocked out Wells in seventy-three seconds was a back number.

Accordingly, the situation was taken in hand in the usual fashion. A British pugilist of something less than commanding eminence was sent to France and pitted against Carpentier, who gave a poor display and obtained the decision with difficulty. Here was proof positive of his decadence. Then the press got to work. Beckett, progressing rapidly from victory to victory, was extolled as invulnerable and invincible. Carpentier's reputation was discounted until hardly a shred of it remained. His two youthful defeats were retold. The public were reminded that he had obtained a decision against Gunboat Smith only on an unintentional foul by that gentleman; and ring reporters solemnly declared their conviction that but for this accident Carpentier could not have lasted another round. I was informed on the strength of private information from "the French colony" that Carpentier had sold the fight and that it was arranged that Beckett should win. Then came a clump of boxing articles, each giving a dozen reasons to show that nothing but a miracle could prevent Beckett from wiping the floor with the exhausted and obsolete Frenchman. I do not know how high the odds were piled at last; but on the morning of the fight every ring-struck sportsman who knew nothing about boxing (and not one in a hundred of the people who read about boxing, or for that matter, who write about it, knows anything worth knowing) had his bet on Beckett. This is a measure of their combined sense.

As to the brutality of the affair, Beckett was chatting to his friends over the ropes without a mark on his face, and with £3,000 in his pocket, before they had stopped kissing Carpentier. There are many industrial pursuits more painful and much more dangerous than boxing. The world now waits breathless for the meeting between Carpentier and Mr. Dempsey.

Suggestions

1. The essays termed Events in this book are distinguished from Experiences by the detachment with which they are written. But their speakers, though not personally involved in the situations they report, are not unmoved by them. In "The Great Fight That Wasn't" both the speaker's detachment and his cuttingly satiric attitude are exemplified in the last sentence of ¶2, with its parody of Tennyson's *In Memoriam, 36*. Show that this attitude is introduced in the description of the "roofed enclosure," identify the principal targets of it, and account for the title of the essay.

2. List the characteristics of Carpentier that give the impression of an extraordinary person, "one born to move assemblies." How is Beckett characterized?

3. Comment on the assertion that boxers are a "sentimental, feminine species, much given to kissing and crying." Use your own examples to attack or defend it.

4. Explain the irony in the comment on the British press and betting ramp: "This is a measure of their combined sense" (¶10).

5. Explain: *Parsifal at Bayreuth, plutocrats, philanthropists, quid, decadence.*

6. Write an essay about a one-sided sporting contest that you have seen, controlling your description by a firm attitude.

7. Write an essay relating the phrase, "two hard-working Britons earning a precarious livelihood by boxing" (¶1), to the last paragraph.

JEMMY BUTTON GETS HIS RIGHTS

HERBERT WENDT ―∘⊰{ *From* IN SEARCH OF ADAM, *Houghton Mifflin Company, 1956.*

The ostensible reason for Captain Robert Fitzroy's voyage to South America was such an unusual one that it alone was bound to appeal to the young Darwin. His Majesty King William's ship *Beagle,* which had hitherto rendered excellent service in surveying operations and hydrography, had received orders to restore three slaves from the remote island of Tierra del Fuego to a life of freedom. This special act of generosity was intended to show the world that Liberal England would in the future no longer be willing to participate in the capture and sale of slaves. The fact that H.M.S. *Beagle* happened also to go on to the Falkland Islands, where Fitzroy hoisted the Union Jack, though England had no particular business in that part of the world, was only a trifling blemish on this admirable enterprise.

The events that led up to the *Beagle*'s proceedings were no less unusual. About the year 1830 the two political parties of England, the conservative Tories and the liberal Whigs, had fallen out badly over the question of slavery. For some considerable time the Slavery Abolition Acts had prohibited the British from engaging in the lucrative "black ivory" trade. But now the Liberal government of Lord Grey, the Prime Minister, and Lord Palmerston, the Foreign Minister, was also demanding the liberation of all colored slaves in the English Crown Colonies. The Tories were against this proposal. But the Whigs succeeded in putting it through and passed a law accordingly.

At this very moment H.M.S. *Beagle* returned from a voyage to Tierra del Fuego, and cast anchor in the Port of London. She had aboard not only Captain Robert Fitzroy and his white crew but also four brown-skinned natives from the island. Fitzroy, an out-and-out Tory, grandson of the Duke of Grafton and, despite his mere five-and-twenty years, already a recognized meteorologist and cartographer, had not the faintest suspicion of Palmerston's new law. He announced without a blush in the Naval Officers' Club that he had brought the four savages with him as slaves, to teach them morals, decency, and the Christian religion. And his sailors supplemented this hair-raising fact, in the taverns round about the West India Docks, by the further appalling statement that one could buy Tierra del Fuego children from their parents for no more than a single mother-of-pearl button.

Hitherto, so far as Captain Fitzroy could remember, no living being had troubled himself in the slightest if an honest seaman had landed in Old England with a few "niggers, or Injuns." At first he couldn't quite understand the point of the scandal that broke out. It was not until he was called to the Home Office and its chief, Viscount Melbourne, dumfounded him with the thunderous accusation of being a brutal slave hunter that he realized he had become involved in a question of high politics.

"Is it a fact," inquired his lordship, "that these Tierra del Fuego people were brought to England against their will?"

"Certainly, my lord," Fitzroy admitted. "I arrested one of them as a public nuisance, because the members of his tribe had been so unchristian as to steal one of my boats. He was baptized aboard by the highly respectable name of York Minster."

"And why did you not afterwards release him, Captain?"

"Because, begging your lordship's pardon, I wished to make him a useful member of society."

Viscount Melbourne raised one eyebrow and asked crossly for details of the other Tierra del Fuego natives. He learned that the second victim, an adolescent girl, had been given the new baptismal name of Fuegia Basket. Fitzroy, according to his own account, had purchased this charming little savage in order to clothe her decently. The third native was a half-grown boy. His name was Jemmy Button.

"Button?" repeated the viscount, filled with uneasy suspicions. "Button? How on earth did you hit on such a name, Captain?"

"Because he cost me a mother-of-pearl button," explained Fitzroy in some embarrassment. "His parents, my lord, were quite satisfied with the bargain."

"A mother-of-pearl button!" groaned his lordship. "It's true, then!"

"Well, yes," Fitzroy replied, somewhat conscience-stricken. "I intended to educate him at my own expense. I beg your forgiveness, my lord. But I don't understand this new law."

Viscount Melbourne was not very interested in the powers of understanding of a man who could offer such an insult to the dignity of humanity. He gave Captain Fitzroy brief and concise instructions, in the name of His Majesty's government, to fit out the *Beagle* for a further voyage and take the four Tierra del Fuego natives forthwith back where he had fetched them from.

"Four?" Fitzroy interrupted. "My lord, there are only three of them. The fourth has just died here in London, unfortunately."

"That only makes matters worse," retorted his lordship with emphasis. There was a short pause. Then he eyed Fitzroy sternly. "You understand, Captain? These three unfortunate people are to be resettled in exactly the same place as they formerly lived in. You will be responsible to me, Captain, for carrying out my instructions to the letter."

"Jemmy won't be very pleased," Fitzroy remarked. "He's taken quite a fancy to me already."

But Jemmy's opinion was not asked. Fitzroy's case was made a precedent. It soon became well known. Before long there was not a Whig in England who was not consumed with the deepest sympathy for Jemmy Button, York Minster, and Fuegia Basket. The preparations for their return to freedom were followed with great emotion and satisfaction.

Fitzroy had to put a good face on the matter. He took aboard a missionary named Matthews, who had been ordered by the Home Office to take up residence at Woolya Bay, Tierra del Fuego, in order to guide Jemmy's cannibal tribe gently and tactfully into the bosom of civilization. The captain had been rather surprised at first that he had not been more severely taken to task and called upon to answer for his infringement of the law. But he soon found out the reason. His Majesty's government still needed him, not only to take charge of the passage to Tierra del Fuego, but also in his capacity as an expert on South American islands and waters. As the *Beagle* was making a voyage to Tierra del Fuego, she might just as well explore some of the localities that interested England. There were the Falkland Islands, for example. They were the subject of dispute between Argentina, Spain, France, American seal hunters, and the Hamburg merchant Louis Vernet. They were quite near Jemmy's native land.

Fitzroy immediately understood this second object of the voyage. So his instructions were to sail to Tierra del Fuego, settle Matthews, the missionary, and the brown pair of lovers, York and Fuegia, somewhere in the wilderness, exchange Jemmy back again for the mother-of-pearl button, then do away with the impossible situation in the Falklands, and finally decide the question of their legal possession. He changed his mind about Viscount Melbourne, who now seemed to him an astute politician who had designed an agreeable mission for him.

But he was not quite so pleased with the third object of the voyage. He had been ordered to take a natural scientist aboard, some learned landlubber or other, who was to collect insects, plants, and minerals in

Tierra del Fuego, on the Patagonian and Chilean coasts, the Falklands, and other islands of equal interest to England. Of course he understood why. If a scientist were aboard, no one would suspect the voyage of any political intention. H.M.S. *Beagle* would be serving the cause of humanity by her voyage and at the same time enriching science. So far, so good. But the fellow sent aboard his ship by Professor Henslow, that twenty-two-year-old bachelor of theology and amateur zoologist, Darwin, was by no means to his taste. He looked just the sort to be frightfully seasick and probably come to a miserable end in the bleak climate of the Strait of Magellan. All the same young Mr. Darwin did have the decency to confess that hardly any natural scientist could ever have started on a voyage so imperfectly equipped as himself, and this admission did win Fitzroy around a little. He sent for the ship's surgeon, Mr. Bynoe, told him to keep an eye on the young fellow, and hoped against hope that all would be well.

On December 27, 1831, the *Beagle* set sail on a southwesterly course into the Atlantic. Thereafter, for a whole year, Darwin had the opportunity to study Jemmy Button, York Minster, and Fuegia Basket and give himself up to serious thoughts about the evolution of human civilization. It is clear from his diary that the three Tierra del Fuego natives, ostensible reasons for a political mission, gave him the first foundations of his subsequent theory of the descent of man. Little Jemmy Button, whose fate had been accidentally illuminated by the searchlight of public interest, thus took his place in the history of natural science.

The three natives soon perceived that they were the center of interest and took prompt advantage of it. They were in high spirits—at any rate at the outset of the voyage—over the prospect of returning to their homes, told astonishing stories about their compatriots, and assumed the airs and graces of prima donnas under the affectionate care of Matthews, the missionary. Fitzroy was obliged from time to time to reprimand them rather sharply. Every such occasion gave him an excuse to grumble over the ill-starred law of the right honorable Lords Grey and Palmerston and to express himself in favor of the retention of the institution of slavery.

Darwin became excited. After all, Fuegia, York, and Jemmy were not simply wild animals, but decently clothed, duly baptized, enlightened human beings, eager to learn, and with as much right to a free life as any white man. The seamy sides of their characters were harmless in comparison with those of the rough sailors from East London and Devonport. Fitzroy only laughed at these observations. He told his sentimental fellow voyager that there was a natural law by which the stronger made his way and used his power. Without slavery, he proceeded, expounding the wisdom of a lifetime, the colonies could make no progress, human society could not be controlled, nor could any culture exist throughout the world.

These were the principles of a scion of the aristocracy. They must have sounded positively obscene to the Whigs. Darwin, nothing if not an objective-minded scientist, had the feeling that there might be something in them. He thought the matter over. A law of Nature? Was Nature really so cruel as to allow the stronger to make a meal of the weaker? Yes, she was. Every glance at a meadow or a pond proved it. What was the object of such behavior? There must, after all, be some kind of sense in the brutal struggle for existence. Mysterious as it might be, it was perhaps extremely important for science. He remembered once more the free competition of forces, advocated by the Whigs and transferred by his grandfather Erasmus to nature. Basically, that was the same idea, the only difference being that competition in that case did not result in the ethical chaos of the jungle but in the rationally grounded selection of superior types for survival. Darwin gasped a little. He felt a sudden sense of relief.

The ticklish problem of the Tierra del Fuego natives still remained obstinate, despite his recognition of this principle. It was clear that the colored races had been defeated by the white in the struggle for survival. But this fact, in the opinion of Darwin as a Christian and a Whig, laid special obligations upon the victor. Man, as distinct from all other creatures, was a moral being. He had been charged in the cradle with the duty of loving his neighbors, even those weaker than himself. This high estimate of mankind that Charles Darwin of Christ's College had conceived was destined to receive a rude shock on the island of Tierra del Fuego.

A year had passed since the start of the expedition by the time the *Beagle* reached Tierra del Fuego and cast anchor in Woolya Bay. The three brown protagonists then had to be returned to the bosoms of their families. They had suddenly grown very silent. They were staring with something like dread at the wild, deeply indented coast. And as soon as they met the first members of their tribe they showed every sign of alarm. Apparently they had quite forgotten, during their contact with civilization, what it was like at home. The wild natives, on the other hand, received the returning travelers without surprise, without, in fact, any sign of emotion. They looked at them, so at least the men of the *Beagle* could not help thinking, in practically the same way as one might inspect a prime joint of meat.

Darwin, too, was much alarmed. He had imagined the natives of Tierra del Fuego to be not very different from Jemmy and Fuegia, a bit more naked and unrefined perhaps, but at any rate recognizably human. The mob he saw rushing out of the woods of Tierra del Fuego consisted of utterly bestial creatures, devoid of all appearance of modesty and morality. It was a horde of savages that tried to steal everything but the fixtures. They might be described as a superior troop of monkeys, the individual members of which, whether male or female, behaved in utterly brutal and indecent fashion. How had civilization been able to bring about such a change in three human beings taken from this rabble of cave dwellers? A sudden thought, sinister and deeply disturbing, shot through Darwin's mind. Had all human beings originally been animals like these natives and only developed true humanity and civilization after a long process of growth?

Darwin fell into reverie while the captain, the missionary, and the crew did all they could to smooth over the return of their protégés. Little Jemmy had taken refuge at Darwin's side. He was trembling from head to foot and staring at his compatriots in wide-eyed terror. He had remembered that it was the custom in Tierra del Fuego to beat sick and weakly members of the tribe to death and devour them. And he had already become so English that the very thought made him feel faint with horror. Darwin, doing his best to console the boy, wondered anxiously what was going to become of Jemmy and the other two natives in this barbarous place. Would they be able to teach the savages what they had learned and start humanizing them? Hardly, he thought, for English habits and customs—as he very soon found—did not suit the primitive conditions of Tierra del Fuego.

A second idea occurred to him, as overpowering as the first. Might it not be that the natives of this island at the end of the world had become bestial, cruel, and greedy on account of the very harshness of nature in these parts and the remorseless struggle for existence? He noted in his diary that since Nature made habit all powerful and its effects hereditary, she had suited the native of Tierra del Fuego to the climate and the produce of that miserable country. How did she do this? By annihilating what was inappropriate and only allowing what held good to survive. It must be the same with animals and plants. They were passed through the sieve of the struggle for existence; this accordingly decided which were to remain and which were to leave the stage.

Then he remembered his Lyell. Environments, it was stated in the *Principles of Geology,* changed in the course of millions of years. The conditions of existence, the rules of the game of the survival of the fittest changed with them. What had formerly been appropriate and passed the severe test of selection would be appropriate no longer and be doomed to disappear. Darwin had a vision of a savage landscape inhabited by prehistoric animals and primitive human beings. He watched them, in his mind's eye, gradually changing because of the cumulative effect of a number of different, extremely small variations: the primitive forms died out one after the other and only those best suited to the new conditions maintained themselves, continuing to propagate, and thus after enormous lapses of time developing into the species of the present day. In the case of Jemmy, Fuegia, and York this process of change had been compressed, under the English sky, to a period of a few months. Would there now be a retrogression? Or did Nature in Tierra del Fuego annihilate, by some deed of violence, what had become foreign to her?

This last question was soon answered. York Minster, being robust, was the first to return to the old way of life. The islanders made the acquaintance of his fists and began to respect him. Since he had learned from the whites all sorts of technical accomplishments into the bargain, he came in a short time to occupy a most important position in the tribe. He paid fewer and fewer visits to the settlement that the missionary Matthews had built for himself and the better behaved of the natives. Fuegia, too, now formally united to him in marriage, began to lead the old savage life again. Both of them, to Matthews' disgust, were very soon going about completely naked, taking part in heathen ceremonies, and acting as though they had quite forgotten England and the *Beagle*.

One day when Jemmy in his smart European clothes was taking a walk at a little distance from the settlement, his former comrade York Minster attacked him, stripped him to his very shirt, and robbed him of all his possessions. Jemmy fled in despair to the missionary's hut, called his compatriots a set of wicked and ignorant rascals, and begged with tears to be allowed to return aboard the *Beagle*. Matthews did his best to comfort the boy. Shortly afterwards he in his turn had such unpleasant experiences with the natives that he came to the conclusion that no sort of missionary work in such a place was likely to succeed, and went off to see Fitzroy.

The captain listened to him with a malicious smile. He made no comment, merely inquiring when Matthews had finished what the reverend gentleman proposed to do about it. The latter was at his wits' end. "Those brigands tried to strip me naked and pull all my hair out," he complained, in great distress. "I think it's a hopeless case. We shall have to abandon the settlement."

"Without the application of a cat-o'-nine-tails," Fitzroy observed imperturbably, "it is impossible to teach such people how to behave. The authorities ought to have realized that in London before we left. It's a thousand pities," he added, "about those three pets of ours."

"It is, indeed," Matthews agreed. He went on diffidently, "So you don't think, Captain, we can take poor Jemmy aboard again?"

"No," replied Fitzroy. "We should be disobeying the government's orders."

Matthews bowed his head, examining the misty landscape of Tierra del Fuego with a melancholy air. He proceeded to have his possessions brought aboard the *Beagle* and took leave of Jemmy Button. However much the boy might plead, he would have to stay with his wicked kindred. Politics took priority over the longing of a little brown native for civilization.

A few months later, after Fitzroy had completed his survey of the most southerly point of South America, the *Beagle* returned to Woolya Bay. Darwin met Jemmy again. The experience crushed him. He saw an emaciated, wretched savage with long, disheveled hair, naked except for a rag of cloth about his loins. There never was such a complete and deplorable change in anyone. Jemmy's opinions had changed, too. He no longer wished to return to England. The reason he gave was a cogent one. Beside him squatted a naked young girl, toward whom Matthews cast a highly censorious eye. The boy, in such English as he still remembered, introduced her as "Jemmy Button's wife." He accepted valuable parting presents. The other natives looked on avidly, ready to seize their share of the booty as soon as the ship departed.

Neither Darwin nor anyone else ever heard what happened to him and the ferocious York. Fuegia Basket met a tragic fate ten years later. In 1842 a sealing vessel anchored off the coast of Tierra del Fuego. The crew were greatly astonished when a strange sort of female native came aboard who could speak a little broken English and showed a childish pleasure at meeting white men again. The seal hunters naturally had not the remotest idea of the identity of their delighted visitor or the story of Fuegia Basket. All they understood was that she was a woman; they treated her accordingly. Fuegia was not strong enough to endure the demands of these robust seamen. She died a few days later. No doubt she had imagined that her return to civilization would work out rather differently.

The humanitarian part of the enterprise, accordingly, failed utterly, though we may add that the Falklands operation on the contrary succeeded. Fitzroy and his learned passenger took different views of the fiasco. The captain considered that his distaste for sentimental nonsense of this kind had been brilliantly justified. Darwin, on the other hand, drew the conclusions of a natural scientist from the affair. He now realized how greatly the characters and peculiarities of animate beings could alter under the influence of environment and the high degree of risk of permanent displacement run by all plants, animals, and human beings in consequence of the struggle for survival. The Tierra del Fuego natives who had been softened by their lives in England could not easily adapt themselves to an existence among savage hordes. They either had to return to primitive ways or perish. Was that really a law of nature? And what followed from it?

While the *Beagle* cruised off the American coast tentative conjectures and flashes of inspiration gradually shaped themselves into a theory in Darwin's mind.

Suggestions

1. "Jemmy Button Gets His Rights" has a narrative structure similar to that of many fictions. The main character is introduced at the end of the first sentence, then apparently forgotten during a *flashback* that accounts for his presence on the *Beagle*. (Notice the transitional sentence at the beginning of ¶2.) The immediate political background is sketched briefly but fully enough to prepare for the important interview between Fitzroy and Melbourne. This interview, presented as a dramatic scene, is the point of departure for the rest of the story.

2. Darwin's theory of evolution, still controversial in some quarters, is not a subject for debate in this essay, which investigates the origin of the theory, not its truth or falsity. With the help of the essay † "Evolution" summarize the beliefs of Darwin that resulted from his voyage on the *Beagle*.

3. Describe the *tone* of the essay with emphasis on the interview between Fitzroy and Melbourne. Is Fitzroy's character further revealed in other passages?

4. List the official reasons for the voyage of the *Beagle*. Is there any evidence that the speaker disapproves of the mixed motives involved?

5. (a) Explain the *irony* of the title.
   (b) "Little Jemmy Button, whose fate had been accidentally illuminated by the searchlight of public interest, thus took his place in the history of natural science." In view of this sentence, can the title be called *paradoxical* as well as ironic?

6. Comment: "The preparations for their return to freedom were followed with great emotion and satisfaction" (¶18).

7. The return of the natives, interpreted by both Fitzroy and Darwin as a fiasco, is an example of how one set of circumstances can be used as "proof" for two entirely different beliefs. Summarize these two views by (a) contrasting the two men and (b) relating the views of the missionary to theirs.

8. Explain: *ostensible, meteorologist, cartographer, protégés, retrogression, cat-o'-nine-tails, censorious.*

9. Write an essay showing the advantages of considering "Jemmy Button Gets His Rights" and † "Evolution" together.

SHARK CLOSE-UPS

J. Y. COUSTEAU
and
FRÉDÉRIC DUMAS

From THE SILENT WORLD, *Harper & Brothers, 1953.*

One day we were finishing a movie sequence on trigger fish when Dumas and I were galvanized with ice-cold terror. It is a reaction unpleasant enough on land, and very lonely in the water. What we saw made us feel that naked men really do not belong under the sea.

At a distance of forty feet there appeared from the gray haze the lead-white bulk of a twenty-five-foot *Carcharodon carcharias,* the only shark species that all specialists agree is a confirmed maneater. Dumas, my bodyguard, closed in beside me. The brute was swimming lazily. In that moment I thought that at least he would have a bellyache on our three-cylinder lungs.

Then, the shark saw us. His reaction was the last conceivable one. In pure fright, the monster voided a cloud of excrement and departed at an incredible speed.

Dumas and I looked at each other and burst into nervous laughter. The self-confidence we gained that day led us to a foolish negligence. We abandoned the body guard system and all measures of safety. Further meetings with sharp-nosed sharks, tiger sharks, mackerel sharks, and ground sharks inflated our sense of shark mastery. They all ran from us. After several weeks in the Cape Verdes, we were ready to state flatly that all sharks were cowards. They were so pusillanimous they wouldn't hold still to be filmed.

One day I was on the bridge, watching the little spark jiggle up and down on the echo-sound tape, sketching the profile of the sea floor nine thousand feet below the open Atlantic off Africa. There was the usual faint signal of the deep scattering layer twelve hundred feet down. The deep scattering layer is an astounding new problem of oceanography, a mystifying physical mezzanine hovering above the bedrock of the sea. It is recorded at two to three hundred fathoms in the daytime and it ascends toward the surface at night.

The phenomenon rises and falls with the cycle of sun and dark, leading some scientists to believe it is a dense blanket of living organisms, so vast as to tilt the imagination. As I watched the enigmatic scrawls, the stylus began to enter three distinct spurs on the tape, three separate scattering layers, one above the other. I was lost in whirling ideas, watching the spark etch the lowest and heaviest layer, when I heard shouts from the deck, "Whales!" A herd of sluggish bottlenosed whales surrounded the *Élie Monnier*.

In the clear water we studied the big dark forms. Their heads were round and glossy with bulbous foreheads, the "bottle" which gives them their name. When a whale broke the surface, it spouted and the rest of the body followed softly, stretching in relaxation. The whale's lips were curved in a fixed smile with tiny eyes close to the tucks of the lips, a roguish visage for such a formidable creature. Dumas skinned down to the harpoon platform under the bow while I stuck a film magazine in the underwater camera. The whales were back from a dive. One emerged twelve feet from Dumas. He threw the harpoon with all his might. The shaft struck near the pectoral fin and blood started. The animal sounded in an easy rhythm and we paid out a hundred yards of harpoon line, tied to a heavy gray buoy. The buoy was swept away in the water—the whale was well hooked. The other whales lay unperturbed around the *Élie Monnier*.

We saw Dumas's harpoon sticking out of the water; then it, the whale and buoy disappeared. Dumas climbed the mast with binoculars. I kept the ship among the whales, thinking they would not abandon a wounded comrade. Time passed.

Libera, the keen-eyed radio man, spotted the buoy and there was the whale, seemingly unhurt, with the harpoon protruding like a toothpick. Dumas hit the whale twice with dum-dum bullets. Red water washed on the backs of the faithful herd, as it gathered around the stricken one. We struggled for an hour to pick up the buoy and tie the harpoon line to the *Élie Monnier*.

A relatively small bottlenosed whale, heavily wounded, was tethered to the ship. We were out of sight of land, with fifteen hundred fathoms of water under the keel, and the whale herd diving and spouting around the ship. Tailliez and I entered the water to follow the harpoon line to the agonized animal.

The water was an exceptional clear turquoise blue. We followed the line a few feet under the surface and came upon the whale. Thin streams of blood jetted horizontally from the bullet holes. I swam toward three other bottlenoses. As I neared them, they turned up their flukes and sounded. It was the first time I had been under water to actually see them diving and I understood the old whaler's word, "sound." They did not dive obliquely as porpoises often do. They sped straight down, perfectly vertical. I followed them down a hundred feet. A fifteen-foot shark passed way below me, probably attracted by the whale's blood. Beyond sight was the deep scattering layer; down there a herd of leviathans grazed; more sharks roamed. Above in the sun's silvery light was Tailliez and a big whale dying. Reluctantly I returned to the ship.

Back on deck I changed into another lung and strapped a tablet of cupric acetate on an ankle and one on my belt. When this chemical dissolves in water it is supposed to repulse sharks. Dumas was to pass a noose over the whale's tail, while I filmed. Just after we went under he saw a big shark, but it was gone before I answered his shout. We swam under the keel of the ship and located the harpoon line.

A few lengths down the line in a depth of fifteen feet we sighted an eight-foot shark of a species we had never before seen. He was impressively neat, light gray, sleek, a real collector's item. A ten-inch fish with vertical black-and-white stripes accompanied him a few inches above his back, one of the famous pilot fish. We boldly swam toward the shark, confident that he would run as all the others had. He did not retreat. We drew within ten feet of him, and saw all around the shark an escort of tiny striped pilots three or four inches long.

They were not following him; they seemed part of him. A thumbnail of a pilot fish wriggled just ahead of the shark's snout, miraculously staying in place as the beast advanced. He probably found there a compressibility wave that held him. If he tumbled out of it, he would be hopelessly left behind. It was some time before we realized that the shark and his courtiers were not scared of us.

Sea legends hold that the shark has poor eyesight and pilot fish guide him to the prey, in order to take crumbs from his table. Scientists today tend to pooh-pooh the attribution of the pilot as a seeing-eye dog, although dissection has confirmed the low vision of sharks. Our experiences lead us to believe they probably see as well as we do.

The handsome gray was not apprehensive. I was happy to have such an opportunity to film a shark, although, as the first wonder passed, a sense of danger came to our hearts. Shark and company slowly circled us. I became the film director, making signs to Dumas, who was co-starred with the shark. Dumas obligingly swam in front of the beast and along behind it. He lingered at the tail and reached out his hand. He grasped the tip of the caudal fin, undecided about giving it a good pull. That would break the dreamy rhythm and make a good shot, but it might also bring the teeth snapping back at him. Dumas released the tail and pursued the shark round and round. I was whirling in the center of the game, busy framing Dumas. He was swimming as hard as he could to keep up with the almost motionless animal. The shark made no hostile move nor did he flee, but his hard little eyes were on us.

I tried to identify the species. The tail was quite asymmetrical, with an unusually long top, or heterocercal caudal fin. He had huge pectorals, and the large dorsal fin was rounded with a big white patch on it. In outline and marking he resembled no shark we had seen or studied.

The shark had gradually led us down to sixty feet. Dumas pointed down. From the visibility limit of the abyss, two more sharks climbed toward us. They were fifteen-footers, slender, steel-blue animals with a more savage appearance. They leveled off below us. They carried no pilot fish.

Our old friend, the gray shark, was getting closer to us, tightening his slowly revolving cordon. But he still seemed manageable. He turned reliably in his clockwise prowl and the pilots held their stations. The blue pair from the abyss hung back, leaving the affair to the first comer. We revolved inside the ring, watching the gray, and tried to keep the blues located at the same time. We never found them in the same place twice.

Below the blue sharks there appeared great tunas with long fins. Perhaps they had been there since the beginning, but it was the first time we noticed them. Above us flying fish gamboled, adding a discordant touch of gaiety to what was becoming a tragedy for us. Dumas and I ransacked our memories for advices on how to frighten off sharks. *"Gesticulate wildly,"* said a lifeguard. We flailed our arms. The gray did not falter. *"Give 'em a flood of bubbles,"* said a helmet diver. Dumas waited until the shark had reached his nearest point and released a heavy exhalation. The shark did not react. *"Shout as loud as you can,"* said Hans Hass. We hooted until our voices cracked. The shark appeared deaf. *"Cupric acetate tablets fastened to leg and belt will keep sharks away if you go into the drink,"* said an Air Force briefing officer. Our friend swam through the copper-stained water without a wink. His cold, tranquil eye appraised us. He seemed to know what he wanted, and he was in no hurry.

A small dreadful thing occurred. The tiny pilot fish on the shark's snout tumbled off his station and wriggled to Dumas. It was a long journey for the little fellow, quite long enough for us to speculate on his purpose. The mite butterflied in front of Dumas's mask. Dumas shook his head as if to dodge a mosquito. The little pilot fluttered happily, moving with the mask, inside which Dumas focused in cross-eyed agony.

Instinctively I felt my comrade move close to me, and I saw his hand held out clutching his belt knife. Beyond the camera and the knife, the gray shark retreated some distance, turned, and glided at us head-on.

We did not believe in knifing sharks, but the final moment had come, when knife and camera were all we had. I had my hand on the camera button and it was running, without my knowledge that I was filming the oncoming beast. The flat snout grew larger and there was only the head. I was flooded with anger. With all my strength I thrust the camera and banged his muzzle. I felt the wash of a heavy body flashing past and the shark was twelve feet away, circling us as slowly as before, unharmed and expressionless. I thought, *Why in hell doesn't he go to the whale? The nice juicy whale. What did we ever do to him?*

The blue sharks now climbed up and joined us. Dumas and I decided to take a chance on the surface. We swam up and thrust our masks out of the water. The *Élie Monnier* was three hundred yards away, under the wind. We waved wildly and saw no reply from the ship. We believed that floating on the surface with one's head out of the water is the classic method of being eaten away. Hanging there, one's legs could be plucked like bananas. I looked down. The three sharks were rising toward us in a concerted attack.

We dived and faced them. The sharks resumed the circling maneuver. As long as we were a fathom or two down, they hesitated to approach. It would have been an excellent idea for us to navigate toward the ship. However, without landmarks, or a wrist compass, we could not follow course.

Dumas and I took a position with each man's head watching the other man's flippers, in the theory that the sharks preferred to strike at feet. Dumas made quick spurts to the surface to wave his arms for a few seconds. We evolved a system of taking turns for brief appeals on the surface, while the low man pulled his knees up against his chest and watched the sharks. A blue closed in on Dumas's feet while he was above. I yelled. Dumas turned over and resolutely faced the shark. The beast broke off and went back to the circle. When we went up to look we were dizzy and disoriented from spinning around under water, and had to revolve our heads like a lighthouse beacon to find the *Élie Monnier*. We saw no evidence that our shipmates had spied us.

We were nearing exhaustion, and cold was claiming the outer layers of our bodies. I reckoned we had been down over a half hour. Any moment we expected the constriction of air in our mouthpieces, a sign that the air supply nears exhaustion. When it came, we would reach behind our backs and turn the emergency supply valve. There was five minutes' worth of air in the emergency ration. When that was gone, we could abandon our mouthpieces and make mask dives, holding our breath. That would quicken the pace, redouble the drain on our strength, and leave us facing tireless, indestructible creatures that never needed breath. The movements of the sharks grew agitated. They ran around us, working all their strong propulsive fins, turned down and disappeared. We could not believe it. Dumas and I stared at each other. A shadow fell across us. We looked up and saw the hull of the *Élie Monnier*'s launch. Our mates had seen our signals and had located our bubbles. The sharks ran when they saw the launch.

We flopped into the boat, weak and shaken. The crew were as distraught as we were. The ship had lost sight of our bubbles and drifted away. We could not believe what they told us; we had been in the water only twenty minutes. The camera was jammed by contact with the shark's nose.

Suggestions

1. Like † "Sea Monsters" in Part 1, "Shark Close-ups" contains bits of scientific information without being a textbook of marine biology. The gathering of these facts may strike you as described with more personal coloring than those of "Sea Monsters"—and as more important than the facts themselves. If so, do you conclude that "Shark Close-ups" should be classified as an Experience rather than an Event? Does it contain either word? Discuss fully.

2. The theme of "Shark Close-ups" is advanced by implication and *indirection,* beginning with the last sentence of ¶1. Later it is modified (¶4) and strengthened by the episode of the fearless sharks. Formulate the theme; can it be extended to include the idea of human arrogance?

3. Point out passages in which the speaker admits his ignorance, and others in which the divers' ignorance is proven by their foolish actions.

4. Explain the relation between the episode of the dying whale and the encounter with the sharks.

5. The whales, sharks, and pilot fish are made real by the style used to describe them. Point out instances of *personification;* of striking *similes.*

6. Write an account of an event that you have witnessed and that suggests a theme similar to the theme of "Shark Close-ups."

7. Write a comparison of "Shark Close-ups" and † "Climbing by the Book," centering it on the dangers described and the speakers' attitudes toward them.

A PINCH OF DUST

BERTON ROUECHÉ *Permission the author;* © *1951 The New Yorker Magazine, Inc.*

Among the several reports and memoranda that came to the attention of Dr. Morris Greenberg, then chief epidemiologist of the Bureau of Preventable Diseases of the New York City Department of Health and now its director, on Wednesday, January 21, 1942, was a note initialed by the head of the Department's Bureau of Records. It was on Dr. Greenberg's desk when he returned from lunch. The message was short, explicit, and altogether flabbergasting. For a moment, Dr. Greenberg could only stare at it. Then he shook himself, picked up the telephone, and called his chief diagnostician, Dr. David A. Singer, who now heads the Bureau's Manhattan division. He told Dr. Singer that he had before him the names of six people whose deaths had recently been reported to the Department, and asked to be provided as quickly as possible with a full medical history of each. Five of the group—four females and a male—had died in Roosevelt Hospital, at Fifty-ninth Street and Ninth Avenue. Their names and death dates were: Bab Miller, December 29th; Juanita Jackson, December 30th; Josephine Dozier, January 1st; Ida Metcalf, January 3rd; and Charles Williams, January 8th. The sixth was a woman named Ruby Bowers. She had died on January 19th, at Bellevue Hospital. All were Negroes, all were unmarried, all had lived in or near the San Juan Hill section west of Columbus Circle, and all were adults, their ages ranging from twenty-five to sixty-one. The cause of death was tetanus.

The abrupt thirst for knowledge that was excited in Dr. Greenberg by this generous set of coincidences was entirely understandable. So was his disconcertion, for tetanus is a disease of gothic ferocity. It has, however, one redeeming quality. It is not communicable. It is invariably the result of a wound into which a bacillus called *Clostridium tetani* has found its way. In the majority of cases, it is introduced by the instrument that inflicts the injury. Although the intestinal tracts of many animals provide a congenial habitat for *Clostridium tetani,* it is also commonly found in soil, especially that rich in manure. The adult organism, like many other bacilli, readily expires when exposed to air and sunlight, but the spores by which it perpetuates itself do not share this attractive trait. They are among the hardiest forms of life. Tetanus spores are impervious to most antiseptics, including the cruelest extremes of heat and cold, and, in the absence of the dark and airless environment that favors their maturation, practically immortal. They are also balefully abundant. Bacteriologists have encountered them on vegetables, in hay, hair, cobwebs, and clothing, in the dust of streets and houses, and even adrift in the air of hospital operating rooms. No wound is too small to admit a multitude of tetanus spores. In fact, the smallest wounds—abrasions and pricks and thready cuts—are sometimes warmly hospitable. There are two reasons for this apparent anomaly. One is that such wounds close rapidly and thus shield the mature or maturing organism from the withering touch of oxygen. The other is that they are nearly always ignored. The cause of tetanus is a toxin that possesses a shattering affinity for the central nervous system. Neither the chemistry of the toxin's generation nor the method by which it reaches its destination is fully understood, but its nature is no mystery. Five hundred times more explosive than strychnine, whose action it somewhat resembles, the toxin elaborated by *Clostridium tetani* is one of the most venomous poisons known to man.

Tetanus is the name generally preferred by physicians for lockjaw.

They consider the latter more apt than adequate. The rigors of tetanus are by no means limited to an inability to move the jaw freely. Constriction of the masseter muscles is merely the characteristic symptom of onset. The physical manifestations of a full-fledged case of tetanus amply reflect the virulence of its cause. They are of such distinctive vigor and variety that the disease was among the first to be recognized as an entity. The accounts of clinical studies made by Hippocrates in the fourth century before Christ include one of a tetanus seizure that is still regarded as a model of acute observation. "The master of a large ship mashed the index finger of his right hand with the anchor," he wrote. "Seven days later a somewhat foul discharge appeared; then trouble with his tongue—he complained he could not speak properly. The presence of tetanus was diagnosed, his jaws became pressed together, his teeth were locked, then symptoms appeared in his neck; on the third day opisthotonos appeared, with sweating. Six days after the diagnosis was made he died."

Opisthotonos is a spine-cracking muscular spasm. Numerous physicians have been inspired to describe the appearance of a patient in opisthotonos, but a Cappadocian named Aretaeus, who conducted a wide and successful practice in Rome in the second century, is usually acknowledged to be its classic delineator. "Opisthotonos," he noted, "bends the patient backward, like a bow, so that the reflected head is lodged between the shoulder blades; the throat protrudes; the jaw sometimes gapes, but in some rare cases it is fixed in the upper one; respiration stertorous; the belly and chest prominent . . . the abdomen stretched, and resonant if tapped; the arms strongly bent back in a state of extension; the legs and thighs are bent together, for the legs are bent in the opposite direction to the hams." Not all victims of tetanus are called upon to experience the excruciation of opisthotonos. More commonly, though no less disastrously, the systematic paralysis that marks the disease is not accompanied by tonic convulsions. Sometimes, however, a spasm the reverse of opisthotonos occurs. Aretaeus's description of this form of tetanic attack is not only definitive but perhaps the most elegiac passage in medical literature. "But if [the sufferers] are bent forward," he wrote, "they are protuberant at the back, the loins being extruded in a line with the back, the whole of the spine being straight; the vertex prone, the head inclining toward the chest; the lower jaw fixed upon the breastbone; the hands clasped together, the lower extremities extended; pains intense; the voice altogether dolorous; they groan, making deep moaning. Should the mischief then seize the chest and the respiratory organs, it readily frees the patient from life; a blessing this, to himself, as being deliverance from pains, distortion, and deformity; and a contingency less than usual to be lamented by the spectators, were he a son or a father. But should the powers of life still stand out . . . the patient is not only bent up into an arch but rolled together like a ball. . . . An inhuman calamity!

An unseemly sight! A spectacle painful even to the beholder! An incurable malady! . . . But neither can the physician, though present and looking on, furnish any assistance as regards life, relief from pain or from deformity. For if he should wish to straighten the limbs, he can only do so by cutting and breaking those of a living man. With them, then, who are overpowered by this disease, he can merely sympathize."

Aretaeus's melancholy view of tetanus has not been rendered seriously obsolete by the accomplishments of modern medicine. Tetanus, once its grip is fixed, is still an essentially incurable malady, with whose victims the physician can for the most part merely sympathize. A remedy effective at any but the earliest stages of the disease has yet to be devised; its treatment is largely confined to the prevention of complications and the moderation of pain, and surviving an attack precipitated by a large number or an undebilitated strain of *Clostridium tetani* is anything but likely. "The outlook in cases of generalized tetanus is always grave," Dr. Warfield M. Firor, visiting surgeon at Johns Hopkins Hospital, in Baltimore, has noted in a recent monograph. "Even in the best hospitals the death rate is frequently more than fifty per cent." In other than the best hospitals, and among those victims to whom no hospital care is speedily available, the death rate is seldom as low as fifty per cent.

Nevertheless, in most parts of the world, tetanus is no longer a very domineering menace. Not for some years has its avoidance been wholly a matter of chance. Since the late nineteenth century, when an extensive inquiry into the mechanics of the disease culminated, in 1889, in the isolation of *Clostridium tetani* by the Japanese bacteriologist Shibasaburo Kitazato, a prophylactic antitoxin (and, more recently, a toxoid that will confer an absolute and a reasonably durable immunity) has been within easy reach. Inoculation against tetanus is now compulsory in the armed forces of all nations, many business concerns throughout the world emphatically commend it to their employees and in an increasing number of countries, among which the United States is outstanding, it is fast becoming an integral part of pediatric routine. For these reasons, and because most physicians are in the habit of administering a prophylactic charge of antitetanic serum whenever they are confronted by a suspicious-looking wound, the disease has been for nearly a generation—in this country, at least—something of a rarity. Its current incidence in the United States is hardly two thousand cases a year. Of these, on the average, only around fifteen turn up in New York City, and they are usually pretty well scattered among the five boroughs. Also, as might be expected from the solitary nature of the disease, they are generally far apart.

The clinical biographies commissioned by Dr. Greenberg on that winter afternoon in 1942 were compiled with the dispatch to which he is accustomed. They reached him the following morning, Thursday, January 22nd, at about ten o'clock. The first of the six on which he happened to fix his eyes was that of Charles Williams. "I visited Roosevelt Hospital today," wrote the operative Dr. Singer had assigned to the job, "and examined the records of Charles Williams. . . . History reveals that he [was] an old colored man, sixty-one years of age, and single. He was admitted to the hospital on January 4, 1942, at 7:00 P.M., with complaints of pain in the back of his neck for the past twenty-four hours and difficulty in swallowing for the past forty-eight hours. History shows that he was a [heroin] addict, having used injections into the skin for the past two years. On examination, the neck was rigid and his pupils reacted sluggishly to light. On January 4, 1942, he was given 100,000 units of tetanus antitoxin. On January 5th, he developed opisthotonos. . . ." Dr. Greenberg didn't bother to read any more of it. Instead, he turned to the next dossier. After a line or two, he let it drop, and glanced sharply at each of the others. A glance was all he needed. It was enough to convince him that he was indeed up against a series of related cases of tetanus. It was also enough to give him an excellent idea of how they must have originated. Like Williams, Bab Miller, Ida Metcalf, Juanita Jackson, Josephine Dozier, and Ruby Bowers had all been firmly addicted to heroin. Dr. Greenberg returned the reports to their folder with a somewhat muted sense of triumph. He was conscious that he had just made a vividly illuminating discovery but scarcely a reassuring one. If, as seemed probable, the six Negroes had contracted the disease from a common source, it might very well be one that was still accessible to others who happened to share their failing.

The task of determining the source of the infection fell to a field epidemiologist whose name, because he is now engaged in private practice and prefers anonymity, shall here be Ernest Clarke. He was not an arbitrary choice. Dr. Clarke was, and is, an investigator of some distinction in the field of tetanus, and it was Dr. Greenberg's expectation that the congeniality of the subject would supply him with an unusual and perhaps a rewarding zest for the task. He knew he would need it. Dr. Clarke accepted his attractive assignment with a rather clearer notion of what he was looking for than of where to find it. It could be anywhere in the warrens of San Juan Hill, and the only known people who might have been able to direct him were dead. On the other hand, he could conceive of just two possible vehicles that would be compatible with the evidence. A contaminated hypodermic needle was one. The other was a contaminated batch of heroin. At the moment, Dr. Clarke was inclined to favor the former. He was aware, however, that it really didn't much matter. One could hardly be less lethal, or elusive, than the other.

Before actively buckling down to the hunt, Dr. Clarke retired to his office and made a series of sedentary casts. At the end of an hour on the telephone, he was satisfied that nothing even suggestive of tetanus had been seen in the past few weeks at any Manhattan hospital except

Bellevue and Roosevelt, and that if something, especially in a drug addict, did appear, he would be promptly informed. Then he dropped in at a restaurant around the corner and had a thoughtful lunch. From there, no livelier course having occurred to him, he headed first for Bellevue and then for Roosevelt. His retracing of the steps of Dr. Singer's agent did not imply a lack of confidence in the agent's ability as a medical historian. He merely hoped that his colleague, in a natural preoccupation with the clinical aspects of the outbreak, had overlooked some biographical detail that would give him a serviceable lead. If he had, Dr. Clarke was soon persuaded, it hadn't been at Bellevue. There was nothing whatever in the recorded history of Ruby Bowers that he did not already know. Still hopeful, though weighted by a new and discomfiting appreciation of his predecessor's thoroughness, Dr. Clarke moved on to Roosevelt. It was a little past two when he presented himself to the librarian of the record room there. He emerged from his studies at three, possessed of only one trifling nugget of additional knowledge. For what it was worth, he now knew that at least two of the six victims were linked by more than race, geography, and misfortune. Ida Metcalf and Josephine Dozier had been friends. During most of 1941, they had shared a room in a lodging house on West Fifty-second Street.

As Dr. Clarke rose to go, the librarian came hurrying over and asked if she could be of any further help. Dr. Clarke said he guessed not—unless, of course, he added wryly, she could conjure up another case of tetanus for him. The librarian gave him a reproachful smile. After all, she remarked, five cases in less than two weeks were— She stopped, looking stunned. As a matter of fact, she said in amazement, it was just possible, if sudden memory served, that she could. Then, sped by a stare from Dr. Clarke, she vanished into the stacks. When she returned, she had another folder in her hand. Dr. Clarke sank back into his chair, crossed his fingers, and opened the folder. Its subject was a woman named Lulu Garcia. She was colored, single, and fifty-three years of age. Her address was 530 West Forty-fifth Street. She had been admitted to the hospital on January 5th for observation, the findings of the examining physician having been provocative but inconclusive. They included headache, nausea, and a stiff jaw and neck. Also, the clinician noted in passing, she was plainly addicted to drugs. That night, the house physician took a look at her, and though what he saw failed to inspire even a tentative diagnosis, he prescribed a liberal dose of tetanus antitoxin. It was not repeated. There was no need. Nine days later, on January 14th, she was judged to be recovered from whatever had ailed her, and discharged. Dr. Clarke reached jubilantly for his hat.

At a quarter to four, Dr. Clarke bounded up the eroded stoop of 530 West Forty-fifth Street. At five, he slowly descended. He hadn't seen Lulu Garcia. She didn't live there any more. She had moved away a week earlier, and he could find nobody in the building who was able, or at any rate willing, to tell him where.

Dr. Clarke's withdrawal from 530 West Forty-fifth Street was only temporary. He was destined to become a familiar figure on the block. Two weeks later, he was still there and still stumped. He had by then had an endless monotony of conversation with every inhabitant of the building and with most of the people who lived next door or across the street. He had talked to the janitor and the rent collector and a dozen delivery boys. He had spent hours of inquisitive loitering among the loiterers in the corner stores and bars and lunchrooms. Twice, driven less by hope than by exasperation, he had made a long and garrulous tour of the other addresses on his list. But nothing had come of any of it. Lulu Garcia was not merely gone; she had vanished without a trace. Toward the end of the second week, Dr. Clarke sought out Dr. Greenberg for a word of counsel. Dr. Greenberg wasn't much help. He had nothing to recommend but persistence. The disappearance of Lulu Garcia, he admitted, was nettling, but, he added optimistically, matters could be a lot worse. The important thing, he reminded his colleague, was that she existed. Dr. Clarke began to wonder, as he glumly resumed his rounds, if she really did. A day or two later, on Saturday, February 7th, he received a telephone call that further tried his resilience. The call, which reached him at home and at breakfast, was from the medical superintendent of Harlem Hospital. He understood that Dr. Clarke had asked to be notified if a case of tetanus with evidence of drug addiction should happen to turn up at Harlem. Well, one had. The victim was a woman named Mildred Stewart. She was twenty-six years old, unmarried, and colored. Her home was on West 140th Street, and she had lain there, ill and alone, for several days. An ambulance summoned by neighbors had brought her to the hospital about an hour before. Dr. Clarke cut in with an impatient volley of thanks. He said he would be right up for a talk with her. The medical superintendent cleared his throat. That, he was sorry to say, would be impossible. The patient was dead.

Monday morning, February 9th found Dr. Clarke back on West Forty-fifth Street again. He had nowhere else to go. An active but uneventful weekend among Mildred Stewart's effects and neighbors had merely confirmed his belief that Lulu Garcia, in spite of her increasingly chimerical aspect, was probably still his only chance of success. It was about ten o'clock when he dropped off a crosstown trolley and made his way up Tenth Avenue to the familiar corner. As he stood there, trying to decide which of his usual haunts was the least hopeless, a man emerged from a nearby areaway, stared at him for a moment, and then raised a beckoning finger. He wanted to ask a question. Wasn't he the fellow who had been asking around for Lulu Garcia? Dr. Clarke took a deep breath and said he certainly was. Was he sure enough a doctor? Dr. Clarke produced his credentials. The man gave them an inscrutable glance. Most people on the block thought different, he said. They thought he was most likely a bill collector or a process server, or even a detective. He himself—he shrugged—he didn't know or care. But he saw no harm in doing a man a favor. It might come back to him someday. Bread on the waters. If Dr. Clarke was interested, Lulu Garcia had a friend or a relative or something named Mrs. Johnson. She lived at 417 West Fifty-second Street.

The house at 417 West Fifty-second Street turned out to be a battered brownstone a few doors west of Ninth Avenue. Mrs. Johnson's apartment was on the fifth floor. A tall, robust woman of indeterminate age opened the door. Dr. Clarke introduced himself and, after explaining that his mission was both urgent and innocuous, said he was seeking a woman named Lulu Garcia. Mrs. Johnson, he understood, was acquainted with her. The woman gazed at him. Then she nodded, and stepped aside to let him enter. "Mrs. Johnson won't be back till later," she said. "But take a seat. I'm Lulu Garcia. What did you want to see me about?"

Dr. Clarke walked into Dr. Greenberg's office at dusk. Dr. Greenberg was just leaving, but at a provocative murmur from Dr. Clarke he discarded his hat, hung up his overcoat, and sat cheerfully down. "Congratulations," he said, and indicated a chair. "Which was it?"

"I don't know," Dr. Clarke said. "I've got a pretty good idea, though. Everything points to the heroin. For one thing, I'm satisfied that it wasn't a contaminated needle. It couldn't have been. Not if we believe Lulu, and I do. She has her own outfit. And so, she says, did Juanita Jackson and Ida Metcalf and Charles Williams. Charles Garcia, I should say. According to Lulu, that was his real name, and she ought to know. It seems they used to be married. And they were still friends. He and Lulu and Juanita and Ida generally took their shots together. The last time was at Lulu's place, somewhere around Christmas, just before they all got sick. And there's another reason for ruling out the needle theory. Lulu flatly denies knowing any of the others. And I believe her. Why should she lie? Why should she admit knowing Ida Metcalf, say, and deny knowing Ruby Bowers unless it was the truth? There'd be no point in it. But they're all linked up. Lulu didn't know Ruby Bowers or Bab Miller or Josephine Dozier or Mildred Stewart, but she had heard of them—from Juanita Jackson. Juanita knew them all. She was what Lulu calls the runaround. They all got their heroin through her."

"And tetanus?" asked Dr. Greenberg.

"Yes, I know," Dr. Clarke said. "Juanita wasn't a real peddler. She just bought a little batch every so often, and resold it—what she could spare of it—to her friends. Well, one of those little batches was contaminated. I'm not entirely guessing. Lulu has an idea that the stuff they had at Christmastime looked different. Dirtier than usual, I gather. So it was probably cut. It was probably cut a good many other times, but I mean by Juanita. Hers was the one that did the damage. Otherwise, we wouldn't have had eight cases of tetanus. We'd have had dozens. I don't know what she cut it with, but you know how those addicts operate. They'll use anything that's handy. My guess is she mixed in a pinch of dust."

"I suppose that's as good a guess as any," Dr. Greenberg said. "Except for one thing. It doesn't explain why Lulu is still alive."

"I was coming to that," Dr. Clarke said. "As a matter of fact, it does. It's about the only explanation that seems to stand up. The last few times Lulu and her friends met, Lulu didn't get a regular shot. She didn't have any money for drugs. All she got, she says, was what she could cadge from the others. And they weren't overly generous. They only gave her just enough to keep her going."

Suggestions

1. "A Pinch of Dust" concerns a piece of medical research, complicated by lack of necessary data and hampered by human suspicion, which is solved by happy strokes of luck and professional persistence. As a literary work it shows that a scientific essay can be as exciting as a detective fiction. The style incorporates both the no-nonsense factual approach (¶1) and the suspenseful technique of revealing only step-by-step progress (¶10). The speaker establishes the semi-official tone of a report, but at appropriate points introduces imaginative details.

2. How is the necessary history of tetanus woven into the narrative? Examine the *transitions* and comment on their effectiveness.

3. Does the speaker establish the relevance of Aretaeus' description of tetanus to modern knowledge about the disease?

4. Describe the style used for the reported case of Mildred Stewart (¶12). Do touches of this same style appear in other sections of the essay?

5. Explain: *balefully, thready, resilience, chimerical, definitive, dossier.*

6. Can you detect the speaker's attitude toward dope addicts in this essay? Why do you think it is not more clearly stated? Point out other attitudes implied toward the persons and events described.

7. Examine the latter half of the essay and point out all the devices used to postpone the climax until the most appropriate time for it.

8. Write an essay based on the process you have gone through to solve a personal problem or to settle a troublesome issue that may have arisen at some job. Examine the process to see if the outcome was caused by a combination of luck and ingenuity.

A HIGHWAY TO THE PACIFIC

HENRY NASH SMITH ──◦◖

Reprinted by permission of the publishers from Henry Nash Smith, VIRGIN LAND: The American West as Symbol and Myth, Cambridge, Mass.: Harvard University Press, © 1950, by The President and Fellows of Harvard College.

Although Jefferson, as we have seen, believed that all North America would eventually be peopled by descendants of the original English colonists, this prospect belonged to a remote and rather dim future. His immediate attitude toward the Far West was in some respects like that of the British authorities toward the Ohio Valley before the Revolution: he thought of it as an area to be occupied by fur traders rather than farmers. He does not seem to have felt that his devout agrarianism was applicable to the area beyond the Mississippi. A certain instinct for order, and perhaps also the attacks of his Federalist opponents, led him to suggest at the time of the Louisiana Purchase that the right bank of the river should be turned into an Indian reservation for at least fifty years. Emigrants should be forbidden to cross the river "until we shall have filled up all the vacant country on this side." [1]

Nevertheless, Jefferson was clearly the intellectual father of the American advance to the Pacific. Early in his career he began collecting materials relating to the vast hinterland which he believed to be included within the original grant to the colony of Virginia. During his five years of diplomatic service in Paris, from 1784 to 1789, as he wrote later, he formed "a pretty full collection of the English, French, and Spanish authors, on the subject of Louisiana." [2] Not content with buying books and compiling notes, he began a long series of efforts to bring about actual exploration of the trans-Mississippi area. In Paris he worked out a plan whereby the Connecticut traveler John Ledyard was to go eastward through Siberia to the Pacific Northwest and thence overland across North America to Virginia, but the venture was frustrated by the Empress Catherine. Back in America as Secretary of State in Washington's cabinet, Jefferson arranged for the French scientist André Michaux to explore the Pacific Northwest under the auspices of the American Philosophical Society. This plan likewise failed when Michaux became in-

[1] *The Writings of Thomas Jefferson,* ed. H. A. Washington, 9 vols. (Philadelphia, 1868–1871), IV, 509 (letter to du Pont de Nemours, Washington, November 1, 1803). [2] *The Writings of Thomas Jefferson,* ed. Andrew A. Lipscomb, 20 vols. (Washington, D. C., 1904–1905), XI, 20 (letter to William Dunbar, March 13, 1804).

152

volved in the filibustering intrigues of the French ambassador Genêt.[3]

After Jefferson's inauguration as President in 1801 he was at last in a position to carry out the projected exploration of the Far West by sending Meriwether Lewis and William Clark up the Missouri and over the Rocky Mountains to the mouth of the Columbia. The ostensible purpose of the expedition was the one mentioned by Jefferson when he sought permission from Madrid for Lewis and Clark to enter Spanish territory: it was a scientific enterprise. But a responsible statesman was not likely to forget that geographical knowledge was a necessary preliminary to economic penetration and eventual political domination. Scientific knowledge was to be sought for the sake of the fur trade. The North West Company of Montreal was expanding westward across Canada; Alexander Mackenzie had reached the Pacific in 1793. British fur traders were already established far down into present Minnesota and the Dakotas. Indeed, as Lewis and Clark found when they wintered from 1804 to 1805 at the Mandan Villages near present Bismarck, North Dakota, the British were in undisturbed control of the fur trade of the upper Missouri.

American trappers had to be encouraged to move into this area as an offset to the British, whose strong economic position might easily lead to the extension of their sovereignty over most of the trans-Mississippi.[4] The best means of inducing American fur companies to enter the area was to make it profitable for them, and this in turn meant finding a better trade route than the British could command. Jefferson pointed out to Congress that the Canadian route along the line of lakes and rivers from Montreal to the Rocky Mountains "could bear no competition with that of the Missouri," which was shorter, offered a continuous water route without portages, and might possibly lead to the Pacific with only a short land carriage over the mountains.[5]

The concrete plans outlined in this famous message to Congress proved unworkable when brought to the test of practice. The prospect of an advance up the Missouri to the area where American fur traders might come to grips with the British faded when the hostility of the Blackfoot Indians effectively closed the waterway. And the effort to find a commercial route over the Continental Divide and down the Columbia to the Pacific failed because of difficulties of terrain. Even Meriwether Lewis was forced to admit that 340 miles of land carriage, 140 miles of it "over tremendous [*sic*] mountains which for 60 miles are covered with eternal snows," would be necessary along the most practicable communication across the continent by way of the Missouri and the Columbia.[6]

But these practical difficulties were of minor consequence beside Jef-

---

[3] *Original Journals of the Lewis and Clark Expedition,* ed. Reuben G. Thwaites, 8 vols. (New York, 1904–1905), VII, 195–197, 202–205.   [4] Jefferson's "Secret Message to Congress," January 18, 1803, *ibid.,* VII, 206–209.   [5] *Ibid.,* VII, 208.   [6] *Ibid.,* VII, 334.

ferson's continental breadth of vision. The importance of the Lewis and Clark expedition lay on the level of imagination: it was drama, it was the enactment of a myth that embodied the future. It gave tangible substance to what had been merely an idea, and established the image of a highway across the continent so firmly in the minds of Americans that repeated failures could not shake it. John Jacob Astor's ambitious plan of establishing trade between the Columbia Valley and the Orient from a base at Astoria was upset by the British navy, which captured the fort during the War of 1812 and supervised a virtually forced sale of the property to the North West Company. But the American fur traders were determined to penetrate the northern Rockies and in the 1820's William Ashley and Jedediah Smith developed an overland route through the Platte Valley and over South Pass.[7] For the next two decades British and American trappers struggled for economic domination of the Northwest. In this contest the Americans were worsted once again. After all, they were fighting the greatest mercantile empire in the world. In the Hudson's Bay Company, which had absorbed the North West Company in 1821, they had an adversary enjoying the advantage of vigorous governmental support as well as the practical experience of more than two centuries of British chartered trading companies. As long as the contest for Oregon remained in the stage of imperial rivalry based on the fur trade, the British proved impregnable.

On the other hand, the discovery of the overland route that became the Oregon Trail had an ultimate consequence of far greater moment than the fur trade. In the late 1830's and early 1840's widespread economic distress in the Mississippi Valley led Westerners to look longingly at the free land and the supposedly better markets of Oregon. When the frontier farmer learned that he could take his family all the way to the Pacific with no more equipment than his rifle, his wagon, and his livestock, his new energies were thrown into the contest against Britain in the Northwest.[8] Within five years after the first significant migration of American settlers to the Willamette Valley the mercantilist colossus of the Hudson's Bay Company gave up and quit. The Treaty of 1846, establishing the boundary where it now is, at the forty-ninth parallel, merely records officially the fact that the American agricultural frontier had been pushed out to Oregon.

Suggestions

1. This brief account of American attempts to forge an overland route to the West abbreviates those long years of struggle, failure, and finally success by tying the account to Thomas Jefferson. He becomes the "in-

[7] Harrison C. Dale, *The Ashley Smith Explorations and the Discovery of a Central Route to the Pacific 1822–1829* (Cleveland, 1918), pp. 36–40, 89–112.

[8] James C. Bell, *Opening a Highway to the Pacific, 1838–1846* (New York, 1921), pp. 183–190.

tellectual father" of the advance despite the failure of two of his plans. Structurally, all elements of the essay cluster about Jefferson to give it coherence.

2. Comment on any sentences or paragraphs that might be said to violate that principle of unity (Jefferson).

3. Analyze Smith's attitude toward Jefferson.

4. Without investigating the historical accuracy of Smith's statements, would you say his references to authorities suggest a *thesis?* a *theme?*

5. Contrast and compare "A Highway to the Pacific" and † "Jemmy Button Gets His Rights." Pay particular attention to (a) narrative technique and (b) tone.

6. Choose an event from American history and write an essay showing how that event may be reconstructed around the figure of one man who played a significant role.

P R O C E S S E S

HOW ROCKS AND MINERALS ARE FORMED

RICHARD M. PEARL

With the permission of McGraw-Hill Book Company, Inc. from HOW TO KNOW THE MINERALS AND ROCKS *by Richard M. Pearl.* © *1955, by Richard M. Pearl.*

The difference between a rock and a mineral should be clearly understood. Rocks are the essential building materials of which the earth is constructed, whereas minerals are the individual substances that go to make up the rocks. Most rocks, therefore, are aggregates of two or more minerals. Thus, granite (a rock) is composed of at least two minerals (quartz and feldspar), though others are almost certain to be present.

If a single mineral exists on a large enough scale, it may also be considered as a rock, because it may then be regarded as an integral part of the structure of the earth. Thus, a pure sandstone or quartzite rock contains only one mineral, quartz, distributed over a wide area. Other single minerals regarded also as rocks by this definition include anhydrite, dolomite, gypsum, magnesite, serpentine, and sulfur—all of which occur in huge beds or masses. Some rocks of this type have a different name from that of the mineral composing them. Thus, the mineral halite makes rock salt; calcite is the constituent of the rock called limestone; and either calcite or dolomite can make up the rock called marble. Kaolinite composes many of the rocks we know as clay. Bauxite has been proved to be really a rocky mixture of several minerals, but many geologists still prefer to call it a mineral.

In addition to these two classifications, rocks include natural glass, though it may be devoid of any actual mineral components. Obsidian, an abundant rock in Mexico and Iceland, is natural volcanic glass. Organic products of the earth, which cannot be called minerals because they are formed from plants and animals, are properly known as rocks. Coal, derived from partly decomposed vegetation, is a rock of this kind.

Seldom will you find a single species of mineral occurring entirely by itself. Like people, minerals have a tendency to be found in the company of others of the same kind, having formed under the same conditions. This is a fact which proves most helpful to the collector, who soon discovers that often the best way to recognize a mineral is by its associations.

Thus, feldspar and quartz occur together in the rock called pegmatite because they originate in the same manner, that is, by the cooling of molten rock of a certain chemical composition and within the limited range of temperature required to form pegmatite. Again, no one can fail to know at a glance that he has a specimen of the zinc ore from Franklin, N. J., when he sees the distinctive combination of red zincite, yellowish-green willemite, black franklinite, and white calcite. These minerals are not found together anywhere else in the world, and each mineral immediately suggests the presence of the others. As another instance, in 1870 a man named DeKlerk was led to the first diamond ever recovered from its original rock when he saw some pebbles of garnet in a dry stream bed in South Africa and realized that the two gems often occur side by side.

Moreover, each group of minerals is related naturally to definite types of rock. This enables us to identify the rock more readily than otherwise. Rocks are not so easy to name as minerals because they grade imperceptibly into one another, but this principle of mineral association is very helpful.

The many rocks which constitute the earth's crust are the result of geologic processes acting during long ages, building up some rocks and breaking down others. The normal rock cycle leads from molten rock to igneous rock, then to sediment and sedimentary rock, followed or preceded by a metamorphic stage. Countless bypaths to this cycle give rocks an infinite variety and prevent them from becoming monotonous to anyone who has gained a speaking acquaintance with them and even a slight knowledge of geology.

Suggestions

1. One of the most important kinds of knowledge concerns the way things are formed, come into being. Hence a great many essays are descriptions of processes, and in them the speaker's chief concern must be to make the reader follow the process in an orderly way, with enough detail supplied so that he can visualize it. Often the thing created by the process must first be clearly defined. "How Rocks and Minerals Are Formed" has a typical title for an essay about a process. But does it concentrate on the process, or on distinguishing between the two things that result from it?

2. The style of the essay is plain and factual, but sometimes a figure of speech is introduced. Point these out, showing how they help to make the process vivid.

3. Characterize the audience that "How Rocks and Minerals Are Formed" addresses. How much technical information does the reader need in order to follow it?

4. Explain how minerals can best be recognized.

5. Examine and discuss devices that give the essay coherence.

6. Write an essay on any process in nature that you are familiar with. It may be something you have recently learned in geology, botany, or zoology. Remember to keep your organization clear and tight.

7. Write an essay explaining the formation of rocks and minerals more extensively.

HOUSE TRAINING A PUPPY

CECIL WIMHURST ---*&{ *From* OBEDIENCE TRAINING FOR YOUR DOG *by Cecil Wimhurst. Reprinted through permission by Dover Publications, Inc., New York 10, New York, ($.65).*

A puppy has been described as a busy little man who spends his time doing jobs around the house, and the accuracy of this definition will not be disputed by anyone who has attempted to teach a pup habits of cleanliness.

It is not difficult to house train a puppy but it requires patience and unremitting watchfulness for the first week. It should take little more than fourteen days to make the puppy trustworthy—and many are trained in much less than this.

The secret is to watch the pup like a cat eyeing the next-door terrier. Snatch him up when he begins to run around in small circles and put him in the garden. Do the same when he runs backwards and forwards with his nose to the ground—he won't be showing an early aptitude for tracking, he'll be a pup with one thought in his mind, and that thought will be detrimental to your dining-room carpet. Get him outside without delay.

Puppies play hard and then flop over and go to sleep. Watch for him to awake and put him outside again. The end of a meal is the signal for another visit to the garden and it is advisable to spend some time with him until you are certain that he is safe to come indoors again.

But mistakes will happen in spite of your vigilance, and there is nothing you can do about it unless you catch the pup in the act. An animal simply does not understand punishment for an action which happened even a few minutes ago and which he has already forgotten. But the time will come when he will misbehave in your presence and you must pick him up, show him his mistake, grumble at him, smack him lightly on the rump, and put him outside. Do not pounce on him roughly or you will frighten him. Pick him up firmly and let the disapproval in your voice be obvious—remember the tone of voice is the thing which counts with a dog. You can call a dog the most shocking things in a kind voice and he'll wag his tail and think he is being complimented.

If this routine is faithfully followed the pup will soon understand that a certain action performed in the house meets with anger, while the same action in the garden is praised, and he'll connect the two sets of circumstances and find the answer. It is a matter of constant watching, never allowing the animal to get away with a wrongful action if he is caught in the act, and always giving him plenty of opportunity to ease himself at frequent intervals.

House training usually breaks down at night when the pup is left to himself. A puppy should not be fed too late and he should have a good run in the garden before being left for the night. However, in spite of this, it is almost impossible to expect him to stay clean throughout the night, while coming down to let him out not only breaks his owner's rest but establishes a bad habit in the puppy and leads him to expect the same attention for the rest of his life. Fortunately, it is a fact that even a very young dog will dislike soiling his bed.

We can make use of this dislike by confining the puppy in a box at night. The box should be large enough to allow him to curl up and stretch in comfort but small enough to discourage strolling about inside. The bottom should be lined with several wads of newspaper and topped with an old blanket which may be thrown away or easily washed.

An old box, obtained for a few cents from any grocer, laid on its side, and with a slatted wood gate, makes an excellent indoor kennel. Smaller-sized boxes may be made for puppies under the size of spaniels.

The puppy should be put inside at night and, for the first night or two, he will very likely object and raise his voice in no uncertain manner. Take no notice, close your ears and ignore him, and he'll soon learn to keep quiet and settle down. In fact, after a few days, he'll recognize the box as his own special domain and resent sleeping anywhere else. It is essential to get the puppy into the open as soon as possible in the morning, but do not make the mistake of opening the door and allowing him to run out. Lift him out of the box and carry him into the garden so that there will be no mistakes on the way to the door. He may wet the box for the first few nights, but this is likely to be the extent of the damage.

Suggestions

1. An essay that explains the proper way of doing a thing implies that the speaker is qualified to give advice (usually on the basis of his experience with his subject) and that the process is worth learning about. "House Training a Puppy" has these implications, and you may find others. Judged by these two principles, how does it emerge?

2. Sometimes the description of a trivial process is made interesting with humor. Can you define the kind of humor present in "House Training a Puppy"? Where does it occur?

3. How does the opening paragraph set the tone for the rest of the essay?

4. What traditional devices are used to unify the middle section on the breakdown of the training? How are these paragraphs (5–7) coherent with those before and after?

5. As directions for practical advice, how complete are Wimhurst's suggestions? What, from your own similar experience, would you add to his?

6. Write an essay giving your own method for housebreaking a pet. If you disagree with any of Wimhurst's procedure, explain your reasons.

7. Write an essay describing the process of teaching a child something new.

A STRAND OF THE WEB BREAKS

JOHN H. STORER

Quoted from THE WEB OF LIFE *by John H. Storer, published 1953 by The Devin-Adair Co., New York 10, New York, © 1953 by John Storer.*

As one looks from a mountaintop across a vast expanse of western forest, it becomes perfectly clear that this blanket of giant trees must be the one dominant factor that controls all the life within it. But scattered through the forest blanket are occasional gray skeletons of dead trees, or patches of rusty color that tell of a dying tree. Like the animals that live beneath them, these trees seldom have a chance to die of old age, for from the time each seedling sprouts it is subject to a constant attack from animals, including insects or smaller living organisms of disease, all seeking to harvest its store of food for their use. These attacks are a normal part of forest life.

Among the attackers is a small, dark-colored beetle, not much over a quarter inch long. It is the bark beetle, that spends much of its life under the bark of the trees. These beetles are permanent residents in many of the pine and spruce forests of the West. The growing forest withstands them through the vigor of its young trees, which can outgrow and repair the damage. Moreover, there seems to be some quality in the sap of vigorous growing trees that repels the beetles, for under normal conditions they will seldom attack a healthy young tree. As the trees become older and their growth slows, the beetles begin their attacks. Under normal conditions, most of those that gain entrance to the tree are killed by woodpeckers, which drill through the bark to get them, sometimes taking up to 95 percent. But the numbers of the woodpeckers are nicely adjusted by hunger to the numbers of the insects that support them, and if this balance is broken it may mean disaster to the whole forest.

In the White River National Forest in Colorado a heavy wind blew down several groups of Englemann spruce trees. It broke many of the tree roots, weakening the flow of sap, but left enough roots in the ground to keep the trees alive. Thousands of beetles gained entrance to these weakened trees and found a paradise to work in; for the underside of each tree, buried in a mat of crushed branches, was protected from the hunting woodpeckers. The most effective of these woodpeckers, the arctic three-toed, hunts this area chiefly in winter, but now, with the fallen trees covered by snow, the beetles were completely safe from their chief enemy and they multiplied.

First they killed the fallen trees. Then the dead trees became a focus of infection for the surrounding forest, as more beetles in search of food attacked the healthy trees nearby. The potent sap of these growing trees drove out the first attackers, but millions more followed, puncturing the bark and weakening the sap flow until later hordes gained easy entrance. These swarms outgrew the appetites of the woodpeckers, whose numbers were adjusted to a normal beetle population.

In a few years the entire forest, covering many thousands of acres, was dead or dying. Four thousand million board feet of timber stood rotting where it died, most of it wasted; for in this rough mountain country it was not worth building roads to bring it out. There was no young, productive forest left to justify the cost of these roads.

The entire forest was doomed, and all the great dependent community of living things had lost its food and shelter. This community too must go, simply because one of its smallest members had escaped its natural controls and found too much prosperity.

A forest killed by beetles will usually be replaced by another forest of the same kind, for the humus under the dead trees still offers a seedbed for new growth. But as the dead trees dry out they become as inflammable as tinder, and a bolt of lightning or a carelessly dropped cigarette may change the whole future of the area. Scattered through this dead forest in Colorado there are great areas of grassland that suggest what has sometimes happened, for these grassy areas were once covered by forest. Forest fires of the past burned the trees and destroyed the humus that had protected the land and stored moisture from rain and snow. This unprotected land faced three possibilities. On a steep slope it might have been eroded away to become a desert such as we have noted earlier. On more level land, where moisture could collect, it could have grown back to forest, following the usual slow steps of natural growth. But because the humus had been destroyed by fire, the soil had lost its capacity to absorb water, and so the grasses, which need less water than trees, were better adapted to take over.

At the borderline between forest and grassland it is often possible to see in action this conflict between trees and grass. The seedling trees spread out into the grass after a few moist seasons, only to die again when the return of drought gives the advantage to the grass, whose root system is proportionately larger and nearer the surface. Here all of the moisture from the scanty rains is captured before it can sink to the tree roots. So, the boundary line between grass and forest tends to stabilize itself, for at this point of near balance the grass, once established, can dominate the trees through its control of the moisture supply, while the trees, once established, can control the grass by their shade.

Suggestions

1. Find one sentence that states the theme and relate it organically to the rest of "A Strand of the Web Breaks." The metaphor on which the essay turns is the web of life. Discuss the relevance of the title to the essay itself. Can you formulate the metaphor with only the information in the essay?

2. Does Darwin's theory of the survival of the fittest (see † "Jemmy Button Gets His Rights") apply to the plant kingdom in "A Strand of the Web Breaks"?

3. Compare the organization of "A Strand of the Web Breaks" with that of † "What Johannes Kepler Accomplished."

4. The first sentence refers to the life sustained by the great trees, and later the speaker mentions that "all the great dependent community of living things" had suffered with the destruction of the forest. Do you consider the generality of these statements a fault in the essay?

5. Write an essay based on personal experience in which you show a principle of plant or animal life working through specific events. The experience might come from a summer job as a forest lookout, a trail crew member, or a camp counselor.

WHAT JOHANNES KEPLER ACCOMPLISHED

ALBERT EINSTEIN

From IDEAS AND OPINIONS *by Albert Einstein.* © *1954 by Crown Publishers, Inc. Used by permission of the publisher.*

In anxious and uncertain times like ours, when it is difficult to find pleasure in humanity and the course of human affairs, it is particularly consoling to think of the serene greatness of a Kepler. Kepler lived in an age in which the reign of law in nature was by no means an accepted certainty. How great must his faith in a uniform law have been, to have given him the strength to devote ten years of hard and patient work to the empirical investigation of the movement of the planets and the mathematical laws of that movement, entirely on his own, supported by no one and understood by very few! If we would honor his memory worthily, we must get as clear a picture as we can of his problem and the stages of its solution.

Copernicus had opened the eyes of the most intelligent to the fact that the best way to get a clear grasp of the apparent movements of the planets in the heavens was by regarding them as movements around the sun conceived as stationary. If the planets moved uniformly in a circle around the sun, it would have been comparatively easy to discover how these movements must look from the earth. Since, however, the phenomena to be dealt with were much more complicated than that, the task was a far harder one. The first thing to be done was to determine these movements empirically from the observations of Tycho Brahe. Only then did it become possible to think about discovering the general laws which these movements satisfy.

To grasp how difficult a business it was even to find out about the actual rotating movements, one has to realize the following. One can never see where a planet really is at any given moment, but only in what direction it can be seen just then from the earth, which is itself moving in an unknown manner around the sun. The difficulties thus seemed practically insurmountable.

Kepler had to discover a way of bringing order into this chaos. To start with, he saw that it was necessary first to try and find out about the motion of the earth itself. This would simply have been impossible if there had existed only the sun, the earth and the fixed stars, but no other planets. For in that case one could ascertain nothing empirically except how the direction of the straight sun-earth line changes in the course of the year (apparent movement of the sun with reference to the fixed stars). In this way it was possible to discover that these sun-earth directions all lay in a plane stationary with reference to the fixed stars, at least according to the accuracy of observation achieved in those days, when there were no telescopes. By this means it could also be ascertained in what manner the line sun-earth revolves round the sun. It turned out that the angular velocity of this motion went through a regular change in the course of the year. But this was not of much use, as it was still not known how the distance from the earth to the sun alters in the course of the year. It was only when they found out about these changes that the real shape of the earth's orbit and the manner in which it is described were discovered.

Kepler found a marvelous way out of this dilemma. To begin with it was apparent from observations of the sun that the apparent path of the sun against the background of the fixed stars differed in speed at different times of the year, but that the angular velocity of this movement was always the same at the same point in the astronomical year, and therefore that the speed of rotation of the straight line earth-sun was always the same when it pointed to the same region of the fixed stars. It was thus legitimate to suppose that the earth's orbit was a self-enclosed one, described by the earth in the same way every year—which was by no means obvious *a priori*. For the adherent of the Copernican system it was thus as good as certain that this must also apply to the orbits of the rest of the planets.

This certainly made things easier. But how to ascertain the real shape of the earth's orbit? Imagine a brightly shining lantern M somewhere in the plane of the orbit. We know that this lantern remains permanently in its place and thus forms a kind of fixed triangulation point which the inhabitants of the earth can take a sight on at any time of year. Let this lantern M be further away from the sun than the earth. With the help of such a lantern it was possible to determine the earth's orbit, in the following way:

First of all, in every year there comes a moment when the earth E lies exactly on the line joining the sun S and the lantern M. If at this moment we look from the earth E at the lantern M, our line of sight will coincide with the line SM (sun-lantern). Suppose the latter to be marked in the heavens. Now imagine the earth in a different position and at a different time. Since the sun S and the lantern M can both be seen from the Earth, the angle at E in the triangle SEM is known. But we also know the direction of SE in relation to the fixed stars through direct solar observations, while the direction of the line SM in relation to the fixed stars was finally ascertained previously. But in the triangle SEM we also know the angle at S. Therefore, with the base SM arbitrarily laid down on a sheet of paper, we can, in virtue of our knowledge of the angles at E and S, construct the triangle SEM. We might do this at frequent intervals during the year; each time we should get on our piece of paper a position of the earth E with a date attached to it and a certain position in relation to the permanently fixed base SM. The earth's orbit would thereby be empirically determined, apart from its absolute size, of course.

But, you will say, where did Kepler get his lantern M? His genius and Nature, benevolent in this case, gave it to him. There was, for example, the planet Mars; and the length of the Martian year—i.e., one rotation of Mars around the sun—was known. It might happen one fine day that the sun, the earth, and Mars lie absolutely in the same straight line. This position of Mars regularly recurs after one, two, etc., Martian years, as Mars has a self-enclosed orbit. At these known moments, therefore, SM always presents the same base, while the earth is always at a different point in its orbit. The observations of the sun and Mars at these moments thus constitute a means of determining the true orbit of the earth, as Mars then plays the part of our imaginary lantern. Thus it was that Kepler discovered the true shape of the earth's orbit and the way in which the earth describes it, and we who come after—Europeans, Germans, or even Swabians, may well admire and honor him for it.

Now that the earth's orbit had been empirically determined, the true position and length of the line *SE* at any moment was known, and it was not so terribly difficult for Kepler to calculate the orbits and motions of the rest of the planets too from observations—at least in principle. It was nevertheless an immense work; especially considering the state of mathematics at the time.

Now came the second and no less arduous part of Kepler's life work. The orbits were empirically known, but their laws had to be deduced from the empirical data. First he had to make a guess at the mathematical nature of the curve described by the orbit, and then try it out on a vast assemblage of figures. If it did not fit, another hypothesis had to be devised and again tested. After tremendous search, the conjecture that the orbit was an ellipse with the sun at one of its foci was found to fit the facts. Kepler also discovered the law governing the variation in speed during rotation, which is that the line sun-planet sweeps out equal areas in equal periods of time. Finally he also discovered that the square of the period of circulation around the sun varies as the cube of the major axes of the ellipse.

Our admiration for this splendid man is accompanied by another feeling of admiration and reverence, the object of which is no man but the mysterious harmony of nature into which we are born. As far back as ancient times people devised the lines exhibiting the simplest conceivable form of regularity. Among these, next to the straight line and the circle, the most important were the ellipse and the hyperbola. We see the last two embodied—at least very nearly so—in the orbits of the heavenly bodies.

It seems that the human mind has first to construct forms independently before we can find them in things. Kepler's marvelous achievement is a particularly fine example of the truth that knowledge cannot spring from experience alone but only from the comparison of the inventions of the intellect with observed fact.

Suggestions

1. Einstein's essay on the German astronomer Kepler (1571–1630) is more than a description of a process; Kepler's investigation of the movement of the planets illustrates (a) his genius, which is worthy of honor, and beyond that (b) the principle behind all human knowledge. The

organization is far more complicated than that of the two preceding essays: it consists of generalization, specific illustration, and greater generalization. The speaker pays tribute to Kepler's accomplishment, gives the detailed account of the process he used in determining the laws governing the planets' movements, and concludes with the suggestion that Kepler's technique enlightens the workings of the human mind itself.

2. Is the essay written to a *thesis* or a *theme*? Formulate the one or the other.

3. Is the account of the stages by which Kepler solved his problem clear and self-contained, or do you think they need graphs or charts for better understanding?

4. Explain: *a priori, the Copernican system, Tycho Brahe, empirical data*.

5. How does the speaker establish his attitude toward Kepler? Does the generalization in the last paragraph in any way modify that attitude?

6. Paying particular attention to the chief problems and how they were solved, write an essay describing the emergence of a notable historical event or scientific principle.

A CANYON IS BORN

EDWIN CORLE

From LISTEN, BRIGHT ANGEL *by Edwin Corle, by permission of Duell, Sloan & Pearce, Inc.*

Almost every visitor to the Grand Canyon, after he has recovered from the shock of the first look, wants to know two things: "When did this happen—and what caused it?"

The answers are simple: It happened twelve million years ago; the river did it.

And the visitor, quite properly, is not satisfied. He wants to know more, and unless he has some knowledge of geology it is not likely that it will ever be very clear to him. To fill this want, the National Park Service has provided a series of lectures, and nature walks, and charts and maps and models, and a library, and a museum. They are all excellently managed, and a visitor who has never heard of geological eras and periods will begin to see daylight if he attends a few talks, and thinks about what he has seen and heard. Nature has prepared a mighty drama. At your feet is the amazing and thrilling story of the history of the earth and the life that populates it. A sensitive mind will be excited, awed, and moved. A great artist is there to perform for you if you will but take it in. You will never be quite the same again—to your advantage. Theodore Roosevelt said that the Grand Canyon was something that every American ought to see. He might have expanded the remark to include everybody on earth. Just seeing it is not quite enough; people ought to understand it. Some do; some don't. But the Park Service is making it easy for those who have a genuine desire to know more.

As we have seen, there was a time when the Grand Canyon didn't exist. This may have been twelve million years ago—or it may have been as much as a hundred million. Since man himself has been on earth only one million years, there are no witnesses as to just when the erosion process of canyon cutting began, or just when the first little trickle of water began to wear its path into the Kaibab limestone. Scientists agree, in general, that twelve to fifteen million years ago would be a fair estimate.

One thing is certain, and that is geological history. The earth built up its steady system of sedimentary deposits up to the last geological era. Then it contrived to wear away the recent strata back to the Permian period. Here it stopped the great denudation. A broad flat plain of limestone existed. A little stream ran west across the plain. Slowly the force that raised the blister on the earth at this spot raised it again. The little stream dug in deeper, and although the limestone plain sloped toward the south, the little stream refused to be thrown from its channel by this tilt. This slope of the land to the south meant, however, that most of the tributaries of the stream would come from the north. Water didn't run uphill, even twelve or fifteen million years ago.

The gash that was cut into the limestone may have been two inches deep. If so, it was probably several inches across. This was the Grand Canyon in its infancy and the little stream was the Colorado River. It is still cutting that gash deeper and wider today and will still be cutting it centuries hence. Today it is a mile deep and varies from ten to twelve miles across at the rim.

As the water erosion and canyon cutting continued, the stream began to turn backwards the pages of geological history. It cut all the way through the Kaibab limestone and hit the Coconino sandstone beneath. This meant that it was a huge canyon, for the limestone goes down into the earth for five hundred and fifty feet. It cut through the underlying soft sandstone and into the Hermit shale. The canyon was then over eleven hundred feet deep. Two Washington Monuments, one on top of the other, would barely have reached the rim from the river. This was nothing to what was to come.

The river, at this time, must have been about as large as it is today.

Wind erosion was helping to recess the side walls. A great earthquake fault, a crack which ran diagonal to the river, proved an ideal course for a side creek coming in from the north, and this side creek eroded a great gash of its own. There were other similar tributary canyons in the process of creation as century after century went around the clock. Rainfall was also helping to widen the main canyon, while in the bottom the surging river, carrying its cutting implements of sand, silt, and rocks of all sizes, went on wearing its bed deeper and deeper into the earth. The stream in the side canyon raced on to keep pace with the river. It cut equally well and it meets the river today deep in the canyon bottom. It is called Bright Angel Creek.

After about six million years of this relentless and unceasing cutting and grinding and boring and drilling, the canyon was half a mile deep and five or more miles across. It was worthy of the name Grand Canyon even then.

But the incessant water, sand, wind, and rain erosion had a long way yet to go. The whole Permian period had been exposed. And the river cut on into the carboniferous limestone, the Redwall. It sheered the Redwall like a knife. It reached the Devonian period—the age of fishes in the Darwinian scale—and it sliced through this in a short time, that is, geologically speaking.

The Silurian period was missing and so was the Ordovician. An earlier erosion, millions of years ago, had removed those two strata. The river never missed them; it cut on into the Cambrian rocks which had once been laid down by the erstwhile Tonto Sea. Here it was exposing to daylight rocks that had been overlaid for five hundred million years. The skeletons of the ancient trilobites with their crablike bodies were exposed along with other marine life of a mysterious ancient world.

And even deeper went the river to the very foundation of the Cambrian rocks and the meeting of the third geological era with the second. Here it turned back the pages of history to the Proterozoic, or more than a billion years.

And finally it cut down to the oldest rocks on earth, rocks that comprised the first crust when the globe was forming a solid surface and the sun had not yet penetrated the mists, rocks that held not the first live thing, but rocks that antedated even life itself. Here, then, at the canyon bottom is the stuff the earth was made of two billion years ago.

It is quite a show.

From the Permian period back to the birth of the globe is what the river and the canyon have to exhibit to anybody who makes the trip from rim to river. Nowhere else on earth can you see such a performance.

And that is not all. The whole pageant is here, not just part of it. For, to the north in Utah, an easy day's drive, is Zion National Park. If you have seen the play called "From Archeozoic to Permian," which the Grand Canyon stages, there is a sequel called the "Fourth Era," which the Painted Desert (which you pass on the way to Utah) and Zion have to present. Here you will be able to see the history of the earth from the Permian period at the Grand Canyon rim through the whole fourth era, the Mesozoic. And there is one more act after that; it is found at Bryce Canyon, also in Utah, not far from Zion. Bryce will show you the last scene, the fifth-era formations, the Cenozoic, and that brings you right up to date. Thus it is possible for a visitor to start the day at Phantom Ranch in the canyon bottom, ascend the Bright Angel Trail to the south rim; drive via the Painted Desert to Zion National Park, and, if he hurries, pull into Bryce Canyon National Park before dark. He will have run the gamut of geological history; he will have passed through every phase of the earth's development; he will have seen the home of every species of life since the first algae swam in the primordial sea; and he will have done it all in the space of one day.

As you stand beside the roaring river at the mouth of Bright Angel Creek you wonder how much farther down into the earth this canyon will go. Where will it be in another million years? The answer is that the river will continue to cut deeper until its pitch toward sea level is sufficiently lowered so that it will no longer be a rushing torrent. At the bottom of Grand Canyon you are still more than two thousand feet above sea level. Thus the river has another two thousand feet of Archean rock to excavate before the force of gravity will be tempered and it will then be a quiet well-behaved river like the Hudson or the Delaware. Does the Archean rock extend down another two thousand feet? Yes, indeed—it extends down another thirty or forty miles, so the river will stop cutting long before it reaches the hot interior of the earth where the sun-stuff of three billion years ago is still molten.

And how long will it take to cut these next two thousand feet? No-body knows. Since man has applied his knowledge to the phenomena at the Grand Canyon, a matter of less than a hundred years, there has been no perceptible change. Man's life span is too short to permit him to see the erosion taking place. He knows it is going on, but the movement, like that of the hour hand of his watch, is too slow for his eye to perceive.

It has been a little over four hundred years since white men first saw the Grand Canyon. And in accordance with geological time which reckons years by the hundreds of millions, man's total time on earth, to say nothing of a mere four hundred years, is not enough to count. Hence to man, change in the physiography of the Grand Canyon is negligible or nonexistent. The canyon looked very much as it does today when Columbus sailed from Spain, when Rome was founded, when Troy fell, when Hammurabi wrote the laws of Babylon. And it will still be the same two thousand years in the future. Man needn't be concerned.

Suggestions

1. Like Einstein's essay on Kepler, Corle's description of the birth of the Grand Canyon is linked with a generalization. The final paragraph states it explicitly, but it is implied throughout: man is a late comer on this planet, his history negligible in terms of years. The cutting and eroding action of the Colorado River demonstrates a power quite out of man's hands—a power more ancient than man's remotest ancestors. The *theme* is stressed by a recurring metaphor, which appears first in "Nature has prepared a mighty drama." The verbs "excited, awed, and moved" are those commonly associated with the impact of drama on man, and the imagery is reinforced by references to literal dramas about the canyon and other geologic attractions in the second half of the essay.

2. How do the first two paragraphs help unify or organize the body of the essay?

3. What is the significance of the shift in tense at the beginning of the second part ("It is quite a show")? Explain the force of the one-sentence paragraph.

4. Comment on the *diction* of "A Canyon Is Born." Does it make the factual information more or less palatable?

5. Write an explanation of some natural phenomenon. Keep your facts straight, remembering to weave them into your essay in an interesting way.

CANNED FISH

ALDOUS HUXLEY

From TOMORROW AND TOMORROW AND TOMORROW *by Aldous Huxley, Harper & Brothers.* © *1955 by Aldous Huxley. Published by Chatto & Windus, Ltd., London, under the title* ADONIS AND THE ALPHABET.

An enormous new building had been added to the cannery. From now on, in straight-line and continuous production, six hundred women would daily convert three hundred and fifty tons of frozen carcasses into seven hundred thousand tins of tuna. Today the new facilities were being dedicated.

It was a solemn occasion. A rostrum had been erected on the wharf outside the factory. Bunting flapped in the fishy breeze. Mayors, senators, vice-governors were on hand to say a few well-chosen words. The new cannery, it appeared, was a triumph not only of technology but also and above all of Private Enterprise, of the American Way of Life. It represented, we were told, two million dollars' worth of faith in the Future, of fidelity to the Past, of belief in Progress, of trust in . . . But listening to eloquence is something I have never been very good at. I looked at my companion, and my companion looked at me. Without a word we rose and tiptoed away.

A friendly engineer offered to show us round the factory. We began with the thawing tanks, into which the ocean-going trawlers discharge their refrigerated cargo. Next came the butchering tables, where the great fish are cleaned, and from which their heads, guts, and tails are spirited away across the street, to a processing plant that transforms them (not without an overpowering stench) into fish meal for poultry. From the butchering tables we moved to the huge pressure cookers, the cooling shelves, the long conveyor belts of stainless steel, the machines for filling the cans, the machines for sealing and sterilizing the cans, the machines for labeling the cans, the machines for packing the cans in cartons.

So far as tunas were concerned, this was a holiday. The factory was empty; our voices reverberated in a cathedral silence. But next door, in the mackerel department, the work of canning was in full swing. Standing at an immensely long workbench, a line of overalled women receded into the dim distance. Beyond the bench was a trough full of rapidly flowing water, and beyond the trough were the conveyor belt and, above it, on a shelf, an inexhaustible reservoir of empty cans. From an upper story, where, invisible to us, the butchering was evidently going on, a wide-mouthed pipe descended perpendicularly. About once every minute a plug was pulled and a cataract came rushing down the pipe. Floating in the water were thousands of cross sections of mackerel. At breakneck speed they were whirled along the trough. As they passed, each woman reached out a gloved hand and dragged ashore as much as she needed for the five or six cans that she would fill before the next discharge. The cross sections were rammed into place—a big chunk, a smaller chunk, a tiny chunk, whatever piece would fit into the three-dimensional jigsaw—and the tightly packed can was placed on the conveyor belt, along which it moved, unhurrying, toward the weighers, the sealers, the sterilizers, labelers and craters. I clocked the performance and found that it took from ten to fifteen seconds to fill a can. Three hundred, on an average, every hour; two thousand four hundred in the course of a working day; twelve thousand a week.

Outside, in the hazy sunshine, a dignitary of some sort was still talking. "Liberty," he declaimed, and a second, distant loud-speaker repeated the overlapping syllables: "Liberty—berty."

Once more the plug was pulled. Another Niagara of water and sliced fish came rushing down the flume.

"Oppor—opportunity," bawled the loud-speakers. "Way of life—of life."

Buried in every language are nodules of petrified poetry, rich and unsuspected veins of fossil wisdom. Consider, for example, the French word *travail*. It is derived from Late Latin *trepalium*, the name of a kind of rack used for punishing criminals or persuading reluctant witnesses. Etymologically, work is the equivalent of torture. In English we preserve the word's original sense in relation to obstetrics (a woman "in travail") and have endowed it with the secondary meaning, not of work, but of wayfaring. Journeys in the Middle Ages were exhausting and dangerous. "Travel" is *trepalium*—torment for tourists.

The word "work" is emotionally neutral; but "toil" and the now obsolete "swink" carry unpleasant overtones. It was the same in the languages of classical antiquity. *Ponos* in Greek and *labor* in Latin signify both "work" and "suffering." "And Rachel travailed," we read in the Book of Genesis, "and she had hard labor." Two words for work, two words for pain. Moreover, when Modern English "labor" carries its primary meaning, it generally stands for work of the most disagreeable kind—compulsory work, as in the case of penal "hard labor," or the heavy, unskilled work which is performed by "laborers."

Backward-looking sentimentalists are never tired of telling us that in the Middle Ages, work was all joy and spontaneous creativity. Then what, one may ask, could have induced our ancestors to equate labor with anguish? And why, when they wanted a name for work, did they borrow it from the torture chamber?

> Who first invented work, and bound the free
> And holiday-rejoicing spirit down
> To the ever-haunting importunity
> Of business in the green fields, and the town—
> To plow, loom, anvil, spade—and, oh! most sad,
> To that dry drudgery of the desk's dry wood?
> Who but the Being unblest, alien from good,
> Sabbathless Satan, he who his unglad
> Task ever plies 'mid rotatory burnings,
> That round and round incalculably reel—
> For wrath divine hath made him like a wheel—
> In that red realm from which are no returnings,
> Where toiling and turmoiling ever and aye,
> He and his thoughts keep pensive working-day.
>
> [Charles Lamb, "Work"]

Lamb was quite right. In every civilization work, for all but a favored few, has always been a thing of hideous dreariness, an infernal monotony of boredom at the best and, at the worst, of discomfort or even sheer anguish. One remembers the description, in *The Golden Ass,* of the animals and humans who worked, while the owner's wife amused herself with magic and adultery, at the flour mill. Men and asses, mules and boys—they were all in travail, all on the *trepalium,* bruised, galled, strained beyond the limits of organic endurance. And the life of laborers in a medieval village, the life of journeymen and apprentices in the workshop of a master craftsman in the town, was hardly less dismal than that of their pre-Christian ancestors. In its beginnings industrialization merely aggravated an already intolerable state of affairs. The physical tortures imposed in the dark satanic mills of Georgian and Early Victorian England were worse, because more systematic, better organized, than the travail of earlier centuries. Thanks to automatic machines and labor laws, thanks to trade unions and the internal-combustion engine, thanks to hoists and belts and humanitarianism, there are now few tasks which actually hurt. The rack has been abolished. But the boredom, the frightful punctuality of wheels returning again and again to the same old position—these remain. Remain under free enterprise, remain under Socialism, remain under Communism.

Under the present technological dispensations the opportunity to escape from the tyranny of repetition comes only to a very small minority. But with the multiplication of fully automatic machines, fully automatic factories, even fully automatic industries, the case will be altered. Some of those now condemned to the task of keeping time with wheels will become the highly skilled doctors and nurses of the new, all-but-human gadgets. The rest will do—what? It remains to be seen. Only one thing seems tolerably certain. Owing to the deplorable lack of quantitative and qualitative uniformity displayed by living organisms, the fish-canning industry will be one of the last to become fully automatic. The technical procedures current today will probably be current, with only trifling modifications, a generation from now. Should we rejoice over this island of stability in a flux of change? Or should we lament? In another twenty-five or thirty years we may be in a position to answer.

And meanwhile what will have happened to the raw material of our industry? What, in a word, will the fish be up to? A generation ago the biologist and the commercial fisherman would have answered, without hesitation: "If they aren't overfished, they will be doing exactly what they are doing now." Times have changed, and today the answer to our question would probably be: "Goodness only knows." For in recent years fishes have been behaving in the most eccentric and indecorous manner. Consider, for example, the European tuna. Forty years ago individual specimens of *Thunnus thynnus* were caught, at certain seasons, in the English Channel and the North Sea; but there was no tuna-packing industry north of Portugal, and the main supply of tinned or salted tunny came from the Mediterranean islands of Sardinia and Sicily. Today there is a flourishing tunny industry in Norway.

And the tuna's is by no means an isolated or exceptional case. Fishes which, not long ago, were thought of as being exclusively tropical, are now caught off the New England coast, and fishes once regarded as natives of the temperate zone have moved into the Arctic. The North Sea has ceased to be the great fishing ground of Western Europe. Today ocean-going trawlers, equipped with freezing units, make long voyages to the coasts of Iceland and northernmost Scandinavia. The Eskimos of Greenland have given up their traditional occupation, the hunting of seals, and have taken instead to fishing for cod. What were once regarded as immutable behavior patterns have changed, almost overnight. The world of fishes is in a state of revolution. Within the next twenty or thirty years the strangest things may happen in that world—with incalculable results for all concerned in the catching and processing of sea food.

This revolution in the watery world of the fish is a consequence of a larger revolution in the earth's atmosphere—a revolution which is changing the climate of the northern hemisphere and is likely to affect profoundly the course of human history during the next few generations or even centuries. The causes of this climatic revolution are obscure, but its effects are manifest. The glaciers are everywhere melting. The snow pack on the mountains has diminished to such an extent that the Jungfrau is now thirty feet lower than it used to be when I was a boy. The Spizbergen Archipelago, which used to be open for shipping for about four months out of the twelve, is now open for eight or nine. Russian icebreakers and cargo ships sail the once impassable seas that wash the northern coasts of the Soviet empire. In Canada and Siberia agriculture is moving steadily into higher and higher latitudes. Plants, birds, and mammals, hitherto unknown in those regions, have now made their entrance and may soon take the place of the cold-loving species which are beginning to find their environment uncomfortably balmy.

This sort of thing, we should remember, has happened before, not merely in the remote geological past, but in quite recent historical times. In the early Middle Ages, Europe (and presumably the rest of the northern hemisphere) enjoyed two or three centuries of most unusual weather. There was enough sunshine in southern England to ripen grapes, and for four or five generations it was possible to drink British wine. Then, about the time of Chaucer, the climate changed again, and for a couple of centuries Europe experienced the rigors of what has been called the Little Ice Age. In Denmark and northern Germany many villages had to be abandoned. In Iceland the cultivation of cereals became impossible, and the fields, in many cases, were covered by the encroaching glaciers. Today the glaciers are in full retreat, and there is every reason to believe that in a few years rye and barley will once more be grown, to the further enrichment of a country which has already profited by the migration to its shores of innumerable fishes fleeing from the increasing warmth of the North Sea.

But if the high latitudes of the northern hemisphere become pleasantly warmer, does it not follow that the low latitudes will grow most *un*pleasantly hotter? There are some indications that this may be actually happening. In Africa, north of the equator, forests are giving place to savannas, and savannas are drying up into deserts. And what of the long, hardly intermitted drought, from which large areas of the American Southwest have recently been suffering? Is this the usual kind of cyclical dry spell, or does it presage a relatively permanent worsening of an arid or semiarid climate? Time alone will show. Meanwhile, if I had a few millions to invest for the benefit of my grandchildren, I would put them all into Canada rather than Texas. "Westward the course of empire takes its way." So wrote the good Bishop Berkeley two centuries ago. Reincarnated today, the philosopher-poet would probably turn his prophetic eyes ninety degrees to the right. Westward no longer, but northward, northward moves the course of empire. The tunas, the pilchards, the sharks and codfish—these forward-looking pioneers have already made the move, or at least are swimming in the right direction. In ever-increasing numbers, men will soon be following their example.

Suggestions

1. If you were asked to write an essay on the origin of words in their relation to acts, the mechanization of labor, and the change in the world's weather, unifying your discussion under a heading as specific as Canned Fish, you would be justified in asking for help. These topics appear to have little in common with one another; yet the problem might be solved by concentration on style and theme. Style can weld together seemingly unrelated topics into a coherent piece of writing. Since style is method it incorporates point of view, diction, tone, sentence structure. The style of "Canned Fish" gives the feeling that all its separate subjects are related to a common theme, though the theme is never stated. The essay suggests that life is change. Can you formulate its theme more specifically?

2. Examine the essay carefully, listing all the shifts in subject. Then try to account for these shifts by hints or self-explanatory passages given in the essay itself.

3. (a) What is the tone of the opening paragraphs? Does the tone change as the essay develops?

(b) Account for the unusual capitalization in ¶2.

4. List the various ways in which the essay achieves a feeling of great space in the factory (¶4).

5. Decide whether the speaker prefers contemporary life to the life of the past.

6. Explain: *nodules, Etymologically, The Golden Ass, Georgian, Jungfrau, savannas.*

7. Write an essay comparing the style with that of † "The Great Fight That Wasn't" or † "Insouciance."

8. Write an essay about a town or region forced to change its means of livelihood. Use this process to suggest a larger theme which stirs your emotions.

D   E   F   I   N   I   T   I   O   N   S

TOLERANCE OF OPPOSITION

From MEET THE U.S.A. © *1952, Institute of International Education, Inc., New York.*

Walk into the legislature of the central government or of any state or city, and you will hear members expounding their theories on a variety of matters such as the desirability of national management of a certain industry (a radical stand in America), the need of lowering or raising taxes, the virtues and defects of a proposed treaty or law. On the surface, the co-existence of such diversity of opinion appears chaotic, but this superficial chaos is an important stage in the procedure of government by proposal, discussion, and vote. Without this stage, public opinion would not be able to develop. Once the vote is counted, however, and the majority has spoken, order will emerge. Minority will follow majority, and majority will tolerate minority. This tradition of tolerance of opposition is the key to the success of American democracy. On the floor of the legislature opponents may be shaking angry fists at each other and even "slinging mud," but you frequently see them later seated together in a restaurant over dinner. Their political opinions may be as incompatible as fire and water, but they can still be friends and do business together. This is not hypocrisy but a valuable asset—tolerance of opposition.

The diversity of American political opinions and factions is no less than that of any European country, but in the United States there are only two parties of nation-wide strength, the Democrats and the Republicans. This gives America political stability, preventing the confusion of political parties such as is found in some countries under parliamentary governments. A strong voice advocating a third party frequently arises in critical moments, but though the effective third party is ever in the perennial laboring stage, it is never born. One reason may be that whenever a new demand arises in the nation and gains strong following, one of the "big two" usually adopts it, leaving the third party without the soil in which to take root. Down to this day no third party has elected a president; at most it has elected a few lonely members of Congress.

Suggestions

1. An essay defining something, especially an abstract term such as *love, democracy,* or *freedom,* must give the term meaning within certain boundaries, enclosing it in a special category so as to set it off from other, similar terms. Most essays of definition are *extended definitions,* for a mere dictionary meaning necessarily omits many implications, explanations, and modifications. The essayist must carry a formal meaning farther than a dictionary can; he wants to clarify, illustrate, and make the definition more real. The technique will vary from essay to essay, though the usual devices are those you have already met in previous groups: analogy, specific example, comparison and contrast, analysis. The organization of "Tolerance of Opposition" differs from the essays that follow it, yet all of them have a common aim: to identify a thing by placing it in its class and differentiating it from similar things.

2. Summarize "Tolerance of Opposition" by showing what term it chiefly defines and which parts of it are most directly related to the definition.

3. The first paragraph is developed from the particular to the general. Is it more effective than it would have been with the scheme reversed? Why?

4. How is the second paragraph related to the first? How does it illustrate the title?

5. Does the speaker approve or disapprove of the lack of a third political party in the United States?

6. Write a "minority opinion" on the statement, "Minority will follow majority, and majority will tolerate minority."

7. Write an extended definition of a third party about which you have heard or read.

8. Write an essay on your opinion about the "key to the success of American democracy." Be sure to make your "key" clearly distinguishable from others similar to it.

SOME AMERICAN TYPES

MAX LERNER ──◦◦✠ *From* AMERICA AS CIVILIZATION. © *1957, by Max Lerner. Reprinted by permission of Simon and Schuster, Inc.*

Seventeenth-century England produced a number of books on *Characters* depicting English society through the typical personality patterns of the era.[1] Trying something of the same sort for contemporary America, the first fact one encounters is the slighter emphasis on a number of character types that stand out elsewhere in Western society: to be sure, they are to be found in America as well, but they are not characteristically American. One thinks of the scholar, the aesthete, the priest or "parson," the "aristocratic" Army officer, the revolutionary student, the civil servant, the male schoolteacher, the marriage broker, the courtesan, the mystic, the saint. Anyone familiar with European literature will recognize these characters as stock literary types and therefore as social types. Each of them represents a point of convergence for character and society. Anyone familiar with American literature will know that it contains stock portraits of its own which express social types. I want to use these traditional types as backdrops and stress some of the social roles that are new and still in process of formation.

Thus there is the *fixer,* who seems an organic product of a society in which the middleman function eats away the productive one. He may be public-relations man or influence peddler; he may get your traffic fine settled, or he may be able—whatever the commodity—to "get it for you wholesale." He is contemptuous of those who take the formal rules seriously; he knows how to cut corners—financial, political, administrative, or moral. At best there is something of the iconoclast in him, an unfooled quality far removed from the European personality types that

[1] See † "What a Character Is," † "A Child," etc.

always obey authority. At worst he becomes what the English call a "spiv" or cultural procurer.

Related to the fixer is the *inside dopester,* as Riesman [2] has termed him. He is oriented not so much toward getting things fixed as toward being "in the know" and "wised up" about things that innocents take at face value. He is not disillusioned because he has never allowed himself the luxury of illusions. In the 1920s and 1930s he consumed the literature of "debunking"; in the current era he knows everything that takes place in the financial centers of Wall Street, the political centers of Capitol Hill, and the communications centers of Madison Avenue—yet among all the things he knows there is little he believes in. His skepticism is not the wisdom which deflates pretentiousness but that of the rejecting man who knows ahead of time that there is "nothing in it" whatever the "it" may be. In short, he is "hep."

Another link leads to the *neutral* man. He expresses the devaluing tendency in a culture that tries to avoid commitments. Fearful of being caught in the crosscurrents of conflict that may endanger his safety or status, he has a horror of what he calls "controversial figures"—and anyone becomes "controversial" if he is attacked. As the fixer and the inside dopester are the products of a middleman's society, so the neutral man is the product of a technological one. The technician's detachment from everything except effective results becomes—in the realm of char-acter—an ethical vacuum that strips the results of much of their meaning.

From the neutral man to the *conformist* is a short step. Although he is not neutral—in fact, he may be militantly partisan—his partisanship is on the side of the big battalions. He lives in terror of being caught in a minority where his insecurity will be conspicuous. He gains a sense of stature by joining the dominant group, as he gains security by making himself indistinguishable from that group. Anxious to efface any unique traits of his own, he exacts conformity from others. He fears ideas whose newness means they are not yet accepted, but once they are firmly established he fights for them with a courage born of the knowledge that there is no danger in championing them. He hates foreigners and immigrants. When he talks of the "American way," he sees a world in which other cultures have become replicas of his own.

It is often hard to distinguish the conformist from the *routineer.* Es-sentially he is a man in uniform, sometimes literally, always symbolically. The big public-service corporations—railroads, air lines, public utilities —require their employees to wear uniforms that will imprint a common image of the enterprise as a whole. City employees, such as policemen and firemen, wear uniforms. Gas-station attendants, hotel clerks, bellhops, must similarly keep their appearance within prescribed limits. Even the sales force in big department stores or the typists and stenographers in

[2] David Riesman wrote *The Lonely Crowd, Faces in the Crowd,* and other works.

big corporations tend toward the same uniformity. There are very few young Americans who are likely to escape the uniform of the Armed Services. With the uniform goes an urge toward pride of status and a routineering habit of mind. There is the confidence that comes of belonging to a large organization and sharing symbolically in its bigness and power. There is a sense of security in having grooves with which to move. This is true on every level of corporate business enterprise, from the white-collar employee to "the man in the gray flannel suit," although it stops short of the top executives who create the uniforms instead of wearing them. Even outside the government and corporate bureaus there are signs of American life becoming bureaucratized, in a stress on forms and routines, on "going through channels."

Unlike the conformist or routineer, the *status seeker* may possess a resourceful energy and even originality, but he directs these qualities toward gaining status. What he wants is a secure niche in a society whose men are constantly being pulled upward or trodden down. Scott Fitzgerald has portrayed a heartbreaking case history of this character type in *The Great Gatsby,* whose charm and energy are invested fruitlesly in an effort to achieve social position. The novels of J. P. Marquand are embroideries of a similar theme, narrated through the mind of one who already has status and is confronted by the risk of losing it. At various social levels the status seeker becomes a "joiner" of associations which give him symbolic standing.

Suggestions

1. "Some American Types," as its title indicates, makes a comment on our society by describing, not individual Americans, but Americans considered as distinguishable classes or kinds. Compare its parts with the English characters in Part 4 of this book.

2. How valid are the distinctions among the fixer, the inside dopester, the neutral, the conformist, the routineer, and the status seeker? Can you formulate a case for making all these types subdivisions of one type? If so, define that one type.

3. Examine and list the specific transitions between paragraphs. Do they successfully unify the essay?

4. Can you think of other significant types of Americans who are omitted from this essay?

5. What is the speaker's implicit criticism of American life? Is his thesis expressed or implied?

6. Consider the Mississippi politicians of † "The Bottom Rail on Top" as a character-type. To which of Lerner's types are they closely related?

7. Lerner supports each of his definitions with specific characteristics and some illustrations. Are some of his definitions stronger than others? Why?

8. Write your own definitions of some American types, using people you have known as illustrations. Members of the college community, students and professors, offer tempting possibilities.

WHAT IS A STUDENT?

HAROLD TAYLOR ⸺⸱⸱◦⸺ *First published in* COLLEGE ENGLISH.
© *1957 by Harold Taylor.*

Not long ago I was forced by circumstances beyond my control to address a group of people on a topic entitled, Education for What? I discovered when I began thinking about it that I had heard every answer to the question, Education for What? known to man. I had heard Education for Citizenship, Education for Responsible Living, for Effective Living, for Democratic Living, for Clean Living, for Clear Thinking, for the American Century, for Americanism, for the Kingdom of Heaven, for Moral Character, for Ethical Conduct, for a Better World, for Success in Love, Marriage, Motherhood, Wifehood, Womanhood, and a Career, Education for the Future, for a World of International Tension, for Western Civilization, for the Atomic Age, for an Age of Neurosis, an Age of Anxiety, and Education for God, for Country, and for Yale. Each "what" had been sponsored with great enthusiasm by those who believed in it. But I do not see how there can be a single aim for education, because I do not see how there can be a single aim for human life.

Yet everyone is now talking as if there were one aim for education. That aim is said to be to produce enough scientific technicians and engineers to match the output of the Soviet Union. The Soviet Union is producing 60,000 more engineers a year than we are; therefore, the argument goes, we need to catch up by turning out that many more of our own. We need to outproduce them in every way, including scientists.

My worry is that we might succeed in doing it. If we continue to try, we might turn every student in the country into either an engineer, or a graduate of a business school, or a graduate with a B.A. degree who has taken only courses which will help him get a good job. Then we will be able to turn to ourselves and to the Soviet Union and to the rest of the world, and with great pride and self-satisfaction and say, as a colleague of mine at Sarah Lawrence said recently: Look, everybody, no mind.

I had the opportunity a year ago in New York to spend an evening with the Soviet Deputy Minister of Education, Madame Dubrovna.

Through an interpreter, I asked about the Soviet curriculum in the universities and colleges. There is no equivalent of the American college in the Soviet Union: there are technical institutes and universities. When I asked if Soviet students studied philosophy, literature, the creative arts in the university, I was told that Marx and Lenin were taught, but no other authors, that music, theatre, dance, poetry were learned in professional academies and did not belong in the university.

Will it make us more, or less, secure if we adopt the Soviet view of education as a combination of propaganda and training for technicians? Will it make us more, or less, secure if we give the highest salaries and the greatest recognition to technical experts, with no one left either to teach the new generation or to discover new forms of knowledge, new values, new works of art, or the new ideas which alone make civilization worth preserving? I don't think that security lies in this direction and I think it is a dangerous and foolish mistake to think of students as potential "trained manpower." We do not need to compete with other countries in the production of domesticated intellects. We need scientists and engineers who are passionate in their love for knowledge and intense in their wish to understand the truth of their world. We need scientists who care first of all for the discovery of truth and the welfare of their fellow-men, and only after that for the techniques of their profession. The great scientists are those who can pry loose the secrets of the universe, who are restless in the presence of the unknown. This, and their talent for using the things they have learned to illuminate the new things they find, is what makes progress in science. There can be no progress in science, and therefore no progress in technology, and therefore no security, until there are scientists and scholars whose first love is in the excitement of discovery and whose deepest satisfactions come from enriching the world with the fruits of their knowledge, no matter what their field of endeavor.

I believe that one of the reasons there is so much public acceptance of the drive toward technical studies is that educators themselves are not paying enough attention to students. This is odd, I must say, since students are the reason for having colleges and universities. In all the plans made for the reform of American higher education in the post-war period, the discussion has been about subjects to be required, tests to be administered, rules to be applied, buildings to be raised, money to be found, numbers of qualified experts to be produced. Certainly these things must be discussed. But it is a dreadful mistake to think of students as anonymous units of mental stuff, to be put into classes, lectured at, examined, and graded as if they were products in a manufacturing plant, to be turned out in thousands for the maintenance of American prosperity and military supremacy.

No wonder people are arguing for using television in higher education.

If higher education merely consists in feeding information to students and grading them on how they manage to hand it back, it would be much better to save the money now spent to build campuses and just pipe in the information to every happy student listener in his own living-room or bar. Among other things, it would certainly help with the parking problem and there would be no need for a building program or even a campus. You would then see the logical outcome of the present system. The faculty, unhampered by the presence of students, would then be able to do their research and sign government contracts, or—if they preferred it—fill the professional journals with more and more technical articles, or even publish fat books on higher education. As General Grant once said about Venice, it would be a great town if they would just drain it.

What kind of teaching, then, can help us to achieve the level of technical competence we must have, and yet develop young men and women who are free and independent, who *want* to think and act for themselves? It seems to me that this is a question of teaching people to find themselves, to establish their own identity, an identity which is theirs and no one else's; it is a question of teaching people to know what they believe, about themselves and their world, about other people, to know who they are, to know what there is in life, what they want from life, and what they want to give to it. All this is involved in the struggle for personal independence.

But what does it mean to be a *student?* To whom is he responsible, and for what?

To be a student and a teacher is an honorable and highly respected position to occupy. In Burma, in Indonesia, in Ceylon, in Africa, to be a student and a teacher is to accept the responsibility for becoming a leader of your country, of being educated to bring your gifts to the country's service at a time when education has not been able to catch up with the incredible demands for educated men and women who can build new countries.

But is the student and the teacher in America in a very different situation? Is there not a shortage of educated and informed leadership in our country? Is the American student not responsible—quite as much as the Burmese student—for putting his education at the service of his country, and not merely putting it at the service of a commercial career? Have we so many teachers that we do not need an infusion of new, enthusiastic educational leaders recruited from among our own students, ready to undertake the excitement of reforming American education?

It needs reform, as we hear every day. But education is only reformed and invigorated by students and teachers who are vigorous, active, lively and interested. We cannot promise our American youth that after a college education they will go straight into a post with the Cabinet or a United Nations delegation. But we can promise them that their presence as informed and interested citizens, aware of political and social issues, is wanted in the government, in education, in politics, in the law, in business, and everywhere else. But it is wanted most in teaching.

In most other countries the student does not go to a university merely to increase his chances of a higher income in later years. He goes to develop those talents which in the view of the university are needed for the continuation of his country's culture. In this country, at this point in the country's material success and prosperity, we hear constantly of the values of an education in raising one's income. It works out, I believe, to around $100,000 more over a life-time for a B.A. degree than without one. But any of your students who have it on their minds should remember not to go on to the Ph.D. or any higher degree. The income seems to fall sharply after the B.A.

Emphasis on the personal advantages of an education has distracted many people from thinking of the true values of higher learning and the true mission of the student.

A student is not a professional athlete, although many universities and a large segment of the watching public act as if he were. He is not a little politician or junior senator looking for angles, getting a good record, getting contacts, and starting his business career in his sophomore year. He is not an amateur promoter, a glad-hander, embryo Rotarian, café-society leader, quiz kid, or man-about-town. He may be some of these or all these for a little while before he grows up, but none of it defines him as a student.

A student is a person who is learning to fulfill his powers and to find ways of using them in the service of mankind. The student at his best has a purity of motive which is the mark of his true function. He wants to know the truth, to know what is good, not merely for his own or for other people's advantage, but in order to achieve his maturity as a student. He is granted the priceless advantage of looking openly at the world to discover its secrets. He is given the rare privilege of withholding his assent to the claims the world makes for its own particular brand of truth, and he can decide what he thinks on the basis of the evidence, not on the basis of pressure, because this is in fact what it means to be a student, and what the world asks the student to be. For a little time before he begins a life which will gradually involve him in more and more commitment to tasks and duties which are not central to the concern with truth and ideals, the student lives in a world of discovery and of possibility where nothing is yet completely settled, where everything, including the achievement of greatness, is still actively possible.

A student must make the most of this time, for it may never come again. If the life of the student does not possess the excitement, the innocence, and the hope of the true inquirer, he may never again experience a time for thoughtful and sensitive attention to the big issues of human life. If he does possess that quality in his life as a student, you can be sure it will remain with him as a way of thinking and acting for the rest of his days.

Suggestions

1. An essay in definition may involve casting off near-definitions or confusing definitions in order to make clear what the term does not mean before declaring what it does. Point out some of the meanings of *student* that "What Is a Student?" rejects.

2. Examine the first eight paragraphs to determine their relevance to the main thesis.

3. Compare the function of the capitalized nouns in the first paragraph with those in † "Canned Fish." Is the tone the same in both?

4. How do the occasional witticisms—of the Sarah Lawrence colleague, of General Grant—help to express the speaker's attitude? Would you call them examples of *hyperbole? analogy?*

5. Discuss the proposal to fit college graduates into governmental service.

6. Can you point out one sentence that is the heart of Taylor's definition of a student?

7. Write a definition of *university* as the term is understood in the Soviet Union.

8. Write an essay about the thesis that "educators themselves are not paying enough attention to students."

9. Write a combined definition and characterization of a student you know who belongs to one of the types mentioned in "What Is a Student?": amateur promoter, glad-hander, embryo Rotarian, café-society leader, quiz kid, man-about-town.

DEFERRED EXCHANGES

HARRY SCHERMAN ··◄{

From THE PROMISES MEN LIVE BY *by Harry Scherman,* © *1948 by Random House, Inc. Reprinted by permission of Random House, Inc.*

Assume that you are a slightly grizzled middle-aged gentleman on his way home from work on a late Saturday afternoon. At the corner of your home street, as you pass a bakeshop with which you have had some pleasant experiences in the past, your eye happens to fall upon a large and tempting cake displayed in the window. It occurs to you at once, unselfishly, that it would be a delightful surprise to the rest of the family if you bought that cake and took it home as a crowning end to the evening meal. You go within and ask the price. The white-capped baker tells you one dollar. You hand him a dollar bill, he carefully wraps up and hands you the cake, both of you murmur something like "Thank you," and out you go.

What has happened? At the least, a simple exchange—a swap of a dollar bill for a cake. Or, to be slightly more sociological, what may be called *an exchange in ownership*. A moment before, you owned the dollar bill, which means pragmatically you could have done whatever you pleased with it; the baker owned the cake and could have done what he pleased with it. Now the baker owns the dollar bill and you the cake. Observe, also, that the transaction is over and done with. This exchange can fairly be called *a completed exchange*.

Let us assume now a slight change in the circumstances.

At the moment the baker tells you the price of the cake is one dollar, you suddenly recollect something: you had been paid by check that afternoon and have only a few coins in your pocket. "Gracious!" you exclaim, "I have no money with me. I'm sorry"—and you proceed to walk out. "That's all right," says the baker, hurriedly. "You can pay me when you come around this way again. You are certainly good for a dollar and a great deal more." Accordingly, he wraps up and hands you the cake, you thank him with real appreciation for his courtesy, and out you go.

In this case, what has happened? An exchange in ownership, also— that is clear; but plainly, up to the point described, a *one-sided* exchange. A moment before, the baker owned the cake; now you own it and within a few hours it will cease to exist. On the other hand, you have not as yet transferred ownership of anything to the baker. With no reflection upon your integrity, it is within the bounds of possibility *that you never will*. You may be stricken with amnesia before you get home, or be killed by a taxicab. All that remains with the baker—is it not true?—is his mere recollection, perhaps enforced for reminder by a scribbled notation somewhere, that you promised to give him one dollar within a day or so. One might say, then, he has exchanged his cake for a promise. But this is hardly an inclusive description of the incident. The whole transaction is better described, it seems, as an exchange of ownership *which has not yet been completed*. One half of it, by mutual understanding, has been *deferred* to an indefinite moment when you again pass by and—if you are not forgetful—hand over a dollar bill to the baker. At that moment the exchange will indeed be closed and completed, like the first one.

This may, therefore, properly be called *a deferred exchange in owner-ship.*

It can be stated as an incontrovertible truth that incompleted, deferred exchanges, of this second type, *make up by far the larger part* of that immense volume of transactions by which the two billion human beings on the planet now manage to keep themselves alive.

More than this: in this simple distinction—between fully completed and temporarily incompleted exchanges—there lies the first key to un-locking a thousand economic mysteries which currently bewilder the average citizen. Unless all the implications of this simple distinction are fully grasped it is impossible to arrive at any satisfactory comprehension, first, of how our so-called advanced civilization has developed into its present forms; and, second, how it *continues* in all its complexity to function.

These are large-scale generalizations, obviously. Assuming for the moment they are well-founded, it seems desirable to examine more closely this little transaction of yours with the baker. For, as we shall soon see, it holds another truth quite as basically important as this difference between completed and temporarily incompleted exchanges.

The first obvious thing to be noticed is that when the baker handed you the cake—himself at the moment receiving a mere promise—he did so with no apparent worry. You, also, took the transaction as quite a matter of course. One might say, then, that this "confidence," on both sides, was the principal motivating factor in the transaction. The word, however, reveals little. Indeed, it is an excellent illustration [of the way in] which words that are commonly used obscure rather than reveal the actualities they ought to convey. The incident cries out for a much fuller explanation than the mere word "confidence" carries. How, for example, did the baker happen to be so sure your promised action would be per-formed? Your certainty on this point might need no explanation. His most assuredly does.

Perhaps he had dealt with you many times before. Possibly, even, at other times you had shown a similar thoughtlessness, had come in without a penny and had unfailingly paid him afterward. At any rate it is certain he had picked up considerable information about you and was thoroughly satisfied in his mind about two things: first, that it was quite within your means at any time to pay him one dollar; and, second, that you were not the type of person likely to cheat him out of a dollar. Your *beaux yeux* alone would not have inspired him to such a quick and unhesitating offer. Would he have so readily relinquished ownership of the cake had he never seen or heard of you before? The question answers itself.

It will be observed, therefore, that the all-important economic question as to *whether or not the transaction should take place* depended upon the baker's certainty about two matters: first, your available resources; and, second, your probable intention to complete the exchange. That is, it was no mere vague, good-natured, mental predisposition in the baker, called "confidence," but *certainty about your very particular solvency and honesty,* that was responsible for the transaction taking place.

While this seems to be getting nearer the actualities in the incident, we still have but a circumscribed picture of it. The baker's state of mind was, of course, a *sine qua non* of the transaction. But, after all, that state of mind had you as its object. His unquestioning faith that you would carry out this simple economic promise demands a little further examination. We have seen it must have arisen either from previous experience with you, or through information he had acquired about you. His faith in your integrity, which was necessary for the transaction to take place at all, could only have been the result of past demonstrations of your integrity.

In other words, the ultimate core of fact to observe about this entire incident is not so much that the baker had an unhesitating "confidence" in you, but that he had reason to have confidence: *that in fact you always did carry out such promises.*

That this distinction is not mere quibbling, but is indeed like a peep-hole in a black curtain through which a vast lighted scene may be beheld, appears immediately when its implications are considered. For there is involved here an explanation of the greater part of the transactions that go on in modern life—what we have called deferred exchanges in ownership. It would be a narrow, almost an unmeaning, picture of our society to say that it is the confidence of men in one another's dependability which is responsible for their taking place. For, as we have seen in your own simple incident, analysis reveals a fact of the most profound social significance: *that this faith arises only because men in their dealings with one another actually do carry out by action the greater part of the economic promises they make.* It is the exception for them to fail to do so.

Suggestions

1. "Deferred Exchanges" is like "Tolerance of Opposition" in several respects. It defines a term more completely than a dictionary can, and its technique consists of specific illustration or examples. But "Deferred Exchanges" is not only longer than the first essay; it is also more complex. The specific illustration here is itself so extended that it becomes the controlling analogy by which the argument progresses. From the first paragraph to the last, that illustration of you at the baker's is kept uppermost. Also, the terms being defined are given more careful, rigorous analysis than those in "Tolerance of Opposition."

2. Point out examples of familiar tone and show its value in the essay.

3. Larger generalizations follow the two examples of the person in the baker's shop. What are they?

4. In addition to *completed exchange* and *deferred exchange,* does this essay involve other definitions?

5. Explain: *amnesia, beaux yeux, incontrovertibly, sine qua non.* Are both foreign phrases used with the same tone?

6. What printing device is used to mark the important places in the essay? Is it necessary?

7. Analyze the last two sentences and write your own essay on those generalizations.

8. Write an extended definition of some social relationship that depends on confidence, as deferred exchanges do. Consider for your topic invitations to dinner, behavior at parties, coffeebreaks at work, applications for jobs.

THE MODERN CLIMATE OF OPINION

CARL BECKER ---⊰{ *From* THE HEAVENLY CITY OF THE EIGHT-EENTH CENTURY PHILOSOPHERS *by Carl Becker.* © *1932, Yale University Press.*

Edit and interpret the conclusions of modern science as tenderly as we like, it is still quite impossible for us to regard man as the child of God for whom the earth was created as a temporary habitation. Rather must we regard him as little more than a chance deposit on the surface of the world, carelessly thrown up between two ice ages by the same forces that rust iron and ripen corn, a sentient organism endowed by some happy or unhappy accident with intelligence indeed, but with an intelligence that is conditioned by the very forces that it seeks to understand and to control. The ultimate cause of this cosmic process of which man is a part, whether God or electricity or a "stress in the ether," we know not. Whatever it may be, if indeed it be anything more than a necessary postulate of thought, it appears in its effects as neither benevolent nor malevolent, as neither kind nor unkind, but merely as indifferent to us. What is man that the electron should be mindful of him! Man is but a foundling in the cosmos, abandoned by the forces that created him. Unparented, unassisted, and undirected by omniscient or benevolent authority, he must fend for himself, and with the aid of his own limited intelligence find his way about in an indifferent universe.

Such is the world pattern that determines the character and direction of modern thinking. The pattern has been a long time in the weaving. It has taken eight centuries to replace the conception of existence as divinely composed and purposeful drama by the conception of existence as a blindly running flux of disintegrating energy. But there are signs that the substitution is now fully accomplished; and if we wished to reduce eight centuries of intellectual history to an epigram, we could not do better than to borrow the words of Aristophanes, "Whirl is king, having deposed Zeus." [1]

Perhaps the most important consequence of this revolution is that we look about in vain for any semblance of the old authority, the old absolute, for any stable foothold from which to get a running start. Zeus, having been deposed, can no longer serve as a first premise of thought. It is true we may still believe in Zeus; many people do. Even scientists, historians, philosophers still accord him the customary worship. But this is no more than a personal privilege, to be exercised in private, as formerly, in Protestant countries, Papists were sometimes permitted to celebrate mass in private chapels. No serious scholar would now postulate the existence and goodness of God as a point of departure for explaining the quantum theory or the French Revolution. If I should venture, as certain historians once did, to expound the thought of the eighteenth century as having been foreordained by God for the punishment of a perverse and stiff-necked generation, you would shift uneasily in your chairs, you would "register" embarrassment, and even blush a little to think that a trusted colleague should exhibit such bad taste. The fact is that we have no first premise. Since Whirl is king, we must start with the whirl, the mess of things as presented in experience. We start with the irreducible brute fact, and we must take it as we find it, since it is no longer permitted to coax or cajole it, hoping to fit it into some or other category of thought on the assumption that the pattern of the world is a logical one. Accepting the fact as given, we observe it, experiment with it, verify it, classify it, measure it if possible, and reason about it as little as may be. The questions we ask are "What?" and "How?" What are the facts and how are they related? If sometimes, in a moment of absent-mindedness or idle diversion, we ask the question "Why?" the answer escapes us. Our supreme object is to measure and master the world rather than to understand it.

Since our supreme object is to measure and master the world, we can make relatively little use of theology, philosophy, and deductive logic— the three stately entrance ways to knowledge erected in the Middle Ages. In the course of eight centuries these disciplines have fallen from their high estate, and in their place we have enthroned history, science, and the technique of observation and measurement. Theology, or something

[1] In *The Clouds* (423 B.C.), a comedy satirizing Socrates.

that goes under that name, is still kept alive by the faithful, but only by artificial respiration. Its functions, the services it rendered in the time of St. Thomas,[2] have been taken over, not as is often supposed by philosophy, but by history—the study of man and his world in the time sequence. Theology in the thirteenth century presented the story of man and the world according to the divine plan of salvation. It provided the men of that age with an authentic philosophy of history, and they could afford to ignore the factual experience of mankind since they were so well assured of its ultimate cause and significance. But in the succeeding centuries men turned more and more to an investigation of the recorded story of mankind, bringing to that enterprise a remarkable attention to detail, an ever greater preoccupation with the factual event. In the light of the mass of irreducible brute facts thus accumulated, the theological vision of man and his world faded into a pale replica of the original picture. In the eighteenth century the clear-cut theological philosophy of history had degenerated into an amiable and gentlemanly "philosophy teaching by example." In the early nineteenth century, history could still be regarded as the Transcendent Idea realizing itself in the actual. In our time, history is nothing but history, the notation of what has occurred, just as it happened. The object of history, according to Santayana,[3] is quite simply "to fix the order of events throughout past times in all places." No respectable historian any longer harbors ulterior motives; and one who should surreptitiously introduce the gloss of a transcendent interpretation into the human story would deserve to be called a philosopher and straightway lose his reputation as a scholar.

I am, of course, using the word *history* in the broad sense. It is to be understood as a method of approach rather than as a special field of study. Literature and language, government and law, economics, science and mathematics, love and sport—what is there that has not in our time been studied historically? Much of what is called science is properly history, the history of biological or physical phenomena. The geologist gives us the history of the earth; the botanist relates the life history of plants. Professor Whitehead[4] has recently illuminated physics by tracing the history of physical concepts. To regard all things in their historical setting appears, indeed, to be an instructive procedure of the modern mind. We do it without thinking, because we can scarcely think at all without doing it. The modern climate of opinion is such that we cannot seemingly understand our world unless we regard it as a going concern. We cannot properly know things as they are unless we know "how they came to be what they are." Nor is it merely, or chiefly, the succession of external events that engages our attention. No doubt St. Thomas was

[2] Aquinas (1225–1274), author of *Theological Compendium* and other works.
[3] George Santayana (1863–1952), Hispano-American philosopher.
[4] Alfred North Whitehead (1861–1947), author of *Science and the Modern World* and other works.

aware that one thing follows another. What is peculiar to the modern mind is the disposition and the determination to regard ideas and concepts, the truth of things as well as the things themselves, as changing entities, the character and significance of which at any given time can be fully grasped only by regarding them as points in an endless process of differentiation, of unfolding, of waste and repair. Let St. Thomas ask *us* to define anything—for example, the natural law—let him ask us to tell him what it *is*. We cannot do it. But, given time enough, we can relate for him its history. We can tell him what varied forms the natural law has assumed up to now. Historical-mindedness is so much a preconception of modern thought that we can identify a particular thing only by pointing to the various things it successively was before it became that particular thing which it will presently cease to be.

Besides the historical approach to knowledge we have another to which we are even more committed—the scientific. As history has gradually replaced theology, so science has replaced philosophy. Philosophy, it is true, has managed, much better than theology, to keep up appearances in the modern world, and at the present moment signs are not wanting of refurbishings going on in its ancient and somewhat dilapidated dwelling. Yet, it is obvious that the undisputed sway which it formerly exercised has long been usurped by natural science. In the hands of St. Thomas, philosophy, with "deductive" logic as its instrument of precision, was a method of building a rational world, its aim being to reconcile experience with revealed truth. But the influences which disposed succeeding generations to examine the facts of human history, induced them also to examine the facts of natural phenomena. The rise of history and of science were but two results of a single impulse, two aspects of the trend of modern thought away from an overdone rationalization of the facts to a more careful and disinterested examination of the facts themselves.

Galileo, for example (not that he was the first by any means), did not ask what Aristotle had said about falling bodies, or whether it was reasonable to suppose that a ten-pound weight would fall to the ground more quickly than a one-pound weight. He applied to this problem the scientific method. He dropped two weights, differing as ten to one, from the leaning tower, and noted the fact that both weights reached the ground at the same time. In such a world as this, he said in effect, this is the way falling bodies behave. If that is not possible in a rational world, then the world we live in is not a rational one. Facts are primary and what chiefly concern us; they are stubborn and irreducible and we cannot get around them. They may be in accord with reason, let us hope that they are; but whether they are so or not is only a question of fact to be determined like any other.

This subtle shift in the point of view was perhaps the most important event in the intellectual history of modern times, but its implications were not at once understood. Philosophy continued to reign, and when in the eighteenth century she added a new word to her title (calling herself natural philosophy [5]), no one noted the fact as ominous. Galileo and his successors were philosophers too, preëminently so, since their marvelous discoveries, based upon observation and experiment, uncovered so many secret places in the world, and by promising to banish mystery from the universe seemed to leave it more obviously rational than they found it. The laws of nature and nature's God appeared henceforth to be one and the same thing, and since every part of God's handiwork could all in good time be reasonably demonstrated, the intelligent man could very well do with a minimum of faith—except, of course (the exception was tremendous but scarcely noticed at the time), faith in the uniform behavior of nature and in the capacity of reason to discover its *modus operandi.*

In the course of the nineteenth century this optimistic outlook became overcast. The marriage of fact and reason, of science and the universal laws of nature, proved to be somewhat irksome, and in the twentieth century it was, not without distress, altogether dissolved. Natural philosophy was transformed into natural science. Natural science became science, and scientists rejected, as a personal affront, the title of philosopher, which formerly they had been proud to bear. The vision of man and his world as a neat and efficient machine, designed by an intelligent Author of the Universe, gradually faded away. Professors of science ceased to speak with any assurance of the laws of nature, and were content to pursue, with unabated ardor, but without any teleological implications whatever, their proper business of observing and experimenting with the something which is the stuff of the universe, of measuring and mastering its stress and movement. "Science," said Lloyd Morgan, "deals exclusively with changes of configuration, and traces the accelerations which are observed to occur, leaving to metaphysics to deal with the underlying agency, if it exist." [6]

It is well known that the result of pursuing this restricted aim (the scientific method reduced to its lowest terms) has been astounding. It is needless to say that we live in a machine age, that the art of inventing is the greatest of our inventions, or that within a brief space of fifty years the outward conditions of life have been transformed. It is less well understood that this bewildering experience has given a new slant to our minds. Fresh discoveries and new inventions are no longer the result of fortunate accidents which we are expected to note with awe. They are all a part of the day's work, anticipated, deliberately intended, and brought to pass according to schedule. Novelty has ceased to excite

[5] I.e. science. The change was ominous because eventually only scientific knowledge would be considered knowledge.
[6] *Interpretation of Nature,* p. 58.

wonder because it has ceased to be novelty; on the contrary, the strange, so habituated have we become to it, is of the very essence of the customary. There is nothing new in heaven or earth not dreamt of in our laboratories; and we should be amazed indeed if tomorrow and tomorrow and tomorrow failed to offer us something new to challenge our capacity for readjustment. Science has taught us the futility of troubling to understand the "underlying agency" of the things we use. We have found that we can drive an automobile without knowing how the carburetor works, and listen to a radio without mastering the secret of radiation. We really haven't time to stand amazed, either at the starry firmament above or the Freudian complexes within us. The multiplicity of things to manipulate and make use of so fully engages our attention that we have neither the leisure nor the inclination to seek a rational explanation of the force that makes them function so efficiently.

In dismissing the underlying agency with a casual shrug, we are in good company. The high priest of science, even more than the common man, is a past master of this art. It is one of the engaging ironies of modern thought that the scientific method, which it was once fondly hoped would banish mystery from the world, leaves it every day more inexplicable. Physics, which it was thought had dispensed with the need of metaphysics, has been transformed by its own proper researches into the most metaphysical of disciplines. The more attentively the physicist looks at the material stuff of the world the less there is to see. Under his expert treatment the substantial world of Newtonian physics has been dissolved into a complex of radiant energies. No efficient engineer or Prime Mover could have designed the world, since it can no longer be fully understood in terms of mechanics. "What is the sense of talking about a mechanical explanation," asks Professor Whitehead, "when you do not know what you mean by mechanics?"[7] We are told that if we ascribe position to anything it ceases to have determinable velocity; if we ascertain its velocity it ceases to have determinable position. The universe is said to be composed of atoms, an atom is said to be composed of a nucleus around which electrons revolve in determinable orbits; but experiments seem to show that an electron may, for reasons best known to itself, be moving in two orbits at the same time. To this point Galileo's common-sense method of noting the behavior of things, of sticking close to the observable facts, has brought us; it has at last presented us with a fact that common sense repudiates.

What can we do? Reason and logic cry out in pain no doubt; but we have long since learned not to bother overmuch with reason and logic. Logic was formerly visualized as something outside us, something existing independently which, if we were willing, could take us by the hand and lead us into the paths of truth. We now suspect that it is something the

[7] *Science and the Modern World*, p. 24.

mind has created to conceal its timidity and keep up its courage, a hocus-pocus designed to give formal validity to conclusions we are willing to accept if everybody else in our set will too. If all men are mortal (an assumption), and if Socrates was a man (in the sense assumed), no doubt Socrates must have been mortal; [8] but we suspect that we somehow knew all this before it was submitted to the test of a syllogism. Logics have a way of multiplying in response to the changes in point of view. First there was one logic, then there were two, then there were several; so that now, according to one authority (if a contributor to the *Encyclopaedia Britannica* who ventures to employ humor can be an authority), the state of logic is "that of Israel under the Judges, every man doeth that which is right in his own eyes." With all due allowance made for mathematical logic (which has to do with concepts, not with facts), and for the logic of probability (which Mr. Keynes [9] assures us has a probable validity), the secure foundations of deductive and inductive logic have been battered to pieces by the ascertainable facts, so that we really have no choice; we must cling to the ascertainable facts though they slay us.

Physicists, therefore, stick to the ascertainable facts. If logic presumes to protest in the name of the law, they know how to square it, so that it complaisantly looks the other way while they go on with illicit enterprises—with the business, for example (it is Sir William Bragg [10] who vouches for it), of teaching "the wave theory of light on Monday, Wednesday, and Friday, and the quantum theory on Tuesday, Thursday, and Saturday." It need not surprise us, then, to learn that physicists make nothing, when it suits their convenience, of regarding nucleus and electron, not as substances, but only as radiations—thus casually dissolving the substantial world into a congeries of repellent and attractive velocities which we are invited to believe in because they can be mathematically identified and made use of. Perhaps, as Professor Jeans [11] suggests, the world we live in was designed by a mathematician. Why not, indeed, if it can be most easily understood in terms of mathematical formulas? We know that two apples plus two apples make four apples. We have always taken it for granted that the apples exist, but we can very well understand that even if no apples are anywhere found it still remains true that two plus two make four. The mathematician gets on just as well without the apples, better indeed, since the apples have other attributes besides number. When sufficiently hard pressed, therefore, the physicist solves his difficulties by turning mathematician. As mathematician he can calculate the velocities that are observed to occur, meantime assuring us that the velocities could readily be attributed to substantial

[8] The basic syllogism in the deductive logic of Aristotle, 384–322 B.C. See † "The Uses and Limitations of Logic."

[9] John Maynard Keynes (1883–1946), author of *A Treatise on Money* and other works.

[10] Either W. L. Bragg (b. 1890) or his father, W. H. Bragg (1862–1942), who in 1915 were jointly awarded the Nobel Prize in physics.

[11] Sir James Jeans (1877–1946), author of *The Universe Around Us* and other works.

electrons, provided substantial electrons with such velocities should ever turn up. There is really no occasion for despair: our world can be computed even if it doesn't exist.

Perhaps I have said enough to suggest that the essential quality of the modern climate of opinion is factual rather than rational. The atmosphere which sustains our thought is so saturated with the actual that we can easily do with a minimum of the theoretical. We necessarily look at our world from the point of view of history and from the point of view of science. Viewed historically, it appears to be something in the making, something which can at best be only tentatively understood since it is not yet finished. Viewed scientifically, it appears as something to be accepted, something to be manipulated and mastered, something to adjust ourselves to with the least possible stress. So long as we can make efficient use of things, we feel no irresistible need to understand them. No doubt it is for this reason chiefly that the modern mind can be so wonderfully at ease in a mysterious universe.

Suggestions

1. "The Modern Climate of Opinion" presents both a definition and a thesis. The thesis, however, is subordinate to an ironic attitude toward a body of facts. One might say that the speaker adopts the manner of the historians he describes, dispassionately observing and recording. Do you accept his thesis? Discuss fully.

2. Is the speaker sympathetic or antagonistic toward the current climate of opinion? Point out passages that reveal his attitude.

3. Explain: Man's intelligence is "conditioned by the very forces that it seeks to understand and to control" (¶1); the modern conception of existence as opposed to the earlier one (¶2); "I am . . . using the word *history* in the broad sense" (¶5). What is peculiar to the modern mind regarding history?

4. Show how the reference to Galileo's experiment helps to prepare for the concluding paragraph.

5. ¶11 says that science has "presented us with a fact that common sense repudiates." Explain; what facts of this kind does the essay mention?

6. According to the last paragraph, why is "Why?" no longer the significant question to ask in determining man's place in his world? Compare this paragraph with the first; how does it reiterate the thesis?

7. Explain: *sentient organism, postulate, omniscient, Zeus, quantum theory, modus operandi, teleological, Freudian complexes, congeries.*

8. Point out and evaluate the success of the allusions to the following: † "Quickened Consciousness," ¶1; *Psalms* 8, 4; *The Declaration of Independence,* first sentence; *Hamlet* I.v; *Judges* 21,25.

9. Evaluate the methods by which the paragraphs of the essay are developed. Is there usually a clear topic sentence? Are the paragraphs mainly developed by many examples from various fields or by a few examples from one field? How are the paragraphs made coherent?

10. Write an essay defining the climate of opinion in your own age-group.

11. If the climate of opinion changes from one century to another, is it possible that changes and variations occur within a single century? Write an essay giving evidence that Becker's "Climate" should be plural.

DEFINING DEFINITION

MONROE C. BEARDSLEY —⧉ © *1960 by Monroe C. Beardsley.*

Much of the time, in our daily life, the language we use to get about in the world and get along with our fellow-creatures is like a windowpane that we habitually look through, but not at. We use words to talk about the world, but we don't talk about the words themselves. When something goes wrong with the windowpane, though—it gets smudged or cracked, so that it dims or distorts the images that pass through it—then we become aware of the glass itself. For the first time, we look at it and wonder what to do about it. The same is true of our language: when something goes wrong with words, so that they no longer transmit our thoughts clearly and efficiently, we have to do something about them. And what we do is clarify their meanings.

Thus, when a new law or ordinance is passed, it is often necessary to include some sentences to specify more exactly than we ordinarily do what the key words are to mean. What precisely constitutes an act of trespass? Under what conditions has indirect aggression occurred? What characteristics make a literary work obscene? Sometimes these explanations are too loose and have to be rewritten; sometimes they are drawn more sharply than they need to be—Connecticut's lottery law, for example, is said to be so strict that it is illegal to toss a coin before a football game, though so far the law has not been invoked on such occasions. Nor is it only laws that need clarifying: a great many disputes arise from disagreements about how words are to be used. You may recall the recent trouble between American and foreign airlines which had agreed, in order to keep costs down, to serve only sandwiches on trans-oceanic flights. It was found that the foreign airlines were luring passengers by heaping substantial and exotic meals on slices of bread and calling these repasts sandwiches. So it became necessary for the International Air Transport Association to obtain an agreement on the meaning of *sandwich*. That proved a somewhat complicated task.

I

There are several methods of clarifying the meaning of a word or phrase (let us, for short, speak of a *term* instead of a *word or phrase*), and any of these methods may, in a broad sense, be called a definition. (1) Sometimes we teach the meaning of the term by uttering it in the presence of the thing it refers to. We show what the hi-fi fan calls *wowing* by putting on a performance, if we have the proper apparatus; we show what *Okefenokee* is the name of by taking someone to the swamp. These acts can be called *definitions by pointing,* or *ostensive definitions.* (2) Sometimes, though we cannot produce a sample of the thing we have in mind, we refer to examples already known to others: the term *picaresque novel* is applied by literary historians to such works as the anonymous *La vida de Lazarillo de Tormes* (c. 1554), *Gil Blas,* by Le Sage, and *Captain Singleton,* by Defoe. This can be called a *definition by examples.* (3) Sometimes we help others understand, at least in part, the meaning of a word by talking about the object or process it refers to, comparing it and contrasting it with other objects or processes. Here, for example, someone is talking about clairvoyance:

> When Subject *K,* stationed in one room, under careful observation, was able to call off twenty-five cards turned up one at a time by Subject *J,* in a different building, and also under careful observation, we regarded it as clear-cut evidence of clairvoyance. He appeared to be able to perceive the cards, though his perception is, of course, not at all like ordinary visual perception, for there could have been no response to light-waves. On the other hand, though different from visual perception, it appeared to eventuate in knowledge of what the cards were, as if he had been able to read them. . . .

Whether this was a case of clairvoyance or of telepathy does not matter here; a person who had never heard the term *clairvoyance* would presumably get some notion of the sort of thing it means from these remarks. And such a clarification of meaning by talking about the thing meant can be called *definition by description* or, more narrowly, *definition by comparison and contrast.*

But though the term *definition* is often used in this broad sense, as equivalent to *clarification of meaning,* it is perhaps best reserved for a more specific and direct method of clarifying meaning. This method consists in offering for the term whose meaning is in doubt another whose meaning is not in doubt—one that can serve as a substitute for the first term, because its meaning is identical. The simplest and most trivial case of such a substitution, of course, is that of one single word for another: *hog* for *pig*, or *dried* for *desiccated*. A clarification of this simple sort can be called a *definition by one-word synonym*, and sometimes it may be helpful, but usually it does not take us very far. The kind of thing that we recognize as a definition in the strictest sense is a statement in which one term is clarified by a longer term that breaks down its meaning or analyzes it: a *presidio* is *a settlement that is fortified and garrisoned*. This tells us that in the meaning of *presidio* there is an implicit reference to (a) being settled, (b) being fortified, and (c) having troops stationed there. If *definition* is to be used in the broad sense, then such a definition as this is called an *analytic definition*. Henceforth, in this context, we shall deal only with analytic definitions, and therefore we can refer to them simply as definitions.

II

A definition, it is now clear, has at least three parts. There is the term we are interested in defining: this is called the *definiendum*. There is the term we use to define it, the *definiens*, or defining term. And there is the link between them: the assertion that they have the same meaning, that to all intents and purposes one can be used in place of the other. Since the definition says that the definiendum and the definiens are to be understood in the same way, anyone who understands the definiens automatically understands the definiendum—once he is provided with the definition.

For a start, it is all right to say that in a definition the definiens and the definiendum have the same meaning—but only for a start, because the term *meaning* can easily give us trouble, too. If we take it in a strict sense, it is pretty clear that no two terms in English have exactly the same meaning—we can always find some subtle differences in the way they are used. Even *pig* and *hog*, which are perhaps about as closely synonymous as you can get, may not be substitutable for each other everywhere. Somehow "The Three Little Hogs" wouldn't be quite the same story. So it might seem that we cannot give any definitions at all, since we can never find perfectly equivalent terms. But the equivalence of meaning that we require for a definition is fortunately more limited, and in this limited sense it is available.

To clarify this limited sense, we must introduce an important distinction between two ways in which words may be said to mean, that is to refer to the world. When we survey the world about us and its contents, we can sum up very abstractly what we find by saying that it is made up of things—where *things* is taken to include every distinguishable and identifiable substantial entity, physical objects, events, animals, people, numbers, and so on. Here, for example, is a xylophone; that is a thing. But what is a xylophone? It is a thing with certain characteristics, a certain size, weight, materials, use, effect, method of performance, and so on. Some of these characteristics are, so to speak, accidental to it—its size, for example, or the material of which the legs are constructed—for it could still be a xylophone whether large or small, whether the legs are steel, copper, or glass. Other characteristics are not accidental, but indispensable to it, if it is to be a xylophone: for example, its bars must be made of wood, rather than metal or glass; for if they were not wood it would be a different instrument, perhaps a celesta, a marimba, or a vibraharp. These indispensable characteristics constitute the xylophon-ishness of the xylophone: they are what make it a xylophone; they are its *defining characteristics.*

We have distinguished (a) the xylophone itself as a physical object, and (b) certain characteristics of the xylophone which it shares with all other xylophones. Now let us consider the word *xylophone* and what it means. Here we must make a corresponding distinction. For in one sense the word means the xylophone itself: it is a common name that applies to all xylophones and to no other objects in the world. But in a second sense it means xylophonishness: a certain set of characteristics, such as having wooden bars. All xylophones, and nothing but xylo-phones, have this entire set of characteristics.

We must distinguish, in short, two kinds or dimensions of meaning. (1) The term *xylophone* comprehends (that is, names) all actual xylo-phones that have ever existed or ever will exist, and this class of xylophones is called the *comprehension* of the term. (2) The term *xylophone* signifies a set of characteristics that any object must have if it is to be correctly called a xylophone, and this set of characteristics is called the *signification* of the term. Most common nouns and noun-phrases have both these dimensions of meaning. But note, first, that a self-contradictory term, such as *competitive monopoly,* comprehends nothing (there is nothing it can be applied to), though it has a signification; and, second, that a proper name, such as *George Washington of Mt. Vernon,* which comprehends a single object rather than a number of objects, has no signification, for it is simply a label attached to a particular person, and does not indicate any of his characteristics.

The signification and comprehension of a term do not exhaust its meaning—there are, for example, connotations to be considered—but the signification is that part of meaning, the central and basic part of it, with which definition is concerned. When it is said that the definiendum and definiens are equivalent in meaning, it is their signification that counts. But even this must be qualified in one important way. For it is clear that many words (unlike *xylophone*) have more than one signification. The signification may vary from context to context: in clothing stores, a *cap* is a flat, soft, peaked headgear, but in toy stores it is a bit of paper enclosing a small quantity of powder, for use in cap pistols. These two sets of characteristics are different indeed. Now it is obviously asking too much of any definition to present more than one signification at a time, and therefore I have in effect given two definitions of *cap*, distinguishing them by a rough indication of the sort of context in which each sense will be found.

So we have found a fourth part to add to our definitions, when necessary—and it often is. Let us put in a parenthetical remark after the definiens, saying what sort of context we are defining the word for. In clothing-store advertisements we can correctly substitute according to one definition, but not according to the other:

> *Cap* (in clothing contexts) has the same signification as *visored, brimless cloth covering for the head.*
> *Cap* (in contexts connected with toys) has the same signification as *small piece of paper enclosing a small quantity of gunpowder, which explodes on percussion.*

These definitions are fairly fussy, and of course we seldom need to be so formal—provided we know what we are doing. Sometimes, however, it is handy to be able to cast a definition in this form, even if we do not present it formally to others, for the form will make clear whether we have followed a very important, but as yet unstated, rule for clarifying terms. The definiens is supposed to be equivalent, that is, identical in signification, to the definiendum, and therefore (in the appropriate context) a substitute for it. That means it must be the same part of speech. If the definiendum is a noun, the definiens must be a noun or noun phrase, and so, too, for verbs, adjectives, adverbs, and phrases and clauses of all kinds.

It won't do, for example, to define *cutting* (in college contexts) as *when a student doesn't turn up in class as he is supposed to.* Try substituting that definiens for *cutting* in "Jones was put on probation for cutting"—it makes no sense. In this example, it is easy to transform the definiens into a substitutable verb form; sometimes, however, it requires a little ingenuity. Can you define the verb *to goof*?

III

Even if you are willing to take the two definitions offered just above as examples of the way definitions look when most properly stated, you may find fault with them in another respect. Are they good definitions? Are they, that is, correct?

Since a definition claims an equivalence between its two terms, it is correct if and only if the two terms really do have that equivalence. Now, suppose the term you are defining is one you have made up, for a certain purpose: "A *temporometer* is a device used on time machines to indicate the rate at which the machine is traveling backward or forward in time." Or suppose it is a well-known word that you wish to give a new signification in a special context: "For the purpose of the present Act, *organization* shall mean any group of two or more people a majority of whom meet together at least once a year"—a definition that gives an unusually broad meaning to the term *organization*. In these sentences there is no expectation, and no claim, that the definiendum has actually been used by anyone in the way described, and so the question of correctness does not arise. The word *temporometer* did not even exist until you created it; and in defining *organization* so broadly you would be deliberately deviating from ordinary usage. Such definitions are arbitrary, and while they are very useful they must be handled with particular care. But ordinarily when we are defining words we are trying, as the dictionary-maker tries, to isolate some meaning that the word already has in certain contexts, and so the definition may be justly criticized if it does not correctly report that meaning.

When a person is unusually gifted at handling words, it is possible to ask him directly whether a given definition is correct: "Would you agree," we might ask, "that the following set of characteristics, namely (a) being an article of headgear, (b) being made of cloth, (c) being brimless, and (d) being visored, are sufficient for an object to be called a *cap,* and also that they must all be present for an object to be so called?" But most of us, particularly in thinking about common words, find it much easier to say what things we apply the term *cap* to (that is, to give examples of the class of things comprehended by this term) than to say exactly why we apply it to them (that is, to analyze the signification). And so it is convenient to have an indirect test of the correctness of any proposed definition.

The test follows from the nature of signification and comprehension. The characteristics in the signification are like the rules of membership in an honorary organization: anything that has these characteristics satisfies the conditions and is automatically admitted to membership in the class. If two terms have the same signification, they must have the same comprehension, that is, apply to the same things, as, for example, do *husband* and *male spouse.* Therefore, if we find that the comprehension of one term does not correspond exactly to the comprehension of another, we can be certain that the terms do not have the same signification, and any definition that claims their equivalence must be incorrect. So this gives us a negative test of correctness: we look to see whether there are things we would call a *husband* but not a *male spouse,* and vice versa; and if we find any such things, we can conclude that the definition needs mending.

Notice, however, that the test does not work in the other direction. For it is possible for two terms to have the same comprehension but different significations. *Evergreen* and *conifer* are popularly used almost interchangeably, though there are evergreen (that is, non-deciduous) trees, like the laurel, that do not bear cones; and there are conifers, like the larch, that are deciduous. Now suppose there were no exceptions, like laurels and larches, and every evergreen was a conifer and every conifer was an evergreen. Then *evergreen* and *conifer* would have exactly the same comprehension, yet they would still have different significations. Hence, if in a definition the definiens and definiendum turn out to coincide in what they comprehend, the definition may still be incorrect, though there is a probability that it is not.

It is convenient to distinguish two ways in which a definition may go wrong, even though some definitions succeed in going wrong both ways at once. First, the definiens may extend beyond the definiendum, by taking in things that the definiens does not comprehend. To define *kettle* as *metal pot for boiling water* would commit this error, for saucepans that are not kettles are used for boiling water, too. This definition is too broad. To make it correct we would have to add to the definiens some reference to a spout. Second, the definiendum may extend beyond the definiens, so that the definiens fails to include some things that the definiendum comprehends. To define *pie* as *pastry with two crusts and fruit filling* is too narrow, for some pies have only one crust, and some pies are filled with other things than fruit. This definition is probably too broad, as well as too narrow, for a good definition of *pie* would have to clarify the meaning of *crust,* in terms of its ingredients and method of cooking. When we give such a definition, we shall find that we have excluded Boston cream pies and Eskimo pies; does this mean that the definition is still too narrow? Since these are so different from the other things called pies, and since Boston cream pies have all the characteristics commonly signified by *cake,* we shall simply have to conclude that *pie* is used with a very different signification in these contexts. A Boston cream pie is no more a pie, in the strict sense, than a bellboy is necessarily a boy or carhops are a variety of hops.

To frame a definition that will avoid these two mistakes, we need a systematic method. And it consists in working out the definition step by step, starting with a large class of things that includes those we are concerned to isolate, and working down. Consider *xylophone* once more. What is a broad class to which xylophones belong? The class of musical instruments. So we may begin our definition:

A xylophone is *a musical instrument that . . .*

Next we make a further subdivision of the general class: let's say, percussion instruments (as distinct from stringed and wind instruments). The characteristic we are taking note of in making this division is the

manner in which the tone is produced. So far, then, we have a *genus*
(musical instruments) and a *species* of that genus (percussion instruments). The *differentiae,* or distinguishing characteristics, of that species
are that they produce their sounds by being struck. Thus:

A xylophone is *a percussion instrument that . . .*

Now some percussion instruments produce tones, others (like snare
drums) do not: so again, if we take percussion instruments as our genus,
we get a species of tone-producing percussion instruments. And these in
turn divide into those that produce one tone (the kettledrum) and those
that produce several. The latter in turn can be divided according to
whether the striking is done by the performer directly, or by a mechanism
(as in a piano). These may in turn be divided according to the material
that is struck. All these distinctions may seem unnecessarily cautious and
pedestrian, and no doubt we could have done the job more rapidly.
Nevertheless, the method is worth illustrating in detail, because there
are other words that we find much more difficult (as well as important)
to define, where every precaution is called for: say, *law, property, investment, price, romanticism, existentialism.* By moving one step at a time,
and checking at each step, we may be sure that the definition is not too
narrow because something essential is left out; and we proceed to the
point where any further subdivision would make the definition too narrow. At that point we have reached a correct definition, which, in the
present example, might be something like this:

> *Xylophone* has the same signification as *percussion instrument containing
> tuned wooden bars, which the player strikes with wooden hammers.*

The method of dividing by genus and differentiae is an ancient method,
and a good one for sorting out the meanings of words. Even in this little
example, perhaps, we come out with a clearer idea than we had before
of what we mean by *xylophone.* When we apply the same technique to
words with more complicated meanings, we can clarify these meanings
tremendously.

Suggestions

1. Since formulating a correct analytic definition is troublesome, "Defining *Definition"* begins by arguing that nevertheless it is sometimes
necessary. Summarize this argument and decide whether it is convincing.

2. Name four kinds of definition and show the limitations (if any) of
each one.

3. List the technical terms in this essay, beginning with *definiendum*
in section II, and define them.

4. Distinguish between the two kinds of meaning with respect to
several terms that are important in your favorite hobby or sport.

5. Find several examples of faulty definition, showing whether the fault of each one is in being too broad or too narrow.

6. Write an anti-lottery law that the toss of a coin at a football game would not infringe.

7. Write analytic definitions of *obscenity, sandwich, to goof, Boston cream pie, carhop.*

8. Write an analytic definition of each of the important terms in the other essays of this section.

9. Criticize these definitions:

Trespassing is when somebody comes on somebody else's property.

Man is a featherless biped.

A bat is a winged mammal that has fur.

An American is a citizen of the United States.

10. Write an essay about a term that has several meanings: e.g. *education, liberal, nature.*

C O M P A R I S O N S

TALENT AND GENIUS

W. SOMERSET MAUGHAM

From THE SUMMING UP *by W. Somerset Maugham.* © *1938 by W. Somerset Maugham. Reprinted by permission of Mr. Maugham, A. P. Watt & Son, Doubleday & Co., Inc., and William Heinemann, Ltd.*

I lived once in a group of young men who had by nature gifts that seemed to me much superior to mine. They could write and draw and compose with a facility that aroused my envy. They had an appreciation of art and a critical instinct that I despaired of attaining. Of these some died without fulfilling the promise I thought they had and the rest have lived on without distinction. I know now that all they had was the natural creativity of youth. To write prose and verse, to hammer out little tunes on the piano and to draw and paint, are instinctive with a great many young persons. It is a form of play, due merely to the exuberance of their years, and is no more significant than a child's building of a castle on the sands. I suspect that it was my own ingenuousness that led me to admire so much the gifts of my friends. If I had been less ignorant I might have seen that the opinions that seemed to me so original were theirs only at second-hand and that their verses and their music owed more to a retentive memory than to a lively imagination. The point I want to make is that this facility is, if not universal, so common that one can draw no conclusions from it. Youth is the inspiration. One of the tragedies of the arts is the spectacle of the vast number of persons who have been misled by this passing fertility to devote their lives to the effort of creation. Their invention deserts them as they grow older, and they are faced with the long years before them in which, unfitted by now for a more humdrum calling, they harass their wearied brain to beat out material it is incapable of giving them. They are lucky when, with what bitterness we know, they can make a living in ways, like journalism or teaching, that are allied to the arts.

Of course it is from among those who possess by nature this facility that the artist is produced. Without it he cannot have talent; but it is only a part of talent. We start by living, each one of us, in the solitariness of our own minds and from the data given us and our communications with other minds we construct the outside world to suit our needs. Because we are all the result of one evolutionary process, and our environment is more or less the same, the constructions we make are roughly similar. For convenience and simplicity we accept them as identical and speak of a common world. The peculiarity of the artist is that he is in some particular different from other men and so the world of his construction is different too. It is this idiosyncrasy that is the better part of his equipment. When the picture he draws of his private world appeals to a certain number of persons, either by its strangeness, its intrinsic interest or its correspondence with their own prepossessions (for none of us is quite the same as his neighbor, only rather like, and not everyone accepts the world common to us all in every respect) his talent will be acknowledged. If he is a writer he will fulfil some need in the nature of his readers and they will lead with him a life of the spirit that satisfies them better than the life circumstances have forced on them. But there are others to whom this idiosyncrasy does not appeal. They have no patience with the world constructed by its instrumentality. It may actually revolt them. Then the artist has nothing to say to them and they will deny his talent.

I do not believe that genius is an entirely different thing from talent. I am not even sure that it depends on any great difference in the artist's natural gifts. For example, I do not think that Cervantes had an exceptional gift for writing; few people would deny him genius. Nor would it be easy in English literature to find a poet with a happier gift than Herrick and yet no one would claim that he had more than a delightful talent. It seems to me that what makes genius is the combination of natural gifts for creation with an idiosyncrasy that enables its possessor to see the world personally in the highest degree and yet with such catholicity that his appeal is not to this type of man or to that type, but to all men. His private world is that of common men, but ampler and more pithy. His communication is universal and though men may not be able to tell exactly what it signifies they feel that it is important. He is supremely normal. By a happy accident of nature seeing life with immense vivacity, as it were at concert pitch, he sees it, with its infinite diversity, in the healthy way that mankind at large sees it. In Matthew Arnold's phrase he sees it steadily and sees it whole. But genius arises once or twice in a century. The lesson of anatomy applies: there is nothing so rare as the normal. It is foolish to do as many do now and call a man a genius because he has written half-a-dozen clever plays or painted a score of good pictures. It is very well to have talent; few people have. With talent the artist will only reach the second class, but that need not disturb him for it contains the names of many whose works have uncommon merit. When you think it has produced such novels as *Le Rouge et le Noir,* such poems as "The Shropshire Lad," such paintings as those of Watteau, there is not much to be ashamed of. Talent cannot reach the utmost heights, but it can show you many an unexpected and delicious view, an unfrequented dell, a bubbling brook or a romantic cavern, on the way that leads to them. The forwardness of human nature is such that it falters sometimes when it is bidden to take the broadest of all surveys of human nature. It will shrink from the splendor of Tolstoi's *War and Peace* to turn with complacency to Voltaire's *Candide.* It would be hard to live always with Michelangelo's ceiling in the Sistine Chapel, but anyone could do with one of Constable's pictures of Salisbury Cathedral.

Suggestions

1. Our everyday tendency to make comparisons can be put to good use in composition. By isolating one thing and its characteristics and setting them alongside another thing and its characteristics, we can see and describe both with greater clarity. What "Talent and Genius" does, most of us do less precisely almost every day: for instance, we evaluate a movie, a person, or a popular tune by distinguishing it from a superior member of its own class: "John is a good club organizer, but we'll never

get another one like Henry." An excellent method, provided the comparison is supported with specific reasons—as Maugham does in distinguishing talent from genius.

Notice the phrase *of its own class*. When two things are compared, the more alike they are the more their differences will stand out. Most comparisons are for this reason statements of both likeness and unlikeness. When the speaker is stressing the first, we may call the comparison an *analogy;* when he stresses the second, we usually say *contrast*. But no contrast is effective unless the two opposed things have much in common.

2. What have talent and genius in common, according to the essay?

3. What are the sources of creativity in many young artists?

4. Does the speaker make a clear distinction between the man of talent and the man of genius? Does he illustrate it with concrete examples? What is his attitude toward the second-best?

5. Examine the concluding sentence. Does it imply something about works of art other than the paintings of Michelangelo and Constable? How does it function in relation to the rest of the essay?

6. Write an essay on the advantages of the second-best, using the organizing principles of both definition and comparison.

7. Write a comparison of two friends who (a) have something in common—a job, a talent, a hobby; or (b) have little in common except your liking for them.

SOUND AND SIGHT

HOWARD TAUBMAN First *printed in* THE NEW YORK TIMES. © *1958, Howard Taubman.*

Let us begin this morning with a proposition so obvious that it hardly needs statement: Music is an aural art. In opera or ballet, it is associated with elements that require the eye. But the sound itself can be apprehended only through the ear. As for works like symphonies, string quartets, and piano sonatas, only the sense of hearing is needed.

Agreed? Of course. Ask any of the thousands of persons in this country who have given up concert-going on the ground that their record collections provide them with all that they seek from music. They will tell you that they have liberated themselves from nuisances, like spending money on tickets, engaging sitters, and bucking traffic. When they want to hear something, they turn on their hi-fi rig. You don't have to look at the performer, do you? What's more, the performance is there to be enjoyed again and again.

These people are wrong. With all the gratitude and respect for the almost incredible richness and variety to be found on records today, it must be emphasized that they are not the same thing as live music. It does not matter how faithfully playing equipment reproduces the sound of the voice or instruments. Nor does the greatness, even the uniqueness, of a performance alter the point, though it is treasurable to have lasting mementoes of the master performers.

No matter how magnificent an interpretation, it is forever frozen in those microgrooves. If you play the same record often enough, you will get to know intimately every detail of the performer's approach. You will be prepared in advance for an inner voice stressed here, a delicious retard made there, a wonderfully built climax. You will be deprived of one of the life-giving forces of music—the freshness of the new and unexpected approach which is inevitable with the flesh-and-blood performer who has not become routinized into a machine himself.

The very possibility of error adds excitement to the living performance. It may be disconcerting to hear a soprano reach for an E flat in alt and have her land somewhere below it. It may be annoying to have a golden horn turn sour. But some of us have grown tired of perfection as it exists in the recording studios where a younger and more agile voice may be borrowed to supply the sure, bright top tones for another singer. There is more adventure in the striving for the difficult than in predictable precision.

Then there is the personality of the performer. He is only human. He responds to people. Often he catches fire from a responsive audience. He charges his music-making with an intensity he did not plan. He plays with a spontaneity he cannot summon up under the eyes of the engineer. He radiates from his person some of the emotions he is trying to express through the music. Suddenly the listener finds it enormously profitable and stimulating to be also a viewer.

Music is aural, but visual impressions affect and complement the aural. Some day television will recall this vivid lesson and make use of it—to its own and our advantage.

Suggestions

1. "Sound and Sight" advances a thesis; it contradicts the belief and practice of "thousands of persons in this country" who prefer records to concert performances. The technique is comparison supported by details that make the thesis persuasive. Explain the importance to the thesis of the proposition that music is more than simply an aural art.

2. Is the essay fair to the arguments of music lovers who prefer recorded over live performances? Do their arguments deserve more than two paragraphs?

3. Show how the parallel sentence structure in ¶6 helps to make the reader side with the concert performer.

4. Using the final sentence as a starting point, write an essay analyzing and comparing live and filmed television shows.

5. Write an essay defending the pleasures of listening to a "perfect" performance on records as against an "imperfect" performance on the concert stage. Illustrate by describing specific performances that you have attended.

GLADSTONE AND LENIN

BERTRAND RUSSELL ·····⊶ﻌﻣ᷄

From UNPOPULAR ESSAYS. © *1950, by Bertrand Russell. Reprinted by permission of Simon and Schuster, Inc. and George Allen & Unwin, Ltd.*

I have known seven Prime Ministers, from my grandfather (who was Prime Minister in 1846) to Mr. Attlee. Far the most unforgettable of those was Gladstone, whom those who knew him always alluded to as "Mr." Gladstone. The only other man known to me in public life that I could regard as his equal in personal impressiveness was Lenin. Mr. Gladstone was embodied Victorianism; Lenin was embodied Marxian formulas—neither quite human, but each with the power of a natural force.

Mr. Gladstone, in private life, dominated by the power of his eye, which was quick and piercing, and calculated to inspire terror. One felt, like a small boy in presence of an old-fashioned schoolmaster, a constant impulse to say "please, Sir, it wasn't me." Everybody felt like this. I cannot imagine a human being who would have ventured to tell him a story even in the faintest degree *risqué;* his moral horror would have frozen the narrator to stone. I had a grandmother who was the most formidable woman I have ever known; other eminent men invariably quailed before her. But once, when Mr. Gladstone was coming to tea, she told us all in advance that she was going to set him right on his Irish policy, of which she strongly disapproved. He came, and I was present throughout, waiting breathlessly for the expected clash. Alas! my grandmother was all softness and said not a syllable to start the lion roaring; no one could have guessed that she disagreed with him about anything.

Far the most terrifying experience of my life was connected with Mr. Gladstone. When I was seventeen, a very shy and awkward youth, he came to stay with my family for the week-end. I was the only "man" in the house, and after dinner, when the ladies retired, I was left *tête-à-tête* with the ogre. I was too petrified to perform my duties as a host, and he did nothing to help me out. For a long time we sat in silence; at last, in his booming bass voice, he condescended to make his one and only remark: "This is very good port they've given me, but why have they given it me in a claret glass?" Since then I have faced infuriated mobs, angry judges, and hostile governments, but never again have I felt such terror as in that searing moment.

Profound moral conviction was the basis of Mr. Gladstone's political influence. He had all the skill of a clever politician, but was sincerely convinced that every one of his maneuvers was inspired by the most noble purposes. Labouchère, who was a cynic, summed him up in the saying: "Like every politician, he always has a card up his sleeve; but unlike the others, he thinks the Lord put it there." Invariably he earnestly consulted his conscience, and invariably his conscience earnestly gave him the convenient answer.

The force of his personality is illustrated by the story—true or false— of his encounter with a drunken man at a meeting. This man, it appears, was of the opposite political party, and interrupted frequently. At last Mr. Gladstone fixed him with his eye, and spake these words: *"May I request the gentleman who has, not once but repeatedly, interrupted my observations by his interjections, to extend to me that large measure of courtesy which, were I in his place and he in mine, I should most unhesitatingly extend to him."* It is said—and I can well believe it—that the man was sobered by the shock, and remained silent the rest of the evening.

Oddly enough, about half of his compatriots, including a great majority of the well-to-do, regarded him as either mad or wicked or both. When I was a child, most of the children I knew were conservatives, and they solemnly assured me, as a well-known fact, that Mr. Gladstone ordered twenty top-hats from various hatters every morning, and that Mrs. Gladstone had to go round after him and disorder them. (This was before the days of telephones.) Protestants supposed him secretly in league with the Vatican; the rich regarded him (with few exceptions) as Mr. Roosevelt was regarded by the most reactionary of the American rich. But he remained serene, because he never doubted that the Lord was on his side. And to half the nation he was almost a god.

Lenin, with whom I had a long conversation in Moscow in 1920, was, superficially, very unlike Gladstone, and yet, allowing for the difference of time and place and creed, the two men had much in common. To begin with the differences: Lenin was cruel, which Gladstone was not; Lenin had no respect for tradition, whereas Gladstone had a great deal; Lenin considered all means legitimate for securing the victory of his party, whereas for Gladstone politics was a game with certain rules that must be observed. All these differences, to my mind, are to the advantage of Gladstone, and accordingly Gladstone on the whole had beneficent effects, while Lenin's effects were disastrous. In spite of all these dissimilarities, however, the points of resemblance were quite as profound. Lenin supposed himself to be an atheist, but in this he was mistaken. He thought that the world was governed by the dialectic, whose instrument he was; just as much as Gladstone, he conceived of himself as the human agent of a super-human Power. His ruthlessness and unscrupulousness were only as to means, not as to ends; he would not have been willing to purchase personal power at the expense of apostasy. Both men derived their personal force from this unshakable conviction of their own rectitude. Both men, in support of their respective faiths, ventured into realms in which, from ignorance, they could only cover themselves with ridicule —Gladstone in Biblical criticism, Lenin in philosophy.

Of the two, I should say that Gladstone was the more unforgettable as a personality. I take as the test what one would have thought of each if one had met him in a train without knowing who he was. In such circumstances Gladstone, I am convinced, would have struck me as one of the most remarkable men I had ever met, and would have soon reduced me to a speechless semblance of agreement. Lenin, on the contrary, might, I think, have seemed to me at once a narrow-minded fanatic and a cheap cynic. I do not say that this judgment would have been just; it would have been unjust, not positively, but by what it would have omitted. When I met Lenin, I had much less impression of a great man than I had expected; my most vivid impressions were of bigotry and Mongolian cruelty. When I put a question to him about socialism in agriculture, he explained with glee how he had incited the poorer peasants against the richer ones, "and they soon hanged them from the nearest tree— ha! ha! ha!" His guffaw at the thought of those massacred made my blood run cold.

The qualities which make a political leader were less obvious in Lenin than in Gladstone. I doubt whether he could have become a leader in quieter times. His power depended upon the fact that, in a bewildered and defeated nation, he, almost alone, had no doubt, and held out hopes of a new sort of victory in spite of military disaster. He seemed to demonstrate his gospel by cold reasoning, which invoked logic as his ally. In this way the passion of his followers came to appear, to them as to him, to have the sanction of science, and to be the very means by which the world was to be saved. Robespierre must have had something of the same quality.

Suggestions

1. "Gladstone and Lenin" illustrates the principle of likeness and contrast explained in the *Suggestions* for † "Talent and Genius." Point out the paragraph devoted to the differences of the two men. Is the main topic of the essay their differences or their similarities?

2. With the help of the library, summarize the influence of Gladstone and Lenin on modern history; and comment on the appropriateness of the allusion to Robespierre in the last sentence.

3. To what extent is the speaker's opinion of Gladstone based on personal experience? to a greater or less extent than his opinion of Lenin?

4. What evidence is there that, even though he calls them equal, he considers Gladstone the more impressive of the two?

5. The tone of the analysis of Gladstone's unique political status (¶4) is *ambiguous*. Describe the ambiguity.

6. Explain: *risqué, tête-à-tête, Vatican, reactionary, dialectic, apostasy.*

7. Write a comparison-contrast of two people, other than personal friends, who have at some time impressed you.

PHYSICAL AND HISTORICAL FACTS

ERNST CASSIRER ⟶ *From* ESSAY ON MAN *by Ernst Cassirer.*
© *1944 by Yale University Press.*

What makes the difference between a physical fact and a historical fact? Both are regarded as parts of one empirical reality; to both we ascribe objective truth. But if we wish to ascertain the nature of this truth, we proceed in different ways. A physical fact is determined by observation and experiment. This process of objectification attains its end if we succeed in describing the given phenomena in mathematical language, in the language of numbers. A phenomenon which cannot be so described, which is not reducible to a process of measurement, is not a part of our physical world. Defining the task of physics Max Planck says that the physicist has to measure all measurable things and to render all unmeasurable things measurable. Not all physical things or processes are immediately measurable; in many, if not most, cases we are dependent on indirect methods of verification and measurement. But the physical facts are always related by causal laws to other phenomena which are directly observable or measurable. If a physicist is in doubt about the results of an experiment he can repeat and correct it. He finds his objects present at every moment, ready to answer his questions. But with the historian the case is different. His facts belong to the past, and the past is gone forever. We cannot reconstruct it; we cannot waken it to a new life in a mere physical, objective sense. All we can do is to "remember" it—give it a new ideal existence. Ideal reconstruction, not empirical observation, is the first step in historical knowledge. What we call a scientific fact is always the answer to a scientific question which we have formulated beforehand. But to what can the historian direct this question? He cannot confront the events themselves, and he cannot enter into the forms of a former life. He has only an indirect approach to his subject matter. He must consult his sources. But these sources are not physical things in the usual sense of this term. They all imply a new and specific moment. The historian, like the physicist, lives in a material world. Yet what he finds at the very beginning of his research is not a world of physical objects but a symbolic universe—a world of symbols. He must, first of all, learn to read these symbols. Any historical fact, however simple it may appear, can only be determined and understood by such a previous analysis of symbols. Not things or events but documents or monuments are the first and immediate objects of our historical knowledge. Only through the mediation and intervention of these symbolic data can we grasp the real historical data—the events and the men of the past.

Before entering into a general discussion of the problem I should like to clarify this point by reference to a specific concrete example. About thirty-five years ago an old Egyptian papyrus was found in Egypt under the débris of a house. It contained several inscriptions which seemed to be the notes of a lawyer or public notary concerning his business—drafts of testaments, legal contracts, and so on. Up to this point the papyrus belonged simply to the material world; it had no historical importance, and, so to speak, no historical existence. But a second text was then discovered under the first which after a closer examination could be recognized as the remnants of four hitherto unknown comedies of Menander. At this moment the nature and significance of the codex changed completely. Here was no longer a mere "piece of matter"; this papyrus had become a historical document of the highest value and interest. It bore witness to an important stage in the development of Greek literature. Yet this significance was not immediately obvious. The codex had to be submitted to all sorts of critical tests, to careful linguistic, philological, literary, and aesthetic analysis. After this complicated process it was no longer a mere thing; it was charged with meaning. It had

become a symbol, and this symbol gave us new insight into Greek culture
—into Greek life and Greek poetry.[1]

All this seems obvious and unmistakable. But, curiously enough,
precisely this fundamental characteristic of historical knowledge has been
entirely overlooked in most of our modern discussions of historical
method and historical truth. Most writers looked for the difference between history and science in the *logic*, not in the *object* of history. They
took the greatest pains to construct a new logic of history. But all these
attempts were doomed to failure. For logic is, after all, a very simple and
uniform thing. It is one because truth is one. In his quest of truth the
historian is bound to the same formal rules as the scientist. In his modes
of reasoning and arguing, in his inductive inferences, in his investigation
of causes, he obeys the same general laws of thought as a physicist or
biologist. So far as these fundamental theoretical activities of the human
mind are concerned we can make no discrimination between the different
fields of knowledge. As regards this problem we must subscribe to the
words of Descartes: "The sciences taken all together are identical with
human wisdom, which always remains one and the same, however applied
to different subjects, and suffers no more differentiation proceeding from
them than the light of the sun experiences from the variety of the things
which it illumines." [2]

No matter how heterogeneous the objects of human knowledge may be,
the forms of knowledge always show an inner unity and a logical homo-
geneity. Historical and scientific thought are distinguishable not by their
logical form but by their objectives and subject matter. If we wanted to
describe this distinction it would not be enough to say that the scientist
has to do with present objects whereas the historian has to do with past
objects. Such a distinction would be misleading. The scientist may very
well, like the historian, inquire into the remote origin of things. Such
an attempt, for instance, was made by Kant. In 1755 Kant developed an
astronomical theory which also became a universal history of the material
world. He applied the new method of physics, the Newtonian method,
to the solution of a historical problem. In so doing he developed the
nebular hypothesis by which he tried to describe the evolution of the
present cosmic order from a former undifferentiated and unorganized
state of matter. This was a problem of natural history, but it was not
history in the specific sense of the term. History does not aim to disclose
a former state of the physical world but rather a former stage of human
life and human culture. For the solution of this problem it can make
use of scientific methods, but it cannot restrict itself only to the data

[1] For details of this discovery see Gustave Lefebre, *Fragments d'un manuscrit de Ménandre,
découverts et publiés* (LeCaire, Impression de l'Institut Français d'Archéologie, 1907).
[2] *The Philosophical Works of Descartes* (Cambridge University Press, 1911), I, 1.

available by these methods. No object whatever is exempt from the laws of nature. Historical objects have no separate and self-contained reality; they are embodied in physical objects. But in spite of this embodiment they belong, so to speak, to a higher dimension. What we call the historic sense does not change the shape of things, nor does it detect in them a new quality. But it does give to things and events a new depth. When the scientist wishes to go back into the past he employs no concepts or categories but those of his observations of the present. He connects the present with the past by following backward the chain of causes and effects. He studies in the present the material traces left by the past. This is, for instance, the method of geology or paleontology. History too has to begin with these traces, for without them it could not take a single step. But this is only a first and preliminary task. To this actual, empirical reconstruction history adds a symbolic reconstruction. The historian must learn to read and interpret his documents and monuments not only as dead remnants of the past but as living messages from it, messages addressing us in a language of their own. The symbolic content of these messages is, however, not immediately observable. It is the work of the linguist, the philologist, and the historian to make them speak and to make us understand their language. Not in the logical structure of historical thought but in this special task, in this special mandate, consists the fundamental distinction between the works of the historian and the geologist or paleontologist. If the historian fails to decipher the symbolic language of his monuments history remains to him a sealed book. In a certain sense the historian is much more of a linguist than a scientist. But he not only studies the spoken and written languages of mankind; he tries to penetrate into the sense of all the various symbolic idioms. He finds his texts not merely in books, in annals or memoirs. He has to read hieroglyphs or cuneiform inscriptions, look at colors on a canvas, at statues in marble or bronze, at cathedrals or temples, at coins or gems. But he does not consider all these things simply with the mind of an antiquary who wishes to collect and preserve the treasures of olden times. What the historian is in search of is rather the materialization of the spirit of a former age. He detects the same spirit in laws and statutes, in charters and bills of right, in social institutions and political constitutions, in religious rites and ceremonies. To the true historian such material is not petrified fact but living form. History is the attempt to fuse together all these *disjecta membra,* the scattered limbs of the past, and to synthesize them and mold them into new shape.

Suggestions

1. "Physical and Historical Facts" moves from a comparison of the two kinds of fact to a definition of history at its conclusion. The definition

serves as a controlling idea or topic sentence for the whole essay. Summarize the idea of the historian advanced here: what is the object of his search?

2. Cassirer was particularly interested in the part played by *symbols* in human culture. Show how this interest enters into his description of the historian's work, and compare "Physical and Historical Facts" with † "The Miracle of Language."

3. Compare the diction of this essay with that of "A Case of Co-Existence," which follows.

4. Explain: *papyrus, philological, heterogeneous, paleontology, cuneiform.*

5. Write a comparison of "Physical and Historical Facts" and † "The Modern Climate of Opinion," concentrating on (a) the concept of logic and (b) the difference between science and history.

A CASE OF CO-EXISTENCE:
Christendom and the Turks

H. R. TREVOR-ROPER

From MEN AND EVENTS *by H. R. Trevor-Roper.* © *1957 by W. A. Evill and A. D. Peters.*

To us the great fact of the fifteenth and sixteenth centuries is the expansion of Europe by the spectacular discovery of new continents; to contemporaries it was its diminution by the spectacular advance of the Turkish Empire. In France, between 1480 and 1609, twice as many books were published upon the Turks as upon America, and the greatest of the observers of Turkey, the Belgian Busbecq, complained that the nations of Christendom were gathering worthless empires at the end of the world while losing the heart of Europe. Throughout the sixteenth century Europeans were alternately fascinated and terrified by the Turks; by their silent, invincible, victorious armies, by their mixture of cruelty and toleration, their system of political slavery, and their private moral virtues. Alternately the rulers of Europe preached crusades and practised appeasement of this terrible enemy, whom only his eastern enemies, first Tamerlane, then the Sophy of Persia, seemed to restrain from swallowing up their whole continent: "When the Turks have settled with Persia," wrote Busbecq, they will fly at our throats, supported by the might of the whole East; how unprepared we are, I dare not say . . . Constantinople, once the rival of Rome, is now laid low in wretched slavery. Who can look on without pity, without reflecting on the mutability of human things? Besides who knows whether the same fate may not now be threatening our own land?

For already, when he wrote, the bastions of Eastern Europe had crumbled: Belgrade had fallen by land and Rhodes by sea; the Turkish armies had conquered the plains of Hungary and their fleets dominated the Western Mediterranean from Algiers.

The Europeans had reason to be fascinated by the Turks, for these new conquerors were unlike any others they had known. They were not a nation: they were a host of peoples, an imperial family, and a system. The Sultan's subjects were of diverse conquered races, his invincible Janissaries had all been Christians, his terrible sea-captains were almost invariably renegades, his technicians, his financiers, his merchants were Christians or Jews. What power had made these men desert their natural traditions and uphold a slave-empire so utterly at variance with European society? For European society was an aristocratic and landed society, a society of hierarchy, heredity, and privilege: the Ottoman Empire knew no aristocracy, no class loyalties, no hereditary privilege outside the Sultan's own family, whose privilege was limited to the alternative of the throne or the bowstring.[1] Wherever the Turks imposed direct rule, the old aristocracies were liquidated and a new social system was implanted on their ruin. In Budapest Busbecq saw the splendid palaces of the Hungarian nobles, recently so powerful, all in ruins; in Bulgaria he found descendants of the royal house married to ploughmen and shepherds; in Constantinople he saw members of the imperial families of Palæologus and Cantacuzene reduced to menial trades. These were the few who had survived the general massacres of the nobility, and Busbecq was one of the few who could see them: for in general the Turks, having conquered a country and imposed their social system, protected it by an iron curtain from profane eyes. Were it not for the all-penetrating power of money, he remarked, "their country would be as inaccessible to foreigners as those lands which are said to be uninhabitable through heat or cold." On crossing the frontier from Vienna to Budapest he felt as if he was entering another world, so different was it from the old Europe of which so lately it had been a part.

A hideous system, Europeans thought; and yet, since it had been accepted willingly by so many of their former subjects, they were obliged to concede its merits, or their defects. Why, they asked, had it so triumphed? The answer stared them in the face. Europe, in the days of

---

[1] I.e. either the Sultan's son succeeded his father or was strangled by the brother who did.

Turkish conquest, had not only been politically divided: it had been full of social unrest. The aristocratic system in Eastern Europe had become intolerable. Landlordism on the continent, colonialism and *monoculture* in the islands, had everywhere bred a mutinous native peasantry ready to welcome the Turk as a deliverer from social bondage. The fifteenth century was an age of peasant revolts, and the feudal oppressions of the Hungarian and Frankish nobles, the Byzantine and Italian "despots," were no more hateful to their subjects than the mercantile rule of the Venetian aristocracy in Salonika, Eubœa, and Cyprus, or of those private capitalist companies—the *Maona* and the Bank of San Giorgio—to which Genoa had surrendered or sold its colonies in Chios, Corsica, and the Crimea. The Hungarian chivalry which went down fighting in the valley of the Danube, the Venetian galleys which watched the loss of Greece and its islands, were the forces of an alien oligarchy whose subjects preferred—or thought they preferred—the Turks. Constantinople itself—a medieval Shanghai controlled by Venetian and Genoese concessionaires—hardly resisted its change of masters. Three years after its fall, a German popular play, the *Türkenspiel,* represented the Sultan coming to Nuremberg as the Messiah of the poor peasants. Eighty-five years later Luther, whose great hymn "Ein feste Burg" ["A Mighty Fortress Is Our God"] may well have been written to inspire an imperial crusade against the Turks, nevertheless declared that the German peasantry, crushed by noble landlords, might well prefer Turkish rule to that of such Christian lords.

Thus, for some two centuries, from the disastrous crusade of Nicopolis in 1396 to the peace of 1606, the aristocratic society of Western Europe, like the liberal society of Western Europe today, looked with apprehension on the portentous new power in the East: a power of huge military strength which, exploiting every social discontent, had advanced into the heart of Europe, imposed a new social system, and protected it behind an iron curtain: a power, moreover, which, by its very success, fascinated many of those who sought to resist it. Half the contemporary books on Turkey are inspired by admiration as well as by fear and hatred. Even the imperial ambassador could not withhold his respect from the civic virtue, the charitableness, the frugality, the public works, and the *carrière ouverte aux talents* [careers-for-the-talented system] which he found in the Ottoman Empire, and grudgingly admitted that slavery, after all, has its social utility. From overpopulated Southern Europe there was a constant stream of emigration to those hospitable lands of opportunity where, it was noted, there were no beggars; and persecuted intellectuals—Jews of Spain and Germany, Protestants of Italy—fled, or dreamed of fleeing, to that tolerant Empire where religion at least was free. To the rulers of Western Europe all this was an added source of alarm. What were they to do? The answer was given by their traditional oracle, the Pope of Rome: Christians unite! Prepare for a crusade against the ideological enemy, the conquering tyrant!

And what did they do in fact? Alas, as Miss Vaughan's learned and closely packed diplomatic narrative shows,[2] they did no such thing. They quarreled among themselves, split Christendom in two, mopped up empires overseas, and while all vying with each other in denouncing the infamous Turk, each secretly made, or sought to make, alliances with him against the others. The King of France, by his alliance, obtained profitable concessions for his subjects and, in return, welcomed a Turkish army in France: "Christian captives were openly sold in Toulon market-place, and while French Protestants were undergoing savage persecution, Turks on French soil turned unmolested to Mecca to pray." The King of Spain taxed his subjects regularly for the crusade and as regularly pocketed the proceeds. Venice for the sake of old markets, England for new, managed and supplied the infidel. Lutheran Germany, suspicious of all papal crusades, insisted that

> to reform our ways and works
> is the best defence against the Turks.

The Jesuits, having once got a footing in Constantinople for the purpose of missionary work, quickly changed their tune and concentrated on the more congenial task of denouncing Protestant and Greek Christians to the common enemy. As for the Pope himself, when it came to the point he always found himself too poor for any action—perhaps even (like Alexander VI) he was in receipt of a Turkish pension. . . . It was all very unedifying and ought, of course, as Busbecq foresaw, to have led to a Turkish conquest of Europe. In fact it did not. Whereas a crusade might have proved as disastrous as the crusade of Nicopolis, this refusal of a crusade led to a long practical co-existence, until suddenly, in the seventeenth century, it became clear that the danger was past. Europe, in full internecine vigor, then observed the decay of the Turkish empire, and having failed to unite against the tyrant in his prime, soon had to unite to prop him up when he had become "the sick man of Europe."

How had it happened? The rise and fall of nations remains a historical mystery which cannot be solved in a paragraph. We know very little of Turkish history, and what we know is almost entirely drawn from the imperfect observation of foreigners: for the Turks themselves have, until recently, been incurious in such matters. As Busbecq wrote, "they have no idea of chronology and dates and make a wonderful mixture and confusion of all the epochs of history." Probably the breakdown was institutional: the collapse of that system of privileged slavery which, under able Sultans, had given a formidable but temporary cohesion to an otherwise

[2] Dorothy Vaughan, *Europe and the Turk* (Liverpool, 1954).

ramshackle empire. Perhaps it was also economic: the Turkish, like the Roman and the Spanish empires, created no new wealth: it lived parasitically on foreign wealth and faltered when that supply ran out. Possibly a complex "liberal" society has, after all, greater staying power, because greater resilience, than a "classless" tyranny. We cannot say. But even so, even if we must leave this deep question open, at least there is one negative conclusion that we can draw from this historical precedent. The theory that the world cannot live "half slave and half free," that a frontal struggle between opposing systems is sooner or later inevitable and might as well be hastened by an ideological crusade, is simply not true. Europe and the Turk, with their opposing ideologies and opposing social systems, faced each other for centuries. There were diplomatic relations and local struggles, as between Christian powers, but there was no crusade, and when the system which had once seemed so formidable began to disintegrate, it was through inner weakness.

Today these facts are worth remembering. Our Marxist historians like to compare the opposition between Bolshevism and the West with the struggle between barbarian Christianity and the decadent pagan empire of Rome. They do so because they know that the barbarians prevailed. Professor Toynbee likes to remember the time when Rome and Carthage faced each other in uncompromising frontal struggle

> *in dubioque fuere utrorum ad regna cadendum*
> *omnibus humanis esset terraque marique*

[. . . and were uncertain under which empire, on land and sea, the whole human race would be thrown.—Lucretius, *Of the Nature of Things* 3, 836–7.]

and his disciple, James Burnham, deduces therefrom the necessity of a preventive crusade.[3] This also was Hitler's view, but it did not prove correct. Thus the doctrinaires seek out the parallel that best suits their doctrine. All historical parallels are imperfect and therefore dangerous; but those who use them would do well to remember one which, being inconvenient, they too often forget: the parallel of co-existence, of Europe and the Turk.

Suggestions

1. Trevor-Roper's essay is an example of extended comparison, or *analogy*, which, though not carried to its ultimate conclusion, is supposed to be close enough to warrant some strong opinions. Its contrast between the people, religions, and cultures of Turkey and medieval Europe leads to an analogy between that struggle and the present cold war between Russia and the West.

[3] Arnold J. Toynbee (b. 1889), author of *A Study of History* and other works; James Burnham (b. 1905), an American professor, author of *The Struggle for the World* and other works.

2. Point out sets of minor comparisons and contrasts in the essay.

3. The speaker gradually suggests and builds up the analogy before drawing it to the reader's attention directly. This method helps to gain more ready acceptance of the analogy when it is spelled out, for it will have been working in the reader's mind before its explicit statement. Show the means by which it is suggested before being stated (e.g. in ¶4).

4. Does the speaker seem to be aware that his thesis will not be readily accepted by other historians?

5. Define the tone in which the Pope's plan of action against the Turks is described (¶4).

6. How carefully does the speaker generalize about stratified and class-less societies in the long view of history? What qualifying terms are used?

7. Write an analysis of Trevor-Roper's thesis, pointing out as many more parallels as you can that will further support it.

8. Write a refutation of his thesis, pointing out many dissimilarities between the historical situation of four centuries ago and our own.

A R G U M E N T S

HISTORY

LEO TOLSTOY *From* WAR AND PEACE, *translation by Constance Garnett.*

The first fifteen years of the nineteenth century present the spectacle of an extraordinary movement of millions of men. Men leave their habitual pursuits; rush from one side of Europe to the other; plunder, slaughter one another, triumph and despair; and the whole current of life is transformed and presents a quickened activity, first moving at a growing speed, and then slowly slackening again. What was the cause of that activity, or from what laws did it arise? asks the human intellect.

The historians, in reply to that inquiry, lay before us the sayings and doings of some dozens of men in one of the buildings of the city of Paris, summing up those doings and sayings by one word—revolution. Then they give us a detailed biography of Napoleon, and of certain persons favorably or hostilely disposed to him; talk of the influence of some of these persons upon others; and then say that this it is to which that activity is due, and these are its laws.

But the human intellect not only refuses to believe in that explanation, but flatly declares that the method of explanation is not a correct one, because in this explanation a smaller phenomenon is taken as the cause of a greater phenomenon. The sum of men's individual wills produced both the revolution and Napoleon; and only the sum of those wills endured them and then destroyed them.

"But whenever there have been wars, there have been great military leaders; whenever there have been revolutions in states, there have been great men," says history.

"Whenever there have been great military leaders there have, indeed, been wars," replies the human reason; "but that does not prove that the generals were the cause of the wars, and that the factors leading to warfare can be found in the personal activity of one man."

Whenever, looking at my watch, I see the hand has reached the figure x, I hear the bells beginning to ring in the church close by. But from the fact that the watch hand points to ten whenever the bells begin to ring, I have not the right to infer that the position of the hands of my watch is the cause of the vibration of the bells.

Whenever I see a steam-engine move, I hear the whistle, I see the valve open and the wheels turn; but I have no right to conclude from that that the whistle and the turning of the wheels are the causes of the steam-engine's moving.

The peasants say that in the late spring a cold wind blows because the oak-buds are opening, and, as a fact, a cold wind does blow every spring when the oak is coming out. But though the cause of a cold wind's blowing just when the oaks are coming out is unknown to me, I cannot agree with the peasants that the cause of the cold wind is the opening of the oak-buds, because the force of the wind is altogether outside the influence of the buds. I see in this simply such a coincidence of events as is common in every phenomenon of life, and I see that however long and minutely I might examine the watch hand, the valve, and the wheel of the steam-engine and the oak-bud, I shall not discover the cause of the bells ringing, of the steam-engine moving, and of the spring wind. To do that I must completely change my point of observation and study the laws of the motion of steam, of the bells, and of the wind. History must do the same. And efforts have already been made in this direction.

For the investigation of the laws of history, we must completely change the subject of observations, must let kings and ministers and generals alone, and study the homogeneous, infinitesimal elements by which masses are led. No one can say how far it has been given to man to advance in that direction in understanding of the laws of history. But it is obvious that only in that direction lies any possibility of discovering historical laws; and that the human intellect has hitherto not devoted to that method of research one millionth part of the energy that historians have put into the description of the doings of various kings, ministers, and generals, and the exposition of their own views on those doings.

Suggestions

1. "History," like the other essays in this group, is an argument, which means that its main point is the advancement of a thesis. It is an extract from the novel *War and Peace;* the title was given to it by the editors of this book. Select three or four phrases from it that would make more precise titles, particularly ones that would suggest its thesis. Which of your choices do you consider the best?

2. State the thesis, showing how it differs from those of Chesterton and Shaw that follow. How many of the three directly contradict one another? (If you have read Ibsen's play *An Enemy of the People,* you may decide that it supports Tolstoy more than it does Shaw.)

3. Discuss the part played by analogies in "History."

4. Explain: ". . . a smaller phenomenon is taken as the cause of a greater phenomenon" (¶3). Is such an explanation necessarily fallacious?

5. Write an essay in which you evaluate the thesis of "History" by applying it to the Revolution, the Civil War, or some other event in American history with which you are familiar.

UNECONOMIC MAN

G. K. CHESTERTON ──◦◦

From THE EVERLASTING MAN *by G. K. Chesterton.* © *1925 by Dodd, Mead & Company, Inc. Reprinted by permission of Dodd, Mead & Company and Miss D. E. Collins.*

The materialist theory of history, that all politics and ethics are the expression of economics, is a very simple fallacy indeed. It consists simply of confusing the necessary conditions of life with the normal preoccupations of life, that are quite a different thing. It is like saying that because a man can only walk about on two legs, therefore he never walks about except to buy shoes and stockings. . . . Cows may be purely economic, in the sense that we cannot see that they do much beyond grazing and seeking better grazing-grounds; and that is why a history of cows in twelve volumes would not be very lively reading. Sheep and goats may be pure economists in their external action at least; but that is why the sheep has hardly been a hero of epic wars and empires thought worthy of detailed narration; and even the more active quadruped has not inspired a book for boys called *Golden Deeds of Gallant Goats* or any similar title. But so far from the movements that make up the story of man being economic, we may say that the story only begins where the motive of the cows and sheep leaves off. It will be hard to maintain that the Crusaders went from their homes into a howling wilderness because cows go from a wilderness to a more comfortable grazing-ground. It will be hard to maintain that the Arctic explorers went north with the same material motive that made the swallows go south. And if you leave things like all the religious wars and all the merely adventurous explorations out of the human story, it will not only cease to be human at all but cease to be a story at all. The outline of history is made of these decisive curves and angles determined by the will of man. Economic history would not even be history.

But there is a deeper fallacy besides this obvious fact that men need not live for food merely because they cannot live without food. The truth is that the thing most present to the mind of man is not the economic machinery necessary to his existence; but rather that existence itself; the world which he sees when he wakes every morning and the nature of his general position in it. There is something that is nearer to him than livelihood, and that is life. For once that he remembers exactly what work produces his wages and exactly what wages produce his meals, he reflects ten times that it is a fine day or it is a queer world, or wonders whether life is worth living, or wonders whether marriage is a failure, or is pleased and puzzled with his own children or remembers his own youth, or in any such fashion vaguely reviews the mysterious lot of man. This is true of the majority even of the wage-slaves of our morbid modern industrialism, which by its hideousness and inhumanity has really forced the economic issue to the front. It is immeasurably more true of the multitude of peasants or hunters or fishers who make up the real mass of mankind. Even those dry pedants who think that ethics depend on economics must admit that economics depend on existence. And any number of normal doubts and day-dreams are about existence; not about how we can live, but about why we do. And the proof of it is simple; as simple as suicide. Turn the universe upside down in the mind and you turn all the political economists upside down with it. Suppose that a man wishes to die, and the professor of political economy becomes rather a bore with his elaborate explanations of how he is to live. And all the departures and decisions that make our human past into a story have this character of diverting the direct course of pure economics. As the economist may be excused from calculating the future salary of a suicide, so he may be excused from providing an old-age pension for a martyr. As he need not provide for the future of a martyr, so he need not provide for the family of a monk. His plan is modified in lesser and varying degrees by a man being a soldier and dying for his own country, by a man being a peasant and especially loving his own land, by a man being more or less affected by any religion that forbids or allows him to do this or that. But all these come back not to an economic calculation about livelihood but to an elemental outlook upon life. They all come back to what a man fundamentally feels, when he looks forth from those strange windows which we call the eyes, upon that strange vision that we call the world.

Suggestions

1. Formulate the theory of history that is attacked in "Uneconomic Man." Then determine from an examination of attitude, tone, and direct statement what proportion of the essay is serious argument and what proportion whimsical reflection. Are the two necessarily opposed? Point out places where the speaker's tone changes.

2. To what extent does the speaker's view of man apply to all men? Do you think the majority are motivated predominantly as he suggests, or as the economic historians suppose?

3. By your own standards Chesterton's paragraphs may seem too long. Can you justify dividing these two long paragraphs into several shorter ones? At what points?

4. Is the analogy of cows and goats more amusing than persuasive?
   (a) What more serious analogy might have been used?
   (b) Why, in the light of the total effect of the essay, would another analogy be less successful?

5. Point out devices in the last six or seven sentences which give the paragraph coherence.

6. Refute some common belief with an argument of your own.

7. Write an essay on an important decision in your life, determining the kinds of motives that caused you to decide as you did.

IBSEN'S ENEMY OF THE PEOPLE

BERNARD SHAW —⚬

From THE QUINTESSENCE OF IBSENISM. *Reprinted by permission of the Public Trustee and The Society of Authors.*

As *An Enemy of the People* contains one or two references to Democracy which are anything but respectful, it is necessary to examine Ibsen's criticism of it with precision. Democracy is really only an arrangement by which the governed are allowed to choose (as far as any choice is possible, which in capitalistic society is not saying much) the members of the representative bodies which control the executive. It has never been proved that this is the best arrangement; and it has been made effective only to the very limited extent short of which the dissatisfaction which it appeases might take the form of actual violence. Now when men had to submit to kings, they consoled themselves by making it an article of faith that the king was always right, idealizing him as a Pope, in fact. In the same way we who have to submit to majorities set up Voltaire's pope, *Monsieur Tout-le-monde* [Mr. Everybody], and make it blasphemy against Democracy to deny that the majority is always right, although that, as Ibsen says, is a lie. It is a scientific fact that the majority, however eager it may be for the reform of old abuses, is always wrong in its opinion of new developments, or rather is always unfit for them (for it can hardly be said to be wrong in opposing developments for which it is not yet fit). The pioneer is a tiny minority of the force he heads; and so, though it is easy to be in a minority and yet be wrong, it is absolutely impossible to be in the majority and yet be right as to the newest social prospects. We would never progress at all if it were possible for each of us to stand still on democratic principles until we saw whither all the rest were moving, as our statesmen declare themselves bound to do when they are called upon to lead. Whatever clatter we may make for a time with our filing through feudal serf collars and kicking off old mercantile fetters, we shall never march a step forward except at the heels of "the strongest man, he who is able to stand alone" and to turn his back on "the damned compact Liberal majority." All of which is no disparagement of parliaments and adult suffrage, but simply a wholesome reduction of them to their real place in the social economy as pure machinery: machinery which has absolutely no principles except the principles of mechanics, and no motive power in itself whatsoever. The idealization of public organizations is as dangerous as that of kings or priests. We need to be reminded that though there is in the world a vast number of buildings in which a certain ritual is conducted before crowds called congregations by a functionary called a priest, who is subject to a central council controlling all such functionaries on a few points, there is not therefore any such thing in the concrete as the ideal Catholic Church, nor ever was, nor ever will be. There may, too, be a highly elaborate organization of public affairs; but there is no such thing as the ideal State. There may be a combination of persons living by the practice of medicine, surgery, or physical or biological research; or by drawing up wills and leases, and preparing, pleading, or judging cases at law; or by painting pictures, writing books, and acting plays; or by serving in regiments and battle ships; or by manual labor or industrial service. But when any of these combinations, through its organizers or leaders, claims to deliver the Verdict of Science, or to act with the Authority of the Law, or to be as sacred as the Mission of Art, or to revenge criticisms of themselves as outrages on the Honor of His Majesty's Services, or to utter the Voice of Labor, there is urgent need for the guillotine, or whatever may be the mode in vogue of putting presumptuous persons in their proper place. All abstractions invested with collective consciousness or collective authority, set above the individual, and exacting duty from him on pretence of acting or thinking with greater validity than he, are man-eating idols red with human sacrifices.

This position must not be confounded with Anarchism, or the idealization of the repudiation of Governments. Ibsen did not refuse to pay the tax collector, but may be supposed to have regarded him, not as the vicar of an abstraction called THE STATE, but simply as the man sent round by a committee of citizens (mostly fools as far as Maximus the Mystic's Third Empire is concerned) to collect the money for the police or the paving and lighting of the streets.

Suggestions

1. Point out two or three sentences showing that the speaker is not arguing for the abolishment of democracy in favor of any other system. Then state his thesis.

2. By recent standards the first paragraph is unduly long. Decide where it could be broken into two or three shorter ones.

3. This essay, which was written in London, denies that the majority is always right. Is this assumed by the governmental system of Britain or of the United States? Explain the role of constitutions in democratic countries.

4. Which sentence in this essay stands most in need of concrete illustrations? Which one is perhaps over-illustrated?

5. Point out several examples of *hyperbole* in the essay and explain their function. Are there any examples of *understatement*?

6. Choose one point from this argument and use it as the subject of your own essay. You may want to disagree, but you will need concrete evidence to support your views.

DECLINE AND FALL

SOLOMON KATZ ---◦⊰

From THE DECLINE OF ROME. © *1955 Cornell University Press. Reprinted by special permission of Cornell University Press.*

From St. Augustine (354–430), in whose lifetime Italy and Rome were overrun by barbarian invaders, to the present, historians, philosophers, and theologians have sought an answer to one of the central problems of history: what caused the decline of the Roman Empire? What were the forces of dissolution? What were the weaknesses in the Roman Empire? What, in the words of the great eighteenth-century historian Edward Gibbon,[1] were "the most important circumstances of its decline and fall: a revolution which will ever be remembered, and is still felt by the nations of the Earth"?

For each generation the question has had a topical as well as a historical interest. Consciously or not, men have sensed in that decline a foreshadowing of the fate of their own civilization and have tried, by seeking the causes of Rome's decline, to escape the same misfortune. Their own basic assumptions about the meaning of history, their own philosophy of history, have inevitably dictated the answers which men have given to the question.

HISTORICAL EXPLANATIONS OF THE DECLINE

To Ammianus Marcellinus (born *c.* 330), the last great Roman historian, a decline in personal morality was the cause of the ills which afflicted the Empire. The more profound mind of St. Augustine saw in the calamities of his day one act in the great unfolding drama of universal history. In *The City of God (De Civitate Dei)*, a work which for more than a thousand years continued to mold the mind of medieval man, Augustine looked beyond the somber present, beyond Rome, beyond the transitory city of the world, to the eternal City of God. The

---

[1] His *Decline and Fall of the Roman Empire* appeared from 1776 to 1778.

earthly city of Rome was passing, not because of the abandonment of the pagan gods for Christianity, as some critics charged, but as the necessary and fortunate preparation for the triumph of the heavenly city where man's destiny was to be attained. The events of Rome's history, therefore, were unrolling as part of the general plan of the universe.

In contrast to this interpretation based upon the Christian faith stands Gibbon's explanation, which was rooted in eighteenth-century rationalist thought. The historian saw the decline not as the preparation for something better, but as a tragedy which he sums up in the sentence: "I have described the triumph of Barbarism and Religion."

In our own times there has been an equally wide range of explanations, each reflecting the crises of the twentieth century: Spengler's belief, expounded in *The Decline of the West,* that history, Egyptian or Roman, follows a predetermined course from birth to childhood and from maturity to old age and death; Rostovtzeff's thesis of the failure of ancient civilization to reach the masses and the resulting conflict between the educated, propertied urban classes and the ignorant and impoverished rural masses to whose level culture declined; and most recently Toynbee's view that a symptom of decay is the failure of a civilization to assimilate its "internal proletariat," those who have no real stake in society, or its "external proletariat," the barbarians on the frontiers.[2]

Confronted with much the same data about the decline of the Empire, writers have offered widely varying interpretations of their meaning. The problem, therefore, is one of abiding interest, as much for what it reveals about historians and their times as for the light it sheds upon history. No more than others can we presume to offer a definite solution to the riddle, but we must at least present the question and analyze some possible answers.

PROBLEMS IN EVALUATING THE DECLINE

The decline of the Roman Empire was neither sudden nor cataclysmic, but was a gradual process extending over several centuries. Many of the disquieting symptoms of decay and disintegration appeared during the third and even the second century A.D., and successive emperors applied force and compulsion in order to maintain the integrity of the Empire. Important as their achievement was, Diocletian and Constantine succeeded only in postponing the collapse of the Roman Empire, not in preventing it. After the death of Constantine in 337, the signs of decay increased, and the world of the fifth and sixth centuries, while it preserved many elements of ancient civilization, was already recognizably medieval. On the soil of the western half of the Roman Empire, Ger-

---

[2] Oswald Spengler, 1880–1936; M. I. Rostovtzeff, *A History of the Ancient World,* 1928; Arnold Toynbee, *A Study of History,* 1947–1957.

manic kingdoms were established; while in the East, Byzantine emperors ruled as heirs to the Romans. Trade continued, but on a diminishing scale, and agriculture was increasingly on the basis of large, self-sufficient estates worked by serfs who were bound to the soil. The pagan cults yielded to Christianity, the Christian church built a strongly centralized administrative system, and classical learning was adapted to Christian needs or was superseded by Christian theology.

Roman armies had been defeated by Germanic invaders before, but the catastrophic defeat of the Romans in 378 at the battle of Adrianople, which will be treated later, was a dramatic proof that the imperial government was unable to offer effective resistance to invasion. This was underscored in 410, when the barbarians occupied and sacked Rome. Finally in 476 Romulus Augustulus, the last Roman emperor in the West, lost his throne, and soon the invaders gained full control of the western half of the Roman Empire. The Empire had experienced other crises in the past and had surmounted them; now it was unable to rally. A government which for centuries had united almost the whole civilized world into one empire was disintegrating. Meanwhile the acceptance of Christianity by the emperors and the vast majority of their subjects was both cause and effect of a profound transformation in the civilization of the ancient world. To this theme Gibbon gave a title which has become traditional: *The Decline and Fall of the Roman Empire.* Closer study has revealed that Gibbon exaggerated the extent of decline: there were elements of vitality as well as signs of decay in the centuries after the Antonine Age. Some historians, indeed, have insisted that there was no real decline, but merely a transformation of civilization. Nevertheless, if from whatever point of view—political, economic, or cultural—we compare the Roman world of the third and fourth centuries with the Empire during the first two centuries, we find indisputable evidence of decline.

Whether we designate what occurred as change or decline, we are concerned with a very complex phenomenon. Many of the explanations have been oversimplified solutions to an immensely difficult problem. Scholars have sometimes selected one factor, for example, the barbarian invasions or the exhaustion of the soil, and have declared it to be the ultimate cause of the decline of the Roman Empire, or they have looked for one common denominator of decline to which they have reduced all other factors. We shall see, however, that the process of decline was due not to a single cause, but to a variety of interacting factors—political, economic, social, cultural, and psychological. To give priority to any one of them is virtually impossible, since each acted with and upon every other factor. At the outset, therefore, we should recognize the principle of multiple causation.

THE DISTINCTION BETWEEN CAUSES AND SYMPTOMS

A more common error arises out of the difficulty of distinguishing between cause and symptom. Many of the alleged causes are actually symptoms of decline due to antecedent causes or conditions, rather than ultimate causes in themselves. Some of the symptoms of decay are obvious: economic collapse, inadequate revenues, insufficient armed forces to defend the Empire, intellectual stagnation. Each of these factors, however, is itself in need of explanation. Each is a symptom of decline and at the same time a cause of further decline, in other words, an effect of an antecedent cause and a cause itself.

An example or two may illustrate the difficulty of differentiating between cause and symptom and between proximate and remote causes. We have seen how Romans or Romanized elements, those who had the largest stake in Roman institutions, came to form a dwindling minority in the army. The barbarization of the army and the civil service and Rome's dependence upon barbarian allies and mercenaries were undoubtedly one of the factors in the decline of Rome. But more and more Germans were admitted into the army and the civil service because Rome desperately needed men to help defend her frontiers and administer her empire. The barbarization of the Empire is, therefore, a symptom of decay, an indication that there was a shortage of manpower in relation to the tasks which had to be performed. What caused that? Was it a declining birth rate, high mortality in wars and epidemics, or increased requirements for men? Each and all may have been remote causes of the barbarization of the Empire, and the process of barbarization was itself both symptom and cause of decline.

Again, the insistent needs of the army and the bureaucracy imposed an enormous burden upon the treasury. The high cost of continuous warfare, the shrinking revenues which followed the loss of provinces, the dislocation of trade as a result of civil war, the depreciation of the coinage—all these had a ruinous effect upon the economic life of the Empire. The methods devised by the imperial government to meet soaring expenses reduced men to the level of slaves of the state, straining to support a costly machinery of defense and administration. Individual and municipal freedom was destroyed by the central government, and with the loss of that freedom initiative and enterprise were paralyzed. Was this a cause of decline? Or did the imperial government adopt the Draconian solution of binding merchants and artisans to their callings, farmers to the land, and city officials to their posts because the emperors believed that only by mobilizing all their resources in this way could they save the Empire? Again we have symptoms of decline which are at the same time causes springing from other causes, each interacting upon the other, each an aspect of the whole causative process. Moreover, some factors, whether they are regarded as causes or symptoms, cannot be measured accurately. By tracing the deterioration of the coinage, we may describe with some precision such physical phenomena as the shrinking supply of precious metal, but we have no yardstick for measuring other aspects of the decline of the Empire, such as apathy or "loss of nerve." We can only infer that they existed both as causes and as symptoms of decline.

SOME UNFOUNDED THEORIES OF THE DECLINE

Some alleged causes may be rejected at once. Thus a major climatic change, an increasing drought caused by the diminution of rainfall, has been held responsible for the decline of ancient civilization. Long spells of dry weather are said to have led to the exhaustion of the soil, poor crops, abandonment of the land, impoverishment, famine, and depopulation. This remains, however, a hypothesis for which no valid evidence from the whole Empire has been adduced. A closely related physical factor, the exhaustion of the soil, has also been suggested. In certain districts, for example, in southern Italy, deforestation and other factors undoubtedly reduced the fertility of the soil, but there is no evidence for a general exhaustion of the soil throughout the Empire, despite primitive methods of fertilizing and farming. On the contrary, Gaul continued to produce bountiful crops in the late Roman Empire, and Egypt, largely dependent upon the flood waters of the Nile, had its fertility renewed annually.

Some scholars have explained the decline of Rome on the basis of biological factors. There are no scientifically acceptable data to support the argument that societies, like individuals, have a life-cycle—birth, growth, maturity, and death—and hence that civilizations like individuals are predestined to die. Nor can we accept the hypothesis that the "best" elements in Roman society were exterminated by wars and revolution or died out because of the disinclination of these members of society to reproduce. We are given neither a satisfactory definition of the "best," nor proof that only the "best" perished. Similarly, one may dispose of the related argument that Rome succumbed because of "race suicide" or "race mixture," that is, that the "superior Roman stock" was overwhelmed by "inferior races" who bred freely while the "best" failed to reproduce. Biologists and anthropologists have demonstrated that there are no superior or inferior races. The decline of Rome has also been attributed to malaria or to the great plague which occurred in the reign of Marcus Aurelius, but malaria was not endemic throughout the Empire, and the effects of the plague, however deadly, might have been overcome were it not for other factors which we shall analyze later. In any event, we cannot be sure that Rome would have been saved by a larger population.

Moralists have suggested that the decline was caused by a slackening of personal morality, but most of the evidence they have presented is from the flourishing years of the early Principate. In the Later Empire, under the influence of the religious revival, morals may actually have been elevated. In any case, most people in both the earlier and the later period seem to have lived decent and sober lives. Even if moral standards had decayed, it would still be necessary to seek an explanation for such an historical phenomenon.

THE ROLE OF SOCIAL CONFLICT

The decline of ancient civilization has been attributed, by Rostovtzeff, to the failure of the upper classes to extend their culture to the rural and urban lower classes.[3] In the end, according to this argument, there was a prolonged social conflict between the urban propertied classes and the rural masses who made up the bulk of the army. The masses put their leaders on the throne, absorbed the higher classes, and lowered standards in general. But there is little evidence that the army was made up of a class-conscious proletariat which hated the urban upper classes. On the contrary, in its greed the army plundered town and country alike. Yet so much of the argument must be granted: that Roman culture had not penetrated sufficiently into the masses, had not inspired them with devotion to a high ideal to which all alike were committed, and that now in a time of mounting difficulties it failed to evoke their active effort and co-operation in its defense.

Another unsatisfactory hypothesis is that the lack of any clear constitutional provision for the succession on the death of an emperor led to military usurpation of power, anarchy, and all its concomitant evils. The method of adoption of an heir to the throne by the incumbent, haphazard as it may have been, worked well during most of the Antonine period. Indeed, the choice of the ablest man available, regardless of family affiliation, worked better than Marcus Aurelius' solution of designating his own son Commodus as emperor.

Finally, the Empire was not suddenly destroyed by the barbarians, although their attack contributed to Rome's decline and eventually they took possession of the western half of the Roman Empire. The pressure of barbarians had been felt by the Romans from very early times, and the invasions of the fifth century were not much more formidable than previous ones which had been repelled. If Rome had not already been weakened internally and demoralized, she might have put up an effective resistance, as she had to earlier onslaughts.

POLITICAL FACTORS

We have rejected certain explanations of the decline of ancient civilization. What factors remain? Among the political factors may be counted

[3] *A History of the Ancient World*, vol. ii.

the failure of the civil power to control the army. We have seen how the troops were preoccupied with making and unmaking emperors and how ambitious generals fought for the throne. The result was military disorganization, which facilitated the advance of the barbarians. We have observed both as a symptom and as a cause of decline the decay of civic vitality, as the emperors interfered more and more with municipal freedom and thus undermined a civilization which had been based upon an association of self-governing city-states. The municipal aristocracy, the backbone of that civilization, was crushed by a harsh and arbitrary despotism and old loyalties were weakened. Cities decayed and eventually many of them disappeared.

What lay behind these changes? It has been suggested that Rome acquired a larger empire than she could control effectively, that imperialism was the basic fault from which stemmed all other weaknesses: an insubordinate army, a top-heavy bureaucracy, political corruption, oppression of individuals and cities, class warfare, the growth of slavery, the influx of alien ideas. The difficulties of defending and governing too large an empire, it has been said, were complicated by primitive methods of transportation and communication. Should the Romans have stopped at the borders fixed by Augustus (31 B.C.–A.D. 14), or at the borders of 133 B.C., or 272 B.C., or 509 B.C.? Each acquisition of territory obviously posed fresh problems, but it was a measure of Rome's greatness that for centuries she solved many of these problems, and a measure of her decline that ultimately she was unable to do so. We must seek if we can some explanation for her failure other than the paradox that her rise caused her decline.

THE END OF EXPANSION

It may be argued, on the contrary, that a basic factor of decline was not overexpansion, but a cessation of expansion. Within the geographical limits set by the emperor Hadrian (117–138), Rome quickly attained the maximum possibilities of exploitation under existing techniques and economic stagnation set in. Since her wealth was no longer replenished by the plunder and resources of new provinces, there was a shift from an economy which had grown with the Empire to a static economy. Meanwhile pressures on the frontiers increased, and the government was compelled to maintain more armed forces and administrative officials than she could afford. Higher taxes, bureaucratic and autocratic controls, and the whole machinery of compulsion followed.

Further expansion, however, would have been neither feasible with the resources of manpower which Rome had available nor immediately profitable. As an alternative the Romans might have extended their domestic markets. But the purchasing power of the mass of the people was always limited, and the requirements of the rich were not sufficient to compensate for the limited demands of the majority of men. It has been suggested that an abundance of cheap slave labor prevented the invention and use of labor-saving machinery which might have produced cheap products and thus stimulated the economy by extending the internal market. Long before the fourth century, however, with the cessation of expansion, slaves were neither readily available nor cheap and there was, in fact, a labor shortage. A more valid explanation of the failure to produce a machine technology was the inability of the impoverished masses to purchase its products. The civil and foreign wars of the third century further dislocated the limited markets, and the economic structure of the Empire was badly shaken. The very measures taken by the government to preserve the Empire weakened and finally paralyzed initiative and enterprise.

THE DISINTEGRATION OF CENTRAL AUTHORITY

We have traced the growth of an inefficient and oppressive financial system which was both cause and result of economic decline. We have seen how the normal requirements of defense and administration and the extraordinary costs of half a century of military anarchy led to higher taxes, depreciation of the coinage, extension of the system of compulsory requisitions and forced labor, and economic chaos. The enforcement of the system called for an ever larger and more elaborate machinery of government and more repressive measures. As men sought to escape the insatiable demands of the state, they were regimented and bound to their classes and callings. The heavy hand of a centralized bureaucracy lay upon everyone, but especially upon the townsfolk. Men lost public spirit as well as individual initiative, and the failure of both was a portent of the decline of ancient civilization. These are some of the aspects of decline, but it must be remembered that in taking these measures the emperors were trying to prop up a structure which was already tottering and that these measures were therefore symptoms as well as causes of decline.

Economic decentralization was another factor. The provincials either had their own industrial skills or quickly developed them. Soon they began to manufacture goods themselves for local and even for imperial markets, and the market for Roman and Italian products shrank as competition from new provincial industries increased. Although the Empire was linked by an excellent system of roads and seaways, the methods of transportation were relatively poor. The normal difficulties of movement from one region to another were intensified by the disorders of a century of crisis. Thus high costs and risks helped promote economic decentralization, and provincial autarchy in turn fostered political dis-integration.

Related to these economic and political developments was the growth of large estates cultivated by slaves and semi-servile *coloni*. The free peasantry, once a major element in the strength of the Roman Empire, sank to the status of dependents. As early as the time of the Gracchi (133–121 B.C.) this evil had been apparent; now the whole process was intensified. In the end it led to the development of more or less self-sufficient large estates which in turn advanced economic decentralization.

INTELLECTUAL AND PSYCHOLOGICAL ASPECTS OF DECLINE

It is extremely difficult to assess the intellectual and psychological aspects of decline, but certain characteristics may be noted. Gibbon and others considered Christianity a major cause of the decline of ancient civilization. To be sure, the Christian attitude of resignation to adversity and the Christian emphasis upon a life to come represented a surrender to the material difficulties which beset men rather than a struggle to overcome them. But this is only a phase of the changing intellectual interests of the ancient world. As a result of the chaos and dislocation of life, there was a growing note of pessimism and despair which led to apathy and inertia. A reflection of this was the shift of interest from the here to the hereafter. We have seen how, under the stress of political, economic, and social ills, men turned to other-worldly religions, the Oriental mystery cults and Christianity. As they lost confidence in the Empire and in their own power to alter conditions, they tried to find inner security as compensation for a world which was grim and uncertain. This groping for salvation in new religions is one aspect of the psychological change; another is the resignation to the misfortunes of this world: to a totalitarian regime, a collapsing economy, and the barbarian invaders themselves. There was a "loss of nerve," as it has been called, a breakdown of morale, a defeatist mentality. Even if they had the means, men no longer had the will to maintain the Empire against invasion and dissolution. An intellectual collapse accompanied and hastened the decline of the Roman Empire.

In the final analysis, it was interaction of many factors, some hidden, some only partly discerned, some obvious, which resulted in the decline of ancient civilization. A nexus of political, social, economic, and psychological factors, each both cause and symptom of decline, accounts for the phenomenon. In time we may have more evidence and other historical methods which may enable us to determine with a greater degree of precision and accuracy the causes of historical events. Meanwhile we may study the facts and seek to establish their meaning, but we cannot always say categorically and definitely how and why great historical phenomena, like the decline of Rome, occurred.

Our description of the maladies which beset Rome must not make us think that all was unrelieved gloom. The foundations of Roman civilization endured and on them medieval civilization was built. In the West the Germanic kingdoms inherited many elements of Roman civilization;

while in the Byzantine East, ancient civilization, adapted to Christian purposes, flourished for a thousand years. Both in the East and West the Christian church assumed many of the functions of Rome. In the period of transition . . . much was preserved and much was salvaged from the ruin of the ancient world. A continuous thread linked the old and the new, and out of the chaos and confusion the medieval world slowly emerged.

Suggestions

1. "Decline and Fall" seems to present all possible answers to its central question, "What caused the decline of the Roman Empire?" The technique of discussing them all, however briefly, helps the reader to decide on the merits of each before reaching the thesis of the essay.

2. What hints are given earlier in the essay that the conclusion will be what it is? Do these hints (a) give direction to the development of the thesis or (b) load the argument in favor of the thesis?

3. Are there enough specific examples to show the difference between the "proximate and remote causes"?

4. Explain: *Draconian, Principate, concomitant, coloni.*

5. Comment on the function of frequent questions throughout the essay.

6. Is the speaker fair in his treatment of "unfounded theories" about Rome's decline?

7. Compare and contrast Katz's method of writing history with the principles set down in † "The Modern Climate of Opinion", † "Physical and Historical Facts", and † "History".

ON OBSTINACY IN BELIEF

C. S. LEWIS ⸺⸼

First read to the Socratic Club of Oxford. © 1955 by The University of the South, Sewanee, Tenn. Reprinted by permission of the author.

Papers have more than once been read to this Society in which a contrast was drawn between a supposedly Christian attitude and a supposedly scientific attitude to belief. We have been told that the scientist thinks it his duty to proportion the strength of his belief exactly to the evidence; to believe less as there is less evidence and to withdraw belief altogether when reliable adverse evidence turns up. We have been told that, on the contrary, the Christian regards it as positively praiseworthy to believe without evidence, or in excess of the evidence, or to maintain his belief unmodified in the teeth of steadily increasing evidence against it. Thus a "faith that has stood firm," which appears to mean a belief immune from all the assaults of reality, is commended.

If this were a fair statement of the case, then the coexistence within the same species of such scientists and such Christians would be a very staggering phenomenon. The fact that the two classes appear to overlap, as they do, would be quite inexplicable. Certainly all discussion between creatures so different would be hopeless. The purpose of this paper is to show that things are really not quite so bad as that. The sense in which scientists proportion their belief to the evidence, and the sense in which Christians do not, both need to be defined more closely. My hope is that when this has been done, though disagreement between the two parties may remain, they will not be left staring at one another in wholly dumb and desperate incomprehension.

And first, a word about belief in general. I do not see that the state of "proportioning belief to evidence" is anything like so common in the scientific life as has been claimed. Scientists are mainly concerned not with believing things but with finding things out. And no one, to the best of my knowledge, uses the word "believe" about things he has found out. The doctor says he "believes" a man was poisoned before he has examined the body; after the examination, he says the man was poisoned. No one says that he believes the multiplication table. No one who catches a thief red-handed says he believes that man was stealing. The scientist, when at work, that is, when he is a scientist, is laboring to escape from belief and unbelief into knowledge. Of course he uses hypotheses or supposals. I do not think these are beliefs. We must look, then, for the scientist's behavior about belief not to his scientific life but to his leisure hours.

In actual modern English usage the verb "believe," except for two special usages, generally expresses a very weak degree of opinion. "Where is Tom?" "Gone to London, I believe." The speaker would be only mildly surprised if Tom had not gone to London after all. "What was the date?" "430 B.C., I believe." The speaker means that he is far from sure. It is the same with the negative if it is put in the form "I believe not." ("Is Jones coming up this term?" "I believe not.") But if the negative is put in a different form it then becomes one of the special usages I mentioned a moment ago. This is of course the form "I don't believe it," or the still stronger, "I don't believe you." "I don't believe it" is far stronger on the negative side than "I believe" is on the positive.

"Where is Mrs. Jones?" "Eloped with the butler, I believe." "I don't believe it." This, especially if said with anger, may imply a conviction which in subjective certitude might be hard to distinguish from knowledge by experience. The other special usage is "I believe" as uttered by a Christian. There is no great difficulty in making the hardened materialist understand, however little he approves, the sort of mental attitude which this "I believe" expresses. The materialist need only picture himself replying, to some report of a miracle, "I don't believe it," and then imagine this same degree of conviction on the opposite side. He knows that he cannot, there and then, produce a refutation of the miracle which would have the certainty of mathematical demonstration; but the formal possibility that the miracle might after all have occurred does not really trouble him any more than a fear that water might not be H and O. Similarly the Christian does not necessarily claim to have demonstrative proof; but the formal possibility that God might not exist is not necessarily present in the form of the least actual doubt. Of course there are Christians who hold that such demonstrative proof exists, just as there may be materialists who hold that there is demonstrative disproof. But then, whichever of them is right (if either is) while he retained the proof or disproof would be not believing or disbelieving but knowing. We are speaking of belief and disbelief in the strongest degree, but not of knowledge. Belief, in this sense, seems to me to be assent to a proposition which we think so overwhelmingly probable that there is a psychological exclusion of doubt, though not a logical exclusion of dispute.

It may be asked whether belief (and of course disbelief) of this sort ever attaches to any but theological propositions. I think that many beliefs approximate to it; that is, many probabilities seem to us so strong that the absence of logical certainty does not induce in us the least shade of doubt. The scientific beliefs of those who are not themselves scientists often have this character, especially among the uneducated. Most of our beliefs about other people are of the same sort. The scientist himself, or he who was a scientist in the laboratory, has beliefs about his wife and friends which he holds, not indeed without evidence, but with more certitude than the evidence, if weighed in the laboratory manner, would justify. Most of my generation had a belief in the reality of the external world and of other people—if you prefer it, a disbelief in Solipsism—far in excess of our strongest arguments. It may be true, as they now say, that the whole thing arose from category mistakes and was a pseudo-problem; but then we didn't know that in the 'Twenties. Yet we managed to disbelieve in Solipsism all the same.

There is, of course, no question so far of belief without evidence. This point was blurred in a previous discussion. There was a confusion between the way in which a Christian first assents to certain propositions and the way in which he afterwards adheres to them. These must be carefully distinguished. Of the second it is true, in a sense, to say that Christians do recommend a certain discounting of apparent contrary evidence, and I will later attempt to explain why. But so far as I know it is not expected that a man should assent to these propositions in the first place without evidence or in the teeth of the evidence. At any rate, if anyone expects that, I certainly do not. And in fact, the man who accepts Christianity always thinks he had good evidence; whether, like Dante, *fisici e metafisici argomenti* [physical and metaphysical arguments], or historical evidence, or the evidence of religious experience, or authority, or all these together. For of course authority, however we may value it in this or that particular instance, is a kind of evidence. All of our historical beliefs, most of our geographical beliefs, many of our beliefs about matters that concern us in daily life, are accepted on the authority of other human beings, whether we are Christians, Atheists, Scientists, or Men-in-the-Street.

It is not the purpose of this paper to weigh the evidence, of whatever kind, on which Christians base their belief. To do that would be to write a full-dress *apologia*. All that I need do here is to point out that, at the very worst, this evidence cannot be so weak as to warrant the view that all whom it convinces are indifferent to evidence. The history of thought seems to make this quite plain. We know, in fact, that believers are not cut off from unbelievers by any portentous inferiority of intelligence or any perverse refusal to think. Many of them have been people of powerful minds. Many of them have been scientists. We may suppose them to have been mistaken, but we must suppose that their error was at least plausible. We might, indeed, conclude that it was, merely from the multitude and diversity of the arguments against it. For there is not one case against religion but many. Some say, like Capaneus in Statius, that it is a projection of our primitive fears, *primus in orbe deos fecit timor:* others, with Euhemerus, that it is all a "plant" put up by wicked kings, priests, or capitalists; others, with Tylor, that it comes from dreams about the dead; others, with Frazer, that it is a by-product of agriculture; others, like Freud, that it is a complex; the moderns that it is a category mistake.[1] I will never believe that an error against which so many and various defensive weapons have been found necessary was, from the outset, wholly lacking in plausibility. All this "post haste and rummage in the land"[2] obviously implies a respectable enemy.

---

[1] "Fear first created gods in the universe," says Capaneus in *The Story of Thebes* (c. 92) by the Roman poet Publius Papinius Statius; the Greek Euhemerus (4th century B.C.) wrote *Sacred History* and other works; the British anthropologist Sir Edward Tylor (1832–1917) wrote *Primitive Culture* and other works; the British anthropologist Sir James G. Frazer (1854–1951) wrote *The Golden Bough* and other works; Sigmund Freud (1856–1939), founder of psychoanalysis, analyzed religious belief in *Moses and Monotheism* and other works.

[2] Shakespeare, *Hamlet* I.i.107.

There are of course people in our own day to whom the whole situation seems altered by the doctrine of the concealed wish. They will admit that men, otherwise apparently rational, have been deceived by the arguments for religion. But they will say that they have been deceived first by their own desires and produced the arguments afterwards as a rationalization: that these arguments have never been intrinsically even plausible, but have seemed so because they were secretly weighted by our wishes. Now I do not doubt that this sort of thing happens in thinking about religion as in thinking about other things; but as a general explanation of religious assent it seems to me quite useless. On that issue our wishes may favor either side or both. The assumption that every man would be pleased, and nothing but pleased, if only he could conclude that Christianity is true, appears to me to be simply preposterous. If Freud is right about the Oedipus Complex the universal pressure of the wish that God should not exist must be enormous, and Atheism must be an admirable gratification to one of our strongest suppressed impulses. This argument, in fact, could be used on the Theistic side. But I have no intention of so using it. It will not really help either party. It is fatally ambivalent. Men wish on both sides: and again, there is fear-fulfilment as well as wish-fulfilment, and hypochondriac temperaments will always tend to think true what they most wish to be false. Thus instead of the one predicament on which our opponents sometimes concentrate there are in fact four. A man may be a Christian because he wants Christianity to be true. He may be an Atheist because he wants Atheism to be true. He may be an Atheist because he wants Christianity to be true. He may be a Christian because he wants Atheism to be true. Surely these possibilities cancel one another out? They may be of some use in analyzing a particular instance of belief or disbelief, where we know the case history, but as a general explanation of either they will not help us. I do not think they overthrow the view that there is evidence both for and against the Christian propositions which fully rational minds, working honestly, can assess differently.

I therefore ask you to substitute a different and less tidy picture for that with which we began. In it, you remember, two different kinds of men, Scientists who proportioned their belief to the evidence, and Christians who did not, were left facing one another across a chasm. The picture I should prefer is like this. All men alike, on questions which interest them, escape from the region of belief into that of knowledge when they can, and if they succeed in knowing they no longer say they believe. The questions in which Mathematicians are interested admit of treatment by a particularly clear and strict technique. Those of the Scientist have their own technique, which is not quite the same. Those of the Historian and the Judge are different again. The Mathematician's proof (at least so we laymen suppose) is by reasoning, the Scientist's by experiment, the Historian's by documents, the Judge's by concurring sworn testimony. But all these men, as men, on questions outside their own disciplines, have numerous beliefs to which they do not normally apply the methods of their own disciplines. It would indeed carry some suspicion of morbidity and even of insanity if they did. These beliefs vary in strength from weak opinion to complete subjective certitude. Specimens of such beliefs at their strongest are the Christian's "I believe" and the convinced Atheist's "I don't believe a word of it." The particular subject matter on which these two disagree does not, of course, necessarily involve such strength of belief and disbelief. There are some who moderately opine that there is, or is not, a God. But there are others whose belief or disbelief is free from doubt. And all these beliefs, weak or strong, are based on what appears to the holders to be evidence; but the strong believers or disbelievers of course think they have very strong evidence. There is no need to suppose stark unreason on either side. We need only suppose error. One side has estimated the evidence wrongly. And even so, the mistake cannot be supposed to be of a flagrant nature; otherwise the debate would not continue.

So much, then, for the way in which Christians come to assent to certain propositions. But we have now to consider something quite different, their adherence to their belief after it has once been formed. It is here that the charge of irrationality and resistance to evidence becomes really important. For it must be admitted at once that Christians do praise such an adherence as if it were meritorious; and even, in a sense, more meritorious the stronger the apparent evidence against their faith becomes. They even warn one another that such apparent contrary evidence—such "trials to faith" or "temptations to doubt"—may be expected to occur, and determine in advance to resist them. And this is certainly shockingly unlike the behavior we all demand of the Scientist or the Historian in their own disciplines. There, to slur over or ignore the faintest evidence against a favorite hypothesis is admittedly foolish and shameful. It must be exposed to every test; every doubt must be invited. But then I do not admit that a hypothesis is a belief. And if we consider the Scientist not among his hypotheses in the laboratory but among the beliefs in his ordinary life, I think the contrast between him and the Christian would be weakened. If, for the first time, a doubt of his wife's fidelity crosses the scientist's mind, does he consider it his duty at once to entertain this doubt with complete impartiality, at once to evolve a series of experiments by which it can be tested, and to await the result with pure neutrality of mind? No doubt it may come to that in the end. There are unfaithful wives; there are experimental husbands. But is such a course what his brother scientists would recommend to him (all of them, I suppose, except one) as the first step he should take and the only one consistent with his honor as a scientist? Or would they, like us, blame him for a moral flaw rather than praise him for an intellectual virtue if he did so?

This is intended, however, merely as a precaution against exaggerating the difference between Christian obstinacy in belief and the behavior of normal people about their non-theological beliefs. I am far from suggesting that the case I have supposed is exactly parallel to the Christian obstinacy. For of course evidence of the wife's infidelity might accumulate, and presently reach a point at which the scientist would be pitiably foolish to disbelieve it. But the Christians seem to praise an adherence to the original belief which holds out against any evidence whatever. I must now try to show why such praise is in fact a logical conclusion from the original belief itself.

This can be done best by thinking for a moment of situations in which the thing is reversed. In Christianity such faith is demanded of us; but there are situations in which we demand it of others. There are times when we can do all that a fellow creature needs if only he will trust us. In getting a dog out of a trap, in extracting a thorn from a child's finger, in teaching a boy to swim or rescuing one who can't, in getting a frightened beginner over a nasty place on a mountain, the one fatal obstacle may be their distrust. We are asking them to trust us in the teeth of their senses, their imagination, and their intelligence. We ask them to believe that what is painful will relieve their pain and that what looks dangerous is their only safety. We ask them to accept apparent impossibilities: that moving the paw further back into the trap is the way to get it out—that hurting the finger very much more will stop the finger hurting—that water which is obviously permeable will resist and support the body—that holding onto the only support within reach is not the way to avoid sinking—that to go higher and onto a more exposed ledge is the way not to fall. To support all these *incredibilia* we can rely only on the other party's confidence in us—a confidence certainly not based on demonstration, admittedly shot through with emotion, and perhaps, if we are strangers, resting on nothing but such assurance as the look of our face and the tone of our voice can supply, or even, for the dog, on our smell. Sometimes, because of their unbelief, we can do no mighty works. But if we succeed, we do so because they have maintained their faith in us against apparently contrary evidence. No one blames us for demanding such faith. No one blames them for giving it. No one says afterwards what an unintelligent dog or child or boy that must have been to trust us. If the young mountaineer were a scientist it would not be held against him, when he came up for a fellowship, that he had once departed from Clifford's rule of evidence[3] by entertaining a belief with strength greater than the evidence logically obliged him to.

---

[3] According to William Kingdon Clifford (1845–1879), it is better to go without belief than to believe on insufficient evidence. See William James, "The Will to Believe," section II.

Now to accept the Christian propositions is *ipso facto* to believe that we are to God, always, as that dog or child or bather or mountain climber was to us, only very much more so. From this it is a strictly logical conclusion that the behavior which was appropriate to them, will be appropriate to us, only very much more so. Mark: I am not saying that the strength of our original belief must by psychological necessity produce such behavior. I am saying that the content of our original belief by logical necessity entails the proposition that such behavior is appropriate. If human life is in fact ordered by a beneficent being whose knowledge of our real needs and of the way in which they can be satisfied infinitely exceeds our own, we must expect *a priori* that His operations will often appear to us far from beneficent and far from wise, and that it will be our highest prudence to give Him our confidence in spite of this. This expectation is increased by the fact that when we accept Christianity we are warned that apparent evidence against it will occur—evidence strong enough "to deceive if possible the very elect." Our situation is rendered tolerable by two facts. One is that we seem to ourselves, besides the apparently contrary evidence, to receive favorable evidence. Some of it is in the form of external events: as when I go to see a man, moved by what I felt to be a whim, and find he has been praying that I should come to him that day. Some of it is more like the evidence on which the mountaineer or the dog might trust his rescuer—the rescuer's voice, look, and smell. For it seems to us (though you, on your premises, must believe us deluded) that we have something like a knowledge-by-acquaintance of the Person we believe in, however imperfect and intermittent it may be. We trust not because "a God" exists, but because *this* God exists. Or if we ourselves dare not claim to "know" Him, Christendom does, and we trust at least some of its representatives in the same way: because of the sort of people they are. The second fact is this. We think we can see already why, if our original belief is true, such trust beyond the evidence, against much apparent evidence, has to be demanded of us. For the question is not about being helped out of one trap or over one difficult place in a climb. We believe that His intention is to create a certain personal relation between Himself and us, a relation really *sui generis* but analogically describable in terms of filial or of erotic love. Complete trust is an ingredient in that relation—such trust as could have no room to grow except where is also room for doubt. To love involves trusting the beloved beyond the evidence, even against much evidence. No man is our friend who believes in our good intentions only when they are proved. No man is our friend who will not be very slow to accept evidence against them. Such confidence, between one man and another, is in fact almost universally praised as a moral beauty, not blamed as a logical error. And the suspicious man is blamed for a meanness of character, not admired for the excellence of his logic.

There is, you see, no real parallel between Christian obstinacy in faith and the obstinacy of a bad scientist trying to preserve a hypothesis although the evidence has turned against it. Unbelievers very pardonably get the impression that an adherence to our faith is like that, because they meet Christianity, if at all, mainly in apologetic works. And there, of course, the existence and beneficence of God must appear as a speculative question like any other. Indeed it is a speculative question as long as it is a question at all. But once it has been answered in the affirmative, you get quite a new situation. To believe that God—at least *this* God—exists is to believe that you as a person now stand in the presence of God as a Person. What would, a moment before, have been variations in opinion, now become variations in your personal attitude to a Person. You are no longer faced with an argument which demands your assent, but with a Person who demands your confidence. A faint analogy would be this. It is one thing to ask *in vacuo* whether So-and-So will join us tonight, and another to discuss this when So-and-So's honor is pledged to come and some great matter depends on his coming. In the first case it would be merely reasonable, as the clock ticked on, to expect him less and less. In the second, a continued expectation far into the night would be due to our friend's character if we had found him reliable before. Which of us would not feel slightly ashamed if, one moment after we had given him up, he arrived with a full explanation of his delay? We should feel that we ought to have known him better.

Now of course we see, quite as clearly as you, how agonizingly two-edged all this is. A faith of this sort, if it happens to be true, is obviously what we need, and it is infinitely ruinous to lack it. But there can be faith of this sort where it is wholly ungrounded. The dog may lick the face of the man who comes to take it out of the trap; but he may only mean to vivisect it in South Parks Road [4] when he has done so. The ducks who come to the call "Dilly, dilly, come and be killed" have confidence in the farmer's wife, and she wrings their necks for their pains. There is that famous French story of the fire in the theatre. Panic was spreading, the spectators were just turning from an audience into a mob. At that moment a huge bearded man leaped through the orchestra onto the stage, raised his hand with a gesture full of nobility, and cried *Que chacun regagne sa place* [Everyone return to his seat]. Such was the authority of his voice and bearing that everyone obeyed him. As a result they were all burned to death, while the bearded man walked quietly out through the wings to the stage door, took a cab which was waiting for someone else, and went home to bed.

That demand for our confidence which a true friend makes of us is exactly the same that a confidence trickster would make. That refusal to trust, which is sensible in reply to a confidence trickster, is ungenerous

[4] I.e. in the physiology and anatomy laboratories of Oxford University.

and ignoble to a friend, and deeply damaging to our relation with him. To be forewarned and therefore fore-armed against apparently contrary appearance is eminently rational if our belief is true; but if our belief is a delusion, this same forewarning and fore-arming would obviously be the method whereby the delusion rendered itself incurable. And yet again, to be aware of these possibilities and yet to reject them is clearly the precise mode, and the only mode, in which our personal response to God can establish itself. In that sense the ambiguity is not something that conflicts with faith so much as a condition which makes faith possible. When you are asked for trust you may give it or withhold it; it is senseless to say that you will trust if you are given demonstrative certainty. There would be no room for trust if demonstration were given. When demonstration is given what will be left will be simply the sort of relation which results from having trusted, or not having trusted, before it was given.

The saying "Blessed are those that have not seen and have believed" [5] has nothing to do with our original assent to the Christian propositions. It was not addressed to a philosopher enquiring whether God exists. It was addressed to a man who already believed that, who already had long acquaintance with a particular Person, and evidence that that Person could do very odd things, and who then refused to believe one odd thing more, often predicted by that Person and vouched for by all his closest friends. It is a rebuke not to scepticism in the philosophic sense but to the psychological quality of being "suspicious." It says in effect, "You should have known me better." There are cases between man and man where we should all, in our different way, bless those who have not seen and have believed. Our relation to those who trusted us only after we were proved innocent in court cannot be the same as our relation to those who trusted us all through.

Our opponents, then, have a perfect right to dispute with us about the grounds of our original assent. But they must not accuse us of sheer insanity if, after the assent has been given, our adherence to it is no longer proportioned to every fluctuation of the apparent evidence. They cannot of course be expected to know on what our assurance feeds, and how it revives and is always rising from its ashes. They cannot be expected to see how the *quality* of the object which we think we are beginning to know by acquaintance drives us to the view that if this were a delusion then we should have to say that the universe had produced no real thing of comparable value and that all explanations of the delusion seemed somehow less important than the thing explained. That is knowledge we cannot communicate. But they can see how the assent, of necessity, moves us from the logic of speculative thought into what might perhaps be called the logic of personal relations. What would, up till

[5] Jesus said it to the doubting Thomas; *Gospel of St. John* 20, 29.

then, have been variations simply of opinion become variations of conduct by a person to a Person. *Credere Deum esse* [Believing God exists] turns into *Credere in Deum* [Believing in God]. And *Deum* here is this God, the infinitely knowable Lord.

Suggestions

1. "It is not the purpose of this paper to weigh the evidence . . . on which Christians base their belief," says the speaker (¶7). What then is his purpose? Perhaps to define the word *belief* precisely, so as to show that "if we consider the Scientist not among his hypotheses in the laboratory but among the beliefs in his ordinary life . . . the contrast between him and the Christian would be weakened" (¶10). Summarize the beliefs in the Scientist's ordinary life that "On Obstinacy in Belief" mentions. Do they weaken the contrast between him and the Christian?

2. Assuming that the speaker does not reach the essence of his argument until ¶7, summarize the first six paragraphs and decide whether their presence can be justified.

3. Point out repetitive devices used to introduce the body of the arguments.

4. List some of the speaker's analogies and evaluate their effectiveness by comparing them with those in † "A Case of Co-Existence."

5. Explain: *Solipsism, apologia, portentous, Oedipus Complex, Theistic, ambivalent, ipso facto, a priori, sui generis, erotic, meanness, in vacuo.*

6. Are there any indications in style or substance showing (a) that this was first a speech and (b) the nature of the audience?

7. Write an essay for or against one of the following:
   "No man is our friend who believes in our good intentions only when they are proved."
   "There is . . . no real parallel between Christian obstinacy in faith and the obstinacy of a bad scientist trying to preserve a hypothesis although the evidence has turned against it."
   "There would be no reason for trust if demonstration were given."

THE MORAL OF *THE RIME* OF *THE ANCIENT MARINER*

LESLIE HOWARD PALMER ⸺ *Reprinted by permission of the author.*

In 1817 Samuel Taylor Coleridge finished his revisions of a poem that he had first completed in 1798. The poem, *The Rime of the Ancient Mariner,* was something of a success for Coleridge; at least his contemporary critics were unanimous in excepting his poem from their general disparagement of his work. Of the poem, *The Monthly Review* said it had "exquisite touches" in spite of the fact that it was "the strangest cock and bull story ever seen on paper." [1]

Clouds of controversy have continued to swirl around this imaginative poem. Critics have tried to determine whether it has a moral or is nothing but a reflection of one of Coleridge's opium dreams. Numerous writers have taken various sides of the issue. This paper will examine only three of the many theories that have gained great prominence. Each of these begins with the same statement by Coleridge, originally published in his *Table Talk:*

> Mrs. Barbauld once told me that she admired The Ancient Mariner very much, but that there were two faults in it—it was improbable, and had no moral. As for the probability, I owned that might admit some question; but as to the want of a moral, I told her that in my own judgment the poem had too much; and that the only, or chief fault, if I might say so, was the obtrusion of the moral sentiment so openly on the reader as a principle or cause of action in a work of such pure imagination. It ought to have had no more moral than the *Arabian Nights* tale of the merchant's sitting down to eat dates by the side of a well, and throwing the shells aside, and lo! a genie starts up, and says that he *must* kill the aforesaid merchant, *because* one of the date shells had, it seems, put out the eye of the genie's son.[2]

From this statement a noted expert on Coleridge, Professor John Livingston Lowes, has decided that though there is "moral and rhythmical harmony" to the story, "Nevertheless, to interpret the drift of 'The Ancient Mariner' as didactic in its intention is to stultify both Coleridge and one's self." [3] Robert Penn Warren has decided the poem has two themes, one of these the theme of sacramental vision, the other that of

---

[1] Walter Graham, "Contemporary Critics of Coleridge, the Poet," *PMLA,* XXXVIII (1923), 282.
[2] *Table Talk,* 31 May 1830, in *Coleridge's Miscellaneous Criticism,* ed. Thomas Middleton Raysor (Cambridge, Mass., 1936), p. 405. Italics in the original.
[3] John Livingston Lowes, *The Road to Xanadu* (Boston, 1927), p. 299.

imagination.[4] The third theory, that of Newton P. Stallknecht, is that Coleridge began the poem with no didactic purpose, but afterward noticed the advantages it offered for a philosophical work.[5] There is truth in each of their theories, but whether any of them grasps the whole purpose of the poem is questionable.

Lowes was so fascinated by the workings of Coleridge's imagination that he wrote a whole book, *The Road to Xanadu,* describing the creation of *The Ancient Mariner.* Although Coleridge had never been to sea, he was able to produce a masterpiece about the sea. There are geographical discrepancies, but Lowes argues that the work is an adventure into the imaginative realm of the supernatural.[6] He believes that Coleridge created *The Ancient Mariner* because of the wonderful story it made, much like the *Arabian Nights* tales with which he was so fascinated.

Robert Penn Warren takes a different stand. He has decided that the incidents in Coleridge's life influenced the writing of *The Ancient Mariner.*[7] By considering letters of the poet written near the time of its creation he has managed to construct a hypothetical tie between it and Coleridge's philosophical beliefs at the time. Warren interprets the poem as an allegory, showing Coleridge's belief in Original Sin.[8]

On the other hand, Newton P. Stallknecht takes the stand that the poet is trying to show the triumph of reason over feeling, the crime and then repentance of a person.[9] The obscurity of the meaning of the death of the albatross is a weak point in his theory, Mr. Stallknecht concedes, but the obscurity is caused by Coleridge's late realization of the meaning the poem could be made to bear.[10]

It can be seen that each critic has a foundation for his beliefs, but we must go back to the original quotation from Coleridge. He did say that the poem had a moral that was pressed upon the reader. He also gave an example from an *Arabian Nights* tale. No one man seems to have considered that Coleridge might have meant what he said. I would like to present my theory as to the moral of the poem, which I believe is in complete agreement with that statement of Coleridge's. My interpretation depends upon the parallel between the merchant's careless act and the careless deed of the Mariner. The merchant carelessly threw aside a shell, thinking little of what he had done until confronted by a genie who punished him severely for such a trivial action. If the merchant could have known, he never would have thrown aside that shell! The

---

[4] Robert Penn Warren, "A Poem of Pure Imagination: An Experiment in Reading," in *The Rime of the Ancient Mariner* (New York, 1946), p. 71.
[5] Newton P. Stallknecht, "The Moral of the Ancient Mariner," *PMLA,* XLVII (1932), 563.
[6] Lowes, pp. 299–300.
[7] Warren, p. 72.
[8] *Ibid.,* p. 81.
[9] Stallknecht, pp. 564–566.
[10] *Ibid.,* p. 564.

Mariner too was to regret his killing of the albatross. His heedless action was to prove disastrous for him. Coleridge's poem has the same theme as the tale of the merchant and the genie, the terrible results of rash action. Coleridge himself said that this was the moral of his work, but literary experts, ranging into the realm of the psychiatric, have attempted to draw some other meaning. It is all right to do this when the author does not reveal the moral, but with *The Rime of the Ancient Mariner* the author has told his purpose.

Other, perhaps even more interesting, aspects of *The Ancient Mariner* are revealed in the writings of Lowes, Warren, and Stallknecht, but the controversy over the poem has always revolved around the moral. Coleridge seems to have tried to help settle any doubts about it, but the storm rages on. At any rate, whether *The Ancient Mariner* has a moral or not, it has achieved lasting fame as the only complete expression of the genius of Samuel Taylor Coleridge.

Bibliography

Coleridge's Miscellaneous Criticism. Edited by Thomas Middleton Raysor. Cambridge, Mass.: Harvard University Press, 1936.

Graham, Walter. "Contemporary Critics of Coleridge the Poet." *PMLA,* XXXVIII (1923), 278–289.

Lowes, John Livingston. *The Road to Xanadu.* Boston: Houghton Mifflin, 1927.

Stallknecht, Newton P. "The Moral of the Ancient Mariner." *PMLA,* XLVII (1932), 559–569.

Warren, Robert Penn. "A Poem of Pure Imagination: an Experiment in Reading," in *The Rime of the Ancient Mariner.* New York: Reynal & Hitchcock, 1946, pp. 59–117.

Suggestions

1. "The Moral of *The Rime of the Ancient Mariner*" attacks the opinions of three other critics. Are its summaries of them as unbiased as † "Decline and Fall" is in its treatment of opposing views? Does Palmer's essay offer sufficient evidence for its own interpretation?

2. Decide whether the speaker has interpreted Coleridge's reply to Mrs. Barbauld correctly.

3. In relation to the subject of the whole essay, how successful is the concluding sentence? Write an essay on the value of an acceptable thesis to the worth of a poem, mentioning the opinion expressed in *The Road to Xanadu.*

4. Read Coleridge's *Rime of the Ancient Mariner* and evaluate the thesis that the poem is concerned with the "terrible results of rash action."

C O M P O S I T E S

THE HELPMATE

H. L. MENCKEN ---⊶ *From* A MENCKEN CHRESTOMATHY, *H. L. Mencken, 1924. Copyright 1924, 1949 by Alfred A. Knopf, Inc.*

Every intelligent woman knows instinctively that the aspirations of her husband are fundamentally inimical to her, and that their realization is apt to cost her her possession of him. What she dreams of is not an infinitely brilliant husband, but an infinitely "solid" one, which is to say, one bound to her irretrievably by the chains of normalcy. It would delight her to see him get to the White House, for a man in the White House is policed as relentlessly as an archbishop. But it would give her a great deal of disquiet to see him develop into a Goethe or a Wagner.

I have known in my time a good many men of the first talent, as talent is reckoned in America, and most of them have been married. I can't recall one whose wife appeared to view his achievements with perfect ease of mind. In every case the lady was full of palpable fear—the product of feminine intuition, *i.e.,* of hard realism and common sense—that his rise shook her hold upon him, that he became a worse husband in proportion as he became a better man. In the logic I can discern no flaw. The ideal husband is surely not a man of active and daring mind; he is the man of placid and conforming mind. Here the good business man obviously beats the artist and adventurer. His rewards are all easily translated into domestic comfort and happiness. He is not wobbled by the admiration of other women, none of whom, however much they may esteem his virtues as a husband, are under any illusion as to his virtues as a lover. Above all, his mind is not analytical, and hence he is not likely to attempt any anatomizing of his marriage—the starting point for the worst sort of domestic infelicity. No man, examining his marriage intelligently, can fail to observe that it is compounded, at least in part, of slavery, and that he is the slave. Happy the woman whose husband is so stupid that he never launches into that coroner's inquest.

Suggestions

1. Essays known in this book as Composites are essays in generalization. They concern not individuals but species—"every intelligent woman," "the typical writer," "today's shopper,"—and they speak not of actions but of characteristic behavior. Of course there are many exceptions, and so the reader must always ask himself whether the speaker is fair to the group about which he generalizes. Thus in reading "The Helpmate" one must decide whether there are so many wives who do not conform to its portrait of them as to make its generalizations absurd, or whether its statements really do apply to wives considered as a class.

2. Point out the concrete examples in "The Helpmate." Do you think there are enough of them to illustrate its general statements?

3. Invent (or cite from history) examples of what the first sentence means by "the aspirations of her husband" and what the last sentence means by "that coroner's inquest." Then formulate the thesis of "The Helpmate." Has it a coherent one?

4. In your opinion, does the speaker side with husbands, with wives, or with neither?

5. Explain: *aspirations, inimical, Goethe, Wagner, palpable, anatomizing.*

6. Write an essay assuming that all marriages resulted in "domestic comfort and happiness." What would be the effects on society?

7. "The Helpmate" refers to intelligent husbands, stupid husbands, and intelligent wives—but fails to mention stupid wives. Write an essay in which you repair this omission, disagreeing with the essay if you choose.

BABES IN CONSUMERLAND

VANCE PACKARD

From THE HIDDEN PERSUADERS, *by Vance Packard.* © *1957, by Vance Packard. Courtesy of David McKay Company, Inc.*

You have to have a carton that attracts and hypnotizes this woman, like waving a flashlight in front of her eyes.
—*Gerald Stahl, executive vice-president, Package Designers Council.*

For some years the DuPont company has been surveying the shopping habits of American housewives in the new jungle called the supermarket.

The results have been so exciting in the opportunities they suggest to marketers that hundreds of leading food companies and ad agencies have requested copies. Husbands fretting over the high cost of feeding their families would find the results exciting, too, in a dismaying way.

The opening statement of the 1954 report exclaimed enthusiastically in display type: "Today's shopper in the supermarket is more and more guided by the buying philosophy—'If somehow your product catches my eye—and for some reason it looks especially good—I WANT IT.' " That conclusion was based on studying the shopping habits of 5,338 shoppers in 250 supermarkets.

DuPont's investigators have found that the mid-century shopper doesn't bother to make a list or at least not a complete list of what she needs to buy. In fact less than one shopper in five has a complete list, but still the wives always manage to fill up their carts, often while exclaiming, according to DuPont: "I certainly never intended to get that much!" Why doesn't the wife need a list? DuPont gives this blunt answer: "Because seven out of ten of today's purchases are decided in the store, where the shoppers buy on impulse!!!"

The proportion of impulse buying of groceries has grown almost every year for nearly two decades, and DuPont notes that this rise in impulse buying has coincided with the growth in self-service shopping. Other studies show that in groceries where there are clerks to wait on customers there is about half as much impulse buying as in self-service stores. If a wife has to face a clerk she thinks out beforehand what she needs.

The impulse buying of pungent-odored food such as cheese, eye-appealing items like pickles or fruit salad in glass jars, and candy, cake, snack spreads, and other "self-gratifying items" runs even higher than average, ninety per cent of all purchases. Other investigators have in general confirmed the DuPont figures on impulse buying. The Folding Paper Box Association found that two-thirds of all purchases were completely or partially on impulse; the *Progressive Grocer* put the impulse figure about where DuPont does: seven out of ten purchases. And *Printer's Ink* observed with barely restrained happiness that the shopping list had become obsolescent if not obsolete.

One motivational analyst who became curious to know why there had been such a great rise in impulse buying at supermarkets was James Vicary. He suspected that some special psychology must be going on inside the women as they shopped in supermarkets. His suspicion was that perhaps they underwent such an increase in tension when confronted with so many possibilities that they were forced into making quick purchases. He set out to find out if this was true. The best way to detect what was going on inside the shopper was a galvanometer or lie detector. That obviously was impractical. The next best thing was to use a hidden motion-picture camera and record the eye-blink rate of the women as they shopped. How fast a person blinks his eyes is a pretty good index of his state of inner tension. The average person, according to Mr. Vicary, normally blinks his eyes about thirty-two times a minute. If he is tense he blinks them more frequently, under extreme tension up to fifty or sixty times a minute. If he is notably relaxed on the other hand his eye-blink rate may drop to a subnormal twenty or less.

Mr. Vicary set up his cameras and started following the ladies as they entered the store. The results were startling, even to him. Their eye-blink rate, instead of going up to indicate mounting tension, went down and down, to a very subnormal fourteen blinks a minute. The ladies fell into what Mr. Vicary calls a hypnoidal trance, a light kind of trance that, he explains, is the first stage of hypnosis. Mr. Vicary has decided that the main cause of the trance is that the supermarket is packed with products that in former years would have been items that only kings and queens could afford, and here in this fairyland they were available. Mr. Vicary theorizes: "Just in this generation, anyone can be a king or queen and go through these stores where the products say 'buy me, buy me.' "

Interestingly many of these women were in such a trance that they passed by neighbors and old friends without noticing or greeting them. Some had a sort of glassy stare. They were so entranced as they wandered about the store plucking things off shelves at random that they would bump into boxes without seeing them and did not even notice the camera although in some cases their face would pass within a foot and a half of the spot where the hidden camera was clicking away. When the wives had filled their carts (or satisfied themselves) and started toward the check-out counter their eye-blink rate would start rising up to a slightly subnormal twenty-five blinks per minute. Then, at the sound of the cash-register bell and the voice of the clerk asking for money, the eye-blink rate would race up past normal to a high abnormal of forty-five blinks per minute. In many cases it turned out that the women did not have enough money to pay for all the nice things they had put in the cart.

In this beckoning field of impulse buying psychologists have teamed up with merchandising experts to persuade the wife to buy products she may not particularly need or even want until she happens to see them invitingly presented. The 60,000,000 American women who go into supermarkets every week are getting "help" in their purchases and "splurchases" from psychologists and psychiatrists hired by the food merchandisers. On May 18, 1956, *The New York Times* printed a remarkable interview with a young man named Gerald Stahl, executive vice-president of the Package Designers Council. He stated: "Psychiatrists say that people have so much to choose from that they want help—they will like the package that hypnotizes them into picking it." He urged food packers to put more hypnosis into their package designing, so that the housewife will stick out her hand for it rather than one of many rivals.

Mr. Stahl has found that it takes the average woman exactly twenty seconds to cover an aisle in a supermarket if she doesn't tarry; so a good package design should hypnotize the woman like a flashlight waved in front of her eyes. Some colors such as red and yellow are helpful in creating hypnotic effects. Just putting the name and maker of the product on the box is old-fashioned and, he says, has absolutely no effect on the mid-century woman. She can't read anything, really, until she has picked the box up in her hands. To get the woman to reach and get the package in her hands designers, he explained, are now using "symbols that have a dreamlike quality." To cite examples of dreamlike quality, he mentioned the mouth-watering frosted cakes that decorate the packages of cake mixes, sizzling steaks, mushrooms frying in butter. The idea is to sell the sizzle rather than the meat. Such illustrations make the woman's imagination leap ahead to the end product. By 1956 package designers had even produced a box that, when the entranced shopper picked it up and began fingering it, would give a soft sales talk, or stress the brand name. The talk is on a strip that starts broadcasting when a shopper's finger rubs it.

The package people understandably believe that it is the package that makes or breaks the impulse sale, and some more objective experts agree. A buyer for a food chain told of his experience in watching women shopping. The typical shopper, he found, "picks up one, two, or three items, she puts them back on the shelf, then she picks up one and keeps it. I ask her why she keeps it. She says, 'I like the package.'" (This was a buyer for Bohack.)

The Color Research Institute, which specializes in designing deep-impact packages, won't even send a package out into the field for testing until it has been given ocular or eye-movement tests to show how the consumer's eye will travel over the package on the shelf. This is a gauge of the attention-holding power of the design.

According to some psychologists a woman's eye is most quickly attracted to items wrapped in red; a man's eye to items wrapped in blue. Students in this field have speculated on the woman's high vulnerability to red. One package designer, Frank Gianninoto, has developed an interesting theory. He has concluded that a majority of women shoppers leave their glasses at home or will never wear glasses in public if they can avoid it so that a package to be successful must stand out "from the blurred confusion."

Other merchandisers, I should add, have concluded that in the supermarket jungle the all-important fact in impulse buying is shelf position. Many sharp merchandisers see to it that their "splurge" items (on which their profit margin is highest) tend to be at eye level.

Most of the modern supermarkets, by the mid-fifties, were laid out in a carefully calculated manner so that the high-profit impulse items would be most surely noticed. In many stores they were on the first or only aisle the shopper could enter. Among the best tempters, apparently, are those items in glass jars where the contents can be seen, or where the food is actually out in the open, to be savored and seen. Offering free pickles and cubes of cheese on toothpicks has proved to be reliable as a sales booster. An Indiana supermarket operator nationally recognized for his advanced psychological techniques told me he once sold a half ton of cheese in a few hours, just by getting an enormous half-ton wheel of cheese and inviting customers to nibble slivers and cut off their own chunks for purchase. They could have their chunk free if they could guess its weight within an ounce. The mere massiveness of the cheese, he believes, was a powerful influence in making the sales. "People like to see a lot of merchandise," he explained. "When there are only three or four cans of an item on a shelf, they just won't move." People don't want the last package. A test by *The Progressive Grocer* showed that customers buy twenty-two per cent more if the shelves are kept full. The urge to conformity, it seems, is profound with many of us.

People also are stimulated to be impulsive, evidently, if they are offered a little extravagance. A California supermarket found that putting a pat of butter on top of each of its better steaks caused sales to soar fifteen per cent. The Jewel Tea Company set up "splurge counters" in many of its supermarkets after it was found that women in a just-for-the-heck-of-it mood will spend just as freely on food delicacies as they will on a new hat. The Coca-Cola Company made the interesting discovery that customers in a supermarket who paused to refresh themselves at a soft-drink counter tended to spend substantially more. The Coke people put this to work in a test where they offered customers free drinks. About eighty per cent accepted the Cokes and spent on an average of $2.44 more than the store's average customer had been spending.

Apparently the only people who are more prone to splurging when they get in a supermarket than housewives are the wives' husbands and children. Supermarket operators are pretty well agreed that men are easy marks for all sorts of impulse items and cite cases they've seen of husbands who are sent to the store for a loaf of bread and depart with both their arms loaded with their favorite snack items. Shrewd supermarket operators have put the superior impulsiveness of little children to work in promoting sales. The Indiana supermarket operator I mentioned has a dozen little wire carts that small children can push about the store while their mothers are shopping with big carts. People think these tiny carts are very cute; and the operator thinks they are very profitable. The small children go zipping up and down the aisles imitating their mothers in impulse buying, only more so. They reach out, hypnotically I assume, and grab boxes of cookies, candies, dog food, and everything else that delights or interests them. Complications arise, of course, when mother and child come out of their trances and together reach the check-out counter. The store operator related thus what happens: "There is usually a wrangle when the mother sees all the things the child has in his basket and she tries to make him take the stuff back. The child will take back items he doesn't particularly care about such as coffee but will usually bawl and kick before surrendering cookies, candy, ice cream, or soft drinks, so they usually stay for the family."

All these factors of sly persuasion may account for the fact that whereas in past years the average American family spent about twenty-three per cent of its income for food it now spends nearly thirty per cent. The Indiana operator I mentioned estimates that any supermarket shopper could, by showing a little old-fashioned thoughtfulness and preplanning, save twenty-five per cent easily on her family's food costs.

The exploration of impulse buying on a systematic basis began spreading in the mid-fifties to many other kinds of products not available in food stores. Liquor stores began organizing racks so that women could browse and pick up impulse items. This idea was pioneered on New York's own "ad alley," Madison Avenue, and spread to other parts of the country. Department and specialty stores started having counters simply labeled, "Why Not?" to promote the carefree, impulsive purchasing of new items most people had never tried before. One store merchandiser was quoted as saying: "Just give people an excuse to try what you are selling and you'll make an extra sale."

One of the most daring ventures into impulse selling was that launched by a Chicago insurance firm, Childs and Wood, which speculated that perhaps even insurance could be sold as an impulse item. So it sets up a counter to sell insurance to passers-by at the department store Carson Pirie Scott and Company. Women who happened to be in that area, perhaps to shop for fur coats or a bridal gown, could buy insurance (life, automobile, household, fire, theft, jewelry, hospital) from an assortment of firms. The experiment was successful and instituted on a permanent basis. Auto, household, and fire insurance were reported to be the most popular impulse items.

Social scientists at the Survey Research Center at the University of Michigan made studies of the way people make their decisions to buy relatively expensive durable items such as TV sets, refrigerators, washing machines, items that are usually postponable. It concluded: "We did *not* find that all or most purchases of large household goods are made after careful consideration or deliberation . . . that much planning went into the purchasing . . . nor much seeking of information. About a quarter of these purchases of large household goods were found to lack practically all features of careful deliberation."

In a study that was made on the purchasing of homes in New London, Connecticut, investigators were amazed that even with this, the most important purchase a family is likely to make in the year if not the decade, the shopping was lethargic and casual. On an average the people surveyed looked at less than a half-dozen houses before making a decision; ten per cent of the home buyers looked at only one house before deciding; nineteen per cent looked at only two houses before choosing one of them.

Dr. Warren Bilkey, of the University of Connecticut, and one of the nation's authorities on consumer behavior, systematically followed a large (sixty-three) group of families for more than a year as they wrestled with various major purchasing decisions. He learned that he could chart after each visit the intensity of two opposing factors, "desire" and "resistance." When one finally overwhelmed the other, the decision, pro or con, was made. He found that these people making major decisions, unlike the ladies in the supermarket, did build up a state of tension within themselves. The longer they pondered the decision, the higher the tension. He found that very often the people became so upset by the indecision that they often threw up their hands and decided to make the purchase just to find relief from their state of tension.

Suggestions

1. Much of the effectiveness of "Babes in Consumerland" depends on its attitude toward both advertising and the shopper. Beginning with the allusion in the title, describe the explicit and implicit attitudes.

2. The bulk of the essay presents facts about impulse buying as revealed by research and supported by results of that research. Do the conclusions extend beyond the point warranted by the evidence?

3. Is there a significant difference between products that "hypnotize" customers and those that create "mounting tension"?

4. Comment: (a) "If a wife has to face a clerk she thinks out beforehand what she needs."
(b) "Supermarket operators are pretty well agreed that men are easy marks for all sorts of impulse items. . . ."

5. Explain the relation of the last six paragraphs to the total essay.

6. Would you make any changes in the final paragraph if you were writing this essay? Why?

7. Write an analysis of "Babes in Consumerland" as an argument.

8. Write an essay on your estimate of yourself as a shopper, keeping in mind both your strengths and weaknesses.

9. Write a comparison-contrast of your shopping methods and those of some member of your family or a neighbor.

10. Write an analysis of the psychology used in advertising on television or in the magazines.

DYING FOR DEAR OLD —

HEYWOOD BROUN —✷{

A young man is being supported by two comrades as he limps across a
field. It would not be stretching a point to call him a boy, as he is just
past nineteen. His face is grimed and bloody and one foot drags behind
him. He is crying. Not because of his injury, mind you, for this is a
deeper hurt. A cause for which he has fought is going down in defeat.
After the grave disaster of this afternoon his team has lost all claim to
the football championship of Cambridge, New Haven, and Princeton,
N. J.

He is young, you say, and will soon get over the tragedy which has
come upon him. I am not so sure of that. I remember the man who
dropped the punt during my Freshman year at Harvard. Everybody
thought Yale would win easily, but the crimson line was holding beyond
all expectations. The score was 0 to 0 and then this man came into the
game. The first play to follow was a punt by the Yale fullback. This man
had the ball squarely in his arms. He dropped it. Down flashed a Yale
end and in six rushes the ball was carried over the line. There was no
further scoring. Yale won.

All this happened in November, and in June there wandered about
the yard an unhappy soul who was known to all his fellows as "the man
who dropped the punt." He was a senior and it may be that graduation
brought some release, although it must have been hard for him to find
a spot in the United States to which the news of his mishap had never
carried. Fate had been harsh to him but not unscrupulous, exactly. He
did drop the punt. The true protagonist of the tragedy was another. He
might have been spared, for at the time his brother dropped the punt
this one had not yet matriculated at Harvard. That made no difference.
The tradition endured. During his four years of college life he was known
universally as "the brother of the man who dropped the punt."

And in all seriousness I advance the surmise that there are middle-
aged men in this country who have been a little embittered and shaken
for thirty years because of the fact that in some critical football game
they acquitted themselves badly. The team on which they played was
beaten.

I don't think this is a fantastic assumption. Unless he grows up to be
President, or defendant in an important murder trial, the college football player is likely to receive far more extensive and searching newspaper

publicity during his undergraduate days than at any other period of his life. He is called upon to face an emotional crisis in his life and to be watched by seventy thousand as he faces it. On the following day several million people will read of what he did. The quarterback who calls for a plunge through center will be publicly denounced as dull-witted if the play is piled up just short of the goal line. To stumble in the spotlight never did anybody any good, and if the man who fails happens to be nineteen years old he may get an ego bruise which will leave him permanently tender. And if he succeeds brilliantly he may be no better off. The American community is cluttered with ineffective young men who gave their souls to learn dropkicking and then found that there was no future in it.

The football player is not permitted to take any big game casually. Emotionalizing his men is accepted by the coach as a necessary part of his functions. "I was assigned to work on a big halfback," a former football star at Harvard told me. "He was a good defensive player but in the early games he didn't seem to show much fire. He was a lonely sort of fellow and it took me some time to find a line to get going on. We talked awhile and he told me that he came from Weston, Massachusetts. I said to him, 'My brother lives in Weston, and when you get in that game tomorrow I want you to play so that he and everybody else in Weston will be proud of you. You don't want to disgrace my brother in Weston, do you?'

"It was perfectly true that I did have a brother in Weston," my football friend continued, "and the angle I took worked all right. In fact it worked a little too well. After I'd been talking about Weston for quite a time this big halfback began to cry. I couldn't get him to stop. He was crying the next morning when we got out to the field and the doctor wouldn't let him attend the talk before the game. The doctor had to walk him up and down the sidelines to get him quieted down. Still he did go in and play a whale of a game."

I've always wanted to get an exact transcript of the parting words of a head coach to his men or his subsequent speech between the halves. I do know one but it was delivered to the squad of a comparatively small college. Just before the North Carolina eleven took the gridiron against Harvard their coach said to his players, "I want you boys to remember that every man on the Harvard team is a Republican."

But in this case oratory failed. The game was a conventional Republican landslide. More effective was an address delivered to another Southern team which invaded the North. On this occasion the coach relinquished his privilege of providing the last words and called an old gentleman into the locker room. And the voice of the veteran rang out like a trumpet call. He spoke of the Civil War and of how the South had held the Yankees back for four years. There was a line not to be split by any Yankee plunger. And the sons of Rebs could do it again. The old man called on the excited youngsters to remember Stonewall Jackson and Robert E. Lee. They remembered and played gloriously but later there was hard feeling, for the discovery was made that the old man had never served with any of the great commanders whom he mentioned but had actually marched with Sherman from Atlanta to the Sea.

Coaches are fond of saying, "I want you boys to fight and to keep on fighting." If asked to explain his precise meaning the coach would undoubtedly answer with complete sincerity, "I told them to play hard." But it does not always work that way. Only too often the instructions are taken all too literally. Football grows cleaner but Spotless Town is still a long march ahead. And when a young man deliberately injures an opposing player by the use of foul tactics there are accessories before the fact. Graduates who insisted loudly that "Dear Old—" must have a winning team, and coaches who said that defeat would sully the honor of the institution, must share in the blame. It isn't possible to rouse impressionable youth right up to the point of being ready to die for "Dear Old—" and not have a few of them, in the heat of battle, come to the decision that some of the foe ought at least to be maimed for the same good cause.

In spite of the stiff penalty provided by the rules, slugging continues. The officials can't see everything. Again and again players are tackled after they have crossed the sidelines and the whistle has blown. Men who are down get jumped upon. To be sure there is a difference between hard football and dirty football. When one watches the big games from way up on the rims of bowls and stadiums he is likely to have a good deal of trouble in detecting just where honest ardor ceases and foul play begins. I have observed, however, that star players tend to get injured a little more often than those of slighter worth. To be sure, the burdens of attack and defense fall more frequently to the stars, but this is not the only reason. Football, even under strict observance of the rules, permits the practice of disarming the enemy by injuring his most conspicuous players.

And in addition to physically dirty play there are other devices not wholly glamorous. A great college coach taught his scrub team to curse the varsity players most foully through an entire week of practice. "It worked well," explained a veteran of that eleven. "When we got into the big game that Saturday I never paid any attention to the names they were calling me. I don't care about being called names like that, but the practice made me used to it. The coach told us not to listen to anything but the signals and to go through with our assignments. They did all the cursing and we won the game."

And if all this is well founded, why is college football looked upon as the very flower and pattern of the highest sporting ideals in America? I don't know why. I like to watch college football and I can get emotional about it, but when I want moral stimulus and confirmation for my faith in the fundamental romanticism of man I go to see professional baseball. There have been scandals in the big leagues and even the most worthy and honest player is paid for his performances on the diamond. That doesn't matter. The distinction between the amateur and the professional cannot be reduced to a simple formula. In any field of endeavor your true and authentic amateur is a man who plays a game gleefully. I have never seen any college player who seemed to get half so much fun out of football as Babe Ruth derives from baseball. Ruth is able to contribute this gusto to his game spontaneously. Nobody makes him a set speech in the dressing room before he embarks to meet his test. The fans will not spell out "N-E-W Y-O-R-K" with colored handkerchiefs to inspirit him. There will be no songs about hitting the line. Indeed, Ruth will not even be asked to die for the cause he represents.

Instead of running out at top speed, Babe Ruth may be observed ambling quite slowly in the general direction of the diamond. He approaches a day's work. This thing before him is a job and it would not be fitting for him to run. But a little later you may chance to see a strange thing happen. The professional ball players take up their daily tasks. Soon, in the cause of duty, Ruth is called upon to move from right center all the way to the edge of the foul line. And now he is running. To the best of my knowledge and belief there is no current gridiron hero who runs with the entire earnestness of Ruth. Once I saw him charge full tilt against the wall of the Yankee Stadium. It was a low wall and Ruth's big body was so inextricably committed to forward motion that a wall was insufficient to quell the purpose inhering in the moving mass. And so his head and shoulders went over the barrier and, after a time, his feet followed. The resulting tumble must have been at least as vicious as any tackle ever visited upon a charging halfback. But for Ruth there was no possibility of time out. He could not ask so much as the indulgence of a sponge or a paper drinking cup. Shaking the disorders out of his spinning head, he tumbled himself back over the wall again and threw a runner out at the plate.

It is my impression that in the savage charge up to the wall and over, Ruth was wholly in the grip of the amateur spirit. If he had stopped short of the terrific tumble his pay would have still continued. To me there is nothing very startling in the fact that young men manage to commit themselves wholeheartedly to sport without hope of financial return. That is a commonplace. Recruiting volunteer workers for any cause is no trouble at all. I grow more sentimental over a quality much rarer in human experience. I give my admiration utterly to that man who can put the full sweep of effort into a job even though he is paid for it.

The bleeding right-tackle making a last stand on the goal line is to me a lesser figure than Walter Johnson staving off the attack of the Giants in the final game of the World's Series. For, as I look at it, the bleeding tackle is fighting merely for the honor and glory of his college. My mind will not accept him as a satisfactory symbol of any larger issue. But when Johnson pitched I felt that the whole samurai tradition was at stake. Once I shook hands with Walter Johnson and he remarked that the late summer had been a handicap for pitchers. Nothing more was said and I got no direct personal emanation from the man which convinced me that I was in the presence of true greatness. It never was the real Johnson but only the fictional one which captured my imagination. He was the Prince of Pitchers and the Strikeout King. From Montana he came to the big leagues to throw a baseball faster than it had ever been thrown before. And as a boy I read of how the hands of his catcher were bruised and maimed by the ordeal of receiving this mighty delivery.

And so Johnson became a demigod, and I am always sad when the gods die. I saw Johnson sicken under torture as the Giants scourged him. I watched him driven to the dugout in defeat. And then I saw him come back from his cavern revivified with all his old magic. This demigod was alive again and before me was played out a solar myth. So it had been with Buddha and Osiris. There is resiliency in the soul of man and he may lie down to bleed awhile and return refreshed. College football is just a game; professional baseball can rise to the height of a religious experience.

And it is a religion with only the scantiest bonds of ritual. It is incumbent upon the faithful to stretch in the seventh inning. Beyond complying with that one easy ceremony, the rooter has no responsibility in this Quaker meeting. If he chooses to sit silent that is permissible. Only when the spirit truly summons him is there any necessity of shouting. And so I find the emotion of a big-league ball game far more genuine and deep rooted than at any college football encounter. All shade and sensitivity is sacrificed in football by the pernicious practice of regimentation. "A long cheer with three Harvards on the end," cries the man in the white sweater through his megaphone. It is entirely possible that at the precise moments he calls upon me and my fellows to declare ourselves there is stored up in none of us more than a short cheer. It may even be that we have no inclination to cheer at all. Still, the duty is heavy upon us and we must render lipservice.

Before the afternoon is done the vilest sort of hypocrisy will be forced upon us. When the team in blue comes out upon the gridiron we shall all be called upon to render them a long cheer and to add three "Yale's" for courtesy. This is in violation of the deeper feelings of the human heart. We wish no success to Yale. At the mass meeting eloquent speakers have pointed out that it is imperative to the honor of Harvard that

Yale shall be turned back from our gates. Already we have sung of our intention to smash, bleach, and ride them down. And here we are called upon to cheer them. It is too distracting. Ambivalency is not a condition which one cares to celebrate at the top of his voice.

The psychology of baseball is much more simple and more honest. The Washington rooter makes no pretense of wishing the Giants well. He pays them the compliment of thorough-going opposition. In the first game of the last World's Series two home runs were made by New York players. It was as if a lace handkerchief had been tossed into the Grand Canyon. This was an aggressive silence. A sincere horror and anguish struck forty thousand people into a muteness which fairly throbbed. They made no dishonest pretense of polite applause but maintained instead an honorable silence.

And yet your baseball player and your baseball fan never take defeat in any such tragic spirit as the football collegian. Finality is so long delayed. The game which is lost may be cancelled by victory on the succeeding day. And all this serves to create in the mind of the impressionable a picture of life more accurate than that which is conveyed by football. Defeat is a portion of every man born into the world. He must learn to accept it and, if he is to amount to much in his community, he must get from every check a certain stimulus to appeal from the decision. There is no use crying over spilt milk because it is no great trouble to run around the corner and get another bottle. As our Salvation Army friends say, "A man may be down but he's never out." That won't do for a football proverb. A team can be both. Princeton, let us say, has just run rings around Harvard. The final whistle has blown. From this there can be no appeal. The issue may not be tried again. The teams will not meet for another year and then many a new figure will be in the lineup of either side. Here is a finality which is disturbing. The Harvard rooters have no recourse except to say that football is not so terribly important and that anyway Harvard still has a better English department.

I arranged that my small son should first come into contact with sport by watching professional baseball. One reason is wholly unconnected with ethics. When he asks questions I am better prepared to answer them. But beyond that I don't want him to think of a game as something which leaves two or three young men stretched on their backs in the wake of every smashing play. I cannot think up any good reason, suitable to his immature years, why these young men should submit to such an ordeal. The chairman of the football committee at a great Eastern University explained to a mass meeting that preparedness was the chief justification for intercollegiate football. He said that unless the young men of America submitted to the arduous discipline and drill of training and the hard knocks of fighting football, we should have no adequate officers for our next war. But I won't want to use that reasoning on my small son. I have tried to enlist him in the determined ranks of those who insist that there will be no next war.

Only once did I ever hear of an official football speech which met with my entire approval. It was made by a Harvard captain. His team had lost to Yale but by a smaller score than was expected. It had been a fast and interesting game. At the dinner when the team broke training the captain said, "We lost to Yale but I think we had a satisfactory season. We have had fun out of football and it seems to me that ought to be the very best reason for playing the game."

A shocked silence followed his remarks. He was never invited to come to Cambridge to assist in the coaching of any future Harvard eleven. His heresy was profound. He had practically intimated that being defeated was less than tragic.

Suggestions

1. Summarize the thesis of "Dying for Dear Old —," showing how it is not only stated several times but also reinforced by the tone and the concrete examples.

2. The tone ranges from the openly sarcastic to the subtly ironic. Locate several spots in the essay that illustrate varying degrees of the comic tone and decide whether each is appropriate to its context.

3. What bits of internal evidence for dating this essay can you find in it?

4. How does the title reinforce the tone?

5. Evaluate the speaker's reasons for taking his small son to a professional baseball rather than a college football game.

6. Comment: "In any field of endeavor your true and authentic amateur is a man who plays a game gleefully."

7. Using your own observations, write a comparison of the amateur and the professional.

8. Write an essay about the relevance of this attack on college football to the situation as you know it today.

LAUGHING AT ANIMALS

KONRAD Z. LORENZ

From KING SOLOMON'S RING *by Konrad Z. Lorenz.* © *1952 by Thomas Y. Crowell Company and Methuen and Company, Ltd. Reprinted by permission. Translation by Marjorie Kerr Wilson.*

It is seldom that I laugh at an animal, and when I do, I usually find out afterwards that it was at myself, at the human being whom the animal has portrayed in a more or less pitiless caricature, that I have laughed. We stand before the monkey house and laugh, but we do not laugh at the sight of a caterpillar or a snail, and when the courtship antics of a lusty greylag gander are so incredibly funny, it is only that our human youth behaves in a very similar fashion.

The initiated observer seldom laughs at the bizarre in animals. It often annoys me when visitors at a Zoo or Aquarium laugh at an animal that, in the course of its evolutionary adaptation, has developed a body form which now deviates from the usual. The public is then deriding things which, to me, are holy: the riddles of the Genesis, the Creation and the Creator. The grotesque forms of a chameleon, a puffer, or an anteater awake in me feelings of awed wonder, but not of amusement.

Of course I have laughed at unexpected drollness, although such amusement is in itself not less stupid than that of the public that annoys me. When the queer, land-climbing fish Periophthalmus was first sent to me and I saw how one of these creatures leaped, not out of the water basin, but on to its edge and, raising its head with its pug-like face towards me, sat there perched, staring at me with its goggling, piercing eyes, then I laughed heartily. Can you imagine what it is like when a fish, a real and unmistakable vertebrate fish, first of all sits on a perch, like a canary, then turns its head towards you like a higher terrestrial animal, like anything but a fish, and then, to crown all, fixes you with a binocular stare? This same stare gives the owl its characteristic and proverbially wise expression, because, even in a bird, the two-eyed gaze is unexpected. But here, too, the humor lies more in the caricature of the human, than in the actual drollness of the animal.

In the study of the behavior of the higher animals, very funny situations are apt to arise, but it is inevitably the observer, and not the animal, that plays the comical part. The comparative ethologist's method in dealing with the most intelligent birds and mammals often necessitates a complete neglect of the dignity usually to be expected in a scientist. Indeed, the uninitiated, watching the student of behavior in operation, often cannot be blamed for thinking that there is madness in his method. It is only my reputation for harmlessness, shared with the other village idiot, which has saved me from the mental home. But in defense of the villagers of Altenberg I must recount a few little stories.

I was experimenting at one time with young mallards to find out why artificially incubated and freshly hatched ducklings of this species, in contrast to similarly treated greylag goslings, are unapproachable and shy. Greylag goslings unquestioningly accept the first living being whom they meet as their mother, and run confidently after him. Mallards, on the contrary, always refused to do this. If I took from the incubator freshly hatched mallards, they invariably ran away from me and pressed themselves in the nearest dark corner. Why? I remembered that I had once let a muscovy duck hatch a clutch of mallard eggs and that the tiny mallards had also failed to accept this foster-mother. As soon as they were dry, they had simply run away from her and I had trouble enough to catch these crying, erring children. On the other hand, I once let a fat white farmyard duck hatch out mallards and the little wild things ran just as happily after her as if she had been their real mother. The secret must have lain in her call note, for, in external appearance, the domestic duck was quite as different from a mallard as was the muscovy; but what she had in common with the mallard (which, of course, is the wild progenitor of our farmyard duck) were her vocal expressions. Though, in the process of domestication, the duck has altered considerably in color pattern and body form, its voice has remained practically the same. The inference was clear: I must quack like a mother mallard in order to make the little ducks run after me. No sooner said than done. When, one Whit-Saturday, a brood of purebred young mallards was due to hatch, I put the eggs in the incubator, took the babies, as soon as they were dry, under my personal care, and quacked for them the mother's call-note in my best Mallardese. For hours on end I kept it up, for half the day. The quacking was successful. The little ducks lifted their gaze confidently towards me, obviously had no fear of me this time, and as, still quacking, I drew slowly away from them, they also set themselves obediently in motion and scuttled after me in a tightly huddled group, just as ducklings follow their mother. My theory was indisputably proved. The freshly hatched ducklings have an inborn reaction to the call-note, but not to the optical picture of the mother. Anything that emits the right quack note will be considered as mother, whether it is a fat white Pekin duck or a still fatter man. However, the substituted object must not exceed a certain height. At the beginning of these experiments, I had sat myself down in the grass amongst the ducklings and, in order to make them follow me, had dragged myself, sitting, away from them. As soon, however, as I stood up and tried, in a standing posture, to lead them on, they gave up, peered searchingly on all sides, but not upwards towards me and it was not long before they began that penetrating piping of abandoned ducklings that we are accustomed simply to call "crying." They were unable to adapt themselves to the fact that their foster-mother had become so tall. So I was forced to move along, squatting low, if I wished them to follow me. This was not very comfortable; still less comfortable was the fact that the mallard mother quacks unintermittently. If I ceased for even the space of half a minute from my melodious "Quahg, gegegegeg, Quahg, gegegegeg," the necks of the ducklings became longer and longer corresponding exactly to "long faces" in human children—and did I then not immediately recommence quacking, the shrill weeping began anew. As soon as I was silent, they seemed to think that I had died, or perhaps that I loved them no more: cause enough for crying! The ducklings, in contrast to the greylag goslings, were most demanding and tiring charges, for, imagine a two-hour walk with such children, all the time squatting low and quacking without interruption! In the interests of science I submitted myself literally for hours on end to this ordeal. So it came about, on a certain Whit-Sunday, that, in company with my ducklings, I was wandering about squatting and quacking, in a May-green meadow at the upper part of our garden. I was congratulating myself on the obedience and exactitude with which my ducklings came waddling after me, when I suddenly looked up and saw the garden fence framed by a row of dead-white faces: a group of tourists was standing at the fence and staring horrified in my direction. Forgivable! For all they could see was a big man with a beard dragging himself, crouching, round the meadow, in figures of eight, glancing constantly over his shoulder and quacking—but the ducklings, the all-revealing and all-explaining ducklings were hidden in the tall spring grass from the view of the astonished crowd.

Jackdaws long remember someone who has laid hands on them and thereby elicited a "rattling" reaction. Therein lay a considerable impediment to the ringing of the young jackdaws reared in my colony. When I took them out of the nest to mark them with aluminium rings, I could not help the older jackdaws seeing me and at once raising their voices to a wild rattling concert. How was I to stop the birds developing a permanent shyness for me as a result of the ringing procedure, a state of affairs which would have been immeasurably detrimental to my work? The solution was obvious: disguise. But what? Again quite easy. It lay ready to hand in a box in the loft and was very well suited for my purpose, although, normally, it was only brought out every sixth of December to celebrate the old Austrian festival of St. Nicholas and the Devil. It was a gorgeous, black, furry devil's costume with a mask covering the whole head, complete with horns and tongue, and a long devil's tail which stuck well out from the body. I wonder what you would think if, on a beautiful June day, you suddenly heard from the gabled roof of a high house a wild rattling noise and, looking up, you saw Satan himself, equipped with horns, tail and claws, his tongue hanging out with the heat, climbing from chimney to chimney, surrounded by a swarm of black birds making ear-splitting rattling cries. I think this whole alarming impression disguised the fact that the devil was fixing, by means of a forceps, aluminium rings to the legs of young jackdaws, and then replacing the birds carefully in their nests. When I had finished the ringing, I saw for the first time that a large crowd of people had collected in the village street, and were looking up with expressions just as aghast as those of the tourists at the garden fence. As I would have defeated my own object by now disclosing my identity, I just gave a friendly wag of my devil's tail and disappeared through the trapdoor of the loft.

The third time that I was in danger of being delivered up to the psychiatric clinic was the fault of my big yellow-crested cockatoo Koka. I had bought this beautiful and very tame bird shortly before Easter, for a considerable sum of money. It was many weeks before the poor fellow had overcome the mental disturbances caused by his long imprisonment. At first he could not realize that he was no longer fettered and could now move about freely. It was a pitiable sight to see this proud creature sitting on a branch, ever and anon preparing himself for flight, but not daring to take off, because he could not believe that he was no longer on the chain. When at last he had overcome this inward resistance he became a lively and exuberant being and developed a strong attachment for my person. As soon as he was let out of the room in which we still shut him up at night-time, he flew straight off to find me, displaying thereby an astonishing intelligence. In quite a short time he realized where I was probably to be found. At first he flew to my bedroom window, and, if I was not there, down to the duck pond; in short he visited all the sites of my morning inspection at the various animal pens in our research station. This determined quest was not without danger to the cockatoo because, if he failed to find me, he extended his search farther and farther and had several times lost his way on such occasions. Accordingly, my fellow workers had strict instructions not to let the bird out during my absence.

One Saturday in June, I got off the train from Vienna at Altenberg station, in the midst of a gathering of bathers, such as often flock to our village at fine week-ends. I had gone only a few steps along the street and the crowd had not yet dispersed when, high above me in the air, I saw a bird whose species I could not at first determine. It flew with slow, measured wing-beats, varied at set intervals by longer periods of gliding. It seemed too heavy to be a buzzard; for a stork, it was not big enough and, even at that height, neck and feet should have been visible. Then the bird gave a sudden swerve so that the setting sun shone for a second full on the underside of the great wings which lit up like stars in the blue of the skies. The bird was white. By Heaven, it was my cockatoo! The steady movements of his wings clearly indicated that he was setting out on a long-distance flight. What should I do? Should I call to the bird? Well, have you ever heard the flight-call of the greater yellow-crested cockatoo? No? But you have probably heard pig-killing after the old method. Imagine pig squealing at its most voluminous, taken up by a microphone and magnified many times by a good loudspeaker. A man can imitate it quite successfully, though somewhat feebly, by bellowing at the top of his voice "O-ah." I had already proved that the cockatoo understood this imitation and promptly "came to heel." But would it work at such a height? A bird always has great difficulty in making the decision to fly downwards at a steep angle. To yell, or not to yell, that was the question. If I yelled and the bird came down, all would be well, but what if it sailed calmly on through the clouds? How would I then explain my song to the crowd of people? Finally, I did yell. The people around me stood still, rooted to the spot. The bird hesitated for a moment on outstretched wings, then, folding them, it descended in one dive and landed upon my outstretched arm. Once again I was master of the situation.

On another occasion, the frolics of this bird gave me quite a serious fright. My father, by that time an old man, used to take his siesta at the foot of a terrace on the south-west side of our house. For medical reasons, I was never quite happy to think of him exposed to the glaring mid-day sun, but he would let nobody break him of his old habit. One day, at his siesta time, I heard him, from his accustomed place, swearing like a trooper, and as I raced round the corner of the house, I saw the old gentleman swaying up the drive in a cramped position, bending forwards, his arms tightly folded about his waist. "In heaven's name, are you ill?" "No," came the embittered response, "I am not ill, but that confounded creature has bitten all the buttons off my trousers while I was fast asleep!" And that is what had happened. Eye-witnesses at the scene of the crime discovered, laid out in buttons, the whole outline of the old professor: here the arms, there the waistcoat, and here, unmistakably, the buttons off his trousers.

One of the nicest cockatoo-tricks which, in fanciful inventiveness, equaled the experiments of monkey or human children, arose from the ardent love of the bird for my mother who, so long as she stayed in the garden in summertime, knitted without stopping. The cockatoo seemed to understand exactly how the soft skeins worked and what the wool was for. He always seized the free end of the wool with his beak and then flew lustily into the air, unravelling the ball behind him. Like a paper kite with a long tail, he climbed high and then flew in regular circles round the great lime tree which stood in front of our house. Once, when nobody was there to stop him he encircled the tree, right up to its summit, with brightly colored woolen strands which it was impossible to disentangle from the wide-spreading foliage. Our visitors used to stand in mute astonishment before this tree, and were unable to understand how and why it had been thus decorated.

The cockatoo paid court to my mother in a very charming way, dancing round her in the most grotesque fashion, folding and unfolding his beautiful crest and following her wherever she went. If she were not there, he sought her just as assiduously as he had been used, in his early days, to search for me. Now my mother had no less than four sisters. One day these aunts, in company with some equally aged ladies of their acquaintance, were partaking of tea in the veranda of our house. They sat at a huge round table, a plate of luscious home-grown strawberries in front of each, and in the middle of the table, a large, very shallow bowl of finest icing sugar. The cockatoo, who was flying accidentally or wittingly past, espied, from without, my mother who was presiding at this festive board. The next moment, with a perilous dive, he steered himself through the doorway, which, though wide, was nevertheless narrower than the span of his wings. He intended to land before my mother on the table where he was accustomed to sit and keep her company while she knitted; but this time he found the runway encumbered with numerous obstacles to flying technique and, into the bargain, he was in the midst of unknown faces. He considered the situation, pulled himself up abruptly in mid-air, hovering over the table like a helicopter, then turning on his own axis, he opened the throttle again and the next second had disappeared. So also had the icing sugar from the shallow bowl, out of which the propeller wind had wafted every grain. And around the table sat seven powdered ladies, seven rococo ladies whose faces, like lepers', were white as snow and who held their eyes tight shut. Beautiful!

Suggestions

1. "Laughing at Animals" is an essay describing events (experiments of a comparative ethologist), with touches of characterization (of both the speaker and his animals) and a process (specific approaches to and results of experiments with mallards, cockatoos, etc.). Examine the essay for elements of other types of essays you are familiar with.

2. Can the first two paragraphs be said to advance a thesis? If not, explain their function in the total essay.

3. What devices are used to unify the various episodes, keeping them from being disconnected stories?

4. Analyze the personification of the cockatoo in the final episode. How is it built up?

5. What evidence is there that the speaker regards his profession, despite the humor that it sometimes provokes, with the utmost seriousness?

6. Describe the reaction of the villagers to the speaker's experiments. Does this reaction remain consistent throughout all episodes?

7. Explain the title, relating it to the subject of the essay.

8. Write an essay about any unusual experiences you have had with pets. Unify it with some generalizations you could draw about either pets or people.

THE WORLD OF THE WHIGS

DAVID CECIL ⟶

From MELBOURNE *by Lord David Cecil.* © *1939, 1954, used by special permission of the publishers, The Bobbs-Merrill Company, Inc. and Constable & Company, Ltd.*

The great Whig country houses of the eighteenth and early nineteenth centuries are among the most conspicuous monuments of English history. Ornate and massive, with their pedimented porticoes, their spreading balustraded wings, they dominate the landscape round them with a magnificent self-assurance. Nor are their interiors less imposing. Their colonnaded entrance halls, whence the Adam staircase sweeps up beneath a fluted dome; their cream and gilt libraries piled with sumptuous editions of the classics; their orangeries peopled with casts from the antique; their saloons hung with yellow silk, and with ceiling and doorways painted in delicate arabesque by Angelica Kauffmann—all combine to produce an extraordinary impression of culture and elegance and established power.

Yet, they are not palaces. There is something easy-going and unofficial about them. Between library and saloon one comes on little rooms, full of sporting prints and comfortable untidiness; the bedrooms upstairs are friendly with chintz and flowered wallpaper. Even the great rooms themselves, with their roomy writing-tables, their armchairs, their tables piled with albums and commonplace books, seem designed less for state occasions than for private life—for leisure and lounging, for intimate talk and desultory reading. And the portraits that glow down from the walls exhibit a similar character. The gentlemen lean back in their hunting coats, the ladies stroll in their parks with spaniels snapping at the ribbons that dangle from the garden hats slung on their arms. In big and in detail these houses convey an effect of splendid naturalness. In this they are typical of the society which was their creator.

The Whig aristocracy was a unique product of English civilization. It was before all things a governing class. At a time when economic power was concentrated in the landed interest, the Whigs were among the biggest landowners: their party was in office for the greater part of the eighteenth century; during this period they possessed a large proportion of the seats in the House of Commons; they produced more ambassadors and officers of state than the rest of England put together. And they lived on a scale appropriate to their power. "A man," said one of their latest representatives, "can jog along on £40,000 a year." And jog very well they did. They possessed, most of them, a mansion in London and two or three in the country; they moved through the world attended by a vast retinue of servants, of secretaries and chaplains, of companions, librarians, and general hangers-on; they never traveled but in their own carriages; they kept open house to a continuous stream of guests, whom they entertained in the baroque and lavish style approved by their contemporaries.

For the elaboration of their life was increased by the period they lived in. The eighteenth century, that accomplished age, did not believe in the artless and the austere. In its view the good man, or, as they would have phrased it, "man of sense and taste," was he whose every activity was regulated in the light of a trained judgment and the experience of the wise in his own and former ages. From his earliest years the Whig nobleman was subjected to a careful education. He was grounded in the classics first by a tutor, then at Eton, then at the University. After this he went abroad for two years' grand tour to learn French and good manners in the best society of the Continent. His sisters learnt French and manners equally thoroughly at home; and their demeanor was further improved by a course of deportment. The Whigs' taste was in harmony with the ideal that guided their education. They learnt to admire the grand style in painting, the "correct" in letters, the Latin tradition in oratory. And in everything they paid strict attention to form. Since life to them was so secure and so pleasant, the Whig aristocrats tended to take its fundamental values very much for granted; they concentrated rather on how to live. And here again their ideal was not an artless one. Their customs, their mode of speech, their taste in decoration, their stylish stiff clothes, are alike marked by a character at once polished and precise, disciplined and florid. If one of them writes a note, it is rounded with a graceful phrase; their most extempore speeches are turned with a flourish of rotund rhetoric.

Yet—and here it is that it differs from those of similar societies on the Continent—theirs was not an unreal life, no Watteau-like[1] paradise of exquisite trifling and fastidious idleness. For one thing it had its roots in the earth. Founded as their position was on landed property, the Whig aristocracy was never urban. They passed at least half the year in their country seats, and there they occupied themselves in the ordinary avocations of country life. The ladies interested themselves in their children and visited the poor; the gentlemen looked after their estates, rode to hounds, and administered from the local bench justice to poachers and pilferers. Their days went by, active, out-of-door, unceremonious; they wore ridingboots as often as silk stockings. Moreover, they were always in touch with the central and serious current of contemporary life. The fact that they were a governing class meant that they had to govern. The Whig lord was as often as not a minister, his eldest son an M.P., his second attached to a foreign embassy, so that their houses were alive with the effort and hurry of politics. Red Foreign Office boxes strewed the library tables; at any time of day or night a courier might come galloping up with critical news, and the minister must post off to London to attend a Cabinet meeting. He had his work in the country too. He was a landlord and magistrate, often a lord lieutenant, while every few years would come a general election when his sons, if not himself, might have to sally forth to stand on the hustings and be pelted with eggs and dead cats by the free and independent electors of the neighboring borough. Indeed his was not a protected existence. The eighteenth century was the age of clubs; and Whig society itself was a sort of club, exclusive, but in which those who managed to achieve membership lived on equal terms—a rowdy, rough-and-tumble club, full of conflict and plain speaking, where people were expected to stand up for themselves and take and give hard knocks. At Eton the little dukes and earls cuffed and bullied one another like street urchins. As mature persons in their country homes, or in the pillared rooms of Brooks's Club, their intercourse continued more politely, yet with equal familiarity, while their House of Commons life passed in a robust atmosphere of combat and crisis and defeat. The Whigs despised the royal family; and there was certainly none of the hush and punctilio of court existence about them. Within the narrow limits of their world they were equalitarians.

Their life, in fact, was essentially a normal life, compounded of the same elements as those of general humanity, astir with the same clamor and clash and aspiration and competition as filled the streets round their august dwellings. Only, it was normal life played out on a colossal stage and with magnificent scenery and costumes. Their houses were homes, but homes with sixty bedrooms, set in grounds five miles round; they fought to keep their jobs, but the jobs were embassies and prime min-

[1] Resembling the paintings of Jean Antoine Watteau, 1684-1721.

isterships; their sons went to the same universities as humbler students, but were distinguished from them there by a nobleman's gold-tasselled mortar-board. When the Duke of Devonshire took up botany, he sent out a special expedition to the East Indies to search for rare plants; Lord Egremont liked pictures, so he filled a gallery with Claudes and Correggios; young Lord Palmerston was offered the Chancellorship of the Exchequer a year or two after entering Parliament.

This curiously blended life produced a curiously blended type of character. With so many opportunities for action, its interests were predominantly active. Most of the men were engaged in politics. And the women—for they lived to please the men—were political too. They listened, they sympathized, they advised; through them two statesmen might make overtures to each other, or effect a reconciliation. But politics then were not the life sentence to hard labor that in our iron age they have become. Parliament sat for only a few months in the year; and even during the session, debates did not start till the late afternoon. The Whigs had the rest of their time to devote to other things. If they were sporting, they raced and hunted; if interested in agriculture, they farmed on an ambitious scale; if artistic, they collected marbles and medals; if intellectual, they read history and philosophy; if literary, they composed compliments in verse and sonorous, platitudinous orations. But the chief of their spare time was given up to social life. They gave balls, they founded clubs, they played cards, they got up private theatricals; they cultivated friendship and every variety, platonic and less platonic, of the art of love. Their ideal was the Renaissance ideal of the whole man, whose aspiration it is to make the most of every advantage, intellectual and sensual, that life has to offer.

In practice, of course, this ideal was not so broad as it sounds. The Whigs could not escape the limitations imposed by the splendor of their circumstances. Like all aristocrats they tended to be amateurs. When life is so free and so pleasant, a man is not likely to endure the drudgery necessary to make himself really expert in any one thing. Even in those affairs of state which took up most of the Whigs' time, they troubled little with the dry details of economic theory or administrative practice. Politics to them meant, first of all, personalities and, secondly, general principles. And general principles to them were an occasion for expression rather than thought. They did not dream of questioning the fundamental canons of Whig orthodoxy. All believed in ordered liberty, low taxation, and the enclosure of land; all disbelieved in despotism and democracy. Their only concern was to restate these indisputable truths in a fresh and effective fashion.

Again, their taste was a little philistine. Aristocratic taste nearly always is. Those whose ordinary course of life is splendid and satisfying find it hard to recognize the deeper value of the exercises of the solitary imagination; art to them is not the fulfilment of the soul, but an ornamental appendage to existence. Moreover, the English nobility were too much occupied with practical affairs to achieve the fullest intellectual life. They admired what was elegant, sumptuous, and easy to understand: portraits that were good likenesses and pleasing decorations, architecture which appropriately housed a stately life. In books, they appreciated acute, wittily phrased observation of human nature, or noble sentiments expressed in flowing periods: Cicero, Pope, Horace, Burke. The strange and the harsh they dismissed immediately. Among contemporary authors they appreciated Jane Austen, condemned Crabbe, for the most part, as sordid and low, and neglected Blake almost entirely. If they had read him, they would not have liked him. For—it is another of their limitations —they were not spiritual. Their education did not encourage them to be; and, anyway, they found this world too absorbing to concern themselves much with the next. The bolder spirits among them were atheists. The average person accepted Christianity, but in a straightforward spirit, innocent alike of mysticism and theological exactitude.

Further, their circumstances did not encourage the virtues of self-control. Good living gave them zest; wealth gave them opportunity; and they threw themselves into their pleasures with an animal recklessness at once terrifying and exhilarating to a modern reader. The most respectable people often drank themselves under the table without shocking anyone. "Colonel Napier came in tonight as drunk as an owl," remarks Lady Sarah Napier of the staid middle-aged gentleman who was her husband. And their drinking was nothing to their gambling. Night after night they played loo and faro from early evening till the candles guttered pale in the light of the risen sun. Lord Stavordale lamented he had not been playing higher, on a night when he won £11,000 in a single hand at hazard. Georgiana, Duchess of Devonshire, cost her husband nearly £1,000,000 in card debts. Rich as they were, they often ruined themselves. The letters of the time are loud with lamentations about the duns coming in and the furniture going out. Nor was their sexual life of a kind to commend them to an austere morality. "I was afraid I was going to have the gout the other day," writes Lord Carlisle to a friend. "I believe I live too chaste: it is not a common fault with me." It was not a common fault with any of them. In fact, an unmarried man was thought unpleasantly queer if he did not keep under his protection some sprightly full-bosomed Kitty Clive or Mrs. Bellamy, whose embraces he repaid with a house in Montpelier Square, a box at the opera, and a smart cabriolet in which to drive her down to Brighthelmstone for a week's amorous relaxation. Nor did he confine himself to professional ladies of pleasure. Even unmarried girls like Lady Hester Stanhope were suspected of having lovers; among married women the practice was too common to stir comment. The historian grows quite giddy as he tries to disentangle the complications of heredity consequent on the free and easy habits of the English aristocracy. The Harley family, children of the Countess of Oxford, were known as the Harleian Miscellany [2] on account of the variety of fathers alleged to be responsible for their existence. The Duke of Devonshire had three children by the Duchess and two by Lady Elizabeth Foster, the Duchess one by Lord Grey; and most of them were brought up together in Devonshire House, each set of children with a surname of its own. "Emily, does it never strike you," writes Miss Pamela Fitzgerald in 1816, "the vices are wonderfully prolific among Whigs? There are such countless illegitimates, such a tribe of children of the mist." It is noteworthy that the author of this lively comment was a carefully brought-up young lady of the highest breeding. The free habits of these days encouraged free speech. "Comfortable girls," remarks a middle-aged lady of her growing nieces, "who like a dirty joke." And the men, as can be imagined, were a great deal freer than the women. For all their polish the Whigs were not refined people in the Victorian sense of the word.

It appears in other aspects of their lives. They could be extremely arrogant, treating their inferiors with a patrician insolence which seems to us the reverse of good breeding. Lady Catherine de Bourgh [3] was not the caricature that an ignorant person might suppose. Fashionable young men of refined upbringing amused themselves by watching fights where the Game Chicken battered the Tutbury Pet into unconsciousness with bare and blood-stained fists. And the pamphlets, the squibs, the appalling political cartoons that lay open in the most elegant drawing-rooms show that the ladies of the day were not squeamish either.

Still, unseemly as some of its manifestations were, one must admit that there is something extremely attractive in this earthy exuberance. And, as a matter of fact, it was the inevitable corollary of their virtues. English society had the merits of its defects. Its wide scope, its strong root in the earth, gave it an astounding, an irresistible vitality. For all their dissipation there was nothing decadent about these eighteenth-century aristocrats. Their excesses came from too much life, not too little. And it was the same vitality that gave them their predominance in public life. They took on the task of directing England's destinies with the same self-confident vigor that they drank and diced. It was this vigor that made Pitt Prime Minister at twenty-four years old,[4] that enabled the Foxites [5] to keep the flag of liberty flying against the united public opinion of a panic-stricken nation. Nor did they let their pleasures interfere with these more serious activities. After eighteen hours of uninterrupted gambling, Charles Fox would arrive at the House of Commons to electrify his

---

[2] The literal Harleian Miscellany is a collection of books and manuscripts, now in the British Museum, assembled by Lord Robert Harley (1661–1724) and his son.

[3] Haughty aunt of Fitzwilliam Darcy in Jane Austen's *Pride and Prejudice*.

[4] Pitt diverged from the Whigs in later life, but he was brought up among them and is, so far, representative of the Whig tradition.—*Cecil's note*.

[5] Followers of Charles James Fox, Member of Parliament from 1768 to 1806.

fellow members by a brilliant discourse on American taxation. Rakes and ladies of fashion intersperse their narratives of intrigue with discussions on politics, on literature, even on morals. For they were not unmoral. Their lapses came from passion, not from principle; and they are liable at any time to break out in contrite acknowledgments of guilt and artless resolutions for future improvement. Indeed it was one of the paradoxes created by their mixed composition that, though they were worldly, they were not sophisticated. Their elaborate manners masked simple reactions. Like their mode of life their characters were essentially natural: spontaneous, unintrospective, brimming over with normal feelings, love of home and family, loyalty, conviviality, desire for fame, hero-worship, patriotism. And they showed their feelings too. Happy creatures! They lived before the days of the stiff upper lip and the inhibited public-school Englishman. A manly tear stood in their eye at the story of a heroic deed; they declared their loves in a strain of flowery hyperbole. They were the more expressive from their very unself-consciousness. It never struck them that they needed to be inarticulate to appear sincere. They were equally frank about their less elevated sentiments. Eighteenth-century rationalism combined with rural common sense to make them robustly ready to face unedifying facts. And they declared their impressions with a brusque honesty, outstandingly characteristic of them. From Sir Robert Walpole, who encouraged coarse conversation on the ground that it was the only form of talk which everyone enjoyed, down to the Duke of Wellington, who described the army of his triumphs as composed of "the scum of the earth, enlisted for drink," the Augustan aristocracy, Whig and Tory alike, said what they thought with a superb disregard for public opinion. For if they were not original they were independent-minded. The conventions which bounded their lives were conventions of form only. Since they had been kings of their world from birth, they were free from the tiresome inhibitions that are induced by a sense of inferiority. Within the locked garden of their society, individuality flowered riotous and rampant. Their typical figures show up beside the muted introverts of today as clear-cut and idiosyncratic as characters in Dickens. They took for granted that you spoke your mind and followed your impulses. If these were odd, they were amused but not disapproving. They enjoyed eccentrics: George Selwyn, who never missed an execution, Beau Brummell, who took three hours to tie his cravat. The firm English soil in which they were rooted, the spacious freedom afforded by their place in the world, allowed personality to flourish in as many bold and fantastic shapes as it pleased.

But it was always a garden plant, a civilized growth. Whatever their eccentricities, the Whig nobles were never provincial and never uncouth. They had that effortless knowledge of the world that comes only to those who from childhood have been accustomed to move in a complex society, that delightful unassertive confidence possible only to people who have never had cause to doubt their social position. And they carried to the finest degree of cultivation those social arts which engaged so much of their time. Here we come to their outstanding distinction. They were the most agreeable society England has ever known. The character of their agreeability was of a piece with the rest of them: mundane, straightforward, a trifle philistine, largely concerned with gossip, not given to subtle analyses or flights of fancy. But it had all their vitality and all their sense of style. It was incomparably racy and spontaneous and accomplished, based solidly on a wide culture and experience, yet free to express itself in bursts of high spirits, in impulses of appreciation, in delicate movements of sentiment, in graceful compliments. For it had its grace—a virile classical grace like that of the Chippendale furniture which adorned its rooms, lending a glittering finish to its shrewd humor, its sharp-eyed observation, its vigorous disquisitions on men and things. Educated without pedantry, informal but not slipshod, polished but not precious, brilliant without fatigue, it combined in an easy perfection the charms of civilization and nature. Indeed the whole social life of the period shines down the perspective of history like some masterpiece of natural art—a prize bloom, nurtured in shelter and sunshine and the richest soil, the result of generations of breeding and blending, that spreads itself to the open sky in strength and beauty.

It was at its most characteristic in the middle of the century; it was at its most dazzling towards its close. by 1780 a new spirit [6] was rising in the world. Ossian had taught people to admire ruins and ravines, Rousseau to examine the processes of the heart; with unpowdered heads and the ladies in simple muslin dresses, they paced the woods meditating, in Cowper-like mood, on the tender influences of nature. Though they kept the style and good sense of their fathers, their sympathies were wider. At the same time their feelings grew more refined. The hardness which had marred the previous age dwindled. Gainsborough, not Hogarth, mirrored the taste of the time; [7] "sensibility" became a fashionable word. For a fleeting moment Whig society had a foot in two worlds and made the best of both of them. The lucid outline of eighteenth-century civilization was softened by the glow of the romantic dawn.

Dawn—but for them it was sunset. The same spirit that tinged them with their culminating glory was also an omen of their dissolution. For the days of aristocratic supremacy were numbered. By the iron laws which

[6] Romanticism: represented in the next sentence by *Fingal* and other prose poems supposedly the work of Ossian, a 3rd century bard, but largely the creations of James Macpherson (1736–1796); by Jean-Jacques Rousseau, author of *The New Eloise* and other works; and by William Cowper (1731–1800), author of *The Task* and other poems.

[7] Thomas Gainsborough (1727–1788) painted society portraits and agreeable landscapes; William Hogarth (1697–1764) is best known for his savage caricatures of the seamy side of London life.

condition the social structure of man's existence, it could last only as long as it maintained an economic predominance. With the coming of the Industrial Revolution this predominance began to pass from the landlords to other ranks of the community. Already by the close of the century go-ahead manufacturers in the north were talking of Parliamentary reform; already, in the upper rooms of obscure London alleys, working-men met together to clamor for liberty, equality, and fraternity. Within forty years of its zenith the Whig world was completely swept away. Only a few survivors lingered on to illustrate to an uncomprehending generation the charm of the past.

Suggestions

1. "The World of the Whigs" pictures 18th century life through a series of vividly representative details; in it a composite impression is built up by particulars. But these particulars lead to larger generalizations, as when the speaker says, "Like all aristocrats they tended to be amateurs" (¶8). What are some other of these larger generalizations? Describe their effect on the total essay.

2. "The World of the Whigs" is a composite definition, its effectiveness depending on many diverse elements. Can you point out character-sketches in it? descriptions of places? an account of an experience?

3. The composite description of an 18th century country house assumes in the reader a knowledge of architecture and interior decoration. If you are unfamiliar with the terms, look them up. How does this passage (¶¶1–2) set the tone for the rest of the essay? How would you characterize the ideal reader of this essay?

4. For what does this composite description (¶1) become a symbol? Is it appropriate, considering the facts given in the rest of the essay?

5. Examine the beginnings of each paragraph to determine transitions. Is a characteristic method used to give the essay coherence?

6. Does the speaker mention enough of the deficiencies of the Whigs to suggest that he is objective? How would you describe his tone?

7. Are any phases of Whig life mentioned but not adequately discussed?

8. Which paragraph near the end seems to you to be a recapitulation of everything mentioned in detail earlier?

9. Discuss the diction of the last two paragraphs. What mood does it suggest?

10. Explain: *hustings, Eton, philistine, loo, faro, corollary, Chippendale,* the sums of English money mentioned.

11. Write a contrast between 18th century life as presented in "The World of the Whigs" and 20th century life as interpreted by †"The Modern Climate of Opinion."

12. Write an essay about a particular historical period familiar to you, giving substance to your general picture by much concrete illustration.

I N D I R E C T I O N S

AN EMINENTLY REASONABLE SUGGESTION
of Incalculable Benefit to the Nation

DONALD MALCOLM   *First printed in* THE NEW REPUBLIC.
© *1958 by Donald Malcolm.*

We were sitting at our desk the other day and thinking of nothing special when, just like that, we discovered a way to end the recession and the Cold War at a single stroke. It seemed hard to believe at first, but subsequent examination of the idea has failed to turn up a flaw of any consequence. It merely requires, for its success, that the citizens of Russia accept, as gifts, all the automobiles this country can produce. And how can they refuse? If there is one impulse that the 20th Century has proved to be common to all mankind, it is the impulse to grip the wheel of a brand-new car and sally forth, with manifold toots of the horn, in search of high adventure. We may take it, therefore, that the cooperation of the Russians is assured. Nor does it seem likely that our own State Department would enter a demurrer. What objection could there possibly be to such a brilliant stroke of diplomacy? As a peaceful and conciliatory gesture, it would be worth a whole Himalaya of Summit meetings.

Then who, we wonder, could object to a plan to provide every Russian with a free automobile? Certainly not the Pentagon, whose experts would be quick to realize that, in times of peace, the auto is a perfect weapon. By means of it, this nation might easily inflict upon its truculent international rival as much damage as it regularly inflicts upon itself, and this is no small thing. Every year in America, traffic accidents kill some 40,000 citizens, or the equivalent of three divisions, and injure about 130,000 others, or the equivalent of three army groups, while doing $5 billion worth of damage.

Perhaps it might be argued that the automobile, despite recent substantial improvements, remains an inferior instrument of destruction as compared, say, to contemporary bombs. But surely this is to argue beside the point. Frightening as they are, these bombs cannot be used, for they must be held in reserve, as a deterrent to aggression. And there is this about deterrence: your opponent is none the worse for it. Deter him today and he will still be there tomorrow, requiring to be deterred again. But once a fellow has been run over, he has, so to speak, been permanently deterred. Thus, to continue testing explosives when we already possess, in the automobile, a weapon whose destructiveness we have thoroughly proved on ourselves, is merely to sacrifice an assured result to a frivolous love of spectacle. For we must remember that no other weapon of comparable destructiveness can be used without arousing some degree of resentment on the part of its victims. Only the motor car has the skill to injure people without losing their good opinion.

But, you may ask, what of the ordinary American citizen, whose taxes must support this colossal enterprise? Well, *what* of him? During the present fiscal year, he has put up more than $40 billion toward a military establishment which, for all its awesome potential, has not achieved a stroke of useful work. Would he not feel better if he had something solid to show for all that money? After all, if a mere fraction of the military budget had been invested in automobiles for the Russians, the money would have earned, by this time, a really substantial return in the way of devastation and good will.

Suggestions

1. As you no doubt have discovered, a thesis sometimes stands a better chance of being accepted (or at least well thought of) if it is disguised as something else—perhaps even its very opposite. "An Eminently Reasonable Suggestion" has the effect of making us smile because of (a) the extravagance of its idea and (b) the tongue-in-cheek manner by which it is proposed—the logic of the argument is itself satirized. This kind of writing, known in this book as Indirection, ranges from broad burlesque to irony and understatement. The oblique approach may lend an essay more force than if its meaning were expressed directly.

2. In an essay of indirection, the reader must be led to the true meaning by the speaker's tone. What do you consider to be the true meaning of "An Eminently Reasonable Suggestion"? How does the title contribute to its tone?

3. List all the possible objects which the speaker may be attacking indirectly, and comment on his *rhetorical questions.*

4. Point out a single sentence that states the topic of the essay—if you can.

5. Explain the odd linking of *devastation* and *good will* in the final sentence.

6. Write an essay, using indirect methods, on some aspect of current living that you dislike.

PARKINSON'S LAW

or The Rising Pyramid

C. NORTHCOTE PARKINSON   *From* PARKINSON'S LAW *by C. Northcote Parkinson.* © *1957 by Houghton Mifflin Company.*

Work expands so as to fill the time available for its completion. General recognition of this fact is shown in the proverbial phrase "It is the busiest man who has time to spare." Thus, an elderly lady of leisure can spend the entire day in writing and dispatching a postcard to her niece at Bognor Regis. An hour will be spent in finding the postcard, another in hunting for spectacles, half an hour in a search for the address, an hour and a quarter in composition, and twenty minutes in deciding whether or not to take an umbrella when going to the mailbox in the next street. The total effort that would occupy a busy man for three minutes all told may in this fashion leave another person prostrate after a day of doubt, anxiety, and toil.

Granted that work (and especially paper work) is thus elastic in its demands on time, it is manifest that there need be little or no relationship between the work to be done and the size of the staff to which it may be assigned. A lack of real activity does not, of necessity, result in leisure. A lack of occupation is not necessarily revealed by a manifest idleness. The thing to be done swells in importance and complexity in a direct ratio with the time to be spent. This fact is widely recognized, but less attention has been paid to its wider implications, more especially in the field of public administration. Politicians and taxpayers have assumed (with occasional phases of doubt) that a rising total in the number of civil servants must reflect a growing volume of work to be done. Cynics, in questioning this belief, have imagined that the multiplication of officials must have left some of them idle or all of them able to work for shorter hours. But this is a matter in which faith and doubt seem equally misplaced. The fact is that the number of the officials and the quantity of the work are not related to each other at all. The rise in the total of those employed is governed by Parkinson's Law and would be much the same whether the volume of the work were to increase, diminish, or even disappear. The importance of Parkinson's Law lies in the fact that it is a law of growth based upon an analysis of the factors by which that growth is controlled.

The validity of this recently discovered law must rest mainly on statistical proofs, which will follow. Of more interest to the general reader is the explanation of the factors underlying the general tendency to which this law gives definition. Omitting technicalities (which are numerous) we may distinguish at the outset two motive forces. They can be represented for the present purpose by two almost axiomatic statements, thus: (1) "An official wants to multiply subordinates, not rivals" and (2) "Officials make work for each other."

To comprehend Factor 1, we must picture a civil servant, called A, who finds himself overworked. Whether this overwork is real or imaginary is immaterial, but we should observe, in passing, that A's sensation (or illusion) might easily result from his own decreasing energy: a normal symptom of middle age. For this real or imagined overwork there are, broadly speaking, three possible remedies. He may resign; he may ask to halve the work with a colleague called B; he may demand the assistance of two subordinates, to be called C and D. There is probably no instance in history, however, of A choosing any but the third alternative. By resignation he would lose his pension rights. By having B appointed, on his own level in the hierarchy, he would merely bring in a rival for promotion to W's vacancy when W (at long last) retires. So A would rather have C and D, junior men, below him. They will add to his consequence and, by dividing the work into two categories, as between C and D, he will have the merit of being the only man who comprehends them both. It is essential to realize at this point that C and D are, as it were, inseparable. To appoint C alone would have been impossible. Why? Because C, if by himself, would divide the work with A and so assume almost the equal status that has been refused in the first instance to B; a status the more emphasized if C is A's only possible successor. Subordinates must thus number two or more, each being thus kept in order by fear of the other's promotion. When C complains in turn of being overworked (as he certainly will) A will, with the concurrence of C, advise the appointment of two assistants to help C. But he can then avert internal friction only by advising the appointment of two more assistants to help D, whose position is much the same. With this recruitment of E, F, G, and H the promotion of A is now practically certain.

Seven officials are now doing what one did before. This is where Factor 2 comes into operation. For these seven make so much work for each other that all are fully occupied and A is actually working harder than ever. An incoming document may well come before each of them in turn. Official E decides that it falls within the province of F, who places a draft reply before C, who amends it drastically before consulting D, who asks G to deal with it. But G goes on leave at this point, handing the file over to H, who drafts a minute that is signed by D and returned to C, who revises his draft accordingly and lays the new version before A.

What does A do? He would have every excuse for signing the thing unread, for he has many other matters on his mind. Knowing now that he is to succeed W next year, he has to decide whether C or D should succeed to his own office. He had to agree to G's going on leave even if not yet strictly entitled to it. He is worried whether H should not have gone instead, for reasons of health. He has looked pale recently—partly but not solely because of his domestic troubles. Then there is the business of F's special increment of salary for the period of the conference and E's application for transfer to the Ministry of Pensions. A has heard that D is in love with a married typist and that G and F are no longer on speaking terms—no one seems to know why. So A might be tempted to sign C's draft and have done with it. But A is a conscientious man. Beset as he is with problems created by his colleagues for themselves and for him— created by the mere fact of these officials' existence—he is not the man to shirk his duty. He reads through the draft with care, deletes the fussy paragraphs added by C and H, and restores the thing back to the form preferred in the first instance by the able (if quarrelsome) F. He corrects the English—none of these young men can write grammatically—and finally produces the same reply he would have written if officials C to H had never been born. Far more people have taken far longer to produce the same result. No one has been idle. All have done their best. And it is late in the evening before A finally quits his office and begins the return journey to Ealing. The last of the office lights are being turned off in the gathering dusk that marks the end of another day's administrative toil. Among the last to leave, A reflects with bowed shoulders and a wry smile that late hours, like gray hairs, are among the penalties of success.

From this description of the factors at work the student of political science will recognize that administrators are more or less bound to multiply. Nothing has yet been said, however, about the period of time likely to elapse between the date of A's appointment and the date from which we can calculate the pensionable service of H. Vast masses of statistical evidence have been collected and it is from a study of this data that Parkinson's Law has been deduced. Space will not allow of detailed analysis but the reader will be interested to know that research began in the British Navy Estimates. These were chosen because the Admiralty's responsibilities are more easily measurable than those of, say, the Board of Trade. The question is merely one of numbers and tonnage. Here are some typical figures. The strength of the Navy in 1914 could be shown as 146,000 officers and men, 3249 dockyard officials and clerks, and 57,000 dockyard workmen. By 1928 there were only 100,000 officers and men and only 62,439 workmen, but the dockyard officials and clerks by then numbered 4558. As for warships, the strength in 1928 was a mere fraction of what it had been in 1914—fewer than 20 capital ships in commission as compared with 62. Over the same period the Admiralty officials had increased in number from 2000 to 3569, providing (as was remarked) "a magnificent navy on land." These figures are more clearly set forth in tabular form.

ADMIRALTY STATISTICS

Year	Capital ships in commission	Officers and men in R.N.	Dockyard workers	Dockyard officials and clerks	Admiralty officials
1914	62	146,000	57,000	3249	2000
1928	20	100,000	62,439	4558	3569
Increase or Decrease	−67.74%	−31.5%	+9.54%	+40.28%	+78.45%

The criticism voiced at the time centered on the ratio between the numbers of those available for fighting and those available only for administration. But that comparison is not to the present purpose. What we have to note is that the 2000 officials of 1914 had become the 3569 of 1928; and that this growth was unrelated to any possible increase in their work. The Navy during that period had diminished, in point of fact, by a third in men and two-thirds in ships. Nor, from 1922 onward, was its strength even expected to increase; for its total of ships (unlike its total of officials) was limited by the Washington Naval Agreement of that year. Here we have then a 78 per cent increase over a period of fourteen years; an average of 5.6 per cent increase a year on the earlier total. In fact, as we shall see, the rate of increase was not as regular as that. All we have to consider, at this stage, is the percentage rise over a given period.

Can this rise in the total number of civil servants be accounted for except on the assumption that such a total must always rise by a law governing its growth? It might be urged at this point that the period under discussion was one of rapid development in naval technique. The use of the flying machine was no longer confined to the eccentric. Electrical devices were being multiplied and elaborated. Submarines were tolerated if not approved. Engineer officers were beginning to be regarded as almost human. In so revolutionary an age we might expect that storekeepers would have more elaborate inventories to compile. We might not wonder to see more draughtsmen on the payroll, more designers, more technicians and scientists. But these, the dockyard officials, increased only by 40 per cent in number when the men of Whitehall increased their total by nearly 80 per cent. For every new foreman or electrical engineer at Portsmouth there had to be two more clerks at Charing Cross. From this we might be tempted to conclude, provisionally, that the rate of increase in administrative staff is likely to be double that of the technical staff at a time when the actually useful strength (in this case, of seamen) is being reduced by 31.5 per cent. It has been proved statistically, however, that this last percentage is irrelevant. The officials would have multiplied at the same rate had there been no actual seamen at all.

It would be interesting to follow the further progress by which the 8118 Admiralty staff of 1935 came to number 33,788 by 1954. But the staff of the Colonial Office affords a better field of study during a period of imperial decline. Admiralty statistics are complicated by factors (like the Fleet Air Arm) that make comparison difficult as between one year and the next. The Colonial Office growth is more significant in that it is more purely administrative. Here the relevant statistics are as follows:

1935	*1939*	*1943*	*1947*	*1954*
372	450	817	1139	1661

Before showing what the rate of increase is, we must observe that the extent of this department's responsibilities was far from constant during these twenty years. The colonial territories were not much altered in area or population between 1935 and 1939. They were considerably diminished by 1943, certain areas being in enemy hands. They were increased again in 1947, but have since then shrunk steadily from year to year as successive colonies achieve self-government. It would be rational to suppose that these changes in the scope of Empire would be reflected in the size of its central administration. But a glance at the figures is enough to convince us that the staff totals represent nothing but so many stages in an inevitable increase. And this increase, although related to that observed in other departments, has nothing to do with the size—or even the existence—of the Empire. What are the percentages of increase? We must ignore, for this purpose, the rapid increase in staff which accompanied the diminution of responsibility during World War II. We should note rather, the peacetime rates of increase: over 5.24 per cent between 1935 and 1939, and 6.55 per cent between 1947 and 1954. This gives an average increase of 5.89 per cent each year, a percentage markedly similar to that already found in the Admiralty staff increase between 1914 and 1928.

Further and detailed statistical analysis of departmental staffs would be inappropriate in such a work as this. It is hoped, however, to reach a tentative conclusion regarding the time likely to elapse between a given official's first appointment and the later appointment of his two or more assistants.

Dealing with the problem of pure staff accumulation, all our researches so far completed point to an average increase of 5.75 per cent per year. This fact established, it now becomes possible to state Parkinson's Law in mathematical form: In any public administrative department not actually at war, the staff increase may be expected to follow this formula—

$$x = \frac{2k^m + 1}{n}$$

k is the number of staff seeking promotion through the appointment of subordinates; l represents the difference between the ages of appointment and retirement; m is the number of man-hours devoted to answering minutes within the department; and n is the number of effective units being administered. x will be the number of new staff required each year. Mathematicians will realize, of course, that to find the percentage increase they must multiply x by 100 and divide by the total of the previous year, thus:

$$\frac{100 (2k^m + 1)}{yn} \%$$

where y represents the total original staff. This figure will invariably prove to be between 5.17 per cent and 6.56 per cent, irrespective of any variation in the amount of work (if any) to be done.

The discovery of this formula and of the general principles upon which it is based has, of course, no political value. No attempt has been made to inquire whether departments ought to grow in size. Those who hold that this growth is essential to gain full employment are fully entitled to their opinion. Those who doubt the stability of an economy based upon reading each other's minutes are equally entitled to theirs. It would probably be premature to attempt at this stage any inquiry into the quantitative ratio that should exist between the administrators and the administered. Granted, however, that a maximum ratio exists, it should soon be possible to ascertain by formula how many years will elapse before that ratio, in any given community, will be reached. The forecasting of such a result will again have no political value. Nor can it be sufficiently emphasized that Parkinson's Law is a purely scientific discovery, inapplicable except in theory to the politics of the day. It is not the business of the botanist to eradicate the weeds. Enough for him if he can tell us just how fast they grow.

Suggestions

1. Consider this sentence in the last paragraph: "No attempt has been made to inquire whether departments *ought* to grow in size." How do you know that the speaker's meaning is just the opposite? How is the sentence related to the satiric point? With this sentence as your guide, look for places in the essay where by indirection the speaker makes the discovery of his law an attack on modern bureaucratic methods.

2. Show that "Parkinson's Law" not only satirizes bureaucracy but is also a *parody* of a certain kind of textbook.

3. The essay is divided into two distinct sections. Find the point of division; then justify the logic behind this arrangement.

4. Discuss the concluding analogy with the botanist and the weeds. What is its implication?

5. Can you discover any flaws in these figures or the conclusions based on them?

6. Decide whether "Parkinson's Law" applies only to public administration or to more ordinary activities as well.

7. Write an essay about the efficiency of an office where you have worked. You may wish to refer to such personal factors as petty jealousies, employer-employee friction, and salary squabbles.

8. Write an analysis of what you consider to be a flagrant example of poor planning in some business or administrative operation, citing specific recommendations for improving it.

THE IRONY OF IT ALL

PETER DE VRIES ⟶

Reprinted by permission of the author. © *1956 The New Yorker Magazine, Inc.*

This was a dinner party I faced with more than the usual reluctance. Besides girding my loins for the five or six hours of continuous conversation to which custom maniacally commits us, I had to steel myself to spend them with a man I couldn't abide—the host. (Why our two households had kept exchanging invitations is one of the mysteries of a social system administered by women, and I do not feel equipped to discuss it.)

An added hazard in all my meetings with this egg had arisen from his being an author, and one who could buy and sell me and everybody I know. I bristle each time I see, on my way to my office job in the city, a fellow-commuter reading one of his novels.

They are no good, those books. But they sell. They have the disproportionate quantities of seaminess that gain authors reputations as realists, and their style is no tax on the brain. They abound in lines like "Behind him he could hear Dumbrowski's heavy breathing" and "With a bellow of mingled rage and pain he came at him." There are more descriptive stencils like "a thickset man with beetling brows" and "a small bird-like woman" than you can shake a stick at, and the frequency of "You mean—?" in his dialogue indicates that he is no pathfinder there, either. Triter still is the lyric strain with which the brutal realism is relieved, being marked by an almost unlimited use of the atmospheric "somewhere": "Somewhere a bird sang," "Somewhere a woman's laughter broke the stillness of the night," and so on. Complexity of characterization is achieved by the sedulous repetition of "part of him." "Part of him wanted to so-and-so, while another part of him wanted to such-and-such." It goes without saying that the "as if in a dream" locution appears on every fourth page. As befits the work of a fearless realist, the aspect of life most abundantly dealt with is sex.

It was this particular exaggeration I was reflecting on as my wife and I drove over to the party at the home of the man in question, whom I will call Dumbrowski because it's so typical of the names he gives his characters. I groped for some thought on which to impale this latter-day obsession with the frequent and physical depiction of passion—an ironic phrase for it, which I felt to be teasing the edge of my mind if not the very tip of my tongue. "Why does he lay sex on so thick?" I finally asked my wife, who was driving the car. I thought a little conversation on the subject might help me snare that elusive conceit. "He and realists of that ilk? They have people in and out of bed like seals in and out of water—affairs right and left, sex day and night. Why is that?"

"Maybe they just don't know the facts of life," she said.

I lapsed into silence, staring ahead through the windshield. We must have gone a mile or more before I turned irritably to her and said, "What the hell are we going there for? You don't like him any better than I do."

She shrugged. "They owed us an invitation."

We slowed and entered the front gate of the house in which we were to spend the evening. I climbed out of the car and made my way unwillingly up the gravel drive to the door.

The house was jammed with guests. Dumbrowski, however, stood out in his pink shirt and black tie, which, in turn, stood out under his light-gray cashmere jacket. He was too tall and too broad-shouldered, I noted, and his hair needed some judicious cutting, like his books. I managed to steer clear of him during the cocktail period and even through dinner, for which the more than thirty guests were distributed among several small tables. After dinner, though, the whole party formed a unified group to which mine host held forth in typical fashion—by which I mean his way of aiming the stem of his pipe at you when making a point, or (another favorite piece of business) swirling his brandy around in a snifter. A man has a perfect right to gaze into a brandy inhaler and swirl the contents around when making an observation, but in that case he ought to get off something better than "I'm sure our ways must seem as odd to them as theirs do to us," and "The burdens of the Presidency are enormous."

I had eaten and drunk heavily, as an alternative to hanging myself from the nearest chandelier, and as a result had the hiccups so badly that for a while I sounded like an outboard motor. Luckily, I found a chair in a remote corner of the living room, and went for the most part unnoticed. At about half-past ten, some cretin, a woman who had just moved to Westport and was socially on the make, asked Dumbrowski to read us a chapter of his work in progress. He modestly refused, and, what with one thing and another, was soon installed with a sheaf of manuscript in his hand and a circle of prisoners around him.

This was a story, he told us as he stoked his pipe preparatory to the reading, about a burnt-out prizefighter who signs for one last fight in an attempt to get enough money to marry a woman he is in love with. He is not only badly beaten but gravely injured, and is taken to the hospital immediately following the bout.

" 'Stramaglia knew that he lay dying,' " Dumbrowski read, in a voice that was low and modulated, yet vibrant with respect for the material. " 'Part of him wanted to die.' " See? " 'Part of him wanted desperately to live. A great weariness assailed him. Somewhere a cart rattled in the corridor. Then he was dimly aware that the door of his room had opened and someone was sitting in the chair beside his bed. He knew without opening his eyes that it was Constanza.' "

A hush fell across the room as, in a pregnant pause of more than usual duration, Dumbrowski took a last suck on his pipe before setting it down in an ashtray at his elbow. There was no denying the emotion generated among his listeners—a tension that made even me momentarily leave off tallying the clichés as they fell from his lips. He continued reading: " ' "Constanza, I have a request to make that may seem strange to you," Stramaglia whispered thickly, "but would you get me my gloves? I'd like to go out with them on." ' "

A snicker escaped me at the same time that a sob caught in my throat. In addition, I wasn't quite over the hiccups, so the resulting moment was one of great confusion indeed. Everyone turned to look at me. Dumbrowski himself raised his head and glanced in my direction, but he resumed reading almost immediately, in an effort to recover what he could of the spell he had been weaving. Fortunately, he was near the end of the chapter, or of the section he had chosen to read, and presently he was putting his manuscript aside, to a ripple of compliments and hand clapping. He acknowledged the applause smilingly, then rose with a brisk "Well so!" and set to work freshening up people's drinks.

I knew that I had got his goat. And I knew, as I'm sure he did, too, that the undercurrent of animosity between us, so long concealed, must break through into open hostility very soon. Dumbrowski, at any rate, took his revenge in short order. A girl of about twenty-five launched a long and detailed account of the trouble she was having finding a job in New York. In the course of it, she asked three or four of the men present, including me, if they couldn't help. I promised to see if there were any openings in my office. "Oh, openings!" she exclaimed, throwing up her hands. "I'm talking about somebody just plain getting me *in*."

Here Dumbrowski slipped in his stiletto. "You mustn't give the poor chap such a time, Nancy," he said. "He doesn't have any of the kind of influence you're talking about—the kind that cuts corners for people. He only just works there himself."

I spent the remainder of the evening spoiling for a fight. I prowled the living room with highball after highball, glaring either at Dumbrowski, who went from strength to strength with one group after another, or at my wife, whom I saw in gay communion with a succession of attentive males. "It's no wonder," I snapped elliptically from behind her as she sat on a sofa waiting for an admirer to trot back with a drink for her. "Next time you go out with me, you'll wear a dress with a top. I mean that." Before she could turn and ask for an exegesis, I was making for a piano, at which I sat for some time picking out chords of an angry and atonal nature. I eased my feelings by reviewing some of my adversary's more blatant shortcomings as an artist, mentally repeating a few of his characteristic effects. "Behind him he could hear Dumbrowski's heavy breathing," I reiterated amusedly to myself, and "You mean—?"

It was toward midnight, when the party was boiling noisily through its climax, that he gave me what I took to be *casus belli*. He was standing nearby with a dapper but gloomy-looking man of about forty, whose name I hadn't caught. As I watched them, it was borne in on me that they were discussing my wife, who was chattering away to several people in the vicinity. The two men nodded and smiled appreciatively. Then Dumbrowski said something that I got only imperfectly but that—under the din, at least—seemed to have something to do with someone's being "picked up without any trouble."

I took a long pull on my drink, rose from the piano bench, and strode over, just as the other man made off. "All right, Dumbrowski," I said. "I heard that."

"Heard what?" he asked.

"Whatever you said. Shall we step outside?"

He glanced into my glass. "Don't you think you've had about enough, old boy?" he asked.

"More than enough. Just slip out through the terrace, shall we?" I suggested, nodding toward a pair of French doors, closed against the autumn night.

"I'm sure I don't know what the devil you're talking about."

"I think you know what I'm talking about, Dumbrowski," I said, fixing him with narrowed eyes.

He paused and took me in speculatively. "You hate my guts, don't you?" he said at last, in low tones.

"I would if you had any. You get 'em, I'll hate 'em."

"Why, you—!" His fists opened and shut at his sides. "I've got guests to think about, but you come back here any time you wish, and by God—"

"How's tomorrow morning?"

"That's fine with me."

"I'll be here with bells on," I said. "That's a promise."

I awoke the next morning, Sunday, at eleven o'clock. My head felt swollen to twice its size, and as though it had been filled with concrete. When I tried to move it, the room swam in a steady circle from floor to ceiling, like the picture on a television set when it is in need of vertical tuning. The condition cleared up after a bit, and I got up and doused myself with cold water, dressed, and went down to the kitchen, where my wife was sitting over a cup of coffee and the *Times*.

"Good morning," I said, drawing on a tweed jacket, for the day was quite nippy.

"What's morning about it?"

I helped myself to a glass of cold orange juice from a pitcher. I drank it standing up, aware of her watching me. "What in heaven's name happened last night?" she asked. (I had stalked out of the party after my skirmish, pausing only long enough to make sure she had transportation home, and gone straight to bed on getting there myself, so these were our first words since then.) "What was that all about between you and Frank?"

"You'd be surprised," I answered acidly, and marched out of the house, making directly for the car, which I had left parked in the driveway, the keys in it.

I sat inside the car reviewing the hazards of living in a society as complex as ours. The memory of my grievances sent my temper flaring again. Should I keep my date with Dumbrowski? Honor—or at least self-respect—demanded that I do. There seemed no alternative. It was as though we had parted with the understanding "Fists, at dawn."

It was closer to noon when I reached the Dumbrowskis'. Nobody was stirring except the maid, who frowned uncertainly when, standing on the porch with my hands in my coat pockets, I asked for the master. She glanced over her shoulder up the vestibule stairway. "Are you expected?" she asked.

I told her that I was. As we talked, I debated with myself whether to leave a message that I had called, and go. Then a second-story window slid open and Dumbrowski's head appeared between the curtains, his face mangled with sleep, and an ice bag on his tousled hair. "Oh—that," he said, remembering. He squinted down through the bright fall sunshine and, with the hand not concerned with steadying the ice bag, gathered the lapels of a bathrobe over his chest.

"I can come back later," I said, squinting back up at him, "if now isn't convenient."

"I'll be down." His head withdrew, and the window slid shut.

I sat on the porch steps to wait, declining the maid's invitation to wait inside. I picked up a handful of gravel from the drive and flicked the stones away one by one with my thumb. After about five minutes, the door behind me opened and Dumbrowski emerged, clad in a black turtleneck sweater and denim slacks. He must have had quite a night (my wife hadn't got home till two o'clock, I learned later), because he looked like something the cat dragged in. I sympathetically murmured something to that effect as I rose to greet him, and repeated my offer to let this go till some other time. "No, let's get it over with," he said doggedly.

"Right," I said, removing my coat as I followed him down the steps to the yard.

We squared away on a width of lawn that was concealed from the house by a group of birches, from which the ground we stood on fell away to a small pond in which the Dumbrowskis had once kept goldfish. We circled one another for a minute or two, our guards up, edging about for the advantage. There was no doubt what that consisted in here; it consisted in remaining above one's opponent.

"This has been brewing for a long time," I observed as we sparred.

"It was bound to come to a head," Dumbrowski agreed. He cocked his forward arm—the right—a bit, and I stiffened my own guard, at the same time thrusting out my chest to give that impression of pectoral strength that is always suggested in photographs of prizefighters.

"We don't cotton to one another, you and I," I went on. "And there you have it."

"You don't like my stuff. I know that."

"It's not my dish of tea."

"I hate that expression," Dumbrowski replied with unexpected violence. "Why don't you come right out and say what you think? Not that I don't know what your dish of tea *is*. That English lot! Twitches and nuances!" Here he reeled off a string of contemporary British novelists who did, with uncanny accuracy, reflect my private reading tastes. "Lint pickers!" he exclaimed in a burst of spirit. "All those hemidemisemiquavers!"

I recognized well enough the animus of the popular artist whom critical approval has bypassed. He was one of those authors read by hundreds of thousands but of whom no one has ever *heard*. They have no *reputation;* they are merely household words. Oh, I knew what was in Dumbrowski's craw all right. But that did not spare me the comparable sting of having my *goût* as a reader under attack. Now I felt the urgent need to strike a blow.

"It's better than that burly realism," I retorted hotly. "And all that sex. Want to know why you chaps slather it on? You don't know the facts of life."

He paused long enough for the exquisite irony of this to sink in—I could sense the shaft going home—then he lowered his head and came at me with a bellow of mingled rage and pain.

I met his charge by adroitly stepping aside, more or less executing what is known in bullfighting as, I believe, a veronica. He stumbled in his plunge and lost his balance, sprawling headlong among the birches. He got to his feet and came for me again. I lunged forward to meet him, and we came together, our arms going like flails. It was amazing how few blows found their mark—practically none at all. This time, I tripped on a rock and stumbled against him, and, interlocked, we danced down the incline toward the goldfish pond. We fetched up short of it only because, at the conclusion of our career down the grass, we clumsily pulled each other down in a jumble of arms and legs. This had the effect of converting the encounter into a wrestling match, and by an accident of the terrain in my favor I landed on top, but so near the water that any atempt to alter our positions might have meant disaster for both of us. So I sat there on Dumbrowski's chest for a bit.

"This will teach you to speak lightly of a lady's name," I panted.

"Ridiculous." He brought the word out between gasps of his own. "Never understood this—fussing over a—compliment paid a woman."

"Compliment?"

He nodded. "Only told Feversham be—sure go talk to *her* if he wanted picking up."

"You mean—?" I said.

He nodded again. "Feversham was depressed. So I told him go talk to her. She picks you right up. Always thought so. Great fun. At least appreciate your taste in *that.*"

I climbed off of him. I turned away and dropped leadenly to the grass in a sitting position. I knew well enough now what was happening, and I offered no resistance. Behind me I could hear Dumbrowski's heavy breathing. Somewhere a car backfired, shattering the morning stillness. As if in a dream, I gave my head a shake and said, "It was all a ghastly mistake."

"I'll accept that."

I could hear him getting to his feet now. When he spanked the dirt from his clothes, it was as if the blows stung my cheeks. But when I turned to look up at him over my shoulder, his face was twisted in a grin of forgiving triumph. Dumbrowski knew that he had won; in his eyes there was that quiet knowledge. There is no need to relate the rest in detail: how part of me hated him while more of me hated myself; how I rose, as if in a trance, to dust off my own clothes; and how, at last, Dumbrowski steered me up the lawn to the house and even into it, my arm in his viselike grip. "Wash up in there," he said, not unkindly. When I emerged from the bathroom he had indicated, he said, "Now come into the kitchen for some coffee."

We sat hunched over our cups of strong black coffee, our arms along the table, facing each other in a new understanding that needed no words. Each treasured within him the satisfaction of having stood up to the other, yet respected the other for having done the same. Somewhere a clock struck—one—and I told Dumbrowski that I had to go. I rose and, shaking his hand, took my leave.

As I strode up the walk to my car, I knew a strange peace—the peace of a man who has faced up to what courage and chivalry demanded, and not flinched. I knew it was the same with Dumbrowski. We would never speak of this again, yet we were strangely cleansed. Part of me regretted the incident—always would—but another deeper part of me would always prize it for the challenge that had come out of it . . . a challenge met. Somewhere a duck quacked. The air was like wine. It was with a high heart that I sprang into my car and drove—home—to the woman I loved.

Suggestions

1. "The Irony of It All" has the movement of a regular narrative—it even has "plot" enough to make it a short story. But the plot, slender itself, is a vehicle for satirizing a particular kind of writer. Far more important than "what happens" is the manner in which the events are related. The title itself is the first clue: it is a *cliché*, and this is an essay about the sloppy kind of writing that depends on a random, thoughtless piling up of clichés. The theme, stated first in the second paragraph, recurs with variations throughout the piece. There is even a slight shift in style, when the more-or-less straightforward account of the earlier half dissolves into a style compounded of the very vice that is under attack. Thus the reader is made ready to accept the satiric digs at the "Dumbrowski" method.

2. Point out the place where "The Irony of It All" shifts into a mock-cliché style.

3. Discuss the connotations of Dumbrowski's names for the speaker's favorite writers.

4. The title has both a literal appropriateness and a thematic relevance. Discuss both.

5. What details show the speaker's progressive stages of drunkenness?

6. Explain: *elliptically, atonal, blatant, pectoral, nuances, slather.*

7. Paying attention to diction, understatement, exaggeration, and sentence structure, study and analyze the following passage: "At about half-past ten, some cretin, a woman who had just moved to Westport and was socially on the make, asked Dumbrowski to read us a chapter of his work in progress. He modestly refused, and, what with one thing and another, was soon installed with a sheaf of manuscript in his hand and a circle of prisoners around him."

8. Write an account of some social affair dominated by a person or experience you disliked. Rely on style rather than direct statement to communicate your attitude.

CYPRUS: THE POLITICAL ANIMALS AT PLAY

C. P. LEE   *Reprinted from* ATHENIAN ADVENTURE *by C. P. Lee, by permission of Alfred A. Knopf, Inc. © 1957 by C. P. Lee.*

Biologists tell me that I am an animal, and although theologians are more flattering, I am inclined to admit the biologists' claim. Politically I am most certainly an animal; I seem to vote according to my glands. Most Americans do, no matter what their pretense. "We've always been Democrats." "I like his smile." "I don't like his mustache." If we offer a more concrete reason, it is usually associated with our self-pride or our pocketbook. "Look at the price of cotton!" "He's a nigger-lover, that's what he is." In this we are simply animal.

But if I am a political animal, I am also politically lethargic. I am not easily politically aroused, and from the number of my fellow Americans who do not bother to vote, I suspect that this is a national characteristic too. Quaint foreigners, I knew, took politics more seriously. Italian deputies spat at one another in the National Assembly, or occasionally stabbed an opponent at the end of a particularly fiery speech (I associated Italians with knives), while the inkpots thrown in the Chambre des Députés in Paris, the slammed desk lids, the screams, the shouts, were proverbial. But these, I assumed, were simply characteristics of lesser breeds without the law, or, to state it more kindly, adolescent republicans, well-intentioned, but not quite civilized. That might come in time. If I thought about Greek politics at all, it was simply to resolve not to think about them. I would be, I knew, objective, by which I really meant that I would not be interested.

Now I knew that the Greek is interested in politics, and I vaguely associated Plato's *Republic* and Aristotle's *Politics* with his political behavior. I must reread them, I said, and perhaps a quick glimpse of modern Greek history would be wise. I began dutifully. "In 1832 by the Convention of London Prince Otho, son of the king of Bavaria, was proclaimed King." War. "In 1862, Prince William George of Schleswig-Holstein was selected by the British government and elected King of the Hellenes." War. King Constantine. War. Deposition. War. King Constantine again. War. Deposition. King George. War. Deposition. War. King George returns. War. King George leaves. Civil war. King Paul. It all seemed rather cyclic. Well, perhaps ignorance would ensure objectivity; perhaps, in fact, they were much the same thing.

But I arrived in 1955, and 1955–6, my Greek friends assured me, was an unusually active political year. Certainly it was active enough, with the death of the dictator prime minister, General Papagos, a new electoral law, a general election, and Cyprus, alas Cyprus, to boot. Nevertheless, I believe my Greek friends were wrong. Every year in Greece is a political year; the Greek political pot, unlike our own, boils annually, and simmers perpetually. The Greek word for city, *polis,* is the root for our word *politics* as well as our word *police,* and I saw the connection on that root's home soil. I was longer in realizing, however, that the connotations of the word *politics* itself have suffered, in the transatlantic crossing, a sea-change, so great that when I used the word I did not mean even vaguely what my Greek friends did. I used it looking in; they used it looking out. The American, I was forced to realize, is a highly unrepresentative political animal, for his wide land, flanked by two seas, has led him to make two assumptions, unspoken, which the majority of mankind is not lucky enough to share.

The first assumption is that "politics" concerns what Americans will do to Americans. If there is any mention of foreign policy, it is to reiterate the firm determination of both parties that what shall be done in that area shall be done by us, to others, and it shall be done overseas. We all know that a radar screen is being built at vast expense across Canada; we all see the signs outside our cities: "In Event of Enemy Attack, This Highway Will Be Closed to Civilian Traffic"—signs a bit weatherbeaten

by now; we all know that city school-children have been given identification tags, bearing their names and blood-types, and we all know why.
But we regard these precautions as the equivalent of a first-aid kit taken
camping. A snake may bite, we realize, but it never has bitten us, and it
probably never will. Symptomatic of adult as well as adolescent concern
over invasion, in this country, is the habit of high-school belles, who
collect boys' identification tags and dangle them from charm-bracelets,
like scalps. (And symptomatic of our lightheaded and lighthearted preparations for attack is the announcement of the committee to select sites
for mass burials, in a city where I once lived. The committee offered this
consolation: in case of a mass burial, the bodies would be borne to the
potter's field by the local high-school football teams!) Such preparations,
then, in the United States seem to us to represent reality no more than
the double feature of horror films at midnight on Halloween.

The second assumption, as deeply felt, is that no matter which party
wins an American election, our lives will go on much the same, although
we may believe that our pocketbooks will thin or fatten accordingly. We
cannot help feeling that not much is at stake except which hog gets to the
trough. Our revealing phrase is "to *play* politics," which suggests to us not
only a shady, but a shadowy, quarrel. The American voter feels himself a
superior bystander, without serious concern for the struggle he watches,
rather like the spectator of the Friday night TV prizefight—fun to watch,
but designed to make us buy somebody's beer, when there are at least
six other brands just as good. What we pride ourselves upon, our decorous
behavior at the polls, our calm acquiescence in the electoral returns, may
be a national strength, but it is a strength which we owe to geography
rather than self-control. "When we conquer our passions," said a French
cynic, "it is because of their weakness, rather than our strength."

I was, then, slow to comprehend the political habits of a less fortunate
nation, whose history is both longer and more eventful than our own, and
whose history will be, it has every reason to expect, eventful all too soon
once more. Every Greek—and every national of most European countries
—lives on a volcano, and knows it. When he votes, he votes with one eye
upon the menace across the border, all too near the polling booth, and
quite likely to be much nearer in the immediate future. He knows, too,
from experience (the adjective which usually accompanies that noun is,
rightly, "bitter"), that this election may change the national way of life,
and change it both drastically and soon.

I tried to put myself in his shoes. Greece, even with its Ionian and
Ægean islands, is not much larger than Tennessee. Greece has five immediate neighbors, Turkey, Bulgaria, Yugoslavia, Albania, and Italy.
Imagine, then, Tennessee with five neighboring states all differing in
language and two differing radically in religion, and a long history of
mutual hatred. Tennessee troops would face corresponding state troops

at the mountain passes into North Carolina, into Virginia at the Bristol Gap, into Kentucky at the Cumberland Gap and along the western border, while other troops faced Georgia and Alabama forces at the major approaches from the Georgia and Alabama plain. They would face each other armed, for even if we ignore centuries of raids back and forth, since 1912 alone each of these states would have invaded Tennessee, or been invaded by her, to gain, or keep, an outlet upon the Tennessee or Mississippi rivers, or to incorporate all who spoke the Tennessee dialect into that state, or to retain Kentucky-speakers within Tennessee. In addition, imagine that fifteen years ago, in a continental struggle for hegemony, New York invaded and occupied Tennessee for over three years. After that time, California, struggling with New York for continental supremacy, came to Tennessee's aid and forced New York's withdrawal. Tennessee, famished, wrecked, flamed into ideological civil war between those Tennesseans who sincerely believed that the state must be radically reorganized upon a basis of state ownership, land reform, etc., and their opponents, who desired capitalism and private enterprise, a return to the *status quo ante*. This civil war lasted five years, and in it some 100,000 Tennesseans were killed in battle, while untold thousands starved. But by 1950, with the assistance of California aid and troops, the armed adherents of state ownership, etc., would have been driven into the mountains behind Knoxville, then wiped out; for the first time in nine years the railroad from Knoxville to Memphis would be in operation. Too, the ships in the Tennessee River, which blocked navigation, would have been removed. In 1956, then, the Tennessee voter goes to the polls in a general election. What will be his state of mind?

Higher taxes, the price of tobacco or cotton, a candidate's mustache are not likely to be paramount. What he will want, first, is either security, or revenge, the *status quo* reinforced, or a violent change. For either goal he knows perfectly well that some arrangement with alien states is necessary. He may wish to keep them out, or to bring his favorite's troops in. He may wish to gang up with several neighbors against another, or he may wish to strengthen an alliance with a distant but powerful state in order that his neighbors will be afraid to gang up on him. He may, of course, believe that entangling alliances are best avoided, that skillful maneuvering, a delicate blackmail of all other states, distant or neighboring, promises most reward, and if he does, he will find many a politician with perfect platform faith in his own cleverness and agility, and with a program deliberately vague, since blackmail is a matter best pursued unhampered by a rigid plan.

The Greek voter—and the European voter in general—does not regard the outcome of the election academically. He does not make the comic election bet; he does not square off at defeat, smile widely for the cameras, and magnanimously shake hands with the winner. For not only have his relatives been killed during the civil war by the party of the man whose hand would be extended, but *he* very well may be. During the civil war, everyone had to register his stand. He is known to have advocated this or that, to have fought with this or that group, to have sympathized with this or that fighting group, and while amnesties have been regularly proclaimed, he remembers former amnesties that failed to protect. It was Robert Benchley who defined the difference between Republicans and Democrats as a slight preponderance of blue-eyed among the former; no European would understand that, even as a joke. Party differences are very real differences, and the voter's own neck, not only his pocket-book, may well be at stake. If one feels that the monarchist party offers protection, not merely against higher taxes, but against a Communist firing-squad, one does not confine one's electoral activity to wearing a button emblazoned "I Like King Paul."

Such, then, is the psychological tempest, personal as well as public, in which the Greek voter approaches the polls. Yet in February 1956, when the general election was held, although the government took the precautions Greek governments had always felt necessary (including a new electoral law which in some mysterious way counted votes in districts likely to be pro-Communist in another fashion from votes cast in districts that were not likely to be)—soldiers at the alert, extra police, automobile traffic banned without special permit for the day—that election was the quietest in Greek memory. The answer is not, unfortunately, that these party quarrels had diminished, but that they had been so overshadowed by a quarrel so dear to every Greek heart, no matter what other political considerations inflamed that organ, that party politics were for once secondary. Every Greek political party wanted Cyprus, and the only issue that mattered was which party had the best chance to get it. The best chance, the Greek electorate decided, lay with the party known to favor a strong alliance with the United States of America, since that country frequently voices its anti-colonialism. That party won; the Greeks did not get Cyprus, and at this time of writing, have not gotten it still. In their anger, they have stoned American buildings, burned American flags, attacked American citizens, in a cycle of riots that began as far back as 1954, when the American Embassy was attacked and seventy-five Athenians were injured. This anger flared up again in September 1955, and riots, with increasing frequency and violence, punctuated that autumn and the following spring and summer, until worse trouble in the Middle East saw them slacken. In Athens, alas, an American is the United States; when a Greek friend says "you" he may mean you individually, but he very often means "your nation." They become much the same thing. "Why don't you. . ." my Greek friends began to ask, and they meant, why doesn't the United States do this or that. So I had to learn about Cyprus, although I reacted in as rebellious and bewildered a fashion as the cowboy accused of the crime in Stephen Crane's "The Blue Hotel," when he "cried out blindly into this fog of mysterious theory: 'I didn't do anythin', did I?' " That, it appeared, was my crime.

I sighed. Well, then, what was the truth about Cyprus? I barely knew where it was. That it was an island in the eastern Mediterranean, that Britain owned it, that Greece meant to have it, I knew, but aside from that, and a vague picture of mountains studded with Crusader castles, garnered from childhood *National Geographics,* my mind was a blank. I knew, too, all too well, its Greek name, "Kypros," which I saw scrawled in chalk or blue or black paint on house fronts, on shop-windows, on columns as I walked the streets of Athens, and the word was all too familiar to me from the radio's constant chatter and the Athenian press.

"You will recall," began Greek friends blandly, and I recognized the phrase, one used by teachers to eradicate ignorance without offense. They did not, in fact, recall much, for two reasons, the first that I knew nothing for them to recall, the second, that they had no intention of arguing their case historically. Their argument was simplicity itself: Cyprus is eighty per cent Greek in language and religion, England promised it to us, and we are going to have it now that they have said we can't. "We'll get it," said George, the humanist, the classics scholar. "You see if we don't!"

"Why don't the English want to give it to you?" I demanded. "That is, if they promised it?"

"They promised it. And now they do not give it because—" He hesitated. "Because," he said triumphantly, "they are pigs!"

"Well, what's turned them into pigs?" I thought to appeal to his training. "Who or what is the Circe here?"

Not even *The Odyssey* quieted him. "They have always been pigs," he spat. I sighed again. The days of Aristotle seemed definitely dead. Perhaps, I thought, a little library work might help me.

"The truth," wrote Oscar Wilde, "is rarely pure and never simple." I shall try to state it, as I see it, as simply as possible. Ancient Greece, as everyone knows, became Roman. As everyone knows, the Roman Empire under Constantine possessed two capitals, and the eastern Empire lasted, ignoring piecemeal conquests by Franks and Arabs, until the conquest of Constantinople in 1453 by the Ottoman Turks. The Byzantine Empire, a conglomeration of languages and ethnic groups, was Roman in name, but largely Greek in language and Greek-Oriental in thought. By 1460 the Turks had extended their conquest to what is now Greece; and by 1570, Cyprus, where a weak Crusader kingdom was extinguished, and by 1669, Crete, where the Venetians had ruled, were Turkish. Until 1821 the Turks ruled modern Greece despite revolts.

In 1821 the Greeks freed a segment of what is now Greece, the peninsula sometimes called the Morea, because of its supposed resemblance to a mulberry leaf, or more commonly the Peloponnesus, the ancient kingdom of Pelops. Aided, for their own reasons, by France and England particularly, the Greeks gradually extended their rule north, wresting from the Turks a valley here, an island there, when the Turks were occupied elsewhere or when allied powers offered aid, military or diplomatic. The Greek frontier was in reality simply the official demarcation of the contemporary battle-lines. Not until 1947, for example, was the present Greek frontier accepted by foreign states. No Greek accepts the present frontier as final. Why should he? It has not been final in the whole of his national history. The Greek dream is, as it always has been, Greek domination of the eastern Mediterranean, with Constantinople as his capital. Modern Greece is, in his eyes, that part of the Byzantine Empire which his efforts have restored, and he has every intention, if the opportunity presents itself, of "liberating" the rest.

He knows now that this chance will probably never come. Greek domination of Constantinople, of Asia Minor, will not occur. Yet it very nearly did occur, not much over twenty-five years ago. At the end of World War I the great chance came. Russia, who traditionally desires the Dardanelles, was in chaos. Europe was exhausted. The Turks had allied themselves with Germany, the loser. Greece, after wavering between a pro-German king and a pro-Western politician, had chosen the victors. By the Treaty of Sèvres a great chunk of European Turkey became Greek, and a great chunk of Asia Minor, around Smyrna, modern Izmir. Much of the population in Asia Minor was Greek and had been since the earliest days; much of the population of Constantinople was also Greek, and had been since the earliest days. Alas, Greek internal politics and international politics clashed. The Greeks wanted more; their young king, son of the deposed pro-German monarch, died, of a bite from his pet monkey, and a national plebiscite recalled the deposed pro-German from exile. The Allied powers refused to sanction his return. The Greeks, piqued, refused to attend a proposed meeting to "reconsider" the treaty by which they had been awarded the former Turkish territory. They simply attacked Turkey, from the bases they now held in former European Turkey and Asia Minor. They reckoned without Mustafa Kemal, then a young officer, born in Salonika before that city became Greek. He drove the Greeks into the sea. While the Greeks were able to keep their booty on the European side of the Bosporus, they lost Asia Minor, and since their excuse for getting it had been its Greek populace, the Turks massacred as many Greeks there as possible, to solve that ethnological problem by genocide, a term a later and more delicate-minded generation was to invent to cloak horror beneath a classical shroud. The Turks had, too, as precedent the massacre of Turks by Greeks during their advance, who in the same reasonable manner sought to ensure the ethnic solidarity of their Asiatic province. The League of Nations arranged an exchange of populations for those still alive, and the Greeks in Turkey, the Turks in

Greece were dumped, with only their portable possessions, into their linguistic motherlands. Some are still alive in both countries; their children in both countries imbibe hatred as happily as milk.

The chance of dominating Asia Minor was gone. The Greeks chose their scapegoats, eight former ministers, tried them on charges ranging from willful treason to extreme negligence amounting to treason, and shot six. Now when the Greek looks about him he sees a strong Turkey, a strong Yugoslavia, a weak Bulgaria, but Russia looming behind her satellite's back, even Albania protected by the Bear. As for Italy, she has already disgorged the territory the Greeks could claim, the twelve islands of which Rhodes is the most important, the Dodecanese. Practically, the dream of empire is gone, and to reiterate a claim to it would bring swift retribution. Not even old-fashioned Greek politicians dare openly to advocate moving north or east. But the passion for empire is there, the passion for expansion, and the passion to save face after the disaster in Asia Minor. So Cyprus, which is certainly Greek ethnically, Cyprus, which a former friend and ally holds, is the goal and the emotional symbol of all this frustrated dream. They can agitate safely for Cyprus, they well know, for much as they hate the British, they do not believe that Britain will bomb Athens, or launch a cannonade against the Piræus in retaliation.

The Greeks have, too, as a strong talking point in a world which likes to think that a nation's word is its bond (though how it can do so in face of all evidence is odd), the fact that English politicians, if not English governments, have promised that Cyprus shall be Greek. The Greeks can be quite clear about the distinction between political speeches and a government promise, but they can also, when it suits them, allow the distinction to blur. England got Cyprus, almost casually, in 1878, when Disraeli was allowed by the Sultan to occupy the island in return for a promise to protect against Russia the Turkish Asiatic coast. Britain, secure in Egypt, viewed Cyprus as simply another bit of Imperial real estate, of small value, but an investment that might come in handy sometime. It did, but before its handiness was apparent, many a British politician, among them young Winston Churchill, advocated openly its presentation to Greece, just as Britain, in 1863, had presented to the new kingdom Corfu and the Ionian islands. But by 1950, just when the Greeks, their satisfaction with the Dodecanese whetting their appetite for more, looked at Cyprus most longingly, Britain had lost Egypt and was losing Suez. By 1950 the pipelines that pour the oil of the Middle East into tankers at Mediterranean ports had been built, by 1950 Israel, new creation, was at odds with the surrounding Arab countries, and Great Britain, dependent upon oil for her economy, was bound by intricate agreements to both. Planes based on Cyprus could range over this troubled region in an hour's time. The British began to build a vast Cypriot base. India free, Malaya touchy, Arabs aroused, Jews belligerent, Egypt restive, with a new awareness of the importance of Middle East oil, Britain looked at Cyprus with new eyes. Moreover, Cyprus, now that Suez was gone, was a symbol of British domination of the Mediterranean. Cyprus was, for Briton and Greek alike, a matter of face. For Great Britain had emerged from World War II impoverished, weakened, and now, in her eyes, the Greeks, who owed the creation of their state, and its preservation, to British aid, were snapping at the lion. The lion bared its teeth.

So much I learned from libraries, but I did not learn it from Greek or Briton. Nations, like individuals, are ill-tempered after a period of strain. The air was filled with righteous self-justifications, with mutual recriminations, hurt surprise until one was ludicrously reminded of a married couple quarreling over the custody of a child, of "I've given you the best years of my life." No one talked sensibly, and in Athens, at least, sensible talk was out of the question. Not one Greek politician dared to suggest moderation, and not one British minister, whether he dared or not, did.

Cyprus is a classic example of the modern power-state's semantic confusion. That state, inevitably, talks loudly of its desire that all subject peoples shall be free to govern themselves, of Four Freedoms, or more, of self-determination, and it talks that way not solely for foreign consumption. It really believes that it means what it is saying, but in the minds of its officials as they speak, and in the minds of its citizens as they hear, certain unspoken and saving clauses are present. "Should it be possible, that is, should no more important considerations overrule this generality, all peoples should be self-governing." That is what the minister means as he speaks and what his compatriots hear. These "important considerations," of course, are the well-being of the speaker and the speaker's state. For that well-being is quite clearly, in that nation's mind, the best possible basis for world peace, which on those terms it sincerely desires. These speeches, pumped abroad by Information Services and Propaganda Bureaus and Commissariats for Culture, are not sheer humbug. They are sermons, which, remember, are always preached at somebody else, sermons which sketch the world in which we would like to live, not the world in which we do live. As such they are valuable, for they keep the ideal alive. So when American politicians wrote and subscribed to the declaration "that all men are created equal . . . endowed . . . with certain unalienable Rights, . . . Life, Liberty . . . " they were expressing a pious hope for the future, not a fact, as they admitted when, in a subsequent document, they insisted that only three-fifths of the population of slave states should be used as a basis for representation in the House. This lofty talk, particularly prevalent in time of war, is a characteristic of all states, but particularly of democratic states, whose electorate must be convinced and constantly reassured that this particular war is being fought for the most righteous of motives.

Unfortunately the listeners abroad swallow such speeches at their literal value, not because they are stupid, but because in this case they wish to believe. When the war is over, and the modern state continues to talk like Wilson and act like Machiavelli, those foreigners affected fail to realize the purity of the power's motives, and the power is astonished by their reproaches. Cannot others see the reasons that at this moment, in this position, former promises cannot be fulfilled? They cannot. They do not wish to see, and moreover, the reasons which would be advanced if the power spoke frankly, would seem to them selfish and crass. They do not, oddly, correlate the speaker's well-being and world peace quite as closely as he is likely to do.

So in the case of Cyprus. Very well, the Greeks disliked the British; one can see why. But why were they so anti-American that even as early as 1954 they mobbed the American Embassy, a riot in which seventy-five Athenians were wounded? Why, in early 1956, was the American flag to be burned, why were American properties destroyed, American sailors attacked on the streets of Athens? Briefly, because the Greeks believed that when we spoke for foreign consumption we meant what we said. About the British, the Greeks had certain reservations, for despite the long friendship, Britain was an imperial power, but the United States . . . Yet we assisted Britain in every way to keep her grip on Cyprus, and we kept on assisting Britain, even as we began a new series of sermons against colonialism. In 1954, for example, the United States assisted Britain in blocking a Greek appeal to the UN that the matter of Cyprus be discussed. Not even a discussion would we permit, and that after all our talk! After that action, a tactless Minister of State for Colonial Affairs, encouraged, the Greeks reasoned, by our attitude, dropped diplomatese and stated bluntly that Cyprus, for reasons of imperial strategy, could "never" hope to determine its own allegiance. Since that speech the island has fought the British with strikes, homemade grenades, and bullets, while the British have fought back with guns, curfews, and raids upon houses and monasteries. As they fought, the Greeks encouraged the Cypriots, with inflammatory broadcasts, technical advice, and probably with clandestine shipments of arms. The last the Greeks naturally deny, but if they could get arms to Cyprus, they got them there.

In August 1955, Great Britain deigned to talk the matter over, at least, but while she invited the Greek Prime Minister to London, she invited his Turkish counterpart too. To the Greeks the invitation to Turkey was a shock. True, twenty per cent of the island's population is Turkish, but that seemed inadequate reason in their eyes. The greater shock was the Turkish announcement that, should Cyprus leave British hands, it must revert to Turkey. She had owned it before Great Britain, and if it left present hands, she must have it back. What that meant to the Greeks is that the British and the Turks were now allies against Greece. The Turks, the ancient enemies, would once more try to enslave Greeks.

On September 6, someone set off a bomb in the Turkish Consulate in Salonika. A Greek, the Turks said; a Turk, said the Greeks officially, or perhaps a renegade Greek in Turkish pay, or perhaps . . . Their imaginations worked overtime. Whoever did it, Turkish mobs, inflamed by press headlines that Mustafa Kemal's birthplace had been destroyed, had by that evening systematically destroyed Greek lives and property in Istanbul and Izmir, that is, in the ancient capital of the Byzantine Empire and the city formerly called Smyrna, where Greek armies had been based in the nineteen-twenties. While the Turkish government stood politely aside, Turks killed Greeks—particularly priests; they desecrated more than seventy Greek churches; they smashed Greek tombs in cemeteries, particularly those of the Ecumenical Patriarchs, Archbishops of Constantinople, traditional heads of the Orthodox Church. It was a clear renewal of traditional hostility, somewhat muffled recently by the mutual fear of Communism, a clear reminder that the Greek dream of expansion in that direction, if not dead, had better die, and a hint of what Greeks could expect if they attempted, through Cyprus, another attack upon the Turkish Asiatic coast. The Turks fear this much less, in fact, than they fear an eventual Communist domination of Greece, and hence a Communist occupation of an island in sight of the Turkish mainland, an island that could block Turkey from her Koranic brethren in Egypt and hamper her communications with the countries of the Arab League.

The United States had backed Britain once. What would she do now? Into Athens poured condolences from church groups, among them American, from governments, but not until September 18 did Dulles speak. As tactless as the British Minister of State for Colonial Affairs, and without his excuse of exasperation, Dulles addressed identical notes to both Greece and Turkey, scolding them for being bad boys, when, after all, both were brothers in NATO and both were receiving American aid. The day after the note was published in Athens, the UN rejected a Greek request that Cyprus be discussed; those voting against the request included the United States, Great Britain, and Turkey; those for, the USSR and Egypt. By nightfall the green uniforms of police massed thick about the American Consulate, the offices of the American Military Mission, and the U. S. Information Service library, an attention British and Turkish properties also enjoyed. Mobs formed, but so rich was the choice of targets, American, British, and Turkish, that they swept uncertainly through the streets, and for the moment the physical damage—and thus to the imperceptive eye the diplomatic damage—seemed slight.

It was at this moment that Andreas called. Andreas was a Cypriot, a student at the University of Athens, in his last year. As a Cypriot, he had certain university fees waived, as well as the entrance examinations, inducements by which the Greeks hope to lure Cypriots away from British universities, to steep them in Greek attitudes so that they may return to

Cyprus as political missionaries. (Students from the Dodecanese islands, so recently returned by Italy, share these privileges, lest they study in Italy and thus maintain culturally the former tie.) Andreas, then, had a form of scholarship which he badly needed, as he received no money from home. He supported himself in Athens by teaching English to Greek officers attached to the British and American military missions, and to students at a private institute.

Before studying in Athens Andreas had spent two years in business in London. In Athens, therefore, he was suspected of being pro-British. At home the British authorities, now that he was in Athens, suspected him of being pro-Greek, and EOKA (National Organization of Cypriot Fighters), an underground society which specializes in anti-British violence, held his allegiance doubtful, to say the least. Moreover, he was studying at the University of Athens English language and literature, which, even if taught in Athens, seemed suspect both to EOKA and the Greeks. He was, then, when I met him, a worried young man.

He was particularly anxious to meet Americans, for although he longed to practice his English, he was no longer able to associate openly with the British. He had been in the habit of stopping every morning at a café near the British Council, the equivalent of our Information Service, to take a coffee with an Englishman who taught at the University, but the police had watched this association, had trailed him home, and informed him that if he continued to enjoy the company of the enemy, his scholarship would be withdrawn. Since I was an American, and we had in America a mutual friend, Andreas even proposed that I take a large apartment, one room of which he could rent. He saw himself in my house under a neutral roof, where he could speak without hesitation and without fear. But political novice though I was, I was already able to prophesy. "You'd better be glad there isn't room here," I warned him. "In three months the Americans will be as unpopular as the British in Greece. Oh," I continued, Cassandra-like, "you wait and see."

In one sense I was wrong, despite the burning of the American flag, the wrecking of American property, the attack upon American servicemen. The anger against both British and Americans remained curiously impersonal; flags might be burned, libraries wrecked, the consular shield ripped from British or American offices, but individuals were rarely molested. When they were, such as the American sailors, the anger seemed directed against the uniform, not the person. But this anger, impersonal though it might remain, was deeper against the British than against the Americans, so much so that at the height of the disturbance, a Greek lady suggested, for my own benefit, that I should wear in my lapel a miniature American flag.

Meanwhile, the Greeks worked overtime to explain that no Greek was to blame for anything. The American fleet, they said, was not in the

Piræus by chance when Makarios was seized; it was there by plan, a scheme of British and Americans to overawe them. Hence the riot. Greeks asserted that a Turk set off the bomb inside the Turkish Consulate at Salonika. Or an Englishman. The purpose? To incite the riots against Greeks in Istanbul and Izmir. An Englishman bombed, they swore, the British Institute in Athens. He did it to make the Greeks look like barbarians. And they know that no Greek Cypriots threw the hand-grenades over the garden wall in Nicosia, in June, which killed the American Vice-Consul and wounded two of his friends. An Englishman did that, or a Turk, to turn America against the Greeks. (The Greek-American press in the United States has solemnly recorded this.) The Greek will accept no responsibility at all if he can avoid it, and he is an expert wiggler. "Poor Greece!" he will say, and his eyes well with tears. "She is unfortunate." And so she is, subject to earthquakes that devastate whole areas, arid, infertile, mountainous, ringed by enemies, over-populated. All these things are true, and it is doubtful if they can be ameliorated, much less corrected. One sympathizes. But the Greeks are also, and for historic reasons this generation cannot control, so in-dividualistic, so ruthlessly opportunistic as they fight to keep alive in this poor, crowded land, that they can be spurred to co-operation only through passion, and that passion must be kept at white-heat. Analysis is improb-able in this atmosphere; self-analysis impossible. Politically, the Greeks move in spurts and in frenzy, and for this human failing they pay a high political and social price.

Americans, of course, are basically the same, but we have been aided by chance. We have felt secure. We have never known, in any great numbers, the fear of actual starvation; there has always been, in our pantry, at least a few beans and a little fat meat. When we did face invasion and starvation, in colonial times, for example, we exhibited exactly the Greek characteristics. We forget that Cotton Mather insisted that Indians were not humans but demons or the descendants of demons, and hence should be destroyed; we forget the slyness, the deceit in colonial dealings with the Indian, the bland assumption that since the colonists were God's chosen, they could do no wrong. With us this was a passing phase, and one sentimentalized by now into thankful Pilgrims inviting noble savages to a feast. We could, and did, grab and expand. The Greeks cannot, and they have festered under these conditions for—at a mini-mum—five hundred years. The Greeks may be right in believing that riches cure most social ills. It is a rich nation that sentimentalizes about living in a house by the side of the road and being a friend to man, the vine-covered cottage with roses round the door, a cottage, if visualized at all, complete with electric kitchen with mechanical garbage disposal, and tiled bath. We are rich, are glad of it, and we ought to be glad of it, but when we thank God that we are made not as other men, we might consider that we had a broad land, weak or distant enemies, and ample natural resources upon which to build.

I did not feel so magnanimous when Andreas told me that the British had bombed the British Institute. I was sharp. "Of all people, Andreas," I scolded, "you ought to know that the English mind doesn't work that way. The last thing an Englishman would think of doing is to bomb English property." The British Institute, Andreas informed me, wasn't British property at all; it was leased from the Greek Ministry of War! But then Andreas was distraught. Both his jobs were gone. His aunt had arrived from Cyprus for a rest cure, his responsibility during her stay, and she was still too nervous to sleep. His cousin, her daughter, had been caught in a street shooting fray in the streets of Paphos (Paphos, where Aphrodite sprang from the waves!), her son had been threatened with death for holding a government, and hence, British, job. She lived for news broadcasts and letters from home, longing for news, afraid of its arrival.

He looked at his watch and glanced at the radio. I nodded permission. We listened to the news. "Every day," he said dully, "I listen, and I hear the name of someone I know. Arrested, shot."

"Andreas," I asked diffidently, "is there nothing that can be done?"

"There was a time when they could have had their bases, gladly. If they had talked to us. . . . Now it is too late. I'll have to go back," he added, "but there will be nothing for me to do except teach English, and I cannot teach that, now, except in a government school. And then, as a teacher in a government school, I shall be a traitor to my countrymen, and so I may be shot. It is not a very nice prospect," he said mildly. "I know it used to happen like that, but I hoped, after all these wars, that it just might turn out differently for me."

In July, after the university year was over, Andreas sailed for Cyprus. I received his letter in Arkansas, remote from a war, remote from a frontier, remote from a sea. I opened it in a garden, under a big oak tree. "Dear Mr. Lee," the letter read, "I am back in Cyprus. When I arrived, I was arrested, with all the other returning students, and for some time we were kept in jail. Now I am released. I am at home, but I am only allowed to leave the house from sunrise to sunset, and I may not walk outside the town. I am reading a good deal. They say that if I take a job as a teacher, perhaps the ban on my movements will be lifted. I am considering the matter."

Considering the matter indeed! If he accepted, another Michaelakis Karaolis might well confine him to a much narrower room. I felt the dog licking my hand. "Oh, go away!" I said crossly, as I thought: "Is there anything I can do?" I knew there was nothing. Then, curious, I looked carefully at the envelope. It had not been censored. The amenities, then, were being observed.

Suggestions

1. As in "The Irony of It All," the title "Cyprus: The Political Animals at Play" is an ironic description of the subject. The essay concerns a situation and a cultural attitude far different from those to which Americans are accustomed. The connotations of "playing politics," common in American discussions, can only be considered ironic when applied to Athenian politics. But the speaker's attitude toward his subject is even more complex. His dominant tone is decidedly serious. The behavior of foreigners is not seen as merely amusing. Beneath the seriousness there is a tone of sardonic humor, which relieves and strengthens the dominant tone. With this secondary tone he can treat Athenians as friends or acquaintances rather than statistical or factual items for a political report; it is this that keeps the essay from becoming a pedantic rehash of history or a newscaster's pretentious analysis of current events. To consider this ironic tone flippant is to miss the important point of the essay and to misread its technique.

2. How effective is the analogy of Greece with Tennessee?

3. Comment on the function of sentence fragments as the author recounts past Greek history (¶3).

4. Discuss: "Americans, of course, are basically the same [as Greeks in political behavior]." Is the analysis of American attitudes toward politics supported by convincing evidence?

5. Does the explanation of the Greek desire for Cyprus strike you as satisfactory?

6. How would you describe the speaker's attitude toward the "modern power-state's semantic confusion"—i.e. the discussion of how a single idealistic proclamation or official policy can have multiple meanings?

7. Does the example of Andreas, which illustrates the last third of the essay, strengthen or weaken the generalizations about other Greeks and Cypriots?

8. Write an analysis of a foreign problem, looking at it if possible with the eyes of the nation concerned. You may wish to use as examples foreign students you have known as well as secondary material in newspapers or in the library.

3

Principles and Practice

Experience with persons, places, events, and processes gives a writer his material; intuition will perhaps lead him to define and compare, and practice at least some of the other methods illustrated in Part 2 of this book. Analyzing the work of professionals, though, makes the writer's experience and intuitive grasp of technique more readily available to him. Now we approach some other ways in which reading can assist him. Since writing begins, or should begin, in thought and emotion, he must study the processes of reasoning and feeling; he must, that is, learn a little about logic and psychology. Further, the writer's medium is words—the language; and so he must not only understand the importance of language as a human instrument but also know, at least in outline, the history of his own language, the American branch of the English trunk. Like most other languages, to divide yet again, American English exists in both oral and written form. *Style* is the quality that language possesses when it is written expertly. And the experts: what have they recorded about the profession of writing? A very great deal from which the apprentice writer can benefit. Finally, since the reader who cannot evaluate gains little from his reading, the writer must be acquainted with methods of literary analysis, or literary criticism, and study its principles in action.

The essays in this part introduce some salient features of these activities, these kinds of knowledge. The first two groups are concerned with matters of thought, language, and style: with deductive-inductive logic and its offspring, scientific thinking; with the emotions in relation to reason; with language, from its importance as a "tool of symbolization" to the particulars of English as it is spoken west of the Atlantic Ocean; with style and certain crimes against style committed by amateurs and professionals. Serious topics, these, but capable of lighter treatment too, as some of the essays show.

"Critics and Creators," the third group, ranges from accounts of the writer's working day to considerations of more speculative questions, such as the role of the reviewer and that of the creative writer in contemporary society. Still other essays, illustrating the activities of the critics, are concerned with a number of problems often debated. For instance: Why study literature? What are the differences among the various literary forms? Why is much contemporary writing hard to understand? These essays look forward to Part 4 of the book, which is a miniature introduction to literature in its traditional sense. They also look back to the earlier sections, since considerations of thought, language, and style are seldom far from their speakers' minds. "Critics and Creators" is thus both a recapitulation and a new beginning.

T H O U G H T

THE USES AND LIMITATIONS OF LOGIC

L. M. MYERS *From* GUIDE TO AMERICAN ENGLISH.
© *1955, Prentice-Hall, Inc.*

The kind of reasoning used in the formation of generalizations is called *inductive*. Properly used, it begins with careful observations of physical phenomena and works up to a systematic explanation of them. This explanation is called a hypothesis. It may be anything from a bare guess to a firm and well tested belief, but it is always subject to re-examination and possible revision when new evidence comes in. For example, many of the hypotheses of Isaac Newton, which for centuries seemed to be absolutely solid, have had to be modified in the light of Einstein's theory of relativity. Newton's system has not been destroyed, it has been refined. For most purposes it still works well enough, but when we are dealing with the great distances found in outer space or the tiny distances found within the atom we find that Einstein's system works better. And of course the time may come when we know enough to modify that.

The inductive method is the one primarily used in the experimental approach to knowledge. The mathematical or logical approach begins from the other end. Whether logic is a branch of mathematics or mathematics is a branch of logic is a question I do not feel competent to settle. At any rate, both mathematicians and logicians proceed by *deductive reasoning*. That is, they begin with general statements assumed to be true and work down from these to more particular statements which must be true if the general ones are.

It is silly to argue about which of these methods is better. They are appropriate for different purposes. A scientist usually forms his hypotheses by a combination of induction and hunches, and he may test them the same way (if he doesn't have any hunches, he may be a good technician, but he'll never get very far except by pure luck). But once he is satisfied with a hypothesis he will say, "All right, let's assume this is true. Now what follows?" It is now time for a stage of deductive reasoning, to open new possibilities. Of course his conclusions must again be checked by observation, and then—and so forth, and so forth. Science moves forward by steps, and it takes two legs to walk.

Deductive logic may be defined roughly as a systematic method of *comparing statements* in such a way that they will produce reliable additional statements. Suppose, for instance, that somebody asks you whether a German-born friend of yours has become a naturalized citizen of the United States. Since you have never heard the matter discussed, you do not immediately know; but you decide to see whether anything you do know will lead you to the correct answer. Is there anything about him that is *characteristic* of either citizens or non-citizens? Among other things, you know that he is employed as an engineer in the State Highway Department, and you remember that in your state only citizens are eligible to hold such jobs. You therefore conclude that he *must be* a citizen. Two bits of information which apparently had nothing to do with each other when you picked them up have been made to produce a third bit of information.

Everybody of even moderate intelligence compares statements in some such way as this; but a good many people do not know how to *test the connections* to see whether the results they get are reliable. Suppose we compare two attempts to prove the same thing:

>   1. All Communists read Marx.
>   Jones reads Marx.
>   Therefore Jones is a Communist.
>   2. Only Communists read Marx.
>   Jones reads Marx.
>   Therefore Jones is a Communist.

Perhaps you see at a glance that the first argument proves nothing at all, while the second is quite sound. However, if you read the newspapers you must realize that millions of people are actually convinced by arguments like the first, so it may be just as well to study the structure of the two arguments. The easiest way to do this is to change the form of the statements so that they can be readily diagramed, and then see what the diagrams indicate.

1. All Communists are readers of Marx.

   This can be diagramed as follows, with the circle marked C standing for Communists, and the circle marked R standing for readers of Marx:

Jones is a reader of Marx.

If we want to add the information in this statement to the diagram we already have, we must put a little circle J for Jones somewhere within the circle marked R for readers. But there is nothing to tell us *where* in the circle it goes—whether it should be within or without the circle marked C for Communists.

We therefore have no basis for deciding whether Jones is a Communist or not.

2. Only Communists are readers of Marx.

This has to be diagramed with the circles in a different relation:

Jones is a reader of Marx.

If we add the information in this statement to the diagram we have just drawn, we must put the little circle for Jones in the medium-sized circle marked R; and if we do this we *inevitably* put it also within the larger circle marked C.

We are therefore justified in drawing the conclusion that Jones is a Communist. If the first two statements are true, the conclusion *must* be true.

SYLLOGISMS

The kind of argument we have been considering is called a *syllogism*. It is the principal device of traditional logic, and very useful if you know how to handle it. There are various types of syllogisms, and it is possible to discuss them at great length and in highly technical terms. But the basic principles are simple, and by using our three circles we can get at these principles much more rapidly and directly than we could with words alone.

A syllogism consists of two statements *assumed to be true,* from which a third statement follows inevitably *if* the first two are true. The first two statements are usually called the *premises,* and the third the *conclusion.* Thus if we say (1) that all college students are intelligent and (2) that Dick is a college student, we can draw the conclusion that Dick is intelligent. Of course if the statements are not true, the conclusion may not be true either; but it is *logically sound.*

THE FIRST STATEMENT

The first statement must show the relation between *two classes.* Typical statements of this kind are:

> All Frenchmen are Europeans.
> Some Irishmen are policemen.
> No Bolivians are Europeans.
> Some Irishmen are not policemen.
> Casey is an Irishman.
> Casey is not a policeman.
> The Spartans were Greeks.

Notice three things about these statements: (1) we may talk of all or part of a class; (2) an individual (Casey) is considered a class by himself; (3) the verb in the statement is always some form of the verb *to be.*

If you have a statement like "John *eats* pie," you have to change it to "John *is* a pie eater" before you can use it in a syllogism. It is then easy to show the relation between the two classes by drawing two circles. There are only a limited number of possible relations. The most obvious are these three:

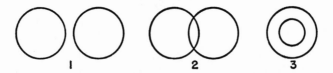

The first of these is simple, reliable, and reversible. It indicates definitely that the two classes do not coincide at all. If the two circles stand for Bolivians and Europeans, this diagram shows not only that no Bolivians are Europeans, but that no Europeans are Bolivians.

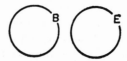

The second is also reversible, but it is not as simple as the first. Suppose we use it to diagram the statement that some Irishmen are policemen.

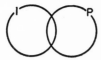

Does it also indicate that some policemen are Irishmen? A glance shows that it does. Since the two classes overlap, some members of each must also be in the other. But this diagram fails to give any reliable information about the parts of the two circles that do *not* overlap. If we want to be really careful, we had better draw it this way:

The solid parts of the two circles indicate our definite information; the dotted parts indicate mere possibilities. Thus the diagram indicates that certainly some *and possibly all* Irishmen are policemen; and that certainly some *and possibly all* policemen are Irishmen. We cannot be sure *from our premise* that either circle actually extends beyond the overlap. Of course we may know as a matter of general information that there are Irishmen who are not policemen and policemen that are not Irishmen; but neither fact follows logically from the statement that some Irishmen are policemen.

We might also draw overlapping circles to indicate that some Irishmen are *not* policemen. To do this accurately we would need a diagram like this:

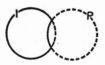

The area within the solid curves indicates the Irishmen who are not policemen. But we cannot tell either whether there are Irishmen who are policemen (in the overlapping area) or policemen who are not Irishmen. In other words, a really accurate diagram might show the circles overlapping, separate, or with the P inside the I. But on the basis of our statement, the only diagram we can draw is one that shows that *at least some* Irishmen are not included in the class of policemen.

The third diagram also has to be considered with care. Suppose we use it to indicate that all Frenchmen are Europeans:

This seems to indicate that there are some Europeans who are *not* Frenchmen. This is true enough, but it is not contained in the statement which our diagram is supposed to illustrate. Therefore we might draw a more careful diagram this way:

This shows that the inner circle *cannot* extend beyond the outer circle; but, as the arrows indicate, it may completely fill the larger one.

For most ordinary purposes we do not have to be as careful as all this; we can draw our circles with solid lines and without arrows. But we should remember to be very careful not to make any assumptions from the parts of circles that could be drawn differently.

There is another thing about the third diagram that deserves special emphasis, because failure to realize it is the most common cause of faulty logic. It can represent either of the following statements.

> *All* Frenchmen are Europeans.
> *Only* Europeans are Frenchmen.

But it does not imply the statement that all Europeans are Frenchmen or that only Frenchmen are Europeans. Remember: (1) the class described by *all* must be represented by the *smaller* circle; (2) the class described by *only* must be represented by the *larger* circle.

THE SECOND STATEMENT

The second statement in a syllogism must show the relation between *one* of the classes in the first statement and a *third* class. The information contained in this statement may then be added to the diagram representing the first statement. We gave examples of this in the two syllogisms, one valid and one invalid, that attempted to show that Jones was a Communist. Other examples will be found in the next paragraph.

THE CONCLUSION

If the diagram representing the first two statements now shows definitely the relation between the third class and the class *not* mentioned in the second statement, a valid conclusion may be drawn. Otherwise the syllogism proves nothing at all.

1. All Norwegians are blonds.
   John is a blond.

   No conclusion possible.

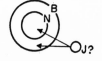

2. All blonds are Norwegians.
   John is blond.

   Conclusion: John is a Norwegian.

3. No marines are cowards.
   Dave is a marine.

   Conclusion: Dave is not a coward.

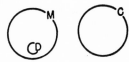

4. Some of his friends are sailors.
   All of his friends are clever people.

   Conclusion: Some sailors are clever
   people.

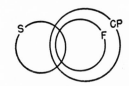

5. Only big men are tackles.
   Dick is a big man.

   No conclusion possible.

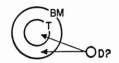

Of course you may be quite capable of testing a syllogism for validity without drawing a picture of it; but if you have to check one it is much easier to do it with the three circles than by learning a large number of rules about *universal negatives, particular affirmatives,* the *laws of conversion,* and the *fallacy of unwarranted distribution.* All you have to do is to draw the first two circles in such a way as to indicate the information in the first statement, add the information contained in the second statement, and see whether the combined diagram proves anything or not.

There is, of course, a good deal more to logic than the study of syllogisms; and I hope I have not given the impression that the whole subject can be condensed into one neat little capsule for handy absorp-tion. But the basic principles of the logical method are illustrated in the material we have examined, and the importance of this method should be obvious. A man who thinks illogically is like one who pays no atten-tion to the difference between the signs for multiplication and division, or addition and subtraction. When he attempts to work out a problem for himself he is completely unreliable. And when he receives information he is likely to be at the mercy of the man who hands it out.

TRUTH AND VALIDITY

If you learn the method shown in the preceding pages you can avoid *illogical conclusions,* because you will have found out a reliable way of tracing the connections between *statements assumed to be true.* But you must resist the temptation to believe that when a conclusion is logically sound or "valid" it is inevitably true. The conclusion is certainly true *only* if the basic statements are certainly true. And this is *never* possible when the statements deal with physical things. This does not mean that logic is useless in dealing with physical things, but only that it must be used with appropriate caution.

A TRUE SYLLOGISM

Examine the following syllogism:

> All squares are rectangles.
> ABCD is a square.
>
> Therefore ABCD is a rectangle.

There is not only a sound syllogism but a perfectly true one, because both squares and rectangles are *pure abstractions created by definition,* and the definition of a rectangle includes the definition of a square. All squares have the same properties *by definition.* It is therefore unnecessary to examine every square that has been conceived or that may be con-ceived in the future to see if its sides and angles are equal; if they are not equal, it is not a square. The same is true of "all rectangles." Re-member, *no square has ever been drawn.* The *figure* ABCD that you see on a blackboard or in a book is not a square, but merely the representa-tion of a square. If you should measure it with very accurate instruments and find that two of the angles were 89 degrees and the other two 91 degrees, you would not have found an exceptional square that violated the rule. You would merely have found a slightly inaccurate *representa-tion* of a square, which is nothing to get excited about.

AN APPROXIMATELY TRUE SYLLOGISM

On the other hand, let us consider the following syllogism:

> All Englishmen are tea-drinkers.
> Derek is an Englishman.
>
> Therefore Derek is a tea-drinker.

This follows the same form as the syllogism about squares and rectangles, and is equally sound from a logical point of view. We may therefore say that *if* the first two statements are true, the conclusion is equally true. But if we examine the argument closely we notice an important difference. Englishmen are *not* created by definition, but by cohabitation. We cannot, therefore, be certain in advance that they are all alike. We are not justified in making a statement about all Englishmen until we have examined them all. If Derek is an Englishman, we have to find out that he is a tea-drinker before we are justified in making the statement that all Englishmen are tea-drinkers. In other words, we have to know that he is a tea-drinker before we can prove that he is a tea-drinker. Our logic does not seem to be getting us very far.

This does not mean that logic is useless when applied to physical things, but only that it never produces hundred per cent certainties in this field as it does when applied to mathematical abstractions. With physical things, logic can give us only probabilities and approximations— but so can measurements. Let us rephrase our syllogism about Derek in such a way as to make it useful.

> A very high proportion of Englishmen are known to be tea-drinkers.
> It is very nearly certain that Derek is an Englishman.
>
> Therefore it is extremely probable that Derek is a tea-drinker.

If we are expecting to have Derek as a house guest, this more elastic syllogism will be useful. In the first place it suggests that we have some tea on hand when Derek comes. It also suggests that we ask him about his taste before we start forcing tea down his possibly unwilling throat. If it turns out that he is an unusual Englishman, we are spared a shock— and maybe we can get a refund on the unopened tea.

THE LIMITATIONS OF LOGIC

The reason that logic cannot be used rigidly with physical things may be explained quite simply. In a class of abstractions *created* by definition, all members are exactly alike, and some characteristics are *inevitably* associated with others. If you prove that something is a circle, you know that the relation of its diameter to its circumference is exactly *pi,* because that's the way circles are. But when we turn to the physical world we find:

1. That the members of a class are never exactly alike. Even if the class has only one member, that one is constantly changing.

2. That the association of characteristics is merely a matter of probability.

Consequently, when a man says "All Syrians (or women or college professors or Fords) are alike," he is not telling the truth, though he may be perfectly sincere. And when he says "Anybody that would do that would steal sheep," he is treating a probability (possibly a pretty good one) as if it were a fact.

There are two obvious temptations to say (and think) things like these. First, it is flattering to the ego to pretend that we know "all about" something. Second, it saves a lot of trouble. If you "know" in advance that all Mexicans are lazy, all Scotsmen stingy, and all politicians dishonest, you are spared the task of finding out about them one by one. Before yielding to these temptations, however, it might be a good idea to consider whether you can afford to yield to them.

It is often said that many fanatics and certain types of lunatics are among the most logical people in the world. You can't find fault with their chains of reasoning, and even their facts are often approximately right. But because they treat approximations and probabilities as absolute certainties, their conclusions are wildly wrong.

THE COMMUNIST THEORY

Perhaps the most terrifying example of logic run wild is the development and spread of communistic theories. Marx's theories are collectively known as dialectical materialism. *Dialectical* is merely another word for logical, and *materialism* indicates that physical things are to be taken as the basis of all thinking. In other words, Marx believed: (1) that logic can be applied directly and exactly to physical things; (2) that by *defining* such things as capitalists and proletarians he somehow exerted such control over them as to make them all exactly, or at least "essentially" alike. He would probably have denied this, but it is implicit in his whole theory. He states very definitely that if people own property and employ labor they *must* act in certain ways, and that their actions will *inevitably* bring about certain results. Moreover, he asserts that the interests of capitalists and proletarians are inevitably opposed.

Now, whatever else he was, Marx was a well-educated and highly intelligent man. His logic is sound throughout. If you take his assumptions as true, you simply cannot avoid his conclusions. And the fact that a great many people do take his assumptions as absolutely true is causing an enormous amount of trouble in the world today.

The basic fallacy of dialectical materialism is not that the assumptions —the things stated to be true—did not happen to be true. It is that they could not *possibly* have been true in a world composed of ever-moving and changing arrangements of particles. Marx examined a certain number of specimens which he classified as capitalists and proletarians, and observed their activities. Up to this point he was acting like a respectable scientist. But then he lost his scientific modesty. He did not say:

This is the way these specimens have been observed to act. We may reasonably expect similar specimens under similar conditions to act in similar ways in the future. But of course if conditions change or new evidence is discovered we shall have to revise our tentative conclusions.

Instead he said in effect:

I have examined these specimens and found out all about them. They are exactly alike in all significant characteristics, and all their successors will be exactly like them. Any minor differences we may disregard as non-essential. No further observations are necessary, because this is the permanent truth. And if further observations seem to contradict my results, or changed conditions seem to modify the actions of later specimens slightly, we must explain the differences away. For instance, if you find a capitalist who does not seem to act like my capitalists, it is merely because he is clever in concealing his nature.

In other words, Marx thought that a definition of a capitalist, like a definition of a circle, could be effectively made to cover unobserved and future specimens. Instead of realizing that definitions of physical things are merely general statements based on past observations, he treated them exactly like definitions of mathematical abstractions. This was not an isolated mistake by Karl Marx; it was a typical example of an attitude which had been almost universal among educated people from Aristotle's time to his own, *but which has now been demonstrated to be completely unsound.* Of course this attitude has by no means disappeared. We are still plagued with plenty of learned people who think that by "defining their terms" they can somehow keep the changing universe in tidy order. But at least we have discovered how to disprove their arguments.

As we have already said, Marx himself was both well-educated and intelligent. If he had lived a century later and been exposed to modern knowledge of the physical universe, his theories might have taken a very different form. But today he has millions of followers who accept his theories quite uncritically as a matter of faith. They are led by thousands who have been trained to follow the kind of logical argument he used—and used extremely well—but who have not been trained to recognize the *limitations of logic.*

The fact is that the whole economic set-up of the twentieth century, especially in America, is quite different from the set-up in nineteenth-century England that Marx observed. His capitalists and proletarians were not quite so uniform as he thought they were, but at least they were on the whole fairly distinct groups, with interests that were often sharply opposed. Our economic classes are about as scrambled as our national blood lines. The workers at the Acme Knitting Mills may be sharply opposed to the owners in a given dispute, but they can hardly be opposed to all capitalists. Between their bank accounts and their insurance policies and a few stocks and bonds salted away here and there, almost all of them are to some extent capitalists themselves. Marx simply hadn't figured on this (how could he—it hardly occurred in his time), and Marx's followers are very much annoyed about the whole situation. They have spent years and years building a bridge across a raging torrent, preparing to lead their people over it and into the promised land. But they haven't noticed that the water has gone down and that people from both sides have been wading across it, fraternizing, intermarrying, and even settling down on islands that have appeared in the middle. It is all very confusing.

LOGIC—HANDLE WITH CARE

It is easy for most of us to accept the statement that the rigid application of Marxian logic to economic facts is a delusion, because we are opposed to Communism anyhow and will believe almost anything that shows it up. But Communists do not have a monopoly on this type of confusion. There are plenty of capitalists, soldiers, educators, and all sorts of other people who are perfectly certain that anything that was "logically proved" some generations ago must still be true today, no matter how much things have changed in the meantime.

There are perhaps even more people who take statements that are actually statistical summaries, only roughly true, and treat them as if they were absolutely reliable. They argue, for instance, that since fresh air is healthy, everybody should sleep with a window open. Their logic is beyond criticism, and perhaps their first premise is ninety per cent accurate; but their conclusion is sometimes unfortunate for children with sinus trouble or hay fever. You can undoubtedly find other examples.

Using sound logic on any practical problem is like using sound mathematics on an engineering problem—if you don't do it, you may go hopelessly astray. But when a good engineer has made his exact calculations, he always allows a reasonable margin of safety, because he realizes two things. There *may* be a factor or so he has not allowed for; and a part that *should* stand a thousand pounds of strain *may* break at five hundred. When we are dealing with the physical universe we never know *all* about anything. And no matter how carefully we define our classes, we can't make their members exactly alike.

Suggestions

1. Summarize the distinction between induction and deduction. Which is the main subject of "The Uses and Limitations of Logic"? Compare the speaker's account of the methods of the scientist, including the importance of hunches, with that given in † "The Method of Scientific Investigation."

2. Explain in your words what a *syllogism* is and summarize the rules governing its premises. Why are the following statements worthless in syllogistic reasoning?
"Henry R. Luce publishes *Time* magazine" (as a major premise).
"American Indians are vanishing, and Tallchief is an American Indian."

3. Show that the following statements yield valid (though possibly untrue) conclusions:
"Alice's boyfriend is a person, and nobody speaks to Alice."
"Santa Claus has a white beard, and anyone with a white beard is fat and jolly."

4. Reduce the reasoning about the German-born friend (¶3) to syllogistic form.

5. Define the sort of behavior that the speaker considers typical of a "respectable scientist," judging by his estimate of Karl Marx. What fallacy is committed by Marx's definitions?

6. Summarize the likeness between deductive logic and mathematics.

7. Explain: *phenomena, hypothesis, abstractions, proletarians, fraternizing.*

8. Write an essay on the place of deductive logic in argumentative writing, drawing your examples from the essays in Part 2, Section 8.

THOUGHT-SAVERS

CURTIS WOODHAM © *1960 by Curtis Woodham.*

It has long been a question whether the study of logic teaches us to avoid fallacies, or teaches us to employ them. Certainly its contribution in the latter respect justifies all the effort demanded by it; it may, indeed, be counted as one of the most significant labor-saving devices that have yet sprung from the human mind. Neither slide-rules nor washing-machines can hold a candle to it. For whereas only a small proportion of the country's high-school graduates enter colleges of engineering, and most women find that the laundry of an average-sized family can be done in one day a week, hard questions requiring some sort of answers turn up every day. Ought the country to maintain a strong air force if it has to borrow money to do so? Are youths of eighteen old enough to vote? Should football players have to pass courses? Very few of us can sidestep these and other knotty problems indefinitely, and when we are brought face-to-face with one of them we have our choice of two alternatives and no more.

Of course, if we like we can strive to think validly about the question before us. But the drain imposed on the brain-cells by this line of action is harrowing—some think positively dangerous. In such an emergency it is easier and safer to fall back on one or more of the fallacies isolated for us by the logicians. When, moreover, we find ourselves defending the indefensible—and who has never let fall such careless assertions as that more powerful cars promote highway safety, or that Southern Ne-groes are happier than Northern ones, and then been forced to uphold it? —in these crises the resort to fallacies is imperative. The affectionate nickname of "Thought-Savers," which their conservation of mental energy has earned for them, is a fair indication of the esteem in which they are universally held.

In referring to logical fallacies as thought-savers I do not have in mind those that form the core of the study of deductive logic—weaknesses in the structure of the syllogism, with whose invention Aristotle is gen-erally credited. For the beginner, at least, to introduce into his argument an undistributed middle, or draw an inference from two negative prem-ises, would either require more mental agility than would have been demanded by valid thought, or else would be to risk immediate detection and resulting disaster. Better to leave these devices to lecturers, editorial-writers, Fourth-of-July orators, and other monologuists, whose audiences cannot conveniently answer back. In the cut-and-thrust of friendly dis-cussion, however, the truly efficient thought-savers are those modes of reasoning—unreasoning, rather—that logicians call the material fallacies —nonsense imbedded in the substance of one's argument.

The principal value of a material fallacy lies not so much in its advancement of your own views as in its probable effect on your opponent. Whereas a false disjunction, if noticed at all, may produce only a faint sneer, while the development of the opposing argument continues unchecked, a well placed material fallacy usually upsets the other's inner equilibrium whether he can identify it or not. The consequent emotional tension makes it hard for him to follow his proper train of thought. If he falls to wrangling about the fallacy, a temptation he is not likely to be able to resist, the game will of course be yours.

The logicians who performed the service of cataloguing these thought-savers (and even equipping some of them with delightful Latin names) have unfortunately never reached agreement as to their exact number. There are, however, ten that seem to be basic, since they turn up in almost every list, and it is with them that the neophyte's study of the subject should commence. Let him commit their names carefully to memory; with one exception the names are descriptive and appropriate, and will aid him immeasurably in calling the right one to mind when the occasion requires it. And since the occasion is everything, since our watchword must ever be "The *right* fallacy on the *right* occasion," the list is here arranged in alphabetical order. By this system, luckily, one of the easiest to understand and remember is made to stand first. This is the

APPEAL TO A BIG STICK

or *Argumentum ad Baculum,* which evidently originated in kindergartens, where such persuasive appeals as "Take that back or I'll knock your ears off" are standard in the daily dialectic. At a more mature level this kind of argument takes a subtler form, as in "If you ever want to be invited to another rush-party, don't for heaven's sake bring up the race question"; and it is said that some professional men abstain from voting because political opinions can't possibly be good for business. To remind a government employee that Congress maintains investigating committees is to make the APPEAL TO A BIG STICK somewhat less subtly. For those in circles where threats are frowned on, it has its uses none the less: it can be silently practised on oneself. For instance, "I'd rather not even think about foreign policy; it always gives me a headache." In discussions of foreign policy the value of an

APPEAL TO A GREAT NAME

or *Argumentum ad Verecundiam*—appeal to reverence—has long been recognized. These may be effectively introduced by such formulas as *The Bible says* or *Shakespeare says.* Logicians often illustrate the APPEAL TO A GREAT NAME by citing the isolationist who reminds us, with perfect truth, that "Washington warned against entangling alliances." The name of Washington is about as great as they come, and when these words of his are quoted it is not much trouble to forget that they were spoken more than a century before 1903, the year the Wright Brothers proved that machines can fly. As a thought-saver, however, this example leaves a little to be desired, because a modicum of thought may have been expended in the choice of a man who had had a great deal of experience with alliances and normally refrained from expressing himself on subjects he knew nothing about. Better to select someone like Bernard Shaw, who is unquestionably a great playwright and never minded expressing himself on anything. If your opponent is rude enough to ask why being the author of the play that *My Fair Lady* is derived from should make anyone an authority on diet, you can always answer, "He lived to be ninety-three, didn't he?" where just living that long sounds like a mark of greatness. The APPEAL TO A GREAT NAME bears some resemblance to

ARGUMENT FROM ANALOGY

since most people reverence common sense (the faculty, says Stuart Chase, that tells us the world is flat) and all good analogies have a homely, familiar, common-sensical air about them. As a thought-saver the ANALOGY has few rivals and no superiors. It is so easy, so *simple* to see that a family which lives beyond its means is headed for trouble. Then isn't it plain that a government with an unbalanced budget is on the road to ruin? An ANALOGY exists, all right, between family and government finances, but there are two emergencies to watch out for when you use this one in a political squabble. Your opponent may realize that no two things in this world are alike in all respects and may interrupt with, "The danger of a family going into debt is that the husband's earning-power lasts only a few years, whereas. . . ." Or he may counter with an ANALOGY of his own: "If your child had polio you wouldn't hesitate to borrow money for his hospital expenses, would you? Now, our schools. . . ." If you are not speaking but merely unthinking about the national debt, you will find either of these ANALOGIES vastly comforting. Mrs. America of 1956, wishing the state to demand skill in cookery of prospective brides, argued before the Oregon legislature as follows: "If a state can require a blood test before marriage, it can certainly pass a law for compulsory cooking tests."[1] It is to be hoped that the legislators were too greatly awed to think of COUNTER-ANALOGIES. If the antagonist does respond in this way, switch the conversation off analogies as rapidly as possible. This may be done by

BEGGING THE QUESTION

or *Petitio Principii,* as in "Well, anyway, governments with huge national debts have always gone under." Since the question at issue is whether deficit financing is wise or foolish, you have "begged" it by speaking as though all hands agreed that the fall of Rome, etc., resulted from borrowing money. If the other man remarks that this country has grown steadily stronger ever since it got started by deficit-financing the Revolution, and our national debt is rather larger now, answer: *"Exceptio*

---

[1] Philadelphia *Bulletin,* 29 June 1956. Notice the lady's grasp of the basic principle, that a cogent analogy touches our love of the homely and down-to-earth.

probat regulam"—the exception proves the rule. The misapplication of this proverb—which properly understood is entirely correct—is the most adroit QUESTION-BEGGING device ever invented. If you see a sign reading GO ON GREEN ONLY at one intersection in a strange town but not at the others, you may reasonably assume that the prohibition is exceptional—else why did they put up a sign about it? The existence of the solitary sign proves the exception, and the exception proves the rule: turns on red normally permitted. Complicated, isn't it? But you don't want a valid example; the proverb is a thought-saver only when used fallaciously, as in your argument about government spending. Here you have *assumed* that the American experience is exceptional and that the reverse of it must be the rule. Why isn't "Issuing bonds makes governments stronger" the rule, and the history of the Confederate States the exception? Should your opponent accuse you of BEGGING THE QUESTION, assert what is generally believed, that that means talking beside the point. He probably won't be sure, and this will confuse him. If so, you will have produced a neat example of

DISTRACTION

by your mention of *talking beside the point,* which is another name for it. (Hence the neatness of the example.) As a thought-saver DISTRACTION follows a principle often usefully applied to exhausting physical labor: when you have washed windows until you are too tired to get them clean, switch to waxing floors or go do the dishes. You may find it impossible to return to the windows later. Likewise your transposition of the argument to the meaning of a logical term may leave fiscal matters permanently behind. DISTRACTION, which may also be practised in solitude, comprehends appeals to emotion for which no other terms exist (*Argumentum ad Baculum* is an appeal to fear), provided they are employed as substitutes for relevant reasoning. An attack on corporation income-taxes which begins satisfactorily with "Have you no pity for the widows and orphans whose only means of livelihood is being eroded?" is spoiled by the suggestion that heirs and heiresses, if their dividends were not taxed at the source, would have more funds to aid in the expansion of industry. This may involve both parties in some actual thinking about ratios of expenditure for consumer and producer goods, etc. DISTRACTION should be reapplied at once: don't you know something disgraceful about your opponent? (See SLURRING, below.) If not, return to the widows' trust-funds and introduce the expression *double taxation.* He may not notice the

EQUIVOCATION

or use of a term in an unstable sense if you lead off with the man who lives in Massachusetts and commutes to a job in New York. When both states tax the man's salary he is clearly a victim of double taxation, and surely your opponent will agree that that is unfair. Now it is your task to show that the widow who pays a tax on dividends derived from a company that has paid an income-tax is being similarly victimized, though of course she pays no tax on the money she did not receive. Here again the danger is that too much cerebration will be expended in exploiting the fallacy. If EQUIVOCATION is to be a true thought-saver we must content ourselves with simpler examples, such as, "Biologists say that man is the highest being on the evolutionary ladder. So women must be inferior— they obviously aren't men." If the double sense of *man* is too well known to make this argument dependable, several words of a more learned character offer possibilities: "I don't trust his politics; he is taking *Liberal* Arts." Such terms as *democracy, happiness,* and *religion*—the more abstract the better—lend themselves to EQUIVOCATION peculiarly well. As a rule the unthinker must carefully sidestep (see DISTRACTION) any request in the following form: "Would you mind giving me a concrete example of what you mean by [*equivocal term*]?" An exception may be made, however, when an opportunity arises for

HASTY GENERALIZATION

(or *Generalizing from One Instance*). Most general statements, if they are to be very useful, must cover such a large number of cases that nobody could possibly examine each one. That *all swans are white* was widely believed until a black one arrived from Australia. Other scientific generalizations have fared better: *Sunlight retards the growth of plant cells* has proved exceedingly useful to botanists, among others, though it is not certain but just immensely probable, since not all the cells that have ever been exposed to the sun have been inspected. This limitation on the trustworthiness of the inductive method opens a rich field for unthought. If scientists can be excused and even admired for dealing in uncertainties, why, after meeting two or three braggarts from Dallas or Houston, should the unthinker not state that all Texans boast? In case of objections, see *Exceptio probat regulam.* Logic tells us that a generalization grows increasingly probable as the number of instances supporting it grows, whereas each new exception weakens it that much more. If generalizing is to be an effective thought-saver this rule must at all costs be forgotten. HASTY GENERALIZATION may also be applied to the search for causes: in which case it is affectionately called

POST HOC ERGO PROPTER HOC

which is unique among thought-savers in that the Latin phrase is the common name and the translation, "After this therefore due to this," is known only to the learned. The fallacy, however, is known to practically everybody. Since HIC (anything) cannot possibly cause HOC (anything that happened before HIC appeared) the temptation to assume the negative contrary is often overwhelming. An example might clarify this point. Suppose you have a friend (call him HIC) who becomes an alcoholic. Then you discover (no matter how) that in his early years his parents kept liquor around, and he knew it (this is HOC). Although (and even *since*) it is not possible that HIC's alcoholism caused his parents to have liquor in the house during his childhood (HOC), what could be more logical than to reverse matters and suppose that (*a*) HOC caused HIC to become an alcoholic, and, further, that (*b*) the universal cause of alcoholism is early exposure to the fumes? This example shows that POST HOC ERGO PROPTER HOC is serviceable for not only casual causal explanations of particular things but also the HASTY GENERALIZATIONS that they readily slide into. Since anything that is caused is caused by a thing or things that happened earlier (not later) than it did, and since the number of things that happened earlier is unlimited, we have only to pick the one we like and unreason that this "anything," because it happened POST HOC (afterward) must have been due to that earlier thing (PROPTER HOC). We thus save ourselves, in the example just given, the trouble of considering that (*a*) any of the other things which happened to HIC from childhood on might have driven him to drink, and (*b*) that nobody knows the causes of alcoholism anyway. POST HOC ERGO PROPTER HOC is thus seen to be a special variety of

SIMPLIFICATION

or BLURRING. Some authorities, including M. C. Beardsley,[2] call this thought-saver *Oversimplification* and restrict it to the various appeals to emotion. But no experienced unthinker fails to introduce fallacies in scaling down complex issues—nor does he confine himself to emotional appeals. Some of the most cogent SIMPLIFICATIONS, it is true, may be recognized by the presence of such stock words and phrases as *What it boils down to, simply, essentially, to put the matter in a nutshell,* and (see ARGUMENT FROM ANALOGY) *it is only common sense that,* all of which appeal to a universal human emotion: *viz.,* dislike of unnecessary brain-work. The point, however, is simply not to feel confined to emotional appeals, valuable though they are in an ancillary role. Excellent results may be obtained by combining them with BLURRING, as in "[The library bond-issue] moves all of us closer and closer to socialism, communism, collectivism or *whatever you want to call it,*"[3] a sentence from an editorial in the Lima, Ohio, *News*[4] which admirably blurs the distinction between

[2] See *Thinking Straight* (Second edition, Prentice-Hall, Inc., Englewood Cliffs, N. J., 1956), p. 325.
[3] Another stock phrase which the Simplifier would do well always to keep in a state of Red Alert.
[4] Quoted in *The Reporter*, 11 June 1959, p. 26.

the economic system of our strongest ally and that of our most formidable adversaries. Another striking aspect of this example is that it opens the way for a rather subtle resort to the last of the ten cardinal thought-savers,

SLURRING THE OPPONENT

or *Argumentum ad Hominem,* which is based on the principle that pork, ham, and bacon are unwholesome because pigpens are muddy. Logic demands that we argue *ad rem,* to the matter before the House. When that begins to require thought, it is desirable to turn one's attention *ad hominem,* to the person voicing the opposed opinion. He may have been expelled from high school, divorced, or arrested for passing a stop-sign. Obviously no attention need be paid to such a character's views about a new wing for the library. This thought-saver complements the APPEAL TO A GREAT NAME: if a high batting-average makes a man a good judge of razor-blades, then weaklings should hardly be permitted to shave. SLURRING must not be confused with challenging the expertness of a witness testifying about a point on which he is supposed to be expert, as when a lawyer alleges that a doctor called by the other side has buried most of his mistakes. It is essential that the slur be unrelated to the question under discussion. In earlier times it was sufficient to call the opponent a *Copperhead,* an *Atheist,* or a *Republican* to disqualify his opinions on any topic from the use of anesthetics in childbirth to the practice of cremation. Nowadays, as in the assault on the library bond-issue, the slur-of-all-work is *Communist.* (The term may be preceded by the phrase *Fifth-Amendment,* a reference to the U. S. Constitution.)

It may seem unnecessarily laborious to commit to memory the names of the ten thought-savers, and to make sure that they are understood at least vaguely. But *A stitch in time saves nine,* and under no circumstances should this step be omitted. Then, having completed his theoretical training, the novice (now a novice no longer) should begin putting his knowledge into practice by working this

EXERCISE

The following oration may have been published in The Congressional Record *of almost any date. Read it, respond to it emotionally, and extract from it at least one example of each kind of thought-saver, giving its Latin as well as its English name if it has one, and estimating approximately how much thought has been saved by each:*

SENATOR PETLIPS: The great foreign-aid boondoggle, known as Operation Rathole, is with us again, like every year, and once again I rise to say let's have done with this endless, fruitless spending of America's wealth on other countries, which in the final analysis amounts to nothing more than handing out lollypops to keep them quiet.

Let me give you some facts. Mr. Macnamara, the International Co-operation Administration's public-works officer in Laos for two years, has admitted to the House Subcommittee on Foreign Operations and Monetary Affairs that he accepted $13,000 in bribes from a construction company in Laos that got most of the building business paid for by U. S. funds, and that he signed "certificates of performance" for $600,000 worth of contracts without checking to see whether any of them had ever been carried out. This shows that foreign aid is riddled with waste and corruption.

And facts show that foreign aid is futile. It generally produces the opposite effect by making foreign countries more resentful of our wealth and less willing to work themselves—hence poorer and unhappier. You don't rehabilitate a lazy bum by giving him handouts. Remember that we gave money to Indonesia, and it was later taken over by a military dictatorship: cause and effect, obviously.

But facts are not really necessary, for the truth goes deeper than facts. Foreign aid is futile and useless for this reason: it will not work, it will not accomplish what it is supposed to accomplish. That is conclusive.

I say let other countries work out their own problems. It is a biological law that the fit always survive, because they have what it takes; left to themselves, the fit—that is, the best people—will rise to the top, without our messing in their internal affairs.

Giving money to other countries in the hope that they will settle down and avoid going Communist is making a bet; it is, in fact, exactly like betting on the horses. Therefore we ought to know what to expect; for who ever made money that way?

Oh, I know there are some silver-tongued orators who will rise to tell you how American money makes the world safe for democracy, but to them I have three replies: First, how many of you have relatives in the vast, sprawling, overgrown bureaucracy that administers all these foreign loans? Don't you think it's pretty selfish to promote them just to keep those jobs alive? Second, what do you think Francis Scott Key, the author of our proud National Anthem, would have said of his land if he knew we were pouring the substance of our wealth down foreign drains? And lastly, if you are so anxious to spend money abroad, you can save on your own states and cities, because I will remember who votes for this Bill, and the next time a Rivers and Harbors Bill comes before my committee, I will see that their favorite pork-barrel items are cut to the bone.

THE METHOD OF
SCIENTIFIC INVESTIGATION

THOMAS HENRY HUXLEY ──◉ *From "Darwiniana," in* COLLECTED ES-
SAYS, *volume II.*

The method of scientific investigation is nothing but the expression of
the necessary mode of working of the human mind. It is simply the mode
at which all phenomena are reasoned about, rendered precise and exact.
There is no more difference, but there is just the same kind of difference,
between the mental operations of a man of science and those of an
ordinary person, as there is between the operations and methods of a
baker or of a butcher weighing out his goods in common scales, and
the operations of a chemist in performing a difficult and complex analysis
by means of his balance and finely graduated weights. It is not that the
action of the scales in the one case and the balance in the other differ
in the principles of their construction or manner of working; but the
beam of one is set on an infinitely finer axis than the other and of course
turns by the addition of a much smaller weight.

You will understand this better perhaps if I give you some familiar
example. You have all heard it repeated, I dare say, that men of science
work by means of induction and deduction, and that by the help of these
operations they, in a sort of sense, wring from Nature certain other things,
which are called natural laws and causes, and that out of these by some
cunning skill of their own they build up hypotheses and theories. And
it is imagined by many that the operations of the common mind can be
by no means compared with these processes, and that they have to be
acquired by a sort of special apprenticeship to the craft. To hear all these
large words, you would think that the mind of a man of science must be
constituted differently from that of his fellow men; but if you will not be
frightened by terms, you will discover that you are quite wrong and
that all these terrible apparatus are being used by yourselves every day
and every hour of your lives.

There is a well-known incident in one of Molière's plays [*The Bourgeois Gentleman*] where the author makes the hero express unbounded
delight on being told that he had been talking prose during the whole
of his life. In the same way I trust that you will take comfort and be
delighted with yourselves on the discovery that you have been acting on
the principles of inductive and deductive philosophy during the same
period. Probably there is not one here who has not in the course of the
day had occasion to set in motion a complex train of reasoning of the

very same kind, though differing of course in degree, as that which a scientific man goes through in tracing the causes of natural phenomena.

A very trivial circumstance will serve to exemplify this. Suppose you go into a fruiterer's shop, wanting an apple—you take up one and on biting it you find it sour; you look at it and see that it is hard and green. You take up another one and that too is hard, green, and sour. The shopman offers you a third; but before biting it you examine it and find that it is hard and green, and you immediately say that you will not have it, as it must be sour, like those that you have already tried.

Nothing can be more simple than that, you think; but if you will take the trouble to analyze and trace out into its logical elements what has been done by the mind, you will be greatly surprised. In the first place, you have performed the operation of induction. You found that in two experiences hardness and greenness in apples went together with sourness. It was so in the first case and it was confirmed by the second. True, it is a very small basis, but still it is enough to make an induction from; you generalize the facts, and you expect to find sourness in apples where you get hardness and greenness. You found upon that a general law, that all hard and green apples are sour; and that, so far as it goes, is a perfect induction. Well, having got your natural law in this way, when you are offered another apple which you find is hard and green, you say, "All hard and green apples are sour; this apple is hard and green, therefore this apple is sour." That train of reasoning is what logicians call a syllogism, and has all its various parts and terms—its major premiss, its minor premiss, and its conclusion. And by the help of further reasoning, which, if drawn out, would have to be exhibited in two or three other syllogisms, you arrive at your final determination, "I will not have that apple." So that, you see, you have in the first place established a law by induction, and upon that you have founded a deduction and reasoned out the special conclusion of the particular case. Well now, suppose, having got your law, that at some time afterwards you are discussing the qualities of apples with a friend: you will say to him, "It is a very curious thing, but I find that all hard and green apples are sour!" Your friend says to you, "But how do you know that?" You at once reply, "Oh, because I have tried them over and over again, and have always found them to be so." Well, if we were talking science instead of common sense, we should call that an experimental verification. And if still opposed, you go further and say, "I have heard from the people in Somersetshire and Devonshire, where a large number of apples are grown, that they have observed the same thing. It is also found to be the case in Normandy and in North America. In short, I find it to be the universal experience of mankind wherever attention has been directed to the subject." Whereupon, your friend, unless he is a very unreasonable man, agrees with you and is convinced that you are quite right in the conclusion you have drawn. He believes, although perhaps he does not know he believes it, that the more extensive verifications are—that the more frequently experiments have been made and results of the same kind arrived at—that the more varied the conditions under which the same results are attained, the more certain is the ultimate conclusion, and he disputes the question no further. He sees that the experiment has been tried under all sorts of conditions as to time, place, and people with the same result; and he says with you, therefore, that the law you have laid down must be a good one and he must believe it.

In science we do the same thing—the philosopher exercises precisely the same faculties, though in a much more delicate manner. In scientific inquiry it becomes a matter of duty to expose a supposed law to every possible kind of verification, and to take care, moreover, that this is done intentionally and not left to a mere accident, as in the case of the apples. And in science, as in common life, our confidence in a law is in exact proportion to the absence of variation in the result of our experimental verifications. For instance, if you let go your grasp of an article you may have in your hand it will immediately fall to the ground. That is a very common verification of one of the best established laws of nature—that of gravitation. The method by which men of science establish the existence of that law is exactly the same as that by which we have established the trivial proposition about the sourness of hard and green apples. But we believe it in such an extensive, thorough, and unhesitating manner because the universal experience of mankind verifies it, and we can verify it ourselves at any time; and that is the strongest possible foundation on which any natural law can rest.

So much, then, by way of proof that the method of establishing laws in science is exactly the same as that pursued in common life. Let us now turn to another matter (though really it is but another phase of the same question), and that is the method by which, from the relations of certain phenomena, we prove that some stand in the position of causes toward the others.

I want to put the case clearly before you, and I will therefore show you what I mean by another familiar example. I will suppose that one of you on coming down in the morning to the parlor of your house finds that a teapot and some spoons which had been left in the room on the previous evening are gone—the window is open, and you observe the mark of a dirty hand on the window-frame, and perhaps, in addition to that, you notice the impress of a hobnailed shoe on the gravel outside. All these phenomena have struck your attention instantly, and before two seconds have passed you say, "Oh, somebody has broken open the window, entered the room, and run off with the spoons and the teapot!" That speech is out of your mouth in a moment. And you will probably add, "I know there has; I am quite sure of it!" You mean to say exactly what you know; but in reality you are giving expression to what is, in all essential particulars, a hypothesis. You do not *know* it at all; it is nothing but a hypothesis rapidly framed in your own mind. And it is a hypothesis founded on a long train of inductions and deductions.

What are those inductions and deductions, and how have you got at this hypothesis? You have observed, in the first place, that the window is open; but by a train of reasoning involving many inductions and deductions, you have probably arrived long before at the general law—and a very good one it is—that windows do not open of themselves; and you therefore conclude that something has opened the window. A second general law that you have arrived at in the same way is that teapots and spoons do not go out of a window spontaneously, and you are satisfied that as they are not now where you left them, they have been removed. In the third place, you look at the marks on the window-sill and the shoe-marks outside, and you say that in all previous experience the former kind of mark has never been produced by anything else but the hand of a human being; and the same experience shows that no other animal but man at present wears shoes with hobnails in them such as would produce the marks in the gravel. I do not know, even if we could discover any of those "missing links" that are talked about, that they would help us to any other conclusion! At any rate the law which states our present experience is strong enough for my present purpose. You next reach the conclusion that as these kinds of marks have not been left by any other animals than men, or are liable to be formed in any other way than by a man's hand and shoe, the marks in question have been formed by a man in that way. You have, further, a general law, founded on observation and experience, and that, too, is, I am sorry to say, a very universal and unimpeachable one—that some men are thieves; and you assume at once from all these premises—and that is what constitutes your hypothesis— that the man who made the marks outside and on the window-sill, opened the window, got into the room, and stole your teapot and spoons. You have now arrived at a *vera causa;* you have assumed a cause which, it is plain, is competent to produce all the phenomena you have observed. You can explain all these phenomena only by the hypothesis of a thief. But that is a hypothetical conclusion, of the justice of which you have no absolute proof at all; it is only rendered highly probable by a series of inductive and deductive reasonings.

I suppose your first action, assuming that you are a man of ordinary common sense and that you have established this hypothesis to your own satisfaction, will very likely be to go off for the police and set them on the track of the burglar, with the view to the recovery of your property. But just as you are starting with this object, some person comes in and on learning what you are about, says, "My good friend, you are going on a great deal too fast. How do you know that the man who really made the marks took the spoons? It might have been a monkey that took them, and the man may have merely looked in afterward." You would probably reply, "Well, that is all very well, but you see it is contrary to all experience of the way teapots and spoons are abstracted; so that, at any rate, your hypothesis is less probable than mine." While you are talking the thing over in this way, another friend arrives, and he might say, "Oh, my dear sir, you are certainly going on a great deal too fast. You are most presumptuous. You admit that all these occurrences took place when you were fast asleep, at a time when you could not possibly have known anything about what was taking place. How do you know that the laws of Nature were not suspended during the night? It may be that there has been some kind of supernatural interference in this case." In point of fact, he declares that your hypothesis is one of which you cannot at all demonstrate the truth, and that you are by no means sure that the laws of Nature are the same when you are asleep as when you are awake.

Well, now, you cannot at the moment answer that kind of reasoning. You feel that your worthy friend has you somewhat at a disadvantage. You will feel perfectly convinced in your own mind, however, that you are quite right, and you say to him, "My good friend, I can only be guided by the natural probabilities of the case, and if you will be kind enough to stand aside and permit me to pass, I will go and fetch the police." Well, we will suppose that your journey is successful, and that by good luck you meet with a policeman; that eventually the burglar is found with your property on his person and the marks correspond to his hand and to his boots. Probably any jury would consider those facts a very good experimental verification of your hypothesis, touching the cause of the abnormal phenomena observed in your parlor, and would act accordingly.

Now in this supposititious case I have taken phenomena of a very common kind in order that you might see what are the different steps in an ordinary process of reasoning, if you will only take the trouble to analyze it carefully. All the operations I have described, you will see, are involved in the mind of any man of sense in leading him to a conclusion as to the course he should take in order to make good a robbery and punish the offender. I say that you are led, in that case, to your conclusion by exactly the same train of reasoning as that which a man of science pursues when he is endeavoring to discover the origin and laws of the most occult phenomena. The process is and always must be the same; and precisely the same mode of reasoning was employed by Newton and Laplace in their endeavors to discover and define the causes of the movements of the heavenly bodies, as you, with your own common sense, would employ to detect a burglar. The only difference is that the nature of the inquiry being more abstruse, every step has to be most carefully watched, so that there may not be a single crack or flaw in your hypothesis. A flaw or crack in many of the hypotheses of daily life may be of little or no moment as affecting the general correctness of the conclusions at which we may arrive; but in a scientific inquiry a fallacy, great or small, is always of importance and is sure to be in the long run constantly productive of mischievous if not fatal results.

Do not allow yourselves to be misled by the common notion that a hypothesis is untrustworthy simply because it is a hypothesis. It is often urged in respect to some scientific conclusion that, after all, it is only a hypothesis. But what more have we to guide us in nine-tenths of the most important affairs of daily life than hypotheses, and often very ill-based ones? So that in science, where the evidence of a hypothesis is subjected to the most rigid examination, we may rightly pursue the same course. You may have hypotheses and hypotheses. A man may say, if he likes, that the moon is made of green cheese: that is a hypothesis. But another man, who has devoted a great deal of time and attention to the subject and availed himself of the most powerful telescopes and the results of the observations of others, declares that in his opinion it is probably composed of materials very similar to those of which our own earth is made up: and that is also only a hypothesis. But I need not tell you that there is an enormous difference in the value of the two hypotheses. That one which is based on sound scientific knowledge is sure to have a corresponding value, and that which is a mere hasty random guess is likely to have but little value. Every great step in our progress in discovering causes has been made in exactly the same way as that which I have detailed to you. A person observing the occurrence of certain facts and phenomena asks, naturally enough, what process, what kind of operation known to occur in nature applied to the particular case, will unravel and explain the mystery? Hence you have the scientific hypothesis; and its value will be proportionate to the care and completeness with which its basis had been tested and verified. It is in these matters as in the commonest affairs of practical life: the guess of the fool will be folly, while the guess of the wise man will contain wisdom. In all cases you see that the value of the result depends on the patience and faithfulness with which the investigator applies to his hypothesis every possible kind of verification.

Suggestions

1. The first sentence of "The Method of Scientific Investigation" states a thesis, but this thesis turns out to be subordinate to the speaker's explanation of the terms applied to the main processes of scientific thought. The readiest method of proving that you understand these terms is to give clear answers to these questions about the thesis:
 (a) By what analogy is it supported in ¶1?
 (b) By what examples is it supported in ¶¶4, 5, and 8?

2. Prove by reference to ¶9 that the law which the shopper establishes in ¶5 is not certain but only probable.

3. Show that in the last sentence of ¶5 *believe* is used as † "On Obstinacy in Belief" says it should not be used.

4. Explain with the help of the last paragraph how the value of a hypothesis should be determined.

5. Explain by contrast: *induction* and *deduction, hypotheses* and *theories;* explain *phenomena, missing links, unimpeachable, experimental verification;* illustrate as many as possible of these by examples found in the essay.

6. Identify: *Newton, Laplace.*

7. Write a description of an occasion on which you had to formulate a general law, guess at the meaning of a puzzling situation, or test a hypothesis. Analyze your mental processes in detail, using as many as possible of the terms listed in No. 5 above.

REASON IN THE EMOTIONAL LIFE

JOHN MACMURRAY ─◦₰{ *From* REASON AND EMOTION *by John Macmurray. Reprinted by permission of Faber and Faber Limited.*

Any enquiry must have a motive or it could not be carried on at all, and all motives belong to our emotional life. Moreover, if the enquiry is to be satisfactorily carried through, the emotion which provides the motive for it must be an adequate one. Now, most scientific enquiries are concerned with subjects which are not themselves highly charged with emotional significance for the personal life of the enquirer. But when we come to study the emotional life itself this is no longer true. We are enquiring into the motive forces of our own living, and one of these is the motive that sustains our enquiry. For this reason, the subject to which I have chosen to direct your attention is one in which the success of our enquiry is profoundly bound up with the motives which lead us to undertake it. I must therefore begin with a warning. The only way to approach the subject with any hope of success is to grasp from the beginning its relation to the broad and general issues of our social life as a whole. It may even be dangerous to examine our own emotional life from the wrong motives. In this connexion any motive is wrong if it is egocentric or self-interested. We must remember particularly that the desire to improve our individual lives is just as self-interested as any other form of egocentricity. It is the individual reference to ourselves which vitiates the motives, not the quality or character of our interest in ourselves. Our objective and our motive, therefore, must be wider than the success or failure, the discomfort or happiness of our private lives. This is not a moral exhortation. I am trying quite simply to state the condition which must underlie any attempt to understand or to deal with our emotional development. The desire to save our own lives is a complete barrier to understanding our own lives. It infects the enquiry with a prejudice from the beginning. In this sphere particularly it is true that he that would save his life shall lose it.

Whether we like it or not, we are all enmeshed in that network of relation that binds us together to make up human society. We are parts of one great process—the process of human history. Yet one of the strongest prejudices to which we are all prone is to make exceptions in our own case, and to look upon ourselves as outside it. It is an obvious illusion. No one, not even an Englishman, can "contract out" of history. We ourselves are events in history. Things do not merely happen to us, they happen through us. We have no existence and no significance merely in ourselves. We have our meaning and our being only "in God"; and part of what that phrase signifies is "in the process of the world." In the bewilderment of these times of change and revolution we are apt to peer out from our different shelters and ask fretfully: "What is happening to us?" It is an irreligious question. It reveals the kind of people we are. If we had instead the kind of minds that asked naturally "What is God doing through us in his world?" we might be well on the way to receiving an answer. Behind the former question, shaping its character, lies an emotional unreason. The latter question has its form dictated by emotional rationality.

What is emotional reason? The question, I imagine, seems a strange one, and that itself is highly significant. Our lives belong to a stage in human development in which reason has been dissociated from the emotional life and is contrasted with it. Reason means to us thinking and planning, scheming and calculating. It carries our thoughts to science and philosophy, to the counting-house or the battlefield, but not to music and laughter and love. It does not make us think of religion or loyalty or beauty, but rather of that state of tension which knits our brows when we apply our minds to some knotty problem or devise schemes to cope with a difficult situation. We associate reason with a state of mind which is cold, detached, and unemotional. When our emotions are stirred we feel that reason is left behind and we enter another world —more colorful, more full of warmth and delight, but also more dangerous. If we become egocentric, if we forget that we are parts of one small part of the development of human life, we shall be apt to imagine that this has always been so and always must be so; that reason is just thinking; that emotion is just feeling; and that these two aspects of our life are in the eternal nature of things distinct and opposite; very apt to come into conflict and requiring to be kept sternly apart. We shall even be in danger of slipping back into a way of thinking from which we had begun to emerge; of thinking that emotion belongs to the animal nature in us, and reason to the divine; that our emotions are unruly and fleshly, the source of evil and disaster, while reason belongs to the divine essence of the thinking mind which raises us above the level of the brutes into communion with the eternal.

Yet, though this seems to be true, it can hardly be the whole truth about the stage of human development to which we belong. For after all, here we are discussing the question. Somehow or other a doubt has arisen, and we have begun to wonder whether we are right in dissociating the two aspects of our experience. We are asking now: "Is this attitude right? *Is* reason a matter of intellect and logical thought? Is it really separated from the emotional life that surges beneath it in the depths? Or is there reason in the emotional life itself?" Thought has begun to doubt its own monopoly of reason. As soon as that doubt enters the very basis of our civilization begins to shake, and there arises, first dimly in the depths of us, but soon penetrating more and more clearly into consciousness, the cry for a new heaven and a new earth. The doubt and the question mark the opening of a new phase in human development.

We must keep that large prospect before the eyes of our imagination when we begin to think about the emotional life. We must not think of it only in relation to our own emotional stresses. All of us, if we are really alive, are disturbed now in our emotions. We are faced by emotional problems that we do not know how to solve. They distract our minds, fill us with misgiving, and sometimes threaten to wreck our lives. That is the kind of experience to which we are all committed. If anyone thinks they are peculiar to the difficulties of his own situation, let him overcome his shyness and talk a little about them to other people. He will discover that he is not a solitary unfortunate. We shall make no headway with these questions unless we begin to see them, and keep on seeing them, not as our private difficulties but as the growing pains of a new world of human experience. Our individual tensions are simply the new thing growing through us into the life of mankind. When we can see them steadily in this universal setting, then and then only will our private difficulties become really significant. We shall recognize them as the travail of a new birth for humanity, as the beginning of a new knowledge of ourselves and of God.

If we are to discover the nature of emotional reason we must first be sure about what we mean by reason in general. It is, in the first place, that which distinguishes us from the world of organic life; which makes us men and women—super-organic. It is the characteristic of personal life. This, however, is only a formal statement. We want to know what are the particular ways in which reason reveals itself in human behavior. One of the most obvious is the power of speech. Another is the capacity to invent and use tools. Another is the power to organize social life. Behind all these there lies the capacity to make a choice of purposes and to discover and apply the means of realizing our chosen ends. We might go on to draw up a list of such peculiarly personal activities; though it would probably not reveal immediately the root from which they all spring. There are, however, certain persistent cultural expressions of human life which are in a special sense characteristic of our rational nature at its best. These are science, art, and religion. This calls attention to one point at least which is highly significant. Whatever is a characteristic and essential expression of human nature must be an expression of reason. We must recognize, then, that if we wish to discover what reason is we must examine religion and art just as much as science. A conception of reason which is applicable to science but not to religion or art must be a false conception, or at least an inadequate one. Now the obvious difference between science on the one hand and art and religion on the other is that science is intellectual while art and religion are peculiarly bound up with the emotional side of human life. They are not primarily intellectual. This at once forces us to conclude that there must be an emotional expression of reason as well as an intellectual one. Thinking is obviously not the only capacity which is characteristically human and personal.

The definition of reason which seems to me most satisfactory is this. Reason is the capacity to behave consciously in terms of the nature of what is not ourselves. We can express this briefly by saying that reason is the capacity to behave in terms of the nature of the object, that is to say, to behave objectively. Reason is thus our capacity for objectivity. When we wish to determine why anything behaves as it does, we normally assume that it behaves in terms of its own nature. This means that we need only find out how it is constituted to understand why it responds to a particular stimulus in a particular way. We are apt to make the same assumption when we are considering how human beings behave. When we do this we are met by a special difficulty which is usually discussed as the difficulty about the freedom of the will. The controversy about free will is insoluble, not because the facts referred to are irreconcilable, but because the problem itself is wrongly conceived. We are looking for something in the inner constitution of the human being to explain the peculiar nature of his behavior. We are still assuming that he must necessarily behave in terms of his own nature, like anything else. It is precisely this assumption that is at fault. Reason is the capacity to behave, not in terms of our own nature, but in terms of our knowledge of the nature of the world outside. Let me give you a simple example. A little boy starts to run across a busy street. His mother sees him from the pavement and sees that he is in imminent danger of running in front of a motor car. Her natural impulse is to call out to him in terror. If she did so she would be acting subjectively in terms of her own natural constitution, responding to a stimulus from the environment. But she does not. She recognizes that to shout to the boy would only increase his danger by distracting his attention, so she suppresses her impulse. Her behavior is rational, because it is determined not by her subjective impulse but by her recognition of the nature of the situation outside her. She acts in terms of the nature of the object.

It is easy to see that science and all the practical applications of science depend upon reason, in the sense in which we have just defined it. Science rests upon the desire to know things in their objective nature. Behind this lies the desire to be able to use what is in the world through a knowledge of its nature, that is to say, the desire to increase our capacity for acting in terms of the nature of the object. The extent to which we can behave in terms of the nature of the world outside us depends, quite obviously, upon the extent of our knowledge of the world outside. Where objective knowledge fails us we can only act subjectively, on impulse. It is thus the effort to create the conditions of rational activity that gives rise to science.

Now, the main difficulty that faces us in the development of a scientific knowledge of the world lies not in the outside world but in our own emotional life. It is the desire to retain beliefs to which we are emotionally attached for some reason or other. It is the tendency to make the wish father to the thought. Science itself, therefore, is emotionally conditioned. If we are to be scientific in our thoughts, then, we must be ready to subordinate our wishes and desires to the nature of the world. So long as we want things to be other than they are we cannot see things as they are or act in terms of their real nature. We color the world with our own illusions. Reason demands that our beliefs should conform to the nature of the world, not to the nature of our hopes and ideals.

In this field, therefore, the discovery of truth must be from the subjective side a process of disillusionment. The strength of our opposition to the development of reason is measured by the strength of our dislike of being disillusioned. We should all admit, if it were put to us directly, that it is good to get rid of illusions, but in practice the process of disillusionment is painful and disheartening. We all confess to the desire to get at the truth, but in practice the desire for truth is the desire to be disillusioned. The real struggle centers in the emotional field, because reason is the impulse to overcome bias and prejudice in our own favor, and to allow our feelings and desires to be fashioned by things outside us, often by things over which we have no control. The effort to achieve this can rarely be pleasant or flattering to our self-esteem. Our natural tendency is to feel and to believe in the way that satisfies our impulses. We all like to feel that we are the central figure in the picture, and that our own fate ought to be different from that of everybody else. We feel that life should make an exception in our favor. The development of reason in us means overcoming all this. Our real nature as persons is to be reasonable and to extend and develop our capacity for reason. It is to acquire greater and greater capacity to act objectively and not in terms of our subjective constitution. That is reason, and it is what distinguishes us from the organic world, and makes us super-organic.

It is precisely the same problem that faces us in the field of morality. Morality, after all, is merely a demand for rational behavior, and its difficulty is only the difficulty of overcoming our own natural bias in favor of ourselves and those we love, and demanding that life shall show us and them special consideration. Morality demands that we should act "in the light of eternity," that is, in terms of things as they really are and of people as they really are, and not in terms of our subjective inclinations and private sympathies.

Now we can attack the main issue. All life is activity. Mere thinking is not living. Yet thinking, too, is an activity, even if it is an activity which is only real in its reference to activities which are practical. Now, every activity must have an adequate motive, and all motives are emotional. They belong to our feelings, not to our thoughts. At the most our thoughts may restrict and restrain, or direct and guide, our actions. They can determine their form but not their substance. Even this they can only do by rousing emotions which check or alter the primary motives. Thought is always subsidiary to activity even when we are not directly aware of it. The rationality that appears in thought is itself the reflection of a rationality that belongs to the motives of action. It follows that none of our activities, not even the activities of thinking, can express our reason unless the emotions which produce and sustain them are rational emotions.

What can it mean, then, to distinguish between rational and irrational feelings? We are in the habit of saying that our feelings are just felt. They can't be either true or false; they just are what they are. Our thoughts, on the other hand, can be true or false. About that we have no difficulty. Yet, if we think carefully, we shall realize that there is no special difference between feelings and thoughts in this respect. Our thoughts are just what we think. We just think them, and they are what they are. How then can they be either true or false? The answer is that their truth or falsity does not lie in them but in a relation between them and the things to which they refer. True thoughts are thoughts which refer properly to reality, and which are thought in terms of the nature of the object to which they refer. Why should our feelings be in any different case? It is true that they are felt and that they are what they are felt to be, just like our thoughts. But they also refer to things outside us. If I am angry I am angry at something or somebody, though I may not always be able to say precisely what it is. Thought is similar. We are often unable to say precisely what it is that we are thinking about, but it is always something. Since our feelings, then, refer to what is outside them, to some object about which they are felt, why should they not refer rightly or wrongly to their object, just like thoughts? Why should they not be proper feelings when they are in terms of the nature of the object, and improper feelings when they are not in terms of the nature of the object? When we put it in this way, we recognize that this is a distinction which we are always making. To a person who is terribly afraid of a mouse we are quite accustomed to say that there is nothing really to be afraid of. Her fear is not in terms of the real nature of the situation. It is subjective. We can acknowledge, therefore, without any difficulty, that feelings can be rational or irrational in precisely the same way as thoughts, through the correctness or incorrectness of their reference to reality. In thinking thoughts we think the things to which the thoughts refer. In feeling emotions we feel the things to which the emotions refer. And, therefore, we can feel rightly or wrongly. The only one of the great philosophers who recognized this parallelism between thought and feeling, and who maintained that our feelings could be true or false, was Plato. He insisted on it both in the *Republic* and in the *Philebus*. This view of Plato's has usually been treated by commentators as a forgivable eccentricity in Plato's thought, like his attitude to art and artists. It seems to me not merely true but of much more profound significance than Plato himself recognized. It is not that our feelings have a secondary and subordinate capacity for being rational or irrational. It is that reason is primarily an affair of emotion, and that the rationality of thought is the derivative and secondary one. For if reason is the capacity to *act* in terms of the nature of the object, it is emotion which stands directly behind activity determining its substance and direction, while thought is related to action indirectly and through emotion, determining only its form, and that only partially.

The chief difficulty in the development of emotional reason lies in the surprising fact that we know relatively little about our own emotional life. We are apt to know more about other people's. It is a commonplace that in all matters which touch us closely it is very difficult to be sure of our own motives. Rather than admit to motives which would injure our self-esteem we prevent them from entering our consciousness or allow them to appear only in forms which disguise and misrepresent their real nature. Modern psychology has been very much concerned to develop various technical methods of overcoming the forces which repress these motives, and its success has been sufficient at least to reveal to what an extent our emotional life is unconscious. But in fact psychoanalysis has only extended and developed a knowledge which we all possess. We continually recognize in other people motives and feelings of which they themselves are quite ignorant. Let me illustrate this by a story of my own invention. It is about three friends, Jane and Josephine and Peter. They are all young. Jane is wealthy and influential. Josephine is a struggling young artist. Both of them are interested in Peter, and Peter is interested in both of them. Josephine has long cherished a desire to continue her art studies in Rome and has applied for a scholarship which would enable her to go. But she is torn between her desire to go abroad and her growing interest in Peter. Jane uses her influence to get the scholarship for Josephine, and succeeds. She carries the good news to Josephine and in great excitement tells her how hard she had worked to get it for her. She is very astonished and hurt to find that Josephine receives the news very coldly and is not properly grateful. At that Jane feels very angry with Josephine.

Jane confides all this to a friend of hers called Peggy. Peggy suggests that the explanation is a simple one. Josephine is feeling sad at having to leave her friends and has been growing very fond of Peter. Jane admits that Josephine is fond of Peter but feels quite sure that that can't be the reason. Josephine, she says, would never allow anything of that kind to interfere with her art. In any case, it is very good for Peter that she should go. Peter is very sensitive and Josephine's artistic temperament plays havoc with his nerves. Jane has often noticed it. Indeed when she was working to get the scholarship for Josephine, she had Peter's welfare in her mind too. Whether Josephine is grateful or not, she doesn't care. She is proud to have been able to serve both her friends.

What was Jane's real motive? All her friends told themselves—and each other—what it was. But did Jane know? Probably not at all. She would have been very hurt if anyone had presumed to enlighten her. At any rate there is no need for me to explain. The point of the story for our present purpose is this: the reasons we give ourselves for our activities, and even more certainly the reasons we give to other people for them, rarely express our real motive, and never the whole of our motive. When we ask ourselves why we behaved as we did, we often find ourselves insisting to ourselves, with a certain inner stress, upon the reasons that we give. That feeling of insistence is always adequate evidence that the real motive is a different one, and one that is hidden from ourselves. Such hidden motives are necessarily subjective. They are necessarily the expression not of reason but of subjective impulses. They cannot be in terms of our conscious recognition of the true nature of the situation.

It is extremely difficult to become aware of this great hinterland of our minds, and to bring our emotional life, and with it the motives which govern our behavior, fully into consciousness. This is peculiarly true of contemporary people. It is not nearly so true of primitive men. The nineteenth century in particular was the climax of a long period of social repression in which the intellectual development of reason was the main effort and the emotional life was considered chiefly as an intrusive force which prevented the achievement of that calmness which is necessary for the proper functioning of thought. But that development itself brings us back at last to the emotional life. The development of science finally must direct its attention to personality itself; and as soon as it does this it is directed upon the emotional sources of all personal activity. It is because it is so difficult for us to bring our unconscious motives into consciousness that at last we find ourselves driven to make the attempt. That is why so much of the interest of contemporary life is centered upon emotional experience. It means the beginning of the task of developing emotional reason in man. In this, as in most things, it is the first step that is the most difficult. Jane's emotional development will begin when she realizes that she was jealous of Josephine and wanted to get her out of the way. The probable effect of this realization will be that she will say to herself "What a horrible little worm I am," and begin to revel in despising herself. Such self-abasement is just as unreasonable, perhaps even more unreasonable, than her previous state of mind. It is a compensation which still enables her to be concerned with herself. It is still childish, immature, and egocentric. Self-pity and self-disgust are just as irrational as self-assertion. The real problem of the development of emotional reason is to shift the centre of feeling from the self to the world outside. We can only begin to grow up into rationality when we begin to see our own emotional life not as the centre of things but as part of the development of humanity.

The field in which emotional reason expresses itself most directly is the field of art. The artist is directly concerned to express his emotional experience of the world. His success depends upon the rationality of his emotions. It is not enough that the artist should express his emotional reaction to the world. If his feelings are merely subjective reactions, his work will be bad. What will make it valuable or significant is the way in which his emotions refer to the world. The artist expresses the nature of the objective world as apprehended in emotion. As a result, our own experience of works of art shows the same distinction between those which affect us subjectively and those which reveal the world to us in its real significance. Some pictures, for instance, we appreciate because they touch off in our minds associations which are pleasant and exciting. They act upon us merely as a stimulus to thoughts and feelings which we enjoy for their own sake. But such pictures are artistically bad. There are others which move us in an entirely different way, because they contain their significance in themselves. They do not set us to enjoy our own feelings. They make us enjoy *themselves,* and they refer us to the significance of the world outside.

These true works of art are more difficult to appreciate. They do something to us, often, if they are contemporary; something that we object to. They involve some disillusionment that we dislike, and they are not immediately exciting. They deny us the opportunity of reveling in our own sensations and force us to be objective. The reason is that objective emotion is not a mere reaction to a stimulus. It is an immediate appreciation of the value and significance of real things. Emotional reason is our capacity to apprehend objective values. This point, important as it is, I have no time to develop at length. I must conclude by drawing your attention to its final expression in our relations with one another. Love, which is the fundamental positive emotion characteristic of human beings, can be either subjective and irrational, or objective and rational. In feeling love for another person, I can either experience a pleasurable emotion which he stimulates in me, or I can love *him.* We have, therefore, to ask ourselves, is it really the other person that I love, or is it myself? Do I enjoy him or do I enjoy myself in being with him? Is he just an instrument for keeping me pleased with myself, or do I feel his existence and his reality to be important in themselves? The difference between these two kinds of love is the ultimate difference between organic and personal life. It is the difference between rational and irrational emotion. The capacity to love objectively is the capacity which makes us persons. It is the ultimate source of our capacity to behave in terms of the object. It is the core of rationality.

Suggestions

1. The heart of "Reason in the Emotional Life" is the speaker's attack on what he says are the modern attitudes toward reason and emotion. "We associate reason with a state of mind which is cold, detached, and unemotional" (¶3), and tend to think emotions evil, reason divine. His own thesis is that "reason is primarily an affair of emotion," the rationality of thought being a secondary matter (¶13). An emotion can be either rational or irrational, and real success in life depends upon developing emotional reason, "The capacity to apprehend objective values" (last ¶). Analyze the definition of reason in ¶7 and its illustrative anecdote; this will make Macmurray's terms clearer.

2. Illustrate and discuss:

". . . all motives belong to our emotional life" (¶1).

"The desire to save our own lives is a complete barrier to understanding our own lives" (¶1).

"Whatever is a characteristic and essential expression of human nature must be an expression of reason" (¶7).

"We feel that life should make an exception in our favor" (¶11).

". . . we know relatively little about our own emotional life" (¶15).

"The real problem of the development of emotional reason is to shift the center of feeling from the self to the world outside" (¶18).

3. Name four ways in which reason has made human life super-organic (¶6). In what three achievements do we see man's rational nature at its best? What distinguishes the first from the other two?

4. Distinguish rational from irrational feelings by examples other than the one given in ¶13. How does the parable of Jane, Josephine, and Peter help you to make this distinction? Analyze the effect on Jane of her first step in self-understanding.

5. Relate the speaker's discussion of love (last ¶) to the distinction you have just made.

6. Write an essay on your own emotions, attacking or defending the view that emotion is "the source of evil and disaster" (¶3).

7. Write an essay showing that "Reason in the Emotional Life" does or does not receive support from † "The Uses and Limitations of Logic" or from † "Thought-Savers."

8. Write a discussion of the statement "All of us, if we are really alive, are disturbed now in our emotions" (¶4) in relation to † "The Curve of Subjectivity."

ON NOT BEING A PHILOSOPHER

ROBERT LYND ⟶

From IT'S A FINE WORLD *by Robert Lynd. Reprinted by permission of Methuen & Co. Ltd.*

"Have you read Epictetus lately?" "No, not lately." "Oh, you ought to read him. Tommy's been reading him for the first time, and is fearfully excited." I caught this scrap of dialogue from the next table in the lounge of a hotel. I became interested, curious, for I had never read Epictetus, though I had often looked at his works on the shelf—perhaps I had even quoted him—and I wondered if here at last was the book of wisdom that I had been looking for at intervals ever since I was at school. Never have I lost my early faith that wisdom is to be found somewhere in a book—to be picked up as easily as a shell from the sand. I desire wisdom as keenly as Solomon did, but it must be wisdom that can be obtained with very little effort—wisdom that can be caught almost by infection. I have no time or energy for the laborious quest of philosophy. I wish the philosophers to perform the laborious quest and, at the end of it, to feed me with the fruits of their labors; just as I get eggs from the farmer, apples from the fruit-grower, medicines from the chemist, so do I expect the philosopher to provide me with wisdom at the cost of a few shillings. That is why at one time I read Emerson and, at another, Marcus Aurelius. To read them, I hoped, was to become wise by reading. But I did not become wise. I agreed with them while I read them, but, when I had finished reading, I was still much the same man that I had been before, incapable of concentrating on the things on which they said I should concentrate or of not being indifferent to the things to which they said I should not be indifferent. Still, I have never lost faith in books, believing that somewhere printed matter exists from which I shall be able to absorb philosophy and strength of character while smoking in an armchair. It was in this mood that I took down Epictetus after hearing the conversation in the hotel lounge.

I read him, I confess, with considerable excitement. He is the kind of philosopher I like, not treating life as if at its finest it were an argument conducted in difficult jargon, but discussing, among other things, how men should behave in the affairs of ordinary life. Also, I agreed with nearly everything he said. Indifference to pain, death, poverty—yes, that is eminently desirable. Not to be troubled about anything over which one has no control, whether the oppression of tyrants or the peril of earthquakes—on the necessity of this also, Epictetus and I are as one. Yet, close as is the resemblance between our opinions, I could not help feeling, as I read, that Epictetus was wise in holding his opinions and that I, though holding the same opinions, was far from wise. For, indeed, though I held the same opinions for purposes of theory, I could not entertain them for a moment for purposes of conduct. Death, pain, and poverty are to me very real evils, except when I am in an armchair reading a book by a philosopher. If an earthquake happened while I was reading a book of philosophy, I should forget the book of philosophy and think only of the earthquake and how to avoid tumbling walls and chimneys. This, though I am the staunchest possible admirer of Socrates, Pliny, and people of that sort. Sound though I am as an armchair philosopher, at a crisis I find that both the spirit and the flesh are weak.

Even in the small things of life I cannot comfort myself like a philosopher of the school of Epictetus. Thus, for example, when he advises us how to "eat acceptably to the gods" and bids us to this end to be patient even under the most incompetent service at our meals, he commends a spiritual attitude of which my nature is incapable. "When you have asked for warm water," he says, "and the slave does not heed you; or if he does heed you but brings tepid water; or if he is not even to be found in the house, then to refrain from anger and not to explode, is not this acceptable to the gods? . . . Do you not remember over whom you rule—that they are kinsmen, that they are brothers by nature, and they are the offspring of Zeus?" That is all perfectly true, and I should like very much to be a man who could sit in a restaurant, smiling patiently and philosophically while the waiter brought all the wrong things or forgot to bring anything at all. But in point of fact bad waiting irritates me. I dislike having to ask three times for the wine-list. I am annoyed when, after a quarter of an hour's delay, I am told that there is no celery. It is true that I do not make a scene on such occasions. I have not enough courage for that. I am as sparing of objurgations as a philosopher, but I suspect that the scowling spirit within me must show itself in my features. Certainly, I do not think of telling myself: "This waiter is my kinsman; he is the offspring of Zeus." Besides, even if he were, why should the offspring of Zeus wait so badly? Epictetus never dined at the —— Restaurant. And yet his patience might have served him even there. If so, what a difference between Epictetus and me! And, if I cannot achieve his imperturbability in so small affairs as I have mentioned, what hope is there of my being able to play the philosopher in presence of tyrants and earthquakes?

Again, when Epictetus expresses his opinions on material possessions and counsels us to be so indifferent to them that we should not object to their being stolen, I agree with him in theory and yet in practice I know I should be unable to obey him. There is nothing more certain than that a man whose happiness depends on his possessions is not happy. I am sure a wise man can be happy on a pittance. Not that happiness should be the aim of life, according to Epictetus or myself. But Epictetus at least holds up an ideal of imperturbability, and he assures us that we shall achieve this if we care so little for material things that it does not matter to us whether somebody steals them or not. "Stop admiring your clothes," he bids us, "and you are not angry at the man who steals them." And he goes on persuasively concerning the thief: "*He* does not know wherein the true good of man consists, but fancies that it consists in having fine clothes, the very same fancy that you also entertain. Shall he not come, then, and carry them off?" Yes, logically I suppose he should, and yet I cannot feel so at the moment at which I find that a guest at a party has taken my new hat and left his old one in its place. It gives me no comfort to say to myself: "*He* does not know wherein the true good of man consists, but fancies that it consists in having my hat." Nor should I dream of attempting to console a guest at a party in my own house with such philosophy in similar circumstances. It is very irritating to lose a new hat. It is very irritating to lose anything at all, especially if one thinks it has been taken on purpose. I feel that I could imitate Epictetus if I lived in a world in which nothing happened. But in a world in which things disappear through loss, theft, and "pinching," and in which bad meals are served by bad waiters in many of the restaurants, and a thousand other disagreeable things happen, an ordinary man might as well set out to climb the Himalayas in walking shoes as attempt to live the life of a philosopher at all hours.

In spite of this, however, most of us cannot help believing that the philosophers were right—right when they proclaimed, amid all their differences, that most of the things we bother about are not worth bothering about. It is easier to believe that oneself is a fool than that Socrates was a fool, and yet, if he was not right, he must have been the greatest fool who ever lived. The truth is, nearly everybody is agreed that such men as Socrates and Epictetus were right in their indifference to external things. Even men earning £10,000 a year and working for more would admit this. Yet, while admitting it, most of us would be alarmed if one of our dearest friends began to put the philosophy of Epictetus into practice too literally. What we regard as wisdom in Epictetus we should look on as insanity in an acquaintance. Or, perhaps, not in an acquaintance, but at least in a near relation. I am sure that if I became as indifferent to money and comfort and all external things as Epictetus, and reasoned in his fashion with a happy smile about property and thieves, my relations would become more perturbed than if I became a successful company promoter with the most materialistic philosophy conceivable. Think, for example, of the reasoning of Epictetus over the thief who stole his iron lamp:

He bought a lamp for a very high price; for a lamp he became a thief, for a lamp he became faithless, for a lamp he became bestial. This is what seemed to him to be profitable!

The reasoning is sound, yet neither individually nor as a society do we live in that contempt of property on which it is based. A few saints do, but even they are at first a cause of great concern to their friends. When the world is normally cheerful and comfortable, we hold the paradoxical belief that the philosophers were wise men, but that we should be fools to imitate them. We are convinced that, while philosophers are worth reading, material things are worth bothering about. It is as though we enjoyed wisdom as a spectacle—a delightful spectacle on a stage which it would be unseemly for the audience to attempt to invade. Were the Greeks and the Romans made differently? Did the admirers of Socrates and Epictetus really attempt to become philosophers, or were they like ourselves, hopeful of achieving wisdom, not by practice but through a magic potion administered by a wiser man than they? To become wise without effort—by listening to a voice, by reading a book—it is at once the most exciting and the most soothing of dreams. In such a dream I took down Epictetus. And, behold, it was only a dream.

Suggestions

1. The subject of "On Not Being a Philosopher" is fairly represented by the speaker's assertion that "though I held the same opinions for purposes of theory, I could not entertain them for a moment for purposes of conduct." (¶2). His attitude toward philosophers appears to be light ridicule—but can it be argued that the essay is an example of indirection, that the real target of its ridicule is the average man? Discuss fully, with particular attention to any passages that you find especially amusing.

2. Identify: Epictetus (naming the school of philosophy to which he belonged), Solomon, Emerson, Marcus Aurelius, Socrates, Pliny.

3. Show why the speaker was excited by his reading of Epictetus.

4. Explain: *jargon, objurgations, imperturbability.*

5. Write an essay on one:

"There is nothing more certain than that a man whose happiness depends on his possessions is not happy" (¶4).

"Not that happiness should be the aim of life, according to Epictetus or myself" (¶4).

"It is easier to believe that oneself is a fool than that Socrates was a fool, and yet, if he was not right, he must have been the greatest fool who ever lived" (¶5).

"What we regard as wisdom in Epictetus we should look on as insanity in . . . a near relation" (¶5).

6. Write an essay comparing the view of human nature implied by "On Not Being a Philosopher" with that of † "Reason in the Emotional Life."

LANGUAGE
AND STYLE

THE MIRACLE OF LANGUAGE

LEWIS MUMFORD   —◦◦◀

From THE CONDUCT OF LIFE. © *1951 by Lewis Mumford. Reprinted by permission of Harcourt, Brace and Company, Inc.*

The growth of conscious purpose and self-direction—all that is implied in the historic concepts of the soul and the person—was made possible by man's special skill in interpreting his own nature and working his experiences into a meaningful and valuable whole, upon which he could draw for future actions and operations. That skill rests upon a special aptitude, embedded in man's very physiology: the ability to form and transmit symbols. Man's most characteristic social trait, his possession of an extra-organic environment and a super-organic self, which he transmits from generation to generation without using the biological mechanism of heredity, is dependent upon his earlier conquest of the word.

During the last century this essential fact about man's nature has been obscured by the false assumption that man is primarily a "tool-using animal." Carlyle called him that long before Bergson suggested that the term Homo Faber, Man the Maker, should replace Homo Sapiens.[1] But man is not essentially distinguished from his animal relatives either by the fact that he lives in groups or performs physical work with tools. Man is first and foremost the self-fabricating animal: the only creature who has not rested content with his biological form or with the dumb repetitions of his animal role. The chief source of this particular form of creativity was not fire, tools, weapons, machines, but two subjective instruments far older than any of these: the dream and the word.

Without dwelling on the function of symbolization, one cannot begin

[1] For an essay by Thomas Carlyle (1795–1881) see † "Goethe's Portrait"; the French philosopher Henri Bergson (1859–1941) wrote *Creative Evolution* and other works.

357

to describe the nature of man or plumb the deepest spring of his crea-
tiveness. That is why I pass over many other attributes, fully taken into
account today by anthropology and psychology, to dwell on man's role
as interpreter. Language, the greatest of all human inventions, is the
most essential key to the truly human. When words fail him, as we find
in the few authenticated cases of wild children reared without the benefit
of human society, man is an animal without a specific life-plan, compelled to imitate the wolfish habits of the animal in whose brood he has
been suckled and reared.

One can, of course, only speculate on the way in which man invented
and perfected the various tools of symbolization. But in the primary
instance of speech, the word was made possible by changes in the bodily
organs including the larynx, the tongue, the teeth, and not least the creation of mobile lips: in the earliest skulls identifiable as man, the ana-
tomists find the speech centers already relatively well developed. The
enlargement of man's powers, through his quicker ability to learn by
trial and correction, demanded a special instrument for dealing with the
multitude of sensations and meanings, suggestions and demands, that
impinged upon him. Every sensation, as Adelbert Ames[2] has experimentally demonstrated, is a prognostic directive to action: hence even
the simplest stimulus must be interpreted, for whether we accept it or
reject it depends not only upon its own nature but upon our purposes
and predispositions and proposals. Even the purest sensation must be
translated and re-ordered, before the organism will in fact see it, hear it,
or answer it. In that response, the entire organism co-operates; and what
is actually seen or heard or felt is only what makes sense in terms of the
organism's immediate purpose or its historic plan of development.

At every moment of his waking existence, man senses, interprets, pro-
poses, acts in a single unified response: but between the starting point
and the end, the intermediate steps of interpretation and planful reor-
ganization are critical, for it is here that error, miscalculation, and frus-
tration may intervene. With the development of language, man created
an instrument of interpretation that gave him a way of traversing the
largest possible field of life. What he took in of the world expressed his
own nature: what he expressed of himself partook of the nature of the
world; for it is only in thought that organism and environment can be
separated.

Now other creatures than man respond to immediate signals: the snarl
of a dog has meaning for another dog, and the upraised white tail of a
doe tells the fawns, as plainly as words, "Follow me!" But man, at a
critical moment in his development, began to invent signs, in the form
of audible words, which represent an event or a situation even when
they are not present. By this act of detachment and abstraction, man
gained the power of dealing with the non-present, the unseen, the remote,

[2] American psychologist (b. 1880), author of *Visual Perception*.

and the internal: not merely his visible lair and his daily companions, but his ancestors and his descendants and the sun and the moon and the stars: eventually the concepts of eternity and infinity, of electron and universe: he reduced a thousand potential occasions in all their variety and flux to a single symbol that indicated what was common to all of them.

Similarly, by kindred means, man was able to give form to and project his inner world, otherwise hidden and private: by words, images, related sounds, it became part of the public world, and thus an "object." This extraordinary labor-saving device, for extracting, condensing, and preserving the most complicated kinds of events, was perhaps another manifestation of the creative uses of his exuberance and vital proliferation. Man's possession of a "useless instrument," his special voice-producing organs, with their wide range of tones, plus a love of repetition, which one observes in the fullest degree in infants, opened up playful possibilities. If man is an inventor or an artist, the first object of his interest is his own body: he falls in love with his own organs long before he seeks to master the outside world.

"We must never forget," the distinguished philologist Jespersen once observed, "that the organs of speech . . . are one of mankind's most treasured toys, and that not only children but also grown people in civilized as well as savage communities, find amusement in letting their vocal cords and tongue and lips play all sorts of games." Out of this original organic overflow, man found too a way to shape a meaningful, orderly world: the world realized in language, music, poesy, and directed thought. The gift of tongues is the greatest of all gifts: in the beginning was the Word.[3]

Speech, human speech, affected a miraculous transformation in human society: by such magic Prospero tamed Caliban and released Ariel.[4] Speech, at first probably inseparable from gesture, exclamatory, disjointed, structureless, purely emotive, laid the foundation for a more complex mechanism of abstractions, the independent structure of language itself; and with language, human culture as an extra-organic activity, no longer wholly dependent upon the stability and continuity of the physical body and its daily environment, became possible. This broke through the boundaries of time and place that limit animal associations.

In the behavior of that perpetual primitive, the human infant, we can follow the original transition from babble to the involuntary reproduction of facial movements, from private gurglings for self-satisfaction to public demands in which a particular tone will be evoked to bring forth a particular response from the mother: the offer of a breast, the production of a dry diaper, the removal of a pricking pin, the reassurance

<hr>

[3] *Gospel of St. John* 1, 1.
[4] As he tells in Shakespeare, *The Tempest* i.ii.

of human companionship. Much of the intercourse between mother and child is the expression, on both sides, of feeling: tenderness, joy, rage, anxiety. Beyond doubt, the introjection and projection of feeling were basic to the whole achievement of language: a point often overlooked by pragmatic or rationalist interpretations.

In the instances of wild children nurtured by animals, we can verify this interpretation: for the ability to form words seems to disappear altogether when the infant's earliest vocalizings are not encouraged by similar vocalizing on the part of those who look after him. With the loss of language man also loses the facility for more complex forms of human behavior: though some of his organic capacities become intensified to animal sharpness, in an extra-sensitive nose or in muscular endurance, the veritably human touch remains absent: above all, the wild child forfeits the capacity to understand or communicate human feeling, thus becoming inferior, not only to other human beings, but to the dog or cat, who have had the benefit of human association, and who have learned the gestures and tones by which human feelings are expressed. Negatively, there is still another way of understanding the specifically human role of language: for psychologists have found that deaf-mutism, even when combated with skillful care, is a greater handicap to intelligence than blindness. Speech, even though accompanied by blindness, opens the path of social co-operation.

In his attempt to associate intelligence with the special faculty for dealing with the geometrical, the mechanical, the non-living, Henri Bergson curiously underestimated the formative effect of language and over-stressed the part played by physical tools and mechanical aptitudes, for he perversely interpreted speech as being lamed by man's rational preoccupation with static objects. On the contrary, language developed far more rapidly and effectively than mechanical tools; and it was probably in origin primarily a means of representing labile feelings and attitudes, the least geometrical part of man's experience. The most important thing for a human being to know, from infancy onward, is whether he is welcome or unwelcome, whether he is being loved and cherished and protected or hated and feared; and the give-and-take of speech, with all its modulations of color and tone, provides these essential clues. Language was not invented by philosophers seeking truth or by scientists seeking to understand the processes of nature, nor yet by mechanics seeking to shape a more adequate tool; nor was it created by methodical bookkeepers seeking to make an inventory of the contents of the world. Language was the outcome of man's need to affirm solidarity with his own kind. Because it was a prime organ, not only of social co-operation, but of sympathetic and dramatic insight, it helped to control and direct all human behavior.

In time, no doubt, language lent itself to many other uses besides communion and fellowship: it gave rise to a sense of "thatness" as well as "we-ness" and furthered causal insight into processes and relationships. Not least, language was a means whereby subjective reactions became externalized, and objective facts became internalized: thus it favored constant intercourse and traffic between the public world and the private world. In every sense, then, speech was man's prime instrument for sharing his private world with his fellows and for bringing the public world home to himself, though in time it was supplemented by the symbols and significants of the other arts. He who could speak the language could be trusted: every word was a password, indicating friend or foe, in-group or out-group; and these practices linger on in establishing identity right down to our own day. The practical and rational offices of language, which now seem to us all-important, must for long have been purely incidental.

The complicated structure, the grammatical and logical subtlety, and the immense variety of even primitive languages drive one to believe that a large part of man's creative activity, perhaps for hundreds of thousands of years, must have concerned itself almost exclusively with the development of intelligible speech, and with secondary means of symbolization through the visual arts; for painting, too, in the Aurignacian caves, shows an exquisite perfection that argues a prolonged period of unremitting effort. No machine that man invented before the twentieth century compares in complexity and refinement with the simplest of human languages. No wonder this superorganic structure transformed the terms of man's self-development.

Beavers can build dams: bees can construct efficient dwellings: the meanest bird has still a surer mechanism for flying and landing than man has yet achieved. But no other creature has come within sight of man in the arts of symbolic communication. Mainly through language man has created a second world, more durable and viable than the immediate flux of experience, more rich in possibilities than the purely material habitat of any other creature. By the same agent, he has reduced the vastness and overpowering multiplicity of his environment to human dimensions: abstracting from its totality just so much as he could handle and control. The very formal qualities of words served as an instrument for understanding and directing the everlasting flow of things: it is because the structure of language and logic is relatively static (Parmenides and Plato) that the unceasing changes and processes of the natural world (Heraclitus) can be interpreted.[5] If meanings changed as quickly as events, no event would have a meaning.

[5] Heraclitus (6th-5th century B. C.) taught that all things are constantly changing; Parmenides (b. 510? B. C.) and Plato (427?–347 B. C.) held that ideas, being exempt from this process, are the only ultimate realities.

Let us make no mistake then: language is far more basic than any other kind of tool or machine. Through man's overdeveloped fore-brain and his overflowing sensory-emotional responses, he came into contact with an ever-enlarging field of action; and through language, he found an economic way of dealing with this complexity and turning every state and activity to the service of meaning. So essential is language to man's humanness, so deep a source is it of his own creativity, that it is by no means an accident in our time that those who have tried to degrade man and enslave him have first debased and misused language, arbitrarily turning meanings inside out. Civilization itself, from the most primitive stage onward, moves toward the continuous creation of a common social heritage, transcending all the peculiarities of race and environment and historic accident, shared over ever wider reaches of space and time. This heritage, apart from environmental modifications, such as roads, canals, and cities, is transmitted largely in symbolic form; and by far the greater part of its symbolization is in spoken and written language. Contrary to the proverb, words make a greater difference than sticks and stones: they are more durable, too.

Suggestions

1. Language is a miracle, this essay maintains, because man's invention of it has given him "an extra-organic environment and a super-organic self"—which ¶2 explains by saying that man has risen above his biological form and "the dumb repetitions of his animal role." Other animals make signs, we are shown in ¶6, but man alone uses symbols, "which represent an event or a situation even when they are not present." Language is thus the basic source of man's creativity, the chief instrument of his progress. To make sure you understand this thesis, analyze each of the quoted phrases and illustrate it from your own experience.

2. Explain and illustrate: ". . . hence even the simplest stimulus must be interpreted" (¶4).

3. According to ¶8, the development of language begins in play and leads to the creation of "a meaningful, orderly world." Discuss fully, mentioning examples of the world that man creates.

4. Show what the development of the human infant tells us about the history of the human race (¶9).

5. When a child reverts to savagery (¶10) what besides language does he lose? What, according to ¶11, is the most important thing for a human being to know? Discuss fully.

6. What is the "second world" referred to in ¶14? Distinguish it from the world mentioned in ¶8.

7. Explain: *exuberance, vital proliferation, labile,* "*thatness,*" "*we-ness,*" *Aurignacian caves.*

8. Write an essay discussing the reference to 20th century dictators in ¶15.

9. Write an essay identifying the proverb mentioned in the last sentence and defending or attacking it.

10. Write an essay comparing the attitude of this essay toward man's emotional life with that expressed in † "Reason in the Emotional Life."

ORIGIN AND GROWTH OF ENGLISH

HAROLD GOAD ···❧ *From* LANGUAGE IN HISTORY *by Harold Goad. Reprinted by permission of Penguin Books Ltd.*

Anglo-Saxon began its literary life in Northern England as the highly inflected offspring of a Low German vernacular, once spoken in the flat lands of the Elbe. When our forefathers landed in Britain they already possessed a few Latin words—such as *wall, street, mile, monger, pound, inch, wine, pepper, butter,* and *cheese*—showing the ways by which Roman civilization had reached them in their continental home, namely by war and trade. After initial massacres they enslaved the remnant of the Britons, especially in the West, and from these our ancestors took over a few monosyllables, mainly concerning the countryside, such as *carr, combe, dun, lough, ouse, cairn,* and *pen* or *ben.* Some of the names of our oldest towns, like those of most of our rivers, date back to Roman or pre- or post-Roman British days—and obviously the old Roman-British civilization with its roads, bridges, dykes, and fortresses was not entirely destroyed. The Celtic races of Britain, like those of France, left practically no written examples of their languages; for writing was a secret art jealously reserved by the Druids; but the Anglo-Saxons had already many myths, songs, and stories with which their "scops" or minstrels would entertain their warriors before they went to sleep.

The Anglo-Saxons left the richest and most revealing of all primitive Teutonic literatures, a legacy which would have been far richer but for the neglectful contempt with which they and their language were regarded by the conquering Normans and Angevins, and by the foreign churchmen whom the Conquest introduced into the seats of authority and learning. Let us consider for a moment the impressions of certain peculiar characteristics which Anglo-Saxon literature makes on our modern mind.

For instance, we note the strength of the monarchical sentiment, the fact that kings and chiefs were regarded not only as invincible champions in battle but also as dispensers of gifts and inexhaustible hospitality to a permanent court of thegns or knights, and to an unlimited number of guest-friends, travellers, and wanderers. Moreover, we note that the King did not reign solely in his own right of primogeniture but was a prince of the royal house, elected by a council of territorial aristocracy, the *witena gemot* or "meeting of the wise." The King was the Defender and Shepherd, though not the Legislator; and, as among the Greeks of Homeric days, he was a kind of high-priest or head of spiritual affairs, who performed the sacrifices to the gods on behalf of the people. So his person was sacred and loyalty to him implied loyalty to those who chose him and to the whole tradition of the race.

Secondly, we note a popular Teutonic respect for earls and lords, or rather for ancient families, which also persists to this day. The thegns or companions of the King were bound to him by the closest ties, pledged to defend and not to survive him if he fell in battle. For the rest, courage and skill in arms were the essential qualities of honor. The word of a free-born Englishman, earl or churl, seems to have been regarded as at least double the value of that of a descendant of the conquered race, let alone that of any foreigner. The jury system was already adumbrated in the open trials of the peoples' courts, and these courts, or moots, held in each village, elected their own "reeve" or *gerefa* and were attended by all the local landowners. There were no doubt in this the seeds of a peculiar confidence in local or self-government and of regard for families, ancient institutions, or firms of old and long-recognized position.

Thirdly, this self-government implied great reverence for *law,* for law resting on inherited custom, and the common conscience as to what is right or fair. It was not a code of written laws imposed by King or State, for even kings were subject to law and ancient tradition which included a respect for a vast number of unwritten codes and customs, many without moral claim, yet enforced by social sanctions to an extent that is often puzzling to other nations. Such secondary codes may well have grown up in the intimacy of the king's hall, where the thegns lived, slept, ate, and drank together and where their observance became a matter of loyalty to the house or class. Certain things, we still say, "are not done." The code is custom and it frequently includes or prescribes a way of doing, which rests on common consent. This respect for custom often leads to an almost excessive caution before "creating a precedent." Anyhow, we respect the law, as few people do in other countries, where the law is regarded merely as the machinery of Government. Apparently the Anglo-Saxon code did not impose any restriction on drinking, which is still regarded abroad as our national vice, or on gambling, even if it should involve the loss of a free man's liberty.

The Anglo-Saxons, like most barbarians, were naturally lazy, though loving sport and war, and their sports would often take the form of fighting. After their wassails they would listen to interminable chanted stories, anecdotes, or riddles, and merry or moralizing songs. In course of time they became husbandmen and farmers, but it is doubtful if the Anglo-Saxon ever knew the deep devotion to the soil, the veritable land-love of the foreign peasant. The Anglo-Saxon loved the wildness of the waste and woodland and the birds and beasts he watched and hunted; and Anglo-Saxon, like most English poetry, contains much simple natural coloring expressed in a host of imaginative synonyms. But the piety of unwearying soil-service, from earliest dawn till late at night, year in, year out, from infancy to age, without ambition or desire for change or holiday, such as inspires the industry of the foreign peasant —this he has seldom known, by reason of some innate restlessness of spirit. The foreign peasant loves his farm for what it can be made by labor to produce, as he loves his wife for the children that she bears him. He is generally very hard-working, almost indefatigable, docile, and long-suffering, neither enterprising nor impatient, too devoted to his farm and family, animals and cronies to care much about education, travel, sport, or politics. He may be forced by poverty to emigrate for years; but he constantly aspires to return, for the spirit of his home is always with him.

As for religion, the Anglo-Saxon seems to have brought with him a pessimistic fatalism, enbodied in a deep respect for a mysterious Fate or Wyrd, to which all living things in earth and heaven were subject. He had his gods—Woden, Tiw, Thunor, and Frig, and he had his magic and superstitions, totems, or mascots; but he does not seem to have had much faith in them. Huntsmen, herdsmen, sailors, and warriors do not build impressive temples, or carry about great sculptured figures, or collect rich paraphernalia of complicated liturgies, the taste for which inspired the decorative and plastic arts in the city-states of Greece and Italy. Such art as our ancestors practised was in the decoration of their weapons and personal ornaments which they frequently covered with intricate designs. Their sacred rites consisted of certain customary seasonal sacrifices under the direction of some specially dedicated person, king or priest, in the name of the whole tribe. There is no evidence that the Anglo-Saxons practised human sacrifice, as the Britons are said to have done. They apparently believed in the immortality of the soul and in eternal leisure, diversified by fighting and feasting, granted to the brave, and in an everlasting obloquy for cowards. They built no temples of carven stones; their holy places were no more than clearings in the forest, sacred trees, or hilltops; they had no taste for such collective efforts in monumental construction as the great circles of orientated boulders which still excite our wonder, as they well might theirs, at Avebury or Stonehenge. For the rest, they had a vast mythology of heroes, valkyries, wizards, witches, giants, dragons, serpents, and other monsters of earth, air, and sea. But their divinities only existed in the stories told about them. As far as we know, they were not embodied in images, statues, pictures, or relics of any material kind. Magic runes, mottoes, or symbols were engraved upon their weapons; rules and proverbs were transmitted from generation to generation in terse alliterative jingles. Above all they loved riddles, over ninety of which are found in the Exeter Book of Anglo-Saxon poetry.

This book is one of four which contain between them practically all that survives of one of the noblest collections of poetry in the world. That so little survives today must be partly due to the destruction of the northern monasteries by the Danes in the eighth and ninth centuries, still more perhaps to the neglect and contempt of the Latin-speaking monks of the twelfth to the early sixteenth centuries during the long depression of English before its late medieval revival as a partly Latin language, and finally to the dispersion or destruction of the monastic libraries at the Reformation.

Enough, however, survives of Old English to show that it is a magnificently virile literature. There is no trace of weakness, surrender, or even of love for woman or yearning for family life in the home with parents or children. The note of hard endurance sounds throughout from first to last. "That [woe] passed away and so will this!" is the refrain of *Deor,* one of the oldest of the poems. Our older literature is intensely realistic in its descriptions of cliffs and headlands, sea-birds, waves, and wonders of the northern seas; and monsters such as Grendel and his mother, whom Beowulf slew, are full of suggestive imaginative power. In such poems as *The Seafarer* and *The Wanderer* is expressed the passion for the sea in all its moods. Then we find the desire for honor, for the rings which were given by their lords as signs not merely of his favor, wealth, and generosity, but of their own prowess, courage, and merit in the eyes of fellow-thegns. With Christianity came, in some part direct from Rome, but far more through Celtic Ireland, Latin schools and monasteries with libraries and the copying of manuscripts, Latin and English. Iona, Lindisfarne, Jarrow, and York; Biscop, Bebe, Egbert, and Alcuin—these names of places and men trace the first lines of Northumbria's learning and literature. The Christian poets began with Caedmon in the seventh century; and these and their successors, such as Cynewulf, chose from the Bible the stories that were most to their taste—the Fall of Satan, the battles of the Israelites, the description and overwhelming of Pharaoh's host in the Red Sea, the moving episode of the sacrifice of Isaac, and many more. One heroine was Judith, another St. Helena, who finds the

Cross and gives occasion for the description of a great parade of her husband Constantine's warriors, for military parades were always popular with Anglo-Saxon poets and their audiences. But the greatest poem of all is *The Dream of the Rood* discovered in an Anglo-Saxon book at Vercelli in the early nineteenth century, in which the Cross, covered with jewels or with blood, tells the poet in a vision of what the Hero of Heroes had to endure when it was set up for Him on Calvary. This is one of the greatest religious poems in the world. English prose comes later than poetry, and from Wessex, after the monasteries of the North had been destroyed; and in spite of constant wars it flourished in the ninth century under the great King Alfred, who found time to translate books, such as the *Pastoralia* of St. Gregory and the *Consolations* of Boethius, and to begin the *English Chronicle* which continued till long after the Norman Conquest and the irruption of the Latin Benedictine monks into the Cathedral schools. The last great prose-writer was Aelfric, who paraphrased much of the Liturgy and Gospels, before the tide of Norman-French and Latin buried the old scholarship for three hundred years.

This early literature had been disciplined and directed by the return of Rome in the last years of the sixth century—Rome in her most realistic and imperialistic form, that is, the Catholic Church. With her there came into our language a large number of Church-Latin or Latinized-Greek words, such as *altar, alms, angel, devil, bishop, cleric, candle, creed, psalm, hymn, anthem, mass, minister, monk, school,* and *priest,* together with names of fruits and flowers, such as *peach* and *cherry, rose* and *lily,* and household words, such as *cup, plate, dish, pan, kettle, cook,* and *kitchen.* But our fathers kept their own Saxon words for brewing: *yeast, malt, beer, ale, mead,* and *wassail.*

On the other hand, the Danes, in compensation for the destruction of Northumbrian civilization, seem to have contributed a great many common words wherein the Old English were assimilated to the Old Norse forms. Among such words are: *get, hit, loose, low, want, take, leg, skin, knife, fellow, husband, sister,* and so on—proving not so much that these new barbarians brought something new into our islands as that they eventually settled down and mingled on equal terms with the earlier settlers and thus influenced the local speech without subduing it or setting up a rival tongue. Another group of their words, connected with natural features, such as *beck, brack, fell, gill, holm, keld, mel, rigg, scough, slack,* and *thwaite,* are chiefly found in the place-names of those districts where their settlements were most numerous. Negatively they had great influence, for by destroying the old literary tradition in the North and East which was the most civilized part of England, they weakened the resistance of Old English as a literary and much-inflected language, with the result that when the three chief dialects gradually emerged again to literature the one that was most completely freed from all such grammatical encumbrances was that of the most impoverished provinces, where destruction had been most complete.

After the Scandinavian came once more the Latin influence upon our national life and tongue. The Normans were descendants of the Vikings, but they had been over a century in France and had adopted the French tongue. During the two centuries of Norman, Angevin, and early-Plantagenet rule, the Old English vocabulary, as used in popular speech, declined to less than one-third of what it once had been. What with the subjection and the impoverishment of the Saxon land-owning classes, the passing of ecclesiastical authority with its schools into the hands of foreign prelates and the substitution of Northern French, first Anglo-Norman and then the Langue d'Oïl, for Anglo-Saxon at the court, the castle, and the towns or cities of the subservient middle classes, Old English ceased to be the language of literature, although written continuously in some provincial schools and monasteries. The vernacular of uneducated people consequently declined. Learned and poetic terms fell out of use and were forgotten, and their place was taken by words borrowed from the current town language of the upper and middle classes. These were chiefly now French-speaking; but all who had dealings with the English were bilingual and thus became the medium for the teaching of French words. Town craftsmen and tradesmen still keep their French names: *carpenter, cutler, grocer, mason, tailor, butcher, draper,* and *barber;* but village craftsmen, such as *smith, wright, miller, baker, skinner,* and *potter* remain English. Meals on the castle table were French, *dinner* and *supper,* with *beef, mutton, veal, pork, bacon,* and *venison;* meals on the cottage board must have been very simple; only *breakfast* and *lunch* are English, which is surely linguistic evidence of the poverty to which our forefathers were reduced. The schools were in the hands of the Church, which taught Latin, or, for the sake of the middle classes, French.

But the Danish, Norman, and still more the Angevin occupations of England did more than this to English. They profoundly affected its grammatical structure in that they deprived the spoken vernaculars of the natural protection that a common written language affords. Even before the Norman Conquest, spoken English had changed and varied from dialect to dialect without any standard orthography or grammar, so that during this partial eclipse of literary English the several distinct declensions of the nouns were assimilated to the one that was most practical, wherein the cases were least easily confused—a declension forming the singular possessive genitive in *es* and the plurals in *as,* which were soon reduced by the common voice to *s.* By fortunate coincidence French plurals, being derived from Latin accusative plurals *os, as,* and *es,* were formed in the same way. Hence with few exceptions such as *oxen, children, brethren, geese, teeth,* and *mice,* English also makes its plurals in *-s* and, unlike French, still sounds this letter.

French—and indeed Vulgar Latin, out of which it had grown—was already an analytic language, forming its cases by the use of prepositions, such as *de, a,* and *dans,* directly derived from its parent tongue. English was always rich in prepositions, rendering many case-endings redundant.

In 1362 English was made the language for pleading in the Courts, although the phraseology of legal pronouncements long remained Old French. Sixteen years later, notwithstanding the great variety of dialects, English became the official speech of Parliament, proving that this was the natural and probably the only language of the Knights of the Shire and the Burgesses, who by this time wanted to speak. So for the amusement and instruction of this new middle class a new type of English literature, romantic and religious, came slowly into life. Among the earliest of these new productions were naturally many translations from the incomparably richer French romantic literature. For example, there is Layamon's paraphrase of Wace's original French account of the early kings of Britain. It was known as *The Brut,* the name of the mythical great-grandson of Aeneas who came as an exile to Britain not so long after the fall of Troy, founded a kingdom, and became the first progenitor of the early kings of Britain. His tale, like those of Wace's original inspirer, Geoffrey of Monmouth, was especially favored by the Angevin dynasty as a counterblast to any exaltation of the achievements of the old Anglo-Saxon line. Layamon's *Brut* appeared as an English epic in the first years of the thirteenth century and contained, not only the story of this mythical personage, but also those of King Arthur, Lear, and Cymbeline. It was thus both knightly and patriotically English, although without reference to the great deeds of any Anglo-Saxon hero-king, such as Athelstan or Alfred, or to King Horn or Havelok the Dane. Soon after, Gospel homilies known as the *Ormulum* were composed by an Augustinian monk named Orm, and later *The Owl and the Nightingale,* a lively discussion in couplets. Robert Mannyng's *Handlyng Synne* was a free translation of a French book by an Englishman, by which example we may see how intimately connected were the two literatures in this period of transition from a French-speaking to an English-speaking aristocracy. If we put ourselves into the place of one of these paraphrasing poets, who, with a French text before him and the French rhymes in his head, was striving to retell the story according to English taste, we can understand that French words and French rhymes would unavoidably come into his work. It was natural that he should adopt an Anglicized form of many of the French words he translated. Indeed one wonders, given the fact that he was probably educated in a Latin or French school, in which French rather than the English dialect was the medium for translating Latin, whether he realized that many words he used were not true English words at all. They were the only names he knew for things or qualities that were not known or spoken of in English villages. Even as late as 1480 Caxton was puzzled in the choice of words he had to make when he was translating a French text of Virgil's *Aeneid* into English. Therein he found many "fayr and strange termes," but he had already been blamed by "gentylmen" for the "over curyous termes in his translacyons which could not be understande of comyn peple and desired to use olde and homely termes." If that was the problem for Caxton, how much more must it have been so over a century earlier in the days before Chaucer? Surely this is a very common linguistic custom in all similar conditions. So, in order to render a French tale into verse to be recited to English listeners, the poet inevitably used a language interlarded with French expressions, all the more naturally because in all the larger cities French had been used in the castle and largely in the market for some two hundred years, so that the English vocabulary was already full of French. Moreover, there was an intermediate class of bailiffs and stewards, of whom it must have been hard to say which of the two languages they used more often. So something like a new language came to birth in this new aristocratic literature—Old English at base, although shorn of almost all its Teutonic inflections, with a large subsidiary French vocabulary of Anglicized French words. This was the language that Chaucer used—Dan Chaucer "welle of English undefyled," as Edmund Spenser called him! But Chaucer can only be called the "welle" in the sense that he is the fullest, deepest, and richest source from which later poets drew, for into that "welle" several earlier less-known streams had poured. We can trace these various springs from the older tongues right back through the fourteenth and thirteenth centuries—in romantic stories with an English turn such as *Sir Gawain and the Green Knight,* in homiletic poems such as *Cleanness* and *Patience,* and in one lovely elegy, *Pearl.* Almost contemporary with these is the great English vision-poem of *Piers Plowman* and the courtly poems of Chaucer, especially his *Troylus and Cryseyde.* At the same time there appears the great prose work of Wyclif, the spiritual ancestor of the Reformers. So French phrases were not woven upon this English warp as ordinary cloth is made, but each thread, that is, each word, was chosen and put in just when and where it was required, because an Old English word was wanting, having been forgotten during the long eclipse of English as a cultured tongue. Moreover, at two different periods French words were taken as from two different sources and thus in some instances two words were derived from the same French root, pronounced and transcribed according to different forms. Again, each French word was Anglicized and adapted as it was taken in, just as were the Latin, Italian, Dutch, Arabic, Greek, Indian, Hindustani, and other words of later centuries.

The Latin words that came through French underwent French improvement, before they were still more improved in London, which in the twelfth and early thirteenth centuries was probably the largest French-speaking city in the world. French coins were at different periods restamped in the Mint of London and reissued as English currency, and similarly French words, not from the French of Paris but from the French of Stratford-atte-Bowe, whence Chaucer's Prioress got hers. Through all such changes in the common language, the Old English skeleton remained, its nouns stripped of inflections and genders, and its verbs of most of the complications of its tenses. Finally, the Middle English terminal *e*, which must have produced a weak and somewhat drawling tune in spoken English, dropped out of hearing and more slowly out of print. This quickening of speech must have implied a great awakening of the people or possibly a passing of the linguistic currency into a more intellectual or cultured class, who used it to speak more definitely and rapidly. However this may be, it cannot be wholly dissociated from the adoption of English in place of French as the language of Parliament according to the decree of Edward III and, I suggest, to a predominance of the Danish strain from East Anglia, whence most of the new-rich merchants came to London at this time. By the end of the fifteenth century, English had once more become a language of culture, fit to carry the history and learning of the time that had hitherto reposed in Latin. Old and famous Latin books had already been put into the plain man's speech by John Trevisa in his popular versions of the *Polychronicon* of Higden (1387) and the *De Proprietatibus Rerum Naturae* of Brother Bartholomeus Anglicus (1398). For the literature of pleasure and delight, the ancestor of our modern fiction, there were Chaucer's translation of the *Roman de la Rose* and his contemporary Gower's poetry. Henceforward, although each of the streams might swell and grow and fertilize new fields for different audiences, the river they formed was one—a true standard English.

The English people had paid a heavy price for their entrance into Latin Europe. They had had to suffer the arrogant rule of the Norman or French barons for three centuries. They resented their servitude to French-speaking masters; they would not have been English if they had not! It was the policy of the wisest of the Norman kings to seek the people's help to control the lawlessness of their own factious barons. Occasionally a bishop such as Thomas Becket or Stephen Langton would earn the people's love by standing up for them against a tyrannical king. But the extinction of what must have been a great and noble literature and the centuries of silence that followed the Conquest is a tragedy for which responsibility must rest with the monks, whose libraries were the only repositories where it might have been preserved, and a proof of their lack of sympathy with the silenced and illiterate people.

Suggestions

1. The history of the English language is divided into three periods, modern English having been used in England and the United States since the 16th century. "Origin and Growth of English" describes the two earlier forms of English: Old English (or Anglo-Saxon), the language of England before the Norman-French conquest of 1066, and Middle English, which became dominant in the 14th century. Outline the essay, showing each of the linguistic influences that affected the creation of Old and Middle English and explaining why modern English is considered a Germanic language.

2. This essay is concerned not with language alone but with what language tells about the people who use it. List the Anglo-Saxon characteristics described in ¶¶3–7. What is the speaker's attitude toward his early ancestors?

3. Describe the speaker's attitude toward Anglo-Saxon poetry. What was its fate (¶8 and ¶16)?

4. Explaining what is meant by "the return of Rome" (¶10), show its influence on English.

5. In the lists of modern English words derived from Saxon, Danish, and Norman French (¶¶11–13), look up the meanings of those with which you are unfamiliar. What contrast exists in our words for craftsmen, foods, and meals?

6. Show why the plurals of most modern English nouns end in *-s* (¶14).

7. Summarize the process by which Middle English was created and became the dominant language of England (¶15).

8. Explain: *vernacular, Druids, Angevins, primogeniture, Teutonic, pessimistic fatalism, liturgies, Vercelli, Wessex, analytic language.*

9. Write an essay on the Anglo-Saxon characteristics identified in your answer to No. 2 above, showing whether you think they are characteristic of modern Englishmen and of Americans.

10. Write an essay showing how illustrations for † "The Miracle of Language" may be found in "Origin and Growth of English."

THE AMERICAN LANGUAGE

H. L. MENCKEN *Reprinted by permission of* THE YALE REVIEW. © *Yale University Press.*

The first Englishman to notice an Americanism sneered at it aloofly, thus setting a fashion that many of his countrymen have been following ever since. He was one Francis Moore, a ruffian who came out to Georgia with Oglethorpe in 1735, and the word that upset him was *bluff,* in the sense of "a cliff or headland with a broad precipitous face." He did not deign to argue against it; he simply dismissed it as "barbarous," apparently assuming that all Englishmen of decent instincts would agree with him. For nearly a century they seem to have done so, and *bluff* lingered sadly below the salt. When it was printed at all in Great Britain it was set off by sanitary quotation marks, or accompanied by other hints of deprecation, as *rubberneck, hot spot,* and *nerts* are accompanied today. But then, in 1830, the eminent Sir Charles Lyell used it shamelessly in the first volume of his monumental *Principles of Geology,* and from that day to this it has been a perfectly respectable if somewhat unfamiliar word in England, with a place in every dictionary.

Its history is the history of almost countless other Americanisms. They have been edging their way into English since early colonial times, and, for more than a century past, in constantly increasing volume, but I can't recall one that didn't have to run a gantlet of opposition in the motherland, at times verging upon the frantic. After the Revolution, that opposition took on the proportions of a holy war. Never an American book came out that the English reviewers did not belabor its vocabulary violently. The brunt of the attack, of course, had to be borne by the poetasters of the era—for example, Joel Barlow, whose *Columbiad* (1807) loosed a really terrifying geyser of abuse. But even the most serious writers got their share—among them, Jefferson, John Marshall, Noah Webster, and John Quincy Adams. Jefferson's crime was that he had invented the verb *to belittle.* It was, one may argue plausibly, a very logical, useful, and perhaps even nifty word, and seventy-five years later the prissy Anthony Trollope was employing it without apology. But when Jefferson ventured to use it in his *Notes on Virginia* (1787) *The London Review* tossed and raged in a manner befitting the discovery of a brace of dueling pistols beneath the cope of the Archbishop of Canterbury, and for several years following, its dudgeon was supported virtuously by most of the other reviews. "What an expression!" roared the *London.* "It may be an elegant one in Virginia, but for our part, all we can do is to *guess* at its meaning. For shame, Mr. Jefferson! Freely, good sir, will we forgive all your attacks, impotent as they are illiberal, upon our national character; but for the future spare—O spare, we beseech you, our mother-tongue!"

The underscoring of *guess* was a fling in passing at another foul Americanism. It was the belief of most Englishmen then, as it is today, that the use of the verb in the sense of *to suppose* or *assume* originated in this country. It is actually to be found, in that meaning precisely, in [Shakespeare's] *Measure for Measure* and *Henry VI;* nay, in Chaucer, Wycliffe, and Gower. But such historical considerations have never daunted the more ardent preservers of the King's English. When a word acquires an American flavor it becomes anathema to them, even though it may go back to Boadicea. *To advocate* offers an instructive example. It appeared in English in the dark backward and abysm of time, but during the eighteenth century it seems to have dropped out of general use, though Burke used it. Towards the end of the century it came into vogue in this country, and soon it made its way back to the land of its birth. It was received with all the honors proper to an invasion of Asiatic cholera. The reviews denounced it as loutish, "Gothic," and against God, and lumped it with *to compromit* and *to happify* as proof that civilization was impossible in America, and would be so forevermore. Even Benjamin Franklin, returning from England in 1789, was alarmed into begging Noah Webster to "reprobate" it, along with *to notice, to progress,* and *to oppose.* There is no record of Noah's reply, but it is most unlikely that he did any reprobating, for when he began to make dictionaries he included all four verbs, and they have been listed in every considerable dictionary published since, whether in this country or in England.

The leader of the heroic struggle to keep Americanisms out of Britain, in its early stages, was the celebrated William Gifford, editor of *The Quarterly Review.* Gifford was a killer in general practice, and his savage assaults on Wordsworth, Shelley, and Keats are still unpleasantly remembered. He was the first magazine editor in history to make the trade pay, and when he died in 1828 he left £25,000 and was buried in Westminster Abbey. One of his major specialties was the villainousness of everything American, from politics to table manners and from theology to speechways. Among the allegations that he either made himself or permitted his contributors to make were these: (*a*) that the Americans employed naked colored women to wait upon them at table, (*b*) that they kidnapped Scotsmen, Irishmen, Hollanders, and Welshmen and sold them into slavery, and (*c*) that they were planning to repudiate the English language altogether, and adopt Hebrew in its place. This last charge, as it flew from tongue to tongue, acquired variorum readings. One of them made the new American language an Indian dialect, another made it Greek, and a third was to the effect that the people of Britain would be forced to acquire Greek, thus leaving English to the wicked will of the barbaric Yankees. It all sounds idiotic today, but in 1814 it was taken quite seriously by many Englishmen. Gifford was a tyrannical editor and so vastly enjoyed slashing his contributors' copy that Southey once denounced him as "a butcherly review-gelder." But anything that was against the damyankee passed his eye unscathed, and he piled up accusations in a manner so shameless that *The North American Review* was moved to protest that if the tirade went on it would "turn into bitterness the last drops of good-will towards England that exist in the United States."

In the early Twenties of that century there was some amelioration, and when Gifford retired from the *Quarterly* in 1824, voices that were almost conciliatory began to be heard. They heaped praises on Niagara Falls, found something to commend in Cooper's *Spy,* and even had kind words for the speed and luxuriousness of American canalboats. But my most diligent researches have failed to unearth anything complimentary to the American language. It continued to be treated as a grotesque and immoral gibberish, full of uncouth terms and at war with all the canons of English. Every British traveller who came to these shores between the War of 1812 and the Civil War had something to say about the neologisms his ears and eyes encountered on his tour, and nearly all were constrained to deplore them. Captain Basil Hall, who was here in 1827 and 1828, went about in a palpitating daze, confounded and outraged by the signs on American places of business. *Clothing Store* he interpreted after long thought, and *Flour and Feed Store* after prayer and soul-searching, but what on earth was a *Leather and Finding Store?* Captain Thomas Hamilton, who followed five years later, found it impossible to penetrate to "the precise import" of *Dry-Goods Store,* and when he encountered an establishment offering *Hollow Ware, Spiders, and Fire-Dogs* he gave up in despair.[1]

Hall was not one to take it lying down. He decided to call upon Noah Webster, whose American Dictionary of the English Language had just come out, to find out what the Yankees meant by using the mother tongue so cruelly. Webster shocked him by arguing stoutly that "his countrymen had not only a right to adopt new words, but were obliged to modify the language to suit the novelty of the circumstances, geographical and political, in which they were placed." The great lexicographer "who taught millions to spell but not one to sin" went on to observe judicially that it was "quite impossible to stop the progress of language—it is like the course of the Mississippi, the motion of which, at times, is scarcely perceptible; yet even then it possesses a momentum

---

[1] Hall (1788–1844) wrote *Travels in North America, in the Years 1827 and 1828;* Hamilton (1789–1842) wrote *Men and Manners in America.*

quite irresistible. Words and expressions will be forced into use in spite of all the exertions of all the writers in the world."

"But surely," persisted Hall, "such innovations are to be deprecated?"

"I don't think that," replied old Noah. "If a word becomes universally current in America, where English is spoken, why should it not take its station in the language?"

"Because," declared Hall with magnificent pertinacity, "there are words enough already."

This heroic dogma is still heard in England, where even native novelties are commonly opposed violently, and not infrequently strangled at birth. There seems to be, in the modern Englishman, very little of that ecstasy in word-making which so prodigiously engrossed his Elizabethan forebears. Shakespeare alone probably put more new words into circulation than all the English writers since Carlyle, and they were much better ones. The ideal over there today is not picturesque and exhilarating utterance, but correct and reassuring utterance, and one of its inevitable fruits is that bow-wow jargon which Sir Arthur Quiller-Couch describes in *On the Art of Writing* as "the medium through which boards of government, county councils, syndicates, committees, commercial firms, express the processes as well as the conclusions of their thought, and so voice the reason of their being." It is, at its worst, at least in accord with what are taken to be the principles of English grammar, and at its best it shows excellent manners and even a kind of mellifluous elegance; indeed, the English, taking one with another, may be said to write much better than we do—at all events by the standards of the schoolmaster. But what they write is seldom animated by anything properly describable as bounce. It lacks novelty, variety, audacity. There is little juice in it. The reader confronted by it is treated politely and lulled pleasantly, but he seldom enjoys the enchantment of surprise. That diligent search for new and racy locutions which occupied so much of the work day of Walt Whitman and William Dean Howells alike, and is practised so assiduously by scores of saucy Andersons and Hemingways, Sandburgs and Saroyans today, is carried on across the ocean by only a few extravagant eccentrics, virtually all of whom—for example, James Joyce and Ezra Pound—are non- and even anti-Englishmen. The hundred-per-cent English writers, save when they stoop to conscious wickedness, seldom depart very far from the jargon of Quiller-Couch. It is by no means a monopoly of the classes he named, nor is it reserved for solemn occasions. I find it also in my favorite English weekly, the *News of the World,* which is devoted principally to sports, the theatres, and the more scabrous varieties of crime, and is probably a far better mirror of England than *The Times.* When the *News of the World* reports the downfall of a rural dean or a raid on a Mayfair night club, the thing is done in a style so tight and brittle that nothing to match it is discoverable in this country, at least outside the pages of *The Homiletic Review*. "When we want to freshen our speech," Mrs. Virginia Woolf was lately saying, "we borrow from American—*poppycock, rambunctious, flip-flop, booster, good mixer.* All the expressive, ugly, vigorous slang which creeps into use among us, first in talk, later in writing, comes from across the Atlantic."

But whether slang or something better, it always encounters opposition —sometimes merely sullen, but at other times extremely violent. At more or less regular intervals, war upon the invasion is declared formally, and there ensues a long uproar, with the papers full of choleric letters to the editor. One such sharpening of activity was loosed when the chief constable of Wallasey, a suburb of Liverpool, reported in alarm that his policemen were being called *cops* by the tougher youngsters of the place, and otherwise insulted with blasphemies picked up from American movies. "*Oh-yeahs,*" he said, "are frequent in answer to charges, and we are promised *shoots-up in the burg* [*sic*] and threatened to be *bumped off.*" Half the amateur publicists who took a hand in the discussion which followed advocated using the cat on the offenders, and the other half demanded that American movies be barred from England as intolerable public menaces, like cattle infected with foot-and-mouth disease. As usual, the debate ended in philological futilities. Was *oh yeah* actually English, even bad English, insane English? Or was it only an American borrowing from one of the dialects of the savage Red Indians, or maybe from Polish, Pennsylvania Dutch, Gullah, Yiddish, or some other such godless and anti-British lingo? No matter! *Oh yeah* continues to flourish from the Lizard to Unst,[2] and with it *cop* flourishes too. The latter, in fact, has swept upward from the level of bad boys baiting constables to that of bishops following their transcendental occasions. Even before the chief constable of Wallasey sounded his cry of "Wolf!" a right reverend father in God had been charged before the Farnham (Surrey) magistrates with applying *speed-cop* on a public road to a member of the *mobile police*. Overhauled in his car, so the testimony went, he had demanded, "Are you a *speed-cop?*" His Lordship denied wtih some heat that he had used the term, or anything else so unseemly, but the magistrates apparently concluded that he must have let it slip, for they took a serious view of his very modest adventure in speeding, fined him £10, and suspended his driving licence for three months. I give his name and dignities as a warning to lesser evildoers. He was the Right Reverend Cyril Henry Gelding-Bird, D. D. (Oxon.), Assistant Bishop of Guildford and Archdeacon of Dorking, and a man previously unknown to the police.

Whenever an Americanism comes publicly into question in England, there are efforts to track down its etymology, and sometimes the theories offered are extremely bizarre. In January, 1935, for example, the London

---

[2] I.e. from the peninsula in Cornwall known as The Lizard, at the southwestern extremity of England, to the northernmost of the Shetland Islands, off the northern coast of Scotland.

Morning Post opened its columns to a furious and fantastic discussion of the verb-phrase, *to get his goat.* I content myself with one of the explanations: "Among the Negroes in Harlem it is the custom for each household to keep a goat to act as general scavenger. Occasionally one man will steal another's goat, and the household débris then accumulates to the general annoyance." The truth is that *to get his goat* seems to be of French origin, and in the form of *prendre sa chèvre,* philological genealogists have traced it back to the year 1585. But whatever is strange and upsetting is put down, in England, to the hellish ingenuity of Americans—save, of course, when genuine Americanisms are claimed as really English. This last happens often enough to give what may be called a cockeyed aspect to the perennial pother. In 1934 even the learned Dr. C. T. Onions, one of the editors of the great Oxford Dictionary, succumbed to the madness by offering to find in the dictionary any alleged Americanism that a reporter for the London *Evening News* could name. The reporter began discreetly with *fresh* (in the sense of *saucy*), *to figure* (in the sense of *to believe* or *conclude*), and *to grill* (in the sense of *to question*), and Dr. Onions duly found them all. But when the reporter proceeded to *bunkum,* the learned editor had to forget conveniently that its progenitor was the thoroughly American *buncombe,* when *rake-off* followed he had to admit that the earliest example in the dictionary was from an American work, and when *boloney* and *nerts* were hurled at him he blew up with a bang.

Here, of course, Dr. Onions and his interlocutor ended on the level of slang, but there is no telling where they would be if they could be translated to the year 2036. *Boloney,* like *to belittle,* has the imprimatur of an eminent tribune of the people, and is quite as respectable, philologically speaking, as *buncombe, gerrymander, pork barrel, filibuster, carpetbagger, gag rule,* or *on the fence.* All these came into American from the argot of politics, and got only frowns from the schoolmarm, but they are all quite sound American today, and most of them have gone into English. As for *nerts,* it seems to be but one more member of an endless dynasty of euphemisms, beginning with *zounds* and coming down to *son-of-a-gun, gee,* and *darn. Darn,* like *nerts,* is an Americanism, and Dr. Louise Pound has demonstrated that it descends from *eternal,* which first turned into *tarnal* and then lost its tail and borrowed the head of *damn.* I have heard a bishop use it freely in private discourse, with a waggish sprinkling of actual *damns. Son-of-a-gun* is now so feeble and harmless that the Italians in America use it as a satirical designation for native Americans, who seem to them to fall far behind the Italian talent for profanity and objurgation. It is, I believe, a just criticism. Some time ago I was engaged by a magazine to do an article on American and English swearwords. After two or three attempts I had to give it up, for I found that neither branch of our ancient Frisian tongue could show anything worthy of serious consideration. The antinomians of England stick to two or three banal obscenities, one of which, *bloody,* is obscene only formally, and we Americans seldom get beyond variations of *hell* and *damn.* A single Neapolitan boatman could swear down the whole population of Anglo-Saxondom.

Bloody is perfectly innocuous in the United States, and it may be innocuous in England also on some near tomorrow—or even more disreputable than it is today. There is no predicting the social career of words. Dr. Leonard Bloomfield says that even "our word *whore,* cognate with the Latin *carus* (dear), must have been at one time a polite substitute for some term now lost." Prophecy fails just as dismally when propriety does not come into question. Shakespeare's numerous attempts to introduce new words, some of them his own inventions and others borrowed from the slang of the Bankside, failed almost as often as they succeeded. He found ready takers for *courtship, lonely, sportive, multitudinous, hubbub,* and *bump,* but his audiences would have none of *definement,* in the sense of description, or of *citizen* as an adjective, and both seem strange and uncouth to us today, though all the others are as familiar and as decorous as *cat* or *rat.* When John Marston used *strenuous* in 1599 it was attacked by Ben Jonson as barbarous, but a dozen years later it had got into Chapman's Homer, and by 1670 it was being used by Milton. It remained perfectly respectable until 1900, when Theodore Roosevelt announced the Strenuous Life. Both the idea and the term struck the American fancy, and in a little while the latter passed into slang, and was worn so threadbare that all persons of careful speech sickened of it. To this day it carries a faintly ridiculous connotation, and is seldom used seriously. But by 1975 it may be restored to the dignity of *psychopath* or *homoousian.* No one can say yes with any confidence, and no one can say no. "Even the greatest purist," observes Robert Lynd,[3] "does not object to the inclusion of *bogus* in a literary English vocabulary, though a hundred years ago it was an American slang word meaning an apparatus for coining false money. *Carpetbagger* and *bunkum* are other American slang words that have naturalized themselves in English speech, and *mob* is an example of English slang that was once as vulgar as *photo.*"

One finds in current American all the characters and tendencies that marked the rich English of Shakespeare's time—an eager borrowing of neologisms from other languages, a bold and often very ingenious use of metaphor, and a fine disdain of the barricades separating the parts of speech. The making of new words is not carried on only, or even principally, to fill gaps in the vocabulary; indeed, one may well agree with Captain Hall that "there are words enough already." It is carried on

---

[3] British essayist, b. 1879; author of *The Art of Letters* and many other works, including † "On Not Being a Philosopher."

because there survives in the American something that seems to have
faded out of the Englishman: an innocent joy in word-making for its
own sake, a voluptuous delight in the vigor and elasticity of the language.
The search for the *mot juste* is an enterprise that is altogether too
pedantic for him; he much prefers to solve his problem by non-Euclidian
devices. *Hoosegow* was certainly not necessary when it appeared, for we
already had a large repertory of synonyms for *jail*. But when the word
precipitated itself from the Spanish *juzgado* somewhere along the Rio
Grande it won quick currency, and in a little while it was on the march
through the country, and soon or late, I suppose, it will produce its
inevitable clipped forms, *hoose* and *gow,* and its attendant adjective
and verb. *Corral,* which entered by the same route in the Forties of the
last century, had hatched a verb before the Civil War, and that verb,
according to Webster's New International (1934), now has four separate
distinct meanings. *Bummer,* coming in from the German, is now clipped
to *bum,* and is not only noun, verb, and adjective but also adverb.
Buncombe, borrowed by the English as *bunkum,* has bred *bunco* and
bunk at home, both of which rove the parts of speech in a loose and easy
way, and the last of which has issue in the harsh verb *to debunk,* still
under heavy fire in England.

The impact of such lawless novelties upon the more staid English of
the motherland is terrific. The more they are denounced as heathen and
outlandish, the quicker they get into circulation. Nor do they prosper
only on the level of the vulgate, and among careless speakers. There are
constant complaints in the English newspapers about their appearance in
the parliamentary debates, and even in discourses from the sacred desk,
and they begin to show themselves also in *belles-lettres,* despite the English dislike of new ways of writing. Their progress, in fact, is so widespread and so insidious that they often pop up in the diatribes that revile
them; the Englishman, conquered at last, can no longer protest against
Americanisms without using them.

Suggestions

1. "The American Language" might be called a satirical history of
English attitudes toward *neologisms.* Summarize its major divisions and
point out some striking examples of its satire. What qualities of British
English does it praise (¶10)? What qualities of American are most admired in it (¶15)? Do neologisms arise because of gaps in the vocabulary?

2. Decide whether "The American Language" is a suitable title for
this essay, inventing a more precise one if you can.

3. The speaker's allusions to *Henry VI,* Chaucer, Wycliffe, Gower,
Boadicea, Shakespeare's *Tempest* I. ii. 50, Burke, Southey, Virginia Woolf,
Marston, and others prove his wide knowledge of English literature.

Identify at least some of these, showing how such allusions give the essay authority.

4. Name and identify several writers of the past century whose style the speaker admires, and explain what they have in common.

5. Define the speaker's attitude toward William Gifford. Is the attack confined to Gifford's views about language?

6. Summarize the influence of politics and of *euphemisms* on American speech, and show that this paragraph (¶13) ends with a digression.

7. Explain: *below the salt, deprecation, poetasters, Gothic, reprobate, amelioration, pertinacity, scabrous, cat, philological, transcendental occasions, imprimatur, argot, antinomians, innocuous, Bankside, mot juste, non-Euclidian, vulgate, belles-lettres.*

8. Compare the style in which "The American Language" is written with the qualities of style that it praises. Comment with the help of your dictionary on such sentences as "It was, one may argue plausibly, a very logical, useful, and perhaps even nifty word, and seventy-five years later the prissy Anthony Trollope was employing it without apology" (¶2).

9. Write an essay on American slang as it is exemplified in "The American Language." Distinguish the examples that are still current from those with which you are unfamiliar, and suggest new examples that you think might be included if the essay were to be rewritten today.

10. Write an essay showing that statements made in † "The Miracle of Language" can be supported with examples found in "The American Language."

THE PROBLEM OF ENGLISH

From A PIECE OF MY MIND *by Edmund
Wilson.* © *1956 by Edmund Wilson
and the American Jewish Committee.
Used by permission of the publishers,
Farrar, Straus, and Cudahy, Inc.*

EDMUND WILSON

As a child, I imagined that a permanent antagonism existed between my
father and me, that I was always, in tastes and opinions, on the opposite
side from him. This was due, I can see, looking back, to a certain intellectual intolerance on my side as well as on his. But he was not an easy
man to talk to: he almost eliminated give-and-take, for his conversation
mostly consisted of either asking people questions in order to elicit
information or telling them what to think. Our dinners at home, when
we had no guests and there were only my parents and I, were likely to
turn into lectures. My mother at her end of the table was—prematurely
—so very deaf that she could not have any real interchange with my
father at the other end, and my conversation with him usually took the
form either of his asking my view of some question, then immediately
squelching this view and setting me right on the subject, or of explaining
at length, but with an expert lucidity, some basic point of law or government. So much did I take for granted our polarization that I was startled
to realize one day that I was imitating my father's signature—my name
was the same as his—which, like his writing in general, was completely
illegible but quite beautiful in a graphic way, as if he had invented a
calligraphy in order to conceal his meaning from everyone except himself. This handwriting had thus also its arrogance as well as its curious
elegance, and I found myself emulating these.

But it was not until after my father's death—in 1923—that I had a
new revelation of the extent of my mimicry of him. In going through
his speeches, briefs, and other papers, I became for the first time aware
how well he had expressed himself. His style had, I saw, a purity quite
exceptional in a public—or quasi-public—figure in New Jersey in the
early nineteen hundreds, and his language was always distinguished by
a silvery quality of clearness—I remember how he used to make fun of
the pompous labored prose of Cleveland—which led me to understand
his enthusiasm for the style of Stevenson, which I myself rather disliked.
I realized now—and again with surprise—that I had been imitating this
literary style as well as his penmanship. For my methods in writing had
seemed to me personal: though I had imitated Shaw, Henry James, and
a number of other writers, I had consciously corrected these tendencies

382

and was unconscious of my principal model. Since I had rarely heard my father in court or listened to his public speeches, I must have picked up his style mainly from his dinner-table lectures.

Some years after my father's death, I began making notes of his vocabulary and his characteristic phrases, and for the first time I took account of how old-fashioned his English was. He would say, for example, "It rains" or "It snows"—as the characters in Jane Austen do—instead of "It is raining," "It is snowing"; "It makes no matter" for "It doesn't matter." He would sometimes correct himself if he fell into the current usage of "*a* hotel" and make it "*an* hotel." He was the only living person I have ever known who used the exclamation "Zounds!" He was incapable of any other profanity, never even said "Good God!" or "Damn!," and his "Zounds" had a nuance of humor, but he did not regard it as a period piece. He was especially fond of such metaphors as "weltering around in a Dead Sea of mediocrity"—something I was warned not to do, when my school marks were not up to scratch—it was the worst fate with which he could threaten me. He was very much annoyed one day when, on our way home from one of his speeches, I undertook to inform him that the word he had wanted to use was *cataclysm,* not *cataclasm. Cataclasm* [break, rupture] was then so archaic that I did not even know it existed and that it differed in meaning from *cataclysm.* I decided, in any case, at the moment of discovering in the writing of his papers the model for my literary style that this model was a valuable heritage, like the table pieces of silver of the Paul Revere silversmith period which had come to me from his side of the family.

Later on, at my prep school—Hill—I had been trained in traditional English by an extremely able English teacher—Dr. John A. Lester—who was himself an Englishman. He drilled us in sentence structure, grammar, the devices of "rhetoric" and prosody, as if we had been studying a foreign language; and we were made to take very seriously—as I have never, indeed, ceased to do—the great Trinity: Lucidity, Force, and Ease. I have valued this training so much that I have always contended that English ought to be taught in this country by Englishmen. But this brings us to the crux of the problem: should Americans attempt to learn British English: and, if so, to what extent? There have been moments when I have seriously wondered whether my pieces of pre-revolutionary silver were adequate for modern use. I have sometimes become so bored with the language in which I wrote articles—the monotony of the vocabulary and the recurrence of routine formulas—that I would find it a great relief to get away from this kind of writing and give myself a freer hand in a play or a piece of fiction in which I could make people talk as contemporary Americans did. I also tried injecting some current slang into my purely critical writing, but I found that this was likely to jar and that I later had to take it out. With my own education based mainly on the literature and language of England, I sometimes envied H. L. Mencken, with his half-German education, which seemed to make it easier for him to play on "the American language." [1] I was then and still am all in favor of the free development and the literary use of a semi-independent American language, but I cannot face without a shrinking the state of things predicted by Mencken, in which illiterate usage would eventually prevail in the United States—so that our grammar would be reduced to, for example, such conjugations—or non-conjugations—as *I was, you was, he was; we was, you was, they was.* It is not so much, however, that our few surviving inflections are important as that the logic of syntax should not be lost. With all the considerable divergence between British and American idiom, the structure of the language is still the same—or ought to be the same, for otherwise we should have no structure: we should get nothing but woolly writing, incapable of expressing anything either elegantly or exactly.

I am aware of the special problems that exist in American public schools—that in localities where most of the pupils are the children of foreign parents, themselves illiterate in their native tongues, the instructor must sometimes be satisfied to teach them any English at all, that to exact from them a standard of correctitude becomes quite out of the question. I know that in some of our schools it is even as much as the teacher can do to avoid being murdered by his more aggressive students. But there ought to be institutions in which the abler kind of student could be taught to handle language competently. In my ideal university, I should have, as a general requirement, most rigorous courses in English, and I should have them all taught by Englishmen. Every student in every department would have to pass examinations in the accurate writing of English. Those specializing in scientific fields as well as the philosophers and historians would have their papers graded—except, of course, the kind that consist of equations—by the teachers in the English department as well as by their other professors, and, although it might be sometimes unfair to make it an invincible rule that no incompetent writer should ever be allowed to graduate, the gradings for precise expression should be given a good deal of importance.

The use of the English language as an instrument for analysis and exposition is one inheritance from England that we cannot afford to scrap. In the sciences, this logical and concrete style—as I have heard a Russian scientist say—possesses certain decided advantages over either German or French, which both, in their respective ways, so much tend to run to abstractions. In English it is easier to follow the argument, to see what the data are and to know what conclusions have been drawn from them in terms of a practical process. It is handier to describe a species, a

[1] See the essay next before this one.

country, a disease, a geological formation; to lay down the rules for a game, to give directions for navigation. In America, we have done a good deal to make a mess of this excellent medium. In my youthful days as an editor, I had once to prepare for publication a series of articles by the late John Dewey [2] on a trip he had made to China. This ought really not to have involved him in obscurity, since he was merely telling what he had seen and the opinions to which it had led him; but when I came to edit the articles, I found that they both called for and resisted revision in a peculiarly exasperating way. It was not only a question here of clarifying the author's statements but of finding out what he meant; and when you did get the sense of his meaning, there was no way of straightening out the language: you would have had to try to give his meaning in a language of a different kind. But John Dewey, as I presently found out—though typical—was not by any means the worst American writer on education. Later on, the liberal weekly for which I worked ran a supplement on this subject, and the articles we received were incredible. How, I wondered, could a man set up as an authority on teaching the young when he was not himself sufficiently well-educated to have mastered the rudiments of writing? As for my experience with articles by experts in anthropology and sociology, it has led me to conclude that the requirement, in my ideal university, of having the papers in every department passed by a professor of English might result in revolutionizing these subjects—if indeed the second of them survived at all.

But even in the "Humanities" department there is a serious crisis in literacy. How can you write about a literary subject—especially some great artisan of speech—when you yourself are hardly articulate, can scarcely express the most commonplace thoughts? At most, you can unearth a few unknown facts, point out some unsuspected sources. If you even, with no knowledge of the literary art, do not attempt anything more interesting than the dreary *"exposition des textes"* [explanation of the texts (being studied)] that has become a kind of standard academic product, you are likely to misread a language which you have never properly learned. Among the products of American teachers of such feeble qualifications, I have encountered some appalling cases. Some years ago—in 1939—I taught at the summer school of one of the biggest—and, I believe, one of the best—of the Western universities. A man who had been giving a course in contemporary English literature had gone abroad for the summer, and I was asked to grade the papers of his students, who had taken their examination after he left. Among the authors studied were Virginia Woolf, Yeats, and Joyce—one of the greatest of English poets and two of the greatest masters of the harmonics of English prose; but the papers of the students dismayed me as a hideous revelation of the

[2] American philosopher (1859–1952), author of *How We Think* and many other works.

abysses of non-education that are possible in the United States. Hardly one of them could write and punctuate a respectable English sentence. One paper—like Molly Bloom's soliloquy[3]—had been poured out with no punctuation except for an occasional full stop. In response to the question: "Explain the symbolism of Yeats's *The Winding Stair*," another of the examinees had written the following answer: "As Yeats goes up the winding stair he has a kind of a feeling like his old aristocratic past is coming back on him again." This was clearly not the fault of the teacher, a highly competent Britisher, well known as a writer on the subjects he was teaching. The failure had occurred further back. The truth was, of course, that such students should never have been allowed to take such a course at all. They ought to have been learning the use of the comma and the difference between a conjunction and a preposition; they ought to have been standing at blackboards diagramming compound sentences. Another incredible example: a young man, the friend of a friend, once brought me for my criticism a manuscript of his poems. So many kinds of liberties are countenanced—in the way of off-rhymes and irregular rhythms—in the writing of modern poetry that I did not at first question these verses from the technical point of view, but I gradually became suspicious, and when I called the attention of the author to bad metrics and impossible rhymes, I discovered not only that he knew nothing of metrics, had never been told that such a thing existed, but that he did not even understand rhyme, not having grasped the principle that it is the syllables with the accent that have to match, that you cannot rhyme *picture* with *pure*. Yet he had been graduated from an Eastern university which, if not very strong in the Humanities, is of excellent reputation and supposed to keep up a decent standard. He had specialized in American literature and had also had a course in Shakespeare, but it had never been explained to him at any point what kind of verse Shakespeare had written; he seemed, in fact, to have read it as prose. As for his own productions, he had simply seen modern poems in the current "avant-garde" magazines, and had tried to turn out something of the kind himself. (This experience has left me with terrible doubts about some of the stuff that is printed as verse in these literary magazines.) I ought to mention that this touching young man had also been going to classes intended for instruction in the writing of verse at the YMHA in New York, where his writings had been subjected to the scrutiny of a not-unknown poet. But, even after this, it remained for me to break it to him that poetry was an art with rules. It was not that he was stupid: on the contrary, I gave him an hour's instruction and found that he could soon identify the various metrical feet of which till that moment he had never heard. Still another student—from the largest university in the East—told me that he "wanted to write" and turned out to be equally ignorant of the me-

[3] The conclusion of James Joyce's *Ulysses* (1922).

dium that Shakespeare used. He was under the impression that blank verse was any verse that did not rhyme. He had taken one of those courses of miscellaneous classics in translation that are a feature of the modern curriculum, and had been through *The Divine Comedy* without being able to say whether it was written in prose or verse. He did not seem even to know whether the English translation was prose or verse. I was not able to tell him, because he did not know the name of the translator.

Suggestions

1. State the thesis of "The Problem of English," showing its relation to the beginning, which describes the speaker's antagonism to his father, and to the conclusion, which is concerned with metrics. Then comment on the tone in which the thesis is advanced.

2. The speaker asks, ". . . should Americans attempt to learn British English. . . ?" (¶4). Describe some distinctions between British and American English.

3. Explain: ". . . we were made to take very seriously—as I have never, indeed, ceased to do—the great Trinity: Lucidity, Force, and Ease" (¶4).

4. Agree or disagree with the opinion that English should in America be taught by Englishmen (¶4 and ¶5). Is there evidence that the speaker is uncertain about it?

5. Explain: *polarization, calligraphy, Zounds, nuance, cataclysm, prosody, avant-garde, YMHA, metrical feet, blank verse, The Divine Comedy.*

6. Write an essay contrasting the opinions expressed in "The Problem of English" with those of † "The American Language."

FENIMORE COOPER'S LITERARY OFFENCES

SAMUEL L. CLEMENS ⸺⸾ *First published in* THE NORTH AMERICAN REVIEW, *July, 1895.*

The Pathfinder and *The Deerslayer* stand at the head of Cooper's novels as artistic creations. There are others of his works which contain parts as perfect as are to be found in these, and scenes even more thrilling. Not one can be compared with either of them as a finished whole.

The defects in both of these tales are comparatively slight. They were pure works of art.—PROF. LOUNSBURY.

The five tales reveal an extraordinary fullness of invention.
. . . One of the very greatest characters in fiction, Natty Bumppo. . . .
The craft of the woodsman, the tricks of the trapper, all the delicate art of the forest, were familiar to Cooper from his youth up.—PROF. BRANDER MATTHEWS.

Cooper is the greatest artist in the domain of romantic fiction yet produced by America.—WILKIE COLLINS.

It seems to me that it was far from right for the Professor of English Literature in Yale, the Professor of English Literature in Columbia, and Wilkie Collins to deliver opinions on Cooper's literature without having read some of it.[1] It would have been much more decorous to keep silent and let persons talk who have read Cooper.

Cooper's art has some defects. In one place in *Deerslayer,* and in the restricted space of two-thirds of a page, Cooper has scored 114 offenses against literary art out of a possible 115. It breaks the record.

There are nineteen rules governing literary art in the domain of romantic fiction—some say twenty-two. In *Deerslayer* Cooper violated eighteen of them. These eighteen require:

1. That a tale shall accomplish something and arrive somewhere. But the *Deerslayer* tale accomplishes nothing and arrives in the air.

2. They require that the episodes of a tale shall be necessary parts of the tale, and shall help to develop it. But as the *Deerslayer* tale is not a tale, and accomplishes nothing and arrives nowhere, the episodes have no rightful place in the work, since there was nothing for them to develop.

3. They require that the personages in a tale shall be alive, except in the case of corpses, and that always the reader shall be able to tell the corpses from the others. But this detail has often been overlooked in the *Deerslayer* tale.

4. They require that the personages in a tale, both dead and alive, shall exhibit a sufficient excuse for being there. But this detail also has been overlooked in the *Deerslayer* tale.

5. They require that when the personages of a tale deal in conversation, the talk shall sound like human talk, and be talk such as human beings would be likely to talk in the given circumstances, and have a discoverable meaning, also a discoverable purpose, and a show of relevancy, and remain in the neighborhood of the subject in hand, and be interesting to the reader, and help out the tale, and stop when the people cannot think of anything more to say. But this requirement has been ignored from the beginning of the *Deerslayer* tale to the end of it.

---

[1] Thomas R. Lounsbury (1836–1915), was a professor at Yale from 1871 to 1906; Matthews (1852–1929) was a professor at Columbia from 1892 to 1924; Collins (1824–1889) wrote *The Moonstone* and many other mystery novels.

6. They require that when the author describes the character of a personage in his tale, the conduct and conversation of that personage shall justify said description. But this law gets little or no attention in the *Deerslayer* tale, as Natty Bumppo's case will amply prove.

7. They require that when a personage talks like an illustrated, gilt-edged, tree-calf, hand-tooled, seven-dollar Friendship's Offering [2] in the beginning of a paragraph, he shall not talk like a negro minstrel in the end of it. But this rule is flung down and danced upon in the *Deerslayer* tale.

8. They require that crass stupidities shall not be played upon the reader as "the craft of the woodsman, the delicate art of the forest," by either the author or the people in the tale. But this rule is persistently violated in the *Deerslayer* tale.

9. They require that the personages of a tale shall confine themselves to possibilities and let miracles alone; or, if they venture a miracle, the author must so plausibly set it forth as to make it look possible and reasonable. But these rules are not respected in the *Deerslayer* tale.

10. They require that the author shall make the reader feel a deep interest in the personages of his tale and in their fate; and that he shall make the reader love the good people in the tale and hate the bad ones. But the reader of the *Deerslayer* tale dislikes the good people in it, is indifferent to the others, and wishes they would all get drowned together.

11. They require that the characters in a tale shall be so clearly defined that the reader can tell beforehand what each will do in a given emergency. But in the *Deerslayer* this rule is vacated.

In addition to these large rules there are some little ones. These require that the author shall

12. *Say* what he is proposing to say, not merely come near it.

13. Use the right word, not its second cousin.

14. Eschew surplusage.

15. Not omit necessary details.

16. Avoid slovenliness of form.

17. Use good grammar.

18. Employ a simple and straightforward style.

Even these seven are coldly and persistently violated in the *Deerslayer* tale.

Cooper's gift in the way of invention was not a rich endowment; but such as it was he liked to work it, he was pleased with the effects, and indeed he did some quite sweet things with it. In his little box of stage-properties he kept six or eight cunning devices, tricks, artifices for his savages and woodsmen to deceive and circumvent each other with, and

[2] The title of an "annual" or "gift-book," written in a stilted, flowery style and immensely popular in the 19th century.

he was never so happy as when he was working these innocent things and seeing them go. A favorite one was to make a moccasined person tread in the tracks of the moccasined enemy, and thus hide his own trail. Cooper wore out barrels and barrels of moccasins in working that trick. Another stage-property that he pulled out of his box pretty frequently was his broken twig. He prized his broken twig above all the rest of his effects, and worked it the hardest. It is a restful chapter in any book of his when somebody doesn't step on a dry twig and alarm all the reds and whites for two hundred yards around. Every time a Cooper person is in peril, and absolute silence is worth four dollars a minute, he is sure to step on a dry twig. There may be a hundred handier things to step on, but that wouldn't satisfy Cooper. Cooper requires him to turn out and find a dry twig; and if he can't do it, go and borrow one. In fact, the Leatherstocking Series ought to have been called the Broken Twig Series.

I am sorry there is not room to put in a few dozen instances of the delicate art of the forest, as practised by Natty Bumppo and some of the other Cooperian experts. Perhaps we may venture two or three samples. Cooper was a sailor—a naval officer; yet he gravely tells us how a vessel, driving toward a lee shore in a gale, is steered for a particular spot by her skipper because he knows of an *undertow* there which will hold her back against the gale and save her. For just pure woodcraft, or sailorcraft, or whatever it is, isn't that neat? For several years Cooper was daily in the society of artillery, and he ought to have noticed that when a cannon-ball strikes the ground it either buries itself or skips a hundred feet or so; skips again a hundred feet or so—and so on, till finally it gets tired and rolls. Now in one place he loses some "females"—as he always calls women—in the edge of a wood near a plain at night in a fog, on purpose to give Bumppo a chance to show off the delicate art of the forest before the reader. These mislaid people are hunting for a fort. They hear a cannon-blast, and a cannon-ball presently comes rolling into the wood and stops at their feet. To the females this suggests nothing. The case is very different with the admirable Bumppo. I wish I may never know peace again if he doesn't strike out promptly and *follow the track* of that cannon-ball across the plain through the dense fog and find the fort. Isn't it a daisy? If Cooper had any real knowledge of Nature's way of doing things, he had a most delicate art in concealing the fact. For instance: one of his acute Indian experts, Chingachgook (pronounced Chicago, I think), has lost the trail of a person he is tracking through the forest. Apparently that trail is hopelessly lost. Neither you nor I could ever have guessed out the way to find it. It was very different with Chicago. Chicago was not stumped for long. He turned a running stream out of its course, and there, in the slush in its old bed, were that person's moccasin tracks. The current did not wash them away, as it would have done in all other like cases—no, even the eternal laws of Nature have to vacate when Cooper wants to put up a delicate job of woodcraft on the reader.

We must be a little wary when Brander Matthews tells us that Cooper's books "reveal an extraordinary fullness of invention." As a rule, I am quite willing to accept Brander Matthews's literary judgments and applaud his lucid and graceful phrasing of them; but that particular statement needs to be taken with a few tons of salt. Bless your heart, Cooper hasn't any more invention than a horse; and I don't mean a high-class horse, either; I mean a clothes-horse. It would be very difficult to find a really clever "situation" in Cooper's books, and still more difficult to find one of any kind which he has failed to render absurd by his handling of it. Look at the episodes of "the caves"; and at the celebrated scuffle between Maqua and those others on the table-land a few days later; and at Hurry Harry's queer water-transit from the castle to the ark; and at Deerslayer's half-hour with his first corpse; and at the quarrel between Hurry Harry and Deerslayer later; and at—but choose for yourself; you can't go amiss.

If Cooper had been an observer his inventive faculty would have worked better; not more interestingly, but more rationally, more plausibly. Cooper's proudest creations in the way of "situations" suffer noticeably from the absence of the observer's protecting gift. Cooper's eye was splendidly inaccurate. Cooper seldom saw anything correctly. He saw nearly all things as through a glass eye, darkly. Of course a man who cannot see the commonest little everyday matters accurately is working at a disadvantage when he is constructing a "situation." In the *Deerslayer* tale Cooper has a stream which is fifty feet wide where it flows out of a lake; it presently narrows to twenty as it meanders along for no given reason, and yet when a stream acts like that it ought to be required to explain itself. Fourteen pages later the width of the brook's outlet from the lake has suddenly shrunk thirty feet, and become "the narrowest part of the stream." This shrinkage is not accounted for. The stream has bends in it, a sure indication that it has alluvial banks and cuts them; yet these bends are only thirty and fifty feet long. If Cooper had been a nice and punctilious observer he would have noticed that the bends were oftener nine hundred feet long than short of it.

Cooper made the exit of that stream fifty feet wide, in the first place, for no particular reason; in the second place, he narrowed it to less than twenty to accommodate some Indians. He bends a "sapling" to the form of an arch over this narrow passage, and conceals six Indians in its foliage. They are "laying" for a settler's scow or ark which is coming up the stream on its way to the lake; it is being hauled against the stiff current by a rope whose stationary end is anchored in the lake; its rate of progress cannot be more than a mile an hour. Cooper describes the ark, but pretty obscurely. In the matter of dimensions "it was little more than a modern canal-boat." Let us guess, then, that it was about one hundred and forty feet long. It was of "greater breadth than common." Let us guess, then, that it was about sixteen feet wide. This leviathan had been prowling down bends which were but a third as long as itself, and scraping between banks where it had only two feet of space to spare on each side. We cannot too much admire this miracle. A low-roofed log dwelling occupies "two-thirds of the ark's length"—a dwelling ninety feet long and sixteen feet wide, let us say—a kind of vestibule train. The dwelling has two rooms—each forty-five feet long and sixteen feet wide, let us guess. One of them is the bedroom of the Hutter girls, Judith and Hetty; the other is the parlor in the daytime, at night it is papa's bed-chamber. The ark is arriving at the stream's exit now, whose width has been reduced to less than twenty feet to accommodate the Indians—say to eighteen. There is a foot to spare on each side of the boat. Did the Indians notice that there was going to be a tight squeeze there? Did they notice that they could make money by climbing down out of that arched sapling and just stepping aboard when the ark scraped by? No, other Indians would have noticed these things, but Cooper's Indians never notice anything. Cooper thinks they are marvelous creatures for noticing, but he was almost always in error about his Indians. There was seldom a sane one among them.

The ark is one hundred and forty feet long; the dwelling is ninety feet long. The idea of the Indians is to drop softly and secretly from the arched sapling to the dwelling as the ark creeps along under it at the rate of a mile an hour, and butcher the family. It will take the ark a minute and a half to pass under. It will take the ninety-foot dwelling a minute to pass under. Now, then, what did the six Indians do? It would take you thirty years to guess, and even then you would have to give it up, I believe. Therefore, I will tell you what the Indians did. Their chief, a person of quite extraordinary intellect for a Cooper Indian, warily watched the canal-boat as it squeezed along under him, and when he had got his calculations fined down to exactly the right shade, as he judged, he let go and dropped. *And missed the house!* That is actually what he did. He missed the house, and landed in the stern of the scow. It was not much of a fall, yet it knocked him silly. He lay there unconscious. If the house had been ninety-seven feet long he would have made the trip. The fault was Cooper's, not his. The error lay in the construction of the house. Cooper was no architect.

There still remained in the roost five Indians. The boat has passed under and is now out of their reach. Let me explain what the five did—you would not be able to reason it out for yourself. No. 1 jumped for the boat, but fell in the water astern of it. Then No. 2 jumped for the boat, but fell in the water still farther astern of it. Then No. 3 jumped for the boat, and fell a good way astern of it. Then No. 4 jumped for the boat, and fell in the water *away* astern. Then even No. 5 made a jump for the boat—for he was a Cooper Indian. In the matter of intellect, the difference between a Cooper Indian and the Indian that stands in front of the cigar-shop is not spacious. The scow episode is really a sublime burst of invention; but it does not thrill, because the inaccuracy of the details throws a sort of air of fictitiousness and general improbability over it. This comes of Cooper's inadequacy as an observer.

The reader will find some examples of Cooper's high talent for inaccurate observation in the account of the shooting-match in *The Pathfinder.*

A common wrought nail was driven lightly into the target, its head having been first touched with paint.

The color of the paint is not stated—an important omission, but Cooper deals freely in important omissions. No, after all, it was not an important omission; for this nail-head is *a hundred yards from* the marksmen, and could not be seen by them at that distance, no matter what its color might be. How far can the best eyes see a common house-fly? A hundred yards? It is quite impossible. Very well; eyes that cannot see a house-fly that is a hundred yards away cannot see an ordinary nail-head at that distance, for the size of the two objects is the same. It takes a keen eye to see a fly or a nail-head at fifty yards—one hundred and fifty feet. Can the reader do it?

The nail was lightly driven, its head painted, and game called. Then the Cooper miracles began. The bullet of the first marksman chipped an edge of the nail-head; the next man's bullet drove the nail a little way into the target—and removed all the paint. Haven't the miracles gone far enough now? Not to suit Cooper; for the purpose of this whole scheme is to show off his prodigy, Deerslayer-Hawkeye-Long-Rifle-Leatherstocking-Pathfinder-Bumppo before the ladies.

"Be all ready to clench it, boys!" cried out Pathfinder, stepping into his friend's tracks the instant they were vacant. "Never mind a new nail; I can see that, though the paint is gone, and what I can see I can hit at a hundred yards, though it were only a mosquito's eye. Be ready to clench!"

The rifle cracked, the bullet sped its way, and the head of the nail was buried in the wood, covered by the piece of flattened lead.

There, you see, is a man who could hunt flies with a rifle, and command a ducal salary in a Wild West show to-day if we had him back with us.

The recorded feat is certainly surprising just as it stands; but it is not surprising enough for Cooper. Cooper adds a touch. He has made Pathfinder do this miracle with another man's rifle; and not only that, but

Pathfinder did not have even the advantage of loading it himself. He had everything against him, and yet he made that impossible shot; and not only made it, but did it with absolute confidence, saying, "Be ready to clench." Now a person like that would have undertaken that same feat with a brickbat, and with Cooper to help he would have achieved it, too.

Pathfinder showed off handsomely that day before the ladies. His very first feat was a thing which no Wild West show can touch. He was standing with the group of marksmen, observing—a hundred yards from the target, mind; one Jasper raised his rifle and drove the center of the bull's-eye. Then the Quartermaster fired. The target exhibited no result this time. There was a laugh. "It's a dead miss," said Major Lundie. Pathfinder waited an impressive moment or two; then said, in that calm, indifferent, know-it-all way of his, "No, Major, he has covered Jasper's bullet, as will be seen if any one will take the trouble to examine the target."

Wasn't it remarkable? How *could* he see that little pellet fly through the air and enter that distant bullet-hole? Yet that is what he did; for nothing is impossible to a Cooper person. Did any of those people have any deep-seated doubts about this thing? No; for that would imply sanity, and these were all Cooper people.

The respect for Pathfinder's skill and for his *quickness and accuracy of sight* [the italics are mine] was so profound and general, that the instant he made this declaration the spectators began to distrust their own opinions, and a dozen rushed to the target in order to ascertain the fact. There, sure enough, it was found that the Quartermaster's bullet had gone through the hole made by Jasper's, and that, too, so accurately as to require a minute examination to be certain of the circumstance, which, however, was soon clearly established by discovering one bullet over the other in the stump against which the target was placed.

They made a "minute" examination; but never mind, how could they know that there were two bullets in that hole without digging the latest one out? for neither probe nor eyesight could prove the presence of any more than one bullet. Did they dig? No; as we shall see. It is the Pathfinder's turn now; he steps out before the ladies, takes aim, and fires.

But, alas! here is a disappointment; an incredible, an unimaginable disappointment—for the target's aspect is unchanged; there is nothing there but that same old bullet-hole!

"If one dared to hint at such a thing," cried Major Duncan, "I should say that the Pathfinder has also missed the target!"

As nobody had missed it yet, the "also" was not necessary; but never mind about that, for the Pathfinder is going to speak.

"No, no, Major," said he, confidently, "that *would* be a risky declaration. I didn't load the piece, and can't say what was in it; but if it was lead, you will find the bullet driving down those of the Quartermaster and Jasper, else is not my name Pathfinder."
A shout from the target announced the truth of this assertion.

Is the miracle sufficient as it stands? Not for Cooper. The Pathfinder speaks again, as he "now slowly advances toward the stage occupied by the females":

"That's not all, boys, that's not all; if you find the target touched at all, I'll own to a miss. The Quartermaster cut the wood, but you'll find no wood cut by that last messenger."

The miracle is at last complete. He knew—doubtless *saw*—at the distance of a hundred yards—that his bullet had passed into the hole *without fraying the edges*. There were now three bullets in that one hole—three bullets embedded processionally in the body of the stump back of the target. Everybody knew this—somehow or other—and yet nobody had dug any of them out to make sure. Cooper is not a close observer, but he is interesting. He is certainly always that, no matter what happens. And he is more interesting when he is not noticing what he is about than when he is. This is a considerable merit.
The conversations in the Cooper books have a curious sound in our modern ears. To believe that such talk really ever came out of people's mouths would be to believe that there was a time when time was of no value to a person who thought he had something to say; when it was the custom to spread a two-minute remark out to ten; when a man's mouth was a rolling-mill, and busied itself all day long in turning four-foot pigs of thought into thirty-foot bars of conversational railroad iron by attenuation; when subjects were seldom faithfully stuck to, but the talk wandered all around and arrived nowhere; when conversations consisted mainly of irrelevancies, with here and there a relevancy, a relevancy with an embarrassed look, as not being able to explain how it got there.
Cooper was certainly not a master in the construction of dialogue. Inaccurate observation defeated him here as it defeated him in so many other enterprises of his. He even failed to notice that the man who talks corrupt English six days in the week must and will talk it on the seventh, and can't help himself. In the *Deerslayer* story he lets Deerslayer talk the showiest kind of book-talk sometimes, and at other times the basest of base dialects. For instance, when some one asks him if he has a sweetheart, and if so, where she abides, this is his majestic answer:

"She's in the forest—hanging from the boughs of the trees, in a soft rain—in the dew on the open grass—the clouds that float about in the blue heaven—the

birds that sing in the woods—the sweet springs where I slake my thirst—and in
all the other glorious gifts that come from God's Providence!"

And he preceded that, a little before, with this:

"It consarns me as all things that touches a fri'nd consarns a fri'nd."

And this is another of his remarks:

"If I was Injun born, now, I might tell of this, or carry in the scalp and boast
of the expl'ite afore the whole tribe; or if my inimy had only been a bear"—
[and so on].

We cannot imagine such a thing as a veteran Scotch Commander-in-
Chief comporting himself in the field like a windy melodramatic actor,
but Cooper could. On one occasion Alice and Cora were being chased by
the French through a fog in the neighborhood of their father's fort:

"Point de quartier aux coquins [No quarter for the rascals]!" cried an eager
pursuer, who seemed to direct the operations of the enemy.
"Stand firm and be ready, my gallant 60ths!" suddenly exclaimed a voice
above them; "wait to see the enemy; fire low, and sweep the glacis."
"Father! father!" exclaimed a piercing cry from out the mist; "it is I! Alice!
thy own Elsie! spare, O! save your daughters!"
"Hold!" shouted the former speaker, in the awful tones of parental agony,
the sound reaching even to the woods, and rolling back in solemn echo.
" 'Tis she! God has restored me my children! Throw open the sally-port; to
the field, 60ths, to the field! pull not a trigger, lest ye kill my lambs! Drive off
these dogs of France with your steel!"

Cooper's word-sense was singularly dull. When a person has a poor ear
for music he will flat and sharp right along without knowing it. He
keeps near the tune, but it is *not* the tune. When a person has a poor
ear for words, the result is a literary flatting and sharping; you perceive
what he is intending to say, but you also perceive that he doesn't *say* it.
This is Cooper. He was not a word-musician. His ear was satisfied with
the *approximate* word. I will furnish some circumstantial evidence in
support of this charge. My instances are gathered from half a dozen pages
of the tale called *Deerslayer*. He uses "verbal" for "oral"; "precision" for
"facility"; "phenomena" for "marvels"; "necessary" for "predetermined";
"unsophisticated" for "primitive"; "preparation" for "expectancy";
"rebuked" for "subdued"; "dependent on" for "resulting from"; "fact"
for "condition"; "fact" for "conjecture"; "precaution" for "caution";
"explain" for "determine"; "mortified" for "disappointed"; "meretricious" for "factitious"; "materially" for "considerably"; "decreasing" for
"deepening"; "increasing" for "disappearing"; "embedded" for enclosed";

"treacherous" for "hostile"; "stood" for "stooped"; "softened" for "replaced"; "rejoined" for "remarked"; "situation" for "condition"; "different" for "differing"; "insensible" for "unsentient"; "brevity" for "celerity"; "distrusted" for "suspicious"; "mental imbecility" for "imbecility"; "eyes" for "sight"; "counteracting" for "opposing"; "funeral obsequies" for "obsequies."

There have been daring people in the world who claimed that Cooper could write English, but they are all dead now—all dead but Lounsbury. I don't remember that Lounsbury makes the claim in so many words, still he makes it, for he says that *Deerslayer* is a "pure work of art." Pure, in that connection, means faultless—faultless in all details—and language is a detail. If Mr. Lounsbury had only compared Cooper's English with the English which he writes himself—but it is plain that he didn't; and so it is likely that he imagines until this day that Cooper's is as clean and compact as his own. Now I feel sure, deep down in my heart, that Cooper wrote about the poorest English that exists in our language, and that the English of *Deerslayer* is the very worst that even Cooper ever wrote.

I may be mistaken, but it does seem to me that *Deerslayer* is not a work of art in any sense; it does seem to me that it is destitute of every detail that goes to the making of a work of art; in truth, it seems to me that *Deerslayer* is just simply a literary *delirium tremens*.

A work of art? It has no invention; it has no order, system, sequence, or result; it has no life-likeness, no thrill, no stir, no seeming of reality; its characters are confusedly drawn, and by their acts and words they prove that they are not the sort of people the author claims that they are; its humor is pathetic; its pathos is funny; its conversations are—oh! indescribable; its love-scenes odious; its English a crime against the language.

Counting these out, what is left is Art. I think we must all admit that.

Suggestions

1. "Fenimore Cooper's Literary Offenses" sets forth eighteen rules that Cooper's novels are said to have broken. Which of these apply to fiction but not to other forms of writing? Which accusations against *The Deerslayer* are supported by examples in the rest of the essay? Do the episodes involving the moccasins and the broken twigs violate any of them?

2. Point out the irony in the sentence following the quotations from Lounsbury, Matthews, and Collins.

3. Referring to *First Letter to the Corinthians* 13, 12, explain: "He saw nearly all things as through a glass eye, darkly."

4. Point out the mistakes—assuming the essay is correct—in the way the following are used in *The Deerslayer: verbal, phenomena, precau-*

tion, meretricious, rejoined, insensible, brevity, mental imbecility, funeral obsequies.

5. Write a comparison of the idea of good fiction expressed in "Fenimore Cooper's Literary Offenses" with that of † "Plagued by the Nature of Truth" or † "The Artist and The World."

CRITICS AND
CREATORS

MODERN BOOK REVIEWING

ALLAN NEVINS ——⊰| *Reprinted by permission of the author.*

There can be no question that book-reviewing has in recent years largely changed its character and become a more democratic craft. A quarter-century past, the best reviews of books were to be found in monthly or weekly magazines. At that time the *Nation* was probably the most influential medium of reviewing published; the *Outlook,* the *Independent,* and other weeklies gave much space to books; and various monthlies had large literary departments. Today the most important book-reviewing is done in newspapers. The weekly *Book Review* of the New York *Times,* the weekly *Books* of the New York *Herald Tribune,* and the book pages of the Chicago *Tribune, Daily News,* and *Sun* are more widely read than any magazine. Many newspapers, following the example of the largest dailies in New York, are publishing a daily column on new books. And whereas reviews were once written chiefly by experts for experts, giving emphasis to scholarly or aesthetic considerations, today they are more likely to be written simply by competent journalists, and to give emphasis to the news value of books—to whatever in them is of interest to the ordinary intelligent man and woman.

This change seems to me wholesome and encouraging. For one reason, it indicates that literature is of more general and popular interest today than it was a generation ago. For another, the deliverance of book-reviewing to lay critics instead of experts has on the whole improved the quality of reviews. They are more likely now than in the past to fulfill the main object of reviewing, which is to give an accurate and interesting impression or picture of the book under consideration.

Book reviews may be conveniently divided into four general groups. To begin with the least important, from the standpoint of the general reader, there is the erudite or scholarly review to be published in a scholarly publication. A book on government will find its most expert treatment in the *Political Science Quarterly,* and one on history in the *American Historical Review.* But these are read only by specialists. In the second place, we often meet the essay-review. This is a disquisition which simply takes a book as a general text, and deals with the whole broad subject which it opens. The writer, for example, takes O'Neill's latest play and writes a column on the modern American theatre, or he takes a book on rugs and writes a neat paper on interior decoration. The third type of review is one written from an aesthetic point of view, and highly critical in nature. It deals only with books which pretend to be a contribution to literature, and judges them by fixed and austere standards. Finally, we find the fourth and for all ordinary purposes by far the most important type of review in what I may call the expository review—that which tries to give an intelligent, accurate, and interesting *portrait* of the book under discussion.

This is the kind of book review, certainly, which it is most useful for novices to cultivate. It treats books primarily as news, and attempts to extract the greatest possible news value from them. Every reviewer, in sitting down to a book, should think it his first duty to *explain* the volume, not to judge it. A little reflection will show him that this is what his readers or auditors expect. When people take up a published review of Chesterton's *Autobiography,* or of Constance Rourke's *Audubon,* do they wish to know what the reviewer thinks of Chesterton or Miss Rourke? In nine instances out of ten, not at all. What they wish to know is what Chesterton says about his own eventful life, with a number of amusing anecdotes and pungent sayings to illustrate his opinions and adventures; or what Miss Rourke says about Audubon, with a summary of her story of that great artist and naturalist, emphasizing the new elements in it.

Or take a still clearer instance—the book upon present-day Europe by Hamilton Fish Armstrong, or that upon the Supreme Court by Morris Ernst. Anyone interested in current affairs is glad to read an intelligent review of these books. But for what purpose?—to learn what the reviewer thinks of the subject or treatment? Only in a slight degree. The main purpose of reading the review will be to find out what Mr.

Armstrong thinks of the struggle between dictatorships and democracies in the present-day world, or what Mr. Ernst thinks of the propriety and feasibility of limiting the power of the Supreme Court. A penetrating, well-balanced, brightly written exposition of the views of either man will instruct and divert the reader.

But what, it may be asked, becomes of criticism if the reviewer furnishes merely an exposition of the contents of a book? To this there are two answers. One is that criticism is implicit in any good summary or exposition. If the reviewer has any ideas at all about the merits of a book, they will color the presentation of its contents. The very arrangement of your exposition, the way in which you emphasize some parts of a book and ignore other parts, is a form of criticism. The other answer is that if the exposition is full and accurate, the reader or auditor of the review will be in a position to furnish his own criticism. Especially is this true of factual books—of history, of travel, of biography, of economics and sociology. And finally, of course, the reviewer is at liberty —having finished his exposition, having given a portrait of the book as he sees it—to add as much formal criticism as he likes. In many instances, the more the better. But he should think of himself, when he sits down to the task, not as a Matthew Arnold or James Russell Lowell passing Olympian judgment, but simply as a book reporter.

A good review is no mere matter of chance, even when we simplify our requirements in this fashion. It requires half a dozen distinct steps. First, it requires careful reading of the volume in hand. This should be done with pencil in hand, and the flyleaves should be used to note down anything and everything of interest—to make the first brief sketch of the book. The second requirement is at least a little reflection upon the contents of the volume. A bald summary will not do. A *portrait* requires selection, emphasis—that is, interpretation. Some vitality should be put into the treatment of the volume; and this vitality will have to come from the reviewer. The third step is to make a careful outline of the review. It may seem a useless bit of trouble to outline anything so brief, but it is not. In the end, the outline of any written work, even of a social letter, will reduce the labor involved, and at the same time greatly improve the product. The fourth step is to take a sheet of paper, and write at the top not only the title of the book and the name of the author and publisher, but also a general title for your paper—a title which sums up the essence of what you have to say. The more imaginative and clever this general title is, the better. The fifth step is to write the review, and if the reading, reflecting, and outlining have been properly done, this is comparatively simple and easy. The review should almost write itself. Finally, the sixth step is to read the written product over, and polish it as much as possible. That done, your review should be really worth reading. It should be a real portrait of the book, and at the same time have some individuality gained from your own personality.

Suggestions

1. "Modern Book Reviewing" first shows what kind of writer now writes book reviews and the kind of audience to whom he addresses them (¶1); then it defines "the main object of reviewing" (¶2). Relate this definition to the division of reviews into four groups (¶3) and explain why the fourth is considered most important. How is the definition modified in the last sentence?

2. Summarize the speaker's two answers to the objection that his theory of reviewing excludes criticism (¶6).

3. Summarize the six steps in writing a review (¶7). Which of them applies to reviewing but not to other kinds of writing?

4. Explain specifically how a good review can reflect the personality of its author as well as giving a portrait of the book.

5. Read the longest book review in a recent issue of one of the newspapers named in ¶1; then write a review of it by the methods recommended in "Modern Book Reviewing."

THE ARTICLE AS ART

NORMAN PODHORETZ — *From* HARPER'S MAGAZINE, *1958.* © *Norman Podhoretz.*

Anyone who has given much attention to postwar American fiction is likely to have noticed a curious fact. Many of our serious novelists also turn out book reviews, critical pieces, articles about the contemporary world, memoirs, sketches—all of which are produced for magazines and which these writers undoubtedly value far lower than their stories and novels.

Indeed, some novelists (and this applies to many poets too) tend to express their contempt or disdain for discursive prose in the very act of writing it. You can hear a note of condescension toward the medium they happen to be working in at the moment; they seem to be announcing in the very construction of their sentences that they have no great use for the prosy requirements of the essay or the review, that they are only dropping in from Olympus for a brief, impatient visit. But just as often—and this is the curious fact I am referring to—the discursive writing of people who think of themselves primarily as novelists turns out to be more interesting, more lively, more penetrating, more intelligent, more forceful, more original—in short, *better*—than their fiction, which they and everyone else automatically treat with greater respect.

Two examples spring immediately to mind: the late Isaac Rosenfeld and the young Negro author, James Baldwin.[1] Rosenfeld, who died of a heart attack in Chicago two years ago at the age of thirty-seven, was immensely gifted, possibly the most gifted writer to appear in America in the last few decades. Born of immigrant parents and raised in a Yiddish-speaking milieu, he came to own the English language by an act of absolute appropriation. He could make it do anything he wanted— sprout lush flora, like a tropical landscape, or walk in stately simplicity as though it had been designed only to express the basic emotions and the most direct and uncomplicated apprehensions of reality. Beyond that, however, he was intelligent and literate, endowed with wide curiosity and a frisky imagination. He was also prolific: for years his name was ubiquitous in the world of the little magazine, with a story here, a review there, an article yet somewhere else. Though he published only one novel, *A Passage from Home,* and a collection of short stories, *King Solomon's Mines,* he regarded himself and was regarded by others as essentially a novelist.

Yet the truth is that he never produced a piece of fiction which drew on the whole range of his talent and sensibility. You got the impression that in order to write a story, this man had to suppress half of what he knew and saw, that he was possessed of a mind and an eye and an imagination which could not get their full play in a dramatic narrative. Though banality of thought and falsity of feeling hardly ever entered his articles and reviews, his fiction frequently suffered from derivativeness, artificiality, and mere cleverness. You would scarcely have suspected even from his novel that Rosenfeld was more than a bright young man who had read Proust and Joyce and saw himself, like a thousand other bright young men, as a creature set apart by his artistic vocation. You would scarcely have suspected him capable of that marvelous posthumous piece published in *Commentary* called "Life in Chicago," in which the smell and feel of a city and its history are rendered to perfection, in which the meaning of that history is defined through a deliciously fanciful theory of the effect on a city of distance from the sea, in which the combination of love and repulsion that a "rootless" American intellectual invariably feels for his home town are superbly expressed, and in which everything —description, analysis, exhortation, and sheer kidding around—converges in the end on a declaration of faith in the supremacy of the arts and what they represent over the prevalent values of modern life. It is a

[1] See † "Stranger in the Village."

declaration all the more moving for its directness and candor, and all the more powerful for coming from someone who knows that he is flying in the face of the contemporary spirit—but who also knows that a man at some point in his life has to stop agonizing over his apparent eccentricities and say, simply and without refinement or embellishment, "This is what I stand for."

This essay gives you more of Chicago, more of what it means to be an artist and an intellectual in America, and more of Rosenfeld himself than *A Passage from Home,* which, as it happens, is also about Chicago, the artist in America, and the soul of Isaac Rosenfeld.

The case of James Baldwin is no less striking. Baldwin has so far published three books—a collection of essays, *Notes of a Native Son,* and two novels, *Go Tell It on the Mountain* and *Giovanni's Room* (his third novel is coming out some time this year). The essays in *Notes of a Native Son* all appeared originally in magazines; a couple of them are literary criticism, one is a movie review, and the others are memoirs relating to various aspects of a Negro's confrontation with the white world both in America and Europe. Taken together they make up the best book I have ever read about the American Negro, a book that conveys a phenomenally keen sense of the special quality of Negro experience today. What distinguishes these pieces, even apart from the clarity, subtlety, and vividness with which they are written, is Baldwin's complex conception of the Negro as a man who is simultaneously like unto all other men and yet profoundly, perhaps irrevocably, different. The nature of the sameness and the nature of the difference are the subject of the book, and he never allows himself to forget the one term while exploring the other.

But it is precisely the loss of complexity that characterizes his novels. *Go Tell It on the Mountain* is a fairly conventional first novel about a Negro boy in Harlem, and though the hero's milieu (especially the religious background of his life) is well delineated, you nevertheless feel that Baldwin is trying to persuade you that there is no real difference between the situation of John Grimes and that of any other sensitive American boy who is at odds with his environment. But there *is* a difference, and it is not merely one of degree—as any reader of *Notes of a Native Son* can tell you.

Similarly with *Giovanni's Room,* which, though it does not deal with Negroes, exhibits the same slurring over of differences in relation to homosexuality. (The white homosexual in America is in the same boat as the oppressed Negro—they are both, as it were, "black" in the eyes of their culture.) Baldwin, in writing about a young American living in Paris who discovers that he is a homosexual, tries very hard to make it appear that a love affair between two men is spiritually and psychologically indistinguishable from a heterosexual romance—which strikes me as at worst an untruth and at best an oversimplification. Here again, then, we have a writer who seems able to produce fiction only at the expense of suppressing half of what he sees and knows, whose discursive prose is richer, more imaginative, and fundamentally more honest than his novels and stories. And with proper qualifications in each case, similar points might be made of James Agee, Mary McCarthy, Elizabeth Hardwick, Randall Jarrell, Leslie Fiedler, and several others.

Now it can, of course, be said that these examples prove nothing—and would still prove nothing even if another twenty were added to them —except that some people are better essayists than novelists. And if I asked why a first-rate essayist should feel obliged to work so hard at turning out second-rate fiction, the answer would be that the novel is to us what drama was to the Elizabethans and lyric poetry to the Romantics, so that an ambitious writer today will naturally make his bid there. In every college in the country, and probably in most of the high schools too, there are kids who want to be novelists when they grow up —who are convinced that a novelist is the most glorious of all things to be, and who are often prepared to make sacrifices in pursuit of this vocation. The aura of sanctity that used to attach to the idea of a poet has now floated over to rest on the head of the novelist—a very congenial switch when we consider that Americans tend to regard poets as sissies and novelists as hard-drinking, hard-loving, hard-fighting men of the world. (Compare the public image of T. S. Eliot and Wallace Stevens to Hemingway's or Faulkner's and you see that the poets and novelists themselves seem driven to play true to type.)

But the prestige of the novel cannot account for the fact that so much good writing about precisely those experiences which are closest to the heart of life in America and which we would suppose to be the proper province of fiction—experiences involving the quest for self-definition in a society where a man's identity is not given and fixed by birth—has been done in our day not in novels but in discursive pieces of one kind or another.

Lionel Trilling made a similar observation in a review of David Riesman's *The Lonely Crowd:*

> People of literary inclinations . . . have a natural jealousy of sociology because it seems to be in process of taking over from literature one of literature's most characteristic functions, the investigation and criticism of morals and manners. Yet it is but fair to remark that sociology has preempted what literature has voluntarily surrendered.

Nor is it academic sociology alone that has "pre-empted what literature has voluntarily surrendered." The reportage done in magazines by professional journalists like Dwight Macdonald, Robert Shaplen, Richard H. Rovere, John Bartlow Martin, and a good many others, has carried on a more exhaustive and more accomplished investigation of our morals and manners than the bulk of contemporary fiction.

The novel form is honored as never before, yet a feeling of dissatisfaction and impatience, irritation and boredom with contemporary serious fiction is very widespread. The general mood was well expressed by Leslie Fiedler, who opened a fiction chronicle in *Partisan Review* not long ago with the complaint that the sight of a group of new novels stimulates in him "a desperate desire to sneak out to a movie. How respectable the form has become," he lamented, "how predictable!" Many other critics have tried to explain the low condition of current fiction by declaring that the novel is "dead," an exhausted genre like the epic and verse drama. But whether or not the novel is dead (and I myself don't believe that it is), one thing is certain: that a large class of readers, with or without benefit of theories about the rise and fall of literary forms, has found itself responding more enthusiastically to what is lamely called "non-fiction" (and especially to magazine articles and even book reviews) than to current fiction.

This is not, of course, a new observation. The popularity of "criticism" —a word often used as a catch-all term for any writing about literature or culture in general—has been deplored even more passionately than the dullness of postwar fiction and poetry, and has been taken as a sign of the sickness of our present condition. Some years ago, Randall Jarrell, in a famous article, christened this period "The Age of Criticism," [2] and complained that nowadays young men were taking to their typewriters not to compose poems but to analyze and explicate the poems of others. Personally, I have never been able to understand why Mr. Jarrell was so eager to have everyone writing poetry; we can, after all, take it pretty much for granted that any young man who has it in him to become a poet *will* become a poet, even in an "Age of Criticism." And I should have thought that the danger was not that the popularity of criticism would rob us of poets but that the prestige of the "creative" would rob us of good critics, who have always been rarer, even today, than good poets.

Writing in the heyday of piety toward the divine faculty of imagination that succeeded the great flowering of English poetry during the first half of the nineteenth century, Matthew Arnold provided the best possible retort to Mr. Jarrell:

> Everybody . . . would be willing to admit, as a general proposition, that the critical faculty is lower than the inventive. But is it true that criticism is really, in itself, a baneful and injurious employment; is it true that all time given to writing critiques on the works of others would be much better employed if it were given to original composition of whatever kind this may

[2] Reprinted in *Poetry and the Age* (Knopf, 1953), pages 70–95.

be? Is it true that Johnson had better have gone on producing more *Irenes* instead of writing his *Lives of the Poets* . . . ? [3]

Arnold's allusion to the distinction between the "critical faculty" and the "inventive" is one that any modern reader would pass over with automatic assent, so accustomed have we all become to thinking in terms of two radically different categories of mind—the imaginative, which is the mind that creates, and the . . . well, there is not even an adequate word for the other kind of mind. "Critical" won't do because it has too restricted a reference; nor will "philosophical" quite serve. The fact is that our attitude reveals itself beautifully in this terminological difficulty: we call everything that is not fiction or poetry "non-fiction," as though whole ranges of human thought had only a negative existence. We would all admit, if pressed, that books like Freud's *The Interpretation of Dreams* or Tocqueville's *Democracy in America* are as much works of the imagination as *Ulysses* or *The Waste Land,* but we tend in the ordinary course of things to identify "imagination" and "creativity" exclusively with the arts and, where literature is concerned, with poetry, the novel, and the drama. This idea is a legacy from nineteenth-century aesthetic theory. Throughout the eighteenth century the word "imagination" (or its synonym, "fancy") was often used pejoratively and sometimes held to be the source of lies and the enemy of reason. Reason was considered the faculty for perceiving truth, and good poetry was regarded as one of its products.

"A poet is not to leave his reason, and blindly abandon himself to follow fancy," declared the critic Thomas Rymer, "for then his fancy might be monstrous, might be singular, and please nobody's maggot but his own; but reason is to be his guide, reason is common to all people, and can never carry him from what is natural."

Even before Coleridge [4] formulated his famous theory of the poetic imagination as the highest mode of apprehending reality and credited poetry with a truth superior to the truths of reason and science, early Romantics like William Blake were pushing toward a doctrine that would justify the claims of the poet against those of the "natural philosophers." By the age of Victoria, the Coleridgean view had swept all before it; nothing is more characteristic of the Victorians than the reverence they felt toward poets and poetry (a reverence, as Mr. Jarrell should have remembered, which led to the production of more bad verse than any other period has ever foisted upon the world). The poet was a saint and a sage: the robust-minded Keats became to the Victorians a delicate aesthete languishing away for the sake of beauty and killed by the cruel barbs of the critics, while Shelley—a man up to his neck in politics and

[3] "The Function of Criticism at the Present Time," ¶5. Samuel Johnson's tragedy *Irene* (1749) deservedly failed; his biographies (1779–1781) contain some of the best literary criticism of his time.
[4] In his *Biographia Literaria* (1817), chap. IV and elsewhere.

causes—was thought of as the wholly spiritual Ariel. The wicked Lord Byron only added to the charm of these images, and the somber Wordsworth was well suited to the role of Olympian wise man.

One of the consequences of this conception of the poetic faculty was to foster the idea that poetry could be written only in a kind of fit of divine inspiration that had nothing to do with intelligence or consciousness or concern with what was going on in the world. And a plausible relation can be traced between that notion and the decline of poetry in the latter part of the nineteenth century. It was the novelists of Victorian England, who had not yet quite achieved the status of "creative" and "imaginative" writers and to whom the smell of vulgarity that had once been associated with the novel still clung—Dickens, George Eliot, Thackeray, James—who represent their age most vitally and powerfully. What strikes one today about Victorian fiction is the scope it provided for the exercise of intelligence, the testing of ideas in the medium of experience, the examination of major contemporary problems. The novel flourished partly because it was such a free, amorphous, sprawling form in which almost anything (except, of course, explicit discussion of sex!) could go: there was no question of George Eliot's having to suppress half of what *she* knew and saw when she sat down to write fiction. And it flourished because it remained in touch with the world around it, while the poets were busy transcending the mundane and the prosaic.

By now we seem to have reached a point where the novel has taken over from poetry as the sanctified genre, and this has coincided (just as with poetry in the nineteenth century) with the aftermath of a great flowering. Proust, Joyce, Lawrence, Mann, Kafka, Hemingway, Faulkner are all behind us; in our eyes they have borne out the claims made for the "art of the novel" by Henry James and others, just as Wordsworth, Byron, Keats, and Shelley won the case for the superiority of the "poetic faculty" at the bar of Victorian judgment.

In a recent book called *The Living Novel* Granville Hicks, whose benign reviews in the *New Leader* have established him as the most promiscuous admirer of new writing since the days of Carl Van Doren, collected essays by ten well-known novelists aimed at refuting the charge that the novel is dead. Most of the essays are bad—bad thinking and bad writing—but they are interesting for what they reveal of the novelist's view of himself today. The dominant note is one of persecution. Mr. Hicks talks about the "enemies of the novel" and says that the novel has always had enemies. Almost all the contributors throw around words like "vision," "intensity," and, of course, "imagination" to distinguish the novel from other kinds of writing. There is a good deal of bitterness against the critics and a strong implication that they are resentful of "creativity." Saul Bellow (who has fared very well at the hands of the critics) says for example:

And so we are told by critics that the novel is dead. These people can't know what the imagination is nor what its powers are. I wish I could believe in their good-natured objectivity. But I can't. I should like to disregard them, but that is a little difficult because they have a great deal of power. . . . And they can be very distracting. But the deadly earnestness with which they lower the boom! On what? after all. On flowers. On mere flowers.

You can't blame Mr. Bellow for being irritated by people who insist that the novel is dead while he is trying to write novels,[5] but it is worth noticing that he does not answer the charge by asserting that good novels are still being produced and then trying to prove it; instead he invokes the name of "imagination" in reverent accents and identifies it with novels (apparently whether they are good or bad), while criticism is a "boom" lowered in metaphorical confusion on the "flowers" around it. Now it would be hard to think of a more infelicitous image for a novel than a flower; novels, if you like, are trees, they are robust and sturdy, not at all delicate. Why should Mr. Bellow have seized on this inept image? Partly to arouse the reader's sense of pathos, I think, but also because the idea of flowers, with its associations of sweetness, fragility, and loveliness, confers an ethereal dignity on the novel.

The idea comes out of the same sort of thinking that was applied to poetry by many Victorians: poetry was delicate, transcendent, special, inspired—anything, in short, but the measured discourse of a keen human sensibility operating on a world of men. But a new element has been added to the Victorian view. Not only does "imagination" now sprout "flowers," and not only does it (as in Coleridge) represent the highest faculty of intellection; it has also become the principle of "life" itself, while mind and consciousness are now seen as having signed a pact with the Angel of Death. The novel is valuable, we gather from Mr. Bellow and some of his colleagues, because it is the only place left in our world where imagination and its correlatives—sensitivity, responsiveness, passion—still function. (The *reductio* of all this can be found in the "spontaneous bop prosody" of Jack Kerouac.[6]) Mr. Hicks goes so far as to say that "there is no substitute now available for the novel, and those who talk about the death of the novel are talking about the death of the imagination."

I am not one of those who talk about the death of the novel, but I do think that it has fallen on bad days. I also think that the fault lies at least partly with these rarefied and incense-burning doctrines of the imagination, which have had the effect of surrendering the novel—to apply a remark of F. R. Leavis on Shelley's theory of inspiration—"to a sensibility that has no more dealings with intelligence than it can help."

[5] E.g. *The Adventures of Augie March* (1953), *Henderson the Rain-King* (1959).
[6] In *On the Road* (1957) and other works.

My own criticism of much contemporary fiction would be precisely that it lacks the only species of imagination worth mentioning—the kind that is vitalized by contact with a disciplined intelligence and a restless interest in the life of the times. And what the novel has abdicated has been taken over by discursive writers. Imagination has not died (how could it?) but it has gone into other channels; these channels are not by any means commensurate with the novel: they are, in fact, *channels* and not the sea. But there is living water in them nevertheless.

What I have in mind—and I cheerfully admit that the suggestion sounds preposterous—is *magazine articles.* I won't call them essays, even though to do so would make the point seem less disreputable and silly, because the type of thing I am referring to is not an essay in the old sense. Strictly speaking, the essay requires an audience that has no doubts about where the relevant subjects of discussion are to be found, and it is therefore written without any need to persuade the reader that he ought to concern himself with this particular question. The magazine article, as they say in the trade, always hangs on a peg; it takes off from an event in the news, a book recently published, a bill in Congress. And even then, with its relevance established in the most obvious way conceivable, it still has to sell itself to a reader who wants to be told why he should bother pushing his way through it when there are so many other claims on his attention. This is a tyrannical condition which can, of course, result in the reduction of all thought to the occasional and the newsworthy. But now and then a writer whose interests and talent go beyond the merely journalistic can be forced into very exciting pieces of work by the necessity to demonstrate the continuing importance of his special concerns by throwing them into the buzz and hum around him.

To my mind, the critical pieces of Lionel Trilling [7] offer perhaps the best example we have of discursive writing that is not only rich in imagination but animated by an uncanny sensitivity to the life from which it springs. Trilling has spent most of his time analyzing books—often remote books—but who has told us more than he about the way we feel and think today? But for the purposes of detailed illustration, I would like to take a less well-known example, an article (published in *Commentary* in 1953) called "The 'Idealism' of Julius and Ethel Rosenberg" by the late Robert Warshow who, like Isaac Rosenfeld, died suddenly at thirty-seven just when his extraordinary powers were developing into full maturity, and who—unlike Rosenfeld—never wrote any fiction.

This article began as a review of the Rosenberg death-house letters which came out around the time the convicted couple went to their execution. Since Warshow was one of those who believed that the world-wide clamor against the death sentence was largely motivated not by

[7] Collected in *The Liberal Imagination* (1950) and *The Opposing Self* (1955).

compassion for the Rosenbergs or a desire to see justice done, but by political anti-Americanism of one shade or another, one might have expected the review to be a pronouncement on the Communist menace. And certainly the crudity and vulgarity of the Rosenberg letters provided enough opportunity for scoring points against them and the movement to which they gave their lives. But Warshow's imagination would not permit him to turn out a simple polemical tract: what he wanted was an insight into the soul of the Rosenbergs, and it took a powerful act of imagination to find the soul of the Rosenbergs in the mass of depersonalized clichés that make up their correspondence. Considering the patent insincerity of their rhetoric, the temptation was great to deny them any human feelings at all. But again, Warshow's imagination would not allow him to fall into that trap. After quoting several particularly grotesque passages in which they discuss their children, Warshow comments:

> The fact that Julius Rosenberg can speak of a lack of toys as the "materials situation" does not in the least permit us to assume that he did not suffer for his children just as much as anyone else would have suffered. Nor does the impudence of Ethel's appeal to her "sister Americans"—whose lives she had been willing to put in danger—diminish in any way the reality of the "stab of longing for my boy." On the whole, the Rosenbergs in dealing with their children sound the authentic tone of parental love in the educated and conscientious middle class, facing each "problem" boldly and without displaying undue emotion, though "of course" not denying the existence of emotion either. . . . This is how we all deal with our children, and surely we are right to do so. If it happens that you must "prepare" the children for their parents' death in the electric chair instead of for having their tonsils out, then doubtless something better is required. But what, for God's sake? Some unique inspiration, perhaps, and the truth. But we cannot blame the Rosenbergs for their failure to achieve an inspiration, and the commitment for which they died—and by which, we must assume, they somehow fulfilled themselves—was precisely that the truth was not to be spoken. Not spoken, not whispered, not approached in the merest hint.

Warshow goes on to show how the literal truth had ceased to exist for the Rosenbergs as a result of their commitment to Communism, and he connects this brilliantly with "the awkwardness and falsity of the Rosenbergs' relations to culture, to sports, and to themselves" that is evident in their letters:

> It is as if these two had no internal sense of their own being but could see themselves only from the outside, in whatever postures their "case" seemed to demand—as if, one might say, they were only the most devoted of their thousands of "sympathizers."

. . . But it is important to observe the dimensions of their failure, how almost nothing really belonged to them, not even their own experience; they filled their lives with the second-hand, never so much as suspecting that anything else was possible. Communism itself—the vehicle of whatever self-realization they achieved—had disappeared for them, becoming only a word to be written in quotation marks as if it represented a hallucination. . . .

In the end, we discover that "they were equally incapable of truth and of falsehood. What they stood for was not Communism as a certain form of social organization, not progress as a belief in the possibility of human improvement, but only their own identity *as* Communists or 'progressives,' and they were perfectly 'sincere' in making use of whatever catchwords seemed at any moment to assert that identity. . . ." It is this, Warshow argues, that makes the Rosenbergs truly representative of the Communism of 1953. But his piece does not really close on a note of analysis or condemnation:

The Rosenbergs thought and felt whatever their political commitment required them to think and feel. But if they had not had the political commitment could they have thought and felt at all?

Well, we cannot dispose of them quite so easily. They did suffer, for themselves and for their children, and though they seem never to have questioned the necessity of their "martyrdom" or the absolute rightness of all they had ever done . . . , they wept like anyone else at the approach of death. . . .

I have quoted at length from this short article in order to let the grace and beauty of Warshow's style speak for themselves. It is a beauty that comes not from ornateness or self-conscious finesse, but from a remarkable fusion of feeling and intelligence: to follow this prose is to follow a language in which analysis cannot be distinguished from emotion. When the rhetoric surges ("But what, for God's sake?") it is not for the sake of sweeping the reader away, but in response to a simultaneous movement of the mind and the heart: the heart has discovered something and the mind springs like a panther to formulate its meaning.

A six-page review of a book in a monthly magazine; a discussion of a controversial political question almost completely forgotten only five years later—yet it turns out to be a piece of imaginative and creative writing as good as any we have seen in this gloomy period, a piece that is at once a moving expression of a man's ability to feel for two human beings who sacrificed themselves to a cause he hated and despised, a brilliant analysis of the Communist mentality, and a profound comment on the nature of sincerity. And the rest of Warshow's work—almost all of it as good as and better than the Rosenberg article—remains buried in magazines, mostly in the highly perishable form of movie reviews.

Why should the magazine article, of all things, have become so important and fertile a genre in our day? Why have so many writers—both "critics" and professional journalists—found it possible to move around more freely and creatively within it than within fiction or poetry? No doubt it has something to do with the spiritual dislocations of the Cold War period, but the essence of the answer, I think, lies in an analogy with architecture. It has often been pointed out that functionalism is more an idea than a reality: the products of functional architecture aren't purely functional at all, since they always contain "useless" elements that are there for aesthetic rather than practical reasons. Yet the fact remains that our sense of beauty today is intimately connected with the sense of usefulness: we consider a building beautiful when it seems to exist not for anyone to enjoy the sight of or to be impressed by, but solely and simply to be used. We think of those glass structures like Lever House in New York or the United Nations or the Manufacturers Trust Company building on Fifth Avenue as practical, in the sense that women call walking shoes practical; they have a kind of no-nonsense look about them, sensible, stripped down to essentials, purged of all superfluous matter.

The same is true of the way we furnish our homes—Scandinavian efficiency is our idea of handsomeness; foam rubber rather than down our idea of comfort; stainless steel rather than silver our notion of elegant cutlery. I would suggest that we have all, writers and readers alike, come to feel temporarily uncomfortable with the traditional literary forms because they don't *seem* practical, designed for "use," whereas a magazine article by its nature satisfies that initial condition and so is free to assimilate as many "useless," "non-functional" elements as it pleases. It is free, in other words, to become a work of art.

This is not, of course, an ideal situation for literature to be in, but nothing can be gained from turning one's eyes away in horror. Certainly the rigid distinction between the creative and the critical has contributed to the growth of a feeling that the creative is "useless." Curiously enough, the very concept of imagination as a special faculty—and of novels and poetry as mysteriously unique species of discourse subject to strange laws of their own—itself implies that art is of no use to life in the world. What we need, it seems to me, is a return to the old idea of literature as a category that includes the best writing on any subject in any form. This idea is the prevailing one in England today, where the best novels (for example those of C. P. Snow or of William Golding[8]) exhibit all the qualities of intelligence and implication in contemporary problems

---

[8] E.g. *The Search* (1934), *The Masters* (1951); *The Inheritors* (1955), *Pincher Martin* (1956), *Free Fall* (1959).

that are so glaringly absent from current American fiction. We need a return to this idea and we need it, I should add, most urgently of all for the sake of fiction and poetry.

Suggestions

1. The thesis of "The Article as Art" is that, the novel having declined in our day, its place is partly being taken by discursive writing. After reviewing the distinction between discursive and non-discursive writing on pages 14–16, analyze several of the quoted passages in this essay and show that they are in fact discursive. According to the essay, who are some of the most interesting writers now contributing articles to magazines?

2. Why are many readers responding less enthusiastically to novels than to "non-fiction" (¶14)?

3. Summarize the speaker's contrast between the vices of Victorian poetic theory and the virtues of the Victorian novel.

4. How does the speaker distinguish magazine articles from essays (¶28)? Does he attach the same meanings to these terms as does "Various Kinds of Writing," pages 3–4?

5. Examine the analogy between literature and architecture (¶39). What is the speaker's attitude toward contemporary taste? Does the analogy strengthen his plea for discursive writing?

6. Explain what "the old idea of literature" was (last ¶) and relate it to the thesis.

7. Explain: *Olympus, prolific, ubiquitous, banality, Proust, Joyce, baneful, Ulysses, The Waste Land, pejoratively, Ariel, amorphous, reductio, depersonalized clichés.*

8. Write a comparison of the speaker's attack on "thinking in terms of two radically different categories of mind" (¶18) and the thesis of † "Reason in the Emotional Life."

9. Using the *Readers' Guide to Periodical Literature,* write an account of an article by one of the writers admired in "The Article as Art."

A WRITER'S DAY

MALCOLM COWLEY ---✥

From THE LITERARY SITUATION *by Malcolm Cowley.* © *1954 by Malcolm Cowley. Reprinted by permission of The Viking Press, Inc.*

Let us picture the working day of a somewhat younger and more typical writer; he might be forty years old and he lives in the country with his wife. The day is one of those when he is starting work on a "piece"— which is anything short intended for magazine publication—or on a new chapter of a longer work. After sitting for half an hour over a second cup of breakfast coffee he goes upstairs to his study. There he takes the typewriter out of its case, puts in a sheet of paper, and writes a first sentence that he has been thinking about all week. But the next sentence isn't clear in his mind and he starts pacing from window to window like a caged animal. He is tempted to escape into the garden, which is getting weedy; perhaps he could think more clearly with a hoe in his hand. Resisting the temptation, he suddenly thinks of another sentence. He is at the typewriter when he hears the telephone ring and hopes the call is for his wife, who answers it—but no, New York is calling person-to-person for the writer. New York turns out to be a buzz of confused conversation, a wait, and then a clear voice saying, "I'm sorry, Miss Maybank has stepped out of the office. We'll have to call you back."

His wife drives off to the village to do the shopping. Watching her go, but not really seeing her, the writer thinks of another sentence and rushes upstairs to set it down. He reads over what he has written, tears the sheet out of the typewriter, and does a revised version of the three sentences; then he goes back to pacing from window to window. He wonders who Miss Maybank is and what she wants him to do. The telephone rings and he goes downstairs, calling out to the empty house, "I'll take it, dear." It is somebody from the school board with a question for his wife. He says, "Just a minute, I'll call her," then remembers that she is in the village. He goes to the kitchen, finds that there is some cold coffee in a pot, and puts it on a burner. The telephone rings again and this time, after another wait, Miss Maybank introduces herself. She is a fact-checker for a magazine and wants to know the source of a quotation that he has used in a forthcoming article. He runs upstairs, goes through his papers, and finds the quotation. Miss Maybank starts to thank him at length, but there is an acrid smell from the kitchen and he has to hang up; the coffee has boiled over. While he is cleaning

414

the stove his wife appears with an armful of groceries, and they get into an argument about the mess he always makes. He goes upstairs, still muttering, and finds that he can write another sentence, but it will be the last that morning.

The mail has come, and he reads it after lunch. It includes a manuscript by an unknown author who begs him to recommend it to a publisher and thanks him profusely in advance, but doesn't enclose postage. There are galley proofs of two novels that their publishers hope he will like and say a few kind words about, to print on the jacket. An almost total stranger wants to be sponsored for a Guggenheim fellowship. The writer has saved one envelope for the last, because it looks as if there might be a check in it, but what he finds is an appeal for funds. He reflects that every established writer is regarded as a sort of unpaid service bureau for the literature industry. Why not incorporate himself and ask for tax exemption as a charitable organization? Unfortunately, he has no organization, not even a secretary to take care of his correspondence. He remembers Oscar Wilde and his remark that he had known scores of young men who came up to London and ruined themselves by answering letters. Nevertheless he composes a rather testy letter to the author of the manuscript, asking him please to send return postage. Then, feeling too drowsy to stay indoors, he goes out to work in the garden. Late in the afternoon, while he is hoeing a row of beans, another sentence occurs to him. He goes back to the typewriter and works fast for twenty minutes, with the words coming easily, but then his wife calls upstairs to remind him that George and Betty are coming for dinner and he'd better get dressed and be ready to mix the cocktails, of which he will drink too many.

Next morning he starts by reading over what he has written. "This won't do at all," he says aloud as he drops the two sheets into the wastebasket; then he plucks them out again and lays them aside for reference. This day, and the two or three that follow, there are fewer interruptions, but now the writer would almost welcome them; his new obstacle is a torpid and recalcitrant mind. He tries to provoke it into activity by lying on the couch in his study and looking fixedly at a point on the ceiling. Thoughts occur to him, but they all seem unpersuasive or unusable. He paces the floor while the typewriter stares at him with its forty-two round keys like so many accusing eyes. "You damn father symbol," he says to it. He escapes the typewriter by working in the garden until he lapses into a state of brute exhaustion. Next day he takes a long walk on a dull road, hoping to hear the right words repeated by an inner voice, in time to his footsteps, but the words aren't right or writable. His appetite is poor, his sleep broken, his temper so bad that his wife keeps out of his way. He begins to worry about paying the bills, with no money coming in, and wonders whether he shouldn't consult a psychoanalyst. But we are talking about a professional writer, not one of the symptomatic artists who might be Dr. Bergler's patients. The professional has obligations to fulfill or a deadline to meet, and he usually ends by meeting it.

Gradually and in part subconsciously the story has been taking shape in his mind as he walked and worried. One afternoon he is surprised to find himself typing away at it. He eats dinner with an abstracted air, replying briefly to his wife's remarks, then goes back to his study. If he is working on a magazine piece he is likely to finish a first draft of it that night, while the conception is fresh in his mind. He seldom retains a clear picture of the hours when he is actually writing; all he remembers afterward is that the typewriter kept up a nervous clatter, with intervals of silence when he walked the floor between paragraphs, and that he filled a big wastebasket with discarded pages. Once when he came back to the room after getting a drink of water he found it foul-smelling and hazy with smoke. Most writers smoke too much when they are working, not so much for the taste of tobacco as for the need to have something in their mouths; those who stop smoking are likely to chew gum or pencils or kitchen matches. This particular writer has filled a big bowl with pipe ashes, and when he finishes the piece at three o'clock his mouth feels as if he had tried to swallow a boiling infusion of bitterweed. Words and phrases keep echoing in his mind; some he decides to change tomorrow, but others are so completely right that they give him a sense of elation. There is a gray light in the window before he falls asleep.

Tomorrow—or rather this afternoon—he will revise what he has written, an easier operation that he usually enjoys; then he will send it to the magazine just in time for the issue that is going to press. The next day he will go fishing, with a good conscience, and the morning after he will start his struggle to write another piece. Magazine writers are like sprinters, always in severe training to run short races; they live in brief cycles of depression and elation. Book writers are like cross-country runners, jogging along at a steady gait. After the first struggle to get started they can work on their projects for a few hours each day, week after week, always knowing that they will start each morning where they left off the night before—unless, or until, they are stopped midway in the book by some new problem that demands another period of silent wrestling with their minds; then they are off again at the steady trot that may continue to the end—though often they find themselves sprinting in the last desperate half-mile.

Suggestions

1. The plan of "A Writer's Day" is announced in the first three or four sentences: it is to be part character-sketch and part process-

description. From your reading of essays in Part Two, point out in it ingredients of both forms of writing. Do they combine successfully to produce a vivid suggestion of the life led by the group described?

2. Compare the picture of the writer, with respect to the techniques used, and any one of the groups described in † "Some American Types." What makes one more successful than the other?

3. What natural device is followed to describe the various stages in the process of writing a "piece"? Are these stages appropriately unified so as to give the essay a proper organization?

4. Describe the speaker's attitude toward the profession of the "younger and more typical writer."

5. What generalizations are drawn from the description of a typical writer at work?

6. Explain what the writer means by calling his typewriter a "father symbol."

7. Write an essay describing your own process of writing an essay for an English composition course.

8. Write a composite essay embodying a process and a characterization about a typical worker, businessman, professional man, or housewife.

PLAGUED BY THE NATURE OF TRUTH

ALAN PRYCE-JONES   *Reprinted by permission of the author and* The New York Times.

Novels get written, not because some writer has a tale to tell, but because he is plagued by the elusive nature of truth. Very few statements, he may say to himself, are neatly and completely true, and those which are thus demonstrably true cover only a small part of life. It can be demonstrably true to say, "My book has sold more than 100,000 copies"; it can never be demonstrably true to say, "I love you more than anyone else in the world." On the other hand, it is the undemonstrable which offers a challenge to literature. And in order to get as close as possible to this elusive thing writers have turned to allegory and symbolism and metaphor. Knowing they can't state, they suggest. That is how poetry, and the telling of tales in poetry and prose, came to be born.

Furthermore, the best novelists have had an ax to grind. Some vision of the truth has been nagging at them and in order to exercise it they have suddenly found themselves writing a novel. Of this, Cervantes is a perfect example. Having begun quite light-heartedly to satirize the tales of chivalry popular in his time, he could not stop his hero, Don Quixote, from developing an independent existence. Truths about love, religion, madness, courage, self-delusion, came flocking in to expand what was conceived as plain satire into a commentary on the whole of life, a commentary which has still not quite been explained away by three centuries of criticism.

That is why the writer whom V. S. Pritchett [1] has called "the ancestor" of English fiction, Fielding, deliberately modeled himself on Cervantes. Fielding, too, was evidently perplexed by the oddness of people. You cannot, he seems to insist, say very much about them; you can only show them in action under varying lights so that the rest of the world can draw its own conclusions. And from the eighteenth century onward, as the novelists of Europe gained experience, they very evidently felt the same.

One kind of writer can coin a general truth in a phrase: Pascal, La Rochefoucauld, Samuel Johnson perhaps. Yet what kind of truth is it? A nugget, a neat homogeneous object. Whereas truths about people, about human relationships, about motives—about daily life, in other words—are far from neat or homogeneous. They spread and divide and contradict each other; often they move too fast to be examined—they only catch a glance. And it is truths like these which set the novelist at work, not wise maxims nor balanced pieces of logic.

The novel is after all from the tree of poetry. It may also return to the condition of poetry, as in Virginia Woolf's *The Waves;* or it may take from poetry the sense of timeless experience which gives an extra dimension to humanity—as, for example, in the role allotted to Egdon Heath in Hardy's *Return of the Native.* Even the formal prose structures of novelists like Jane Austen are governed by laws the precision and economy of which are essentially poetic, and it is noticeable that the poems and the novels written in any one place and time always have a certain affinity to each other. When experimental poetry is in the air, so is experimental fiction—poetry usually a little ahead. For you will not find novelists, however powerful, flying clean in the face of the poets who surround them; each revolutionary step, such as the Romantic Movement, or Realism, or Surrealism, has been inaugurated by poets and then developed by novelists.

Still, the revolution and the development go on, generation by generation. And so the novelist can never feel that everything has been said, or any aspect of the truth uncovered with finality. The search involves

---

[1] English writer of fiction and criticism, b. 1900; author of *Mr. Beluncle* (1951), *Books in General* (1953), and other works.

different approaches, different techniques, different considerations, but all directed to the same end: to get as near as possible to a central truth about human beings. In fact, the novelists of the world can be compared to players in a game of clock-golf. They putt their little balls from all around the circle, but always aimed at a central hole. The essential point is that there is no way of getting toward the truth except by aiming at it with a novelist's eye. The radio can't do it: there is not enough elbow room, not enough privacy. The cinema can't do it because it can never afford to dawdle. Everything in the cinema has to be a little crisper than life, a little larger and quicker.

So long, then, as people wish to explore the truth about themselves, novels are likely to be written. And since people change, novels will change with them. There are no Henry James characters left in the world—or if there are they prefer to keep quiet; there is no one to get himself into a Meredith, or Bennett, or Galsworthy situation. The Somerset Maugham traveler and the Huxley conversationalist are both looking rather odd; the gay sparks of Evelyn Waugh's *Decline and Fall* were quenched within the year. Which simply amounts to saying that the middle and upper-class kinds of life about which the majority of novels have been written are being annihilated or frightened underground.

What remains is life of a kind far harder to write about. It contains, to begin with, no normal state anywhere to which exceptional states can be referred. Everyone, in all countries, is living to some extent abnormally; and to make these states objectively comprehensible needs the genius of a Dostoevsky or a Dickens. Novels threaten to become spineless accumulations of anecdote; instead of digging for truth writers skim over the daily surface of life, pointing and exclaiming as they go. It is reasonable to hope, however, that just round the corner something better is waiting. A new Stendhal, a new Gogol, a new Swift, may at any moment flash up and dispel a little of the uncomprehending astonishment which the mid-twentieth century feels whenever it thinks about itself.

Suggestions

1. Explain the assertion that Cervantes and Fielding were "perplexed" (¶3); then account for the title, "Plagued by the Nature of Truth."

2. Using the Index of Authors in *Familiar Quotations* or a similar work, list several maxims by Pascal, Rochefoucauld, and Johnson that you find appealing. What is supposedly the weakness of these statements (¶4)?

3. Why does the speaker think the novel is on the brink of drastic change (¶7)? What does he think is wrong with the novel now (¶8)?

4. Discuss:

". . . there is no way of getting toward the truth except by aiming at it with a novelist's eye" (¶6).

"Everyone, in all countries, is living to some extent abnormally" (¶8).

". . . the uncomprehending astonishment which the mid-twentieth century feels whenever it thinks about itself" (¶8).

5. Explain: *exorcise, homogeneous, affinity, Surrealism.*

6. Write a comparison of the views about poetry and the novel expressed in † "The Article as Art" and in this essay.

7. Write a definition and evaluation of the meaning the word *truth* has in this essay. Is it at any time equivalent to *fact?*

THE ART OF FICTION

From WRITERS AT WORK: THE PARIS REVIEW INTERVIEWS, *ed. Malcolm Cowley.* © *1958 by* THE PARIS REVIEW. *Reprinted by permission of the Viking Press, Inc.*

**GEORGES SIMENON
and CARVEL COLLINS**

SIMENON: Just one piece of general advice from a writer has been very useful to me. It was from Colette.[1] I was writing short stories for *Le Matin,* and Colette was literary editor at that time. I remember I gave her two short stories and she returned them and I tried again and tried again. Finally she said, "Look, it is too literary, always too literary." So I followed her advice. It's what I do when I write, the main job when I rewrite.

INTERVIEWER: What do you mean by "too literary"? What do you cut out, certain kinds of words?

SIMENON: Adjectives, adverbs, and every word which is there just to make an effect. Every sentence which is there just for the sentence. You know, you have a beautiful sentence—cut it. Every time I find such a thing in one of my novels it is to be cut.

INTERVIEWER: Is that the nature of most of your revision?

SIMENON: Almost all of it.

INTERVIEWER: It's not revising the plot pattern?

SIMENON: Oh, I never touch anything of that kind. Sometimes I've changed the names while writing: a woman will be Helen in the first

[1] Pen-name of Sidonie Gabrielle Claudine Goudeket, 1872–1954; see † " 'Prrou'."

chapter and Charlotte in the second, you know; so in revising I straighten this out. And then, cut, cut, cut.

INTERVIEWER: Is there anything else you can say to beginning writers?

SIMENON: Writing is considered a profession, and I don't think it is a profession. I think that everyone who does not *need* to be a writer, who thinks he can do something else, ought to do something else. Writing is not a profession but a vocation of unhappiness. I don't think an artist can ever be happy.

INTERVIEWER: Why?

SIMENON: Because, first, I think that if a man has the urge to be an artist, it is because he needs to find himself. Every writer tries to find himself through his characters, through all his writing.

INTERVIEWER: He is writing for himself?

SIMENON: Yes. Certainly.

INTERVIEWER: Are you conscious there will be readers of the novel?

SIMENON: I know that there are many men who have more or less with more or less intensity the same problems I have and who will be happy to read the book to find the answer—if the answer can possibly be found.

INTERVIEWER: Even when the author can't find the answer do the readers profit because the author is meaningfully fumbling for it?

SIMENON: That's it. Certainly. I don't remember whether I have ever spoken to you about the feeling I have had for several years. Because society today is without a very strong religion, without a firm hierarchy of social classes, and people are afraid of the big organization in which they are just a little part, for them reading certain novels is a little like looking through the key-hole to know what the neighbor is doing and thinking—does he have the same inferiority complex, the same vices, the same temptations? This is what they are looking for in the work of art. I think many more people today are insecure and are in a search for themselves.

There are now so few literary works of the kind Anatole France[2] wrote, for example, you know—very quiet and elegant and reassuring. On the contrary, what people today want are the most complex books, trying to go into every corner of human nature. Do you understand what I mean?

INTERVIEWER: I think so. You mean this is not just because today we think we know more about psychology but because more readers need this kind of fiction?

SIMENON: Yes. An ordinary man fifty years ago—there are many problems today which he did not know. Fifty years ago he had the answers. He doesn't have them any more.

[2] Pen-name of Jacques Anatole François Thibault, 1844–1924; author of *The Crime of Sylvester Bonnard* and many other works.

INTERVIEWER: A year or so ago you and I heard a critic ask that the novel today return to the kind of novel written in the nineteenth century.

SIMENON: It is impossible, completely impossible, I think. (*Pausing*) Because we live in a time when writers do not always have barriers around them, they can try to present characters by the most complete, the most full expression. You may show love in a very nice story, the first ten months of two lovers, as in the literature of a long time ago. Then you have a second kind of story: they begin to be bored; that was the literature of the end of the last century. And then, if you are free to go further, the man is fifty and tries to have another life, the woman gets jealous, and you have children mixed in it; that is the third story. We are the third story now. We don't stop when they marry, we don't stop when they begin to be bored, we go to the end.

INTERVIEWER: In this connection, I often hear people ask about the violence in modern fiction. I'm all for it, but I'd like to ask why you write of it.

SIMENON: We are accustomed to see people driven to their limit.

INTERVIEWER: And violence is associated with this?

SIMENON: More or less. (*Pausing*) We no longer think of a man from the point of view of some philosophers; for a long time man was always observed from the point of view that there was a god and man was the king of creation. We don't think any more that man is the king of creation. We see man almost face to face. Some readers still would like to read very reassuring novels, novels which give them a comforting view of humanity. It can't be done.

INTERVIEWER: Then if the readers interest you it is because they want a novel to probe their troubles? Your role is to look into yourself and—

SIMENON: That's it. But it's not only a question of the artist's looking into himself but also of looking into others with the experience he has of himself. He writes with sympathy because he feels that the other man is like him.

INTERVIEWER: If there were no readers you would still write?

SIMENON: Certainly. When I began to write I didn't have the idea my books would sell. More exactly, when I began to write I did commercial pieces, stories for magazines and things of that kind—to earn my living, but I didn't call it writing. But for myself, every evening, I did some writing without any idea that it would ever be published.

INTERVIEWER: You probably have had as much experience as anybody in the world in doing what you have just called commercial writing. What is the difference between it and non-commercial?

SIMENON: I call "commercial" every work, not only in literature but in music and painting and sculpture—any art—which is done for such-and-such a public or for a certain kind of publication or for a particular collection. Of course, in commercial writing there are different grades. You may have things which are very cheap and some very good. The books of the month, for example, are commercial writing; but some of them are almost perfectly done, almost works of art. Not completely, but almost. And the same with certain magazine pieces; some of them are wonderful. But very seldom can they be works of art, because a work of art can't be done for the purpose of pleasing a certain group of readers.

INTERVIEWER: How does this change the work? As the author you know whether or not you tailored a novel for a market, but looking at your work from the outside only, what difference would the reader see?

SIMENON: The big difference would be in the concessions. In writing for any commercial purpose you have always to make concessions.

INTERVIEWER: To the idea that life is orderly and sweet, for example?

SIMENON: And the view of morals. Maybe that is the most important. You can't write anything commercial without accepting some code. There is always a code—like the code in Hollywood, and in television and radio. For example, there is now a very good program on television, it is probably the best for plays. The first two acts are always first-class. You have the impression of something completely new and strong, and then at the end the concession comes. Not always a happy end, but something comes to arrange everything from the point of view of a morality or philosophy—you know. All the characters, who were beautifully done, change completely in the last ten minutes.

INTERVIEWER: In your non-commercial novels you feel no need to make concessions of any sort?

SIMENON: I never do that, never, never, never. Otherwise I wouldn't write. It's too painful to do it if it's not to go to the end.

INTERVIEWER: You have shown me the manila envelopes you use in starting novels. Before you actually begin writing, how much have you been working consciously on the plan of that particular novel?

SIMENON: As you suggest we have to distinguish here between consciously and unconsciously. Unconsciously I probably always have two or three, not novels, not ideas about novels, but themes in my mind. I never even think that they might serve for a novel; more exactly, they are the things about which I worry. Two days before I write a novel I will consciously take up one of those ideas. But even before I consciously take it up I will first find some atmosphere. Today there is a little sunshine here. I will remember such and such a spring, maybe a spring in some small Italian town or some place in the French provinces or in Arizona, I don't know, and then, little by little, a small world will come into my mind, with a few characters. Those characters will be taken partly from people I have known and partly from pure imagination—you know, it's a complex of both. And then the idea I had before will come and stick around them. They will have the same problem I have in my mind myself. And the problem—with those people—will give me the novel.

INTERVIEWER: This is a couple of days before?

SIMENON: Yes, a couple of days. Because as soon as I have the beginning I can't bear it very long; so the next day I will take my envelope, take my telephone book for names, and take my town map—you know, to see exactly where things happen. And two days later I begin writing. And the beginning will be always the same; it is almost a geometrical question: I have such a man, such a woman, in such surroundings. What can happen to them to oblige them to go to their limit? That's the question. It will be sometimes a very simple incident, anything which will change their lives. Then I write my novel chapter by chapter.

INTERVIEWER: What has gone on the planning envelope? Not an outline of the action?

SIMENON: No, no. I know nothing about the events when I begin the novel. On the envelope I put only the names of the characters, their ages, their families. I know nothing whatever about the events which will occur later. Otherwise it would not be interesting to me.

INTERVIEWER: When do the incidents begin to form?

SIMENON: On the eve of the first day I know what will happen in the first chapter. Then, day after day, chapter after chapter, I find what comes later. After I have started a novel I write a chapter each day, without ever missing a day. Because it is a strain, I have to keep pace with the novel. If, for example, I am ill for forty-eight hours I have to throw away the previous chapters. And I never return to that novel.

INTERVIEWER: When you did commercial fiction, was your method at all similar?

SIMENON: No. Not at all. When I did a commercial novel I didn't think about that novel except in the hours of writing it. But when I am doing a novel now I don't see anybody, I don't speak to anybody, I don't take a phone call—I live just like a monk. All the day I am one of my characters. I feel what he feels.

INTERVIEWER: You are the same character all the way through the writing of that novel?

SIMENON: Always, because most of my novels show what happens around one character. The other characters are always seen by him. So it is in this character's skin I have to be. And it's almost unbearable after five or six days. That is one of the reasons my novels are so short; after eleven days I can't— It's impossible. I have to— It's physical. I am too tired.

INTERVIEWER: I should think so. Especially if you drive the main character to his limit.

SIMENON: Yes, yes.

INTERVIEWER: And you are playing this role with him, you are—

SIMENON: Yes. And it's awful. That is why, before I start a novel—this may sound foolish here but it is the truth—generally a few days before the start of a novel I look to see that I don't have any appointments for eleven days. Then, I call the doctor. He takes my blood pressure, he checks everything. And he says "O.K."

Suggestions

1. Georges Simenon (b. 1903) is a Belgian novelist who now lives in Lakeville, Connecticut. Consult the library for details of his career, noticing especially his success at various kinds of writing, and if possible read two of his novels (all of which are short) that illustrate his distinction between commercial and serious fiction (¶32). Summarize the traits of novels that Simenon would condemn as "commercial" and those that he thinks distinguish his best work.

2. Point out the evidence that Simenon does not consider works of art communications.

3. Since Simenon considers one kind of writing painful, why does he do it? Why does he think there is a demand for these novels?

4. Discuss:

"Writing is not a profession but a vocation of unhappiness" (¶9).

". . . many more people today are insecure and are in a search for themselves" (¶17).

"We see man almost face to face" (¶26).

5. Write a comparison of Simenon's attitude toward magazine articles (¶32) and that of † "The Article as Art."

6. Write a comparison of the process which causes Simenon to write (¶40) and novelists' motives described in † "Plagued by the Nature of Truth."

7. Write an essay on Simenon's attitude toward radio and television (¶36), illustrating with a television play you have recently seen.

THE DRAMA

From THE THEATRE *by Stark Young.*
Reprinted by permission of the author
and Hill and Wang, Inc.

STARK YOUNG

The play is the most important element in the theater. Sometimes the acting or the décor will count for more than the play, but it is the play in most cases that gives the idea on which the whole is built and that creates the dominant quality of the whole effect. It is the play that contributes the guiding mind, the essential idea which the director, however great an artist he may be, tries to express through the theatrical medium that he works in. From the play the actors draw their chief notion of the characters they create. From the play as a rule the designer takes his start, however short he may come of it or how far go beyond. And it is the play that endures where scenery fades and rots, the pattern of the color and the miracle of the lighting long since forgotten.

This is especially true in our English theater.[1] We have no solid body of tradition and nothing of what you might call a theater world, not in the serious theater at least; nor have we any system of revivals of the same play throughout a season or from season to season. In the theater of revues and musical comedies it is different, what is done in a certain kind of scene will be repeated in another scene of the same kind; there is a language of gesture, dance, and gag that keeps going and alive quite as much as the words of the pieces do and sometimes more than the words. But in our serious theater what survives is words. A play remains as a text, and the gestures and movement that were once a part of it are lost, and in a very few seasons after a production would have to be entirely re-created.

A play consists, obviously, of plot, characters, dialogue. Of these the theater of modern times has centered on character as the revealing element, as that part of drama by which most is expressed. Most people at present would go so far as to say that character is the all-important and first consideration in a drama; it is almost a commonplace to say so. Such a theory would be expected. It falls in with our general drift toward detail instead of finality of outline and with our general spinelessness and weak touch. It is like the color, the shading, the mood in so much modern painting, all very well in their way, but something more of pattern and robust composition added to it would be a better sign of strength. Great character creation is a fine thing, obviously; but it is

[1] I.e. the theatres of Britain and the United States.

426

just as obvious that much fiddling and fooling and faking comes easy to character writing, and that such writing is always in danger of running into mere psychological patter and subdivision on subdivision without reality of any kind.

In the greatest plays the permanent value rests, on the whole, on both plot and characterization; in plays below the highest grade it rests sometimes on one, sometimes on the other, though in modern plays of this rank it is characterization on which the permanent value is based. It is true also that in many a modern play what interests us almost entirely is the characters, just as in modern buildings what may interest us is some quality or special element presented. But this does not mean that such a play might not hold its place longer or such a building not be more important architecturally if these characters roundly achieved a plot to sum up themselves and their actions, and if these special partial elements achieved a significant outline and architectural mass.

Great character creation is a fine thing in a drama, but the sum of all its characters is the story that they enact. Aristotle puts the plot at the head of the dramatic elements; of all these he thinks plot the most difficult and the most expressive. And he is right. Not that every plot stands first, or any and every plot is more important than the characters in the play; any plot counts only in so far as it is expressive. But the fact remains, nevertheless, that the plot is the most important of all the elements in drama because of them all it can be most completely expressive of the characteristic idea behind the play. And by this process:

The artist has an idea, an essential quality, a content, to express in terms of a play. Ready at hand he has, as means of expression, the life or atmosphere or manners portrayed, the sentiments, thoughts, and emotional reactions characteristic of human beings; he can work in terms of these and of his characters, their actions, and the plot or story. He puts his idea into each of these terms, as the human characteristic is expressed in the various parts of a man's body. Of these terms the most important —because they express most to us—are character, action, and plot. A man's character is most apparent in what he does or does not do; our character appears in our actions. The dramatist discovers creative actions, actions expressive of his characters. A plot in a play derives from these actions brought into combination, as they meet and cross one another, in the world of life that they embody and express. If the characters express themselves in their actions, and the sum of their actions implies the plot, it follows that the plot includes, or can at least include, them both, and can be therefore of all the elements in the play the most inclusive, and therefore most largely and completely expressive of the play's essential idea or quality.

People go on telling us, nevertheless, that the plot is secondary, and they prove it, if by no other argument, by citing the supposedly well-known fact that there are only a few plots, after all, for dramatists to use. Thirty-six plots there are in all, according to the scholars, we are told. This business about few plots, or thirty-six plots, goes back almost a century and a half to Gozzi's famous category.[2] But Gozzi said nothing of plots, he said thirty-six situations. Schiller, so Goethe tells us, thought Gozzi had allowed too small a number, but when he came to count, he could not find so many. Georges Polti in his book, *Les 36 Situations Dramatiques,* developed Gozzi's idea. But the point here is that, while the number of situations may be so limited, the plots to be woven around them are innumerable. And a plot, moreover, does not mean a mere loose story, but a story in its exact dramatic gradations.

So common is the prejudice in favor of character as the leading element in drama that you can hear the characters spoken of as creation, the plot as invention. A foolish distinction; compared to the characters in a play the plot is only creation in larger terms, since the author starts with qualities which he creates into characters, whom, in turn, he creates into actions and these actions into a plot; so that the plot is only an extension of his creation. In a poor example plot may appear as mere invention because of its lack of connection with the characters, in which case it seems only a vehicle for them, or merely tagged on to keep things going. Or it may appear as mere invention because of its final expressiveness; the artist might seem merely to have come upon it, as men come upon the force of steam or the use of electricity. But the more inclusive and expressive the plot the more the degree of creation. In a good play the plot is the most inseparable element in it; in such a case there is no locale, character, or action that would mean the same if isolated to itself and seen without the plot. The plot is the most elusive element in a play to regard in itself because the hardest to isolate, to see separately; and at the same time it is the most distinct and the most final in its effect. The plot is the ultimate element by which we can discern the essential character of each individual play as distinguished from all other plays. This point, despite the critical theories about character and plot, will be proved at once by any history of dramatic literature. In any account of a series of plays the historian will finally distinguish one from another by a statement of their plots.

Is then the plot of *Othello* its most important element? Yes. The characters exist, they act; they have a certain relationship among themselves as embodiments of human nature and of the dramatist's ideas; the sum of their relationships and actions determines the plot. Is the plot of *Le Misanthrope* the most important element in it? No. But that only amounts to saying that Molière was not able to create a plot that would completely embody his idea, which he was obliged to express

---

[2] Count Carlo Gozzi (1720–1806), Italian playwright, wrote *Fable of The Love of Three Oranges, King Turandote,* and other works.

largely through his characters, who exist in their quality rather than in what they do, and that even then his achievement has been admired more as literature than theater. Chekhov's *Three Sisters* on the other hand is theater, as experiment has proved, but the idea is most expressed through character and atmosphere, unless we say, as I should, that what the people in it do not do constitutes a kind of negative plot that counts more than anything else in our impression of the play.

What impresses me most about the work of Mr. Eugene O'Neill is his power at his best to create a plot outline that in itself has shape, idea. In this respect *The Hairy Ape* of all his plays comes first. In that play the story itself is a simple line that in itself expresses the entire idea. Hank, the Stoker, exploded from that job into the world, tries to join the I. W. W., he is kicked out of that, he goes into the great ape's cage and is crushed to death—neither man nor beast has a place for him. So completely expressive is the pattern of this plot that neither the characters nor the dialogue seem essential to the idea. It may be said, too, that Mr. Eugene O'Neill's great gift is most evident in the bold figure of his plots. His men and women are often mere symbols or type puppets to carry out the action, and what they say is often type speech in dialogue that is obviously to serve the purposes of the story or dramatic theme. The strong stir of life that this dramatist can often arouse derives from the fact that he gives us the sense of action and of an intense current of emotion rather than of close and detailed observation or individual character likeness. A part of his reputation is due to the ease with which people can convey the idea of one of his plays by recounting the mere bare plot.

Fables, whose life is long when they are good, are all plot. In a fable like that of The Prodigal Son [3] the characters are wholly action; we know nothing of them but what taken all together they did; we know nothing but the plot, and this expresses the whole idea. The history of great fables as the undying vehicles of ideas proves their consummate worth. And finally, to leave art and come to actual men and women, we can say that in the case of a man like St. Francis of Assisi it is largely his genius for doing things wonderfully expressive of himself and his idea that makes him to this day so real to us; and, furthermore, we may say that there is no character in history who is not most remembered by his story.

Of the four moods in drama, tragedy, comedy, farce, and melodrama, the tragic must always be greater than any other because it most of all brings to bear upon the atom of our human life the infinite universe; and because it includes more of our life, which, whatever happy emphasis it may have had in its long course, is grounded in the tragic, it begins in another's pain and ends in death. All things pushed to their bounds

[3] *Gospel of St. Luke* 15, 11–32.

are tragic, for despite the wills and passionate desires that we exert upon them, they have an end at last and at last are taken from us. The tragic in drama has had many definitions, the struggle of the individual will against eternal law, the struggle of the good with the good, and so on, as we may see in any primer of the subject. In older styles the image of tragedy is always death, the death of the hero is the conclusion of the struggle. It was upon the shock of death that the famous metaphysical comfort of the philosophers ensued, the state in which we rise above the ordinary considerations of personal advantage and contemplate the whole, with our passions quieted, our tempers purged, our spirits lifted with the sense of wisdom gained. In later forms the tragic can be death, as in [Ibsen's] *Ghosts,* or the closed passage in [Chekhov's] *Three Sisters,* mere negation and defeat of life. Or it can be what it is in Pirandello's *Henry IV,* the victory of life over the man's will to permanence, the man's betrayal by that life that had made him what he was and what he willed to remain.

All these definitions and images are at bottom a description of a defeat of life, a defeat of the human inner life trying to find itself and its due form. In all tragedies we see the conflict of wills; we see elements of human life that are set against one another, both good in so far as they are alive, but one by its disproportionate amount destroying the other. In one of the greatest tragedies this failure extends even to the drama itself. A part of the universal melancholy of Shakespeare's play consists in the fact that the dramatist never succeeded in finding a dramatic form that could completely express his idea; even as a play *Hamlet* expresses tragic defeat.

Aristotle speaks of tragedy as dealing with superior persons. We could not say that in our modern drama, but we can say that tragedy deals with elements of living that are superior because they are more intense. Comedy exhibits a less intense life but sets it against a scale of social values by which individual desire or excess may appear disproportionate and hence ridiculous. Both comedy and tragedy might be included in the gift of a great dramatic poet, as Plato in the *Symposium* says by way of his Socrates, who forces Aristophanes and Agathon to admit, much against their Greek inclinations, that a great tragic power in a poet ought to include the comic. Humor in social comedies is measured in its importance by the extent to which it becomes revealing. The lowest form in comedy is the joke, the pun, the witticism stuck in for its own sake and put into the mouths of any character regardless. Of these are the wise-cracks of Broadway and the epigrams of Oscar Wilde. Next comes the piece of humor that is comic in itself but much more so because of its comment on the character that says it. Sheridan's Sir Anthony Absolute[4] abounds in such humor. The highest form of humor is that which

[4] In *The Rivals* (1775).

finds expression in all the terms of the comedy, in the character, the action, and the place in the play's design at which it occurs. In [Molière's] *Tartuffe* the spot at which Orgon's mother refuses to believe ill of the hypocrite even after he has been exposed is perfect comic detail. It reveals the old woman's inmost self; it comments on hypocrisy and what that works in people's minds; and at this stage of the plot it shows Orgon himself what he was like at the beginning.

The technical charm of a good comedy of manners can be likened to modeling in relief, where the limits are fixed and where within a depth of an inch the values are caught and the implications achieved. In that finest scene in any English comedy of manners, that in which Congreve's Millamant consents to marry Mirabell,[5] the dazzling quality of the writing derives from the fact that within their limits of banter and epigram Congreve has given us the sense of two noble natures, of true passion, of intense concern, without ever losing for a second his scale, his touch, his airy key; with the waving of a fan he manages to imply the winds that blow through the vast world of life.

In romantic comedy at its best that "swift perception of similarities" which we call wit takes on yet happier revelations. It becomes incandescent; the similarities extend into felicitous imagination, we have poetic comedy, wings that fly out of the window of the social drawing room, songs that forget the limits of a sane society. Lower down the scale comes ordinary romantic comedy, the sentimental humor with which we are familiar. The essence of all romantic comedy high and low is its freedom from that more exact measure by which social comedy gets its values. The essence of the romantic is possibility, the liberty of adorable escape.

To call a play a farce is nothing against it. Some of the best comic dramas are farces. Bernard Shaw often writes what is at bottom brilliant cerebral farce and Pirandello's theater is farce or, to be more exact, is *commedia dell' arte*[6] in which the familiar characters are ideas, abstract and unreal as Harlequin or Columbine, with the brain as the public square where their lively actions take place. One of the traits of farce and melodrama—which parallels farce—is exaggeration, as every one knows, the heightening beyond probability or possibility that each may employ when it chooses. But this exaggeration is only a phase of what is their essential difference from comedy and tragedy, which is their freedom from the stricter conditions. Their flight is reckless, they are the playwright's trip to the moon. Farce is free to disregard those limits within which the sweet sanity and humor of comedy appear. Melodrama is free to avoid the tragic finality, to evade its conclusion. Farce is closer than comedy is to tragedy because of its stretch beyond the bounds of

[5] *The Way of the World* (1700) IV.i.
[6] Ancient form of Italian low comedy with standardized characters.

a social measure and good sense. Melodrama is closer to comedy than tragedy is because it need bother with the final truth only so much as it chooses. Both farce and melodrama take the cash and let the credit go; they eat their cake and have it too.

Alongside these dramatic forms runs the perennial drama of sentiment, plays that fall under almost any head so long as it is not disagreeably important. The abilities, as Goldsmith said, that can hammer out a novel are fully sufficient for a sentimental play. You need "only to raise the characters a little," give "the hero a riband," the heroine a title, and "mighty good hearts" to them, with a pathetic scene or two, and a new set of scenery. For these dramas we may remember the French proverb for actors—*pour les sots acteurs Dieu créa les sots spectateurs* [for silly actors God made silly spectators]—and say that for simple-minded art God made simple-minded occasions.

There is one point we recognize too little about all dramas, whether tragedy, comedy, farce, or melodrama. This is the truth of structure, by which I mean the degree to which the structure of a drama is a part of its idea, as the height of a table is a part of its truth; I mean that in drama structure and tone are, as they are in music and architecture, expressive elements. In a drama there is a certain final expression that lies in the sheer order of its development, in its proportions, in the emphasis of its parts. The exact spot in *Macbeth* at which Fleance escapes, the spot at which is sprung the ironic surprise of the last of the witches' prophecies, and thereafter the ensuing speed of the exposition and of the dénouement, all establish a large part of what Shakespeare desires to express.

The superiority of Molière over all other writers of comedy consists not in any words or single character so much as in his tone. The greatness of Molière's plays lies in their tone. His tone appears not so much in anything said or done in the course of a play, and not so much in the characters created, as in the distribution of accents, the sequence of parts, and the management by which Molière makes things more or less insignificant when set together; he contrives an order and combination that will itself help to express his idea. Many a drama from the Latin mind, from the French or Italian or Spanish, is lost to us on just this basis; we cannot judge it because so much of it is expressed in its structural proportion and tone, and these are languages that we often fail to understand. On one hand we find in them no mention of God, aspiration, or soul, none of that conscientious perturbation, vagueness, or solemn concern that gives us the impression of profundity or seriousness. On the other we understand nothing of what is said through the structure and tone; and so we grant the author's vivacity but deny his depth.

Suggestions

1. "The Drama" argues in its first part that of all the many persons needed for the production of a play, the playwright is the most important; and that the most important part of the playwright's work is the creation of a plot. Its second part distinguishes the four "moods" of drama: tragedy, comedy, farce, and melodrama. Summarize the speaker's definitions of these, deciding whether the element of plot is prominent enough in each one to support his thesis about its pre-eminence.

2. The speaker's contention that character is less important than plot is supported by an analogy: "A man's character is most apparent in what he does or does not do; our character appears in our actions" (¶7). If the two are so closely related, is it possible to say that either is more important than the other? Or is the thesis made convincing by the examples that follow, such as the discussions of *The Misanthrope* and *The Hairy Ape?* Discuss fully.

3. Explain the "foolish distinction" (¶9) and the importance to the argument of the allusions to The Prodigal Son and St. Francis of Assisi (¶12).

4. Summarize the speaker's argument that the greatest plays are tragedies (¶13), explaining how he would modify Aristotle's definition of the tragic hero (¶14).

5. Distinguish farce from comedy and melodrama from tragedy (¶17).

6. Decide whether the speaker's admiration for tone (last ¶) can be reconciled with the importance he assigns to plot.

7. Explain: *décor, I. W. W., cerebral, dénouement, conscientious perturbation, vivacity.*

8. Identify: Aristotle, Schiller, Molière, Chekhov, Ibsen, Pirandello, Aristophanes, Agathon, Oscar Wilde, Goldsmith.

9. After reading † *The Man of Destiny,* write an essay showing that it does or does not uphold the theories that "The Drama" advances.

10. Write an essay on a movie or television play that you have recently seen, discussing the success of its plot in rendering its theme.

THE CURVE OF SUBJECTIVITY

LAWRENCE DURRELL

From KEY TO MODERN POETRY, *by Lawrence Durrell. Reprinted by permission of the author. © Lawrence Durrell.*

The chief characteristic of art today, if we are to judge by the reactions of the common man, is its obscurity. Everybody complains about obscurity in poetry, in painting, in music. I do not suggest that in some cases the complaint is unjustified. But we should remember that the really original work of art in any age seems obscure to the general public. From a certain point of view it would be true to say that no great work of art finds an appreciative public waiting for it. The work creates its own public, slowly and painfully. A work of art is born as an intellectual foundling. What is interesting to notice is that often the art-specialists themselves are caught napping. It was André Gide, you remember, who first saw Proust's great novel [*Remembrance of Things Past*] while he was working as a reader for a firm of publishers. He turned it down without any hesitation. Perhaps you remember Leigh Hunt's verdict on Blake as "an unfortunate madman whose mildness alone prevented him from being locked up." [1] Wordsworth also thought Blake mad, and yet it was he who wrote: "Every great and original writer, in proportion as he is great and original, must himself create the taste by which he is to be judged." [2]

Perhaps, however, the obscurity and difficulty of modern poetry might be better understood if we could discover its pedigree among the ideas which have influenced the contemporary artist. What are they? Let us mark off a piece of the historical time-track and see whether we cannot establish some significant relationships within the margin of, say, a hundred years. If we spread out the events and ideas of this period—if we sift out the gravel and examine one or two of the heavier objects which remain in the sieve—we might reach a few conclusions, however tentative. Of course to use the historical method often leads one into oversimplifications—but you have been warned of these already.

To try and draw the family tree of the contemporary artist is not by any means an easy matter. It is like drawing a map of the Gulf Stream. It is quite easy to mark out the greater currents and to plot the general direction of their movements, but we would not be surprised to discover that within the greater currents there were cross-currents and even

---

[1] It was the verdict of Leigh Hunt's brother, Robert: Geoffrey Keynes, *Blake Studies*, p. 86.

[2] Wordsworth said the idea was Coleridge's (*Wordsworth's Literary Criticism*, ed. N. C. Smith, p. 195). He thought the madness of Blake more interesting than the sanity of Byron or Scott (Henry Crabb Robinson, *Blake, Coleridge, Wordsworth, Lamb, &c.*, ed. E. J. Morley, p. 18).

counter-currents flowing in arbitrary directions. This is where the critic gets cold feet and with reason. But there is no help for it—he must embark on his journey in the cockle-shell of thought, prepared for a stormy passage.

But in order to bring the subject of this enquiry down to laboratory level let me provide you with a couple of corpses to dissect. I have chosen two poems, one written in 1840 or thereabouts, and the other in 1920. Both are famous anthology pieces, and they are probably well known to you. If you lay them side by side you will at once notice a remarkable thing. They are all but identical in subject-matter. Both are written in the first person singular. Both present a sort of autobiography through the lips of an old man, a hero, who sits before his house, thinking about death. The similarity of the poems is indeed so striking that we could hardly select anything better to study. Would it be possible, by making use of the sharply contrasted material and style of these two poems, to risk a rash judgment about the world of 1840 as compared with that of 1920? Could the change of values between the two be traced which, so to speak, modified the subject matter of the first poem and allowed it to become the second? It would be worth trying perhaps.

The first of the poems is "Ulysses" by Lord Tennyson, the second is "Gerontion" by T. S. Eliot.[3] In either case we have an old man's reflections upon past life and approaching death. Would it be stretching a point to consider the first as the hero of the Victorian Age and the second as the contemporary hero? I think not. Examined in the light of this idea the similarities between the two are almost as exciting as the differences. Both demonstrate the autobiographical method. Both present one with a definite attitude to life and to death. Both sum up the views of an old hero upon the age he represents.

Tennyson's broad classical manner and his simple syntax stand for a world of clear thinking and precise relations. Eliot's hero, however, allows the contents of memory and reflection to pass through him and emerge in a series of oracular statements, often apparently without any form and with only a superficial resemblance to grammatical proportion. "Gerontion" is rather like a series of ticker-tape messages coming in from some remote stock-room, and being recorded haphazardly one after the other. Memory, reflections, desire—they all seem inextricably tangled up, and in order to sort them out we shall have to do far more work than would be necessary to reduce and understand the content of "Ulysses."

But leave the technical aspect on one side for a moment and let us see what differences exist between the actual things said by the two old men. How does the attitude of Gerontion differ from that of Ulysses? The most obvious difference seems to be between Ulysses' activity, his master-

[3] They are printed on pp. 652 and 658.

ful bearing in the face of time, and Gerontion's passivity. Gerontion is a victim. Ulysses is still the master of his fate. He dominates his world— that grave classical world which was founded upon the idealism and classicism of the Victorians. Bravery, nobility, dignity are the keynotes to his attitude. Gerontion shares none of these qualities. "Here I am," he says, "an old man in a dry month, being read to by a boy, waiting for rain." He disclaims any right to be considered a hero. If there were any great battles, he did not see them: "I was neither at the hot gates nor fought in the warm rain nor knee-deep in the salt marsh, heaving a cutlass, bitten by flies, fought."

Ulysses seems to have escaped the disillusion of Gerontion. His hunger is for more life: "Life piled on life were all too little," he says, and adds: "All times I have enjoyed greatly, have suffered greatly . . . I cannot rest from travel: I will drink life to the lees." Gerontion, however, replies to this: "I have lost my passion: why should I need to keep it since what is kept must be adulterated?"

Ulysses feels a part of the historic fabric: "I am become a name . . . much have I seen and known; cities of men and manners, climates, councils, governments, myself not least, but honored of them all." He is not proud or complacent. He is simply fully aware of himself and alive at all points. Gerontion on the other hand has no such sense of himself as a part of historic progress: "History has many cunning passages," he whines, "contrived corridors and issues, deceives with whispering ambitions, guides us by vanities . . . gives when our attention is distracted . . . Gives too late what's not believed in, or if still believed, in memory only, reconsidered passion." History, then, is for him something that deludes and tricks. His voice is the voice of someone who has been deceived by the world, let down by it. Ulysses has faced and dominated it.

As for knowledge, the contrast in attitude between the two old men is even more definite. Ulysses' "gray spirit yearning in desire to follow knowledge like a sinking star, beyond the utmost bound of human thought" is matched by the question of Gerontion: "After such knowledge, what forgiveness? . . . We have not reached conclusion, when I stiffen in a rented house." He cannot bring himself to exclaim, as Ulysses does: " 'Tis not too late to seek a newer world." For Gerontion the boundaries of human thought and hope have narrowed down to these "thoughts of a dry brain in a dry season." The thoughts of an old man "driven by the Trades to a sleepy corner." In the face of the Greek heroism and daring of Ulysses he can only mutter:

> Think
> Neither fear nor courage saves us. Unnatural vices
> Are fathered by our heroism. Virtues
> Are forced upon us by our impudent crimes.
> These tears are shaken from the wrath-bearing tree.

I have said enough to show, I hope, that we are faced by a tremendous difference in values when we consider these two poems side by side. Something radical seems to have happened to the hero's idea of himself between 1840 and 1920. History might be able to offer us some clues.

Now if we re-read "Gerontion" with half the attention that a company director gives to a stock-report we may be able to trace other preoccupations. You must not imagine, however, that I am attempting any very profound analysis of this fine poem. I have ignored the technical and linguistic features of it for the time being. Later I hope to discuss why Gerontion speaks as he does. But for the moment it is enough to consider the poem as a piece of simple autobiography, and to try and find out a bit more of the circumstances of Gerontion's life. His speech is rather difficult to follow at times but he does seem to imply a number of things about himself that are worth our attention.

You have seen how securely grounded in his world Ulysses is. He does not, to give one example, fear for the succession of his son. He is simply bored with old age, bored with the inactivity he is forced to endure. He longs to resume his youthful, adventurous life.

What of Gerontion? "My house," he says, "is a decayed house, and the jew squats on the window sill, the owner." Later on in the poem he mentions that it is a rented house. We know that house as a symbol stands for more than four walls and a roof. A house means property, succession, home, and family order. It also, by association, stands for children. Surely we may read into this passage a pre-occupation with the break-up of a social order, together with a far-reaching sense of insecurity about the values upon which that order was once founded.

> Signs are taken for wonders. "We would see a sign!"
> The word within a word, unable to speak a word,
> Swaddled with darkness. In the juvescence of the year
> Came Christ the tiger.

It is revelation and not more knowledge that Gerontion appears to be waiting for; later comes the phrase "to be eaten, to be divided, to be drunk" and it reminds us of the Christian sacrament. Yet with a sudden ironic turn Eliot brings before us a gallery of *personae* such as one might only see in some small Florentine pension, or perhaps in a Bloomsbury boarding-house for foreign students. "Mr. Silvero . . . who walked all night in the next room; by Hakagawa, bowing among the Titians." These, he seems to say, are the creatures for whom Christ commanded his sacrament to be conducted. They are mere shadows of men he has met on his travels. Yet these figures are to Gerontion what the "peers" of Ulysses were once. "The great Achilles" and the rest. They are mythological shapes which inhabit the subjective world of Gerontion. Ulysses and Achilles were world-figures. They belonged to racial myth. But the myth is dead and for Gerontion only these depersonalized masks remain in his memory.

Something very mysterious has happened to the firm classical order of things, and to the heroic nature of man. In "Gerontion" everything seems to be called into question, not only the doctrine of his age but the knowledge, the morals, and, on the social plane, the security of family life and natural succession. "I have no ghosts," he says. As the poem progresses in its unformal yet rhythmical way you begin to realize that it expresses a very deep-seated sense of insecurity and intellectual exhaustion, together with a strong condemnation of the moral order under which the modern hero has to live. History leads nowhere. Human identity seems to be empty of any joy. Compare these statements, with their mounting flavor of disenchantment, with the marvellous closing lines of "Ulysses" which express faith and affirmation in the human condition:

> The long day wanes: the slow moon climbs: the deep
> Moans round with many voices. Come, my friends,
> 'Tis not too late to seek a newer world.
> Push off, and sitting well in order smite
> The sounding furrows; for my purpose holds
> To sail beyond the sunset, and the baths
> Of all the western stars, until I die.
> It may be that the gulfs will wash us down:
> It may be we shall touch the Happy Isles,
> And see the great Achilles, whom we knew.
> Though much is taken, much abides; and though
> We are not now that strength which in old days
> Moved earth and heaven; that which we are, we are;
> One equal temper of heroic hearts,
> Made weak by time and fate, but strong in will
> To strive, to seek, to find, and not to yield.

"Gerontion," however, ends very much as it began. "Thoughts of a dry brain in a dry season." There is no way forward, the poem says, after it has enumerated those thoughts of a dry brain. Gerontion is in an intellectual *impasse*. He cannot advance. He can only sit and think of the past until his memories

> Protract the profit of their chilled delirium,
> Excite the membrane, when the sense has cooled,
> With pungent sauces, multiply variety
> In a wilderness of mirrors.

What is the secret of this loss of faith, of this negation? You may perhaps think that in putting such a question I am taking unpardonable liberties with my material. Who can say whether the difference in the two poems does not reflect purely temperamental idiosyncrasies? Tennyson was a hero-worshipper, while T. S. Eliot was, at the time he wrote "Gerontion," a cynic. There may be something to be said for this view. Obviously temperament and subject-matter play a very important part in the poems. Yet if poems reflect their age at all we may be able to dig under the surface for their cosmological content, and leave the personal data to look after itself. It is certainly true that the later poems of Tennyson also became pessimistic—yet the gap between his technique and that of Eliot remains as wide. Can we trace historic origins for the change? Can we, by following up the changes of thought and belief within the last hundred years, find some sort of clue to the exhausted subjectivity of the contemporary hero? I think we can.

The problem is where to begin—for both in the arts and sciences the last hundred years has been one of the most momentous epochs in human history. Between 1840 and 1900 lie sixty years characterized by tremendous intellectual upheavals, tremendous changes in beliefs and values. Let us take a simple example.

The Victorians believed, among other things, that time had begun less than 6,000 years ago. Moses, they thought, was only separated from the first man by a few generations. In the Bampton Lecture of 1859 George Rawlinson gravely suggested that Moses' mother, Jochebed, had probably met Jacob, who could have known Noah's son Shem. Shem was probably acquainted with Methuselah, who had been for 243 years a contemporary of Adam. Adam himself had been made on the sixth day after the beginning of Time. The earth, according to the Victorians, had been created about 4,000 B.C. by God, and was more or less as we see it today, except that the perfect life we had been meant to lead on it had been corrupted by the Fall.

It is very hard to put ourselves in the position of people who believed this sort of thing. For us geology tells a different story. But geology is a science still in its infancy. When it first arose and questioned the facts of *Genesis* the assertions made by its followers seemed positively blasphemous. Yet its assertions gained ground. It became obvious that the account of creation given in *Genesis* would not bear close examination. The shock was a considerable one, and the whole age was filled with clamoring voices, with quarrels and speculations centering about the discoveries of geology. In 1857 the first remains of Neanderthal Man came to light. Then came the publication of Darwin's *Origin of Species,* which made man not the noblest member of the animal kingdom but simply a term in the evolutionary series. This idea caused perhaps the greatest shock of all. It was, needless to say, most bitterly contested both from inside the Church and from outside it. Yet the effect of this idea upon the Victorian Age cannot be overestimated. Man had been dethroned. He was no longer the noblest animal. Sherwood Taylor in a recent article on the beliefs of the Victorian Age says:

> For lack of clear thinking in these matters many lost their faith completely. Some felt that the historicity of the scriptural Adam was overthrown, and the doctrine of the fall and the need for redemption with it: and so came to lose belief in the Christian scheme. Others felt that the Bible had been shown to be untrue in some points and therefore no longer carried any assurance of authenticity. . . . I myself have little doubt that in England it was geology and the theory of evolution that changed us from a Christian to a pagan nation. The overt reaction of the age to geology was theological but its influence extended to every phase of thought. It completed in fact the revolution that Copernicus began.

The history of man, then, was suddenly expanded into a region of time so remote that the Victorians might be forgiven for finding the idea terrifying. Lyell, the greatest geologist, suggested that man was 100,000 years old. When you think that the art and morality of Europe were based upon the Bible you can imagine how deep a shock all this was. But it was not all.

History began to expand in another direction, helped this time by archeology. In 1874 Schliemann's excavations at Mycenae were begun. You will remember that the poems of Homer were considered mere poetical fantasies. Schliemann was later to prove that Troy existed. In 1895 Sir Flinders Petrie was at work upon ancient remains in Egypt, while in 1899 Sir Arthur Evans began work upon what was to turn out to be a new civilization, until then unknown, called the Minoan civilization. Ancient cultures were coming to the surface, and the chill wind of religious scepticism was blowing hard. First it was the civilization of Europe which began to look remote and tiny set against the historical perspectives opened up. Secondly the history of man on earth, as explained by geologists, began to appear of negligible importance.

In 1897, in an essay upon literature, Professor J. W. Hales wrote:

> Science has certainly been in part responsible for the growth of a spirit of materialism, and has caused those who do not share that spirit to examine themselves and remould their arguments. Science has therefore tended to depress many who, without accepting materialistic opinions, have been affected by the march of thought. On the whole we may say that science has tended to positivism, agnosticism, and in a word to a negative view of things spiritual.

The characteristics of the Victorian Age, then, centered about this intellectual battle between the forces of reason and the forces of revelation: between theology with its demands on belief, and the new scientific materialism with its collection of disturbing facts. The temper of the age was violent, as we may see by the reception accorded to Darwin's book. It created a sensation. All the forces of established religion were brought to bear upon it. It was commonly objected that such criticisms of the Bible were a wanton unsettlement of the faith of simple people, and in 1864, five years after the appearance of *The Origin of Species*, the Oxford Declaration on Inspiration and Eternal Punishment was signed by eleven thousand members of the clergy. This was a curious document. According to Archbishop Tait the effect of this declaration was that "all questions of physical science should be referred to the written words of Holy Scripture."

Meanwhile, however, archeology went its own way, and among its discoveries we should perhaps record the first example of Paleolithic Cave Art. But we should also hasten to mention that the first studies in anthropology were beginning to occupy the thoughts of scholars about this time. The effect of a book like Frazer's *The Golden Bough*—an inquiry into the origins of religious belief—cannot be over-estimated; and side by side with anthropological speculation came the first attempts to deal with Jesus as a historical figure. The biographical *Jesus* of Renan had caused almost the same storm in Europe as *The Origin of Species* in England.

The narrow iron-bound theology of the Victorian simply could not accommodate all the facts which were piling up in the laboratories of the scientists. It was all very well to appeal to belief. The age, with its materialist bias and its young utilitarian science, thought that reason would be a surer guide in human affairs. "Scientific proof" became one of the watchwords of the day.

Tennyson's "Ulysses" you may remember, burned "to follow knowledge like a sinking star, beyond the utmost bound of human thought." It was a desire which found an echo in every Victorian heart, and it was to be gratified in the most literal sense by the scientists of the next century. For the trouble with scientific thought today is that it does appear to have reached something like the boundary-line of human thought—the boundary-line of its conceptual abilities.

There are several others aspects of the Victorian Age which deserve mention. So far I have tried to stick to those which altered the concept of history in time. But while we cannot stay to treat any of these great systems in detail, we should not forget to add to them the name of Marx, written in the margin of our note-books. *Das Kapital* was written in 1867. Though Marxism was the ugly duckling among the philosophies fathered on us by scientific rationalism, yet the evolution of social ideas and reforms is an important part of the Victorian picture, though not absolutely vital to our own research on "Ulysses." I would prefer to turn to Logical Positivism for a moment as a part of the Victorian inheritance. Auguste Comte, who propounded this philosophy, was born

in 1798. He believed that every science followed a clearly defined historical curve and might be divided up into three stages of belief. In the first,
the animistic stage, people believed that the universe was ruled over by
the personifications of various deities: Gods, Goddesses, Nymphs, etc.
In the second stage these mythical conceptions became depersonified and
were replaced by conceptual entities like "force," "gravity," and other
such mechanical ideas. In the third or positive stage even these mechanical ideas would die out and would be replaced with a purely negative
attitude towards phenomena. The idea of natural forces would die out
and science would no longer offer us explanations of why things happened: it would simply content itself with keeping a log of happenings
and of studying them within a provisional frame of thought.

Now the philosophy of scientific materialism which played so great
a part in the Victorian outlook had taken over the full equipment of
forces, levers, pulleys, and laws, bequeathed to it by Newton.

Ranged against the forces of this mechanistic philosophy we find
representatives of many differing camps, both religious and æsthetic.
They saw with alarm that the scientist in his arrogance was setting up
shop as a theologian. Up till now the mechanical universe postulated
by the mechanist had left elbow-room for the Deity. But the materialists
of "Ulysses' " age were beginning to question whether God could not
be replaced by some hypothetical first cause—some purely chemical
force which set the whole business off. Assailed on all fronts by science,
geology, archeology, theology fought on doggedly but without avail.
The age was a materialistic age and its God was reason.

"Ulysses" of course ante-dates this period by a decade or two. But you
can see from his style that his world has not been threatened as yet,
has not been afflicted with doubt and despair. I would like to suggest
that a good deal of the despair in "Gerontion" comes of a realization that
the world has gone off the rails. Food, as you know, takes time to reach
the stomach; and I suggest that Gerontion expresses all the disillusion
of the 1890's.

The effect of these ideas upon the Victorian world has been very well
expressed by Sherwood Taylor:

> The whole of the literature, art, and philosophy of the past was based
> on the axioms that the changes of the world were a drama enacted on the
> unchanging scene of nature by unchanging man—a little lower than the
> angels and immeasurably above the beasts who had no understanding. The
> art, literature, and morality of Europe were based on the Bible, understood
> in the old simple way. The later Victorians, isolated in vast deserts of space
> and time, with God seemingly removed to the dim status of a remote
> Architect of the World, could no longer feel themselves one with those who
> dwelt contentedly in the little universe of past ages. . . . And so the
> Victorian moved out of man's ancestral home, with its temples, palaces,

cottages, and cathedrals, golden with age, tenderly formed by the hands of the masters, into a fine new city of science—so convenient, so hygienic, so reasonably planned—but devoid of human tenderness and ancient beauty. This loss has never been repaired and man today is still a displaced person in a land he has yet to make his home.

I could not hope for a clearer summing up of the message we find implicit in Gerontion's attitude. It is a message which afterwards received amplification in [Eliot's] *Waste Land*, which has had such a great effect upon the poetic tradition in England. The whole fabric of the poem is shot with reminiscences of history, poetry, myth, all tangled up as they are in "Gerontion." The central message is, of course, disillusion. Gerontion himself might easily have figured in *The Waste Land*. He is written in the same tone of voice.

> And it is not by any concitation
> Of the backward devils.
> I would meet you upon this honestly.
> I that was near your heart was removed therefrom
> To lose beauty in terror, terror in inquisition.
> I have lost my passion: why should I need to keep it
> Since what is kept must be adulterated?
> I have lost my sight, smell, hearing, taste and touch:
> How should I use them for your closer contact?

But do not think that "Gerontion" is simply and solely a revolt against Victorian materialism. That would be a ridiculous over-simplification. Materialism itself was not a new enemy, though it was most firmly entrenched behind the new discoveries of science. But the general philosophy of materialism was, I suppose, a legacy left to us by Hobbes,[4] which received a new impetus from the discoveries of applied science.

Hobbes believed that the whole world consisted simply of matter and motion, and that the only reality was matter. Man was an animal with a body made of matter while his thoughts and emotions arose from the purely mechanical motions of the atoms with which he was constructed.

It followed from this of course that when the scientist managed to break down matter to its smallest part he would find it something substantial, something solid however small, a piece of matter. This is what the early Victorians believed. But there was a surprise in store for them.

There is only one other aspect of Victorian science which is important to grasp, and that is the relation it assumed to exist between subject and object, observer and observed. In the so-called exact sciences subject and object were taken to be two distinct things: so that a description of

[4] Thomas Hobbes (1588–1679), author of *Human Nature*, *Leviathan*, and other works.

any part of the universe was considered a judgment quite independent of the observer—or of any subjective conditions in which he found himself. Science claimed an ABSOLUTE OBJECTIVITY in its judgments about the world.

This view of the subject-object relationship was only discarded in the light of Einstein's Relativity Theory which was born some twenty years later. This is a fact which is vital to our understanding of the age we live in, and the literature which characterizes that age. You will understand me when I say that "Ulysses" is an objective poem and "Gerontion" a subjective one. In "Ulysses" the camera is, so to speak, facing outwards to the world, recording the fears and preoccupations of the hero objectively; "Gerontion" is exactly the opposite. The camera, if I may repeat the metaphor, is focused inward upon the secret hopes and fears of the old hero. It is a moving picture of the processes of the unconscious at work. In Tennyson's poem we deduce the inner state of the hero from his statements about things outside himself. Eliot's poem demands something more. It is a detective story in little, and we must all the time be watching for clues and hints if we are to understand what is going on.

The subject-object relationship is one that is worth some thought. If we mark off the hundred years which separate us from the writers whose work betrays a Semantic Disturbance—I am thinking of Rimbaud, Laforgue, Lewis Carroll, Nietzsche and others of the same *genre*—we see, I think, a gradually increasing curve of subjectivity, through, let us say, Dickens, Tolstoy, Dostoievski, Proust, Joyce. The vision of the artist seems to be gradually turning inward upon himself. Perhaps we can see this state of affairs in the general cosmology of the age also, if we follow out the curve of knowledge, through Victorian materialism, agnosticism, and classical objectivity until we reach the present day.

Suggestions

1. The thesis of "The Curve of Subjectivity" is that the obscurity of modern art results from the changed personality of man, a change caused by historical events. The essay is illustrated by a contrast between the heroes of two poems. With the help of the essay, characterize Ulysses and Gerontion after you have read the poems. Is it correct in saying that Ulysses is a man of faith, whose outlook is objective, and that Gerontion's subjectivity is related to his loss of faith?

2. Explain why the speaker considers the past century "one of the most momentous epochs in human history" (¶18), listing some of his most striking examples. Does he consider these more important than the mechanical inventions of this epoch?

3. Explain how the outlook of Gerontion is summarized in Sherwood Taylor's essay (¶35).

4. Discuss: "Science claimed an ABSOLUTE OBJECTIVITY in its judgments about the world" (¶40). What has supposedly happened to this claim?

5. Explain: *Florentine pension, Bloomsbury, idiosyncrasies, animistic, Relativity Theory, Semantic Disturbance.*

6. Identify: Blake, Rimbaud, Laforgue, Lewis Carroll, Nietzsche.

7. With special attention to the summary of positivism (¶30), write a comparison of the modern temper as it is described in this essay and in † "The Modern Climate of Opinion."

8. After reading the modern poems in Part 4 of this book, write an analysis of the one, not by T. S. Eliot, that you think best supports the thesis of "The Curve of Subjectivity."

WHY DO WE TEACH POETRY?

ARCHIBALD MACLEISH ──◦⊰| *Reprinted by permission of the author.* © THE ATLANTIC MONTHLY.

There is something about the art of poetry which induces a defensive posture. Even in the old days when the primacy of poetry was no more challenged than the primacy of Heaven, which is now also challenged, the posture was habitual. If you published your reflections on the art in those days you called them a *Defense*.[1] Today, when the queen of sciences is Science,[2] you do not perhaps employ that term but you mean it. It is not that the gentlemen at the long table in the Faculty Club whose brains have been officially cleared to serve as depositories of scientific secrets of the eighth and thirteenth classes are patronizing in their manner. They are still gentlemen and therefore still modest no matter how great their distinction or how greatly certified. But one knows one's place. One knows that whereas the teachers of science meet to hear of new triumphs which the newspapers will proudly report, the teachers of poetry meet to ask old questions—which no one will report: such questions as, why teach poetry anyway in a time like this?

It is a relief in this general atmosphere to come upon someone who feels no defensiveness whatever: who is perfectly certain that poetry ought to be taught now as at any other time and who is perfectly certain also that he knows why. The paragon I have in mind is a young friend

[1] E.g. Sir Philip Sidney's *Apology for Poetry* (1595), P. B. Shelley's *Defense of Poetry* (1821).
[2] And not philosophy, as was formerly said.

of mine, a devoted teacher, who was recently made headmaster of one of the leading American preparatory schools, and who has been taking stock, for some time past, of his curriculum and his faculty. Poetry, as he sees it, ought to be taught "as a most essential form of human expression as well as a carrier throughout the ages of some of the most important values in our heritage." What troubles him is that few teachers, at least in the schools he knows, seem to share his conviction. He is not too sure that teachers themselves have "an abiding and missionary faith in poetry" which would lead them to see it as a great clarifier—a "human language" capable of competing with the languages and mathematics and science.

But though teachers lack the necessary faith, the fault, as my young friend sees it, is not wholly theirs. The fault is the fault of modern criticism, which has turned poetry into something he calls "poetry itself" —meaning, I suppose, poetry for poetry's sake. "Poetry itself" turns out to be poetry with its meanings distilled away, and poetry with its meanings distilled away is difficult if not impossible to teach in a secondary school—at least *his* secondary school. The result is that secondary school teachers have gone back, as to the lesser of two evils, to those historical and anecdotal practices sanctified by American graduate schools in generations past. They teach "poets and not poetry." With the result that "students become acquainted with poets from Homer to MacLeish" (quite a distance no matter how you measure it!) "but the experience doesn't necessarily leave them with increased confidence in what poetry has to offer." I can well believe it.

The reason why modern criticism has this disastrous effect, the reason why it produces "an almost morbid apathy toward 'content' or 'statement of idea,' " is its excessive "preoccupation with aesthetic values." Modern criticism insists that poems are primarily works of art; and when you insist that poems are primarily works of art you cannot, in my friend's view, teach them as carriers "throughout the ages of some of the most important values in our heritage." What is important about Homer and Shakespeare and the authors of the Bible is that they were "realists with great vision . . . whose work contains immensely valuable constructions of the meaning of life"; and if you talk too much about them as artists, those constructions of the meaning of life get lost.

Now this, you will observe, is not merely another walloping of the old horse who was once called the New Criticism. It goes a great deal farther. It is a frontal attack upon a general position maintained by many who never accepted the New Criticism or even heard of it. It is an attack upon those who believe—as most poets, I think, have believed—that a poem *is* primarily a work of art and must be read as a work of art if it is to be read at all. It is a high-minded and disinterested attack delivered for the noblest of purposes, but an attack notwithstanding—and an effective one.

What it contends is that an approach to poetry which insists that a poem is a work of art blocks off what the poem has to say, whereas what the poem has to say is the principal reason for teaching it. What the argument comes down to, in other words, is the proposition that it is a mistake, in teaching poetry, to insist that poetry is art, because, if you do so insist, you will not be able to bring your students to the meaning of the poem, the idea of the poem, what the poem has to tell them about man and world and life and death—and it is for these things the teaching of the poem is important.

Now, I can understand this argument and can respect the reasons for making it. Far too many of those who define poetry in exclusively artistic terms use their definition as a limiting and protective statement which relieves them of all obligation to drive the poem's meanings beyond the meanings of the poem: beyond the mere translation of the symbols and metaphors and the classical or other references—the whole apparatus of *explication du texte* [explanation of the text itself]. Far too many, indeed, of those who have to do with literature generally in our time, and particularly with modern literature, consider that meanings in any but a literary (which includes a Freudian) sense are not only outside, but beneath, their proper concern—that the intrusion of questions of morality and religion into the world of art is a kind of trespass and that works of literary art not only should but *can* be studied in a moral vacuum. Literature in the hands of such teachers is well on the way to becoming again that "terrible queen" which the men of the nineties raised above life and which Yeats, when he outgrew the men of the nineties, rejected.

But although I can understand this argument, and although I can respect its reasons, and although I believe it raises a true issue and an important issue, I cannot accept it; for it rests, or seems to me to rest, on two quite dubious assumptions. The first is the assumption, familiar in one form or another to all of us, that the "idea" of a work of art is somehow separable from the work of art itself. The most recent—and most egregious—expression of this persistent notion comes from a distinguished Dean of Humanities in a great institution of learning who is reported by the New York *Times* to have argued in a scholarly gathering that "the idea which the reader derives from Ernest Hemingway's *The Old Man and The Sea* comes after the reader has absorbed some 60,000 words. This takes at least an hour. . . . A similar understanding could come after a few minutes study of a painting by a skillful artist." Precisely, one imagines, as the Doré illustrations gave one the "idea" of the *Inferno* in a few easy looks!

II

It is the second assumption, however, which divides me most emphatically from my young friend. For the second assumption seems to be that *unless* idea and work of art are distinguished from each other in the teaching of a poem, the idea—and so the effectiveness of the teaching—will be lost. At this point my friend and I part company. I am ready, and more than ready, to agree that it is for the meanings of life that one reads (and teaches) poetry. But I am unable to see how there can be a distinction between a poem as a conveyer of such meanings and a poem as a work of art. In brief, the distinction between art and knowledge which is made throughout my friend's argument seems to me wholly without foundation. That it is a distinction almost universally recognized in our epoch I know well enough. Science makes it. Poetry makes it. And the world agrees with both. "Whatever can be *known*," says Bertrand Russell, "can be known by means of science." Poetry, say its professors, has no "messages" to deliver. And no one dissents from either. The exclusive proprietary right of science to know and to communicate knowledge is not only commonly recognized in our civilization: in a very real sense it is our civilization. For the characteristic of our civilization —that which distinguishes it from the civilizations which have preceded it—is the characteristic which knowledge-by-science has conferred upon it: its abstractness.

But though the agreement is general, the proposition is not one I can accept. I argue that the apologists for science are not justified in claiming, nor the apologists for poetry in admitting, the sole right of science to know. I insist that poetry is also capable of knowledge; that poetry, indeed, is capable of a kind of knowledge of which science is not capable; that it is capable of that knowledge *as poetry;* and that the teaching of poetry as poetry, the teaching of poem as work of art, is not only not incompatible with the teaching of poetry as knowledge but is, indeed, the only possible way of teaching poetry as knowledge.

To most of us, brought up as we have been in the world of abstractions which science has prepared for us, and in the kind of school which that world produces—schools in which almost all teaching is teaching of abstractions—the notion of poetry as knowledge, the notion of art as knowledge, is a fanciful notion. Knowledge by abstraction we understand. Science can abstract ideas about apple from apple. It can organize those ideas into knowledge about apple. It can then, by some means, introduce that knowledge into our heads—possibly because our heads are abstractions also. But poetry, we know, does not abstract. Poetry presents. Poetry presents the thing as the thing. And that it should be possible to *know* the thing *as the thing it is*—to *know* apple *as* apple—this we do not understand; this, the true child of the time will assure you, cannot be done. To the true child of abstraction you can't know apple as apple. You can't know tree as tree. You can't know man as man. All you can *know* is a world dissolved by analyzing intellect into abstraction—not a world composed by imaginative intellect into itself. And the result, for the generations of abstraction, is that neither poetry nor art can be a means to knowledge. To inspiration, yes: poetry can undoubtedly lead to that—whatever it is. To revelation, perhaps: there may certainly be moments of revelation in poetry. But to knowledge, no. The only connection between poetry and knowledge we can see is the burden of used abstractions—adages and old saws—which poetry, some poetry, seems to like to carry—adages most of which we knew before and some of which aren't even true.

But if all this is so, what then is the "experience of art"—the "experience of poetry"—which all of us who think about these things at all have known? What is the experience of *realization* which comes over us with those apples on a dish of Cézanne's or those three pine trees? What is the experience of realization which comes over us with Debussy's *Nuages?* What is the experience of realization which comes over us when Coleridge's robin sits and sings

> Betwixt the tufts of snow on the bare branch
> Of mossy apple-tree, while the nigh thatch
> Smokes in the sun thaw; . . .

or when his eave-drops fall

> Heard only in the trances of the blast,
> Or if the secret ministry of frost
> Shall hang them up in silent icicles,
> Quietly shining to the quiet Moon.
> ["Frost at Midnight," lines 68–74]

And if all this is so, why does one of the most effective of modern definitions of poetry (Arnold's in his letter to Maurice de Guérin) assign to that art the peculiar "power of so dealing with *things* as to awaken in us a wonderfully full, new, and intimate sense of them and of our relation with them"?

The answer is, of course, that the children of abstraction are wrong—and are impoverished by their error, as our entire time is impoverished by it. They are wrong on both heads. They are wrong when they think they *can* know the world through its abstractions: nothing can be known through an abstraction but the abstraction itself. They are wrong also when they think they *cannot* know the world as the world: the whole achievement of art is a demonstration to the contrary. And the reason they are wrong on both heads is the reason given, quite unintentionally, by Matthew Arnold. They are wrong because they do not realize that all true knowledge is a matter of relation: that we *really* know a thing only when we are filled with "a wonderfully full, new, and intimate sense of it" and, above all, of "our relation with" it. This sense—this *knowledge* in the truest meaning of the word knowledge—art can give but abstraction cannot.

There are as many proofs as there are successful works of art. Take, for obvious example, that unseen mysterious phenomenon, the wind. Take any attempt, by the familiar processes of abstraction, to "know" the wind. Put beside it those two familiar lines of George Meredith:—

> Mark where the pressing wind shoots javelin-like
> Its skeleton shadow on the broad-backed wave!
> ["Modern Love" 43, lines 1–2]

What will be the essential difference between the two? Will it not be that the first, the analytical, statement is or attempts to be a wholly objective statement made without reference to an observer (true everywhere and always), whereas an observer—*one's self* as observer!—is involved in the second? And will not the consequential difference be that a relation involving one's self is created by the second but not by the first? And will not the end difference be that the second, but not the first, will enable us to know the thing itself—to know what the thing is *like*?

It would be quite possible, I suppose, to semanticize this difference between knowledge by poetry and knowledge by abstraction out of existence by demonstrating that the word, know, is being used in two different senses in the two instances, but the triumph would be merely verbal, for the difference is real. It is indeed the realest of all differences, for what it touches is the means by which we come at reality. How are we to find the knowledge of reality in the world without, or in the shifting, flowing, fluid world within? Is all this a task for the techniques of abstraction—for science as it may be or as it is? Is it through abstraction alone that we are to find what is real in our experience of our lives—and so, conceivably, what is real in ourselves? Or do we need another and a different way of knowing—a way of knowing which will make that world out there, this world in here, available to us, not by translating them into something else—into abstractions of quantity and measure—but by bringing us ourselves to confront them as they are—man and tree face to face in the shock of recognition, man and love face to face?

The question, I beg you to see, is not what we *ought* to do. There is no ought. A man can "live" on abstractions all his life if he has the stomach for them, and many of us have—not the scientists only, but great numbers of the rest of us in this contemporary world, men whose days are a web of statistics, and names, and business deals, held together by the parentheses of a pair of commuting trains with three Martinis at the close. The question is not what we ought to do. The question is what we have the choice of doing—what alternatives are open to us.

And it is here and in these terms that the issue presents itself to the teacher of poetry.

III

Colleges and universities do not exist to impose duties but to reveal choices. In a civilization like ours in which one choice has all but overwhelmed the other, a civilization dominated by abstraction, in which men are less and less able to deal with their experience of the world or of themselves unless experience and self have first been translated into abstract terms—a civilization like a foreign language—in such a civilization the need for an understanding of the alternative is urgent. What must be put before the generation of the young is the possibility of a knowledge of experience *as* experience, of self *as* self; and that possibility only the work of art, only the poem, can reveal. That it is so rarely, or so timidly, presented in our schools is one of the greatest failures of our educational system. Young men and young women graduate from American schools and colleges by the hundreds of thousands every year to whom science is the only road to knowledge, and to whom poetry is little more than a subdivision of something called "literature" —a kind of writing printed in columns instead of straight across the page and primarily intended to be deciphered by girls, who don't read it either.

This sort of thing has consequences. Abstractions are wonderfully clever tools for taking things apart and for arranging things in patterns but they are very little use in putting things together and no use at all when it comes to determining what things are *for*. Furthermore, abstractions have a limiting, a dehumanizing, a dehydrating effect on the relation to things of the man who must live with them. The result is that we are more and more left, in our scientific society, without the means of knowledge of ourselves as we truly are or of our experience as it actually is. We have the tools, all the tools—we are suffocating in tools—but we cannot find the actual wood to work or even the actual hand to work it. We begin with one abstraction (something we think of as ourselves) and a mess of other abstractions (standing for the world) and we arrange and rearrange the counters, but who we are and what we are doing we simply do not know—above all what we are doing. With the inevitable consequence that we do not know either what our purpose is or our end. So that when the latest discoveries of the cyclotron are reported we hail them with the cry that we will now be able to control nature better than ever before—but we never go on to say for what purpose, to what end, we will control her. To destroy a city? To remake a world?

It was something of this kind, I imagine, that Adlai Stevenson had in mind when he startled a Smith Commencement last spring by warning his newly graduated audience of prospective wives that the "typical

Western man—or typical Western husband—operates well in the realm
of means, as the Roman did before him. But outside his specialty, in
the realm of ends he is apt to operate poorly or not at all. . . . The
neglect of the cultivation of more mature values," Mr. Stevenson went
on, "can only mean that his life, and the life of the society he determines, will lack valid purpose, however busy and even profitable it
may be."

As he has so often done before, Mr. Stevenson there found words for
an uneasiness which has been endemic but inarticulate in the American
mind for many years—the sense that we are getting nowhere far too fast
and that, if something doesn't happen soon, we may arrive. But when he
came to spell out the causes for "the neglect of the cultivation of more
mature values" Mr. Stevenson failed, or so it seems to me, to identify
the actual villain. The contemporary environment in America, he told
his young listeners, is "an environment in which 'facts,' the data of the
senses, are glorified and value judgments are assigned inferior status as
'mere matters of opinion.' It is an environment in which art is often regarded as an adornment of civilization rather than a vital element of it,
while philosophy is not only neglected but deemed faintly disreputable
because 'it never gets you anywhere.' " It is true that philosophy is
neglected, and even truer that art is regarded in this country generally
as it seems to be regarded by the automobile manufacturers of Detroit:
as so much enamel paint and chromium to be applied for allegedly
decorative purposes to the outside of a car which would run better without it. But the explanation is not, I think, that we set facts—even facts
in quotation marks—above values, or that we glorify the data of the
senses, unless one means by that latter phrase not what the senses tell us
of the world we live in but what the statistics that can be compiled out
of the data of the senses would tell us if we were ever in touch with our
senses.

In few civilizations have the senses been less alive than they are with
us. Look at the cities we build and occupy—but look at them!—the
houses we live in, the way we hold ourselves and move; listen to the
speaking voices of the greater part of our women. And in no civilization,
at least in recorded time, have human beings been farther from the *facts*
if we mean by that word, facets of reality. Our indifference to ends is the
result of our obsession with abstractions rather than facts: with the ideas
of things rather than with things. For there can be no concern for ends
without a hunger for reality. And there can be no hunger for reality
without a sense of the real. And there can be no sense of the real in the
world which abstraction creates, for abstraction is incapable of the real:
it can neither lay hold of the real itself nor show us where to find it. It
cannot, that is to say, create the *relation* between reality and ourselves
which makes *knowledge* of reality possible, for neither reality nor our-

selves exist in abstraction. Everything in the world of abstraction is object. And, as George Buttrick pointedly says, *we* are not objects: we are subjects.

IV

But all this is a negative way of saying what a defender of poetry should not be afraid of saying positively. Let me say it. We have lost our concern with ends because we have lost our touch with reality and we have lost our touch with reality because we are estranged from the means to reality which is the poem—the work of art. To most members of our generation this would seem an extravagant statement but it is not extravagant in fact and would not have seemed so in another time. In ancient China the place of poetry in men's lives was assumed as matter of course; indeed, the polity was based on it. The three hundred and five odes or songs which make up the Song-word Scripture survived to the fourth century B.C., when Confucius is said to have collected them because they were part of the government records preserved in the Imperial Archive. For thousands of years the examinations for the Chinese civil service were examinations in poetry, and there is no record that the results were more disappointing to the throne than examinations of a different character might have been. Certainly there is no record that a Chinese civil servant ever attempted to deny an honor student in a military academy his commission in the imperial army *or* navy because he was friendly with his own mother [3]! Idiocies which the study of science and of other abstractions in contemporary institutions of naval education in the United States seem to nourish were apparently cauterized from the mind by the reading of poems.

It was not for nothing that Confucius told his disciples that the three hundred and five songs of the Song-word Scripture could be boiled down to the commandment: "Have no twisty thoughts." You cannot have twisty thoughts if you are real and if you are thinking about real things. But if a mother is merely a biological event to you and if you yourself are merely a military event called an admiral, anything may happen: you may make your country ridiculous, humiliate a promising boy, and deprive the navy of a good officer, all in the twisted belief that you are being a wise man and a patriot.

One can see, not only in the three hundred and five songs, but in Chinese poetry of other periods, what Confucius meant. Consider two Chinese poems of the second century B.C. and the sixth of our era, both written by Emperors. The first is a poem of grief—of the sense of loss of someone loved: a poem therefore of that inward world of feeling, of emotion, which seems to us most nearly ourselves and which, because it

[3] In August 1955 the United States government refused an ensign's reserve commission to Midshipman Eugene Landy because he had been "extremely close" to his mother, a former Communist.

is always in flux, always shifting and changing and flowing away, is, of all parts of our experience of our lives, most difficult to know. We cannot know it through science. We cannot know it by knowing things *about* it—even the shrewdest and most intelligent things, helpful though they may be to us in other ways. We cannot know it either by merely feeling it—by uttering its passing urgencies, crying out "I love" meaning "I think of myself as loving" or sobbing "I grieve" meaning "I think of myself as grieving." How then can we know it?

The Emperor Wu-ti wrote (this is Arthur Waley's beautiful translation):—

> The sound of her silk skirt has stopped.
> On the marble pavement dust grows.
> Her empty room is cold and still.
> Fallen leaves are piled against the doors.
>
> Longing for that lovely lady
> How can I bring my aching heart to rest?

Four images, one of sound, two of sight, one of feeling, each like a note plucked on a stringed instrument. Then a question like the chord the four would make together. And all at once we *know*. We know this grief which no word could have described, which any abstraction the mind is capable of would have destroyed. But we know more than this grief: we know our own—or will when it shall visit us—and so know something of ourselves.

The second is a poem of that emotion, that feeling, which is even more difficult to know than grief itself. The second is a poem of delight: youth and delight—the morning of the world—the emotion, of all emotions, most difficult to stop, to hold, to see. "Joy whose hand is ever at his lips bidding adieu" [John Keats, "Ode on Melancholy," lines 22–23]. How would you *know* delight in yourself and therefore yourself delighting? Will the psychiatrists tell you? Is there a definition somewhere in the folios of abstraction by which we attempt to live which will capture it for you? The Emperor Ch'ien Wen-ti (again Waley's translation) knew that there is only one mirror which will hold that vanishing smile: the mirror of art, the mirror of the poem:—

> A beautiful place is the town of Lo-yang:
> The big streets are full of spring light
> The lads go driving out with harps in their hands:
> The mulberry girls go out to the fields with their baskets
> Golden whips glint at the horses' flanks,
> Gauze sleeves brush the green boughs.
> Racing dawn and the carriages come home—
> And the girls with their high baskets full of fruit.

In this world within, you see, this world which is ourselves, there is no possibility of knowing by abstracting the meaning out—or what we hope will be the meaning. There we must know things *as* themselves and it must be *we* who know them. Only art, only poetry, can bring about that confrontation, because only art, only poetry, can show us what we are and ourselves confronting it. To be ignorant of poetry is to be ignorant therefore of the one means of reaching the world of our experience of the world. And to be ignorant of *that* world is to be ignorant of who and what we are. And to be ignorant of who and what we are is to be incapable of reality no matter what tools we have, or what intelligence, or what skills. It is this incapacity, this impotence, which is the tragedy of the time we live in. We are spiritually impotent because we have cut ourselves off from the poem. And the crowning irony is that it is only in the poem that we can know how impotent we have become.

Why do we teach poetry in this scientific age? To present the great alternative not to science but to that knowledge by abstraction which science has imposed. And what is this great alternative? Not the "messages" of poems, their interpreted "meanings," for these are abstractions also—abstractions far inferior to those of science. Not the explications of poetic texts, for the explication of a poetic text which goes no farther ends only in abstraction.

No, the great alternative is the poem as itself, the poem as a poem, the poem as a work of art—which is to say, the poem in the context in which alone the work of art exists: the context of the world, of the man and of the thing, of the infinite relationship which is our lives. To present the great alternative is to present the poem not as a message in a bottle, and not as an object in an uninhabited landscape, but as an action in the world, an action in which we ourselves are actors and our lives are known.

Suggestions

1. The speaker's answer to the question "Why Do We Teach Poetry?" can be readily stated: because poems present a kind of knowledge that is indispensable, especially in a scientific age. But he disagrees to some extent with other persons who value poems, and if the essay is to be fully understood these distinctions must be made clear. Summarize the passages that attack the assumptions of (a) teachers who confine themselves to *explication du texte* (¶6), (b) the headmaster (¶¶7–8), (c) Adlai Stevenson (¶18). To which of these attacks does the speaker return at the end?

2. The basic contrast of the essay is between two ways of knowing the world: that of science and that of art. Describe the speaker's attitude toward each one (see ¶15 especially).

3. Point out the irony in ¶3.

4. After reading MacLeish's poem about poetry, † "Ars Poetica," decide whether it is consistent with the idea of poetry suggested in ¶6 and ¶10 of this essay.

5. Discuss and illustrate:

"They are wrong when they think they *can* know the world through its abstractions. . . ." (¶11)

"Colleges and universities do not exist to impose duties but to reveal choices" (¶15).

". . . that inward world of feeling, of emotion, which seems to us most nearly ourselves and which, because it is always in flux . . . is, of all parts of our experience of our lives, most difficult to know" (¶22).

6. The speaker defines knowledge as dependent on the relation between reality and ourselves (¶ 19). Show how the poems of Wu-ti and Ch'ien Wen-ti, quoted in the last section, are used to support this view.

7. Explain: *paragon, disinterested, Freudian, cyclotron, endemic.*

8. Identify: Doré, *Inferno,* Bertrand Russell, Cézanne, Debussy's *Nuages.*

9. Write a comparison of the theory of knowledge presented here with that of John Macmurray, quoted on page 19.

10. Choose a poem from Part 4 of this book and write a defense of it, showing whether you would use the arguments presented in "Why Do We Teach Poetry?"

THE ARTIST AND THE WORLD

JOYCE CARY

From ART AND REALITY *by Joyce Cary.* © *1958 by Arthur Lucius Michael Cary and David Alexander Ogilvie, executors of the estate of Joyce Cary.*

This is an attempt to examine the relation of the artist with the world as it seems to him, and to see what he does with it. That is to say, on the one side with what is called the artist's intuition, on the other with his production, or the work of art.

My only title to discuss the matter is some practical knowledge of two arts.[1] I know very little about aesthetic philosophy, so I shall try, as far as possible, to speak from practical experience.

---

[1] An accomplished painter, Joyce Cary (1888–1957) also wrote *The Horse's Mouth* and other widely read novels.

It is quite true that the artist, painter, writer, or composer starts always with an experience that is a kind of discovery. He comes upon it with the sense of a discovery; in fact, it is truer to say that it comes upon *him* as a discovery. It surprises him. This is what is usually called an intuition or an inspiration. It carries with it always the feeling of directness. For instance, you go walking in the fields and all at once they strike you in quite a new aspect: you find it extraordinary that they should be like that. This is what happened to Monet as a young man.[2] He suddenly saw the fields, not as solid flat objects covered with grass or useful crops and dotted with trees, but as color in astonishing variety and subtlety of gradation. And this gave him a delightful and quite new pleasure. It was a most exciting discovery, especially as it was a discovery of something real. I mean, by that, something independent of Monet himself. That, of course, was half the pleasure. Monet had discovered a truth about the actual world.

This delight in discovery of something new in or about the world is a natural and primitive thing. All children have it. And it often continues until the age of twenty or twenty-five, *even* throughout life.

Children's pleasure in exploring the world, long before they can speak, is very obvious. They spend almost all their time at it. We don't speak of their intuition, but it is the same thing as the intuition of the artist. That is to say, it is direct knowledge of the world as it is, direct acquaintance with things, with character, with appearance, and this is the primary knowledge of the artist and writer. This joy of discovery is his starting point.

Croce,[3] probably the most interesting of the aesthetic philosophers, says that art is simply intuition. But he says, too, that intuition and expression are the same thing. His idea is that we can't know what we have intuited until we have named it, or given it a formal character, and this action is essentially the work of art.

But this is not at all the way it seems to an artist or a writer. To him, the intuition is quite a different thing from the work of art. For the essential thing about the work of art is that it is work, and very hard work too. To go back to the painter. He has had his intuition, he has made his discovery, he is eager to explore it, to reveal it, to fix it down. For, at least in a grown, an educated man, intuitions are highly evanescent. This is what Wordsworth meant when he wrote of their fading into the light of common day.[4]

I said the joy of discovery often dies away after twenty years or so. And this is simply a truth of observation; we know it from our own experience. The magic object that started up before our eyes on a spring day in its own individual shape, is apt, in the same instant, to turn into

2 Claude Monet (1840–1926), the French Impressionist painter.
3 Benedetto Croce (1866–1952), whose works are known collectively as *Philosophy of the Spirit.*
4 "Ode: Intimations of Immortality from Recollections of Early Childhood," Part v.

simply another cherry tree, an ordinary specimen of a common class. We have seen it and named it pretty often already. But Housman, as poet, fixed his vision of the cherry tree [5] before it had changed into just another tree in blossom.

Housman fixed it for himself and us, but not by an immediate act, indistinguishable from the intuition. He had to go to work and find words, images, rhyme, which embodied his feeling about the tree, which fixed down its meaning for him, so that he could have it again when he wanted it, and also give it to us. He made a work of art, but he made it by work.

So for the painter, when he has his new, his magic landscape in front of him; he has to fix it down. And at once he is up against enormous difficulties. He has only his paints and brushes, and a flat piece of canvas with which to convey a sensation, a feeling, about a three-dimensional world. He has somehow to translate an intuition from real objects into a formal and ideal arrangement of colors and shapes, which will still, mysteriously, fix and convey his sense of the unique quality, the magic of these objects in their own private existence. That is to say, he has a job that requires thought, skill, and a lot of experience.

As for the novelist, his case is even worse. He starts also with his intuition, his discovery; as when Conrad, in an Eastern port, saw a young officer come out from a trial, in which he had been found guilty of a cowardly desertion of his ship and its passengers after a collision. The young man had lost his honor and Conrad realized all at once what that meant to him, and he wrote *Lord Jim* to fix and communicate that discovery in its full force.

For that he had to invent characters, descriptions, a plot. All these details, as with the painter, had to enforce the impression, the feeling that he wanted to convey. The reader had to *feel,* at the end of the tale, "That is important, that is true." It's no good if he says, "I suppose that is true, but I've heard it before." In that case Conrad has failed, at least with that reader. For his object was to give the reader the same discovery, to make him feel what it meant to that young man to lose his honor, and how important honor is to men.

And to get this sharp and strong feeling, the reader must not be confused by side issues. All the scenes and characters, all the events in the book, must contribute to the total effect, the total meaning. The book must give the sense of an actual world with real characters. Otherwise they won't engage the reader's sympathy; his feelings will never be concerned at all.

But actual life is not like that; it doesn't have a total meaning, it is simply a wild confusion of events from which we have to select what we think significant for ourselves. Look at any morning paper. It makes no

---

[5] In "Loveliest of Trees, the Cherry Now," by A. E. Housman (1859–1936).

sense at all—it means nothing but chaos. We read only what we think important; that is to say, we provide our own sense to the news. We have to do so because otherwise it wouldn't be there. To do this, we have to have some standard of valuation, we have to know whether the political event is more important than a murder, or a divorce than the stock market, or the stock market than who won the Derby.

The writer, in short, has to find some meaning in life before he gives it to us in a book. And his subject-matter is much more confused than that of a painter. Of course, in this respect, everyone is in the same boat. Everyone, not only the writer, is presented with the same chaos, and is obliged to form his own idea of the world, of what matters and what doesn't matter. He has to do it, from earliest childhood, for his own safety. And if he gets it wrong, if his idea does not accord with reality, he will suffer for it. A friend of mine, as a child, thought he could fly and jumped off the roof. Luckily he came down in a flower-bed and only broke a leg.

This seems to contradict what I said just now about the chaos which stands before us every morning. For the boy who failed to fly did not suffer only from bad luck. He affronted a law of gravity, a permanent part of a reality objective to him. As we know very well, underneath the chaos of events, there are laws, or if you like consistencies, both of fact and feeling. What science calls matter, that is to say, certain fixed characteristics of being, presents us with a whole framework of reality which we defy at our peril. Wrong ideas about gravity or the wholesomeness of prussic acid are always fatal.

So, too, human nature and its social relations present certain constants. Asylums and jails are full of people who have forgotten or ignored them. On the other hand, we can still comprehend and enjoy paleolithic art and Homer. Homer's heroes had the same kind of nature as our own.

These human constants are also a part of reality objective to us, that is, a permanent character of the world as we know it. So we have a reality consisting of permanent and highly obstinate facts, and permanent and highly obstinate human nature. And human nature is always in conflict with material facts, although men are themselves most curious combinations of fact and feeling, and actually require the machinery of their organism to realize their emotions, their desires and ambitions. Though the ghost could not exist without the machine which is at once its material form, its servant, its limitation, its perfection, and its traitor, it is always trying to get more power over it, to change it.

Men have in fact obtained more power over matter, but to change it is impossible. It may be said that all works of art, all ideas of life, all philosophies are "As if," but I am suggesting that they can be checked with an objective reality. They might be called propositions for truth and their truth can be decided by their correspondence with the real. Man can't change the elemental characters. If you could, the world would probably vanish into nothing. But because of their very permanence, you can assemble them into new forms. You can build new houses with the bricks they used for the oldest Rome, because they are still bricks. For bricks that could stop being bricks at will would be no good to the architect. And a heart that stopped beating at its own will would be no good to the artist. The creative soul needs the machine, as the living world needs a fixed character, or it could not exist at all. It would be merely an idea. But by a paradox we have to accept, part of this fixed character is the free mind, the creative imagination, in everlasting conflict with facts, including its own machinery, its own tools.

Suggestions

1. "The Artist and the World" addresses itself to two important questions: How does a work of art come into being? and, What is its value? To the second question it offers several interrelated answers: the work of art gives form and therefore permanence to a part of the chaos of reality; it evokes appropriate feelings from the reader or spectator; it thereby endows him with knowledge of the objective world. Point out the passage in which each of these assertions is made and relate the examples (Monet, Housman, etc.) to the proper parts of the argument.

2. Show by examples of your own what kind of thing the artist preserves (¶¶7–11).

3. Explain the analogies between the artist's work and (a) the reading of a newspaper (¶14); (b) construction with Roman bricks (last ¶).

4. What seeming contradiction is referred to in ¶16? How is it resolved—if at all?

5. Paraphrase the sentence beginning "Though the ghost could not exist without the machine . . ." (¶18).

6. Explain: *evanescent, prussic acid, paleolithic art, Homer, elemental characters.*

7. Write an essay on the similarity of views expressed in "The Artist and the World" and † "The Art of Fiction" or † "Reason in the Emotional Life."

LITERATURE AND GROWING UP

ROBERT B. HEILMAN

Some years ago, in a university in which I was then teaching, I had to help score several thousand English placement tests for freshmen each fall. This drudgery had one advantage for the scorer: he might be able to spot some of the better students and snatch them for his own sections —provided, of course, that he knew what the score was, that is, what the score meant. I soon learned that of the seven parts in the test, only two seemed to identify important potentialities of mind (I do not speak of technical proficiency) that made the student especially desirable—namely, the two parts that were to test (1) his vocabulary and (2) his ability to read. You could forget about his spelling, grammar, punctuation, etc.; he might have high scores in these and still have only a mechanical or orderly, but still unalerted, mind. But let him have a good score in vocabulary and reading, and you had a mind that had begun to develop its liveliness, its flexibility, and even its depth. The owner of the mind was already moving toward the mastery of verbal symbols which is essential in a political order where wide communication has to precede and go along with all kinds of group action. But beyond the utilitarian competence, he was also pretty likely to be the better reader of imaginative literature. And for that reason, you, the instructor, instinctively felt him to be a little closer to general maturity than his fellow who had developed less skill or no skill in the comprehension of literature.

To say this much is to pose the general problem of the relation of literary experience to the achievement of adulthood (and, to continue the political reference, to the adulthood without which a democracy cannot survive). I am rather inclined to trust this feeling of the instructor that his good reader had come a little closer to maturity and perhaps to wisdom than the others. A skeptic might argue that all they are doing is sharing a pleasure, and I grant that the sharing of a pleasure may confer upon the pleasure an independent value. But there are pleasures and pleasures; some are corrupt, some are cathartic, some are neutral, and some, I believe we may say, serve to "humanize" those who experience the pleasure. It is my conviction that the pleasures of imaginative reading—the imaginative exercise under the guidance of the extraordinary and yet disciplined imagination which is the mark of the artist—are of that sort: they help bring out a potential humanity, lead the individual toward his full status as a human being—in a word, help him to mature or grow up. By growing up, clearly I mean the realizing of certain qualities or attitudes that are potentially present in man but that have to be cultivated if he is to become truly "human." I think, for instance, of the kind of awareness he has of himself and of human reality generally, and the kind of feelings he has: how closely do the awareness and the feelings correspond to reality?

LITERATURE AS "FEELING KNOWLEDGE"

Into the humanizing or maturing of the human being many influences must go, I need hardly say: many disciplines of the mind and heart. In this essay I speak of only one of these influences: the coming into a certain knowledge of humanity of which, I suggest, the literary imagination is an important instrument. The literary imagination makes it possible to know immediately and concretely, and with even a breath-taking fullness, what it is like to be a human being. It provides an inside, thoroughgoing experience of human reality that I will call a "feeling knowledge"—a term that I shall use frequently. It provides this feeling knowledge in two dimensions, in breadth and in depth. By breadth I mean knowledge of difference—of human beings different from oneself, of different impulses, different feelings, different intellectual and moral attitudes. One cannot respect difference without experiencing it, knowing it with that inside "feeling knowledge" that I believe imaginative literature gives. Knowing difference is one approach to knowledge of the human being and of the human situation as a whole. Too much of the time we pay lip service to difference while really acting as if the only virtue were sameness. We might avoid this inconsistency if we thought of difference not in terms of specific incongruities that are repellent or inaccessible to us but simply as the sum of all the diverse ways in which human nature manifests itself. This literary exploring of difference you may call vicarious experience if you will; the term does not make me feel defensive. Most modes of daily life are inevitably so constricting that any vicariousness may be an enlargement, an extension of the living of which the individual is capable. Granted, it depends on what he's being vicarious about, or who with. If we yield only to the temptation to shed our earthly weight and balloon up to high-cloud adventures with the latest luscious starlet from Hollywood, we may be less likely to grow up than to blow up.

The literary imagination offers its feeling knowledge of humanity also in depth. Here I use *depth* to mean the additional reality that lies beneath the surface of an action, the double motive, the conflict of purposes, the clash of different values. ("Depth psychology" offers one kind of formal exploration of realities always present in literature.) Othello wants to indulge his revengeful violence against Desdemona, but he also wants to feel that he is acting justly, like a court. Cordelia proudly refuses to compete with her sisters in a verbal grab for Lear's royal estates, but by this act of honorable pride she gives the game up to her calculating sisters and makes possible dreadful suffering and many deaths. Oedipus the King wants to detect the hidden crime, but he also wants to retain intact his pride in his intelligence and his sense of personal integrity and royal power. Conrad's Lord Jim wants to act nobly and gloriously, but his very dream of heroism is undermined by his instinct for self-preservation. George Eliot's heroes—Tom Tulliver and Adam Bede—want to be good men, but in their pursuit of the good they can become hard and overbearing. Robert Penn Warren's heroes act in the name of an ideal and yet find their actions contaminated.

The human being to whom imaginative reading gives a feeling for and a knowledge of such duality in motive and experience is on the road to that awareness of human reality which is one of the ways of fulfilling his own humanness. For it is not mature, and it may even be anti-human, to know human beings only in terms of a very simple black-and-white view of their moving impulses and of their desire and fulfillment. The more simply I can think of human truth, the easier it is to drop people into handy compartments, to make them conform to rules that suit these compartments, and above all things to deceive myself about what I am up to, about the purity of my own motives. I am suggesting, really, that the sense of human complication which is one gift from literary experience is an approach to self-knowledge, to seeing oneself in perspective, to recognizing one's doubleness of motive without falling into the opposite extreme of regarding all appearances of good as contemptible self-deceptions. Even a young person, it seems to me, cannot work through such self-deceptions as those of Macbeth without having a door opened, if ever so narrowly, on his own share in the self-deceptiveness which is in the human character. The reader of literature must say, *not* "There, but for the grace of God, go I," but instead, "There, by the grace of the artist, go I."

Gaining perspective on oneself is, alas, not quite so easy as saying "Know thyself" to someone else, and it would be no service to literature to intimate that it will move in quickly to solve what has long remained almost insoluble. Such a floral tribute, such a rhapsody can do no good. For the quest of perspective or maturity, we must keep clear, has to buck a number of powerful forces. First, there is a dangerous concept of the human being that has a large but not fully perceived influence in American life. Second, there is a decided disinclination to self-knowledge which knows no national boundaries. Third, there is an equally extensive weakness for certain self-protective patterns of feeling that fog up the perspective. And finally, there are certain questionable ideas about the nature of a democratic order. I will look at all of these, but most fully at the third.

THE MATURER OF HUMANITY

Take the young man I had in Freshman English last fall who wrote that he was going to get ahead in life by, as he put it, "selling himself." He had so little perspective on himself that he did not know that he was talking a dangerous slave language, that is, reducing himself to a non-human commodity that could be moulded into whatever the market would buy, nor was he willing to be persuaded that this was true. He was strongly under the influence of that anti-human element in our culture which wants to view man merely as an economic unit. That element is therefore bound, though perhaps unknowingly, to oppose the kinds of imaginative activity which will enable the individual to see himself in perspective and know that he is taking the part of a slave. In this way, an American concept of the human being blocks the road to perspective.

Second, the young man's road was blocked by his share in that human tendency—we all share in it—to fight off self-knowledge. Most of us think the ten commandments are needed only by the sad sack next door and make every effort we can to remain blind to our own deft ways of managing uncommandmentlike conduct. Here, of course, I can discuss self-ignorance only in terms of its relation to literary experience. For my young man, literary experience meant only contact with popular literary and art forms, where human conduct is normally so stereotyped, so fitted to naive expectations, that its effect is to deepen and confirm ignorance of oneself. I wish not to give out with one more blast against commercial fiction and movies but to note factually the obscurantist quality of art in which we always identify ourselves with an obvious good and the good always wins. In that realm there are no ironies of character, no disconcerting depths; the hero suffers no inner surprises and no real disasters. In popular art, Oedipus is secure, all of a piece, unchallenged in his superb self-confidence; he unfolds the crime, roots out the plague, and finds wrongdoing only in others. In this pulp-slick-and-vistavision view of life we are kept cozily young and ignorant forever, the folds of the never-changing story pattern insulating us against the shock of bumping unexpectedly into any human reality.

In fact, one of the wonderful ironies of our culture is that on the one hand we proliferate an enormous and unprecedented popular art which is founded on the individual's passion to remain ignorant of the facts of psychic and moral life; while on the other hand we proliferate an enormous and unprecedented family of professions supposed to supply us with self-knowledge—vocational counseling, marriage counseling, personality testing, aptitude testing, psychological consulting and advising, and the vast brotherhood of psychiatric activities, from mental-health seminars to psychiatric social work to psychiatry for all income groups.

On the one hand our technology encourages mass habits of self-disguise; on the other we strain our resources to create habits of self-inspection.

Besides bucking the economic view of man in America and the general human addiction to self-ignorance, the quest of perspective through imaginative literature runs into a third form of opposition (on which I shall spend most of my time)—namely, the fact that we all want to go on not only *thinking* but also *feeling* in the same ways we have always felt. Feeling is habit-forming, and in art this leads to second-rate literature, by which I mean the literature of habit, printed dope sold across the counter at any drugstore. You remember W. H. Auden's distinction. Second-rate literature, he insists, makes the reader say, "That's just the way I always felt." But first-rate literature makes him say, "Until now, I never knew how I felt. Thanks to this experience, I shall never feel the same way again." To learn to have, and to live with, new feelings, puzzling feelings, even disturbing feelings, is another avenue to maturity.

Let us explore further the relation between literary experience and the realm of feeling. I suggest that without the correctives supplied by good artists, even our so-called "good feelings" can get out of line. To make this point, let me pick up my basic phrase, "feeling knowledge." By this I mean the insight that is possessed at once through the mind that discerns the general or formulatable truth, and through the emotions that accompany and that in a sense make possible our entry into and our participation in the specific human actions that literature presents. This full knowledge falls between the general formulae of organized knowledge and the particular masses of unorganized experience, and it draws something from both of these at once. Insofar as it has an intellectual aspect, we might think of it as "philosophical"; insofar as it is not intellectual or propositional, we may say that we possess it through "sympathy" and "understanding." Now though both of these words imply a kind of knowing that is essential to maturing, the trouble is that both sympathy and understanding can fail to jell and can become simply emotional self-indulgence. We can get a crying jag from, or get blind drunk on, feeling that is not properly aged. I can think of three forms of sympathy which, instead of being a wisely compassionate intuition of what humanity is, degenerate into nothing but a pleasurable exercising of our simplest emotional machinery. One of these is to "understand" the cause or source of a human action so thoroughly that we forget the quality of the act; we know so well why poor Otto murdered his wife that we forget that he murdered her. The opposite, but equally popular, form of sentimentality is self-indulgence in outrage and indignation; everywhere we see wrongs that we demand, righteously and angrily, to have put down. *We* always feel rightly; those *others,* wrongly. As a character says in Christopher Fry's *The Dark Is Light Enough,* "Any side can accuse the other/And feel virtuous without the hardships of virtue." What an admirable definition of this kind of sentimentality—"feel virtuous without the hardships of virtue." It is the moral trap on the course of every reformer, especially the reformer who cries out loudly against evils a long way from home. The third form of sentimental sympathy lies in the quick material charity which conceals a deep self-satisfaction; in the happy handout paid for by gratitude; in the tear-washed response to the brother-can-you-spare-a-dime appeal. Any charitableness, I acknowledge, may be the key to moral growth; but conduct with a charitable form, the easy giving of *things,* may be without adult sympathy, may be condescension sugarcoated with a tip, may be the front for a warm rush of self-congratulatory feeling, rather than the interplay of discrimination and emotional response which is at the heart of mature understanding.

A while back we saw that popular literature, considered in relation to knowledge, is a powerful strengthener of self-ignorance. Now, considered in relation to feeling, popular literature simply serves to make us sure that we love and hate and feel virtuous according to conventional rules that ignore the complexity of life. But literature of quality, I believe, ministers to sympathy and understanding without making them too easy and without getting sloppy about it. It engages sympathy, but keeps the object of sympathy in full perspective. It elicits at once warmth of feeling and coolness of judgment. It does not merely set you afloat on a wash of feeling, which is the way of sentimentality, or set you up high and dry on the judgment seat of principle, which is the way of lecture and homily. It draws you in but it holds you out; even while you are empathically engaged, you remain a contemplative onlooker.

Take the central action of *Pride and Prejudice,* the clash and the love affair of Elizabeth Bennet and Darcy. Surely every reader is drawn into an immediate sympathy with Elizabeth the heroine; yet Jane Austen does not permit this sympathy to become sentimental by being no more than a gush of feeling for a person who is right but wronged. The reader is compelled to recognize that Elizabeth is also wrong and has to be righted. The very warmth of her family loyalty leads her into misconceptions, unfairness, injustice, and, above all, moral complacency. To understand her fully is to have an experience in the training of human feeling that should make for adulthood. Darcy also contributes importantly to this training, for the portrait of him compels the reader to go beyond the rather immature pleasure of hating snobbery (most of us resent only the snobbery of others, but cling devotedly to our own in the conviction that it is our critical acuteness in action) and to take into account also his ability to see both others and himself sharply. What we feel through him, even before we place it intellectually, is the double direction which pride can take in the human being—becoming, on the one hand, snobbery and arrogance, and, on the other, sense of responsibility. If with

Elizabeth we begin with what we might call simple sympathy, and find this made more mature by the judgment of her which we must make, with Darcy we start as distant, unfriendly judge, but find our simple judgment made more mature by the understanding sympathy exacted of us by his emerging moral quality. In this respect how nicely he is contrasted with Elizabeth's father, the sharp-tongued Mr. Bennet, whose ironic observations at the expense of his not very bright family we invariably join with in enthusiastic sympathy. But then we are forced into a revision of feeling. For we recognize that his delightful irony is made possible by his distance from his family, and that it is this very distance which under the stress of a practical crisis takes the form of moral irresponsibility.

What looks in some ways like a very straightforward story, I am trying to say, is a subtle trainer of feelings away from sentimental self-indulgence—simple love and hate—toward an emotional grasp of human reality. This discipline of feeling, if I may so call it, is managed in a different way by Shakespeare's treatment of Falstaff. If you look at Falstaff only in the light of principle, you are pretty likely to condemn him as a lying and brazen phony, as critics have done. If you regard him only with sympathetic feeling, you are pretty likely to become totally immersed in his humor and vitality, as other critics have done. But Shakespeare does not permit a careful reader the comfort of either of these simple and limited attitudes. On the contrary, I believe, he compels us to be joyfully at one with Falstaff, and at the same time to reject him. Unless one were a pedantic moralizer, it would be impossible not to feel the contagion of that exuberant, witty, and zestful personality; and unless one were sentimentally unbalanced (which is more frequent than being mentally unbalanced, and much more dangerous, because more likely to be taken for a virtue), it would be equally impossible not to identify his ethical carelessness and his scandalous irresponsibility. To come to grips with that full personality made up of coexistent forces that drive us to contradictory responses is to be inducted into some understanding of humanity, or at least into the exploration of its perennial problems. But surely it brings one into a sharper awareness of himself, of the Falstaffian in himself: of all that laughing, juicy energy, tricky and yet animal (that is, both buoyant and cynical), that has as yet found no guidance but that of immediate self-interest; in a word, of the core of that youthfulness which is a good some of the time, some of which is a good all of the time, but which, as a total recipe for existence, must find some leavening or be set aside for more durable forms of the human confrontation of life. To place Falstaff should be a step in growing up.

What I have been trying to do, really, is to set down as precisely as I can what I think literature ought to be doing for those who read it.

I can't prove that literature works as a ripener of knowledge and feeling; above all, I can never prove that any single work has such and such an effect. If literature is, as I believe, a maturer of humanity, that value is the sum of a continuous experiencing of books. The more that experiencing goes on, the more it should contribute to the flexible but penetrating awareness of the human situation, sometimes gay, sometimes grave, that we call wisdom.

THE ELEMENT OF FAITH

It is clear that I have not been stating demonstrable propositions. I have rather been talking about a kind of faith. I suggest that, in whatever role one comes to literature, he has to come with a kind of faith. My own may not be the ultimate one. Others may find a deeper one. But one thing I am sure of: a reader with the wrong kind of faith will miss the boat entirely.

If he disbelieves or is apologetic, he is obviously lost. If he secretly thinks that literature isn't quite "real" or up-to-date or practical, he is lost. Or he may have positive beliefs that don't go deep enough. If he thinks that literature is simply a direct ally of good citizenship or good behavior generally, he is lost. If he thinks of it as a dainty dish to come only at the end of a solid meal of a more fundamental nourishment, he is lost. He is lost, too, if he thinks of it as the specific vitamin that produces highbrows, as the caviar of artists and other special souls, as the Waikiki Beach of those who don't have plane fare, or as the costume jewelry that goes with what the culturally well-dressed person wears. And he is lost if he thinks that the only contemporary literature is being written in the middle of the twentieth century; this provincialism of time is worse than the pedantry that values only the past. The cult of the present, of being up-to-date, is the plausible and often seductive false front of the very thin philosophical idea that nothing is permanently true and that all the seeker after truth can ever do is to hang on to the popular fashion of thought at any given moment.

Behind all the specific faiths that the reader needs lies a basic creed that will help protect him against most misconceptions that he may fall into. He needs to believe in human constants which reappear, no matter what their challenging diversity of dress, in all periods. This very diversity of dress, though it may in some ways hamper new readers, may also help them: the surface unfamiliarity may help reduce the exclusively emotional involvement that can make the literary experience only a state of heightened excitement, make it all feeling and no knowledge. The more mature the work, the more contemporary it is, or at least the more capable of being made contemporary. The problem is to find the contemporariness, that is, the human constants that lie beneath all the different forms, styles, and idioms. I have no doubt that new readers, despite youth and inexperience, are capable of responding to the images of themselves and their kind—to their differences and their new depths —as they are refracted in the multiple mirrors of literary artists.

How does one get people, especially young people, to look into these mirrors in the first place? The problem is a tough one, but we can never escape a commitment to try to solve it. For one thing, I admit that I think we are lost if we surrender unconditionally to the popular "doctrine of interest," which says in effect that we can work only through whatever the boy is already interested in doing or reading, be this the principles of fishing or the cure of the carburetor. But it is no further from no reading to good reading than it is from, say, flies and rods to Caroline Gordon's *Aleck Maury, Sportsman,* or from souped-up motors to the sharp-minded chauffeur in Shaw's *Man and Superman.* The idea that knowledge follows interest is a scandalous half-truth; I suggest that it is a better-than-half-truth that *interest follows knowledge,* that what you are interested in is what you know something about. If a youngster knows very little about anything but sports and hotrods and hence is interested in little of the large subjects in which he is capable of being interested and in which grown-up human beings have to be interested— if such a boy is to be encouraged to announce what he isn't interested in and to believe that what he isn't interested in is a good guide to what he shan't study, the game is up. What's more, it is morally questionable to let an ignoramus think that the lack of interest which results from ignorance justifies an infinite prolongation of the ignorance. Interest isn't, like hunger or sex, instinctive; it is created by man's increasing contact with the world around him. It is a current generated by the friction of experience, and that friction needn't be a lucky accident or something that we hope will just happen some time. It can be induced and ought to be induced; i.e., there are things that people should be, and must be, interested in. We have to bring literary experience to the youngsters, and I think we can believe that for most of those with normal human equipment, the contact with what they need to be interested in will generate a workable modicum of interest.

This is the *push* method. Besides this, there is a *pull* or suction method. It is said that when the father of Montaigne, the essayist, wanted to encourage his son to read the Latin poets, he told the young man that he could have free rein in the library—except for those books on the top shelves that were not suitable for a boy of his age to read. This was the Latin poetry section of the library, and under this stimulating pro-hibition, Montaigne put himself through a good course in classical verse, and not in translation, either. Could we make some use of the forbidden-fruit principle, leading children into temptation to deliver them from the evil of ignorance? I suppose our puritanism would not countenance it, for we like to take our prohibitions literally and not, in the manner of playful maidens, as metaphors for invitation. Yet the Montaigne legend might stimulate a pedagogical imagination to uncover new ways to corrupt the ignorant with the vice of learning.

If you lead the colt to water but can't make him drink, you can try another trick: you can surround the poor animal with water troughs and wait for him to get thirsty. You may of course be stuck with a camel in horse's clothing, but this won't happen every time you try this trough medicine. My wife and I have found that in encouraging our son to read we get some results by just having books lying around rather conspicuously. Though he is perhaps inclined more to good fellowship than to good scholarship, he does pick up books and read them—very frequently the books we ourselves are reading. Can institutions work it this way—having books lying around invitingly, temptingly, virtually tripping the customers up, teasing them to an exercise of freedom? I don't know. But I do know that the tempting freedom has to be real, not too much padded with protection and uplift. Risk is necessary to let the readers get the actual feel of life.

Some time ago we found our teenaged son picking up and reading Saul Bellow's rather pungent picaresque novel, *The Adventures of Augie March*. When our boy proposed writing a report on it, his teacher said (at least, so our boy reported), "All right, if that's the kind of book your parents want you to read." Well, I thought, it isn't that I positively want him to read a book with a fair peppering of naughty scenes, but that I am glad to have him read something in which there is some real zest of life instead of stereotyped romance and a bargain-counter optimism. In fact, I'd go further and say that if he is going to take a literary plunge into sex before the ideal age (whatever the ideal age is), he better do it in the words of someone who can write, as Bellow can, and who can write about other things too, as Bellow can, instead of in the tired words of dead-end artists who compose erotic masterpieces for undercover distribution in the men's room only. It is not only a little knowledge which is a dangerous thing; all knowledge is a dangerous thing. At any time it may lead to disgust or shock or cynicism or revolt or the illusion of knowing more than one does or the trying vanity of the precocious brat who wears his reading list like a football letter or a diamond ring or a purple heart. But knowing too much too soon is a lesser evil than knowing practically nothing too long.

LITERATURE AND DEMOCRACY

I will conclude by making one reference to the role of literature in our society. I closed my first section by suggesting that there are four obstacles in the way of the humanizing experience of literature. The fourth of these, which I now come to, I called "certain questionable ideas about the nature of a democratic order." I will start this by stating my belief that the kind of literary experience of which I have spoken seems to me to be necessary to nourish the democratic imagination. Though democracy, that abused word, is sometimes used to imply a mode of life in which the commonplace is both expectable and gratifying and in which the very idea of standards of distinction seems pretentious, democracy, it seems to me, cannot claim a genealogically sound kinship to reality unless it is based on the supposition that a majority of men are capable of learning the kind of discrimination that will tend to make the good and the true prevail.

It does not matter very much whether many people simply get what they want instead of just one person getting it (monarchy) or a few persons (oligarchy) or a special class (aristocracy); it does not matter, that is, if "what they want" is regarded as the sole end, without reference to the quality of what they want; the chief justification of democracy would seem to be that the majority are more likely than one, or a few, or a special class, to want the right thing—the thing that preserves and strengthens rather than the immediate and transitory gratification. This is really a fascinating and daring vision—the vision of the multitude as the true abiding-place of socially and morally creative discrimination. And after this preliminary definition, we can ask: what is the relation of the study of literature to this vision? Or, as it is sometimes put, what reading is suitable for a democracy? The answer is this, I think: that any literature is good for a democracy which contributes in any way to powers of discrimination—to a perception of the realities of human action, of the impulses and values that human action embodies, of the kind of individual and group choices that diminish and destroy or that create and conserve. That is the business of reading in a democracy—to minister to the powers of human discrimination.

This is simply to say that any mature literature which is suitable for any mature or potentially mature audience is suitable, and desirable, for a democracy. Unless I am wrong, this needs emphasis. For I have the uncomfortable feeling, from what I pick out of the air, that it is sometimes thought that we should be resigned to democracy as the political and social form of an extremely limited humanity, and that therefore the proper reading for a democracy is something "practical" (whatever that means), or typical, or local, or familiar in raw material, or political-propagandist, or not too hard, or not too old, or not too "pessimistic" (whatever that means), and above all things, not concerned with a monarchic or aristocratic order where life is artificial and rarefied and has no relation to the solid and earthly realities that we sturdy democratists live by. I must say that I think that to be not only nonsense, but dangerous nonsense. If seriously applied, it would cut from our reading not only most of the profound works of world literature, but innumerable works with the difference in perspective necessary to modify our own complacency and provincialism.

I find myself particularly shocked, for instance, by some of the attitudes to Henry James; indeed, even in a graduate seminar on James that I happen to know about, a number of participants seemed to feel that James study was perhaps an acceptable academic exercise but really had no tangible relation to the basic realities of our own day—as if James's insistent preoccupation with states of consciousness, with conscience, with moral perception and reality could ever be unrelated to any kind of mature human existence. We have a dangerous totalitarianism of our own: it is the totalitarianism of subsistence (it may be called "subsistentialism"), by which the totality of life consists of making a living and then of making more of a living, but never of making the most of living. But the totality of life goes beyond making a living and includes other things which we will ignore at our peril. If we were seeking an insight into the relation between the personal and the political ideal, between individual passion and organizational sanction, I do not know to what better source of feeling knowledge we could go than James's *The Princess Casamassima;* or if we were concerned with the relation between the personal and the social ideal, between the instinctive and the dogmatic, than *The Bostonians;* or if our problem were the modes of good and evil, than *The Turn of the Screw.*

Briefly, I think we need to escape from a popularized form of thought, according to which all life is felt chiefly as a perpetual negation: as a battle against certain entrenched and repressive political, social, and philosophic interests. This rasping negativism of attitude is widespread enough so that, in one form or another, one is constantly running into it. It is ultimately responsible, I think, for misconceptions of James as well as for other untenable literary ideas, such as the idea that there is no relevance to our own lives in literature written in other political and social frameworks and therefore not at all concerned with subsistence, private enterprise, and the two-party system. But the time of writing and the external structure of life are of little importance; what counts is the insight into human reality. Of that we can never get enough, especially when our problem is not to break down but to build up. By its nature, literature should be one of the allies of the human imagination in its constructive and reconstructive roles. If it can contribute to the growing up of the individual, perhaps it can do the same for a society. That result will not be amiss.

Suggestions

1. Account for the title and the speaker's belief in the necessity of "feeling knowledge": that is, formulate the thesis of "Literature and Growing Up."

2. Summarize four hindrances to self-knowledge (¶6). To which of these are modern Americans peculiarly liable?

3. Explain the "obscurantist quality" that the speaker detects in popular literature (¶8) and the irony of modern culture to which he then refers. Why might this irony disappear if the difference between first-rate and second-rate literature (¶10) were better understood?

4. Show that feeling knowledge is both philosophical and emotional, and summarize the dangers of sentimental sympathy (¶11).

5. Account for the subheading "The Element of Faith" (before ¶16). Besides a lack of faith, what wrong faiths can prove disastrous to a student of literature?

6. Explain the difference between the "push" and "pull" methods of inducing interest in literature (¶¶19–20).

7. In the speaker's view, what is the chief justification of democracy (¶24)? Relate this view to his faith in the value of literature.

8. Explain: *potentialities, utilitarian, cathartic, incongruities, vicarious, homily, "subsistentialism."*

9. Write an essay comparing the beliefs about the value of literature expressed in † "Why Do We Teach Poetry?", † "The Artist and the World," and "Literature and Growing Up."

4

Forms of Literature

⚜

T H E   C L A S S I C   E S S A Y

☤

The French verb meaning "to test, try out" is *essayer,* and the form of writing known as the essay was invented and baptized by a Frenchman, Michel de Montaigne, between 1571 and 1580. Montaigne's *Essais* were, he said, tests of his judgment, which he would try out even on topics that he did not understand. Most of the characteristics of what came to be called the informal essay appear in Montaigne's. Typically, they begin with an anecdote which leads on to reflections about human experience. The allusions and quotations, especially classical ones, with which they are studded seem to say that men change little from one era to the next. The style is colloquial, often humorous, paradoxical, and, above all, digressive; life, thought Montaigne, was too serious to be taken seriously. Many of his choices of topics are whimsical, even trivial, yet his tendency is always discreetly didactic. Like most essayists since, he believed that the lessons of his own experience would fit other people's; his theme is the likenesses and differences of human beings. "If we were not alike," he observed, "we could not tell man from beast; if we were not different, we could not tell one man from another."

The *Essais* were soon to cross over to England and become naturalized there in the translation of John Florio (1603). Meanwhile they had doubtless suggested to Francis Bacon a name for his own published reflections on human life and affairs: *Essays or Counsels Civil and Moral,* which began appearing in 1597. Bacon's essays lack the charm that Montaigne's derive from their wealth of anecdote, colloquial style, and whimsical humor. Yet Bacon excels in conciseness and organization; his topics are weightier, his "counsels" more profound.

Although Montaigne and Bacon between them marked out the high road for the essay, other developments were soon to follow. Sometimes Montaigne's illustrative anecdote would grow into a fully rounded narrative—but these essays point forward to the short story. In others, a single character would predominate—but these foreshadow the "portrait" or "profile." Other essayists were to take a poem or a point of style as their topics—but critical essays are somewhat technical, appealing to a specialized interest. And even more strongly does this description apply to Locke's *Essay Concerning the Human Understanding,* a two-volume treatise of epistemology. As to essays in verse, only those of Pope have escaped mortality. In the hands of its most characteristic practitioners—Cowley, Addison and Steele, Johnson and Goldsmith, Lamb and Hazlitt, Emerson and Arnold—the essay has been fundamentally what Montaigne and Bacon made it: a short prose work, adorned with anecdotes and allusions, in which the essayist tries out his judgment on general questions of human nature and conduct.

OF IDLENESS

(1580)

MICHEL DE MONTAIGNE ---⚶{ *Translations of Montaigne's essays © 1960 by M. W. Daniel.*

Just as we see that neglected fields, if they are rich and fertile, bring forth a hundred thousand kinds of wild, useless grasses, and that to keep them in order it is necessary to plow and sow them regularly for our use; and as we see that women by themselves produce mere shapeless lumps of flesh,[1] for if they are to have proper, natural offspring they must receive another's seed: so is it with our minds. When not occupied on a definite subject that bridles and directs them, they run about in unruly fashion, this way and that, in the cloudy pasture of the imagination.

> As when from water in an urn of bronze
> A flickering light, shot from the imaged sun
> Or moon's reflection, gleams from side to side,
> Then rises in the air and strikes at last
> The laquearia of the highest roof.
> [Vergil, *Aeneid* 8, 22]

In this restless condition there is no fancy too foolish for minds to conceive.

> Like sick men's dreams, creating empty shapes.
> [Horace, *Art of Poetry* 7]

The mind with no established goal gets lost, for to be in every place, as is said, is to be in no place.

> He who lives everywhere, Maximus, lives nowhere.
> [Martial, *Epigrams* 7, 73]

When I recently retired to my own house, having decided as firmly as I could to avoid everything except spending what little was left of my life in relaxation and solitude, I imagined I could do my mind no greater favor than to let it commune with itself in total idleness, to

---

[1] A superstition found in Plutarch, *Advice on Marriage* 48.

pause and settle down—which I hoped it could do more easily from then on, as it had become more poised and mature. But I find—

> Idleness always leads to varying thoughts—
> [Lucan, *Pharsalia* 4, 704]

that on the contrary, like a runaway horse it is more taken up with itself than it ever was with others, and gives birth to so many fantastic monsters, one after the other, without method, without design, that in order to study their strangeness and absurdity at my leisure I have begun putting them down on paper, hoping eventually to make my mind ashamed of itself.

OF SMELLS

(1580)

It is said of some people, such as Alexander the Great, that by some extraordinarily rare quirk for which Plutarch and others sought the explanation, their sweat gave off an agreeable odor. But the body's normal tendency is just the opposite, and the best possible condition for it is not to smell at all. The sweetness of even the purest breath can have no greater merit than being free of offensive odor, like the breath of perfectly healthy children. That is why, says Plautus,

> The woman who smells not smells good:
> [*Mostellaria* I, 3]

the most perfect smell for a woman is not to smell at all, as her behavior is said to smell best when it is unnoticed and noiseless. And as for the fine foreign scents, it is right to look with suspicion on those who use them and to assume that they are used to cover up some natural defect of these people. Hence the witticism of the ancient poets, "To smell good is to stink"—

> You laugh, Coracinus, at our not smelling.
> But rather than smell good I would not smell.
> [Martial, *Epigrams* 6, 55]

And in another place,

> Posthumus, the man who smells always good smells bad.
>   [*Ibid.* 2, 12]

Nevertheless, I love to be surrounded with good smells, and beyond measure I hate bad ones, which I detect from farther away than anybody else does:

> For, Polypus, I have a keener flair
> For the rank goat-smell of an armpit's hair
> Than hounds that track the wild boar to his lair.
>   [Horace, *Epodes* 12, 4]

The simplest, most natural smells are to me the most agreeable ones. And this applies mainly to ladies. The Scythian women, in the most complete barbarism, powder and cake their entire bodies and faces after bathing with an aromatic drug that is native to their soil; and having removed this coating they come to their men smooth and perfumed.

No matter what the smell, it is amazing how it fastens itself to me and how inclined my skin is to soak it up. It is a mistake to complain that nature has given man no means of carrying smells to his nose; they carry themselves. But for me in particular this work is done by my mustache, which is a bushy one. If I bring my gloves or my handkerchief near it the odor stays in it throughout the day. It reveals where I have been. The close kisses of youth—savory, greedy, sticky—used to linger in it for hours afterward. And yet I find I am not very susceptible to epidemic diseases, which are spread at social gatherings and spring from the contagion of the air; and I have escaped those of my lifetime, of which several varieties have occurred in our cities and armies. Books tell us that Socrates alone of all men, though he never left Athens during outbreaks of the plague that so often tormented that city, was never the worse for it.

I think doctors could get more use out of smells than they do, for I have often observed that they affect me and influence my spirits according to their properties. This makes me agree with the theory that the introduction of incense and perfumes into churches, an ancient practice found among all nations and religions, was aimed at delighting us, at alerting and purifying our faculties, the better to prepare us for contemplation.

I wish that, in order to have estimated it, I might have participated in the art of those cooks who know how to mingle foreign odors with the flavor of food—an art particularly noticed among the servants of that King of Tunis who in our time landed at Naples for a conference with the Emperor Charles. They served him dishes so generously stuffed with aromatic drugs that a peacock and two pheasants came to a hundred ducats, prepared by their method; and when carved, these filled not only the dining-hall but every room in the palace and even the houses nearby with an agreeable fragrance that did not fade away for some time.

My chief concern in choosing lodgings is to avoid bad-smelling, heavy air. Those fine cities, Venice and Paris, forfeit some of the regard I have for them, because of their sour smells—the one of its swamps, the other of its mud.

HOW THE MIND ENTANGLES ITSELF

(1580)

It is entertaining to imagine a mind exactly poised between two desires that are equally strong. There is no doubt but what it will never make a choice, for choosing and preferring demand unequal value; and if anyone with an equal craving for food and drink were put between the bottle and the ham he would doubtless die of thirst and hunger. The Stoic philosophers solve the problem of where the choice between two identical things originates, and how it happens that from a large number of coins, though all alike and affording no reason for our preference, we take one instead of another, by saying that this movement of ours is extraordinary and irregular, coming to us from an outside, accidental, indeterminate impulse.

It is more likely, I think, that we meet nothing in which there is not some difference, however slight, and that there is always something which appeals more to the sight or else to the touch, though we may not notice it. Similarly, if we imagine a string of equal strength throughout, it is impossible by every impossibility that it should break—for where would it begin to give? And for it to break all over, at the same time, is not in nature.

If along with this we consider those geometrical theorems which prove conclusively that a thing contained may be bigger than the container, and the center of a circle as big as the circumference, and which show two lines forever approaching one another but never meeting; and the philosopher's stone; and squaring the circle—if we consider all these propositions in which reasoning and experience conflict, we may perhaps find support for this daring statement of Pliny's: "Nothing is certain except uncertainty, and nothing more pitiful or conceited than man." [1]

Suggestions

1. Summarize the account of the origin of the essay given in "Of Idleness." Do you find in it specimens of "strangeness and absurdity"? Compare "Of Smells" and "How the Mind Entangles Itself" in this respect, citing some examples of what "Of Idleness" calls "fantastic monsters."

2. "Of Smells" is not a perfectly unified essay, no doubt because parts of it were written at different times. Point out some inconsistencies in it.

3. Decide whether the quotation from Pliny makes a reasonable conclusion for "How the Mind Entangles Itself."

4. Identify: Alexander the Great, Plutarch, Socrates, the Stoic philosophers, the philosopher's stone.

5. Write a characterization of Montaigne based on these three essays.

OF STUDIES

(1597)

FRANCIS BACON, LORD VERULAM

Studies serve for delight, for ornament, and for ability. Their chief use for delight is in privateness and retiring; for ornament, is in discourse; and for ability, is in the judgment and disposition of business. For expert men can execute, and perhaps judge of particulars, one by one; but the general counsels, and the plots and marshalling of affairs come best from those that are learned. To spend too much time in studies is sloth; to use them too much for ornament is affectation; to make judgment wholly by their rules is the humor of a scholar. They perfect nature, and are perfected by experience: for natural abilities are like natural plants, that need pruning by study; and studies themselves do give forth directions too much at large, except they be bounded in by experience.

---

[1] *Natural History* 2, 7. The Latin sentence was inscribed on the ceiling of Montaigne's library.

Crafty men contemn studies, simple men admire them, and wise men use them; for they teach not their own use; but that is a wisdom without them and above them, won by observation. Read not to contradict and confute, nor to believe and take for granted, nor to find talk and discourse, but to weigh and consider. Some books are to be tasted, others to be swallowed, and some few to be chewed and digested; that is, some books are to be read only in parts; others to be read, but not curiously; and some few to be read wholly, and with diligence and attention. Some books also may be read by deputy, and extracts made of them by others; but that would be only in the less important arguments and the meaner sort of books; else distilled books are, like common distilled waters, flashy things. Reading maketh a full man; conference a ready man; and writing an exact man. And, therefore, if a man write little, he had need have a great memory; if he confer little, he had need have a present wit; and if he read little, he had need have much cunning, to seem to know that he doth not. Histories make men wise; poets, witty; the mathematics, subtle; natural philosophy, deep; moral, grave; logic and rhetoric, able to contend. *Abeunt studia in mores* [Studies develop into habits].

Nay, there is no stone or impediment in the wit but may be wrought out by fit studies, like as diseases of the body may have appropriate exercises. Bowling is good for the stone and reins, shooting for the lungs and breast, gentle walking for the stomach, riding for the head, and the like. So if a man's wit be wandering, let him study the mathematics; for in demonstrations, if his wit be called away never so little, he must begin again. If his wit be not apt to distinguish or find difference, let him study the school men; for they are *cymini sectores* [hair-splitters]. If he be not apt to beat over matters, and to call up one thing to prove and illustrate another, let him study the lawyers' cases. So every defect of the mind may have a special receipt.

OF MARRIAGE AND SINGLE LIFE

(1612)

He that hath wife and children hath given hostages to fortune, for they are impediments to great enterprises, either of virtue or mischief. Certainly the best works, and of greatest merit for the public, have proceeded from the unmarried or childless men, which both in affection and means have married and endowed the public. Yet it were great reason that those that have children should have greatest care of future times, unto which they know they must transmit their dearest pledges.

Some there are who, though they lead a single life, yet their thoughts do end with themselves, and account future times impertinences. Nay, there are some other that account wife and children but as bills of charges. Nay more, there are some foolish rich covetous men that take a pride in having no children, because they may be thought so much the richer. For perhaps they have heard some talk, "Such an one is a great rich man," and another except to it, "Yea, but he hath a great charge of children," as if it were an abatement to his riches. But the most ordinary cause of a single life is liberty, especially in certain self-pleasing and humorous minds, which are so sensible of every restraint, as they will go near to think their girdles and garters to be bonds and shackles.

Unmarried men are best friends, best masters, best servants, but not always best subjects, for they are light to run away, and almost all fugitives are of that condition. A single life doth well with churchmen, for charity will hardly water the ground where it must first fill a pool. It is indifferent for judges and magistrates, for if they be facile and corrupt, you shall have a servant five times worse than a wife. For soldiers, I find the generals commonly in their hortatives put men in mind of their wives and children; and I think the despising of marriage amongst the Turks maketh the vulgar soldier more base. Certainly wife and children are a kind of discipline of humanity; and single men, though they be many times more charitable, because their means are less exhaust, yet, on the other side, they are more cruel and hard-hearted (good to make severe inquisitors), because their tenderness is not so oft called upon. Grave natures, led by custom and therefore constant, are commonly loving husbands, as was said of Ulysses, *Vetulam suam praetulit immortalitati* [He preferred his old wife to immortality].

Chaste women are often proud and froward, as presuming upon the merit of their chastity. It is one of the best bonds, both of chastity and obedience, in the wife if she think her husband wise, which she will never do if she find him jealous. Wives are young men's mistresses, companions for middle age, and old men's nurses, so as a man may have a quarrel to marry when he will. But yet he was reputed one of the wise men that made answer to the question when a man should marry: "A young man not yet, an elder man not at all."

It is often seen that bad husbands have very good wives; whether it be that it raiseth the price of their husbands' kindness when it comes, or that the wives take a pride in their patience. But this never fails, if the bad husbands were of their own choosing, against their friends' consent; for then they will be sure to make good their own folly.

OF TRUTH

(1625)

What is truth? said jesting Pilate and would not stay for an answer.[1] Certainly there be that delight in giddiness, and count it a bondage to fix a belief, affecting free-will in thinking as well as in acting. And though the sects of philosophers of that kind be gone, yet there remain certain discoursing wits which are of the same veins, though there be not so much blood in them as was in those of the ancients. But it is not only the difficulty and labor which men take in finding out of truth, nor again, that when it is found it imposeth upon men's thoughts that doth bring lies in favor; but a natural though corrupt love of the lie itself. One of the later schools of the Grecians examineth the matter and is at a stand to think what should be in it, that men should love lies; where neither they make for pleasure, as with poets; nor for advantage, as with the merchant, but for the lie's sake. But I cannot tell: this same truth is a naked and open daylight that doth not show the masks and mummeries and triumphs of the world half so stately and daintily as candlelights. Truth may perhaps come to the price of a pearl, that showeth best by day, but it will not rise to the price of a diamond or carbuncle, that showeth best in varied lights. A mixture of a lie doth ever add pleasure. Doth any man doubt, that if there were taken out of men's minds vain opinions, flattering hopes, false valuations, imaginations as one would, and the like, but it would leave the minds of a number of men poor shrunken things, full of melancholy and indisposition, and unpleasing to themselves? One of the fathers, in great severity, called poesy *vinum daemonum* [devils' wine] because it filleth the imagination, and yet it is but with the shadow of a lie. But it is not the lie that passeth through the mind, but the lie that sinketh in and settleth in it that doth the hurt, such as we spake of before.

But howsoever these things are thus in men's depraved judgments and affections, yet truth, which only doth judge itself, teacheth that the inquiry of truth, which is the love-making or wooing of it, the knowledge of truth, which is the presence of it, and the belief of truth, which is the enjoying of it, is the sovereign good of human nature. The first creature of God, in the works of the days, was the light of the sense; the last was the light of reason; and his Sabbath work ever since is the illumination of his Spirit. First he breathed light upon the face of the matter, or chaos; then he breathed light into the face of man; and still he breatheth and inspireth light into the face of his chosen. The poet

[1] *Gospel of St. John* 18, 38.

that beautified the sect [1] that was otherwise inferior to the rest saith yet excellently well: "It is a pleasure to stand upon the shore and to see ships tossed upon the sea; a pleasure to stand in the window of a castle and to see a battle, and the adventures thereof below; but no pleasure is comparable to the standing upon the vantage ground of truth" (a hill not to be commanded, and where the air is always clear and serene) "and to see the errors, and wanderings, and mists, and tempests, in the vale below": so always that this prospect be with pity, and not with swelling or pride. Certainly it is heaven upon earth to have a man's mind move in charity, rest in providence, and turn upon the poles of truth.

To pass from theological and philosophical truth to the truth of civil business, it will be acknowledged even by those that practise it not, that clear and round dealing is the honor of man's nature, and that mixture of falsehood is like alloy in coin of gold and silver, which may make the metal work the better, but it embaseth it. For these winding and crooked courses are the goings of the serpent, which goeth basely upon the belly and not upon the feet. There is no vice that doth so cover a man with shame as to be found false and perfidious; and therefore Montaigne saith prettily, when he inquired the reason why the word of the lie should be such a disgrace and such an odious charge. Saith he, "If it be well weighed, to say that a man lieth is as much as to say that he is brave towards God and a coward towards men." For a lie faces God and shrinks from man. Surely the wickedness of falsehood and breach of faith cannot possibly be so highly expressed, as in that it shall be the last peal to call the judgments of God upon the generations of men, it being foretold that when Christ cometh "he shall not find faith upon the earth."

Suggestions

1. Summarize the advice about reading given in "Of Studies," citing your own examples of the three kinds of books. Can too much time be spent in study? Point out sentences in the essay that support your answer.

2. Paraphrase these assertions in "Of Marriage and Single Life": "He that hath wife and children hath given hostages to fortune"; "A single life doth well with the churchmen; for charity will hardly water the ground where it must first fill a pool"; "It is often seen that bad husbands have very good wives; whether it be that it raiseth the price of their husband's kindness when it comes; or that the wives take a pride in their patience." Would you suppose their author to have been a bad husband, a good husband, or a bachelor?

3. Define Bacon's attitude toward Pilate. Compare the meaning of *truth* here with its meaning in † "Plagued by the Nature of Truth."

4. Write an essay with the same title as one of Bacon's.

[1] The Epicureans. See Lucretius, *Of the Nature of Things* 2, Proem.

5. Write a comparison of Bacon's character with Montaigne's as their essays reveal them.

WHAT A CHARACTER IS

(1614)

SIR THOMAS OVERBURY

If I must speak the schoolmaster's language, I will confess that character comes from this infinite mood χαράξω, that signifieth to engrave, or make a deep impression. And for that cause, a letter (as A.B.) is called a character.

[They are] those elements which we learn first, leaving a strong seal in our memories.

Character is also taken from an Egyptian hieroglyphic for an impress or short emblem, in little comprehending much.

To square out a character by our English level, it is a picture (real or personal) quaintly drawn, in various colors, all of them heightened by one shadowing.

It is a quick and soft touch of many strings, all shutting up in one musical close; it is wit's descant on any plain song.

AN AMORIST

(1614)

Is a man blasted or planet-strooken and is the dog that leads blind Cupid; when he is at the best his fashion exceeds the worth of his weight. He is never without verses and musk confects, and sighs to the hazard of his buttons. His eyes are all white, either to wear the livery of his mistress' complexion or to keep Cupid from hitting the black. He fights with passion and loseth much of his blood by his weapon; dreams, thence his paleness. His arms are carelessly used, as if their best use was nothing but embracements. He is untrussed, unbuttoned, and ungartered, not out of carelessness, but care; his farthest end being but going to bed. Sometimes he wraps his petition in neatness, but he goeth not alone; for then he makes some other quality moralize his affection, and his trimness is the grace of that grace. Her favor lifts him up as the sun moisture; when he disfavors, unable to hold that happiness, it falls down in tears. His fingers are his orators, and he expresseth much of himself upon some instrument. He answers not, or not to the purpose, and no marvel, for he is not at home. He scotcheth time with dancing with his mistress, taking up of her glove, and wearing her feather; he is confined to her color and dares not pass out of the circuit of her memory. His imagination is a fool, and it goeth in a pied coat of red and white. Shortly he is translated out of a man into folly; his imagination is the glass of lust and himself the traitor to his own discretion.

A GOOD WIFE

(1614)

Is a man's best movable, a scion incorporate with the stock, bringing sweet fruit; one that to her husband is more than a friend, less than a trouble; an equal with him in the yoke. Calamities and troubles she shares alike; nothing pleases her that doth not him. She is relative in all; and he without her but half himself. She is his absent hands, eyes, ears, and mouth; his present and absent all. She frames her nature unto his howsoever: the hyacinth follows not the sun more willingly. Stubbornness and obstinacy are herbs that grow not in her garden. She leaves tattling to the gossips of the town and is more seen than heard. Her household is her charge; her care to that makes her seldom non-resident. Her pride is but to be cleanly and her thrift not to be prodigal. By her discretion she hath children, not wantons; a husband without her is a misery in man's apparel; none but she hath an aged husband, to whom she is both a staff and a chair. To conclude, she is both wise and religious, which makes her all this.

A YOUNG GENTLEMAN OF THE UNIVERSITY

(1628)

Is one that comes there to wear a gown and to say hereafter, he has been at the university. His father sent him thither because he heard there were the best fencing and dancing schools; from these he has his education, from his tutor the oversight. The first element of his knowledge is to be shown the colleges and initiated in a tavern by the way, which hereafter he will learn of himself. The two marks of his seniority is the bare velvet of his gown and his proficiency at tennis, where when he can once play a set, he is a freshman no more. His study has commonly handsome shelves, his books neat silk strings, which he shows to his father's man and is loth to untie or take down for fear of misplacing. Upon foul days for recreation he retires thither and looks over the pretty book his tutor reads to him, which is commonly some short history or a piece of Euphormio [1]; for which his tutor gives him money to spend next day. His main loitering is at the library, where he studies arms and books of honor and turns a gentleman critic in pedigrees. Of all things he endures not to be mistaken for a scholar, and hates a black suit though it be made of satin. His companion is ordinarily some stale fellow that has been notorious for an ingle to gold hatbands,[2] whom he admires at first, afterwards scorns. If he have spirit or wit he may light of better company and may learn some flashes of wit, which may do him knight's service in the country hereafter. But he is now gone to the inns-of-court,[3] where he studies to forget what he learned before, his acquaintance and the fashion.

A PLODDING STUDENT

(1628)

Is a kind of alchymist or persecutor of nature, that would change the dull lead of his brain into finer metal, with success many times as unprosper-

---

[1] Pen-name of John Barclay (1582–1621), who wrote *Argenis* and other novels in Latin.
[2] Crony of aristocratic students.
[3] *I.e.*, to become a lawyer.

ous, or at least not quitting the cost, to wit, of his own oil and candles. He has a strange forced appetite to learning, and to achieve it brings nothing but patience and a body. His study is not great but continual, and consists much in the sitting up till after midnight in a rug-gown and night-cap, to the vanquishing perhaps of some six lines; yet what he has, he has perfect, for he reads it so long to understand it till he gets it without book. He may with much industry make a breach into logic and arrive at some ability in an argument; but for politer studies he dare not skirmish with them, and for poetry accounts it impregnable. His invention is no more than the finding out of his papers and his few gleanings there; and his disposition of them is as just as the bookbinder's, a setting or gluing of them together. He is a great discomforter of young students by telling them what travail it has cost him, and how often his brain turned at philosophy, and makes others fear studying as a cause of duncery. He is a man much given to apothegms, which serve him for wit, and seldom breaks any jest but which belonged to some Lacedæmonian or Roman in Lycosthenes.[1] He is like a dull carrier's horse that will go a whole week together but never out of a foot-pace; and he that sets forth on the Saturday shall overtake him.

A CHILD

(1628)

JOHN EARLE

Is a man in a small letter, yet the best copy of Adam before he tasted of Eve or the apple; and he is happy whose small practice in the world can only write his character. He is nature's fresh picture newly drawn in oil, which time and much handling dims and defaces. His soul is yet a white paper unscribbled with observations of the world, wherewith, at length, it becomes a blurred note-book. He is purely happy, because he knows no evil nor hath made means by sin to be acquainted with misery. He arrives not at the mischief of being wise, nor endures evils to come by foreseeing them. He kisses and loves all and, when the smart of the rod is past, smiles on his beater. Nature and his parents alike dandle him, and tice him on with a bait of sugar to a draught of wormwood. He plays yet, like a young 'prentice the first day, and is not come to his task of melancholy. All the language he speaks yet is tears, and they serve him well enough to express his necessity. His hardest labor is his tongue, as if he were loth to use so deceitful an organ; and he is best company with it when he can but prattle. We laugh at his foolish sports, but his game is our earnest; and his drums, rattles, and hobby-horses but the emblems and mocking of man's business. His father hath writ him as his own little story, wherein he reads those days of his life that he cannot remember and sighs to see what innocence he has outlived. The older he grows, he is a stair lower from God; and, like his first father, much worse in his breeches. He is the Christian's example and the old man's relapse; the one imitates his pureness, and the other falls into his simplicity. Could he put off his body with his little coat, he had got eternity without a burden and exchanged but one heaven for another.

Suggestions

1. Show how "An Amorist" expresses its attitude toward its subject by detailing his appearance, possessions, and actions.

2. Decide whether the speaker's idea of a Good Wife in fact makes her "equal with [her husband] in the yoke."

3. Define the attitude toward the adult world expressed in "A Child," and paraphrase this sentence: "Nature and his parents alike dandle him, and tice him on with a bait of sugar to a draught of wormwood."

4. Explain the irony of the title "A Young Gentleman of the University." How does your conception of this type differ from that of the essay? For which of the Young Gentleman's activities can modern equivalents be readily found?

5. Point out the traits of the Plodding Student that make you sympathize with him, and those that disgust you. Which attitude predominates in the essay?

6. List a number of character-types that you could describe humorously and concretely in essays modeled on those in this book.

7. Drawing your examples from the work of Overbury and Earle, write an essay expanding Overbury's description of what a "character" is.

8. Write an essay comparing the tone of Overbury with that of Earle. Which writer is more caustic?

¹ Pen-name of the German scholar Conrad Wolfhart.

OF OBSCURITY

(1668)

ABRAHAM COWLEY

> *Nam neque divitibus contingunt gaudia solis,*
> *Nec vixit male, qui natus moriensque fefellit.*

> God made not pleasures only for the rich,
> Nor have those men without their share too lived,
> Who both in life and death the world deceived.

This seems a strange sentence thus literally translated, and looks as if it were in vindication of the men of business (for who else can deceive the world?); whereas it is in commendation of those who live and die so obscurely that the world takes no notice of them. This Horace calls deceiving the world, and in another place uses the same phrase,

> *Secretum iter et fallentis semita vitæ.*

> The secret tracks of the deceiving life.

It is very elegant in Latin, but our English word will hardly bear up to that sense; and therefore Mr. Broom translates it very well,

> Or from a life, led as it were by stealth.

Yet we say, in our language, a thing deceives our sight, when it passes before us unperceived, and we may say well enough out of the same author,

> Sometimes with sleep, sometimes with wine we strive,
> The cares of life and troubles to deceive.

But that is not to deceive the world but to deceive ourselves, as Quintilian says, *vitam fallere;* to draw on still and amuse and deceive our life, till it be advanced insensibly to the fatal period and fall into that pit which nature hath prepared for it. The meaning of all this is no more than that most vulgar saying, *Bene qui latuit, bene vixit,* He has lived well who has lain well hidden. Which, if it be a truth, the world (I'll swear) is sufficiently deceived; for my part I think it is and that the pleasantest condition of life is *in incognito*. What a brave privilege is it to be free from all contentions, from all envying or being envied, from receiving and from paying all kind of ceremonies! It is, in my mind, a very delightful pastime for two good and agreeable friends to travel up and down together in places where they are by nobody known nor know anybody. It was the case of Æneas and his Achates when they walked invisibly about the fields and streets of Carthage; Venus herself

> A veil of thickened air around them cast,
> That none might know or see them as they passed.

The common story of Demosthenes' confession that he had taken great pleasure in hearing of a tanker-woman [water-carrier] say as he passed, "This is that Demosthenes," is wonderful ridiculous from so solid an orator. I myself have often met with that temptation to vanity (if it were any), but am so far from finding it any pleasure that it only makes me run faster from the place, till I get, as it were, out of sight-shot. Democritus relates, and in such a manner as if he gloried in the good fortune and commodity [advantage] of it, that when he came to Athens nobody there did so much as take notice of him; and Epicurus lived there very well, that is, lay hid many years in his gardens, so famous since that time, with his friend Metrodorus; after whose death, making in one of his letters a kind commemoration of the happiness which they two had enjoyed together, he adds at last that he thought it no disparagement to those great felicities of their life that in the midst of the most talked-of and talking country in the world, they had lived so long, not only without fame, but almost without being heard of. And yet within a very few years afterward there were no two names of men more known or more generally celebrated. If we engage into a large acquaintance and various familiarities, we set open our gates to the invaders of most of our time; we expose our life to a quotidian ague of frigid impertinencies, which would make a wise man tremble to think of. Now, as for being known much by sight and pointed at, I cannot comprehend the honor that lies in that. Whatsoever it be, every mountebank has it more than the best doctor, and the hangman more than the lord chief justice of a city. Every creature has it both of nature and art, if it be any ways extraordinary. It was as often said, "This is that Bucephalus," or, "This is that Incitatus,"[1] when they were led prancing through the streets, as "This is that Alexander" or "This is that Domitian"; and truly, for the latter, I take Incitatus to have been a much more honorable beast than his master, and more deserving the consulship than he the empire. I love and commend a true good fame because it is the shadow of virtue, not that it doth any good to the body which it accompanies, but 'tis an

[1] Favorite horses of Alexander the Great and the Emperor Caligula (not Domitian). Caligula is said to have wished to make Incitatus a consul.

efficacious shadow and, like that of St. Peter, cures the diseases of others. The best kind of glory, no doubt, is that which is reflected from honesty, such as was the glory of Cato and Aristides; but it was harmful to them both and is seldom beneficial to any man whilst he lives; what it is to him after his death I cannot say, because I love not philosophy merely notional and conjectural, and no man who has made the experiment has been so kind as to come back to inform us. Upon the whole matter, I account a person who has a moderate mind and fortune, and lives in the conversation of two or three agreeable friends, with little commerce in the world besides, who is esteemed well enough by his few neighbors that know him, and is truly irreproachable by anybody, and so after a healthful, quiet life, before the great inconveniences of old age, goes more silently out of it than he came in (for I would not have him so much as cry in the exit); this innocent deceiver of the world, as Horace calls him this *muta persona* [character with no lines], I take to have been more happy in his part than the greatest actors that fill the stage with show and noise, nay, even than Augustus himself, who asked with his last breath whether he had not played his farce very well.

Suggestions

1. Explain the meaning of the title "Of Obscurity," showing that the topic of the essay is two kinds of men. List and identify the Greeks and Romans who are said to exemplify each kind. Which passages tell most about the author?

2. Explain the pun: ". . . if it be a truth, the world (I'll swear) is sufficiently deceived" (¶4).

3. Cowley's essay "Of Myself" contains the statement, "But God laughs at a man who says to his soul, Take thy ease." Decide whether it is consistent with the thesis of "Of Obscurity."

4. Write an essay comparing "Of Obscurity" with † "The Village."

5. Write an essay attacking or defending Cowley's idea of happiness. Might it be said that he makes a virtue of necessity?

WHAT IS A POET?

(1688)

SIR WILLIAM TEMPLE

The true and natural source of poetry may be discovered by observing to what god this inspiration was ascribed by the ancients—which was Apollo, or the sun, esteemed among them the god of learning in general, but more particularly of music and of poetry. The mystery of this fable means, I suppose, that a certain noble and vital heat of temper, but especially of the brain, is the true spring of these two arts or sciences: this was that celestial fire which gave such a pleasing motion and agitation to the finds of those men that have been so much admired in the world, that raises such infinite images of things so agreeable and delightful to mankind; by the influence of this sun are produced those golden and inexhausted mines of invention which have furnished the world with treasures so highly esteemed and so universally known and used in all regions that have yet been discovered. From this arises that elevation of genius which can never be produced by any art or study, by pains or by industry, which cannot be taught by precepts or examples, and therefore is agreed by all to be the pure and free gift of heaven or of nature, and to be a fire kindled out of some hidden spark of the very first conception.

But though invention be the mother of poetry, yet this child is, like all others, born naked, and must be nourished with care, clothed with exactness and elegance, educated with industry, instructed with art, improved by application, corrected with severity, and accomplished with labor and with time before it arrives at any great perfection or growth. It is certain that no composition requires so many several ingredients or of more different sorts than this, nor that to excel in any qualities there are necessary so many gifts of nature and so many improvements of learning and of art. For there must be a universal genius of great compass as well as great elevation; there must be a sprightly imagination or fancy, fertile in a thousand productions, ranging over infinite ground, piercing into every corner, and by the light of that true poetical fire discovering a thousand little bodies or images in the world, and similitudes among them unseen to common eyes, and which could not be discovered without the rays of that sun.

Besides the heat of invention and liveliness of wit, there must be the coldness of good sense and soundness of judgment to distinguish between things and conceptions which, at first sight or upon short glance, seem

494

alike; to choose among infinite productions of wit and fancy which are worth preserving and cultivating, and which are better stifled in the birth or thrown away when they are born, as not worth bringing up. Without the forces of wit all poetry is flat and languishing; without the succors of judgment it is wild and extravagant. The true wit of poesy is that such contraries must meet to compose it: a genius both penetrating and solid; in expression both delicacy and force; and the frame or fabric of a true poem must have some things both sublime and just, amazing and agreeable. There must be a great agitation of mind to invent, a great calm to judge and correct; there must be upon the same tree and at the same time both flower and fruit. To work up this metal into exquisite figure there must be employed the fire, the hammer, the chisel, and the file. There must be a general knowledge both of nature and of the arts, and, to go the lowest there can be, there are required genius, judgment, and application; for without this last all the rest will not serve turn, and none ever was a great poet that applied himself much to anything else.

When I speak of poetry I mean not an ode or an elegy, a song or a satire, nor by a poet the composer of any of these, but of a just poem; and, after all I have said, it is no wonder there should be so few that appeared in any parts or any ages of the world, or that such as have should be so much admired and have almost divinity ascribed to them and their works.

Whatever has been among those who are mentioned with so much praise or admiration by the ancients, but are lost to us and unknown any further than their names, I think no man has been so bold among those that remain to question the title of Homer and Virgil, not only to the first rank, but to the supreme domination in this state, and from whom, as the great lawgivers as well as princes, all the laws and orders of it are or may be derived. Homer was without dispute the most universal genius that has been known in the world, and Virgil the most accomplished. To the first must be allowed the most fertile invention, the richest vein, the most general knowledge, and the most lively expression; to the last, the noblest ideas, the most just institution, the wisest conduct, and the choicest elocution. To speak in the painter's terms, we find in the works of Homer the most spirit, force, and life; in those of Virgil, the best design, the truest proportions, and the greatest grace. The coloring in both seems equal, and indeed is in both admirable. Homer had more fire and rapture, Virgil more light and swiftness, or at least the poetical fire was more raging in one, but clearer in the other, which makes the first more amazing and the latter more agreeable. The ore was richer in one, but in the other more refined and better alloyed to make up excellent work. Upon the whole I think it must be confessed that Homer was of the two, and perhaps of all others, the vastest and sublimest and most wonderful genius, and that he has been generally so esteemed there cannot be a greater testimony given than what has been by some observed: that not only the greatest masters have found in his works the best and truest principles of all their sciences and arts, but that the noblest nations have derived from them the original of their several races, though it be hardly yet agreed whether his story be true or a fiction. In short, these two immortal poets must be allowed to have so much excelled in their kinds as to have exceeded all comparison, to have even extinguished emulation, and in a manner confined true poetry not only to their languages but to their very persons. And I am apt to believe so much of the true genius of poetry in general and of its elevation in these two particulars, that I know not whether, of all the numbers of mankind that live within the compass of a thousand years, for one man that is born capable of making such a poet as Homer or Virgil there may not be a thousand born capable of making as great generals of armies or ministers of state as any the most renowned in story.

I do not here intend to make a further criticism upon poetry, which were too great a labor, nor to give rules for it, which were as great a presumption. Besides, there has been so much paper blotted upon these subjects in this curious and censuring age that it is all grown tedious or repetitious. The modern French wits (or pretenders) have been very severe in their censures and exact in their rules, I think to very little purpose, for I know not why they might not have contented themselves with those given by Aristotle and Horace and have translated them rather than commented upon them, for all they have done has been no more; they seem by their writings of this kind rather to have valued themselves than improved anybody else. The truth is there is something in the genius of poetry too libertine to be confined to so many rules, and whoever goes about to subject it to such constraints loses both its spirit and grace, which are ever native and never learned even of the best masters. It is as if, to make excellent honey, you should cut off the wings of your bees, confine them to their hive or their stands, and lay flowers before them such as you think the sweetest and likeliest to yield the finest extraction; you had as good pull out their stings and make arrant drones of them. They must range through fields as well as gardens, choose such flowers as they please, and by proprieties and scents they only know and distinguish. They must work up their cells with admirable art, extract their honey with infinite labor, and sever it from the wax with such distinction and choice as belongs to none but themselves to perform or to judge.

It would be too much mortification to these great arbitrary rulers among the French writers, or our own, to observe the worthy productions that have been formed by their rules, the honor they have received in the world, or the pleasure they have given mankind. But to comfort them, I do not know there was any great poet in Greece after the rules of that art laid down by Aristotle, nor in Rome after those by Horace, which yet none of our moderns pretend to have outdone. Perhaps Theocritus and Lucan may be alleged against this assertion, but the first offered no further than at idyls or eclogues, and the last, though he must be avowed for a true and happy genius and to have made some very high flights, yet he is so unequal to himself, and his muse is so young that his faults are too noted to allow his pretenses. *Feliciter audet* [he dares and is lucky] is the true character of Lucan, as of Ovid, *lusit amabiliter* [he frolicked delightfully]. After all, the utmost that can be achieved, or I think pretended by any rules in this art, is but to hinder some men from being very ill poets but not to make any man a very good one. To judge who is so, we need go no further for instruction than three lines of Horace:

> Ille meum qui pectus inaniter angit,
> Irritat, mulcet, falsis terroribus implet,
> Ut magus, et modo me Thebis, modo ponit Athenis.

He is a poet,

> Who vainly anguishes my breast,
> Provokes, allays, and with false terror fills,
> Like a magician, and now sets me down
> In Thebes, and now in Athens.

Whoever does not affect and move the same present passions in you that he represents in others, and at other times raises images about you as a conjurer is said to do spirits, transports you to the places and the persons he describes, cannot be judged to be a poet, though his measures are never so just, his [metrical] feet never so smooth, or his sounds never so sweet.

Suggestions

1. The style of "What Is a Poet?" is highly figurative, resembling the style of poetry in that without these striking metaphors the speaker could scarcely have expressed his meaning as exactly as he does. His first metaphor develops from the Greek myth of Apollo: it is no accident, he thinks, that Apollo was the god of both poetry and the sun, for *fire* is the essential endowment of the poet. Summarize the literal meaning of this metaphor as nearly as you can.

2. Show how the fire-metaphor is succeeded by the metaphor of the child in ¶2, and how the former returns in the comparison of Homer and Virgil (¶5).

3. If *poetry* does not here mean odes, elegies, songs, or satires (¶4), what kind of poet is being defined? List all the gifts that such a poet must have.

4. Name an example of each kind of poem referred to in No. 3.

5. Describe the speaker's attitude toward rules for writing poems (¶6), showing how it is expressed partly by the simile of the bees. How was classical poetry supposedly affected by the appearance of Aristotle's *Poetics* and Horace's *Ars Poetica?*

6. Point out the irony in the first sentence of ¶7.

7. List the ways in which poems may affect their readers (last ¶). Which of these are essential for true poetry, which merely pleasant?

8. Write a comparison of the definitions of poetry in "What Is a Poet?" and † "Why Do We Teach Poetry?" Which essay assigns to it a position of greater importance?

LAUGHTER

(1711)

JOSEPH ADDISON

Ride si sapis [Laugh, if you're wise].
Martial, *Epigrams* 2, 41.

Mr. Hobbes, in his *Discourse of Human Nature* [IX, ¶13], which in my humble opinion is much the best of all his works, after some very curious observations upon laughter, concludes thus: "The passion of laughter is nothing else but sudden glory arising from some sudden conception of some eminency in ourselves by comparison with the infirmity of others, or with our own formerly. For men laugh at the follies of themselves past when they come suddenly to remembrance, except they bring with them any present dishonor."

According to this author, therefore, when we hear a man laugh excessively, instead of saying he is very merry we ought to tell him he is very proud. And indeed, if we look into the bottom of this matter, we shall meet with many observations to confirm us in his opinion. Everyone laughs at somebody that is in an inferior state of folly to himself. It was formerly the custom for every great house in England to keep a tame fool dressed in petticoats, that the heir of the family might have

an opportunity of joking upon him and diverting himself with his ab-
surdities. For the same reason idiots are still in request in most of the
courts of Germany, where there is not a prince of any great magnificence
who has not two or three dressed, distinguished, undisputed fools in
his retinue whom the rest of the courtiers are always breaking their jests
upon.

The Dutch, who are more famous for their industry and application
than for wit and humor, hang up in several of their streets what they
call the sign of the gaper: that is, the head of an idiot dressed in a cap
and bells and gaping in a most immoderate manner. This is a standing
jest in Amsterdam.

Thus everyone diverts himself with some person or other that is below
him in point of understanding, and triumphs in the superiority of his
genius while he has such objects of derision before his eyes. Mr. Dennis
has very well expressed this in a couple of humorous lines which are a
part of a translation of a satire in Monsieur Boileau:

> Thus one fool lolls his tongue out at another
> And shakes his empty noddle at his brother.

Mr. Hobbes's reflection gives us the reason why the insignificant people
above-mentioned are stirrers up of laughter among men of a gross taste.
But as the more understanding part of mankind do not find their risibility affected by such ordinary objects, it may be worth the while to
examine into several provocations in men of superior sense and knowledge.

In the first place, I must observe that there is a set of merry drolls
whom the common people of all countries admire and seem to love so
well *that they could eat them,* according to the old proverb. I mean
those circumforaneous [wandering] wits whom every nation calls by the
name of that dish of meat which it loves best. In Holland they are
termed *Pickled Herrings;* in France, *Jean Pottages;* in Italy, *Maccaronies;*
and in Great Britain, *Jack Puddings.* These merry wags, from whatsoever
food they receive their titles, that they may make their audiences laugh
always appear in a fool's coat and commit such blunders and mistakes
in every step they take and every word they utter as those who listen to
them would be ashamed of.

But this little triumph of the understanding, under the disguise of
laughter, is nowhere more visible than in that custom which prevails
everywhere among us on the first day of April, when everybody takes
it in his head to make as many fools as he can. In proportion as there
are more follies discovered so there is more laughter raised on this day
than on any other in the whole year. A neighbor of mine who is a
haberdasher by trade, and a very shallow, conceited fellow, makes his

boast that for these ten years successively he has not made less than a hundred April Fools. My landlady had a falling out with him about a fortnight ago for sending every one of her children upon some "sleeveless errand," as she terms it. Her eldest son went to buy a halfpennyworth of inkle at a shoemaker's, the eldest daughter was dispatched half a mile to see a monster, and in short, the whole family of innocent children made April Fools. Nay, my landlady herself did not escape him. This empty fellow has laughed upon these conceits ever since.

This art of wit is well enough when confined to one day in a twelvemonth, but there is an ingenious tribe of men sprung up in late years who are for making April Fools every day in the year. These gentlemen are commonly distinguished by the name of *Biters,* a race of men that are perpetually employed in laughing at those mistakes which are of their own production.

Thus we see, in proportion as one man is more refined than another, he chooses his fool out of a lower or higher class of mankind, or to speak in a more philosophical language, that secret elation and pride of heart which is generally called laughter arises in him from comparing himself with an object below him, whether it so happens that it be a natural or an artificial fool. It is indeed very possible that the persons we laugh at may in the main of their characters be much wiser men than ourselves; but if they would have us laugh at them they must fall short of us in those respects which stir up this passion.

I am afraid I shall appear too abstracted in my speculations if I show that when a man of wit makes us laugh it is by betraying some oddness or infirmity in his own character, or in the representation which he makes of others, and that when we laugh at a brute, or even at an inanimate thing, it is at some action or incident that bears a remote analogy to any blunder or absurdity in reasonable creatures.

But to come into common life: I shall pass by the consideration of those stage coxcombs that are able to shake a whole audience, and take notice of a particular sort of men who are such provokers of mirth in conversation that it is impossible for a club or merry-meeting to subsist without them. I mean those honest gentlemen who are always exposed to the wit and raillery of their well-wishers and companions, that are pelted by men, women, and children, friends and foes, and in a word stand as butts [targets] in conversation for everyone to shoot at that pleases. I know several of these butts who are men of wit and sense, though by some odd turn of humor, some unlucky cast in their person or behavior, they have always the misfortune to make the company merry. The truth of it is, a man is not qualified for a butt who has not a good deal of wit and vivacity, even in the ridiculous side of his character. A stupid butt is only fit for the conversation of ordinary people; men of wit require one that will give them play and bestir himself in the absurd part of his behavior. A butt with these accomplishments frequently gets the laugh of his side and turns the ridicule upon him that attacks him. Sir John Falstaff was a hero of this species, and gives a good description of himself in his capacity of a butt, after the following manner: "Men of all sorts," says that merry knight, "take a pride to gird at me. The brain of man is not able to invent anything that tends to laughter more than I invent, or is invented on me. I am not only witty in myself, but the cause that wit is in other men." [1]

Suggestions

1. Summarize the thesis of "Laughter" and mention several of its supporting examples as well as modern equivalents for them. Then attack or defend the thesis. Does the essay sufficiently distinguish wit from humor?

2. Explain: *risibility, sleeveless errand, conceits, raillery.*

3. Write an essay comparing the speaker's explanation of why we laugh at animals (¶10) with that of † "Laughing at Animals."

4. If you have read Shakespeare's *King Henry IV*, write an essay showing that the reference to Falstaff strengthens or weakens the speaker's thesis.

5. Write an essay testing the thesis of "Laughter" by a group of cartoons that you consider funny.

ALEXANDER SELKIRK

(1713)

SIR RICHARD STEELE

> *Talia monstrabat relegens errata retrorsum* [Such things he showed as he retraced his former wanderings].
> Virgil, *Aeneid* 3, 690.

Under the title of this paper [*The Englishman*] I do not think it foreign to my design to speak of a man born in Her Majesty's dominions, and relate an advenure in his life so uncommon that it is doubtful whether the like has happened to any of human race. The person I speak of is

[1] In Shakespeare, *2 Henry IV* I.ii.

Alexander Selkirk, whose name is familiar to men of curiosity from the fame of his having lived four years and four months alone in the island of Juan Fernandez. I had the pleasure frequently to converse with the man soon after his arrival in England in the year 1711. It was matter of great curiosity to hear him, as he is a man of good sense, give an account of the different revolutions in his own mind in that long solitude. When we consider how painful absence from company for the space of but one evening is to the generality of mankind, we may have a sense how painful this necessary and constant solitude was to a man bred a sailor and ever accustomed to enjoy and suffer, eat, drink, and sleep, and perform all offices of life, in fellowship and company. He was put ashore from a leaky vessel, with the captain of which he had had an irreconcilable difference; and he chose rather to take his fate in this place than in a crazy vessel, under a disagreeable commander. His portion was a seachest, his wearing clothes and bedding, a firelock, a pound of gunpowder, a large quantity of bullets, a flint and steel, a few pounds of tobacco, a hatchet, a knife, a kettle, a Bible and other books of devotion, together with pieces that concerned navigation, and his mathematical instruments. Resentment against his officer, who had ill-used him, made him look forward on this change of life as the more eligible one, till the instant in which he saw the vessel put off; at which moment his heart yearned within him and melted at the parting with his comrades and all human society at once. He had in provisions for the sustenance of life but the quantity of two meals, the island abounding only with wild goats, cats, and rats. He judged it most probable that he should find more immediate and easy relief by finding shell-fish on the shore than seeking game with his gun. He accordingly found great quantities of turtles, whose flesh is extremely delicious, and of which he frequently ate very plentifully on his first arrival till it grew disagreeable to his stomach, except in jellies. The necessities of hunger and thirst were his greatest diversions from the reflection on his lonely condition. When those appetites were satisfied, the desire of society was as strong a call upon him, and he appeared to himself least necessitous when he wanted everything; for the supports of his body were easily attained, but the eager longings for seeing again the face of man during the interval of craving bodily appetites were hardly supportable. He grew dejected, languid, and melancholy, scarce able to refrain from doing himself violence, till by degrees, by the force of reason, and frequent reading of the Scriptures, and turning his thoughts upon the study of navigation, after the space of eighteen months he grew thoroughly reconciled to his condition. When he had made this conquest, the vigor of his health, disengagement from the world, a constant, cheerful, serene sky, and a temperate air made his life one continual feast, and his being much more joyful than it had before been irksome. He, now taking delight in everything, made the hut in which he lay, by ornaments which he cut down from a spacious wood on the side of which it was situated, the most delicious bower, fanned with continual breezes and gentle aspirations of wind, that made his repose after the chase equal to the most sensual pleasures.

I forgot to observe that during the time of his dissatisfaction monsters of the deep, which frequently lay on the shore, added to the terrors of his solitude; the dreadful howlings and voices seemed too terrible to be made for the human ears; but upon the recovery of his temper he could with pleasure not only hear their voices but approach the monsters themselves with great intrepidity. He speaks of sea-lions, whose jaws and tails were capable of seizing or breaking the limbs of a man if he approached them; but at that time his spirits and life were so high, and he could act so regularly and unconcerned, that merely from being un-ruffled in himself he killed them with the greatest ease imaginable; for observing that though their jaws and tails were so terrible, yet the animals being mighty slow in working themselves round, he had nothing to do but place himself exactly opposite to their middle and as close to them as possible, and he dispatched them with his hatchet at will.

The precaution which he took against want, in case of sickness, was to lame kids when very young, so as that they might recover their health but never be capable of speed. These he had in great numbers about his hut; and when he was himself in full vigor, he could take at full speed the swiftest goat running up a promontory, and never failed of catching them but on a descent.

His habitation was extremely pestered with rats, which gnawed his clothes and feet when sleeping. To defend him against them, he fed and tamed numbers of young kitlings [wildcats], who lay about his bed and preserved him from the enemy. When his clothes were worn out he dried and tacked together the skins of goats, with which he clothed himself, and was inured to pass through woods, bushes, and brambles with as much carelessness and precipitance as any other animal. It happened once to him that, running on the summit of a hill, he made a stretch to seize a goat, with which under him he fell down a precipice and lay helpless for the space of three days, the length of which time he measured by the moon's growth since his last observation. This manner of life grew so exquisitely pleasant that he never had a moment heavy upon his hands; his nights were untroubled and his days joyous, from the practice of temperance and exercise. It was his manner to use stated hours and places for exercises of devotion, which he performed aloud in order to keep up the faculties of speech and to utter himself with greater energy.

When I first saw him, I thought, if I had not been let into his character and story, I could have discerned that he had been much separated from company, from his aspect and gesture; there was a strong but cheerful seriousness in his look and a certain disregard to the ordinary things about him, as if he had been sunk in thought. When the ship which brought him off the island came in, he received them with the greatest indifference, with relation to the prospect of going off with them, but with great satisfaction in an opportunity to refresh and help them. The man frequently bewailed his return to the world, which could not, he said, with all its enjoyments, restore him to the tranquility of his solitude. Though I had frequently conversed with him, after a few months' absence he met me in the street, and though he spoke to me, I could not recollect that I had seen him; familiar converse in this town had taken off the loneliness of his aspect and quite altered the air of his face.

This plain man's story is a memorable example that he is happiest who confines his wants to natural necessities; and he that goes further in his desires increases his wants in proportion to his acquisitions; or to use his own expression, "I am now worth £800, but shall never be so happy as when I was not worth a farthing."

Suggestions

1. Trace the changes in Selkirk's emotions during his first months on the island. How is this sequence paralleled in ¶2?

2. Decide whether ¶1 should be broken into shorter paragraphs, and whether ¶4 fails in unity.

3. Define the speaker's attitude toward Selkirk. How is the last sentence of ¶5 related to it?

4. Explain: *Juan Fernandez, firelock, necessitous, intrepidity, inured, precipitance.*

5. Write an essay on the last sentence, deciding whether the particulars of Selkirk's life on the island prepare for it adequately.

A MODEST PROPOSAL

FOR PREVENTING THE CHILDREN OF POOR PEOPLE IN IRELAND FROM BEING
A BURDEN TO THEIR PARENTS OR COUNTRY, AND FOR MAKING THEM BENEFICIAL
TO THE PUBLIC

(1729)

JONATHAN SWIFT

It is a melancholy object to those who walk through this great town
[Dublin] or travel in the country, when they see the streets, the roads,
and cabin-doors crowded with beggars of the female sex, followed by
three, four, or six children, all in rags and importuning every passenger
for an alms. These mothers, instead of being able to work for their honest
livelihood, are forced to employ all their time in strolling to beg sustenance for their helpless infants, who, as they grow up, either turn
thieves for want of work, or leave their dear native country to fight for
the Pretender [1] in Spain, or sell themselves to the Barbadoes [as planta-
tion laborers].

I think it is agreed by all parties that this prodigious number of children in the arms, or on the backs, or at the heels of their mothers, and
frequently of their fathers, is, in the present deplorable state of the kingdom, a very great additional grievance; and, therefore, whoever could
find out a fair, cheap, and easy method of making these children sound,
useful members of the commonwealth would deserve so well of the
public as to have his statue set up for a preserver of the nation.

But my intention is very far from being confined to provide only for
the children of professed beggars; it is of a much greater extent and shall
take in the whole number of infants at a certain age, who are born of
parents in effect as little able to support them as those who demand our
charity in the streets.

As to my own part, having turned my thoughts for many years upon
this important subject and maturely weighed the several schemes of our
projectors,[2] I have always found them grossly mistaken in their com-
putation. It is true, a child just dropped from its dam may be supported
by her milk for a solar year with little other nourishment; at most, not
above the value of two shillings, which the mother may certainly get, or
the value in scraps, by her lawful occupation of begging; and it is exactly at one year old that I propose to provide for them in such a man-

---

[1] James Stuart, son of James II, who had been dethroned in 1688.
[2] Proposers of plans—of whom Swift had been one.

ner as, instead of being a charge upon their parents or the parish, or wanting food and raiment for the rest of their lives, they shall, on the contrary, contribute to the feeding and partly to the clothing of many thousands.

There is likewise another great advantage in my scheme, that it will prevent those voluntary abortions and that horrid practice of women murdering their bastard children, alas, too frequent among us! sacrificing the poor innocent babes, I doubt [suspect], more to avoid the expense than the shame, which would move tears and pity in the most savage and inhuman breast.

The number of souls in this kingdom being usually reckoned one million and a half, of these I calculate there may be about two hundred thousand couple whose wives are breeders; from which number I subtract thirty thousand couple who are able to maintain their own children (although I apprehend there cannot be so many, under the present distresses of the kingdom); but this being granted, there will remain a hundred and seventy thousand breeders. I again subtract fifty thousand, for those women who miscarry or whose children die by accident or disease within the year. There only remain a hundred and twenty thousand children of poor parents annually born. The question therefore is, How this number shall be reared and provided for? which, as I have already said, under the present situation of affairs is utterly impossible by all the methods hitherto proposed. For we can neither employ them in handicraft or agriculture; we neither build houses (I mean in the country) nor cultivate land: they can very seldom pick up a livelihood by stealing till they arrive at six years old, except where they are of towardly parts [promising talents]; although I confess they learn the rudiments much earlier, during which time they can, however, be properly looked upon only as probationers, as I have been informed by a principal gentleman in the county of Cavan, who protested to me that he never knew above one or two instances under the age of six, even in a part of the kingdom so renowned for the quickest proficiency in that art.

I am assured by our merchants that a boy or a girl before twelve years old is no salable commodity; and even when they come to this age they will not yield above three pounds, or three pounds and half-a-crown at most, on the exchange; which cannot turn to account either to the parents or kingdom, the charge of nutriment and rags having been at least four times that value.

I shall now, therefore, humbly propose my own thoughts, which I hope will not be liable to the least objection.

I have been assured by a very knowing American of my acquaintance in London that a young healthy child, well nursed, is, at a year old, a most delicious, nourishing, and wholesome food, whether stewed, roasted, baked, or boiled; and I make no doubt that it will equally serve in a fricassee or a ragout.

I do therefore humbly offer it to public consideration that of the hundred and twenty thousand children already computed, twenty thousand may be reserved for breed, whereof only one-fourth part to be males; which is more than we allow to sheep, black-cattle, or swine; and my reason is that these children are seldom the fruits of marriage, a circumstance not much regarded by our savages [3]; therefore one male will be sufficient to serve four females. That the remaining hundred thousand may, at a year old, be offered in sale to the persons of quality and fortune through the kingdom; always advising the mother to let them suck plentifully in the last month, so as to render them plump and fat for a good table. A child will make two dishes at an entertainment for friends; and when the family dines alone, the fore or hind quarter will make a reasonable dish and, seasoned with a little pepper or salt, will be very good boiled on the fourth day, especially in winter.

I have reckoned, upon a medium, that a child just born will weigh twelve pounds and in a solar year, if tolerably nursed, will increase to twenty-eight pounds.

I grant this food will be somewhat dear, and therefore very proper for landlords, who, as they have already devoured most of the parents, seem to have the best title to the children.

Infants' flesh will be in season throughout the year, but more plentifully in March, and a little before and after: for we are told by a grave author, an eminent French physician, that fish being a prolific diet, there are more children born in Roman Catholic countries about nine months after Lent than at any other season; therefore, reckoning a year after Lent, the markets will be more glutted than usual because the number of Popish infants is at least three to one in this kingdom; and therefore it will have one other collateral advantage, by lessening the number of Papists among us.

I have already computed the charge of nursing a beggar's child (in which list I reckon all cottagers, laborers, and four-fifths of the farmers) to be about two shillings per annum, rags included; and I believe no gentleman would repine to give ten shillings for the carcass of a good fat child, which, as I have said, will make four dishes of excellent nutritive meat, when he has only some particular friend or his own family to dine with him. Thus the squire will learn to be a good landlord and grow popular among his tenants; the mother will have eight shillings net profit and be fit for work till she produces another child.

Those who are more thrifty (as I must confess the times require) may

---

[3] I.e. promiscuity is common among the Irish poor—"our savages" as opposed to the American variety.

flay the carcass, the skin of which, artificially dressed, will make admirable gloves for ladies and summer-boots for fine gentlemen.

As to our city of Dublin, shambles may be appointed for this purpose in the most convenient parts of it, and butchers, we may be assured, will not be wanting; although I rather recommend buying the children alive, then dressing them hot from the knife, as we do roasting pigs.

A very worthy person, a true lover of his country, and whose virtues I highly esteem, was lately pleased, in discoursing on this matter, to offer a refinement upon my scheme. He said that many gentlemen of this kingdom, having of late destroyed their deer, he conceived that the want of venison might be well supplied by the bodies of young lads and maidens not exceeding fourteen years of age nor under twelve; so great a number of both sexes in every country being now ready to starve for want of work and service; and these to be disposed of by their parents, if alive, or otherwise by their nearest relations. But with due deference to so excellent a friend and so deserving a patriot, I cannot be altogether in his sentiments; for as to the males, my American acquaintance assured me, from frequent experience, that their flesh was generally tough and lean like that of our schoolboys, by continual exercise, and their taste disagreeable; and to fatten them would not answer the charge. Then as to the females, it would, I think, with humble submission, be a loss to the public, because they soon would become breeders themselves: and besides, it is not improbable that some scrupulous people might be apt to censure such a practice (although indeed very unjustly) as a little bordering upon cruelty; which, I confess, has always been with me the strongest objection against any project, how well soever intended.

But in order to justify my friend, he confessed that this expedient was put into his head by the famous Psalmanazar, a native of the island Formosa, who came from thence to London above twenty years ago; [4] and in conversation told my friend that in his country when any young person happened to be put to death, the executioner sold the carcass to persons of quality as a prime dainty; and that in his time the body of a plump girl of fifteen, who was crucified for an attempt to poison the emperor, was sold to his imperial majesty's prime minister of state and other great mandarins of the court, in joints from the gibbet, at four hundred crowns. Neither indeed can I deny that if the same use were made of several plump young girls in this town, who, without one single groat to their fortunes, cannot stir abroad without a chair [5] and appear at playhouse and assemblies in foreign fineries which they never will pay for, the kingdom would not be the worse.

Some persons of a desponding spirit are in great concern about that vast number of poor people who are aged, diseased, or maimed; and I

[4] "George Psalmanazar," real name unknown, published a spurious *Description* of Formosa in 1704. He was French.
[5] I.e. without being carried in a sedan chair.

have been desired to employ my thoughts, what course may be taken to ease the nation of so grievous an encumbrance. But I am not in the least pain upon that matter, because it is very well known that they are every day dying, and rotting, by cold and famine, and filth and vermin, as fast as can be reasonably expected. And as to the young laborers, they are now in almost as hopeful a condition: they cannot get work, and consequently pine away for want of nourishment to a degree that if at any time they are accidentally hired to common labor, they have not strength to perform it; and thus the country and themselves are happily delivered from the evils to come.

I have too long digressed, and therefore shall return to my subject. I think the advantages by the proposal which I have made are obvious and many, as well as of the highest importance.

For first, as I have already observed, it would greatly lessen the number of Papists, with whom we are yearly overrun, being the principal breeders of the nation as well as our most dangerous enemies; and who stay at home on purpose to deliver the kingdom to the Pretender, hoping to take their advantage by the absence of so many good Protestants,[6] who have chosen rather to leave their country than stay at home and pay tithes against their conscience to an Episcopal curate.

Secondly, The poorer tenants will have something valuable of their own, which by law may be made liable to distress and help to pay their landlord's rent; their corn and cattle being already seized and money a thing unknown.

Thirdly, Whereas the maintenance of a hundred thousand children from two years old and upward cannot be computed at less than ten shillings a piece per annum, the nation's stock will be thereby increased fifty thousand pounds per annum, besides the profit of a new dish introduced to the tables of all gentlemen of fortune in the kingdom who have any refinement in taste. And the money will circulate among ourselves,[7] the goods being entirely of our own growth and manufacture.

Fourthly, The constant breeders, besides the gain of eight shillings sterling per annum by the sale of their children, will be rid of the charge of maintaining them after the first year.

Fifthly, This food would likewise bring great custom to taverns, where the vintners will certainly be so prudent as to procure the best receipts for dressing it to perfection and, consequently, have their houses frequented by all the fine gentlemen, who justly value themselves upon their knowledge in good eating: and a skilful cook who understands how to oblige his guests will contrive to make it as expensive as they please.

Sixthly, This would be a great inducement to marriage, which all wise nations have either encouraged by rewards or enforced by laws and

[6] Irish Dissenters, taxed for the support of the official Church though not members of it.
[7] Instead of going to England to pay for imports.

penalties. It would increase the care and tenderness of mothers toward their children, when they were sure of a settlement for life to the poor babes, provided in some sort by the public, to their annual profit or expense. We should see an honest emulation among the married women, which of them could bring the fattest child to the market. Men would become as fond of their wives during the time of their pregnancy as they are now of their mares in foal, their cows in calf, their sows when they are ready to farrow; nor offer to beat or kick them (as is too frequent a practice), for fear of a miscarriage.

Many other advantages might be enumerated. For instance, the addition of some thousand carcasses in our exportation of barreled beef; the propagation of swine's flesh and improvement in the art of making good bacon, so much wanted among us by the great destruction of pigs, too frequent at our table; which are no way comparable in taste or magnificence to a well-grown, fat, yearling child, which, roasted whole, will make a considerable figure at a lord mayor's feast or any other public entertainment. But this, and many others, I omit, being studious of brevity.

Supposing that one thousand families in this city would be constant customers for infants' flesh, besides others who might have it at merry-meetings, particularly at weddings and christenings, I compute that Dublin would take off annually about twenty thousand carcasses; and the rest of the kingdom (where probably they will be sold somewhat cheaper) the remaining eighty thousand.

I can think of no one objection that will possibly be raised against this proposal, unless it should be urged that the number of people will be thereby much lessened in the kingdom. This I freely own, and it was indeed one principal design in offering it to the world. I desire the reader will observe that I calculate my remedy for this one individual kingdom of Ireland and for no other that ever was, is, or I think ever can be upon earth. Therefore let no man talk to me of other expedients: of taxing our absentees at five shillings a pound: of using neither clothes nor household furniture except what is our own growth and manufacture: of utterly rejecting the materials and instruments that promote foreign luxury: of curing the expensiveness of pride, vanity, idleness, and gaming in our women: of introducing a vein of parsimony, prudence, and temperance: of learning to love our country, in the want of which we differ even from Laplanders and the inhabitants of Topinamboo [8]: of quitting our animosities and factions, nor acting any longer like the Jews, who were murdering one another at the very moment their city was taken: of being a little cautious not to sell our country and conscience for nothing: of teaching landlords to have at least one degree of mercy toward their

[8] Part of Brazil, supposedly inhabited by cannibals.

tenants: lastly, of putting a spirit of honesty, industry, and skill into our shopkeepers; who, if a resolution could now be taken to buy only our native goods, would immediately unite to cheat and exact upon us in the price, the measure, and the goodness, nor could ever yet be brought to make one fair proposal of just dealing, though often and earnestly invited to it.

Therefore I repeat, let no man talk to me of these and the like expedients till he has at least some glimpse of hope that there will be ever some hearty and sincere attempt to put them in practice.

But as to myself, having been wearied out for many years with offering vain, idle, visionary thoughts, and at length utterly despairing of success, I fortunately fell upon this proposal; which, as it is wholly new, so it has something solid and real, of no expense and little trouble, full in our own power, and whereby we can incur no danger in disobliging ENGLAND. For this kind of commodity will not bear exportation, the flesh being of too tender a consistence to admit a long continuance in salt, although perhaps I could name a country which would be glad to eat up our whole nation without it.

After all, I am not so violently bent upon my own opinion as to reject any offer proposed by wise men, which shall be found equally innocent, cheap, easy, and effectual. But before something of that kind shall be advanced in contradiction to my scheme and offering a better, I desire the author or authors will be pleased maturely to consider two points. First, as things now stand, how they will be able to find food and raiment for a hundred thousand useless mouths and backs. And, secondly, there being a round million of creatures in human figure throughout this kingdom, whose whole subsistence put into a common stock would leave them in debt two millions of pounds sterling, adding those who are beggars by profession, to the bulk of farmers, cottagers, and laborers, with the wives and children who are beggars in effect; I desire those politicians who dislike my overture and may perhaps be so bold as to attempt an answer, that they will first ask the parents of these mortals whether they would not at this day think it a great happiness to have been sold for food at a year old, in the manner I prescribe, and thereby have avoided such a perpetual scene of misfortunes as they have since gone through, by the oppression of landlords, the impossibility of paying rent without money or trade, the want of common sustenance, with neither house nor clothes to cover them from the inclemencies of the weather, and the most inevitable prospect of entailing the like or greater miseries upon their breed for ever.

I profess in the sincerity of my heart that I have not the least personal interest in endeavoring to promote this necessary work, having no other motive than the public good of my country by advancing our trade, providing for infants, relieving the poor, and giving some pleasure to the rich. I have no children by which I can propose to get a single penny, the youngest being nine years old and my wife past child-bearing.

Suggestions

1. Perhaps the most famous specimen of *irony* in the language, "A Modest Proposal" is often interpreted as simply an attack on England. Making your own definition of *irony*, show from ¶18 and other passages that the essay has other targets as well. Do you consider the title itself ironic?

2. List the specific ills of Ireland that in the speaker's opinion necessitate drastic remedies.

3. Show how ¶12 supports an ironic rather than a literal interpretation, and that toward its conclusion the essay becomes less ironic and more literal.

4. Explain: *prolific diet, flay, shambles, Papists, tithes, emulation.*

5. Write a characterization of the speaker, with particular attention to ¶16 and the last sentence.

6. Write an essay in which you establish the existence of a bad condition (such as congestion of traffic in your home town) and propose an ironic remedy for it.

7. Write an essay comparing "A Modest Proposal" with † "An Eminently Reasonable Suggestion" or some other essay in its section of Part 2.

TOPICS FOR WRITING

(1753)

SAMUEL JOHNSON

It is often charged upon writers that with all their pretensions to genius and discoveries, they do little more than copy one another, and that compositions obtruded upon the world with the pomp of novelty contain only tedious repetitions of common sentiments, or at best exhibit a transposition of known images and give a new appearance of truth only by some slight difference of dress and decoration.

The allegation of resemblance between authors is indisputably true, but the charge of plagiarism, which is raised upon it, is not to be allowed with equal readiness. A coincidence of sentiment may easily happen without any communication, since there are many occasions in which all reasonable men will nearly think alike. Writers of all ages have had the same sentiments because they have in all ages had the same objects of speculation; the interests and passions, the virtues and vices of mankind, have been diversified in different times only by unessential and casual varieties. And we must therefore expect in the works of all those who attempt to describe them such a likeness as we find in the pictures of the same person drawn in different periods of his life.

It is necessary, therefore, that before an author be charged with plagiarism—one of the most reproachful though perhaps not the most atrocious of literary crimes—the subject on which he treats should be carefully considered. We do not wonder that historians, relating the same facts, agree in their narration; or that authors, delivering the elements of science, advance the same theorems and lay down the same definitions. Yet it is not wholly without use to mankind that books are multiplied and that different authors lay out their labors on the same subject; for there will always be some reason why one should, on particular occasions or to particular persons, be preferable to another. Some will be obscure; some will please by their style and others by their method, some by their embellishments and others by their simplicity, some by closeness and others by diffusion.

The same indulgence is to be shown to the writers of morality: right and wrong are immutable; and those, therefore, who teach us to distinguish them, if they all teach us right, must agree with one another. The relations of social life and the duties resulting from them must be the same at all times and in all nations. Some petty differences may be, indeed, produced by forms of government or arbitrary customs, but the general doctrine can receive no alteration.

Yet it is not to be desired that morality should be considered as interdicted to all future writers; men will always be tempted to deviate from their duty, and will therefore always want a monitor to recall them; and a new book often seizes the attention of the public without any other claim than that it is new. There is likewise in composition, as in other things, a perpetual vicissitude of fashion; and truth is recommended at one time to regard by appearances which at another would expose it to neglect. The author, therefore, who has judgment to discern the taste of his contemporaries, and skill to gratify it, will have always an opportunity to deserve well of mankind by conveying instruction to them in a grateful vehicle.

There are likewise many modes of composition by which a moralist may deserve the name of an original writer: he may familiarize his sys-

514 Forms of Literature

tem by dialogues after the manner of the ancients, or subtilize it into a series of syllogistic arguments; he may enforce his doctrine by seriousness and solemnity, or enliven it by sprightliness and gaiety; he may detain the studious by the artful concatenation of a continued discourse, or relieve the busy by short strictures and unconnected essays.

To excel in any of these forms of writing will require a particular cultivation of the genius. Whoever can attain to excellence will be certain to engage a set of readers whom no other method would have equally allured; and he that communicates truth with success must be numbered among the first benefactors to mankind.

The same observation may be extended likewise to passions: their influence is uniform, and their effects nearly the same in every human breast. A man loves and hates, desires and avoids, exactly like his neighbor; resentment and ambition, avarice and indolence, discover themselves by the same symptoms in minds a thousand years from one another.

Nothing, therefore, can be more unjust than to charge an author with plagiarism merely because he assigns to every cause its natural effect, and makes his personages act as others in like circumstances have always done. There are conceptions in which all men will agree, though each derives them from his own observation. Whoever has been in love will represent a lover impatient of every idea that interrupts his meditations on his mistress, retiring to shades and solitude that he may muse without disturbance on his approaching happiness, or associating himself with some friend that flatters his passion, and talking away the hours of absence upon his darling subject. Whoever has been so unhappy as to have felt the miseries of long-continued hatred will, without any assistance from ancient volumes, be able to relate how the passions are kept in perpetual agitation by the recollection of injury and meditations of revenge; how the blood boils at the name of the enemy, and life is worn away in contrivances of mischief.

Every other passion is alike simple and limited if it be considered only with regard to the breast which it inhabits; the anatomy of the mind, as that of the body, must perpetually exhibit the same appearances; and though by the continued industry of successive inquirers new movements will be from time to time discovered, they can affect only the minuter parts and are commonly of more curiosity than importance.

It will now be natural to inquire by what arts are the writers of the present and future ages to attract the notice and favor of mankind. They are to observe the alterations which time is always making in the modes of life, that they may gratify every generation with a picture of themselves. Thus love is uniform, but courtship is perpetually varying. The different arts of gallantry which beauty has inspired would of themselves be sufficient to fill a volume; sometimes balls and serenades, sometimes a tournament and adventures, have been employed to melt the hearts of ladies who in another century have been sensible of scarce any other merit than that of riches, and listened only to jointures and pin-money. Thus the ambitious man has at all times been eager of wealth and power, but these hopes have been gratified in some countries by supplicating the people and in others by flattering the prince. Honor in some states has been only the reward of military achievements; in others it has been gained by noisy turbulence and popular clamors. Avarice has worn a different form, as she actuated the usurer of Rome and the stock-jobber of England; and idleness itself, how little soever inclined to the trouble of invention, has been forced from time to time to change its amusements and contrive different methods of wearing out the day.

Here then is the fund from which those who study mankind may fill their compositions with an inexhaustible variety of images and allusions, and he must be confessed to look with little attention upon scenes thus perpetually changing who cannot catch some of the figures before they are made vulgar by reiterated descriptions.

It has been discovered by Sir Isaac Newton that the distinct and primigenial colors are only seven, but every eye can witness that from various mixtures in various proportions infinite diversifications of tints may be produced. In like manner the passions of the mind, which put the world in motion and produce all the bustle and eagerness of the busy crowds that swarm upon the earth; the passions from whence arise all the pleasures and pains that we see and hear of, if we analyze the mind of man, are very few; but those few, agitated and combined as external causes shall happen to operate, and modified by prevailing opinions and accidental caprices, make such frequent alterations on the surface of life that the show, while we are busied in delineating it, vanishes from the view, and a new set of objects succeed, doomed to the same shortness of duration with the former. Thus curiosity may always find employment, and the busy part of mankind will furnish the contemplative with the materials of speculation to the end of time.

The complaint, therefore, that all topics are preoccupied is nothing more than the murmur of ignorance or idleness by which some discourage others and some themselves; the mutability of mankind will always furnish writers with new images, and the luxuriance of fancy may always embellish them with new decorations.

Suggestions

1. "Topics for Writing" defends modern authors from an accusation frequently brought against them: that of plagiarism. Summarize the defense, showing what the speaker concedes to be the weakness of many writings.

2. Show that the speaker is much more an absolutist about right and wrong than he is about literary fashions (¶¶4–5).

3. List the speaker's examples of human passions, attacking or defending his belief that "their effects [are] nearly the same in every human breast" (¶8).

4. Paraphrase the second half of the last sentence, showing its connection with the color-analogy and the rest of the preceding paragraph.

5. Explain: *obtruded, embellishment, diffusion, immutable, interdicted, concatenation, stock-jobber, primigenial.*

6. Write an essay, rich in contemporary examples, on one of the topics mentioned in ¶11: love, courtship, ambition, honor, or avarice.

7. Basing your essay on a recent well-known literary work, attack or defend the thesis that topics for writing are always abundant.

ON THE USE OF LANGUAGE

(1759)

OLIVER GOLDSMITH

The manner in which most writers begin their treatises on the Use of Language is generally thus: "Language has been granted to man in order to discover his wants and necessities, so as to have them relieved by society. Whatever we desire, whatever we wish, it is but to clothe those desires or wishes in words, in order to fruition; the principal use of language, therefore," say they, "is to express our wants, so as to receive a speedy redress."

Such an account as this may serve to satisfy grammarians and rhetoricians well enough, but men who know the world maintain very contrary maxims; they hold, and I think with some show of reason, that he who best knows how to conceal his necessities and desires is the most likely person to find redress, and that the true use of speech is not so much to express our wants as to conceal them.

When we reflect on the manner in which mankind generally confer their favors, we shall find that they who seem to want them the least are the very persons who most liberally share them. There is something so attractive in riches that the large heap generally collects from the smaller; and the poor find as much pleasure in increasing the enormous mass as the miser who owns it sees happiness in its increase. Nor is there in this anything repugnant to the laws of true morality. Seneca himself allows that in conferring benefits the present should always be suited to the dignity of the receiver. Thus the rich receive large presents and are thanked for accepting them. Men of middling stations are obliged to be content with presents something less; while the beggar, who may be truly said to want indeed, is well paid if a farthing rewards his warmest solicitations.

Every man who has seen the world and has had his ups and downs in life, as the expression is, must have frequently experienced the truth of this doctrine and must know that to have much, or to seem to have it, is the only way to have more. Ovid finely compares a man of broken fortune to a falling column; the lower it sinks, the greater weight it is obliged to sustain. Thus when a man has no occasion to borrow, he finds numbers willing to lend him. Should he ask his friend to lend him a hundred pounds, it is possible, from the largeness of his demand, he may find credit for twenty; but should he humbly only sue for a trifle, it is two to one whether he might be trusted for twopence. A certain young fellow at George's [Coffee-house], whenever he had occasion to ask his friend for a guinea, used to prelude his request as if he wanted two hundred, and talked so familiarly of large sums that none could ever think he wanted a small one. The same gentleman, whenever he wanted credit for a new suit from his tailor, always made a proposal in laced clothes; for he found by experience that if he appeared shabby on these occasions, Mr. Lynch had taken an oath against trusting; or what was every bit as bad, his foreman was out of the way and would not be at home these two days.

There can be no inducement to reveal our wants except to find pity, and by this means relief; but before a poor man open his mind in such circumstances, he should first consider whether he is contented to lose the esteem of the person he solicits, and whether he is willing to give up friendship only to excite compassion. Pity and friendship are passions incompatible with each other, and it is impossible that both can reside in any breast for the smallest space without impairing each other. Friendship is made up of esteem and pleasure; pity is composed of sorrow and contempt: the mind may for some time fluctuate between them, but it never can entertain both together.

Yet let it not be thought that I would exclude pity from the human mind. There is scarcely any who are not in some degree possessed of this pleasing softness; but it is at best but a short-lived passion and seldom affords distress more than transitory assistance. With some it scarcely lasts from the first impulse till the hand can be put into the pocket; with others it may continue for twice that space, and on some of extraordinary sensibility I have seen it operate for half an hour. But last as it may, it generally produces but beggarly effects; and where, from this motive, we give farthings, from others we give pounds. In great distress we sometimes, it is true, feel the influence of tenderness strongly; when the same distress solicits a second time, we then feel with diminished sensibility, but, like the repetition of an echo, every new impulse becomes weaker, till at last our sensations lose every mixture of sorrow and degenerate into downright contempt.

Jack Spindle and I were old acquaintance; but he's gone. Jack was bred in a counting-house, and his father, dying just as he was out of his time, left him a handsome fortune and many friends to advise with. The restraint in which he had been brought up had thrown a gloom upon his temper, which some regarded as an habitual prudence, and from such considerations, he had every day repeated offers of friendship. Those who had money were ready to offer him their assistance that way; and they who had daughters, frequently, in the warmth of affection, advised him to marry. Jack, however, was in good circumstances; he wanted neither money, friends, nor a wife, and therefore modestly declined their proposals.

Some errors in the management of his affairs and several losses in trade soon brought Jack to a different way of thinking; and he at last thought it his best way to let his friends know that their offers were at length acceptable. His first address was therefore to a scrivener, who had formerly made him frequent offers of money and friendship at a time when, perhaps, he knew those offers would have been refused.

Jack, therefore, thought he might use his old friend without any ceremony, and as a man confident of not being refused, requested the use of a hundred guineas for a few days, as he just then had an occasion for money. "And pray, Mr. Spindle," replied the scrivener, "do you want all this money?" "Want it, Sir," says the other, "if I did not want it, I should not have asked for it." "I am sorry for that," says the friend; "for those who want money when they come to borrow, will want money when they should come to pay. To say the truth, Mr. Spindle, money is money nowadays. I believe it is all sunk in the bottom of the sea, for my part; and he that has got a little is a fool if he does not keep what he has got."

Not quite disconcerted by this refusal, our adventurer was resolved to apply to another, whom he knew to be the very best friend he had in the world. The gentleman whom he now addressed received his proposal with all the affability that could be expected from generous friendship. "Let me see, you want a hundred guineas: and pray, dear Jack, would not fifty answer?" "If you have but fifty to spare, Sir, I must be contented." "Fifty to spare! I do not say that, for I believe I have but twenty about me." "Then I must borrow the other thirty from some other friend." "And pray," replied the friend, "would it not be the best way to borrow the whole money from that other friend, and then one note will serve for all, you know. Lord, Mr. Spindle, make no ceremony with me at any time; you know I'm your friend, when you choose a bit of dinner or so.——You, Tom, see the gentleman down. You won't forget to dine with us now and then. Your very humble servant."

Distressed but not discouraged at this treatment, he was at last resolved to find that assistance from love which he could not have from friendship. Miss Jenny Dismal had a fortune in her own hands, and she had already made all the advances that her sex's modesty would permit. He made his proposal, therefore, with confidence, but soon perceived, "No bankrupt ever found the fair one kind." Miss Jenny and Master Billy Galloon were lately fallen deeply in love with each other, and the whole neighborhood thought it would soon be a match.

Every day now began to strip Jack of his former finery; his clothes flew piece by piece to the pawnbrokers, and he seemed at length equipped in the genuine mourning of antiquity. But still he thought himself secure from starving; the numberless invitations he had received to dine, even after his losses, were yet unanswered; he was therefore now resolved to accept of a dinner because he wanted one; and in this manner he actually lived among his friends a whole week without being openly affronted. The last place I saw poor Jack was at the Rev. Dr. Gosling's. He had, as he fancied, just nicked the time, for he came in as the cloth was laying. He took a chair without being desired and talked for some time without being attended to. He assured the company that nothing procured so good an appetite as a walk to White Conduit House, where he had been that morning. He looked at the table-cloth and praised the figure of the damask; talked of a feast where he had been the day before, but that the venison was overdone. All this, however, procured the poor creature no invitation, and he was not yet sufficiently hardened to stay without being asked; wherefore, finding the gentleman of the house insensible to all his fetches, he thought proper at last to retire and mend his appetite by a walk in the Park.

You then, O ye beggars of my acquaintance, whether in rags or lace; whether in Kent Street or in the Mall; whether at Smyrna or St. Giles's; might I advise you as a friend, never seem in want of the favor you solicit. Apply to every passion but pity for redress. You may find relief from vanity, from self-interest, or from avarice, but seldom from compassion. The very eloquence of a poor man is disgusting; and that mouth which is opened ever for flattery is seldom expected to close without a petition.

If, then, you would ward off the gripe of poverty, pretend to be a stranger to her, and she will at least use you with ceremony. Hear not my advice, but that of Offellus.[1] If you be caught dining upon a halfpenny

---

[1] Nec meus hic sermo est, sed quem praecepit Offellus [This is not my idea, but what Offellus taught].—Horace, *Satires* 2, 2.

porringer of peas, soup, and potatoes, praise the wholesomeness of your frugal repast. You may observe that Dr. Cheyne has prescribed peas broth for the gravel [2]; hint that you are not one of those who are always making a god of your belly. If you are obliged to wear a flimsy stuff in the midst of winter, be the first to remark that stuffs are very much worn at Paris. If there be found some irreparable defects in any part of your equipage, which cannot be concealed by all the arts of sitting cross-legged, coaxing, or darning, say, that neither you nor Sampson Gideon [3] were ever very fond of dress. Or, if you be a philosopher, hint that Plato and Seneca are the tailors you choose to employ; assure the company that men ought to be content with a bare covering, since what is now the pride of some was formerly our shame. Horace will give you a Latin sentence fit for the occasion:

> Toga, quæ defendere frigus,
> Quamvis crassa, queat.
> [A toga that, though coarse, can keep
> out the cold.]

In short, however caught do not give up, but ascribe to the frugality of your disposition what others might be apt to attribute to the narrowness of your circumstances, and appear rather to be a miser than a beggar. To be poor and to seem poor is a certain method never to rise. Pride in the great is hateful, in the wise it is ridiculous; beggarly pride is the only sort of vanity I can excuse.

Suggestions

1. Show how the thesis of "On the Use of Language" is supported by the analogy of the fallen column (¶4). How does the essay begin, according to the methods described in Part 1 of this book?

2. Discuss the irony in the speaker's attitude toward (a) needy persons, (b) the fashionable London world.

3. Explain: *treatises, farthing, scrivener, redress, stuffs, frugality.*

4. Write an essay on one:
   "Pity and friendship are passions incompatible with each other. . . ." (¶5).

   ". . . they who had daughters frequently, in the warmth of affection, advised him to marry" (¶7).

   ". . . if you be a philosopher, hint that Plato and Seneca are the tailors you choose to employ. . . ." (¶14).

---

[2] George Cheyne (1671–1743) recommended a vegetable diet in such works as *The Natural Method of Curing the Diseases of the Body* (1742).
[3] A rich broker, notorious for his slovenly clothes.

WRITING SELF-TAUGHT

(1771)

BENJAMIN FRANKLIN

An ingenious tradesman, Mr. Matthew Adams, who had a pretty collection of books and who frequented our printing-house took notice of me, invited me to his library, and very kindly lent me such books as I chose to read. I now took a fancy to poetry and made some little pieces; my brother, thinking it might turn to account, encouraged me and put me on composing occasional ballads. One was called *The Lighthouse Tragedy* and contained an account of the drowning of Captain Worthilake with his two daughters; the other was a sailor's song on the taking of Teach (or Blackbeard) the pirate. They were wretched stuff, in the Grub-street-ballad style; and when they were printed he sent me about the town to sell them. The first sold wonderfully, the event, being recent, having made a great noise. This flattered my vanity; but my father discouraged me by ridiculing my performances and telling me verse-makers were generally beggars. So I escaped being a poet, most probably a very bad one; but as prose writing has been of great use to me in the course of my life and was a principal means of my advancement, I shall tell you how in such a situation I acquired what little ability I have in that way.

There was another bookish lad in the town, John Collins by name, with whom I was intimately acquainted. We sometimes disputed; and very fond we were of argument and very desirous of confuting one another, which disputatious turn, by the way, is apt to become a very bad habit, making people often extremely disagreeable in company by the contradiction that is necessary to bring it into practice; and thence, besides souring and spoiling the conversation, is productive of disgusts and perhaps enmities where you may have occasion for friendship. I had caught it by reading my father's books of dispute about religion. Persons of good sense, I have since observed, seldom fall into it, except lawyers, university men, and men of all sorts that have been bred at Edinburgh.[1]

A question was once somehow or other started between Collins and me of the propriety of educating the female sex in learning, and their abilities for study. He was of opinion that it was improper and that they were naturally unequal to it. I took the contrary side, perhaps a little

---

[1] I.e. educated at its university.

for dispute's sake. He was naturally more eloquent, had a ready plenty of words, and sometimes, as I thought, bore me down more by his fluency than by the strength of his reasons. As we parted without settling the point and were not to see one another again for some time, I sat down to put my arguments in writing which I copied fair and sent to him. He answered and I replied. Three or four letters of a side had passed when my father happened to find my papers and read them. Without entering into the discussion he took occasion to talk to me about the manner of my writing; observed that, though I had the advantage of my antagonist in correct spelling and pointing (which I owed to the printing-house), I fell far short in elegance of expression, in method, and in perspicuity, of which he convinced me by several instances. I saw the justice of his remarks and thence grew more attentive to the manner in writing, and determined to endeavor at improvement.

About this time I met with an odd volume of *The Spectator.*[2] It was the third. I had never before seen any of them. I bought it, read it over and over, and was much delighted with it. I thought the writing excellent and wished if possible to imitate it. With this view I took some of the papers and, making short hints of the sentiment in each sentence, laid them by a few days, and then, without looking at the book, tried to complete the papers again by expressing each hinted sentiment at length, and as fully as it had been expressed before, in any suitable words that should come to hand. Then I compared my *Spectator* with the original, discovered some of my faults, and corrected them. But I found I wanted a stock of words, or a readiness in recollecting and using them, which I thought I should have acquired before that time if I had gone on making verses, since the continual occasion for words of the same import but of different length, to suit the measure, or of different sound for the rhyme, would have laid me under a constant necessity of searching for variety and also have tended to fix that variety in my mind and make me master of it. Therefore I took some of the tales and turned them into verse, and after a time, when I had pretty well forgotten the prose, turned them back again. I also sometimes jumbled my collections of hints into confusion and after some weeks endeavored to reduce them into the best order, before I began to form the full sentences and complete the paper. This was to teach me method in the arrangement of thoughts. By comparing my work afterwards with the original I discovered my faults and amended them; but I sometimes had the pleasure of fancying that, in certain particulars of small import, I had been lucky enough to improve the method or the language, and this encouraged me to think I might possibly in time come to be a tolerable English writer, of which I was extremely ambitious.

[2] By Steele and Addison. See † "Alexander Selkirk" and † "Laughter."

Suggestions

1. The last sentence of "Writing Self-Taught" suggests that Franklin sometimes bettered the arrangement of the *Spectator* essay on which he was working. After carefully rereading his account, rewrite it in the third person with its topics in this order: (a) his father's criticisms of his writing, (b) the bad influence on it of his arguments with Collins, (c) the good influence of his attempts at poetry, (d) the means by which he improved. Then ask another writer to compare your version with the original.

2. In your rewriting substitute synonyms for these terms: *pretty, occasional ballads, Grub Street, Edinburgh, pointing, perspicuity, sentiment.*

3. Rewrite † "Laughter" or † "Alexander Selkirk" according to Franklin's method.

4. Write an essay on "the propriety of educating the female sex in learning, and their abilities for study" (¶3).

5. With the help of the library write a detailed explanation of Franklin's statement that "prose writing has been of great use to me in the course of my life and was a principal means of my advancement" (¶1).

ON PEDANTRY

(1816)

WILLIAM HAZLITT

The power of attaching an interest to the most trifling or painful pursuits, in which our whole attention and faculties are engaged, is one of the greatest happinesses of our nature. The common soldier mounts the breach with joy; the miser deliberately starves himself to death; the mathematician sets about extracting the cube root with a feeling of enthusiasm; and the lawyer sheds tears of admiration over Coke upon Littleton.[1] It is the same through human life. He who is not in some measure a pedant, though he may be a wise, cannot be a very happy man.

[1] Part I of Sir Edward Coke's *Institutes,* published in 1628.

The chief charm of reading the old novels is from the picture they give of the egotism of the characters, the importance of each individual to himself, and his fancied superiority over everyone else. We like, for instance, the pedantry of Parson Adams, who thought a schoolmaster the greatest character in the world and that he was the greatest schoolmaster in it. We do not see any equivalent for the satisfaction which this conviction must have afforded him in the most nicely graduated scale of talents and accomplishments to which he was an utter stranger. When the old-fashioned Scotch pedagogue turns Roderick Random round and round, and surveys him from head to foot with such infinite surprise and laughter, at the same time breaking out himself into gestures and exclamations still more uncouth and ridiculous, who would wish to have deprived him of this burst of extravagant self-complacency? When our follies afford equal delight to ourselves and those about us, what is there to be desired more? We cannot discover the vast advantage of "seeing ourselves as others see us." [2] It is better to have a contempt for anyone than for ourselves!

One of the most constant butts of ridicule, both in the old comedies and novels, is the professional jargon of the medical tribe. Yet it cannot be denied that this jargon, however affected it may seem, is the natural language of apothecaries and physicians, the mother-tongue of pharmacy! It is that by which their knowledge first comes to them, that with which they have the most obstinate associations, that in which they can express themselves the most readily and with the best effect upon their hearers; and though there may be some assumption of superiority in all this, yet it is only by an effort of circumlocution that they could condescend to explain themselves in ordinary language. Besides, there is a delicacy at bottom; as it is the only language in which a nauseous medicine can be decorously administered, or a limb taken off with the proper degree of secrecy. If the most blundering coxcombs affect this language most, what does it signify, while they retain the same dignified notions of themselves and their art, and are equally happy in their knowledge or their ignorance? The ignorant and pretending physician is a capital character in Molière: and, indeed, throughout his whole plays the great source of the comic interest is in the fantastic exaggeration of blind self-love, in letting loose the habitual peculiarities of each individual from all restraint of conscious observation or self-knowledge, in giving way to that specific levity of impulse which mounts at once to the height of absurdity, in spite of the obstacles that surround it, as a fluid in a barometer rises according to the pressure of the external air! His characters are almost always pedantic, and yet the most unconscious of all

[2] Burns, "To a Louse," stanza 8.

others. Take, for example, those two worthy gentlemen, Monsieur Jourdain and Monsieur Pourceaugnac.[3]

Learning and pedantry were formerly synonymous, and it was well when they were so. Can there be a higher satisfaction than for a man to understand Greek and to believe that there is nothing else worth understanding? Learning is the knowledge of that which is not generally known. What an ease and a dignity in pretensions founded on the ignorance of others! What a pleasure in wondering, what a pride in being wondered at! In the library of the family where we were brought up stood the *Fratres Poloni* [4]; and we can never forget or describe the feeling with which not only their appearance but the names of the authors on the outside inspired us. Pripscovius, we remember, was one of the easiest to pronounce. The gravity of the contents seemed in proportion to the weight of the volumes; the importance of the subjects increased with our ignorance of them. The trivialness of the remarks, if ever we looked into them—the repetitions, the monotony, only gave a greater solemnity to the whole, as the slowness and minuteness of the evidence adds to the impressiveness of a judicial proceeding. We knew that the authors had devoted their whole lives to the production of these works, carefully abstaining from the introduction of anything amusing or lively or interesting. In ten folio volumes there was not one sally of wit, one striking reflection. What, then, must have been their sense of the importance of the subject, the profound stores of knowledge which they had to communicate! "From all this world's encumbrance they did themselves assoil." [5] Such was the notion we then had of this learned lumber; yet we would rather have this feeling again for one half-hour than be possessed of all the acuteness of Bayle or the wit of Voltaire!

It may be considered as a sign of the decay of piety and learning in modern times that our divines no longer introduce texts of the original Scriptures into their sermons. The very sound of the original Greek or Hebrew would impress the hearer with a more lively faith in the sacred writers than any translation, however literal or correct. It may be even doubted whether the translation of the Scriptures into the vulgar tongue was any advantage to the people. The mystery in which particular points

[3] A good-natured man will always have a smack of pedantry about him. A lawyer who talks about law, *certioraris, noli prosequis,* and silk gowns, though he may be a blockhead, is by no means dangerous. It is a very bad sign (unless where it arises from singular modesty) when you cannot tell a man's profession from his conversation. Such persons either feel no interest in what concerns them most, or do not express what they feel. "Not to admire anything" is a very unsafe rule. A London apprentice who did not admire the Lord Mayor's coach would stand a good chance of being hanged. We know but one person absurd enough to have formed his whole character on the above maxim of Horace, and who affects a superiority over others from an uncommon degree of natural and artificial stupidity.—*Hazlitt's note.* The two characters are found in Molière's comedies *The Bourgeois Gentleman* and *Mr. Pourceaugnac.*

[4] A nine-volume commentary on the New Testament, whose title runs, in part, *Bibliotheca Fratrum Polonorum, quos Unitarios vocant, instructa operibus omnibus F. Socini, J. Crellii, J. Slichtingii, A. Bucowietz, et J. L. Wolzogenii. . . .* [Amsterdam,] *post annum, . . . 1656.* The works of Samuel Przipcovius [*sic*], form the ninth volume, 1692.

[5] Spenser, *The Fairie Queene* I, iv, 20.

of faith were left involved gave an awe and sacredness to religious opinions: the general purport of the truths and promises of revelation was
made known by other means; and nothing beyond this general and
implicit conviction can be obtained, where all is undefined and infinite.

Again, it may be questioned whether, in matters of mere human
reasoning, much has been gained by the disuse of the learned languages.
Sir Isaac Newton wrote in Latin; and it is perhaps one of Bacon's fopperies that he translated his works into English. If certain follies have
been exposed by being stripped of their formal disguise, others have
had a greater chance of succeeding by being presented in a more pleasing
and popular shape. This has been remarkably the case in France (the
least pedantic country in the world), where the women mingle with
everything, even with metaphysics, and where all philosophy is reduced
to a set of phrases for the toilette. When books are written in the prevailing language of the country, everyone becomes a critic who can read.
An author is no longer tried by his peers. A species of universal suffrage
is introduced in letters, which is only applicable to politics. The good
old Latin style of our forefathers, if it concealed the dullness of the
writer, at least was a barrier against the impertinence, flippancy, and
ignorance of the reader. However, the immediate transition from the
pedantic to the popular style in literature was a change that must have
been very delightful at the time. Our illustrious predecessors, the *Tatler*
and *Spectator*,[6] were very happily off in this respect. They wore the public favor in its newest gloss, before it had become tarnished and common—
before familiarity had bred contempt. It was the honeymoon of author-
ship. Their Essays were among the first instances in this country of
learning sacrificing to the graces, and of a mutual understanding and
good-humored equality between the writer and the reader. This new
style of composition, to use the phraseology of Mr. Burke, "mitigated
authors into companions, and compelled wisdom to submit to the soft
collar of social esteem."[7] The original papers of the *Tatler*, printed on
a half sheet of common foolscap, were regularly served up at breakfast-
time with the silver tea-kettle and thin slices of bread and butter; and
what the ingenious Mr. Bickerstaff wrote overnight in his easy chair, he
might flatter himself would be read the next morning with elegant applause by the fair, the witty, the learned, and the great, in all parts of this
kingdom, in which civilization had made any considerable advances.
The perfection of letters is when the highest ambition of the writer is to
please his readers and the greatest pride of the reader is to understand
his author. The satisfaction on both sides ceases when the town becomes
a club of authors, when each man stands with his manuscript in his hand
waiting for his turn of applause, and when the claims on our admiration
are so many, that, like those of common beggars, to prevent imposition

[6] Periodicals consisting of essays by Steele (who used the name Bickerstaff), Addison, and others. See page 522.
[7] In *Reflections on the Revolution in France.*

they can only be answered with general neglect. Our self-love would be quite bankrupt if critics by profession did not come forward as beadles to keep off the crowd, and to relieve us from the importunity of these innumerable candidates for fame by pointing out their faults and passing over their beauties. In the more auspicious period just alluded to an author was regarded by the better sort as a man of genius, and by the vulgar, as a kind of prodigy; insomuch that the Spectator was obliged to shorten his residence at his friend Sir Roger de Coverley's, from his being taken for a conjuror.[8] Every state of society has its advantages and disadvantages. An author is at present in no danger of being taken for a conjuror!

Suggestions

1. Referring to the last sentence of ¶1, account for the title "On Pedantry" and summarize the speaker's attitude.

2. State the speaker's two reasons for his attitude toward medical jargon.

3. Show that the speaker's defense of Greek and of the *Bibliotheca Fratrum Polonorum* is *paradoxical.* Can the same be said of his remarks about translation of The Bible?

4. Account for the speaker's envy of Addison and Steele and for his ironies at the expense of contemporary critics and authors.

5. Identify or explain: Parson Adams, Roderick Random, Bayle, Voltaire, Newton; *circumlocution, coxcombs, fopperies.*

6. Assuming it is true that "The perfection of letters is when the highest ambition of the writer is to please his readers and the greatest pride of the reader is to understand his author," write an essay on the present literary situation.

THE GENTLE GIANTESS

(1822)

CHARLES LAMB

The Widow Blacket, of Oxford, is the largest female I ever had the pleasure of beholding. There may be her parallel upon the earth, but

---

[8] In No. 131 of *The Spectator.*

surely I never saw it. I take her to be lineally descended from the maid's aunt of Brainford, who caused Master Ford such uneasiness.[1] She hath Atlantean shoulders; and, as she stoopeth in her gait—with as few offences to answer for in her own particular as any of Eve's daughters—her back seems broad enough to bear the blame of all the peccadilloes that have been committed since Adam.

She girdeth her waist—or what she is pleased to esteem as such—nearly up to her shoulders; from beneath which, that huge dorsal expanse in mountainous declivity emergeth. Respect for her alone preventeth the idle boys, who follow her about in shoals whenever she cometh abroad, from getting up and riding. But her presence infallibly commands a reverence. She is indeed, as the Americans would express it, something awful. Her person is a burthen to herself no less than to the ground which bears her. To her mighty bone, she hath a pinguitude [fatness] withal which makes the depth of winter to her the most desirable season.

Her distress in the warmer solstice is pitiable. During the months of July and August she usually renteth a cool cellar, where ices are kept, whereinto she descendeth when Sirius rageth. She dates from a hot Thursday—some twenty-five years ago. Her apartment in summer is pervious to the four winds. Two doors in north and south direction and two windows fronting the rising and the setting sun, never closed, from every cardinal point catch the contributory breezes. She loves to enjoy what she calls a quadruple draught. That must be a shrew zephyr that can escape her. I owe a painful face-ache, which oppresses me at this moment, to a cold caught sitting by her one day in last July, at this receipt of coolness. Her fan in ordinary resembles a banner spread, which she keepeth continually on the alert to detect the least breeze.

She possesseth an active and gadding mind totally incommensurate with her person. No one delighteth more than herself in country exercises and pastimes. I have passed many an agreeable holiday with her in her favorite park at Woodstock. She performs her part in these delightful ambulatory excursions by the aid of a portable garden chair. She setteth out with you at a fair foot-gallop, which she keepeth up till you are both well breathed, and then she reposeth for a few seconds. Then she is up again for a hundred paces or so, and again resteth; her movement on these sprightly occasions being something between walking and flying. Her great weight seemeth to propel her forward, ostrich-fashion. In this kind of relieved marching I have traversed with her many scores of acres on those well-wooded and well-watered domains.

Her delight at Oxford is in the public walks and gardens, where, when the weather is not too oppressive, she passeth much of her valuable time. There is a bench at Magdalen [College], or rather situated between the

---

[1] In Shakespeare, *Merry Wives of Windsor* IV. ii.

frontiers of that and ——'s College (some litigation latterly about repairs
has vested the property of it finally in ——'s), where at the hour of noon
she is ordinarily to be found sitting—so she calls it by courtesy—but in
fact pressing and breaking of it down with her enormous settlement, as
both those foundations—who, however, are good-natured enough to wink
at it—have found, I believe, to their cost. Here she taketh the fresh air,
principally at vacation times, when the walks are freest from interruption
of the younger fry of students. Here she passeth her idle hours, not idly
but generally accompanied with a book—blessed if she can but intercept
some resident Fellow (as usually there are some of that brood left behind
at these periods) or stray Master of Arts (to most of whom she is better
known than their dinner-bell), with whom she may confer upon any
curious topic of literature.

I have seen these shy gownsmen, who truly set but a very slight value
upon female conversation, cast a hawk's eye upon her from the length
of Magdalen Grove and warily glide off into another walk—true monks
as they are, and ungently neglecting the delicacies of her polished converse for their own perverse and uncommunicating solitariness!

Within doors her principal diversion is music, vocal and instrumental,
in both which she is no mean professor. Her voice is wonderfully fine;
but, till I got used to it, I confess it staggered me. It is for all the world
like that of a piping bullfinch; while, from her size and stature, you
would expect notes to drown the deep organ. The shake, which most
fine singers reserve for the close or cadence, by some unaccountable
flexibility, or tremulousness of pipe, she carrieth quite through the
composition; so that her time to a common air or ballad keeps double
motion like the earth—running the primary circuit of the tune and still
revolving upon its own axis. The effect, as I said before, when you are
used to it is as agreeable as it is altogether new and surprising.

The spacious apartment of her outward frame lodgeth a soul in all
respects disproportionate. Of more than mortal make, she evinceth withal
a trembling sensibility, a yielding infirmity of purpose, a quick suscepti-
bility to reproach, and all the train of diffident and blushing virtues
which for their habitation usually seek out a feeble frame, an attenuated
and meagre constitution. With more than man's bulk, her humors and
occupations are eminently feminine. She sighs—being six foot high. She
languisheth—being two feet wide. She worketh slender sprigs upon
the delicate muslin, her fingers being capable of molding a Colossus.
She sippeth her wine out of her glass daintily—her capacity being that
of a tun of Heidelberg. She goeth mincingly with those feet of hers,
whose solidity need not fear the black ox's pressure.

Softest and largest of thy sex, adieu! By what parting attribute may
I salute thee, last and best of the Titanesses—Ogress fed with milk instead of blood; not least, or least handsome, among Oxford's stately

structures—Oxford, who in its deadest time of vacation can never properly be said to be empty, having thee to fill it.

Suggestions

1. Show that the title, "The Gentle Giantess," is *paradoxical* and that
the paradox is developed by the speaker's attitude as ¶1 foreshadows it.

2. Name the topics of the four following paragraphs, showing how the
humor of the essay depends upon its concentration on a few of Mrs.
Blacket's traits.

3. List the most striking contrasts established in ¶¶7–9.

4. Explain: *Atlantean, dorsal, Sirius, pervious, litigation, Colossus,
tun, Titanesses.*

5. Write a comparison of "The Gentle Giantess" and † "Dream Children," deciding whether they conform to your idea of an essay.

GOETHE'S PORTRAIT

(1832)

THOMAS CARLYLE

Reader! thou here [in *Fraser's Magazine*] beholdest the Eidolon of Johann
Wolfgang von Goethe. So looks and lives, now in his eighty-third year,
afar in the bright little friendly circle of Weimar, "the clearest, most
universal man of his time." Strange enough is the cunning that resides
in the ten fingers, especially what they bring to pass by pencil and pen!
Him who never saw England, England now sees: from Fraser's "Gallery"
he looks forth here, wondering, doubtless, how *he* came into such a
"Lichtstrasse, lightstreet," or galaxy; yet with kind recognition of all
neighbors, even as the moon looks kindly on lesser lights, and, were
they but fish-oil cressets, or terrestrial Vauxhall stars (of clipped tin),
forbids not their shining.—Nay, the very soul of the man thou canst
likewise behold. Do but look well in those forty volumes of "musical
wisdom," which, under the title of *Goethes Werke,* Cotta of Tübingen,
or Black and Young of Covent Garden,—once offer them a trifle of
drink-money,—will cheerfully hand thee: greater sight, or more profitable, thou wilt not meet with in this generation. The German language,

it is presumable, thou knowest; if not, shouldst thou undertake the study thereof for that sole end, it were well worth thy while.

Croquis, a man otherwise of rather satirical turn, surprises us, on this occasion, with a fit of enthusiasm. He declares often, that here is the finest of all living heads; speaks much of blended passion and repose; serene depths of eyes; the brow, the temples, royally arched, a very palace of thought;—and so forth.

The Writer of these Notices is not without decision of character, and can believe what he knows. He answers Brother Croquis, that it is no wonder the head should be royal and a palace; for most royal work was appointed to be done therein. Reader! within that head the whole world lies mirrored, in such clear ethereal harmony as it has done in none since Shakespeare left us: even *this* rag-fair of a world, wherein thou painfully strugglest, and (as is like) stumblest,—all lies transfigured here, and revealed authentically to be still holy, still divine. What alchemy was that: to find a mad universe full of scepticism, discord, desperation; and *transmute* it into a wise universe of belief, and melody, and reverence! Was not *there* an *opus magnum,* if one ever was? This, then, is he who, heroically doing and enduring, has accomplished it.

In this distracted Time of ours, wherein men have lost their old lodestars, and wandered after night-fires and foolish will-o'-wisps; and all things, in that "shaking of the nations," have been tumbled into chaos, the high made low, and the low high; and ever and anon some duke of this, and king of that, is gurgled aloft, to float there for moments; and fancies himself the governor and head-director of it all, and *is* but the topmost froth-bell, to burst again and mingle with the wild fermenting mass: in this so despicable Time, we say, there was nevertheless (be the bounteous Heavens ever thanked for it!) *two great men* sent among us. The one, in the island of St. Helena now sleeps "dark and lone, amid the Ocean's everlasting lullaby"; the other still rejoices in the blessed sunlight, on the banks of the Ilme.

Great was the part allotted each, great the talent given him for the same; yet, mark the contrast! Bonaparte walked through the war-convulsed world like an all-devouring earthquake, heaving, thundering, hurling kingdom over kingdom; Goethe was as the mild-shining, in-audible Light, which, notwithstanding, can again make that Chaos into a Creation. Thus too, we see Napoleon, with his Austerlitzes, Waterloos, and Borodinos, is quite gone; all departed, sunk to silence like a tavern-brawl. While this other!—*he* still shines with his direct radiance; his inspired words are to abide in living hearts, as the life and inspiration of thinkers, born and still unborn. Some fifty years hence, his thinking will be found translated, and ground down, even to the capacity of the diurnal press; acts of parliament will be passed in virtue of him:—this man, if we will consider of it, is appointed to be ruler of the world.

Reader! to thee thyself, even now, he has one counsel to give, the secret of his whole poetic alchemy: GEDENKE ZU LEBEN. Yes, "think of living"! Thy life, wert thou the "pitifulest of all the sons of the earth," is no idle dream, but a solemn reality. It is thy own; it is all thou hast to front eternity with. Work, then, even as he has done, and does,— LIKE A STAR, UNHASTING, YET UNRESTING. *Sic valeas* [So farewell].

Suggestions

1. Summarize the speaker's reasons for his attitude toward Goethe, pointing out the comparisons that make his estimate as precise as possible. Are his reasons for admiring Napoleon made equally clear?

2. Explain: *Eidolon, Weimar, cressets, opus magnum, St. Helena.*

3. With the help of the library, write an essay approving or disapproving of the speaker's admiration for Goethe.

4. Write an essay comparing "Goethe's Portrait" as a *hortatory* essay with † "The Man and the Masses."

LITERATURE OF KNOWLEDGE AND LITERATURE OF POWER

(1848)

THOMAS DE QUINCEY

What is it that we mean by *literature?* Popularly, and amongst the thoughtless, it is held to include everything that is printed in a book. Little logic is required to disturb *that* definition. The most thoughtless person is easily made aware that in the idea of *literature* one essential element is—some relation to a general and common interest of man, so that what applies only to a local or professional or merely personal interest, even though presenting itself in the shape of a book, will not belong to literature. So far the definition is easily narrowed; and it is as easily expanded. For not only is much that takes a station in books not literature, but, inversely, much that really *is* literature never reaches a station in books. The weekly sermons of Christendom, that vast pulpit literature which acts so extensively upon the popular mind—to warn, to uphold, to renew, to comfort, to alarm—does not attain the sanctuary of libraries in the ten-thousandth part of its extent. The drama, again, as for instance the finest of Shakespeare's plays in England and all leading Athenian plays in the noontide of the Attic stage,[1] operated as a literature on the public mind, and were (according to the strictest letter of that term) *published* through the audiences that witnessed their representation, some time before they were published as things to be read; and they were published in this scenical mode of publication with much more effect than they could have had as books during ages of costly copying or of costly printing.

Books, therefore, do not suggest an idea co-extensive and interchangeable with the idea of literature, since much literature, scenic, forensic, or didactic (as from lectures and public orators), may never come into books, and much that does come into books may connect itself with no literary interest. But a far more important correction, applicable to the common vague idea of literature, is to be sought, not so much in a better definition of literature, as in a sharper distinction of the two functions which it fulfils. In that great social organ which, collectively, we call literature, there may be distinguished two separate offices, that may blend and often do so, but capable, severally, of a severe insulation and naturally fitted for reciprocal repulsion. There is, first, the literature of *knowledge,* and, secondly, the literature of *power.* The function of the first is to teach; the function of the second is to move: the first is a rudder; the second an oar or a sail. The first speaks to the mere discursive understanding; the second speaks ultimately, it may happen, to the higher understanding, or reason, but always through affections of pleasure and sympathy. Remotely it may travel towards an object seated in what Lord Bacon calls dry light;[2] but proximately it does and must operate—else it ceases to be a literature of power—on and through that humid light which clothes itself in the mists and glittering iris [rainbow] of human passions, desires, and genial emotions. Men have so little reflected on the higher functions of literature as to find it a paradox if one should describe it as a mean or subordinate purpose of books to give information. But this is a paradox only in the sense which makes it honorable to be paradoxical. Whenever we talk in ordinary language of seeking information or gaining knowledge, we understand the words as connected with something of absolute novelty. But it is the grandeur of all truth which can occupy a very high place in human interests that it is never absolutely novel to the meanest of minds: it exists eternally, by way of germ or latent principle, in the lowest as in the highest, needing to be developed but never to be planted. To be capable of transplantation is the immediate criterion of a truth that ranges on a lower scale. Besides which, there is a rarer thing

---

[1] C. 490–407 B.C., the time of Aeschylus, Sophocles, and Euripides.
[2] Heraclitus the Obscure said: *The dry light was the best soul.* Meaning, when the faculties intellectual are in vigor, not wet nor, as it were, blooded by the affections. Bacon, *Apophthegms New and Old.—De Quincey's note.*

than truth, namely power or deep sympathy with truth. What is the effect, for instance, upon society, of children? By the pity, by the tenderness, and by the peculiar modes of admiration which connect themselves with the helplessness, with the innocence, and with the simplicity of children, not only are the primal affections strengthened and continually renewed, but the qualities which are dearest in the sight of heaven—the frailty, for instance, which appeals to forbearance, the innocence which symbolizes the heavenly, and the simplicity which is most alien from the worldly—are kept up in perpetual remembrance, and their ideals are continually refreshed. A purpose of the same nature is answered by the higher literature, viz., the literature of power. What do you learn from *Paradise Lost?* Nothing at all. What do you learn from a cookery-book? Something new, something that you did not know before, in every paragraph. But would you therefore put the wretched cookery-book on a higher level of estimation than the divine poem? What you owe to Milton is not any knowledge, of which a million separate items are still but a million of advancing steps on the same earthly level; what you owe is power, that is, exercise and expansion to your own latent capacity of sympathy with the infinite, where every pulse and each separate influx is a step upwards, a step ascending as upon a Jacob's ladder from earth to mysterious altitudes above the earth. All the steps of knowledge, from first to last, carry you further on the same plane but could never raise you one foot above your ancient level of earth; whereas the very first step in power is a flight, is an ascending movement into another element where earth is forgotten.

Were it not that human sensibilities are ventilated and continually called out into exercise by the great phenomena of infancy, or of real life as it moves through chance and change, or of literature as it recombines these elements in the mimicries of poetry, romance, etc., it is certain that, like any animal power or muscular energy falling into disuse, all such sensibilities would gradually droop and dwindle. It is in relation to these great moral capacities of man that the literature of power, as contra-distinguished from that of knowledge, lives and has its field of action. It is concerned with what is highest in man; for the Scriptures themselves never condescended to deal by suggestion or cooperation with the mere discursive understanding: when speaking of man in his intellectual capacity, the Scriptures speak, not of the understanding, but of "the understanding heart," [3] making the heart—that is, the great intuitive (or non-discursive) organ, to be the interchangeable formula for man in his highest state of capacity for the infinite. Tragedy, romance, fairy tale, or epopee, all alike restore to man's mind the ideals of justice, of hope, of truth, of mercy, of retribution, which else (left to the support of daily life in its realities) would languish for want of

[3] With which God endowed Solomon; *1 Kings* 3, 12.

sufficient illustration. What is meant, for instance, by *poetic justice?*
It does not mean a justice that differs by its object from the ordinary justice of human jurisprudence, for then it must be confessedly
a very bad kind of justice; but it means a justice that differs
from common forensic justice by the degree in which it attains
its object, a justice that is more omnipotent over its own ends, as
dealing, not with the refractory elements of earthly life, but with the
elements of its own creation and with materials flexible to its own purest
preconceptions. It is certain that, were it not for the literature of power,
these ideals would often remain amongst us as mere arid notional forms;
whereas, by the creative forces of man put forth in literature, they gain
a vernal life of restoration and germinate into vital activities. The commonest novel, by moving in alliance with human fears and hopes, with
human instincts of wrong and right, sustains and quickens those affections. Calling them into action, it rescues them from torpor. And hence
the pre-eminency, over all authors that merely teach, of the meanest that
moves, or that teaches, if at all, indirectly by moving. The very highest
work that has ever existed in the literature of knowledge is but a provisional work, a book upon trial and sufferance, and *quamdiu bene se
gesserit* [(tolerated) so long as it behaved well]. Let its teaching be even
partially revised, let it be but expanded, nay, even let its teaching be
but placed in a better order, and instantly it is superseded. Whereas the
feeblest works in the literature of power, surviving at all, survive as
finished and unalterable among men. For instance, the *Principia* of Sir
Isaac Newton was a book militant on earth from the first. In all stages of
its progress it would have to fight for its existence: first, as regards absolute truth; secondly, when that combat was over, as regards its form, or
mode of presenting the truth. And as soon as a La Place or anybody else
builds higher upon the foundations laid by this book, effectually he
throws it out of the sunshine into decay and darkness; by weapons won
from this book he superannuates and destroys this book, so that soon
the name of Newton remains as a mere *nominis umbra* [shadow of a
name], but his book as a living power has transmigrated into other forms.

Now on the contrary the *Iliad,* the *Prometheus* of Æschylus, the *Othello*
or *King Lear,* the *Hamlet* or *Macbeth,* and the *Paradise Lost* are not
militant but triumphant forever, as long as the languages exist in which
they speak or can be taught to speak. They never can transmigrate into
new incarnations. To reproduce these in new forms or variations, even
if in some things they should be improved, would be to plagiarize. A
good steam-engine is properly superseded by a better. But one lovely
pastoral valley is not superseded by another, nor a statue of Praxiteles
by a statue of Michael Angelo. These things are separated, not by im-
parity, but by disparity. They are not thought of as unequal under the
same standard, but as different in kind, and, if otherwise equal, as equal

under a different standard. Human works of immortal beauty and works of nature in one respect stand on the same footing: they never absolutely repeat each other, never approach so near as not to differ; and they differ not as better and worse, or simply by more and less; they differ by undecipherable and incommunicable differences, that cannot be caught by mimicries, that cannot be reflected in the mirror of copies, that cannot become ponderable in the scales of vulgar comparison.

Suggestions

1. Literature of knowledge, according to this essay, succeeds if it communicates new truth; literature of power, on the other hand, exists to promote "deep sympathy with truth." One speaks to the *discursive* understanding, the other to a *non-discursive* faculty. (Decide whether the italicized terms have approximately the same meanings as in Part 1 of this book.) Which does the speaker consider to be the higher faculty? Agree or disagree.

2. Distinguish poetic justice from ordinary justice, showing the importance of this distinction to the speaker's thesis.

3. Explain what is meant by the statement that unlike Newton's *Principia,* the *Iliad* and other works of power "are not militant but triumphant forever" (last ¶).

4. Explain: *forensic, didactic, reciprocal repulsion, paradox, Jacob's ladder, epopee, ponderable.*

5. Summarizing the speaker's contrast between *Paradise Lost* and a cookbook, write an essay defending or attacking the view that from such works as *Paradise Lost* we learn "Nothing at all." If possible, base your argument on a literary work mentioned in the essay.

THE VILLAGE

(1854)

HENRY DAVID THOREAU

After hoeing, or perhaps reading and writing, in the forenoon, I usually bathed again in the pond,[1] swimming across one of its coves for a stint,

[1] Thoreau had built a hut on the north shore of Walden Pond, near Concord, Mass., and lived alone there for twenty-six months beginning 4 July 1845.

and washed the dust of labor from my person, or smoothed out the last wrinkle which study had made, and for the afternoon was absolutely free. Every day or two I strolled to the village to hear some of the gossip which is incessantly going on there, circulating either from mouth to mouth or from newspaper to newspaper, and which, taken in homeo-pathic doses, was really as refreshing in its way as the rustle of leaves and the peeping of frogs. As I walked in the woods to see the birds and squirrels, so I walked in the village to see the men and boys; instead of the wind among the pines I heard the carts rattle. In one direction from my house there was a colony of muskrats in the river meadows; under the grove of elms and buttonwoods in the other horizon was a village of busy men, as curious to me as if they had been prairie-dogs, each sitting at the mouth of its burrow, or running over to a neighbor's to gossip. I went there frequently to observe their habits. The village appeared to me a great news room; and on one side, to support it, as once at Redding & Company's on State Street, they kept nuts and raisins, or salt and meal and other groceries. Some have such a vast appetite for the former com-modity, that is, the news, and such sound digestive organs, that they can sit forever in public avenues without stirring, and let it simmer and whisper through them like the Etesian winds, or as if inhaling ether, it only producing numbness and insensibility to pain—otherwise it would often be painful to hear—without affecting the consciousness.

I hardly ever failed, when I rambled through the village, to see a row of such worthies, either sitting on a ladder sunning themselves, with their bodies inclined forward and their eyes glancing along the line this way and that, from time to time, with a voluptuous expression, or else lean-ing against a barn with their hands in their pockets, like caryatides, as if to prop it up. They, being commonly out of doors, heard whatever was in the wind. These are the coarsest mills, in which all gossip is first rudely digested or cracked up before it is emptied into finer and more delicate hoppers within doors. I observed that the vitals of the village were the grocery, the bar-room, the post-office, and the bank; and, as a necessary part of the machinery, they kept a bell, a big gun, and a fire-engine at convenient places; and the houses were so arranged as to make the most of mankind, in lanes and fronting one another, so that every traveller had to run the gantlet, and every man, woman, and child might get a lick at him. Of course, those who were stationed nearest to the head of the line, where they could most see and be seen, and have the first blow at him, paid the highest prices for their places; and the few strag-gling inhabitants in the outskirts, where long gaps in the line began to occur, and the traveller could get over walls or turn aside into cow-paths, and so escape, paid a very slight ground or window tax. Signs were hung out on all sides to allure him; some to catch him by the appetite, as the tavern and victualing cellar; some by the fancy, as the dry-goods store and the jeweler's; and others by the hair or the feet or the skirts, as the barber, the shoemaker, or the tailor. Besides, there was a still more terrible standing invitation to call at every one of these houses, and company expected about these times. For the most part I escaped wonderfully from these dangers, either by proceeding at once boldly and without deliberation to the goal, as is recommended to those who run the gantlet, or by keeping my thoughts on high things, like Orpheus, who, "loudly singing the praises of the gods to his lyre, drowned the voices of the Sirens and kept out of danger." Sometimes I bolted suddenly, and nobody could tell my whereabouts, for I did not stand much about gracefulness, and never hesitated at a gap in a fence. I was even accustomed to make an irruption into some houses, where I was well entertained, and after learning the kernels and very last sieveful of news—what had subsided, the prospects of war and peace, and whether the world was likely to hold together much longer—I was let out through the rear avenues, and so escaped to the woods again.

It was very pleasant, when I stayed late in town, to launch myself into the night, especially if it was dark and tempestuous, and set sail from some bright village parlor or lecture room, with a bag of rye or Indian meal upon my shoulder, for my snug harbor in the woods, having made all tight without and withdrawn under hatches with a merry crew of thoughts, leaving only my outer man at the helm, or even tying up the helm when it was plain sailing. I had many a genial thought by the cabin fire "as I sailed." I was never cast away nor distressed in any weather, though I encountered some severe storms. It is darker in the woods, even in common nights, than most suppose. I frequently had to look up at the opening between the trees above the path in order to learn my route, and, where there was no cart-path, to feel with my feet the faint track which I had worn, or steer by the known relation of particular trees which I felt with my hands, passing between two pines for instance, not more than eighteen inches apart, in the midst of the woods, invariably, in the darkest night. Sometimes, after coming home thus late in a dark and muggy night, when my feet felt the path which my eyes could not see, dreaming and absent-minded all the way, until I was aroused by having to raise my hand to lift the latch, I have not been able to recall a single step of my walk, and I have thought that perhaps my body would find its way home if its master should forsake it, as the hand finds its way to the mouth without assistance. Several times, when a visitor chanced to stay into evening, and it proved a dark night, I was obliged to conduct him to the cart-path in the rear of the house, and then point out to him the direction he was to pursue, and in keeping which he was to be guided rather by his feet than his eyes. One very dark night I directed thus on their way two young men who had been fishing in the pond. They lived about a mile off through the woods and were quite used to the route. A day or two after, one of them told me that they wandered about the greater part of the night, close by their own premises, and did not get home till toward morning, by which time, as there had been several heavy showers in the meanwhile and the leaves were very wet, they were drenched to their skins. I have heard of many going astray even in the village streets, when the darkness was so thick that you could cut it with a knife, as the saying is. Some who live in the outskirts, having come to town a-shopping in their wagons, have been obliged to put up for the night; and gentlemen and ladies making a call have gone half a mile out of their way, feeling the sidewalk only with their feet, and not knowing when they turned. It is a surprising and memorable, as well as valuable experience, to be lost in the woods any time. Often in a snow-storm, even by day, one will come out upon a well-known road and yet find it impossible to tell which way leads to the village. Though he knows that he has travelled it a thousand times, he cannot recognize a feature in it, but it is as strange to him as if it were a road in Siberia. By night, of course, the perplexity is infinitely greater. In our most trivial walks we are constantly, though unconsciously, steering like pilots by certain well-known beacons and headlands, and if we go beyond our usual course we still carry in our minds the bearing of some neighboring cape; and not till we are completely lost, or turned round—for a man needs only to be turned round once with his eyes shut in this world to be lost— do we appreciate the vastness and strangeness of nature. Every man has to learn the points of the compass again as often as he awakes, whether from sleep or any abstraction. Not till we are lost, in other words not till we have lost the world, do we begin to find ourselves, and realize where we are and the infinite extent of our relations.

One afternoon, near the end of the first summer, when I went to the village to get a shoe from the cobbler's, I was seized and put into jail, because, as I have elsewhere related, I did not pay a tax to, or recognize the authority of, the State which buys and sells men, women, and children, like cattle, at the door of its senate-house. I had gone down to the woods for other purposes. But wherever a man goes men will pursue and paw him with their dirty institutions, and, if they can, constrain him to belong to their desperate odd-fellow society. It is true, I might have resisted forcibly with more or less effect, might have run "amok" against society; but I preferred that society should run "amok" against me, it being the desperate party. However, I was released the next day, obtained my mended shoe, and returned to the woods in season to get my dinner of huckleberries on Fair Haven Hill. I was never molested by any person but those who represented the State. I had no lock nor bolt but for the desk which held my papers, not even a nail to put over my latch or windows. I never fastened my door night or day, though I was to be absent several days; not even when the next fall I spent a fortnight in the woods of Maine. And yet my house was more respected than if it had been surrounded by a file of soldiers. The tired rambler could rest and warm himself by my fire, the literary amuse himself with the few books on my table, or the curious, by opening my closet door, see what was left of my dinner, and what prospect I had of a supper. Yet, though many people of every class came this way to the pond, I suffered no serious inconvenience from these sources, and I never missed anything but one small book, a volume of Homer, which perhaps was improperly gilded, and this I trust a soldier of our camp has found by this time. I am convinced that if all men were to live as simply as I then did, thieving and robbery would be unknown. These take place only in communities where some have got more than is sufficient while others have not enough. The Pope's Homers [2] would soon get properly distributed.

> Nec bella fuerunt,
> Faginus astabat dum scyphus ante dapes.

> Nor wars did men molest,
> When only beechen bowls were in request.
> [Tibullus, *Elegies* I. x. 8–9]

" You who govern public affairs, what need have you to employ punishments? Love virtue, and the people will be virtuous. The virtues of a superior man are like the wind; the virtues of a common man are like the grass; the grass, when the wind passes over it, bends."

Suggestions

1. Presenting a contrast between life in society and solitude, "The Village" suggests its attitude toward the first by means of several satiric comparisons (news and ether gossipers and mills, the traveller and a captive running the gantlet) and its attitude toward the second by asserting the value of darkness and getting lost in the woods. Summarize these, showing clearly what, according to the speaker, a person gains when he is lost.

2. Though the speaker's resentment against society's "dirty institutions" may seem violent, defend him by identifying the institution to which he has just referred (¶3). Why does he decide not to run amok against society?

3. Interpret: ". . . I never missed anything but . . . a volume of Homer, which perhaps was improperly gilded, and this I trust a soldier of our camp has found by this time."

4. Explain: *homeopathic, Etesian winds, caryatides, irruption, abstraction.*

[2] The lost book was a volume of Alexander Pope's translation of *The Iliad* (1715–1720).

5. Defend or attack the ideal of government suggested by the last quotation. Do you consider the speaker an optimist or a pessimist?

6. Write a characterization of the speaker, showing whether you regard his outlook as a test of your tolerance.

THE GREAT STYLE

(1858)

JOHN RUSKIN

It seems to me, and may seem to the reader, strange that we should need to ask the question, "What is poetry?" Here is a word we have been using all our lives, and I suppose with a very distinct idea attached to it; and when I am now called upon to give a definition of this idea, I find myself at a pause. What is more singular, I do not at present recollect hearing the question often asked, though surely it is a very natural one; and I never recollect hearing it answered or even attempted to be answered. In general, people shelter themselves under metaphors, and while we hear poetry described as an utterance of the soul, an effusion of Divinity, or voice of nature, or in other terms equally elevated and obscure, we never attain anything like a definite explanation of the character which actually distinguishes it from prose.

I come, after some embarrassment, to the conclusion that poetry is "the suggestion by the imagination of noble grounds for the noble emotions." I mean by the noble emotions those four principal sacred passions —Love, Veneration, Admiration, and Joy (this latter especially if unselfish); and their opposites—Hatred, Indignation (or Scorn), Horror, and Grief, this last when unselfish becoming Compassion. These passions in their various combinations constitute what is called "poetical feeling" when they are felt on noble grounds, that is, on great and true grounds. Indignation, for instance, is a poetical feeling, if excited by serious injury; but it is not a poetical feeling if entertained on being cheated out of a small sum of money. It is very possible the manner of the cheat may have been such as to justify considerable indignation; but the feeling is nevertheless not poetical unless the grounds of it be large as well as just. In like manner, energetic admiration may be excited in certain minds by a display of fireworks or a street of handsome shops; but the feeling is not poetical, because the grounds of it are false and therefore ignoble. There is in reality nothing to deserve admiration either in the firing of packets of gunpowder or in the display of the stocks of warehouses. But admiration excited by the budding of a flower is a poetical feeling, because it is impossible that this manifestation of spiritual power and vital beauty can ever be enough admired.

Farther, it is necessary to the existence of poetry that the grounds of these feelings should be *furnished by the imagination.* Poetical feeling— that is to say, mere noble emotion—is not poetry. It is happily inherent in all human nature deserving the name, and is found often to be purest in the least sophisticated. But the power of assembling by *the help of the imagination* such images as will excite these feelings is the power of the poet or literally of the "Maker."

Now this power of exciting the emotions depends of course on the richness of the imagination and on its choice of those images which, in combination, will be most effective or, for the particular work to be done, most fit. And it is altogether impossible for a writer not endowed with invention to conceive what tools a true poet will make use of, or in what way he will apply them, or what unexpected results he will bring out by them; so that it is vain to say that the details of poetry ought to possess, or ever do possess, any *definite* character. Generally speaking, poetry runs into finer and more delicate details than prose; but the details are not poetical because they are more delicate, but because they are employed so as to bring out an affecting result. For instance, no one but a true poet would have thought of exciting our pity for a bereaved father by describing his way of locking the door of his house:

> Perhaps to himself at that moment he said,
> "The key I must take, for my Ellen is dead";
> But of this in my ears not a word did he speak;
> And he went to the chase with a tear on his cheek.
> [Wordsworth, "The Childless Father"]

In like manner, in painting it is altogether impossible to say beforehand what details a great painter may make poetical by his use of them to excite noble emotions; and we shall, therefore, find presently that a painting is to be classed in the great or inferior schools, not according to the kind of details which it represents, but according to the uses for which it employs them.

It is only farther to be noticed that infinite confusion has been introduced into this subject by the careless and illogical custom of opposing painting to poetry, instead of regarding poetry as consisting in a noble use, whether of colors or words. Painting is properly to be opposed to *speaking or writing,* but not to *poetry.* Both painting and speaking are methods of expression. Poetry is the employment of either for the noblest purposes.

This question being thus far determined, we may proceed with our paper in *The Idler*.[1]

"It is very difficult to determine the exact degree of enthusiasm that the arts of Painting and Poetry may admit. There may, perhaps, be too great indulgence as well as too great a restraint of imagination; if the one produces incoherent monsters, the other produces what is full as bad, lifeless insipidity. An intimate knowledge of the passions, and good sense, but not common sense, must at last determine its limits. It has been thought, and I believe with reason, that Michael Angelo sometimes transgressed those limits; and, I think, I have seen figures of him of which it was very difficult to determine whether they were in the highest degree sublime or extremely ridiculous. Such faults may be said to be the ebullitions of genius; but at least he had this merit, that he never was insipid; and whatever passion his works may excite, they will always escape contempt.

"What I have had under consideration is the sublimest style, particularly that of Michael Angelo, the Homer of painting. Other kinds may admit of this naturalness, which of the lowest kind is the chief merit; but in painting, as in poetry, the highest style has the least of common nature."

From this passage we gather three important indications of the supposed nature of the Great Style. That it is the work of men in a state of enthusiasm. That it is like the writing of Homer; and that it has as little as possible of "common nature" in it.

First, it is produced by men in a state of enthusiasm. That is, by men who feel *strongly* and *nobly*; for we do not call a strong feeling of envy, jealousy, or ambition, enthusiasm. That is, therefore, by men who feel poetically. This much we may admit, I think, with perfect safety. Great art is produced by men who feel acutely and nobly; and it is in some sort an expression of this personal feeling. We can easily conceive that there may be a sufficiently marked distinction between such art and that which is produced by men who do not feel at all, but who reproduce, though ever so accurately, yet coldly, like human mirrors, the scenes which pass before their eyes.

Secondly, Great Art is like the writing of Homer, and this chiefly because it has little of "common nature" in it. We are not clearly informed what is meant by common nature in this passage. Homer seems to describe a great deal of what is common—cookery, for instance, very carefully in all its processes. I suppose the passage in the *Iliad* which, on the whole, has excited most admiration is that which describes a wife's

---

[1] A periodical conducted by Samuel Johnson. Sir Joshua Reynolds wrote the number for October 20, 1759, from which Ruskin's quotation comes.

sorrow at parting from her husband and a child's fright at its father's helmet [2]; and I hope, at least, the former feeling may be considered "common nature." But the true greatness of Homer's style is, doubtless, held by our author to consist in his imaginations of things not only uncommon but impossible (such as spirits in brazen armor or monsters with heads of men and bodies of beasts), and in his occasional delineations of the human character and form in their utmost, or heroic, strength and beauty. We gather then on the whole that a painter in the Great Style must be enthusiastic, or full of emotion, and must paint the human form in its utmost strength and beauty, and perhaps certain impossible forms besides, liable by persons not in an equally enthusiastic state of mind to be looked upon as in some degree absurd. This I presume to be Reynolds's meaning, and to be all that he intends us to gather from his comparisons of the Great Style with the writings of Homer. But if that comparison be a just one in all respects, surely two other corollaries ought to be drawn from it, namely, first, that these Heroic or Impossible images are to be mingled with others very unheroic and very possible; and, secondly, that in the representation of the Heroic or Impossible forms, the greatest care must be taken in *finishing the details,* so that a painter must not be satisfied with painting well the countenance and the body of his hero, but ought to spend the greatest part of his time (as Homer the greatest number of verses [3]) in elaborating the sculptured pattern on his shield.

Suggestions

1. Paraphrasing the definition of *poetry* in "The Great Style" (¶2), criticize it by the principles suggested in † "Defining Definition." Does the definition exclude works of prose—e.g. *War and Peace* or some other novel you have read? Ruskin later said that rhythm should have been included in it. Agree or disagree.

2. Defend or attack the speaker's examples of noble and less noble emotions (¶2).

3. Explain the importance of homely details even in works written in "the great style" (last ¶).

4. Explain: *effusion, ebullitions, insipid, corollaries.*

5. Write a comparison of "The Great Style" and † "Topics for Writing" as to their views on the importance of the emotions in life and in literature.

6. Write an essay on the definitions of poetry suggested by † "What Is a Poet?," † "Literature of Knowledge and Literature of Power," and "The Great Style."

---

[2] The characters are Andromache, Hector, and Astyanax (VI. 390–502).
[3] *Iliad* XVIII. 478–608.

THE MAN AND THE MASSES

(1860)

RALPH WALDO EMERSON

Although this garrulity of advising is born with us, I confess that life is rather a subject of wonder than of didactics. So much fate, so much irresistible dictation from temperament and unknown inspiration enters into it, that we doubt we can say anything out of our own experience whereby to help each other. All the professions are timid and expectant agencies. The priest is glad if his prayers or his sermon meet the condition of any soul; if of two, if of ten, 'tis a signal success. But he walked to the church without any assurance that he knew the distemper, or could heal it. The physician prescribes hesitatingly out of his few resources the same tonic or sedative to this new and peculiar constitution which he has applied with various success to a hundred men before. If the patient mends he is glad and surprised. The lawyer advises the client, and tells his story to the jury, and leaves it with them, and is as gay and as much relieved as the client if it turns out that he has a verdict. The judge weighs the arguments and puts a brave face on the matter, and since there must be a decision, decides as he can and hopes he has done justice and given satisfaction to the community, but is only an advocate after all. And so is all life a timid and unskilful spectator. We do what we must, and call it by the best names. We like very well to be praised for our action, but our conscience says, "Not unto us." 'Tis little we can do for each other. We accompany the youth with sympathy and manifold old sayings of the wise to the gate of the arena, but 'tis certain that not by strength of ours, or of the old sayings, but only on strength of his own, unknown to us or to any, he must stand or fall. That by which a man conquers in any passage is a profound secret to every other being in the world, and it is only as he turns his back on us and on all men and draws on this most private wisdom, that any good can come to him. What we have therefore to say of life is rather description, or if you please, celebration, than available rules.

Yet vigor is contagious, and whatever makes us either think or feel strongly, adds to our power and enlarges our field of action. We have a debt to every great heart, to every fine genius, to those who have put life and fortune on the cast of an act of justice, to those who have added new sciences, to those who have refined life by elegant pursuits. 'Tis the fine souls who serve us, and not what is called fine society. Fine society is only a self-protection against the vulgarities of the street and the

545

tavern. Fine society, in the common acceptation, has neither ideas nor aims. It renders the service of a perfumery or a laundry, not of a farm or factory. 'Tis an exclusion and a precinct. Sydney Smith said, "A few yards in London cement or dissolve friendship." It is an unprincipled decorum; an affair of clean linen and coaches, of gloves, cards, and elegance in trifles. There are other measures of self-respect for a man than the number of clean shirts he puts on every day. Society wishes to be amused. I do not wish to be amused. I wish that life should not be cheap but sacred. I wish the days to be as centuries, loaded, fragrant. Now we reckon them as bank-days, by some debt which is to be paid us or which we are to pay, or some pleasure we are to taste. Is all we have to do to draw the breath in and blow it out again? Porphyry's definition is better: "Life is that which holds matter together." The babe in arms is a channel through which the energies we call fate, love, and reason visibly stream. See what a cometary train of auxiliaries man carries with him; of animals, plants, stones, gases, and imponderable elements. Let us infer his ends from this pomp of means. Mirabeau said, "Why should we feel ourselves to be men, unless it be to succeed in everything, everywhere? You must say of nothing, *That is beneath me,* nor feel that anything can be out of your power. Nothing is impossible to the man who can will. *Is that necessary? That shall be:*—this is the only law of success." Whoever said it, this is in the right key. But this is not the tone and genius of the men in the street. In the streets we grow cynical. The men we meet are coarse and torpid. The finest wits have their sediment. What quantities of fribbles, paupers, invalids, epicures, antiquaries, politicians, thieves, and triflers of both sexes might be advantageously spared! Mankind divides itself into two classes: benefactors and malefactors. The second class is vast, the first a handful. A person seldom falls sick but the bystanders are animated with a faint hope that he will die—quantities of poor lives, of distressing invalids, of cases for a gun. Franklin said, "Mankind are very superficial and dastardly: they begin upon a thing, but meeting with a difficulty, they fly from it discouraged; but they have capacities, if they would employ them." Shall we then judge a country by the majority, or by the minority? By the minority, surely. 'Tis pedantry to estimate nations by the census, or by square miles of land, or other than by their importance to the mind of the time.

Leave this hypocritical prating about the masses. Masses are rude, lame, unmade, pernicious in their demands and influence, and need not to be flattered but to be schooled. I wish not to concede anything to them, but to tame, drill, divide, and break them up, and draw individuals out of them. The worst of charity is that the lives you are asked to preserve are not worth preserving. Masses! the calamity is the masses. I do not wish any mass at all, but honest men only; lovely, sweet, accomplished women only; and no shovel-handed, narrow-brained, gin-drinking million stockingers or lazzaroni at all. If government knew how, I should like to see it check, not multiply the population. When it reaches its true law of action, every man that is born will be hailed as essential. Away with this hurrah of masses, and let us have the considerate vote of single men spoken on their honor and their conscience. In old Egypt it was established law that the vote of a prophet be reckoned equal to a hundred hands. I think it was much underestimated. "Clay and clay differ in dignity," as we discover by our preferences every day. What a vicious practice is this of our politicians at Washington pairing off! as if one man who votes wrong going away could excuse you, who mean to vote right, for going away; or as if your presence did not tell in more ways than in your vote. Suppose the three hundred heroes at Thermopylæ had paired off with three hundred Persians; would it have been all the same to Greece, and to history? Napoleon was called by his men *Cent Mille* [One Hundred Thousand]. Add honesty to him, and they might have called him Hundred Million.

Nature makes fifty poor melons for one that is good, and shakes down a tree full of gnarled, wormy, unripe crabs before you can find a dozen dessert apples; and she scatters nations of naked Indians, and nations of clothed Christians, with two or three good heads among them. Nature works very hard and only hits the white once in a million throws. In mankind she is contented if she yields one master in a century. The more difficulty there is in creating good men, the more they are used when they come. I once counted in a little neighborhood and found that every able-bodied man had say from twelve to fifteen persons dependent on him for material aid, to whom he is to be for spoon and jug, for backer and sponsor, for nursery and hospital, and many functions besides. Nor does it seem to make much difference whether he is bachelor or patriarch; if he do not violently decline the duties that fall to him, this amount of helpfulness will in one way or another be brought home to him. This is the tax which his abilities pay. The good men are employed for private centers of use, and for larger influence. All revelations, whether of mechanical or intellectual or moral science, are made not to communities but to single persons. All the marked events of our day, all the cities, all the colonizations, may be traced back to their origin in a private brain. All the feats which make our civility were the thoughts of a few good heads.

Meantime this spawning productivity is not noxious or needless. You would say this rabble of nations might be spared. But no, they are all counted and depended on. Fate keeps everything alive so long as the smallest thread of public necessity holds it on to the tree. The coxcomb and bully and thief class are allowed as proletaries, every one of their vices being the excess or acridity of a virtue. The mass are animal, in pupilage, and near chimpanzee. But the units whereof this mass is composed are neuters, every one of which may be grown to a queen-bee. The rule is, we are used as brute atoms until we think: then we use all the rest. Nature turns all malfeasance to good. Nature provided for real needs. No sane man at last distrusts himself. His existence is a perfect answer to all sentimental cavils. If he is, he is wanted, and has the precise properties that are required. That we are here is proof we ought to be here. We have as good right and the same sort of right to be here as Cape Cod or Sandy Hook have to be there.

To say then, the majority are wicked, means no malice, no bad heart in the observer, but simply that the majority are unripe, and have not yet come to themselves, do not yet know their opinion. *That,* if they knew it, is an oracle for them and for all. But in the passing moment the quadruped interest is very prone to prevail; and this beast-force, whilst it makes the discipline of the world, the school of heroes, the glory of martyrs, has provoked in every age the satire of wits and the tears of good men. They find the journals, the clubs, the governments, the churches, to be in the interest and the pay of the devil. And wise men have met this obstruction in their times, like Socrates, with his famous irony; like Bacon, with lifelong dissimulation; like Erasmus, with his book, *The Praise of Folly;* like Rabelais, with his satire rending the nations. "They were the fools who cried against me, you will say," wrote the Chevalier de Boufflers to Grimm; "aye, but the fools have the advantage of numbers, and 'tis that which decides. It is of no use for us to make war with them; we shall not weaken them; they will always be the masters. There will not be a practice or an usage introduced of which they are not the authors."

Suggestions

1. "The Man and the Masses" opens with a meditation on life's mystery, which leads to a restatement of Emerson's most famous doctrine, that of self-reliance. Show the relation between this doctrine and the speaker's attitude toward society (¶2).

2. Summarize the ways in which the speaker supports his attack on the masses. In ¶5, does he show signs of relenting? Decide whether the words "the majority are unripe" (¶6) summarize his attitude as a whole.

3. Show that despite the disclaimer in ¶1, "The Man and the Masses" is a *hortatory* essay.

4. Identify the persons whose achievements are admired in the conclusion.

5. Explain: *garrulity, didactics, epicures, stockingers, lazzaroni, Thermopylae, proletaries, acridity, dissimulation.*

6. Write an essay on one:

"I wish the days to be as centuries, loaded, fragrant" (¶2).

"Shall we then judge a country by the majority, or by the minority?" (¶2)

"All revelations . . . are made not to communities but to single persons" (¶4).

". . . in the passing moment the quadruped interest is very prone to prevail" (¶6).

QUICKENED CONSCIOUSNESS

(1873)

WALTER PATER

Λέγει που Ἡράκλειτος ὅτι πάντα χωρεῖ καὶ οὐδὲν μένει.

[Heraclitus somewhere says that all things flow and nothing remains.
—Plato, *Cratylus*.]

To regard all things and principles of things as inconstant modes or fashions has more and more become the tendency of modern thought. Let us begin with that which is without—our physical life. Fix upon it in one of its more exquisite intervals—the moment, for instance, of delicious recoil from the flood of water in summer heat. What is the whole physical life in that moment but a combination of natural elements to which science gives their names? But these elements, phosphorus and lime and delicate fibers, are present not in the human body alone: we detect them in places most remote from it. Our physical life is a perpetual motion of them—the passage of the blood, the wasting and repairing of the lenses of the eye, the modification of the tissues of the brain by every ray of light and sound—processes which science reduces to simpler and more elementary forces. Like the elements of which we are composed, the action of these forces extends beyond us; it rusts iron and ripens corn. Far out on every side of us those elements are broadcast, driven by many forces; and birth and gesture and death and the springing of violets from the grave are but a few out of ten thousand resultant combinations. That clear, perpetual outline of face and limb is but an image of ours, under which we group them—a design in a web, the actual threads of which pass out beyond it. This at least of flame-like our life has, that it is but the concurrence, renewed from moment to moment, of forces parting sooner or later on their ways.

Or if we begin with the inward whirl of thought and feeling, the whirlpool is still more rapid, the flame more eager and devouring. There it is no longer the gradual darkening of the eye and fading of color from the wall—the movement of the shoreside, where the water flows down indeed, though in apparent rest—but the race of the mid-stream, a drift of momentary acts of sight and passion and thought. At first sight experience seems to bury us under a flood of external objects, pressing upon us with a sharp and importunate reality, calling us out of ourselves in a thousand forms of action. But when reflection begins to act upon those objects they are dissipated under its influence; the cohesive force seems suspended like a trick of magic; each object is loosed into a group of impressions—color, odor, texture—in the mind of the observer. And if we continue to dwell in thought on this world, not of objects in the solidity with which language invests them, but of impressions unstable, flickering, inconsistent, which burn and are extinguished with our consciousness of them, it contracts still further; the whole scope of observation is dwarfed to the narrow chamber of the individual mind. Experience, already reduced to a swarm of impressions, is ringed round for each one of us by that thick wall of personality through which no real voice has ever pierced on its way to us, or from us to that which we can only conjecture to be without. Every one of those impressions is the impression of the individual in his isolation, each mind keeping as a solitary prisoner its own dream of a world.

Analysis goes a step farther still, and assures us that those impressions of the individual mind to which, for each one of us, experience dwindles down, are in perpetual flight; that each of them is limited by time, and that as time is infinitely divisible, each of them is infinitely divisible also; all that is actual in it being a single moment, gone while we try to apprehend it, of which it may ever be more truly said that it has ceased to be than that it is. To such a tremulous wisp constantly reforming itself on the stream, to a single sharp impression, with a sense in it—a relic more or less fleeting—of such moments gone by, what is real in our life fines itself down. It is with this movement, with the passage and dissolution of impressions, images, sensations, that analysis leaves off—that continual vanishing away, that strange, perpetual weaving and unweaving of ourselves.

Philosophiren, says Novalis, *ist dephlegmatisiren, vivificiren* [To philosophize is to shake off apathy, come alive]. The service of philosophy, of speculative culture, toward the human spirit is to rouse, to startle it into sharp and eager observation. Every moment some form grows perfect in hand or face; some tone on the hills or the sea is choicer than the rest; some mood of passion or insight or intellectual excitement is irresistibly real and attractive for us—but for that moment only. Not the fruit of experience, but experience itself, is the end. A counted number of pulses only is given to us of a variegated, dramatic life. How may we see in them all that is to be seen in them by the finest senses? How shall we pass most swiftly from point to point and be present always at the focus where the greatest number of vital forces unite in their purest energy?

To burn always with this hard, gemlike flame, to maintain this ecstasy, is success in life. In a sense it might even be said that our failure is to form habits: for, after all, habit is relative to a stereotyped world, and meantime it is only the roughness of the eye that makes any two persons, things, situations, seem alike. While all melts under our feet, we may well catch at any exquisite passion, or any contribution to knowledge that seems by a lifted horizon to set the spirit free for a moment, or any stirring of the senses, strange dyes, strange colors, and curious odors, or work of the artist's hands, or the face of one's friend. Not to discriminate every moment some passionate attitude in those about us, and in the brilliancy of their gifts some tragic dividing of forces on their ways, is, on this short day of frost and sun, to sleep before evening. With this sense of the splendor of our experience and of its awful brevity, gathering all we are into one desperate effort to see and touch, we shall hardly have time to make theories about the things we see and touch. What we have to do is to be forever curiously testing new opinions and courting new impressions, never acquiescing in a facile orthodoxy of Comte, or of Hegel, or of our own. Philosophical theories or ideas, as points of view, instruments of criticism, may help us to gather up what might otherwise pass unregarded by us. "Philosophy is the microscope of thought." The theory or idea or system which requires of us the sacrifice of any part of this experience, in consideration of some interest into which we cannot enter, or some abstract theory we have not identified with ourselves, or what is only conventional, has no real claim upon us.

One of the most beautiful passages in the writings of Rousseau is that in the sixth book of the *Confessions,* where he describes the awakening in him of the literary sense. An undefinable taint of death had always clung about him, and now in early manhood he believed himself smitten by mortal disease. He asked himself how he might make as much as possible of the interval that remained; and he was not biased by anything in his previous life when he decided that it must be by intellectual excitement, which he found just then in the clear, fresh writings of Voltaire. Well! we are all *condamnés,* as Victor Hugo says [in *Les Misérables*]: we are all under sentence of death but with a sort of indefinite reprieve—*les hommes sont tous condamnés à mort avec des sursis indéfinis* [men are all condemned to death with indefinite reprieves]; we have an interval, and then our place knows us no more. Some spend this interval in listlessness, some in high passions; the wisest—at least among "the children of this world"[1]—in art and song. For our one chance lies in expanding that interval, in getting as many pulsations as possible into the given time. Great passions may give us this quickened sense of life, ecstasy and sorrow of love, the various forms of enthusiastic activity, disinterested or otherwise, which come naturally to many of us. Only be sure it is passion—that it does yield you this fruit of a quickened, multiplied consciousness. Of this wisdom, the poetic passion, the desire of beauty, the love of art for art's sake, has most; for art comes to you professing frankly to give nothing but the highest quality to your moments as they pass, and simply for those moments' sake.

Suggestions

1. "Quickened Consciousness" represents perpetual change as the chief quality of life—life in the physical sense and still more the life of the mind and feelings—so that life "fines itself down" to a few sharp impressions. Thus the value of culture to the human spirit is "to rouse, to startle it into sharp and eager observation." Compare this view to the idea of poetry advanced by † "Literature of Knowledge and Literature of Power."

2. Summarize the speaker's definitions of success and failure, and his distrust of philosophies (¶5).

3. Account for the title, "Quickened Consciousness," showing what the speaker thinks is the value of art in human life (last ¶).

4. Discuss in writing: "To burn always with this hard, gemlike flame, to maintain this ecstasy, is success in life" (¶5).

5. Write a comparison of "Quickened Consciousness" and † "The Great Style," deciding whether they agree in their attitudes toward the emotions and toward art.

[1] *Gospel of St. Luke* 16, 8.

THE SAVING REMNANT

(1885)

MATTHEW ARNOLD

No doubt to most of us, if we had been there to see it, the kingdom of Ephraim or of Judah, the society of Samaria and Jerusalem, would have seemed to contain a great deal else besides dissolute grandees and foolish common people. No doubt we should have thought parts of their policy serious, and some of their alliances promising. No doubt, when we read the Hebrew prophets now, with the larger and more patient temper of a different race and an augmented experience, we often feel the blame and invective to be too absolute. Nevertheless, as to his grand point, Isaiah, I say, was right. The majority in the Jewish state, whatever their guides and flatterers might think or say, the majority were unsound, and their unsoundness must be their ruin.

Isaiah, however, does not make his remnant confine itself, like Plato's, to standing aside under a wall during this life and then departing in mild temper and good hope when the time for departure comes; Isaiah's remnant saves the state. Undoubtedly he means to represent it as doing so. Undoubtedly he imagines his Prince of the house of David who is to be born within a year's time, his royal and victorious Immanuel, he imagines him witnessing as a child the chastisement of Ephraim and the extirpation of the bad majority there; then witnessing as a youth the chastisement of Judah and the extirpation of the bad majority there also; but finally, in mature life, reigning over a state renewed, preserved, and enlarged, a greater and happier kingdom of the chosen people.

Undoubtedly Isaiah conceives his remnant in this wise; undoubtedly he imagined for it a part which, in strict truth, it did not play, and could not play. So manifest was the nonfulfilment of his prophecy, taken strictly, that ardent souls feeding upon his words had to wrest them from their natural meaning, and to say that Isaiah directly meant something which he did not directly mean. Isaiah, like Plato, with inspired insight foresaw that the world before his eyes, the world of actual life, the state and city of the unsound majority, could not stand. Unlike Plato, Isaiah announced with faith and joy a leader and a remnant certain to supersede them. But he put the leader's coming, and he put the success of the leader's and the remnant's work, far, far too soon; and his conception in this respect is fantastic. Plato betook himself for the bringing in of righteousness to a visionary republic in the clouds; Isaiah—and it is the immortal glory of him and of his race to have done

553

so—brought it in upon earth. But Immanuel and his reign, for the eighth century before Christ, were fantastic. For the kingdom of Judah they were fantastic. Immanuel and the remnant could not come to reign under the conditions there and then offered to them; the thing was impossible.

The reason of the impossibility is quite simple. The scale of things, in petty states like Judah and Athens, is too small; the numbers are too scanty. Admit that for the world, as we hitherto know it, what the philosophers and prophets say is true: that the majority are unsound. Even in communities with exceptional gifts, even in the Jewish state, the Athenian state, the majority are unsound. But there is "the remnant." [1] Now the important thing, as regards states such as Judah and Athens, is not that the remnant bears but a small proportion to the majority; the remnant always bears a small proportion to the majority. The grave things for states like Judah and Athens is that the remnant must in positive bulk be so small and therefore so powerless for reform. To be a voice outside the state, speaking to mankind or to the future, perhaps shaking the actual state to pieces in doing so, one man will suffice. But to reform the state in order to save it, to preserve it by changing it, a body of workers is needed as well as a leader—a considerable body of workers, placed at many points, and operating in many directions. This considerable body of workers for good is what is wanting in petty states such as were Athens and Judah. It is said that the Athenian state had in all but 350,000 inhabitants. It is calculated that the population of the kingdom of Judah did not exceed a million and a quarter. The scale of things, I say, is here too small, the numbers are too scanty, to give us a remnant capable of saving and perpetuating the community. The remnant, in these cases, may influence the world and the future, may transcend the state and survive it; but it cannot possibly transform the state and perpetuate the state: for such a work it is numerically too feeble.

Plato saw the impossibility. Isaiah refused to accept it, but facts were too strong for him. The Jewish state could not be renewed and saved, and he was wrong in thinking that it could. And therefore I call his grand point this other, where he was altogether right: that the actual world of the unsound majority, though it fancied itself solid, and though most men might call it solid, could not stand. Let us read him again and again, until we fix in our minds this true conviction of his, to edify us whenever we see such a world existing: his indestructible conviction that such a world, with its prosperities, idolatries, oppression, luxury, pleasures, drunkards, careless women, governing classes, systems of policy, strong alliances, shall come to nought and pass away; that nothing can save it. Let us do homage, also, to his indestructible conviction that

[1] *Isaiah* 10, 20, etc.

states are saved by their righteous remnant, however clearly we may at the same time recognize that his own building on this conviction was premature.

That, however, matters to us little. For how different is the scale of things in the modern states to which we belong, how far greater are the numbers! It is impossible to overrate the importance of the new element introduced into our calculations by increasing the size of the remnant. And in our great modern states, where the scale of things is so large, it does seem as if the remnant might be so increased as to become an actual power, even though the majority be unsound. Then the lover of wisdom may come out from under his wall, the lover of goodness will not be alone among the wild beasts. To enable the remnant to succeed, a large strengthening of its numbers is everything.

Here is good hope for us, not only, as for Plato's recluse, in departing this life, but while we live and work in it. Only, before we dwell too much on this hope, it is advisable to make sure that we have earned the right to entertain it. We have earned the right to entertain it only when we are at one with the philosophers and prophets in their conviction respecting the world which now is, the world of the unsound majority; when we feel what they mean, and when we go thoroughly along with them in it. Most of us, as I have said already, would by no means have been with them when they were here in life, and most of us are not really with them now. What is saving? Our institutions, says an American; the British Constitution, says an Englishman; the civilizing mission of France, says a Frenchman. But Plato and the sages, when they are asked what is saving, answer: "To love righteousness, and to be convinced of the unprofitableness of iniquity." And Isaiah and the prophets, when they are asked the same question, answer to just the same effect: that what is saving is to "order one's conversation right"; to "cease to do evil"; to "delight in the law of the Eternal"; and to "make one's study in it all day long." [2]

The worst of it is that this loving of righteousness and this delighting in the law of the Eternal sound rather vague to us. Not that they are vague really; indeed, they are less vague than American institutions, or the British Constitution, or the civilizing mission of France. But the phrases sound vague because of the quantity of matters they cover. The thing is to have a brief but adequate enumeration of these matters. The New Testament tells us how righteousness is composed. In England and America we have been brought up in familiarity with the New Testament. And so, before Mr. Bradlaugh on our side of the water [3] and the Congress of American Freethinkers on yours banish it from our

---

[2] *Psalms* 50, 23; *Isaiah* 1, 16; *Psalms* 119, 70 and 174; *Psalms* 1, 2.
[3] Charles Bradlaugh (1833–1891), free thinking Member of Parliament, asserted his right to affirm, rather than swear on the Bible.

556	*Forms of Literature*

education and memory, let us take from the New Testament a text showing what it is that both Plato and the prophets mean when they tell us that we ought to love righteousness and to make our study in the law of the Eternal, but that the unsound majority do nothing of the kind. A score of texts offer themselves in a moment. Here is one which will serve very well: "Whatsoever things are true, whatsoever things are elevated, whatsoever things are just, whatsoever things are pure, whatsoever things are amiable, whatsoever things are of good report; if there be any virtue, and if there be any praise; have these in your mind, let your thoughts run upon these." [4] That is what both Plato and the prophets mean by loving righteousness and making one's study in the law of the Eternal.

Now the matters just enumerated do not come much into the heads of most of us, I suppose, when we are thinking of politics. But the philosophers and prophets maintain that these matters and not those of which the heads of politicians are full do really govern politics and save or destroy states. They save or destroy them by a silent, inexorable fatality, while the politicians are making believe, plausibly and noisily, with their American institutions, British Constitution, and civilizing mission of France. And because these matters are what do really govern politics and save or destroy states, Socrates maintained that in his time he and a few philosophers, who alone kept insisting on the good of righteousness and the unprofitableness of iniquity, were the only real politicians then living.

I say, if we are to derive comfort from the doctrine of *the remnant* (and there is great comfort to be derived from it), we must also hold fast to the austere but true doctrine as to what really governs politics, overrides with an inexorable fatality the combinations of the so-called politicians, and saves or destroys states. Having in mind things true, things elevated, things just, things pure, things amiable, things of good report; having these in mind, studying and loving these, is what saves states.

In these United States you are fifty millions and more. I suppose that, as in England, as in France, as everywhere, so likewise here, the majority of people doubt very much whether the majority is unsound; or rather they have no doubt at all about the matter, they are sure that it is not unsound. But let us consent to remain to the end in the ideas of the sages and prophets whom we have been following all along; and let us suppose that in the present actual stage of the world, as in all the stages through which the world has passed hitherto, the majority is and must be in general unsound everywhere—even in the United States. Where is the failure? I have already, in the past, speculated in the abstract about you perhaps too much. But I suppose that in a democratic community

[4] *Letter to the Philippians* 4, 8—with a few words changed.

like this, with its newness, its magnitude, its strength, its life of business, its sheer freedom and equality, the danger is in the absence of the discipline of respect; in hardness and materialism, exaggeration and boastfulness; in a false smartness, a false audacity, a want of soul and delicacy. "Whatsoever things are *elevated*"—whatsoever things are nobly serious, have true elevation—that perhaps, in our catalogue of maxims which are to possess the mind, is the maxim which points to where the failure of the unsound majority, in a great democracy like yours, will probably lie. At any rate let us for the moment agree to suppose so. And the philosophers and the prophets, whom I at any rate am disposed to believe, and who say that moral causes govern the standing and the falling of states, will tell us that the failure to mind whatsoever things are elevated must impair with an inexorable fatality the life of a nation, just as the failure to mind whatsoever things are just, or whatsoever things are amiable, or whatsoever things are pure, will impair it; and that if the failure to mind whatsoever things are elevated should be real in your American democracy, and should grow into a disease and take firm hold on you, then the life of even these great United States must inevitably suffer and be impaired more and more, until it perish.

Then from this hard doctrine we will betake ourselves to the more comfortable doctrine of *the remnant*. "The remnant shall return," shall "convert and be healed" [5] itself first, and shall then recover the unsound majority. And you are fifty millions and growing apace. What a remnant yours may be, surely! A remnant of how great numbers, how mighty strength, how irresistible efficacy! Yet we must not go too fast, either, nor make too sure of our efficacious remnant. Mere multitude will not give us a saving remnant with certainty. The Assyrian Empire had multitude, the Roman Empire had multitude; yet neither the one nor the other could produce a sufficing remnant any more than Athens or Judah could produce it, and both Assyria and Rome perished like Athens and Judah.

But you are something more than a people of fifty millions. You are fifty millions mainly sprung, as we in England are mainly sprung, from that German stock which has faults indeed—faults which have diminished the extent of its influence, diminished its power of attraction and the interest of its history, and which seems moreover just now, from all I can see and hear, to be passing through a not very happy moment, morally, in Germany proper. Yet of the German stock it is, I think, true, as my father said more than fifty years ago, that it has been a stock "of the most moral races of men that the world has yet seen, with the soundest laws, the least violent passions, the fairest domestic and civil virtues." [6] You come, therefore, of about the best parentage which

---

[5] *Isaiah* 10, 21; 6, 10.

[6] In his journal, 9 June 1828; A. P. Stanley, *The Life and Correspondence of Thomas Arnold*, II, 321.

a modern nation can have. Then you have had, as we in England have also had, but more entirely than we and more exclusively, the Puritan discipline. Certainly I am not blind to the faults of that discipline. Certainly I do not wish it to remain in possession of the field forever, or too long. But as a stage and a discipline, and as means for enabling that poor inattentive and immoral creature, man, to love and appropriate and make part of his being divine ideas, on which he could not otherwise have laid or kept hold, the discipline of Puritanism has been invaluable; and the more I read history, the more I see of mankind, the more I recognize its value. Well, then, you are not merely a multitude of fifty millions; you are fifty millions sprung from this excellent Germanic stock, having passed through this excellent Puritan discipline, and set in this enviable and unbounded country. Even supposing, therefore, that by the necessity of things your majority must in the present stage of the world probably be unsound, what a remnant, I say—what an incomparable, all-transforming remnant—you may fairly hope with your numbers, if things go happily, to have!

Suggestions

1. "The Saving Remnant" is an essay about the fall of nations. Summarize the conditions in Athens and Judah that Plato and Isaiah considered dangerous, and account for the title by explaining their hope that their nations would be saved. Why are these hopes called "fantastic" (¶3)?

2. Does the speaker consider such hopes fantastic when applied to a modern state? Does he think that the numerical ratio of majority and remnant is fixed or changing? Discuss fully.

3. Describe the speaker's attitude toward politicians; toward the United States. Summarize the "hard doctrine" and the "more comfortable doctrine" (¶12).

4. Explain: *chastisement, extirpation, inexorable, efficacy, Puritanism.*

5. With the help of † "Decline and Fall," write a review of the speaker's beliefs about the fall of nations.

6. Write an essay defending or attacking Thomas Arnold's attitude toward the Germans.

7. Write a comparison of the views expressed in "The Saving Remnant" and † "The Man and the Masses."

EVOLUTION

(1894)

THOMAS HENRY HUXLEY

It may be safely assumed that, two thousand years ago, before Cæsar
set foot in southern Britain, the whole countryside visible from the
windows of the room in which I write was in what is called "the state of
nature." Except, it may be, by raising a few sepulchral mounds, such as
those which still, here and there, break the flowing contours of the
downs, man's hands had made no mark upon it; and the thin veil of
vegetation which overspread the broad-backed heights and the shelving
sides of the coombs was unaffected by his industry. The native grasses
and weeds, the scattered patches of gorse, contended with one another for
the possession of the scanty surface soil; they fought against the droughts
of summer, the frosts of winter, and the furious gales which swept, with
unbroken force, now from the Atlantic, and now from the North Sea, at
all times of the year; they filled up, as they best might, the gaps made in
their ranks by all sorts of underground and overground animal ravagers.
One year with another, an average population, the floating balance of
the unceasing struggle for existence among the indigenous plants, maintained itself. It is as little to be doubted that an essentially similar state
of nature prevailed, in this region, for many thousand years before the
coming of Cæsar; and there is no assignable reason for denying that it
might continue to exist through an equally prolonged futurity, except
for the intervention of man.

Reckoned by our customary standards of duration, the native vegetation, like the "everlasting hills" [1] which it clothes, seems a type of permanence. The little Amarella Gentians, which abound in some places today,
are the descendants of those that were trodden underfoot by the prehistoric savages who have left their flint tools about, here and there;
and they followed ancestors which, in the climate of the glacial epoch,
probably flourished better than they do now. Compared with the
long past of this humble plant, all the history of civilized men is but an
episode.

Yet nothing is more certain than that, measured by the liberal scale
of time-keeping of the universe, this present state of nature, however it
may seem to have gone and to go on forever, is but a fleeting phase of

[1] *Genesis* 49, 26.

her infinite variety, merely the last of the series of changes which the earth's surface has undergone in the course of the millions of years of its existence. Turn back a square foot of the thin turf, and the solid foundation of the land, exposed in cliffs of chalk five hundred feet high on the adjacent shore, yields full assurance of a time when the sea covered the site of the "everlasting hills"; and when the vegetation of what land lay nearest was as different from the present flora of the Sussex downs as that of Central Africa now is. No less certain is it that, between the time during which the chalk was formed and that at which the original turf came into existence, thousands of centuries elapsed, in the course of which the state of nature of the ages during which the chalk was deposited passed into that which now is by changes so slow that, in the coming and going of the generations of men, had such witnessed them, the contemporary conditions would have seemed to be unchanging and unchangeable.

But it is also certain that before the deposition of the chalk a vastly longer period had elapsed, throughout which it is easy to follow the traces of the same process of ceaseless modification and of the internecine struggle for existence of living things; and that even when we can get no further back, it is not because there is any reason to think we have reached the beginning, but because the trail of the most ancient life remains hidden or has become obliterated.

Thus that state of nature of the world of plants, which we began by considering, is far from possessing the attribute of permanence. Rather its very essence is impermanence. It may have lasted twenty or thirty thousand years, it may last for twenty or thirty thousand years more, without obvious change; but, as surely as it has followed upon a very different state, so it will be followed by an equally different condition. That which endures is not one or another association of living forms, but the process of which the cosmos is the product, and of which these are among the transitory expressions. And in the living world, one of the most characteristic features of this cosmic process is the struggle for existence, the competition of each with all, the result of which is the selection, that is to say, the survival of those forms which, on the whole, are best adapted to the conditions which at any period obtain; and which are, therefore, in that respect and only in that respect, the fittest.[2] The acme reached by the cosmic process in the vegetation of the downs is seen in the turf, with its weeds and gorse. Under the conditions, they have come out of the struggle victorious, and by surviving have proved that they are the fittest to survive.

[2] That every theory of evolution must be consistent not merely with progressive development, but with indefinite persistence in the same condition and with retrogressive modification, is a point which I have insisted upon repeatedly from the year 1862 till now. See *Collected Essays*, vol. ii. pp. 461–89; vol. iii. p. 33; vol. viii. p. 304. In the address on "Geological Contemporaneity and Persistent Types" (1862), the paleontological proofs of this proposition were, I believe, first set forth,—*Huxley's note.*

That the state of nature, at any time, is a temporary phase of a process of incessant change, which has been going on for innumerable ages, appears to me to be a proposition as well established as any in modern history. Paleontology assures us, in addition, that the ancient philosophers who, with less reason, held the same doctrine, erred in supposing that the phases formed a cycle, exactly repeating the past, exactly foreshadowing the future, in their rotations. On the contrary, it furnishes us with conclusive reasons for thinking that, if every link in the ancestry of these humble indigenous plants had been preserved and were accessible to us, the whole would present a converging series of forms of gradually diminishing complexity, until, at some period in the history of the earth, far more remote than any of which organic remains have yet been discovered, they would merge in those low groups among which the boundaries between animal and vegetable life become effaced.

The word *evolution,* now generally applied to the cosmic process, has had a singular history and is used in various senses. Taken in its popular signification it means progressive development, that is, gradual change from a condition of relative uniformity to one of relative complexity; but its connotation has been widened to include the phenomena of retrogressive metamorphosis, that is, of progress from a condition of relative complexity to one of relative uniformity.

As a natural process, of the same character as the development of a tree from its seed, or of a fowl from its egg, evolution excludes creation and all other kinds of supernatural intervention. As the expression of a fixed order, every stage of which is the effect of causes operating according to definite rules, the conception of evolution no less excludes that of chance. It is very desirable to remember that evolution is not an explanation of the cosmic process but merely a generalized statement of the method and results of that process. And, further, that, if there is proof that the cosmic process was set going by any agent, then that agent will be the creator of it and of all its products, although supernatural intervention may remain strictly excluded from its further course.

So far as that limited revelation of the nature of things which we call scientific knowledge has yet gone, it tends, with constantly increasing emphasis, to the belief that not merely the world of plants but that of animals, not merely living things but the whole fabric of the earth, not merely our planet but the whole solar system, not merely our star and its satellites but the millions of similar bodies which bear witness to the order which pervades boundless space and has endured through boundless time are all working out their predestined courses of evolution.

With none of these have I anything to do, at present, except with that exhibited by the forms of life which tenant the earth. All plants and animals exhibit the tendency to vary, the causes of which have yet to be ascertained; it is the tendency of the conditions of life, at any given time, while favoring the existence of the variations best adapted to them, to oppose that of the rest and thus to exercise selection; and all living things tend to multiply without limit, while the means of support are limited; the obvious cause of which is the production of offspring more numerous than their progenitors, but with equal expectation of life in the actuarial sense. Without the first tendency there could be no evolution. Without the second, there would be no good reason why one variation should disappear and another take its place; that is to say, there would be no selection. Without the third, the struggle for existence, the agent of the selective process in the state of nature, would vanish.

Granting the existence of these tendencies, all the known facts of the history of plants and of animals may be brought into rational correlation. And this is more than can be said for any other hypothesis that I know of. Such hypotheses, for example, as that of the existence of a primitive, orderless chaos, of a passive and sluggish eternal matter molded with but partial success by archetypal ideas, of a brand-new world-stuff suddenly created and swiftly shaped by a supernatural power [8] receive no encouragement, but the contrary, from our present knowledge. That our earth may once have formed part of a nebulous cosmic magma is certainly possible, indeed seems highly probable; but there is no reason to doubt that order reigned there as completely as amidst what we regard as the most finished works of nature or of man. The faith which is born of knowledge, finds its object in an eternal order, bringing forth ceaseless change, through endless time, in endless space; the manifestations of the cosmic energy alternating between phases of potentiality and phases of explication. It may be that, as Kant suggests, every cosmic magma predestined to evolve into a new world has been the no less predestined end of a vanished predecessor.

Suggestions

1. "Evolution" begins by suggesting a belief that it will later destroy: the belief that "the state of nature" is permanent. Summarize the evidence against this belief, and show how the thesis of the essay is supported by its beginning.

2. Define the meaning of *fittest* in the phrase *survival of the fittest* (¶5).

3. Explain the error made by ancient philosophers who believed in evolution (¶6).

4. Show that believing in evolution does not rule out believing in a creator (¶8).

5. Explain the relations between evolution and the tendency of living things to vary, to exercise selection, and to multiply without limit (¶10).

---

[8] I.e. those respectively of Lucretius, Plato, and *Genesis*.

6. Explain: *downs, internecine, paleontology, transitory, retrogressive metamorphosis, potentiality, explication.*

7. Write an essay on the speaker's "faith born of knowledge" (last ¶), agreeing or disagreeing with the objection that his faith makes life meaningless.

8. Write a comparison of the similar views expressed in "Evolution," † "The Modern Climate of Opinion," and † "Quickened Consciousness."

T H E   S H O R T   S T O R Y

If the telling of stories is incalculably old, the emergence of the short story as a literary form scarcely more than a century ago must nevertheless have been influenced by the direction that the personal essay had taken. In † "On the Use of Language" or † "Dream Children" the necessary elements of action, character, and setting are already present, waiting to be made more dramatic and less expository. Whether from this cause or not, short stories—like novels— are normally mixtures of two kinds of writing: passages of narrative summary alternate in them with scenes presented in detail.

Every story is in one sense told from the same point of view. It purports to be a summary of an action already known to its teller, who seems, as we read, to be reviewing it for the sake of expressing his feelings about it. Fiction, in Suzanne Langer's term, is "virtual history," which means that the kind of illusion it creates is the illusion of a past. All four stories in this book, for instance, though not even remotely chosen for the similarity of their first sentences, open with references to times distinctly earlier than the times at which we imagine their being told. Like all other prose fictions, to be sure, they include detailed scenes which we probably regard as occurring while we read them, and it is also true that these scenes are the parts which impress us most. Yet even they are characterized by verbs in the past tense, and when we have finished we see the dramatic scenes as parts of patterns that had been completed before the telling began. Accordingly the teller, though his feelings and judgments are presented more discreetly than in the essay, plays an essential part in the total impression that a story makes.

In another and more technical sense, however, stories differ markedly in the points of view through which they are told. This consideration derives its importance from the reader's skepticism. "Why should I believe it?" he asks. "On whose authority is it told?" Two methods of narration are "natural": it is natural to tell a story as a personal experience—to tell it, that is, in the first person. But it is equally natural to tell it as a historian, in the third person, and reveal the hidden thoughts and feelings of the characters as freely as one is able to invent them. Both methods, though, have their drawbacks. If the first-person point of view is more immediate, it is also more restrictive; and the freedom of the other is a dangerous freedom, for in reality nobody knows the thoughts and feelings of anyone except himself. For these reasons a great many stories—perhaps the majority nowadays—are told in the third person, with the teller restricting himself to the point of view of one character. The reader of a story must make himself aware of the teller's choice of point of view, for it heavily influences the meaning with which he charges his narrative. Each of the four stories that follow illustrates one of the major possibilities. Virtually all stories are told in one of these ways, just as all of them present happenings that involve human beings (or else animals or chimeras treated as though they were human), all involve places as well as actions and characters, and all are climaxed either with some significant change in the characters' conditions or else with a revelation, an insight, of which the characters were not capable earlier.

Despite these likenesses, short stories have increasingly tended to divide into two groups, which may be called stories of plot and stories of feeling. A story of plot, turning upon exciting, unexpected actions, is betrayed by its stock characters and its teller's stereotyped attitudes. Practised readers can exhaust such a story on a first encounter and are unlikely to wish to return to it. A story of feeling, on the other hand, develops its characters and settings more significantly. It may seem plotless, for it will tend to emphasize contrast rather than conflict: its *dénouement* a moment of revelation. The novelty will reside in its characterizations and in the depth of the teller's feelings. These are the stories that are read and reread, for they refuse to surrender the whole of their meanings on a merely casual acquaintance.

THE ECLIPSE

ELIZABETH ENRIGHT *From* UNIVERSITY OF KANSAS CITY RE-VIEW, *March 1957.*

That January morning in 1925 was clear and cold. At seven-thirty the rising bell rang with its usual hellish brusqueness, and I huddled deeper in my bed trying to pretend sleep back again—trying to pretend, as I did every morning, that I need not get up until I wished. My three roommates were groaning lumps under the covers. The room was freezing; our breath was steam on the air, and the water in the glass beside my bed had turned to ice.

It was Nydia's turn to close the windows, but it was only after repeated insults and commands from the rest of us that she finally had the fortitude to hurl back the covers and make a majestic sprint, like a young Demeter in pajamas, to the casement windows.

"God!" she said, banging them shut. "Sweet God Almighty!" and she lunged back into bed.

Marcia reared up on her elbow and reached for her glasses. "God," she agreed. Then she yawned on a note of resignation and put her feet out, searching for her fur slippers which peered like a pair of hamsters from under the bed. "Well, kids, it has to be done," she said. Marcia had the twin advantages over the rest of us of being the most sensible and the most sophisticated. Many boys had kissed her and she had been invited to the Dartmouth Carnival.

Nydia, with her sapphire eyes, was the most beautiful; and Terry, who at this hour of the morning was still only a hump and a pigtail in her bed, was the richest, and was further set apart from the rest of us by the fact that she was seriously in love and was loved in return. She was always receiving letters with such messages on the envelope-flaps as "Wait and Hope," or "Darkest before Dawn," for her love was starcrossed; her parents thought her far too young for serious romance, and perhaps her wealth was an obstacle, too.

As for me, I was the least sophisticated and the least sensible, the least beautiful and the least rich; also I was not in love. However, I thought fairly well of myself none the less; the huge aurora borealis of adolescent hope assured me that some day I would obtain these five major requirements with very little trouble. They would just happen to me nicely when the time came.

Marcia slip-slapped back from the bathroom, looking well-scrubbed and smelling of toothpaste.

"O.K., kids, up!" she said tersely. The two characteristics mentioned, added to the fact that she was a trifle older than the rest of us, endowed her with a quality of leadership, almost of generalship, and sometimes she could be ruthless. Now, for instance, she stooped and stripped the covers away from Nydia. "Get up," she repeated, "today's the great day."

Seeing that peace was at an end I leaped out of bed, and from Terry came signs of slow upheaval. Terry had brought four fur coats to school, and two of them—the beaver, and the leopard with the red fox collar— were draped on her bed as coverlets. More than any of us she hated to get up in the morning, and often we contrived to sneak her breakfast to her, but today this was out of the question.

"Who wants to see the damned old eclipse, anyway," she grumbled. But she grumbled amiably; she was never really cross. She reached for the leopard coat and put it on over her nightgown, then thrust her plump feet into the high-heeled patent leather pumps she preferred to bedroom slippers.

Nydia dressed silently. She was always silent and remote before breakfast. I shivered and complained volubly, and Marcia, butting her head into one of her many sweaters, replied with comments deploring but philosophical.

The breakfast bell rang too soon. It always did. After that we were allowed five minutes leeway, and every day it was chaos and scuffle. This morning even Terry was goaded to haste.

"Where are my shoes, where are my damn shoes—oh, here . . . what did I put them on the bureau for?" she moaned distractedly.

Only Marcia was ready in plenty of time, neat in her skirt and sweater, her argyle-patterned wool stockings and saddle shoes. Nydia daringly applied some Roger & Gallet pink pomade to her lips, then rubbed it off again. She gave herself one last cold passionate look in the mirror and made a hook-shaped gesture with the palm of each hand against the blond sickle of hair that pressed against each cheek. At her side, sharing the mirror, I struggled with my own hair which I had pinned up for the first time a few months before. After weeks of practice I had succeeded in arranging it so that it looked more like cloth than hair. It was wrapped around my head in broad turban-bands. No hat would fit over it, and my scalp was stung with hairpins all day long, but I thought it looked handsome and unusual, though I cannot remember that anyone ever concurred in this opinion.

"Girls! Girls!" cried the house mother, looking in at the door. "This is absolutely your last chance! Hurry!"

I cursed my turban of hair which, this morning, had turned out lopsided and rakish, but there was no time to change it. I plunged after my roommates who were already jostling and thundering down the stairs to the dining-room where, for once, we could all enjoy a leisurely breakfast without thought of classes. Since there was to be a half-holiday in the universe, it was suitable that we should have one, too.

After breakfast was the time to straighten the rooms. We all made our own beds, and mine, when finished, looked rather lumpish due to the fact that the copy of *Wuthering Heights* that I had been reading the night before, by flashlight under the covers, was still in the bed. It is possible that the flashlight was there, too, though I have forgotten.

Each week one of us was delegated to do all the sweeping and dusting of the room, and this week it was my turn. My roommates departed heartlessly and I was left alone.

The room was large, with a bow of leaded casement windows and a window seat. The house and grounds had once been the estate of an heiress, and there was a certain grandeur about the size of everything, and the bathrooms were extremely luxurious for a boarding school. Most of the luxury and grandeur ended there, however. In our room there were two immense bureaus, and four narrow metal beds on which no two bedspreads were the same color or pattern. On the bureaus, among hair brushes and bottles of the kind of perfume people give teenagers, the rather flattered photographs of parents and younger brothers looked out self-consciously. On the window seat there was a portable Victrola (we called it a "Vic"), a stack of records, many magazines, and a few stuffed animals. In the cabinet beneath the window seat there was, as I knew well, a jug of cider, which instead of turning hard was turning disappointingly to vinegar; there were several boxes of soda crackers, and a jar of Hyppolite marshmallow whip with a spoon in it. There may have been a bitten dill pickle in waxed paper—there often was—and there was almost certainly a pound box of salted peanuts. Tucked far back out of sight, beside the copy of *Flaming Youth* and Balzac's *Contes Drolatiques,* there was a package of cigarettes and some matches.

I cranked up the Victrola and put on a record of the "Hymn to the Sun," from the *Coq d'Or.* It was the most wonderful music in the world. When that was finished I put on a record of Ukulele Ike singing "I Can't Get the One I Want," and it was just as wonderful. Listening happily I went about the business of straightening the bureau-tops, blowing the dust off vigorously, and arranging toilet articles in a sort of pious symmetry. When I brought out the broom and carpet sweeper I realized for the hundredth time how fortunate we were. To the furnishing of our room Terry's mother had contributed a huge pink Oriental rug with a fine delicate pattern and the bloom of silk. It must have been very valuable; old Mrs. Purchase, a lady of culture who had endowed the school with a library and then come along to see that it was taken care of, was always creeping in to study the rug and shake her head, and once we had even found her down on her knees with a bottle of Carbona, cleaning off a spot. Aside from its beauty and its silky warmth to our bare soles, we appreciated it for another reason. As I moved about on it now, making casual swipes with the carpet sweeper, the whole rosy expanse crunched and crepitated gently under my feet, for in its passive way the rug had saved us many minutes of time and much dull traffic with dustpans.

In the middle of the morning the bell rang again, sounding strange at this unaccustomed hour, but we all knew what it meant and began getting out our sweaters and galoshes.

"Who wants to see the damned old eclipse, anyway," said Terry again, pulling on the leopard coat. "We'll just stand around freezing for *hours* and *hours.*"

"Well, I prefer it to *Julius Caesar*," I said. "I certainly prefer it to *physics!*" The truth was that I felt the wildest excitement at the prospect of seeing a total eclipse, but thought it would be naïve to say so.

Nydia and I each borrowed a fur coat from Terry; Marcia had her own coonskin one, made just like a college boy's without any shape at all. Terry borrowed a hat from Nydia and I loaned one to Marcia, and she loaned me an extra sweater and Nydia borrowed my angora mittens. We all wore our galoshes unbuckled because that was the way to wear them, and when we walked down the stairs we jingled like a detachment of cavalry.

Outdoors a procession of station wagons had been commandeered from the parents of day pupils. An air of revelry prevailed, causing the younger children to leap in the air and squeal. I would have liked to leap and squeal myself, but of course I didn't.

Finally, after the usual delay and confusion, we were packed into our appointed places in the station wagons, and the journey began. The world was white with fallen snow, and we looked deep, deep into the bare-boned woods that edged the road. I remember the jovial metallic snack-snack-snack of the tire chains, and the starling chittering of the younger children in the car behind.

Miles away we stopped at the foot of a great bald hill where the view was said to be the best in the region.

"You mean we're going to *climb* the thing?" said Terry. She detested exercise, and her techniques for evading basketball practice were formidable.

"I bet I'll be winded," Nydia murmured with pride. She had been known to smoke as many as seven cigarettes in one day.

We toiled up the broad flank of the hill through deep snow. Our unbuckled galoshes clapped and clattered and caught at the hems of our skirts; snow slopped over the tops of them. Erratic as squirrels, the younger children darted and zigzagged, while the teachers and parents, their overshoes sensibly fastened, forged steadily ahead with the Spartan philosophical gait peculiar to adults on an outing with children.

Luckily the day was fair, though already a strangeness had come into the light, like the light in dreams, and it was bitterly cold. The dome of the hill, when we reached it, was immense—a vast rounded plain. Against the waste of white the scattered groups of people seemed diminished and at the same time sharpened in outline; adjuncts to nature, like the figures in Breughel snow-pieces.

Mr. Muller, the science teacher, had built a fire up there. He and Mr. Ripley, the math teacher, were squatted beside it, smoking pieces of glass. My feelings about Mr. Muller were mixed. Every December for the last three years I had taken the part of Mary in the school Nativity play, and Mr. Muller was always Joseph. Three times he had led me across the wilderness of the assembly room, in front of the thrilling, rustling audience, to the door of the secretary's office where we were denied shelter for the night, and from there up the broad staircase to Bethlehem on the landing. Here we disappeared for a moment and then, curtains parting, I was seen beside the manger wearing a gilded buckram halo and gazing earnestly into a 150-watt Mazda bulb. The world would be green for an hour afterward, and I remember feelings of exaltation and gratified ego; but somehow I could not help wishing that somebody else, not Mr. Muller, might have been Joseph.

He and Mr. Ripley handed out the pieces of blackened glass and strips of exposed negative. We had been warned not to look at the sun without one of these protections, and now, holding up my sooty glass, I took my first look.

The sun was in crescent, an imitation of the moon, a humble step down from power. It looked no different from the several partial eclipses I had seen in my life, and I was disappointed.

The younger children played in the snow and screamed. Nydia giggled with Tom Frank, one of our classmates, and Marcia, in low tones, was giving advice to Hank McCurdy, another classmate. She loved to give advice, especially to boys. Terry paced to and fro, lost in her own thoughts.

The light was weakening and weakening and the cold growing: a deathly cold. We began to stamp and beat our hands together, and when a thermos of hot cocoa was produced there were cheers.

"Why couldn't it be coffee!" murmured sophisticated Marcia.

Whenever I looked at the sun through the black glass it had grown narrower; and finally it was little more than a sickle of reddish light. Then less. Less . . . Still less.

And now the miracle took place. I dropped my glass. Across the snow, suddenly, ran streamers of shadow and iridescent light, wavering bands turning and turning in an unimaginable wheel of rays. What was happening? There was a startling impression of swiftness, as if something —someone?—hastened forward to a climax. The sky darkened abruptly.

A great still coldness dropped onto the world and all around its edge there was a band of orange light, like the instant before sunrise on all the horizons of the earth at once.

"Look up! Look, look, look," whispered Terry.

In the deep sky where there had been a sun, we saw a ring of white silver; a smoking ring, and all the smokes were silver, too; gauzy, fuming, curling, unbelievable. And who had ever seen the sky this color! Not in earliest morning nor at twilight, never before had we seen or dreamed this strange immortal blue in which a few large stars now sparkled as though for the first time of all.

At some point I glanced for an instant at those nearest me. I had never seen before, nor have I since, the expression of total awe on the faces of a crowd; all turned upward, arrested, self-forgotten, like the faces of revelation in old religious paintings.

There were tears on Terry's cheeks, I remember, and Carla Cudlipp, a fat pragmatical girl, was on her knees in the snow in an attitude of prayer. Even Miss Lagrange, a battle axe if ever one lived, was trembling all over like a frightened child.

But I watched them for no longer than a second; it was more important to watch, to try to memorize, that marvelous smoking circle of light, where all too soon the blinding edge of crescent appeared and one could look no longer, and had no wish to look.

We were quiet going down the hill again; even the younger children were quiet: "Gosh," said Marcia, and sighed. It seemed as suitable a comment as any.

All of us were frozen with cold, subdued, spotted with soot. The world once more was muted in the queer dream-light. Nothing seemed familiar.

"But suppose you'd never seen the sun set in your life," said Nydia suddenly. "Suppose you'd never seen a rainbow. It would be the same thing; you'd be just as—as dumbfounded. You know, you'd get this same terrific kick out of it. I mean it's not a phenomenon or God or anything, it's just that the moon gets in front of the sun once in a while; just a natural thing. It's only that you hardly ever get to *see* it."

"Yes, but gosh, when you do see it, it makes everything else seem more wonderful," I said. "It's as though they let you in on the secret for a minute or two; I mean it's sort of as though they let you remember how it all works and how *wonderful* it is!"

But it was beyond my powers to express what it meant. I fell silent, trying to recapture in memory the exact impression, the exact sensation, of that instant when the universe had seemed to open like a door before me, or my own eyes to open and behold for the first time.

We felt that we had been away for months. Everything in our room, when we returned, looked childish, trivial, and cheap.

Marcia hurled her coat on the bed, smoothed her sweater down on her hips, sighed.

"I know! Let's have a snack before lunch," she said, brightening. Then she went to the cabinet and brought out the box of crackers and the marshmallow whip, settling comfortably on her bed with them, spreading the crackers with a lavish hand. She held one out to me. I had not realized I was so hungry, and went on eating when the others had stopped, although I knew it would be a matter of minutes until the lunch bell rang.

Nydia went to the mirror and refreshed herself at her own reflection for a while, then she turned to the Victrola, cranked it up, and put on a record called "Brown Eyes Why Are You Blue?" Recklessly, she reached in the cabinet and brought out a cigarette, lighted it, and began dancing slowly with her eyes closed, as if asleep. She had learned, by diligent application, to hold the smoke in her mouth for a long time and then let it out gradually through her nostrils, and she did this now. She looked very worldly. I sat watching her as I crunched steadily through the box of soda crackers.

Terry, oblivious of all, was writing yet another somber letter to her Jack—(she had written three the day before)—and Marcia was polishing her nails with a buffer; the pearl ring she had been given on her sixteenth birthday gleamed and winked rhythmically.

There was a noise in the hall outside our room and Nydia's blue eyes flew open. She stubbed out the cigarette on the sole of her shoe, tossed it into the waste basket, and stood a moment listening, holding her breath and fanning away the smoke. Then she laughed.

"Come on, Lib," she said to me, holding out her hands. "Let's dance, you need the practice, you're still terrible. I'll lead."

Humbly and doggedly I did my best to follow. Terry looked up and smiled at us vaguely from her remote place. Marcia watched my feet. "Try not to trudge," she said.

Little by little we were curing ourselves of wonder, and the universe shrank back to its small customary size.

Suggestions

1. "The Eclipse," closest of the stories in this book to the personal essay, is told from the point of view of the first-person participant. Though limited in this way, it moves freely back and forth between the innocent outlook of the speaker as a schoolgirl and the keener insight brought by the passing of time. The double point of view matches the story's central contrast, between the commonplace details of everyday life and the wonder of a total eclipse of the sun. Together they suggest that the theme is the passage from childhood to maturity—even though

the girl's vision that day lasted only a little while. Do you consider the point of view well suited to the expression of this theme?

2. If "The Eclipse" is to be anything more than a mere personal reminiscence, it must bring the reader to sympathize with the girls' astonishment, culminating perhaps in the exclamation, "It's as though they let you in on the secret for a minute or two. . . ." (Notice the contrast between the speaker's apathy about the Nativity play and her excitement about this secret.) This effect, if it is brought off, results jointly from the descriptions of the eclipse itself and of the crowd of people who witness it. Evaluate its success, considering that the reader, without necessarily being moved himself, must believe that under those circumstances the characters would react as they are said to do.

3. The tone of "The Eclipse" mingles light satire with affectionate sympathy. Point out several examples of both, including the speaker's attitude toward herself as a young girl. Then show the connection between the tone and the point of view.

4. In the introductory paragraphs we saw that a story combines passages of narrative summary with scenes presented in detail. As scenes have the effect of close-ups, they are best confined to the parts of the story that most deserve emphasis. Evaluate "The Eclipse" in this respect.

5. The last ten words of the story belong to its "essay" part, for they make a generalization about ordinary life. Write a comparison of your own experience and life as shown in "The Eclipse."

6. A story may conclude, as we have seen, with an important change in the circumstances of the characters, or with a new insight into the nature of experience. Write an essay on this distinction, using "The Eclipse" for illustration.

BEYOND THE SCREEN

HOWARD NEMEROV

First printed in THE SEWANEE REVIEW, © *1957, 1959 by Howard Nemerov. Reprinted by permission of Simon and Schuster, Inc.*

This is a story about something that happened in the early days of television, just after the time at which it was exceptional to have a set, and just before the time at which it was eccentric not to. You will remember how in those days many people used to show an extreme ethical delicacy and sensitivity about the value of television, before they too bought their sets and settled down in front of them like the rest of us.

Andrew Stonecroft was one such, and at this time he had just achieved his object of moving out of New York and into Westchester—not the landscaped and half-timbered Westchester, though, but the somewhat ruggeder and less expensively pastoralized part nearer the Hudson. The modern house which he had had built, a long, low building of gray field-stone and board, with a steeply slanted roof, represented the closest possible adjustment between his income and the size of his family; he and his wife had one child, a seven-year-old boy named Stephen, and another at this time five months on the way. The house also had a study, den, or library, which could be used as a guestroom, or rather guest space, since the architect, a friend of Andrew's from college days, did not believe in the old-fashioned idea of *rooms* but saw a house rather as "organized space," "a machine for living," with adjustable partitions everywhere substituted for walls and doors. This somewhat fluid conception had much disturbed Andrew at first; he had been raised more or less in the country, in a small village in Massachusetts, and a door had for him the value of a moral distinction (he particularly remembered how his own father would shut himself away on a Sunday afternoon in a study protected from the rest of the household by a corridor and two doors), but when he raised his objections he found Janet and the architect full of rational arguments. The architect pointed out that people did not live that way any more, that it had been demonstrably an unhappy and inefficient way of "using the space," that families nowadays shared things more than they used to. When Andrew gave the example of his father, the architect laughed.

"And look at you," he said. "Do you really want your kid to grow up like you?"

Janet said, "You'll be in New York all day long, five days a week. Stephen will be in school. I've got to live in the place, and keep it swept up together." And she showed how easily the vacuum cleaner would roll from one part of the "space" to another.

The most convincing argument, though it was never spoken aloud, was that the architect was doing the job at a greatly reduced fee out of friendship, in return for which he must naturally be given the chance for a practical demonstration of his own ideas. Andrew wondered whether they were really his own; it all looked, on the blueprints and drawings at any rate, like pages from *Vogue*.

Yet when the building actually went up and he was able to have a true impression of its cleanly and pleasant interior proportions, the crisp efficiency of furnishings and cabinets built into the walls, the easy availability of everything from everywhere within his house, Andrew became convinced that quite truly a new way of life was opening out before him; he could imagine them all, on a winter night before the fine double fireplace, Janet sewing (for instance), himself and Stephen building a model airplane or with heads bent together over the boy's arithmetic problems, the high-fidelity phonograph filling the air with good music, not loud, even a trifle distant, from three properly spaced loud-speakers; it did seem as though there were a charming harmony to be expected from all these activities thus conducted in freedom which did not require the expense of loneliness.

And so it turned out. They moved up when Stephen got out of school in June. Andrew and Janet were delighted with their efficiency in arranging everything so that they might enjoy the summer in the new place, and they did enjoy it. Stephen made friends rapidly, for the neighborhood was delightfully populous without being at all crowded; their two acres were so well screened with stands of pine and birch as to give no view at all, from the lawn, of the two adjacent houses which were, however, close enough for a comfortable sociability and in case of emergencies. By this time Andrew and Janet were aware of the fact that they were to have a new child, but when they confessed their uneasiness about "the space" to the architect, who naturally came to spend a weekend in his creation, he delighted them by pointing out an overlooked advantage in this type of construction—that an "annex" could be built on inexpensively, anywhere almost.

"It's free to grow as you grow," he told them.

Meanwhile, there was no television; Andrew, compliant about all else, was stubborn about that, and Janet for the time being did not make an issue of it.

"Though I don't see what you've got against it," she said sometimes.

"I don't want my child—my children, for that matter—to grow up on that stuff," he would reply. "Stephen will get more out of books, like any civilized person."

"He goes down to watch almost every day with the Stennis boys, and at Joey Capes' house," Janet said. "And he can't invite them back, that's all."

"Now you're talking like an ad in the papers," Andrew said angrily. "Our child is decently clothed, properly fed, we don't beat him or even make him work around the house to teach him how tough the world is, as the Capes do with Joey. But because we don't have one of these damn boxes we are 'depriving' him, you'd think, of life itself. I refuse to be shamed into buying one, and that's absolutely the end."

And so it was, "absolutely the end," for the time being anyhow, though even Andrew sometimes wondered if he really had anything against television beyond, perhaps, an instinctive or inbred puritanical resistance to the passivity it commanded. And those aerials, which he saw in ever-increasing numbers when he drove into town in the mornings, appeared to him as the sign of a social identity he found (and was obscurely ashamed of finding) repulsive. He clipped from a newspaper once an item to the effect that many people, it had been discovered, were installing these aerials on their roofs without buying television sets to go with them, and, showing this to Janet, he said, "That's what it comes to in the end."

II

If there was one thing less suited than another to the Stonecrofts' modern house, or to the style which was felt to go with it, that thing was a wheelchair, and that is exactly what they got. Janet's widowed mother had a heart attack in July, and by mid-August was established in the guest space for a convalescence of indeterminate length; there was some resentment over this, as much from Janet as from her husband, but the situation did not really allow of argument.

Mrs. Parker was a gaunt but massive woman, with hair of a color Andrew had always thought of as battleship gray. An active woman formerly, a leader in her church and community, she was now condemned to a passive life, which she endured with some difficulty. Stifled and suppressed energies emanated from her, which, with her size, made the house seem smaller than it was. The poor lady doubtless realized the somewhat stereotyped nature of her situation, and even tried to make jokes to Andrew about having a mother-in-law in the place; but it quickly became apparent that she had, and needed, an iron determination to be quiet, give no more trouble than necessary, and express none of her disapproval of modern architecture and a churchless generation which brought up its children without God. This determination, like most iron objects, would not bend, but any break would be irreparable.

The television set came as a matter of course with other of her personal possessions from the house which she had put up for sale.

"Mother is used to having one," Janet said, "and now that she can't go out of the house it's practically a necessity for her; they even have church services on Sundays."

"Now I'm depriving people of the right to worship, am I?" asked Andrew severely; but he conceded nevertheless that it would not be fair to prevent Mrs. Parker from enjoying her own television set, even though in his house.

Nevertheless, the large blond box stood in the living space, the aerial lying beside it, for several days while Janet tried to get a serviceman to install it.

"These people aren't interested in you," she told Andrew, "if you don't buy the set from them in the first place. They keep telling me they've more work than they can possibly handle, or that their own customers come first—they behave worse than the butchers did during the war."

Finally Andrew agreed to put the aerial up himself. "If you can wait for the weekend," he added, feeling somewhat uneasy about climbing up on the roof.

So on the Saturday afternoon, wearing old clothes and having assembled about his person a number of wrenches, screwdrivers and pliers, Andrew began to sort out the bits and pieces of the aerial. Mrs. Parker sat in her wheelchair watching him, and Stephen too looked on, ready to give his advice. It was a very hot day toward the end of August.

It had never occurred to Andrew that the aerial must penetrate the house at some point, and he found it gave him considerable pain of mind, after they had decided where the machine must stand, to take a brace and bit and actually bore a hole through the wall of his own home: the inner wall, the insulating wool, the outer wall. One did not realize, he thought, how thin one's walls really were, and how close the outside of things was to the inside. But he did it, anyhow, and threaded the wire through.

"Now what in heaven's name is this?" he asked, turning to his mother-in-law with an iron spike with a porcelain fitting at the end. He was already somewhat exasperated, for he had never been mechanically minded or clever with his hands, and anticipated with some anxiety having to climb up even on their fairly low roof; ladders frightened him.

"Oh, that's very important," Mrs. Parker replied. "You mustn't leave that out of the circuit—is that the word? It's a lightning arrester. You run the wire through that china bit and push the stake into the ground outside. It goes between the aerial and the set, and the man who installed it at home told me that it protects you against storms. Without it, he said, the lightning could travel down the wire and turn the set into one lump of molten glass and metal. It could probably kill anyone in the room."

"I see," Andrew said, thinking of the set fused into "one lump of molten glass and metal."

"Lightning happens when two clouds bang together," Stephen said. "They have electricity in them. The Russians store it up in bottles and use it later," he added.

"I don't think they do, Stephen," Andrew said.

"They do; it was on television," Stephen insisted. "The Black Raider stole some to give to the United States."

"Okay, Stephen," said Andrew, dragging the light but cumbersome aerial out the door.

"Don't forget the arrester," Mrs. Parker called after him, and he came back for it.

The arrester proved a simple enough matter; you merely threaded the aerial wire through two terminals which you then clamped; all you had to do after that was thrust the iron spike into the earth. Andrew looked at it dubiously; it seemed a very simple device, and very small, for warding off a bolt of lightning, but he supposed the people who made it knew what they were about.

The aerial was a good deal less simple. Janet and Stephen stood on the ground below while Andrew went up the ladder, laid the aerial on the roof, dragged the ladder up after him, and propped it against the chimney. For a while it seemed as though he would need a third hand, and twice he lost his temper and told Janet and Stephen to go inside, that he would let them know when he was finished—but they continued to stand there. At last he had the contraption bound securely to the chimney, though.

"I'll leave the ladder here," he said, "till we see if the thing needs to be turned."

And, pleased with himself, he came down onto the roof, from which, on account of the slope of the land, it was not more than six or seven feet to the ground. Andrew took this in a casual jump, but his right foot came down on a loose stone, there was a perfectly audible crack! and three hours later, after Dr. Arnstamm had come and driven him to the hospital for X rays, it turned out that he had broken the outer metatarsal; a simple fracture, fortunately, which hardly needed setting, but which would keep him confined for two or three weeks at least. It hurt terribly, though, when the shock wore off, and after he had been placed with care on the bed Janet had to make an extra pitcher of martinis for the wounded, disconsolate, and angered hero. But the television set, to Andrew's great surprise when he thought of it, worked very well.

III

Because of the simple nature of his injury, Andrew was allowed to get by without a cast—"on condition you're very careful," the doctor said, adding that the cast would be most irksome, especially in this hot weather—"it would begin to itch." For this reason it was a week before he could rise up and move around, even awkwardly, on crutches, and during this time the television had established its routine in the household. Luckily, Stephen's school began too, which kept him away from the set during most of the day, except on weekends; on account of Mrs. Parker, too, he was allowed to invite friends in for viewing only from five till six-thirty. Mrs. Parker, however, sat in front of that window on the world from early morning till bedtime, and Janet contended this was a good thing.

"It keeps her out of my hair, poor Mother," she said to Andrew, who during this week experienced the television only as a vague rumor and murmur from beyond his bedroom, which had a door but not a very thick one. "It gives her something to think about."

"And what does she think about it?" Andrew asked not very pleasantly. His week in bed exasperated him as it would any healthy man who moreover, on such occasions, begins to have guilty suspicions that his *hard day at the office,* of which he normally makes so much, is mere malingering compared with what his wife goes through, and that if he were suddenly to inherit several million dollars he would continue nevertheless to go downtown every morning, simply to get out of his own home. In short, he had begun to think, in a general way, as people do when confined much alone, about the nature of life "as a whole" and about his own place in it, and he wanted nothing more desperately than to get up, get back to work, and put these thoughts out of the way forever.

It was, in fact, to avert such thoughts that during the week following, being able to move around some on his crutches, Andrew took to watching the television set a good deal himself, though most of the time with a grudging and glowering expression on his face. He would swing through to the kitchen in the morning for coffee; then, on the way back, he would prop himself between one crutch and the wall and sneer meanly at the cheerful news editor on the screen, to whom also he occasionally would make comments.

"Don't tell me about your soap, chum," he would say, or, for instance about the weather forecast, "There you are, grinning away and giving me the word, but you're wrong, dead wrong." But he did not move away, and presently Janet would turn on him.

"Sit down and watch, if you're going to watch. Don't stand right in the way."

Andrew then would sit down, sulky and tentative, in a deep armchair right next to where his mother-in-law had already wheeled herself for the day's viewing; and, as it turned out, there he would stay, with his foot up on a pouffe which Janet brought, glumly watching one program after another.

"I knew you'd like it, dear, once you gave it a chance," Mrs. Parker said once, and her son-in-law thereupon refused to speak to her for one whole day.

"You're being ridiculous," Janet said that night. "I know it's hard for you being cooped up at home, but think what it is for me. And you don't need to be rude to Mother. If you don't like television, go into the bedroom and read."

"I don't want to read," he replied, "and I don't want to think."

The weather continued day after day the same; it had gained official status as a heat wave, and there were jokes about it on the television.

Another week, and Andrew was able to get about with a cane. His temper improved, for he rather admired the image of himself as an old man leaning on a stick, and Dr. Arnstamm had said he could probably return to work the Monday following. Then a rather terrible thing happened.

Stephen was sent home from school on Wednesday morning, near noon. He was in tears, but they were tears of rage, and he would say nothing of what had happened beyond some confused story of injury, wrath, and condemnation. Janet phoned the principal, and came from the phone white-faced, nervous; Stephen had been suspended from school for the rest of the week; in the playground that morning he had hit a little girl on the head, with a rock. The little girl was seriously hurt. Oh, she would recover, probably she would suffer no permanent damage, though it was too early to tell about concussion; but there it was. Stephen had hit her on the head with a rock.

The television set had to be turned off while they questioned Stephen, who, however, would tell them nothing more than that "there was a fight." Throughout the interrogation he continued to cry, more and more sullenly.

"Listen, Steve," Andrew said a number of times, "tell me plainly, son —did you do that? Did you hit this little girl with a rock?"

"There was a fight," Stephen said. "Everybody was fighting around."

"But *did* you hit the girl—you yourself, I mean—with a stone or anything like that?"

"Answer your father, Stephen," Janet said.

"We were fighting," Stephen said.

"Children these days aren't taught the difference between right and wrong," Mrs. Parker said.

"All right, Mother," Janet said sharply, and Andrew gave the old lady a terrible look.

Janet phoned the little girl's mother.

"I'm terribly sorry about what happened to little Alma," she began, and had to hold the phone away from her ear; the others could plainly hear the high cackle of the other woman's views, though the words were indistinguishable.

"I'm sorry you feel you have to take that attitude," Janet was finally able to put in, her icy voice contrasting with the redness of her face, "and of course I'm deeply sorry for what happened to your little girl, but I'm not yet convinced that it was absolutely all Stephen's fault."

Another burst of outrage clattered out of the phone.

"Since you are so utterly wanting in charity—" Janet announced when she next got the chance; but she was too late; the other receiver went down with a loud clack.

Janet began to walk up and down, squeezing her hands together.

"How terrible," she repeated again and again, "how brutal, how vile—"

Andrew hobbled to the phone and called the principal of the school again.

"Look here, Mr. Blanchard," he began in a very reasonable voice, after introducing himself, "it's been hard for us to get anything coherent from Stephen about all this sad business, but surely it can't have been all his fault. There was a pretty general row; he's told us that. I'm in favor of some reasonable punishment if the boy has done wrong, but for a seven-year-old kid to be suspended from school is—"

"Mr. Stonecroft," the principal said, breaking in, his voice remote and impersonal in the black receiver, "I don't think I've ever been accused of being a severe or punitive person. We do have our discipline to keep up, and we usually keep it up quite successfully. We simply will not have behavior of this sort at the school; most of our children are good-natured, kindly boys and girls, a little rough of course now and then— but things of this nature, hitting people with rocks, simply can't be permitted to happen. If an example must be made, be sure I will make it as I see fit."

"Do you mean to tell me," Andrew said in a most quiet voice, "that you have arbitrarily elected to punish *my* son because there was a general fight in the playground? Is that what you mean by making an example?"

"Your son was undoubtedly guilty," the principal replied. "His own home-room teacher saw the incident. Let me advise you, Mr. Stonecroft, that you should take this opportune warning—you could scarcely do better than use this period of suspension to institute the kind of home discipline without which a mere school cannot hope to have any effect."

"Now you listen to me," said Andrew.

"Please listen to me first, sir. You are new to this neighborhood, and of course you're welcome here. You came from the city, and I can understand that your boy may have received a rougher sort of education in city schools than we have here . . ."

Andrew listened in silence for some moments after this before putting down the phone without saying goodbye.

"Juvenile delinquency," he announced somewhat breathlessly to Janet. "He actually used the words *juvenile delinquency.*"

Janet and Andrew stared at Stephen, who was curled up in the arm-chair, worn out with tears.

"There, dear," said Mrs. Parker, leaning from her wheelchair to pat his head, "you can stay home with Granny and watch the set this week."

"It's time for lunch, anyhow," Janet said.

"Could you turn on the set, Jan, before you go?" asked Mrs. Parker pleasantly.

IV

The remainder of that week was horrifying. In the first place, the weather continued hot, hot and damp. Andrew twice tried to get out and limp around the grounds alone, but after a few minutes of this his foot caused him so much pain that he went indoors again and sat before the television set, which he watched now out of a kind of helpless despair, like a gambler who, having lost most of his property, hurls the rest after it with a sort of insane gaiety before shooting himself.

Mrs. Parker sat in her wheelchair, Andrew next to her, Stephen on the floor in front of them. There had been a desperate move organized at first to punish Stephen by depriving him of his television rights; but this meant, in their "living space," that Mrs. Parker (not to mention Andrew himself) was being punished; the set had to be turned off. Stephen sulked bitterly, and played father and mother off against each other until he trapped Janet into an exasperated permission to go watch the set, if he must; whereupon Andrew flew into a fit of temper having to do with the nature of discipline.

"If you keep him from the television," Janet explained wearily, "someone has to keep him amused, and I'm usually the one."

"It's just that if I say a thing," he said back, "you must not—must not—go and say the opposite."

"You and your discipline," she said; "you're punishing yourself, if you want to know. You want to watch the tiny screen yourself, and you hate yourself for it."

"Just you go psychoanalyze someone else for a change," he said, since he felt there was some truth in what she said. Then he added, in more reasonable tones, "What gets me is that the boy isn't even sorry; he doesn't seem to realize what he's done."

"Watching or not watching the television isn't connected with what he's done," Janet retorted. "And he is sorry—I'm sure he is. Aren't you sorry, Stephen?"

"I'm sorry, Mommy and Daddy," Stephen said in a small voice.

"You should be ashamed of yourselves, quarreling in front of the child," Mrs. Parker said.

"Stevie, look at me, look in my eyes," Andrew said. "Do you understand that you did something wrong, something real bad, when you hit Alma?"

"Yes, Dad."

"Something you must never do—never? You understand that?"

"Yes, Dad."

"Look me in the eyes, now, Son. You promise never to do anything like that again?"

"Yes, Dad."

"All right, then. You may watch the television."

"If the child is not being properly brought up in his own faith," Mrs. Parker said, "how can he be expected to know good from bad? I've not wanted to say anything all these weeks, because I'm a guest here and an unwanted guest, too—and an unwilling one, I'll let you know that, too. But I've seen what I've seen, and if you want to know God's truth, the pair of you, you've been punished, and you are lucky the punishment was no heavier than it was."

"I don't want to know God's truth," said Andrew savagely, "and when I do, I'll go ask God for it."

"For shame—in front of the child," cried Mrs. Parker.

"Now that is absolutely enough, from both of you," said Janet. "Just one little bit more of that sort of thing, and *I* leave."

So the television set was turned on.

v

On Sunday morning the weather was hot again. The news announcer predicted, however, that the hot spell would definitely break that day. Showers and thunderstorms, a cold front, were forecast for New York City, eastern New York and New England.

"You've been wrong before, chum, and you could be wrong again," said Andrew to the man on the screen.

There followed a succession of religious services, Catholic and Protestant. Mrs. Parker usually turned off the Catholic service, but today, for Stephen, she kept it on.

"It is all about Jesus just the same," she said. "The little differences can come in later."

"Jesus, Son," Andrew said in a plain, toneless, pedagogic voice, "is a man who lived long long ago. Some people believe this man was really a god. Others—like your mother and myself—think that he was only a very good man."

"Was he nice?" asked Stephen.

"Yes, he was very nice," said Janet somewhat tensely, leaning over the counter from the kitchen space.

"Jesus loves all little boys and girls," Mrs. Parker said.

"Is he dead?" Stephen asked.

"Yes," said Andrew exactly as Mrs. Parker said, "No, he is in heaven."

"Do they have television in heaven?" asked Stephen, leaving Andrew a little at a loss. Mrs. Parker replied that they had everything in heaven, and then they all watched in silence for a little while.

The Catholic service was followed by a Protestant discussion group, which talked about the breakup of the family in the modern world.

"If you're bored, Son, you can go out and play," Andrew said. "Any time, you know."

The group on the screen, two oldish men and two middle-aged ladies, congratulated themselves and one another upon a successful family life.

"You listen to that and mark it well," said Mrs. Parker to Andrew. He had left off replying to this kind of thing, out of a sense that the old lady did it only to needle him, and she had become correspondingly bolder.

Stephen did not seem to get bored at all; he watched everything impartially, with bug-eyed attention.

He doesn't understand any of it, Andrew thought. When the novelty wears off he won't bother with this stuff.

After the Protestants came a children's program, a circus, which Andrew found quite fascinating, and after that a Western story.

Janet brought a sandwich lunch in, and sat down herself.

"I think it is going to storm at last," she said. "Big clouds are piling up down over the Hill."

Another religious program, hymn-singing and a sermon, followed the Western.

"Methodists," said Mrs. Parker in some disgust.

"Almost time for the football game, though," Andrew said. It was the thing he looked forward to already; the season had started yesterday, with a college game, and today there would be the first pro game, the New York Giants vs. the Pittsburgh Steelers.

"Oh—" said Mrs. Parker, to indicate that she was bravely concealing her disappointment about something.

"Mother likes to watch 'Window on the World' on Channel three," Janet said.

"And what is 'Window on the World'?" he asked.

"Ah, well." Janet was a trifle vague. "They just show films of what various sorts of people do all over the world."

"Last week they showed pearl divers in Japan," said Mrs. Parker, "and how automobiles are made, on an assembly line—you know, all sorts of things of that kind."

Andrew had been about to make some protest concerning his right to watch a football game if he cared to. But he saw what this would involve him in: further argument, more ill temper and discontent; and besides—his deeply moral nature told him—it would do him good to deprive himself of this trivial pleasure; there would be other football games. Once he had decided to give in, moreover, it became a moral point with him to do so pleasantly, and without seeming to struggle over it.

"Fine with me," he said, smiling. "We'll have a look at this 'Window on the World,' eh, Son?"

Stephen did not reply.

"It's very good for children," Mrs. Parker said. "It's an educational program. Especially while he's out of school," she added.

"He'll get educated when he goes back to school," said Andrew with a sweet-and-sour expression.

"Yes, both you men get out of the hoosegow tomorrow, don't you?" Janet said. "Will you like being back at school, Steve?"

Stephen continued to watch the hymn-singing.

"I said, Steve, will you like being back at school?" Janet asked more sharply.

"Yes," Stephen said without turning around.

"O Lord, my rock and my redeemer," cried the mixed choir; and then, after several very rapid advertisements, expressed so urgently that the people speaking might have been jerked from the microphone by an invisible hand, came "Window on the World."

The narrator of this program was a pleasant-faced, portly and somewhat scholarly-looking man of middle age. He wore thick-rimmed glasses, which he would sometimes take off and twiddle elegantly in his fingers. He had a deep voice, and spoke softly, casually, and in a friendly way which pleased Andrew despite a determination not to be taken in by what he thought of as "this professional bedside manner." If people were really as friendly as this gent sounds, he thought, the world would be a wonderful place, the way one sometimes thought it was when one was a child.

This narrator spoke a few pleasant, random words, talked about the weather for a moment or so, saying how good it was that this heat wave was breaking up all over the eastern seaboard, how his own garden needed the rain as much as anyone's, and so on. About his garden he was humorously modest. "I may not have a green thumb," he said, "but I sure have a black and blue foot—planted a shovel right on it the other evening."

He probably lives in the St. Regis hotel, Andrew thought, but all the same he could not help being rather charmed with the man's way of doing things.

After a little of this kind of talk, the narrator stepped aside and the screen flickered for a moment, then revealed the first episode. It was the Changing of the Guard at Buckingham Palace, the entire ceremony, with only its inactive periods cut out, so that it was not only real, it was better than real; Andrew remembered watching the real thing during the war and being bored by the length of time in which both the incoming and the outgoing guards stood at ease while their officers walked up and down whispering. But here on the screen everything was martial, musical, clipped, and precise; the sound caught even the metal click of heels on the stone, and even the echo of this thrilling military noise from the stone walls of the parade yard. And there followed a parade of the Horse Guards in the Mall.

"You should see it in color, Son," Andrew said, touching Stephen's shoulder. "The way it really is, with the red coats, golden breastplates, the way those bay horses shine in the sun. You'll see it one day."

The boy turned and smiled at his father for the first time in four days. Andrew felt affectionate and grateful.

The narrator spoke a bit more, then faded out on a gracious wave of his hand, like a magician, to show them something of the life of a big farm in the Middle West. The farmer himself, a seamed, bitten, shrewd, yet kindly face, showed them over his land, with not acres but it seemed miles of grain waving in the sun and then bending to a violent storm which the camera splendidly captured. It was at this moment or thereabouts, oddly, that they heard the first distant noise of thunder outside the house.

"It will storm, after all," Janet said.

"Of course," said Andrew, but with a smile. "They control it from the studio."

The narrator returned to say a few more words. He spoke again, casually, with no attempt to be dramatic—to ham it up, as Andrew would have said—about the vastness and variety of the world. Then he faded away, with the promise of strange things to come, and because these were late films his voice continued, giving the commentary informally which ordinarily would have been prepared in advance and recorded with the film.

The thunder sounded a trifle louder outside, and the image on the screen jerked, flickered, and jumped with distant lightnings.

"I hope Mother's lightning arrester works," Janet said.

"We're lucky to have it," said Mrs. Parker, "or we would have to turn the set off."

The cameras now showed them a confused, milling throng of white-robed black people on an evidently limitless grass plain. The narrator said that they were privileged to witness something few white people had ever seen, the incoronation of the King and Queen of the Wabuga peoples of West Africa. And indeed the camera, evidently mounted on a truck, moved bumpily through the great crowd until it arrived at a clear space near the center. Here enthroned among dignitaries sat the monarch and his wife, both of them handsome, dignified, with shining black skins, and dressed in the richest brocaded silks or satins; the King, a young man, wore several large medals as well.

They were able to witness the whole ceremony, which the narrator explained to them: how the bishop—since this was a Christian nation for all the color of their skins—brought the consecrated crown upon a cushion, how he would anoint the King but not the Queen with the holy oil, how all the people would bow down before the Lord's Anointed.

"You will see," the narrator continued, "in a few moments—you will see a rather terrible thing which marred the religious part of the ceremony. Our cameras managed to catch this thing—this moment of history, you might call it—just as it was actually happening."

Like a field of wheat before the storm, those thousands of white robes knelt just then; the camera swung over the field to catch this movement.

"Now watch the upper left corner of your screens," the narrator said, still in a casual voice but with a touch more urgency. "Here he comes."

A boy, or a young man, was riding unsteadily on a bicycle, his white robe tucked up around his waist; he rode down an alley between crowds of kneeling people. The camera turned to look at the royal couple and the bishop, who stood poised with the crown high in the air, then switched back to the boy. A few people had risen up and were waving at him, and then some were shaking their fists, but he rode on toward the central space.

"They are warning him to get off and kneel down," the narrator said rather neutrally.

Now some people took off after the boy, and a few of them made throwing gestures.

"Those are stones they are throwing," the narrator said. "Probably you can't see them on your screens. Stones."

Now some of the white-robed figures had caught up with the boy, who either threw down his cycle or was knocked off it. He began to run.

"The outraged worshipers stoned the young man to death," the narrator said, and they watched a cloud, a wave, of white robes break over the running boy and bring him down; then there followed a violent rippling of cloth over the mob at that place; then the cameras turned back to the King and Queen of the Wabuga, there was a flickering of the film where some interval of confusion probably had been cut, and the coronation went on its way, the narrator explaining as before.

"Tch, tch," went Mrs. Parker. "That poor fellow. He should have known better."

Andrew said in a choked voice, "Mother, this really happened. They killed that child right in front of our eyes."

"Well, I know," Mrs. Parker said, "but after all, I suppose they have their—what do you call them?—taboos, don't they?"

"He said they were Christians," Andrew said.

"Is heaven like that?" Stephen asked. Andrew could only stare at him.

"He means the white robes," Janet said.

The narrator reappeared now, his grave, kindly face comforting. But he did not choose to talk about what they had just been shown. Instead he said a few words about what "Window on the World" would show them next Sunday.

Andrew got up and hobbled outdoors on his cane. He felt confused and outraged, unable to think clearly, and certainly unable to say a word to anyone in the house. He wondered if the New York Giants were beating the Pittsburgh Steelers.

There was going to be a storm, that was certain now. Great dark clouds towered high in the southwest over Appletree Hill, the brilliant anvil shining in the sunlight above them. Thunder, though still a little ways off, rumbled almost continuously, there were brief, indefinite flickers of lightning, and he felt already a few drops of rain. The heat wave was over.

Andrew hobbled slowly around the house, not much caring if he got wet or not. What did he care about? he asked himself, and replied that he surely did not care if one black boy got knocked off by his own people. Only something, something to do with his having watched this episode, this moment of history, as the narrator had called it, seemed to him more atrocious perhaps than the thing itself. To have helplessly witnessed that death on the screen in the security of his own living room— or living space, as he sardonically remembered to call it, *Lebensraum*— that was horrifying to him, and presented to him an image of his life as mean and cowardly.

The thunder banged, suddenly close, as though nearly overhead, and sudden lightning opened the entire sky, it seemed.

"O God of Battles," Andrew said with irrelevant violence. "The Lord is a Man of War," he remembered from his early days, and, from the famous battle hymn, "He is trampling out the vineyards where the grapes of wrath are stored." But none of all this comforted him or released in him feelings which remained obscure and intense.

His eye fell upon the lightning arrester sticking in the ground near the back wall. He disconnected the terminals, freed the aerial wire, and with a gay gesture of violence hurled the iron spike as far away as he was able, into the bushes.

Take your chance along with everyone else, he said to himself, and limped back into the house, already feeling both ridiculous and timid.

His family remained before the television set, which now showed for a long, still instant the image of a television set. The announcer declared that television set to be without fault.

"We won't even show you a picture on the new Universal," he proclaimed, "because you wouldn't be able to see it properly on the set you have now."

Andrew limped back to his chair and sat down.

"What's on next?" he asked, hearing the thunder crackle and roar while the air even in the room seemed to darken.

Suggestions

1. Beyond the television screen lies life itself, and this is a satirical story about the tendency of Americans to insulate themselves from reality by such means as modern architecture (opening up *a new way of life*) and "viewing." A person who has a *window on the world* is evidently set apart from the world's life, like Mrs. Parker after her heart attack. Life as shown on the screen is *better than real*. Personal though the speaker's attitude is, "Beyond the Screen" is given an utterly realistic surface by the wealth of familiar contemporary objects that, sociologically

considered, are status-symbols (like the aerials on houses that contain no sets) and that symbolically support the story's satire. The *dénouement, as* in "The Eclipse," is not a change in the characters' condition but a moment of revelation. The two stories differ, however, in point of view. That of "Beyond the Screen" is the third-person limited: only the feelings and thoughts of Andrew Stonecroft are shown to us directly, the other characters being seen from outside. The technique and the tone— Andrew is presented with a mixture of pity and amusement—support each other just as the different point of view in "The Eclipse" supports its attitude toward its main character. (Since Andrew is viewed more distantly, it is unlikely that either story could be told with the point of view of the other.) At the end of "Beyond the Screen," to what extent has everything returned to its original condition?

2. Point out details which imply that the family is closed off from reality: e.g. Stephen's ideas about the Russians, Andrew's use of the set as a means of avoiding thought. Then show how reality intrudes into their closed-in world, noticing particularly the ironic use of television in the action, and the repetition of the phrase *terrible thing.* Why is it essential for Stephen's weapon to be a rock?

3. Isolate the exact moment of Andrew's revelation. By what symbolic action is it underscored? Which sentence in section II foreshadows it?

4. Explain: *The poor lady doubtless realized the somewhat stereotyped nature of her situation* (section II). Write an essay on the possibility that the story is amusing because the situations of all the characters are stereotyped. Do you consider the *characterizations* stereotyped? If so, does the story suffer accordingly?

5. Write an essay showing that Andrew's understanding of his life is either permanent or only temporary.

6. Write an essay on the attitude toward television expressed in "Beyond the Screen."

LEGEND OF THE TWO SWIMMERS

ROBIE MACAULEY — *From* THE END OF PITY. © *1957 by Robie Macauley. Reprinted by permission of McDowell, Obolensky Inc.*

Everyone must have a worthless uncle; it is a part of life.

At ten I knew all there was to know about remittance men and black-sheep younger sons shipped off to Australia. It seemed significant that no one in the family ever mentioned such a thing and I was certain that, if I watched carefully enough, one morning I would find a letter dropped through the slot onto the faded blue of the hall carpet, addressed in an unfamiliar hand and carrying a foreign postmark.

I was certain then that I would discern a strained look on my grand-mother's face, or a trace of tears. My father would upset his coffee cup at the table and shout for no reason. I had begun to read the indecent language of signs, a child's first corruption.

There would be tense consultations behind closed doors. One day I would come across a picture in an album, the face cut out, or a silk hat in the attic, marked with unknown initials.

The months passed and letters with a foreign postmark came—but only from a friend of my father's vacationing in England. I never found the picture in the album nor the silk hat in the attic. The front door never opened to the sudden sight of a tall man in dark clothes with a wicked familiar-unfamiliar face. By the end of that year I had finished the shelf of old paperback novels in the basement and had begun to forget all about that uncle.

In dull truth I did have an uncle—he lived only four blocks away and owned half interest in a small, failing dry-goods store in a bad neighbor-hood. Under the shadeless bulbs hanging from the tin ceiling, he fussed around among the counters piled with Big Yank and Oshkosh B'Gosh boys' corduroy knickers, caps stuffed with tissue paper—marked down from $1.98—and canvas gloves. The air in that place was a weight on the lungs, loaded with the smell of cheap new cloth. The shadows in the rear hid only bareness and a roll-top desk, for everything Mr. Rood and my uncle had in stock was piled on the front counters. "Come in out of the rain, boy," Uncle would say as I stood reluctantly in the doorway on my way home from school on a Friday afternoon.

My mother was dead three years; my father was, most likely, on one of his business trips; and Mrs. Fahey, my grandmother's iron nurse, had said at least three times this morning, "I won't have them kids under-foot around the house this week-end." My grandmother ruled, but Mrs. Fahey made the common law in the house.

It was not so much that I would be bored and lonely. As I opened the door to the jangle of the brass bell above it, I knew that I entered the world of worn linoleum on kitchen floors, sooty front porches, smells of cabbage cooking, back yards full of washing, darned socks, pinched pennies, overdue rent, angry protests and angry silences—the gravelly downhill slide of the poor.

In my grandmother's house I felt rich and good. In the cold persistent mist of my aunt and uncle's company, I felt sad and pauperized. I had begun to divide things clearly not so much between good and evil, but between good and bad.

A year or two ago I would have gone along willingly enough, squabbled with the Polish neighbor's two boys, contentedly mooned over an old picture book in the living room while the clock hands slowly drifted toward Sunday night. Going there now seemed like the act of becoming my uncle's son. What was it like to be dumpy, ineffective, getting bald, needing money? I knew. I felt it already in myself.

My mother had lain complaining and bedridden in the little house on Jefferson Street for over two years. When she was gone, my sister and I cried at the funeral, but it was more of an exorcism than a death. We moved in with my grandmother—with her temper and her money. My father seemed to work longer and was away more often. We seldom saw him and when we did it was like too much candy all at once. "He is becoming a very successful man," my grandmother told us. "Like your grandfather. You should be proud of him." We sensed a secret reproach to my mother and our fading loyalty stiffened for a moment. But Mother had always been a reproach to *us*—she suffered so much and we were so selfish. It was often brought home to us how selfish we were. Her painful smile had seemed to live in the room long after she disappeared.

My grandmother was the colonel of the family; she assumed we had a regimental duty to live up to, not unpayable debts of tears. She was the drillmaster of our ideas; our silly feelings she conceded us and left alone. One Sunday a few months after we had come to live in her house, she made my father take me to the "upstairs parlor" to explain, in a way, what she meant.

It was by far the pleasantest room in the house, and though dusted daily, almost never used. Long windows the whole length of the south wall made it a reservoir of sunlight. Beneath them were oblong wicker baskets of ferns, a tame jungle two feet high. To the left of the hearth was the glass showcase with all its trophies.

On its shelves silver divers poised gracefully for the double jackknife that would never follow. Crossed oars that would never touch the water lay on polished plaques; medals of different shapes and sizes glinted at my eyes out of silk-lined boxes. Obscurer mementos filled the lower shelf—a copper pocket-piece, a pipe and pouch, seashells, a leather-bound picture album, a framed sketch of gulls, a box with a silver dolphin on the lid. To me it was an undistinguished hoard. On the center shelf there was a black silk object of some kind, lying there like a small discolored puddle.

Abruptly my father said, "Over here. Come look at them." The spirits of the room, the two champions life-sized and piratical, posed above the fireplace.

Their bare arms were folded on their chests, like great oars momentarily shipped. There was an impressive curve of chest muscle under the short-sleeved swimming jerseys. Their heads were tipped back at the same slightly scornful angle and their black eyes, even through the dull filter of time and the lens, showed total confidence, like a lost trait of man, the sense of absolute monarchy. It persisted for a few moments. Then, like one of those trick geometrical drawings that will change before the eye, the picture would change and you saw only two young men in striped swimming suits staring dourly.

They had identical moustaches like startling pairs of wings, thick eyebrows, my grandmother's heavy cheekbones and her Welsh head; they were, I heard, her dead brothers, Owen and Lloyd.

My father shuffled reverently through the pile of picture postcards from the table drawer. Tebb's Beach, Florida, 1902. A million dollars has changed the name and the landscape since then. A ramshackle boarding house-hotel on a fine beach, backed by scrub jungle. *A splendid place,* my father said, quoting, *a mite lonesome. Just fishermen and a few boarders. Wonderful sunshine.*

Yesterday we saw an Indian ninety-eight years old. Still smokes seven cigars a day—he fought in the Seminole war and they left him for dead in the swamp. Big pink shells here, most beautiful you ever saw. We gathered some, are sending a basketful. Is it snowing in Michigan? We hear there is ice and snow. Sometimes we go out with the fishermen. Owen is getting wonderfully good at the Trudgen stroke. Yesterday we swam for three hours. We had our picture made and we shall send it to you. Give our love to Nettie and Mama.

There wasn't much more to the story, just a glimpse in a letter of the two sunburnt young men on the beach one morning, taking off shoes and robes and preparing to go into the water. Owen, who was the younger, must have tired after a while, it said, and came in to sit on the beach. Someone saw him there for a moment, wringing out the little black silk skullcap he always wore while swimming. Evidently Lloyd stayed out in the water and evidently after a little while Owen looked up to see a shark-blade cutting near him and then his brother must have been gone.

Owen must not have waited, my father said. When the man from the hotel happened along the beach a half hour or so later, the beach was empty and the sea was empty too. Owen must not have hesitated for a moment.

That was not quite the end, he said, because they found the skullcap. It was lying in the sand in the afternoon sun, quite dry by this time.

My father said I was always to remember how Owen had never paused or waited. It may not seem like anything very much to you at your age because you are so young. And it may sound very simple, but it isn't at all simple and you should think about what I'm telling you. There will be times when you yourself will be called just as Uncle Owen was and then you must remember him. When you are older you will understand.

In his voice there was a terrible undertow of pride and I felt it dragging me down. I tried to think of just what it was that had happened and I thought that two young men had gone swimming in the ocean twenty-five years ago and had disappeared. My father stood in the sunlight in his gray suit and tried to tell me about sharks and oceans in a place where he had never been. But I could hear the urgency in his voice and I felt that he was really talking about something that had to be paid back, a strange debt not of money which would keep us poor all of our lives.

"Do you understand?" he demanded, unsatisfied.

I felt shameful and small because, try as I would, I could think of no answer. What kept coming into my head was a warning sign that said, "Watch out for sharks!" and finally I just hung my head and lied, "Yes."

As time went on I began to understand, or thought I did, and I strove to make up for my failure by covering the swimmers in imagination with doubled glory. I would spend hours in the room, lying on the window-seat in the sun reading or idly examining the souvenirs.

"Come in out of the rain, boy," my live uncle said again and I stopped in the doorway. It was not raining. The late afternoon sun, half-tangled in long rags of clouds, shone momentarily down on the street. With his poor joke dropping from his lips, my uncle stood in the middle of his shop and life gathered dust around him.

One day he had confessed why he made jokes like this. "I found out in the army I wasn't strong enough to fight and I was too fat to run, so I took up telling jokes." It was the truth; I had never heard a grown man say anything so spineless. When he was nineteen, he said, he ran away and joined the army. First they taught him to take care of horses and then they taught him to cook. The World War was just one pan of hash after the other. He came home, borrowed money from my grandmother, lost it, borrowed again to go halves in the shop, was losing it again.

Grandmother's soldierly kindness was qualified by her high blood pressure and occasional tempers that glowed and smoked like a coal fire and sent off poisonous fumes. There were times when she could not bear the thought of children in her house; her own had betrayed her so. Annette, her daughter, a beautiful girl by family standards, had turned traitor at the age of nine and died. My father's older brother Will, a pale figure not easily recalled, had got himself killed at Belleau Wood. My Uncle Clinton turned money into dry goods and dry goods into debts, and there it was. My father, who was at least getting somewhere, went completely out of her mind. On those days my sister had to stay in her room and not make any noise and I was sent off to my uncle with $1.75 for board.

I played with the Wisnewski boys down the street until we fought bitterly. Thereafter I moped around the house. My aunt urged me to read the Bible and my uncle took me for walks in the woods. We walked along the river road, which began on the other side of the railway tracks, and he showed me how to make a willow whistle. I said, "What good's a willow whistle? That's for little kids." He told me some army stories and I took interest; then I was bored. They had no gunpowder in them. They were all about what the first sergeant said to the chief cook about the stew. He liked to potter around the woods, with a city man's interest in birds' eggs that had fallen out of trees and the sight of a rabbit. He had a noisy little dog named Butch who sometimes went with us.

The one thing I liked to do was to go fishing with him; and during the summer, when I was pawned off on Aunt and Uncle for weeks at a time, we would often go out for an afternoon on the river. We used bamboo poles and angleworms for bait. He dropped things in the water, rocked the boat, then went to sleep while his line slowly wound around an oar. Still he had marvelous luck. He caught many fish—mostly bullheads and catfish that had to be thrown back again.

I liked those somnolent afternoons when I had nothing at all to live up to. I could see French cliffs rise up on the far side of the river as I lay with my arms over the gunwale. I thought we drifted past the estuary of the Tagus and there was Africa on the horizon. I dozed and saw a blue sea with a black fin splitting the water a long way out and came to myself with a shock, asking myself if I wouldn't hesitate, wouldn't wait a minute until it was too late.

The trouble was, I felt, that this very instant was traveling in me like an air bubble in a vein and I could never foretell the moment it would reach the heart. When my father had talked to me, for the first time in my life I had doubted him and thus had doubted myself. I wondered if when Owen was a boy my great-grandfather had told him one day he would see a fin in the water and that he mustn't hesitate or wait even a second. I tried to imagine him telling Owen that. Boys die young and become their fathers.

I looked at my uncle, asleep on the back seat of the rowboat, his face sagging peacefully under his sagging hat. I wondered if he had ever heard the story, or if it meant anything to him.

Then one day I brought the subject up. He fixed the angleworm carefully on the hook and yawned. "Mother never did get over the death of those two darn fools," he said.

"Fools?" I said, shocked. "They were as brave as anybody can be and Owen went to save . . ."

"I know, I know," he said. "That's the way people talked. I say it was lack of good sense. Hadn't got brains enough to stay on dry land or a boat at least. Then go swimming around in shark waters. One got himself eat up, then the other one got himself eat up, too. Darn fools, I say."

At first I was too angry to speak, then when I looked again I saw it was only sluggish Uncle Clint bending over his bait pail and I realized it wasn't even necessary to forgive him.

When the cold water in the bottom of the boat would reach his foot, he would wake up. "Bail for dear life, men," he would say, "the ship is going down." The boat was an old one, paintless and splintery. He had found it one day half submerged in some rocky shallows down the river. He had dragged it ashore, nailed tin strips over the most obvious holes, caulked it, had given the bottom a coat of tar. He loved it in the same way he loved my aunt, who sustained him on the muddy waters of day to day, but who might sometime disappear and leave him to drown.

He was very much afraid of deep water. It must have been the earliest thing that set him apart from the rest of the family, of which Owen and Lloyd had been natural products. Almost all of the men had been skilful swimmers. My father, who never let me have such a dangerous thing as a bicycle, would point out the deepest part of the lake and dare me to swim to it. When I told my uncle about the swimming lessons I was taking from a professional, he pinched his nose and cast his eyes up, as if he were sinking hopelessly among the fish.

Our slow leak he regarded as a monster of the deep. Sometimes he would give up an hour's fishing and drifting because of an extra inch in the bottom of the boat.

"I couldn't be expected to save you," he would say, rowing for the shore.

"*I* can swim pretty well," I would say defiantly. The phlegmatic old Grand River seemed safe as a sidewalk—safer.

He had no very good place to tie the boat and so we just pulled it up on a sandy strip where he had put down a stake with a chain. Then we took our basket and our poles and started back along the river road.

The most agreeable spot in the world, I thought, with woods on one hand and an outpost line of huge trees along the waterside, a great green arcade in summer, it had been claimed by squatters and their shacks. Once it was fashionable to have a boat and a cottage down here, but now people went north or west to the lakes. Bristly mongrel dogs stod by the doors of mimic chalets with sinking roofs and crumbling lines of gingerbread. Four—five—six children's faces were piled in a pyramid inside a window. A man in a ragged leather jacket refused to answer hello, just took another swing with his axe. Some of the places were recently built huts, actually projecting over the riverside slope and supported there by a crazywork of long poles. Underneath them, like the droppings of a tethered animal, were tin cans, newspapers, ash piles, old tires, broken bottles.

Darkness dropped out of the air; it had already dimmed the city by the time we reached our street. My uncle hummed a tune. I walked pigeon-toed and lagged behind, nursing a wish like a bruise. A hundred seventeen steps from the corner, ten steps down the walk, four steps up to the porch; he reached for the knob.

I hung back, kicking the risers. The thought of that house with its long bare hours between bed and bed stunned me. In the hall, my uncle gave a three-note whistle and Butch came running. "Angel, we're home!" he shouted.

At dinner—fried mush and boiled cabbage were nearly inevitable— he talked about our afternoon as if remembering the striking events of history—"Just then a grand trout jumped in the air about fifteen feet away from us. Oh, it was a thrilling moment." He discussed manners and morals —"Six kids, a hound dog, and an old car. No curtains on the windows, no running water but the river, and still enough money to buy gas for an old car . . ."

Mute and unimpressed, Aunt finished her food and poured the coffee. When he had drunk his cup dry, my uncle began to rise, but it was only a poor habitual try. My aunt raised her eyes and stared at him. Saturday night meant prayers and bath for all good Christians. We bowed our heads.

"Forgive us for what we have left undone . . . guide our steps in the right pathways . . . make us better and stronger to withstand temptation in the week to come . . ." As she worked into the substance of her appeal, she became more fervent, more obscure, more biting. She referred obliquely to those who, though not unblessed by the hand of the Lord and having plenty of the goods of this earth—though how they expected to get through the eye of the needle she wouldn't presume to say—refused to help others needier than themselves and acted as if water was just as thick as blood. She worked around to those who sometimes through pure chuckle-headedness neglected to do certain unspecified things they ought to do while their nearest and dearest suffered as a result. My uncle dozed.

Ordinarily she did not scold or complain but went silently on with her work, her mouth like a seam; she was a different woman when she prayed. I listened and was scared at her tone. It came from a hollow distance. Even though its mixture of sarcasm, anger, bitterness, and sorrow confused me, I could recognize it. It was low and muffled through the thickness of many walls, but it came unmistakably from the torture chamber itself.

When she was silent again, Uncle raised his head, yawned, and said, "That was fine, Angel." He went into the living room and she began gathering up the plates.

That summer, the summer of which I am speaking, approached. My sister in a white dress played in the piano recital in the school auditorium and all remarked that she didn't make one mistake. I practiced my curve at the playground and pinned a picture of Lefty Grove over my dresser. My father went to Kansas City on business. My grandmother began to feel the heat approaching and predicted it would be the worst summer on record. School let out. I was banished to my uncle's. Uncle came home at night, slumped, and my aunt put a dishpan full of cool water next to his chair for him to soak his feet. He stared at the water and said, "We can't do it, Angel. It's no use." A man came to see him in the evening and they sat out on the porch for a long time. When I was in bed, I could hear their voices rise occasionally above the ziz-ziz-ziz of the tree toads and I heard my uncle ask, "Foreclosure?"

The summer clouds piled high over the river like marble monuments. I tried my crawl stroke in the river (this was forbidden) and watched the grainy water slide over my arms. On the bank one of the river kids, a solemn child in a patched dress, stood and stared.

My uncle hadn't the heart to go fishing much. Aunt's Saturday-night prayers increased in violence and developed in mystery. June turned into July. The lawns burned brown and crisp like shredded breakfast food. My friends were away at camps or cottages and I no longer wanted to go down to the river alone. From the swing on my uncle's porch I watched the clouds transform themselves and move away. I longed for fall, school, a disaster, anything.

In the course of time, it became Sunday morning of the first week in August. My father was home again, my grandmother was in a fit of well-being, and my exile was over. I was to go back to the other house the same day. Belly down, among the comic strips, I lay in squalid comfort on the worn rug. There was, thank God, no Sunday school in summer. My uncle lolled in his plump chair and surveyed the world as it came, printed, before his eyes. He muttered comments on it. The clock struck nine, shortly ten.

Aunt came home from church with a queer look. We heard her feet on the porch and then she came into the room and stood looking at us. "I'm going to see Mrs. Banning this afternoon," she finally said, but it wasn't what she was thinking.

Slowly she began to pull off one of her gloves, staring in apparent pain at her hand, exactly as if she were in the process of stripping the whole skin from it.

"You must ask today," she said in the voice of her prayers.

Uncle was alarmed. He looked up at her with a deserter's look. His glance roved to the window; he tried to raise the newspaper in front of his face again, but the inexorable skinning stopped him.

The glove came off at last with a final little snap and he jumped—it was as if we had all expected to see white bone. He said hurriedly, "I'll try. Yes, today's the day and I certainly will consider going to ask. They can't refuse me, can they, Angel?" He sighed. The newspaper began to cut him off again. Aunt stood quietly and began on the left hand. For some long-drawn minutes we could hear the same soft stripping sound. Only her fingers worked.

At last my uncle jumped out of his chair and yelled, "Stop!" He was breathing heavily and his thready hair was flying. He yelled, "Don't get so excited!" and rushed upstairs where we could hear him crashing his dresser drawers. He reappeared in a coat and tie and hooked his straw hat off the hall rack as he hit the bottom of the stairs. "Come on, son," he said, grabbing my arm and pulling me protesting to the door. As we went stumbling down the steps, I looked back and saw my aunt sitting in a chair with wet eyes and her hands buried in her dress. She looked beaten.

On the way over we marched and did not speak. When we came into the cool living room, I saw my father and shouted, "Dad!" In a cold voice he said, "Go upstairs and play. We've got business." Then I noticed my grandmother, Mr. Rood, and a stranger in a dark suit. The men were sitting in the shadow on the far side of the room while my grandmother, all by herself, garrisoned the nearer end. Her hand opened and closed on a little ivory stick.

I resented it, but my only choice was to go through the glass doors into the parlor—a room overfurnished with a stupefying taste. I went upstairs, wandered in and out of rooms, and finally found myself in the swimmers' room. I stood before the fireplace looking up at them. Nothing had changed. "Play the game! Keep the faith! Grasp the nettle!" they said silently. It was all very easy, all very well, I thought. It was in their bones and muscles. It was only in my head. I was frightened. Then I thought—times change. For all I knew sharks were killed by some kind of machine nowadays. It didn't help. I stood in despair for a long time.

When I heard a clock striking in the hall, I finally went slowly downstairs. I crept through the parlor up to the glass doors and looked in. They were still talking. My father stood in front of the fireplace, his arms half extended in his usual gesture of irritation. My grandmother's face had petrified—the horrible calm before she opened her mouth. She must have said something to Mr. Rood already because he sat heaped in his chair like a pile of worn-out clothes. Only the stranger seemed detached. With one eye in a squint, he calmly looked across the room at a china figurine of a camel perched on the whatnot. He looked as if he might be ready to take a shot at it.

My uncle looked as if he had been boiled. His face was red and puffed with his eyes bubbled, his mouth sunken. On the other side of the glass, my grandmother was saying, "Last time was really the last time, Clinton; you know it."

"Mother, just think what you're saying," Uncle pled.

"We have thought," said my father harshly. "We have thought and we can't do it." I saw him turn his back.

And he was right to do so because my uncle was crying. In his horrible little fat-man way he was crying and tears ran down his cheeks. It was unbearable for me and I had to go into the room to distract their attention, even though it might make my grandmother angry. I had to stop the beating. But I would never be seen with my uncle again. I would run away and get a job as a cabin boy on a ship.

"Well," said my father pleasantly, "you're back. Now why don't you go for a walk with your Uncle Clint? He hasn't been feeling well, you see. He'll bring you back in time for dinner." It was the last thing I had expected.

"I won't go with him," I said.

My father came over and took me by the shoulder with a strong hand. "You will go," he said abruptly. "We've had enough trouble for one day." He did not say this as if it were meant for me, but to all in general. As we were going out, I heard him say to my uncle in a confidential tone, "Don't worry, Clint. I'll do the best I can." I couldn't understand what was happening.

When we were outside, Uncle stood on the walk and looked back at the front windows of the house while words seemed to thaw in his throat. "So that's the way the land lies, hm? So that's it? For your own good, they say. Well, if you ask me . . ." I didn't know what to expect. I stood and listened to him mutter.

He looked down at me and said, "You got some better place to go?"

I shook my head. He looked queer and choked and we walked along with very slow steps.

Finally he laughed and said, "Let's go down by the river. Yes, the river's the place for me today." He suddenly started to stride and I had to half run to keep up with him.

The streets were quiet; in the heat of Sunday afternoon the houses dozed behind their screens of trees. We crossed the railroad tracks and finally got to the river road, which was cool and deserted. The sun through the leaves made yellow sketches and signatures in the dust of it. My uncle looked anxiously around and I felt his desperation. He broke off a willow twig and made a few random slashes at it with his knife, looked at me, dropped it.

We walked some more. Abruptly he said, "Do you want to take the boat out on the river?"

I nodded. He said in the same voice, "It may be the last time."

"Why is it the last time?" I said. "Why the last time, Uncle Clint?" But he didn't answer. We turned around the bend in the road by the big willow and started down the little track that led to our mooring place.

When we had gone about twenty yards, we began to hear a woman's voice in shrill ups and downs beyond the bushes. We could not hear what she was saying. I ran ahead to see what it was. In a minute I burst through the bushes and saw her. She was calmly sitting on the middle thwart of *our* boat.

Worse than that, she was holding an oar and awkwardly trying to pole the boat away from shore while a girl about my age, but small, like a skinny monkey, had just finished untying the rope. My uncle gasped behind me. "Robbers!" I said. "Look, Uncle Clint."

The woman turned quickly; she had long rusty hair and a rusty face with chipped features—like notches in an axe blade. She was wearing some plaid thing that looked as if it had been torn off a table and hastily stitched around her. The girl swiftly hopped around, twisted over the side into the boat, crouched behind the gunwale and gave us a look out of the same face, though younger, more furtive, and even more ignorant.

My uncle stood gaping as his ship was stolen. I could have counted ten. I yelled, "That's our boat. Come back here, you." I knew I would have to do it myself. I jumped for the trailing rope at the bow. He came along behind me with undecided steps.

As I reached, I saw something happening. Slowly, out of six inches of mushy bottom, out of the shallow water, high into the air in a great trailing slimy arc, the oar was rising. The wide-eyed woman seemed to be clinging to it rather than propelling it. I scrambled sidewise as fast as I could.

Such ponderous soggy haymakers are too futile to hit anything in this world—except Uncle, who was fated. He had come up behind me; I said, "Duck," but as always, he did not fail to fail.

The end of the oar smacked him squarely on the chin, filled the air with a great burst of slime, pitched him backward three feet into a clump of rushes, and buried itself with a spout in the river bottom again. He put his hand up experimentally to his eyes.

I was scrabbling for a stone; "A fast one low and inside, just like Lefty's," I prayed as it left my hand. Not very fast, low and outside, it merely hit a tin plate we'd nailed over a leak in the side of the boat. It hit with a loud *clack!*

They were out in the stream already gathering a sluggish momentum from the current. My uncle said feebly, "That's enough. Stop." Reluctantly I gave up the idea of clearing the decks with my high hard one, and went over to him. It occurred to me then that he was probably badly wounded.

He groaned and got to his knees, while I splashed some water over his face, which ran in red and black ribbons down his white shirt front. "Oh God," he said. "Is my nose still there?" It was. "Count my eyes," he directed.

"You've only got some blood on your chin," I said. "The rest is just mud. Open your mouth. You've got one, no, I think two front teeth out." He groaned again. I put my hands under his arm and tried to help him as he got to his feet. "You're all right," I said anxiously. "It's only one or two teeth."

"One," he said grimly, and spat it out.

While he was splashing some more water on his face, I recovered the oar and hid it in the bushes. I was already beginning to think about pursuit, recovery, revenge. They couldn't get far with one oar. If we worked carefully along the shore—but just beyond us the trees came right down to the river and it was beyond them that the boat had now disappeared. Uncle responded to my schemes with a weak "Ehh, uh," and attended to his face. He was holding his jaw and his lower lip had begun to rise into a purplish sausage.

He followed me aimlessly as I made a way through the bushes. Over my shoulder, I kept saying things to make him come on—"If you'd only pulled back just half a foot . . . they can't row, they can't get far . . ." He didn't answer.

We went on for about twenty or thirty minutes and it seemed hopeless. There was nobody in the woods and the river was empty; the bushes tore at my trouser legs. At last I knew that we had lost them. Uncle came up alongside me, nursing his hurt mouth in his handkerchief. "I'm going home and put some ice on this. We'll have to give up." He said it almost pleadingly.

"But the boat," I said. "We'll never get it back again, you know that." I was perfectly detached and not selfish. I had just decided that I was through with him and the boat and the river forever, but I was trying to save something abstract. I could not see him ruined completely in one short day. I could not stand to think of him sitting at the table tonight while my aunt was praying and he thought, The boat is gone for good. He shook his head feebly at me and I knew I had lost.

So we trudged back up to the road again while I thought bitterly of running ahead and leaving him alone. Just as I was deciding, we came opposite the place where the old pilings from a former landing dock stuck up in the river. I heard a yell and a sound of splashing. I knew and I began to run.

I cut through the bushes quickly and got down to the river bank again. When I got there, I saw what I knew I was going to see—it was the unexpectedness of the completely expected. Out from the shore about fifteen feet was our boat with the rusty woman and the girl in it. They had evidently hit against one of the stumps and, as Uncle had always predicted, the boat was at last stubbornly sinking.

She was thrashing around frantically in her wet tablecloth, trying to scoop water over the side, trying to push with the remaining oar, slapping at the girl, screaming directions. When she saw me, she wailed, "We can't swim!" Then she yelled, "Your damn boat's full of leaks."

I was so winded I could only stand and watch with a feeling that this contemptible day had finally justified itself. I *had* wanted something terrible to happen. Everybody who involved himself with Uncle, even to steal from him, was going to suffer. I was getting out.

The boat lurched; the woman screamed again; Uncle arrived, running like a car on two cylinders.

He didn't ask anything, but pushed by me to see better. The next thing I saw was his clumsy lunge into the river, knees pumping, heels skidding on the slippery mud; then brown sprays of water shooting up over his pants legs. His mind had gone—I knew it, but what could I do? "Come back! Come back! Where're you going?" I said, but he sloshed on with surprising speed. He caught the nearest black pier stump in the crook of his arm and grabbed for the next one further out; he was doing a comic swim, half out of the water. He sank to the level of his belt, then to his shoulders, and the water bounced furiously around him. Then all at once I was thoroughly frightened—because he was not frightened. "Come back!" I yelled frantically. "Uncle, *you can't swim.*"

He had his arm hooked around the last old piling and he was reaching out to grab the gunwale of the boat. It lurched just then and he caught it; he managed to drag it towards him a few inches. His chin dipped under water and he let go of the boat as he reared his head backwards. I saw his eyes open, white and wide, and I knew that I was wrong. He was strangling with fear.

I started forward alarmed, but at the same moment Uncle had succeeded in grasping the woman's wrist in one hand and pulling her toward him. She was holding the girl in one arm and Uncle inched them over the side of the boat as they weakly fought against each other and him. They hung for a moment on the slanting gunwale, then disappeared together in a great spew of water and plaid cloth.

But in a moment his head emerged, an uncertain island around which they wrapped their arms. But underneath the panicky mess of grasping hands, wet hair, muddy faces, and cloth, a slow dogged engine was bringing them in to shore.

There was a slopping sound from behind them and I looked up. The boat gave a last pitch in the lazy current, slid sideways, and vanished.

And here my uncle, too, vanishes from my recollections. He had ceased to take any place in my memory the moment he stepped on shore, as if my mind has let him sink at the exact moment of his success. I do not remember if he was triumphant or cast down. We must have walked home together, but I cannot remember it; and we must have said something or other about what had happened, but nothing remains.

Nothing remains of him except a few hearsay memories—I walked by his shop some weeks later and saw the windows plastered with signs advertising a sale. A fat man with curly black hair stood in the doorway cleaning out his ear with his little finger. My father did speak of his brother Clint sometimes and, I believe, sent him money after he had moved away.

That is all, or would have been all if it had not been for my father, who never lost his taste for moral fancies and noble illustrations.

Years later, in October, 1943, to be exact, I was a member of a regiment specially trained for amphibious operations. We were waiting at an east coast port of embarkation. The bleak barracks town lay under a gray sky and the days went by in a routine of preparation, apprehension, and boredom.

There was nothing to do except line up for inoculations, play cards, check your equipment over again, lie on your bunk for hours tracing the water stains on the beaverboard ceiling. The water stains on those ceilings are remarkable because many of them look like drawings of ships going down, men struggling in the water, or figures suddenly disemboweled. All of the worst deaths known to the world are painted there.

On the Saturday before we were to leave, our last mail arrived, forwarded from our former camp. All I had was a letter from my father and a small package.

The letter began with his usual cheerful sententiousness. On the second page, it went on to say ". . . now I am sending you a memento of your uncle, who, as you remember, was a most courageous man. You might wish to have it with you both as a kind of family souvenir and as a reminder of someone who . . ." I stopped reading and the day came back.

I saw vividly the brown sluggish waters of the river with my uncle's terrified face bucking up and down in them, just as he reached for the gunwale of the foundering rowboat, the ridiculous sputtering, swollen face that against all the probabilities of nature was going forward.

But as far as I knew, my father had never known much of anything about this, or, if he had known, would have dismissed it. It seemed impossible that he could have found anything he could call a "memento." I knew that I now had the only memento of that day. I spent some time recalling it.

At last I opened the package he had sent. In it there lay a small half circle of faded black silk. I took it out and handled it and for a long time I sat turning it over in my fingers, unable to connect it with anything. It was only after some minutes that I recognized it as a small, faded silk skullcap, of course.

Suggestions

1. "Legend of the Two Swimmers" takes the narrator back to the age of ten, even earlier than the age of the main character in † "The Eclipse." Both stories are told in the first person, but here the point of view is that of the first-person observer. His influence on the action is negligible; the events are important only as they register on his consciousness. In so quiet and reflective a story a surprise ending is difficult to bring off, and the force of the last sentence measures the strength of the illusion that has been created. The reality of the story arises from the pointed contrast of the two houses between which the boy's child-

hood is divided. In later years he sees his boyhood as corrupt, because of his simplicity in preferring his grandmother's mansion of romantic illusions to the house of his uncle—ineffective, spineless, and above all, "needing money." At that early age he was shocked when his uncle pronounced the two swimmers "darn fools," and only at the end, when he is waiting to be shipped abroad and sees the waterstains as "All the worst deaths known to the world," does he understand Uncle Clint's moral superiority.

2. In a story of reflection, concerned with the impact of events on an observer's consciousness, the style is of special importance. Discuss the style of "Legend of the Two Swimmers" with particular attention to the many similes.

3. The story is also one of character, differing in this respect from † "Beyond the Screen." Characterize the persons in it who are fully developed, showing how the speaker's attitudes toward them changes. E.g. would he have thought when he was ten that his father had a "taste for moral fancies and noble illustrations"?

4. Explain the reference to "a child's first corruption" in ¶2. What other expressions show that the speaker regards his earlier self without admiration?

5. Point out the most effective dramatic scenes in the story, showing the importance in them of vivid visual details.

6. Write an essay on the possibility that the theme of "Legend of the Two Swimmers" is the contrast between reality and illusion. Analyze its title as part of your discussion.

7. Write an essay on the similarities or differences between the family relationships in this story and those in your own family.

THE STATE OF GRACE

MARCEL AYMÉ

Translation by Norman Denny. From ACROSS PARIS AND OTHER STORIES *by Marcel Aymé.* © *1947 by Librairie Gallimard. Reprinted by permission of Harper & Brothers, Librairie Gallimard, and The Bodley Head.*

In the year 1939 the best Christian in the Rue Gabrielle, and indeed in all Montmartre, was a certain Monsieur Duperrier, a man of such piety, uprightness, and charity that God, without awaiting his death, and while he was still in the prime of life, crowned his head with a halo which never left it by day or by night. Like those in Paradise this halo, although made of some immaterial substance, manifested itself in the form of a whitish ring which looked as though it might have been cut out of fairly stiff cardboard, and shed a tender light. M. Duperrier wore it gratefully, with devout thanks to Heaven for a distinction which, however, his modesty did not permit him to regard as a formal undertaking in respect of the hereafter. He would have been unquestionably the happiest of men had his wife, instead of rejoicing in this signal mark of the Divine approval, not received it with outspoken resentment and exasperation.

"Well really, upon my word," the lady said, "what do you think you look like going round in a thing like that, and what do you suppose the neighbors and the tradespeople will say, not to mention my cousin Léopold? I never in my life saw anything so ridiculous. You'll have the whole neighborhood talking."

Mme. Duperrier was an admirable woman, of outstanding piety and impeccable conduct, but she had not yet understood the vanity of the things of this world. Like so many people whose aspirations to virtue are marred by a certain lack of logic, she thought it more important to be esteemed by her concierge than by her Creator. Her terror lest she should be questioned on the subject of the halo by one of the neighbors or by the milkman had from the very outset an embittering effect upon her. She made repeated attempts to snatch away the shimmering plate of light that adorned her husband's cranium, but with no more effect than if she had tried to grasp a sunbeam, and without altering its position by a hair's-breadth. Girdling the top of his forehead where the hair began, the halo hung low over the back of his neck, with a slight tilt which gave it a coquettish look.

The foretaste of beatitude did not cause Duperrier to overlook the consideration he owed to his wife's peace of mind. He himself possessed too great a sense of discretion and modesty not to perceive that there were grounds for her disquiet. The gifts of God, especially when they wear a somewhat gratuitous aspect, are seldom accorded the respect they deserve, and the world is all too ready to find in them a subject of malicious gossip. Duperrier did his utmost, so far as the thing was possible, to make himself at all times inconspicuous. Regretfully putting aside the bowler hat which he had hitherto regarded as an indispensable attribute of his accountant's calling, he took to wearing a large felt hat, light in color, of which the wide brim exactly covered the halo provided he wore it rakishly on the back of his head. Thus clad, there was nothing startlingly out-of-the-way in his appearance to attract the attention of the passer-by. The brim of his hat merely had a slight phosphorescence which by daylight might pass for the sheen on the surface of smooth felt. During office hours he was equally successful in avoiding the notice of his employer and fellow-workers. His desk, in the small shoe factory in Ménilmontant where he kept the books, was situated in a glass-paned cubbyhole between two workshops, and his state of isolation saved him from awkward questions. He wore the hat all day, and no one was sufficiently interested to ask him why he did so.

But these precautions did not suffice to allay his wife's misgivings. It seemed to her that the halo must already be a subject of comment among the ladies of the district, and she went almost furtively about the streets adjoining the Rue Gabrielle, her buttocks contracted and her heart wrung with agonizing suspicions, convinced that she heard the echo of mocking laughter as she passed. To this worthy woman, who had never had any ambition other than to keep her place in a social sphere ruled by the cult of the absolute norm, the glaring eccentricity with which her husband had been afflicted rapidly assumed catastrophic proportions. Its very improbability made it monstrous. Nothing would have induced her to accompany him out of doors. The evenings and Sunday afternoons which they had previously devoted to small outings and visits to friends were now passed in a solitary intimacy which became daily more oppressive. In the living-room of light oak where between meals the long leisure hours dragged by, Mme. Duperrier, unable to knit a single stitch, would sit bitterly contemplating the halo, while Duperrier, generally reading some work of devotion and feeling the brush of angels' wings, wore an expression of beatific rapture which added to her fury. From time to time, however, he would glance solicitously at her, and noting the expression of angry disapproval on her face would feel a regret which was incompatible with the gratitude he owed to Heaven, so that this in its turn inspired him with a feeling of remorse at one remove.

So painful a state of affairs could not long continue without imperiling the unhappy woman's mental equilibrium. She began presently to complain that the light of the halo, bathing the pillows, made it impossible for her to sleep at nights. Duperrier, who sometimes made use of the divine illumination to read a chapter of the Scriptures, was obliged to concede the justice of this grievance, and he began to be afflicted with a sense of guilt. Finally, certain events, highly deplorable in their consequences, transformed this state of unease into one of acute crisis.

Upon setting out for the office one morning, Duperrier passed a funeral in the Rue Gabrielle, within a few yards of their house. He had become accustomed, outrageous though it was to his natural sense of courtesy, to greet acquaintances by merely raising a hand to his hat; but being thus confronted by the near presence of the dead he decided, after thinking the matter over, that nothing could relieve him of the obligation to uncover himself entirely. Several shopkeepers, yawning in their doorways, blinked at the sight of the halo, and gathered together to discuss the phenomenon. When she came out to do her shopping Mme. Duperrier was assailed with questions, and in a state of extreme agitation uttered denials whose very vehemence appeared suspect. Upon his return home at midday her husband found her in a state of nervous crisis which caused him to fear for her reason.

"Take off that halo!" she cried. "Take it off instantly! I never want to see it again!"

Duperrier gently reminded her that it was not in his power to remove it, whereupon she cried still more loudly:

"If you had any consideration for me you'd find some way of getting rid of it. You're simply selfish, that's what you are!"

These words, to which he prudently made no reply, gave Duperrier much food for thought. And on the following day a second incident occurred to point to the inevitable conclusion. Duperrier never missed early-morning Mass, and since he had become endowed with the odor of sanctity he had taken to hearing it at the Basilica of the Sacré-Cœur. Here he was obliged to remove his hat, but the church is a large one and at that hour of the morning the congregation was sufficiently sparse to make it a simple matter for him to hide behind a pillar. On this particular occasion, however, he must have been less circumspect than usual. As he was leaving the church after the service an elderly spinster flung herself at his feet crying, "St. Joseph! St. Joseph!," and kissed the hem of his overcoat. Duperrier beat a hasty retreat, flattered but considerably put out at recognizing his adorer, who lived only a few doors away. A few hours later the devoted creature burst into the apartment, where Mme. Duperrier was alone, uttering cries of—"St. Joseph! I want to see St. Joseph!"

Although somewhat lacking in brilliant and picturesque qualities, St. Joseph is nevertheless an excellent saint: but his unsensational merits, with their flavor of solid craftsmanship and passive goodwill, seem to have brought upon him some degree of injustice. There are indeed persons, some of the utmost piety, who, without even being conscious of it, associate the notion of naïve complaisance with the part he played in the Nativity. This impression of simple-mindedness is further enhanced by the habit of superimposing upon the figure of the saint the recollection of that other Joseph who resisted the advances of Potiphar's wife. Mme. Duperrier had no great respect for the presumed sanctity of her husband, but this fervor of adoration which with loud cries invoked him by the name of St. Joseph seemed to her to add the finishing touch to his shame and absurdity. Goaded into a state of almost demented fury, she chased the visitor out of the apartment with an umbrella and then smashed several piles of plates. Her first act upon her husband's return was to have hysterics, and when finally she had regained her self-control she said in a decided voice:

"For the last time I ask you to get rid of that halo. You can do it if you choose. You know you can."

Duperrier hung his head, not daring to ask how she thought he should go about it, and she went on:

"It's perfectly simple. You only have to sin."

Uttering no word of protest, Duperrier withdrew to the bedroom to pray.

"Almighty God," he said in substance, "you have granted me the highest reward that man may hope for upon earth, excepting martyrdom. I thank you, Lord, but I am married and I share with my wife the bread of tribulation which you deign to send us, no less than the honey of your favor. Only thus can a devout couple hope to walk in your footsteps. And it so happens that my wife cannot endure the sight or even the thought of my halo, not at all because it is a gift bestowed by Heaven but simply because it's a halo. You know what women are. When some unaccustomed happening does not chance to kindle their enthusiasm it is likely to upset all the store of rules and harmonies which they keep lodged in their little heads. No one can prevent this, and though my wife should live to be a hundred there will never be any place for my halo in her scheme of things. Oh God, you who see into my heart, you know how little store I set by my personal tranquillity and the evening slippers by the fireside. For the rapture of wearing upon my head the token of your goodwill I would gladly suffer even the most violent domestic upheavals. But, alas, it is not my own peace of mind that is imperiled. My wife is losing all taste for life. Worse still, I can see the day approaching when her hatred of my halo will cause her to revile Him who bestowed it upon me. Am I to allow the life-companion you chose for me to die and damn her soul for all eternity without making an effort to save her? I find myself today at the parting of the ways, and the safe road does not appear to me to be the more merciful. That your spirit of infinite justice may talk to me with the voice of my conscience is the prayer which in this hour of my perplexity I lay at your radiant feet, oh Lord."

Scarcely had Duperrier concluded this prayer than his conscience declared itself in favor of the way of sin, making of this an act of duty demanded by Christian charity. He returned to the living-room, where his wife awaited him, grinding her teeth.

"God is just," he said, with his thumbs in the armholes of his waistcoat. "He knew what he was doing when he gave me my halo. The truth is that I deserve it more than any man alive. They don't make men like me in these days. When I reflect upon the vileness of the human herd and then consider the manifold perfections embodied in myself

I am tempted to spit in the faces of the people in the street. God has rewarded me, it is true, but if the Church had any regard for justice I should be an archbishop at the very least."

Duperrier had chosen the sin of pride, which enabled him, while exalting his own merits, in the same breath to praise God, who had singled him out. His wife was not slow to realize that he was sinning deliberately and at once entered into the spirit of the thing.

"My angel," she said, "you will never know how proud I am of you. My cousin Léopold, with his car and his villa at Vesinet, is not worthy to unloose the latchet of your shoe."

"That is precisely my own opinion. If I had chosen to concern myself with sordid matters I could have amassed a fortune as easily as any man, and a much bigger one than Léopold's, but I chose to follow a different road and my triumph is of another kind. I despise his money as I despise the man himself and all the countless other half-wits who are incapable of perceiving the grandeur of my modest existence. They have eyes and see not."

The utterance of sentiments such as these, spoken at first from half-closed lips, his heart rent with shame, became within a short time a simple matter for Duperrier, a habit costing him no effort at all. And such is the power of words over the human mind that it was not long before he accepted them as valid currency. His wife, however, anxiously watching the halo and seeing that its lustre showed no sign of diminishing, began to suspect that her husband's sin was lacking in weight and substance. Duperrier readily agreed with this.

"Nothing could be more true," he said. "I thought I was giving way to pride when in fact I was merely expressing the most simple and obvious of truths. When a man has attained to the uttermost degree of perfection, as I have done, the word pride ceases to have any meaning."

This did not prevent him from continuing to extol his merits, but at the same time he recognized the necessity for embarking upon some other form of sin. It appeared to him that gluttony was, of the Deadly Sins, the one most suited to his purpose, which was to rid himself of the halo without too far forfeiting the goodwill of Heaven. He was supported in this conclusion by the recollection, from his childhood days, of gentle scoldings for excessive indulgence in jam or chocolate. Filled with hope, his wife set about the preparation of rich dishes whose variety enhanced their savor. The Duperriers' dinner-table was loaded with game, pâté, river-trout, lobster, sweets, pastries, and vintage wines. Their meals lasted twice as long as hitherto, if not three times. Nothing could have been more hideous and revolting than the spectacle of Duperrier, his napkin tied round his neck, his face crimson and his eyes glazed with satiation, loading his plate with a third helping, washing down roast and stuffing with great gulps of claret, belching, dribbling sauce and gravy, and perspiring freely under his halo. Before long he had developed such a taste for good cooking and rich repasts that he frequently rebuked his wife for an over-cooked joint or an unsuccessful mayonnaise. One evening, annoyed by his incessant grumbling, she said sharply:

"Your halo seems to be flourishing. Anyone would think it was growing fat on my cooking, just as you are. It looks to me as though gluttony isn't a sin after all. The only thing against it is that it costs money, and I can see no reason why I shouldn't put you back on vegetable soup and spaghetti."

"That's enough of that!" roared Duperrier. "Put me back on vegetable soup and spaghetti, will you? By God, I'd like to see you try! Do you think I don't know what I'm doing? Put me back on spaghetti, indeed! The insolence! Here am I, wallowing in sin just to oblige you, and that's the way you talk. Don't let me hear another word. It would serve you right if I slapped your face."

One sin leads to another, in short, and thwarted greed, no less than pride, promotes anger. Duperrier allowed himself to fall into this new sin without really knowing whether he was doing it for his wife's sake or because he enjoyed it. This man who had hitherto been distinguished by the gentleness and equability of his nature now became given to thunderous rages; he smashed the crockery and on occasions went so far as to strike his wife. He even swore, invoking the name of his Creator. But his outbursts, growing steadily more frequent, did not save him from being both arrogant and gluttonous. He was, in fact, now sinning in three different ways, and Mme. Duperrier mused darkly on God's infinite indulgence.

The fact is that the noblest of virtues can continue to flourish in a soul sullied by sin. Proud, gluttonous, and choleric, Duperrier nevertheless remained steeped in Christian charity, nor had he lost anything of his lofty sense of duty as a man and a husband. Finding that Heaven remained unmoved by his anger, he resolved to be envious as well. To tell the truth, without his knowing it, envy had already crept into his soul. Rich feeding, which puts a burden on the liver, and pride, which stirs the sense of injustice, may dispose even the best of men to envy his neighbor. And anger lent a note of hatred to Duperrier's envy. He became jealous of his relations, his friends, his employer, the shopkeepers of the neighborhood, and even the stars of sport and screen whose photographs appeared in the papers. Everything infuriated him, and he was known to tremble with ignoble rage at the thought that the people next door possessed a cutlery service with silver handles, whereas his own were only of bone. But the halo continued to glow with undiminished brightness. Instead of being dismayed by this, he concluded that his sins were lacking in reality, and he had no difficulty in reasoning that his supposed gluttony did not in fact exceed the natural demands of a healthy appetite, while his anger and his envy merely bore witness to a lofty craving for justice. It was the halo itself, however, which furnished him with the most solid arguments.

"I'm bound to say I would have expected Heaven to be a little more fussy," his wife said. "If all your gluttony and boasting and brutality and malice have done nothing to dim your halo, it doesn't look as though I need worry about *my* place in Paradise."

"Hold your jaw!" roared the furious man. "How much longer have I got to listen to your nagging? I'm fed up with it. You think it funny, do you, that a saintly character like myself should have to plunge into sin for the sake of your blasted peace of mind? Stow it, d'you hear me?"

The tone of these replies was clearly lacking in that suavity which may rightly be looked for in a man enhaloed by the glory of God. Since he had entered upon the paths of sin Duperrier had become increasingly given to strong language. His formerly ascetic countenance was becoming bloated with rich food. Not only was his vocabulary growing coarse, but a similar vulgarity was invading his thoughts. His vision of Paradise, for example, had undergone a notable transformation. Instead of appearing to him as a symphony of souls in robes of cellophane, the dwelling-place of the elect came to look more and more like a vast dining-room. Mme. Duperrier did not fail to observe the changes that were overtaking her husband and even to feel some anxiety for the future. Nevertheless, the thought of his possible descent into the abyss still did not outweigh in her mind the horror of singularity. Rather than an enhaloed Duperrier she would have preferred a husband who was an atheist, a debauchee, and as crude of speech as her cousin Léopold. At least she would not then have to blush for him before the milkman.

No especial decision was called for on the part of Duperrier for him to lapse into the sin of sloth. The arrogant belief that he was required at the office to perform tasks unworthy of his merits, together with the drowsiness caused by heavy eating and drinking, made him naturally disposed to be idle; and since he had sufficient conceit to believe that he must excel in all things, even the worst, he very soon became a model of indolence. The day his indignant employer sacked him, he received the sentence with his hat in his hand.

"What's that on your head?" his employer asked.

"A halo," said Duperrier.

"Is it indeed? And I suppose that's what you've been fooling around with when you were supposed to be working?"

When he told his wife of his dismissal, she asked him what he intended to do next.

"It seems to me that this would be a good moment to try the sin of avarice," he answered gaily.

Of all the Deadly Sins, avarice was the one that called for the greatest

effort of willpower on his part. To those not born avaricious it is the
vice offering the fewest easy allurements, and when it is adopted on principle there is nothing to distinguish it, at least in the early stages, from
that most sterling of all virtues, thrift. Duperrier subjected himself to
severe disciplines, such as confining himself to gluttony, and thus succeeded in gaining a solid reputation for avarice among his friends and
acquaintances. He really liked money for its own sake, and was better
able than most people to experience the malicious thrill which misers
feel at the thought that they control a source of creative energy and prevent it from functioning. Counting up his savings, the fruit of a hitherto
laborious existence, he came by degrees to know the hideous pleasure of
harming others by damming a current of exchange and of life. This
outcome, simply because it was painfully achieved, filled Mme. Duperrier
with hope. Her husband had yielded so easily to the seductions of the
other sins that God, she thought, could not condemn him very severely
for an innocent, animal surrender which made him appear rather a
victim deserving of compassion. His deliberate and patient progress
along the road of avarice, on the other hand, could only be the fruit of a
perverse desire which was like a direct challenge to Heaven. Nevertheless,
although Duperrier became miserly to the point of putting trouser-
buttons in the collection-bag, the brilliance and size of the halo remained
unimpaired. This new setback, duly noted, plunged husband and wife
into despair.

Proud, gluttonous, angry, envious, slothful, and avaricious, Duperrier
felt that his soul was still perfumed with innocence. Deadly though they
were, the six sins he had thus far practised were nevertheless such as a
first communicant may confess to without despairing. The deadliest of
all, lust, filled him with horror. The others, it seemed to him, might be
said to exist almost outside the sphere of God's notice. In the case of
each, sin or peccadillo, it all depended on the size of the dose. But lust,
the sin of the flesh, meant unqualified acceptance of the Devil's work.
The enchantments of the night were a foretaste of the burning shades of
Hell, the darting tongues were like the flames of eternity, the moans of
ecstasy, the writhing bodies, these did but herald the wailing of the
damned and the convulsions of flesh racked by endless torment. Duperrier
had not deliberately reserved the sin of the flesh to the last: he had simply refused to contemplate it. Mme. Duperrier herself could not think of
it without disquiet. For many years the pair had lived in a state of
delicious chastity, their nightly rest attended, until the coming of the
halo, by dreams as pure as the driven snow. As she thought of it, the recollection of those years of continence was a source of considerable annoyance to Mme. Duperrier, for she did not doubt that the halo was the
result. Plainly that lily-white nimbus could be undone by lust alone.

Duperrier, after obstinately resisting his wife's persuasions, at length allowed himself to be overborne. Once again his sense of duty cast out fear. Having reached the decision he was embarrassed by his ignorance; but his wife, who thought of everything, bought him a revolting book in which all the essentials were set forth in the form of plain and simple instruction. The night-time spectacle of that saintly man, the halo encircling his head, reading a chapter of the abominable work to his wife, was a poignant one indeed. Often his voice trembled at some infamous word or some image more hideously evocative than the rest. Having thus achieved a theoretical mastery of the subject, he still delayed while he considered whether this last sin should be consummated in domestic intimacy or elsewhere. Mme. Duperrier took the view that it should all be done at home, adducing reasons of economy which did not fail to weigh with him; but having considered all the pros and cons he concluded that he had no need to involve her in vile practices which might be prejudicial to her own salvation. As a loyal husband he valiantly resolved that he alone should run the risks.

Thereafter Duperrier spent most of his nights in disreputable hotels where he pursued his initiation in company with the professionals of the quarter. The halo, which he could not conceal from these wretched associates, led to his finding himself in various odd situations, sometimes embarrassing and sometimes advantageous. In the beginning, owing to his anxiety to conform to the instructions in his manual, he sinned with little exaltation but rather with the methodical application of a dancer learning a new step or figure of choreography. However, the desire for perfection to which his pride impelled him soon achieved its lamentable reward in the notoriety which he gained among the women with whom he consorted. Although he came to take the liveliest pleasure in these pursuits, Duperrier nevertheless found them expensive and was cruelly afflicted in his avarice. One evening on the Place Pigalle he made the acquaintance of a creature twenty years of age, already a lost soul, whose name was Marie-Jannick. It was for her, so it is believed, that the poet Maurice Fombeure wrote the charming lines:

C'est Marie-Jannick	*[That's Marie-Jannick*
De Landivisiau	*Of Landivisiau,*
Qui tue les moustiques	*Who kills mosquitoes*
Avec son sabot.	*With her wooden shoe.]*

Marie-Jannick had come from Brittany six months previously to go into service as maid-of-all-work in the home of a municipal councillor who was both a socialist and an atheist. Finding herself unable to endure the life of this godless household, she had given notice and was now courageously earning her living on the Boulevard de Clichy. As was to be expected, the halo made a deep impression on that little religious soul. To Marie-Jannick, Duperrier seemed the equal of St. Yves and St.

Ronan, and he, on his side, was not slow to perceive the influence he had over her and to turn it to profit.

Thus it is that on this very day, the 22nd February of the year 1944, amid the darkness of winter and of war, Marie-Jannick, who will shortly be twenty-five, may be seen walking her beat on the Boulevard de Clichy. During the black-out hours the stroller between the Place Pigalle and the Rue des Martyrs may be startled to observe, floating and swaying in the darkness, a mysterious circle of light that looks rather like a ring of Saturn. It is Duperrier, his head adorned with the glorious halo which he no longer seeks to conceal from the curiosity of all and sundry; Duperrier, burdened with the weight of the seven Deadly Sins, who, lost to all shame, supervises the labors of Marie-Jannick, administering a smart kick in the pants when her zeal flags, and waiting at the hotel door to count her takings by the light of the halo. But from the depths of his degradation, through the dark night of his conscience, a murmur yet rises from time to time to his lips, a prayer of thanksgiving for the absolute gratuity of the gifts of God.

Suggestions

1. Among many other things "The State of Grace" shows that a story need not be realistic in order to achieve shrewd insights into the realities of human nature. In a master's hands fantasy can create the illusion of reality just as well as narratives confined to everyday happenings, characters, and objects. The narrator of "The State of Grace" is *omniscient,* all-knowing: he takes us directly into the feelings and thoughts of both Duperrier and Mme. Duperrier. Why realistic stories generally avoid this liberty may be understood by noticing its perfect appropriateness to a story that boasts of its own improbability. A writer who upsets the usual order of nature by endowing his protagonist with a halo may fittingly assume the godlike ability to see into the minds and hearts of all his characters. Fantasies answer the question, "If the impossible should happen, what would probably follow so as to shed light on the underlying nature of things?" Evaluate "The State of Grace" by this standard.

2. Characterize Duperrier and his wife; to what extent are the changes in them only superficial? What general comment on humanity is suggested by each of the seven sections following Duperrier's first prayer? E.g. what is a miser's greatest thrill?

3. Explain: *concierge, circumspect, complaisance, pâté, choleric, ascetic, peccadillo, choreography.*

4. Explain: *The gifts of God, especially when they wear a somewhat gratuitous aspect, are seldom accorded the respect they deserve. . . .* (¶4) Write an essay discussing the truth of this passage.

5. Defining your terms precisely, write an essay on the cynical view of human nature expressed in "The State of Grace."

6. The most interesting question about "The State of Grace," of course, is whether its cynicism extends to religious matters. Write an essay about this question after considering it carefully: e.g. what is the speaker's attitude toward Mme. Duperrier's *lack of logic,* mentioned in ¶3? Include a comment on the last eight words of the story, showing that it has or has not a strong enough climax.

T H E   D R A M A

"Every drama must present a conflict," wrote Bernard Shaw in the Preface to the volume containing *The Man of Destiny.* "The end may be reconciliation or destruction; or, as in life itself, there may be no end; but the conflict is indispensable: no conflict, no drama." What was said about the dramatic scenes in short stories applies even more urgently to plays. Described in very general terms, all conflicts are the same: one character conceives a purpose and another character (or some other force) opposes it. These cross-purposes, as Shaw himself remarks, are not hard to arrange; what distinguishes the best plays is, first, that their minor conflicts are joined to the major ones in some significant way, and second, that all of them suggest some meaning beyond themselves—provide, that is, an illumination of the characters and situations that make up the play.

When a reader of short stories opens a volume of plays that are in any way comparable, he may find the new experience both bewildering and more fascinating. On the one hand, he must draw his own conclusions, however limited his choices are, for only very rarely does a play offer instructions on what its reader is to think and feel. The author of a short story may tell who the main character is, what his strengths and weaknesses are, and even whether his destiny is happy or unhappy. But the playwright remains inaudible and invisible. His exposition is restricted to the few facts essential to an understanding of the situation at the beginning—and most of this information has to be smuggled in. The action must, on the whole, imply its own significance, and this necessity suggests one important reason why drama finds conflict indispensable. In moments of tension, when a person's purpose is threatened, he drops the mask; the way he *really* is comes into view, and it is then possible to make accurate judgments about his motives and his moral quality.

If plays thus tend to leave much of their meaning unspoken, they may on the other hand offer a skilful reader experiences that are more immediate and more stirring. For the illusion created by a story, as we have seen, is of a past; its dramatic scenes are subordinate to a total impression that, as the speaker has already grasped it before he begins his narration, has necessarily already happened. But the tense of drama is the future, the future fulfilling itself in the present, and so at any moment the outcome is in suspense. "Comedy or tragedy?" we ask, following the easy-going classification that, despite our teachers' warnings, seems to fit any play at all. The answer depends upon whether the outcome is favorable or unfavorable for the characters with whom we sympathize—and that, of course, cannot be known until "The curtain steals down and hides them."

THE MAN OF DESTINY

BERNARD SHAW ──◀{

From PLAYS, PLEASANT AND UNPLEASANT, *first produced in 1896. Reprinted by permission of The Society of Authors, London.*

CHARACTERS

in the order of their appearance

Giuseppe Grandi, *the innkeeper*   A French Lieutenant
General Napoleon Bonaparte   The Strange Lady

The twelfth of May, 1796, in north Italy, at Tavazzano, on the road from Lodi to Milan.

The best quarters at Tavazzano are at a little inn, the first house reached by travellers passing through the place from Milan to Lodi. It stands in a vine-

yard; and its principal room, a pleasant refuge from the summer heat, is open so widely at the back to this vineyard that it is almost a large veranda. The bolder children, much excited by the alarums and excursions of the past few days, and by an irruption of French troops at six o'clock, know that the French commander has quartered himself in this room, and are divided between a craving to peep in at the front windows, and a mortal dread of the sentinel, a young gentleman-soldier who, having no natural moustache, has had a most ferocious one painted on his face with boot blacking by his sergeant. As his heavy uniform, like all the uniforms of that day, is designed for parade without the least reference to his health or comfort, he perspires profusely in the sun; and his painted moustache has run in little streaks down his chin and round his neck, except where it has dried in stiff japanned flakes and had its sweeping outline chipped off in grotesque little bays and headlands, making him un- speakably ridiculous in the eye of History a hundred years later, but monstrous and horrible to the contemporary north Italian infant, to whom nothing would seem more natural than that he should relieve the monotony of his guard by pitchforking a stray child up on his bayonet, and eating it uncooked. Never- theless one girl of bad character, in whom an instinct of privilege with soldiers is already stirring, does peep in at the safest window for a moment before a glance and a clink from the sentinel sends her flying. Most of what she sees she has seen before: the vineyard at the back, with the old winepress and a cart among the vines; the door close on her right leading to the street entry; the landlord's best sideboard, now in full action for dinner, further back on the same side; the fireplace on the other side with a couch near it; another door, leading to the inner rooms, between it and the vineyard; and the table in the middle set out with a repast of Milanese risotto, cheese, grapes, bread, olives, and a big wickered flask of red wine.

The landlord, Giuseppe Grandi, she knows well. He is a swarthy vivacious shrewdly cheerful black-curled bullet headed grinning little innkeeper of 40. Naturally an excellent host, he is in the highest spirits this evening at his good fortune in having as his guest the French commander to protect him against the licence of the troops. He actually sports a pair of gold earrings which would otherwise have been hidden carefully under the winepress with his little equip- ment of silver plate.

Napoleon, sitting facing her on the further side of the table, she sees for the first time. He is working hard, partly at his meal, which he has discovered how to dispatch in ten minutes by attacking all the courses simultaneously (this practice is the beginning of his downfall), and partly at a military map on which he from time to time marks the position of the forces by taking a grape- skin from his mouth and planting it on the map with his thumb like a wafer. There is no revolutionary untidiness about his dress or person; but his elbow has displaced most of the dishes and glasses; and his long hair trails into the risotto when he forgets it and leans more intently over the map.

GIUSEPPE: Will your excellency—

NAPOLEON (*intent on his map, but cramming himself mechanically with his left hand*): Don't talk. I'm busy.

GIUSEPPE (*with perfect good humor*): Excellency: I obey.

NAPOLEON: Some red ink.

GIUSEPPE: Alas! excellency, there is none.

NAPOLEON (*with Corsican facetiousness*): Kill something and bring me its blood.

GIUSEPPE (*grinning*): There is nothing but your excellency's horse, the sentinel, the lady upstairs, and my wife.

NAPOLEON: Kill your wife.

GIUSEPPE: Willingly, your excellency; but unhappily I am not strong enough. She would kill me.

NAPOLEON: That will do equally well.

GIUSEPPE: Your excellency does me too much honor. (*Stretching his hand towards the flask*) Perhaps some wine will answer your excellency's purpose.

NAPOLEON (*hastily protecting the flask, and becoming quite serious*): Wine! No: that would be waste. You are all the same: waste! waste! waste! (*He marks the map with gravy, using his fork as a pen.*) Clear away. (*He finishes his wine; pushes back his chair; and uses his napkin, stretching his legs and leaning back, but still frowning and thinking.*)

GIUSEPPE (*clearing the table and removing the things to a tray on the sideboard*): Every man to his trade, excellency. We innkeepers have plenty of cheap wine: we think nothing of spilling it. You great generals have plenty of cheap blood: you think nothing of spilling it. Is it not so, excellency?

NAPOLEON: Blood costs nothing: wine costs money. (*He rises and goes to the fireplace.*)

GIUSEPPE: They say you are careful of everything except human life, excellency.

NAPOLEON: Human life, my friend, is the only thing that takes care of itself. (*He throws himself at his ease on the couch.*)

GIUSEPPE (*admiring him*): Ah, excellency, what fools we all are beside you! If I could only find out the secret of your success!

NAPOLEON: You would make yourself Emperor of Italy, eh?

GIUSEPPE: Too troublesome, excellency: I leave all that to you. Besides, what would become of my inn if I were Emperor? See how you enjoy looking on at me whilst I keep the inn for you and wait on you! Well, I shall enjoy looking on at you whilst you become Emperor of Europe, and govern the country for me. (*As he chatters, he takes the cloth off deftly without removing the map, and finally takes the corners in his hands and the middle in his mouth, to fold it up.*)

NAPOLEON: Emperor of Europe, eh? Why only Europe?

GIUSEPPE: Why, indeed? Emperor of the world, excellency! Why not? (*He folds and rolls up the cloth, emphasizing his phrase by the steps of the process.*) One man is like another (*fold*): one country is like another (*fold*): one battle is like another. (*At the last fold, he slaps the cloth on the table and deftly rolls it up, adding, by way of peroration*) Conquer one: conquer all. (*He takes the cloth to the sideboard, and puts it in a drawer.*)

NAPOLEON: And govern for all; fight for all; be everybody's servant under cover of being everybody's master. Giuseppe.

GIUSEPPE (*at the sideboard*): Excellency?

NAPOLEON: I forbid you to talk to me about myself.

GIUSEPPE (*coming to the foot of the couch*): Pardon. Your excellency is so unlike other great men. It is the subject they like best.

NAPOLEON: Well, talk to me about the subject they like next best, whatever that may be.

GIUSEPPE (*unabashed*): Willingly, your excellency. Has your excellency by any chance caught a glimpse of the lady upstairs?

NAPOLEON (*sitting up promptly*): How old is she?

GIUSEPPE: The right age, excellency.

NAPOLEON: Do you mean seventeen or thirty?

GIUSEPPE: Thirty, excellency.

NAPOLEON: Good looking?

GIUSEPPE: I cannot see with your excellency's eyes: every man must judge that for himself. In my opinion, excellency, a fine figure of a lady. (*Slyly*) Shall I lay the table for her collation here?

NAPOLEON (*brusquely, rising*): No: lay nothing here until the officer for whom I am waiting comes back. (*He looks at his watch, and takes to walking to and fro between the fireplace and the vineyard.*)

GIUSEPPE (*with conviction*): Excellency: believe me, he has been captured by the accursed Austrians. He dare not keep you waiting if he were at liberty.

NAPOLEON (*turning at the edge of the shadow of the veranda*): Giuseppe: if that turns out to be true, it will put me into such a temper that nothing short of hanging you and your whole household, including the lady upstairs, will satisfy me.

GIUSEPPE: We are all cheerfully at your excellency's disposal, except the lady. I cannot answer for her; but no lady could resist you, General.

NAPOLEON (*sourly, resuming his march*): Hm! *You* will never be hanged. There is no satisfaction in hanging a man who does not object to it.

GIUSEPPE (*sympathetically*): Not the least in the world, excellency: is there? (*Napoleon again looks at his watch, evidently growing anxious.*) Ah, one can see that you are a great man, General: you know how to wait. If it were a corporal now, or a sub-lieutenant, at the end of three minutes he would be swearing, fuming, threatening, pulling the house about our ears.

NAPOLEON: Giuseppe: your flatteries are insufferable. Go and talk outside. (*He sits down again at the table, with his jaws in his hands and*

*his elbows propped on the map, poring over it with a troubled ex-
pression.*)

GIUSEPPE: Willingly, your excellency. You shall not be disturbed. (*He
takes up the tray and prepares to withdraw.*)

NAPOLEON: The moment he comes back, send him to me.

GIUSEPPE: Instantaneously, your excellency.

A LADY'S VOICE (*calling from some distant part of the inn*): Giusep-pe!
(*The voice is very musical, and the two final notes make an ascending interval.*)

NAPOLEON (*startled*): Who's that?

GIUSEPPE: The lady, excellency.

NAPOLEON: The lady upstairs?

GIUSEPPE: Yes, excellency. The strange lady.

NAPOLEON: Strange? Where does she come from?

GIUSEPPE (*with a shrug*): Who knows? She arrived here just before your
excellency in a hired carriage belonging to the Golden Eagle at
Borghetto. By herself, excellency. No servants. A dressing bag and
a trunk: that is all. The postillion says she left a horse at the
Golden Eagle. A charger, with military trappings.

NAPOLEON: A woman with a charger! French or Austrian?

GIUSEPPE: French, excellency.

NAPOLEON: Her husband's charger, no doubt. Killed at Lodi, poor fellow.

THE LADY'S VOICE (*the two final notes now making a peremptory descend-
ing interval*): Giuseppe!

NAPOLEON (*rising to listen*): That's not the voice of a woman whose husband was killed yesterday.

GIUSEPPE: Husbands are not always regretted, excellency. (*Calling*) Coming, lady, coming. (*He makes for the inner door.*)

NAPOLEON (*arresting him with a strong hand on his shoulder*): Stop. Let
her come.

VOICE: Giuseppe!! (*Impatiently.*)

GIUSEPPE: Let me go, excellency. It is my point of honor as an innkeeper
to come when I am called. I appeal to you as a soldier.

A MAN'S VOICE (*outside, at the inn door, shouting*): Here, someone. Hollo!
Landlord! Where are you? (*Somebody raps vigorously with a whip
handle on a bench in the passage.*)

NAPOLEON (*suddenly becoming the commanding officer again and throwing Giuseppe off*): My man at last. (*Pointing to the inner door*) Go.
Attend to your business: the lady is calling you. (*He goes to the fireplace and stands with his back to it with a determined military air.*)

GIUSEPPE (*with bated breath, snatching up his tray*): Certainly, excellency.
(*He hurries out by the inner door.*)

THE MAN'S VOICE (*impatiently*): Are you all asleep here?

The other door is kicked rudely open. A dusty sub-lieutenant bursts into the room. He is a tall chuckle-headed young man of 24, with the complexion and style of a man of rank, and a self-assurance on that ground which the French Revolution has failed to shake in the smallest degree. He has a thick silly lip, an eager credulous eye, an obstinate nose, and a loud confident voice. A young man without fear, without reverence, without imagination, without sense, hopelessly insusceptible to the Napoleonic or any other idea, stupendously egotistical, eminently qualified to rush in where angels fear to tread, yet of a vigorous babbling vitality which bustles him into the thick of things. He is just now boiling with vexation, attributable by a superficial observer to his impatience at not being promptly attended to by the staff of the inn, but in which a more discerning eye can perceive a certain moral depth, indicating a more permanent and momentous grievance. On seeing Napoleon, he is sufficiently taken aback to check himself and salute; but he does not betray by his manner any of that prophetic consciousness of Marengo and Austerlitz, Waterloo and St. Helena, or the Napoleonic pictures of Delaroche and Meissonier, which later ages expect from him.

NAPOLEON (*watch in hand*): Well, sir, you have come at last. Your instructions were that I should arrive here at six and find you waiting for me with my mail from Paris and with despatches. It is now twenty minutes to eight. You were sent on this service as a hard rider with the fastest horse in the camp. You arrive a hundred minutes late, on foot. Where is your horse?

THE LIEUTENANT (*moodily pulling off his gloves and dashing them with his cap and whip on the table*): Ah! where indeed? That's just what I should like to know, General. (*With emotion*) You don't know how fond I was of that horse.

NAPOLEON (*angrily sarcastic*): Indeed! (*With sudden misgiving*) Where are the letters and despatches?

THE LIEUTENANT (*importantly, rather pleased than otherwise at having some remarkable news*): I don't know.

NAPOLEON (*unable to believe his ears*): You don't know!

LIEUTENANT: No more than you do, General. Now I suppose I shall be court-martialed. Well, I don't mind being court-martialed; but (*with solemn determination*) I tell you, General, if ever I catch that innocent-looking youth, I'll spoil his beauty, the slimy little liar! *I'll* make a picture of him. *I'll*—

NAPOLEON (*advancing from the hearth to the table*): What innocent-looking youth? Pull yourself together, sir, will you; and give an account of yourself.

LIEUTENANT (*facing him at the opposite side of the table, leaning on it with his fists*): Oh, I'm all right, General: I'm perfectly ready to give an account of myself. I shall make the court-martial thoroughly understand that the fault was not mine. Advantage has been taken of the better side of my nature; and I'm not ashamed of it. But with all respect to you as my commanding officer, General, I say again that if ever I set eyes on that son of Satan, I'll—

NAPOLEON (*angrily*): So you said before.

LIEUTENANT (*drawing himself upright*): I say it again. Just wait until I catch him. Just wait: that's all. (*He folds his arms resolutely and breathes hard, with compressed lips.*)

NAPOLEON: I am waiting, sir. For your explanation.

LIEUTENANT (*confidently*): You'll change your tone, General, when you hear what has happened to me.

NAPOLEON: Nothing has happened to you, sir: you are alive and not disabled. Where are the papers entrusted to you?

LIEUTENANT: Nothing happened to me! Nothing!! He swore eternal brotherhood with me. Was that nothing? He said my eyes reminded him of his sister's eyes. Was that nothing? He cried—actually cried— over the story of my separation from Angelica. Was that nothing? He paid for both bottles of wine, though he only ate bread and grapes himself. Perhaps you call that nothing. He gave me his pistols and his horse and his despatches—most important despatches—and let me go away with them. (*Triumphantly, seeing that he has reduced Napoleon to blank stupefaction*) Was *that* nothing?

NAPOLEON (*enfeebled by astonishment*): What did he do that for?

LIEUTENANT (*as if the reason were obvious*): To show his confidence in me, of course. (*Napoleon's jaw does not exactly drop; but its hinges become nerveless.*) And I was worthy of his confidence: I brought them all back honorably. But would you believe it? when I trusted him with *my* pistols, and *my* horse, and *my* despatches—

NAPOLEON: What the devil did you do that for?

LIEUTENANT: I'm telling you: to show my confidence in him. And he betrayed it! abused it! never came back again! The thief! the swindler! the heartless treacherous little blackguard! You call that nothing, I suppose. But look here, General: (*again resorting to the table with his fists for greater emphasis*) you may put up with this outrage from the Austrians if you like; but speaking for myself personally, I tell you that if ever I catch—

NAPOLEON (*turning on his heel in disgust and irritably resuming his march to and fro*): Yes: you have said that more than once already.

LIEUTENANT (*excitedly*): More than once! I'll say it fifty times; and what's more, I'll do it. You'll see, General. *I'll* show my confidence in him, so I will. *I'll*—

NAPOLEON: Yes, yes, sir: no doubt you will. What kind of man was he?

LIEUTENANT: Well, I should think you ought to be able to tell from his conduct the kind of man he was.

NAPOLEON: Psha! What was he like?

LIEUTENANT: Like! He was like—well, you ought to have just seen the fellow: that will give you a notion of what he was like. He won't be like it five minutes after I catch him; for I tell you that if ever—

NAPOLEON (*shouting furiously for the innkeeper*): Giuseppe! (*To the Lieutenant, out of all patience*) Hold your tongue, sir, if you can.

LIEUTENANT (*plaintively*): I warn you it's no use trying to put the blame on me. How was I to know the sort of fellow he was? (*He takes a chair from between the sideboard and the outer door; places it near the table; and sits down.*) If you only knew how hungry and tired I am, you'd have more consideration.

GIUSEPPE (*returning*): What is it, excellency?

NAPOLEON (*struggling with his temper*): Take this—this officer. Feed him; and put him to bed, if necessary. When he is in his right mind again, find out what has happened to him and bring me word. (*To the Lieutenant*) Consider yourself under arrest, sir.

LIEUTENANT (*with sulky stiffness*): I was prepared for that. It takes a gentleman to understand a gentleman. (*He throws his sword on the table.*)

GIUSEPPE (*with sympathetic concern*): Have you been attacked by the Austrians, lieutenant? Dear! dear! dear!

LIEUTENANT (*contemptuously*): Attacked! I could have broken his back between my finger and thumb. I wish I had, now. No: it was by appealing to the better side of my nature: that's what I can't get over. He said he'd never met a man he liked so much as me. He put his handkerchief round my neck because a gnat bit me, and my stock was chafing it. Look! (*He pulls a handkerchief from his stock. Giuseppe takes it and examines it.*)

GIUSEPPE (*to Napoleon*): A lady's handkerchief, excellency. (*He smells it.*) Perfumed.

NAPOLEON: Eh? (*He takes it and looks at it attentively.*) Hm! (*He smells it.*) Ha! (*He walks thoughtfully across the room, looking at the handkerchief, which he finally sticks in the breast of his coat.*)

LIEUTENANT: Good enough for him, anyhow. I noticed that he had a woman's hands when he touched my neck, with his coaxing fawning ways, the mean effeminate little hound. (*Lowering his voice with thrilling intensity*) But mark my words, General. If ever—

THE LADY'S VOICE (*outside, as before*): Giuseppe!

LIEUTENANT (*petrified*): What was that?

GIUSEPPE: Only a lady upstairs, lieutenant, calling me.

LIEUTENANT: Lady!

VOICE: Giuseppe, Giuseppe: where *are* you?

LIEUTENANT (*murderously*): Give me that sword. (*He snatches up the sword and draws it.*)

GIUSEPPE (*rushing forward and seizing his right arm*): What are you thinking of, lieutenant? It's a lady: don't you hear? It's a woman's voice.

LIEUTENANT: It's *his* voice, I tell you. Let me go. (*He breaks away and rushes to the edge of the veranda, where he posts himself, sword in hand, watching the door like a cat watching a mousehole.*)

It opens; and the Strange Lady steps in. She is tall and extraordinarily graceful, with a delicately intelligent, apprehensive, questioning face: perception in the brow, sensitiveness in the nostrils, character in the chin: all keen, refined, and original. She is very feminine, but by no means weak: the lithe tender figure is hung on a strong frame: the hands and feet, neck and shoulders, are useful vigorous members, of full size in proportion to her stature, which perceptibly exceeds that of Napoleon and the innkeeper, and leaves her at no disadvantage with the lieutenant. Only, her elegance and radiant charm keep the secret of her size and strength. She is not, judging by her dress, an admirer of the latest fashions of the Directory [1]; *or perhaps she uses up her old dresses for travelling. At all events she wears no jacket with extravagant lapels, no Greco-Tallien sham chiton, nothing, indeed, that the Princesse de Lamballe might not have worn. Her dress of flowered silk is long-waisted, with a Watteau pleat behind, but with the paniers reduced to mere rudiments, as she is too tall for them. It is cut low in the neck, where it is eked out by a creamy fichu. She is fair, with golden brown hair and grey eyes.*

She enters with the self-possession of a woman accustomed to the privileges of rank and beauty. The innkeeper, who has excellent natural manners, is highly appreciative of her. Napoleon is smitten self-conscious. His color deepens: he becomes stiffer and less at ease than before. She is advancing in an infinitely well-bred manner to pay her respects to him when the lieutenant pounces on her and seizes her right wrist. As she recognizes him, she becomes deadly pale. There is no mistaking her expression: a revelation of some fatal error, utterly unexpected, has suddenly appalled her in the midst of tranquillity, security, and victory. The next moment a wave of angry color rushes up from beneath the creamy fichu and drowns her whole face. One can see that she is blushing all over her body. Even the lieutenant, ordinarily incapable of observation, can see a thing when it is painted red for him. Interpreting the blush as the involuntary confession of black deceit confronted with its victim, he addresses her in a loud crow of retributive triumph.

LIEUTENANT: So I've got you, my lad. So you've disguised yourself, have you? (*In a voice of thunder, releasing her wrist*) Take off that skirt.

---

[1] I.e. those of the period 1795–1799, when a committee of five men, known as the *Directoire*, ruled France. The next sentence satirizes the adaptation of Greek costume made fashionable by the wife of the Revolutionary leader Jean Lambert Tallien. The Princesse de Lamballe, intimate friend of Queen Marie Antoinette, had been murdered four years earlier. The Lady's pleat resembles those in the paintings of Antoine Watteau (1684–1721).

GIUSEPPE (*remonstrating*): Oh, lieutenant!

LADY (*affrighted, but highly indignant at his having dared to touch her*): Gentlemen: I appeal to you. (*To Napoleon*) You, sir, are an officer: a general. You will protect me, will you not?

LIEUTENANT: Never you mind him, General. Leave me to deal with him.

NAPOLEON: With *him!* With whom, sir? Why do you treat this lady in such a fashion?

LIEUTENANT: Lady! He's a man! the man I showed my confidence in. (*Raising his sword*) Here, you—

LADY (*running behind Napoleon and in her agitation clasping to her breast the arm which he extends before her as a fortification*) Oh, thank you, General. Keep him away.

NAPOLEON: Nonsense, sir. This is certainly a lady (*she suddenly drops his arm and blushes again*); and you are under arrest. Put down your sword, sir, instantly.

LIEUTENANT: General: I tell you he's an Austrian spy. He passed himself off on me as one of General Masséna's staff this afternoon; and now he's passing himself off on you as a woman. Am I to believe my own eyes or not?

LADY: General: it must be my brother. He is on General Masséna's staff. He is very like me.

LIEUTENANT (*his mind giving way*): Do you mean to say that you're not your brother, but your sister? the sister who was so like me? who had my beautiful blue eyes? It's a lie: your eyes are not like mine: they're exactly like your own.

NAPOLEON (*with contained exasperation*): Lieutenant: will you obey my orders and leave the room, since you are convinced at last that this is no gentleman?

LIEUTENANT: Gentleman! I should think not. No gentleman would have abused my confid—

NAPOLEON (*out of all patience*): That will do, sir: do you hear? Will you leave the room? I order you to leave the room.

LADY: Oh pray let me go instead.

NAPOLEON (*drily*): Excuse me, madam. With all possible respect for your brother, I do not yet understand what an officer on General Masséna's staff wants with my letters. I have some questions to put to you.

GIUSEPPE (*discreetly*): Come, lieutenant. (*He opens the door.*)

LIEUTENANT: I'm off. General: take warning by me: be on your guard against the better side of your nature. (*To the lady*) Madam: my apologies. I thought you were the same person, only of the opposite sex; and that naturally misled me.

LADY (*recovering her good humor*): It was not your fault, was it? I'm so glad you're not angry with me any longer, lieutenant. (*She offers her hand.*)

LIEUTENANT (*bending gallantly to kiss it*): Oh, madam, not the lea— (*Checking himself and looking at it*) You have your brother's hand. And the same sort of ring!

LADY (*sweetly*): We are twins.

LIEUTENANT: That accounts for it. (*He kisses her hand.*) A thousand pardons. I didn't mind about the despatches at all: that's more the General's affair than mine: it was the abuse of my confidence through the better side of my nature. (*Taking his cap, gloves, and whip from the table and going*) You'll excuse my leaving you, General, I hope. Very sorry, I'm sure. (*He talks himself out of the room. Giuseppe follows him and shuts the door.*)

NAPOLEON (*looking after them with concentrated irritation*): Idiot!

The Strange Lady smiles sympathetically. He comes frowning down the room between the table and the fireplace, all his awkwardness gone now that he is alone with her.

LADY: How can I thank you, General, for your protection?

NAPOLEON (*turning on her suddenly*): My despatches: come! (*He puts out his hand for them.*)

LADY: General! (*She involuntarily puts her hand on her fichu as if to protect something there.*)

NAPOLEON: You tricked that blockhead out of them. You disguised yourself as a man. I want my despatches. They are there in the bosom of your dress, under your hands.

LADY (*quickly removing her hands*): Oh, how unkindly you are speaking to me! (*She takes her handkerchief from her fichu.*) You frighten me. (*She touches her eyes as if to wipe away a tear.*)

NAPOLEON: I see you don't know me, madam, or you would save yourself the trouble of pretending to cry.

LADY (*producing an effect of smiling through her tears*): Yes, I do know you. You are the famous General Buonaparte. (*She gives the name a marked Italian pronunciation; Bwawna-parr-te.*)

NAPOLEON (*angrily, with the French pronunciation*): Bonaparte, madam, Bonaparte. The papers, if you please.

LADY: But I assure you— (*He snatches the handkerchief rudely.*) General! (*indignantly.*)

NAPOLEON (*taking the other handkerchief from his breast*): You lent one of your handkerchiefs to my lieutenant when you robbed him. (*He looks at the two handkerchiefs.*) They match one another. (*He smells them.*) The same scent. (*He flings them down on the table.*) I am waiting for my despatches. I shall take them, if necessary, with as little ceremony as I took the handkerchief.

LADY (*in dignified reproof*): General: do you threaten women?

NAPOLEON (*bluntly*): Yes.

LADY (*disconcerted, trying to gain time*): But I don't understand. I—

NAPOLEON: You understand perfectly. You came here because your Austrian employers calculated that I was six leagues away. I am always to be found where my enemies don't expect me. You have walked into the lion's den. Come! you are a brave woman. Be a sensible one: I have no time to waste. The papers. (*He advances a step ominously.*)

LADY (*breaking down in the childish rage of impotence and throwing herself in tears on the chair left beside the table by the lieutenant*): *I* brave! How little you know! I have spent the day in an agony of fear. I have a pain here from the tightening of my heart at every suspicious look, every threatening movement. Do you think everyone is as brave as you? Oh, why will not you brave people do the brave things? Why do you leave them to us, who have no courage at all? I'm not brave: I shrink from violence: danger makes me miserable.

NAPOLEON (*interested*): Then why have you thrust yourself into danger?

LADY: Because there is no other way: I can trust nobody else. And now it is all useless: all because of you, who have no fear because you have no heart, no feeling, no— (*She breaks off and throws herself on her knees.*) Ah, General, let me go: let me go without asking any questions. You shall have your despatches and letters: I swear it.

NAPOLEON (*holding out his hand*): Yes: I am waiting for them.

She gasps, daunted by his ruthless promptitude into despair of moving him by cajolery. She looks up perplexedly at him, racking her brains for some device to outwit him. He meets her regard inflexibly.

LADY (*rising at last with a quiet little sigh*): I will get them for you. They are in my room. (*She turns to the door.*)

NAPOLEON: I shall accompany you, madam.

LADY (*drawing herself up with a noble air of offended delicacy*): I cannot permit you, General, to enter my chamber.

NAPOLEON: Then you shall stay here, madam, whilst I have your chamber searched for my papers.

LADY (*spitefully, openly giving up her plan*): You may save yourself the trouble. They are not there.

NAPOLEON: No: I have already told you where they are (*pointing to her breast.*)

LADY (*with pretty piteousness*): General: I only want to keep one little private letter. Only one. Let me have it.

NAPOLEON (*cold and stern*): Is that a reasonable demand, madam?

LADY (*encouraged by his not refusing point-blank*): No: but that is why you must grant it. Are your own demands reasonable? thousands of lives for the sake of your victories, your ambitions, your destiny! And what I ask is such a little thing. And I am only a weak woman, and you a brave man. (*She looks at him with her eyes full of tender pleading, and is about to kneel to him again.*)

NAPOLEON (*brusquely*): Get up, get up. (*He turns moodily away and takes a turn across the room, pausing for a moment to say, over his shoulder*) You're talking nonsense; and you know it. (*She sits down submissively on the couch. When he turns and sees her despair, he feels that his victory is complete, and that he may now indulge in a little play with his victim. He comes back and sits beside her. She looks alarmed and moves a little away from him; but a ray of rallying hope beams from her eye. He begins like a man enjoying some secret joke.*) How do you know I am a brave man?

LADY (*amazed*): You! General Buonaparte (*Italian pronunciation.*)

NAPOLEON: Yes, I, General Bonaparte (*emphasizing the French pronunciation.*)

LADY: Oh, how can you ask such a question? you! who stood only two days ago at the bridge at Lodi, with the air full of death, fighting a duel with cannons across the river! (*Shuddering*) Oh, you do brave things.

NAPOLEON: So do you.

LADY: I! (*With a sudden odd thought*) Oh! Are you a coward?

NAPOLEON (*laughing grimly and slapping his knees*): That is the one question you must never ask a soldier. The sergeant asks after the recruit's height, his age, his wind, his limb, but never after his courage.

LADY (*as if she had found it no laughing matter*): Ah, you can laugh at fear. Then you don't know what fear is.

NAPOLEON: Tell me this. Suppose you could have got that letter by coming to me over the bridge at Lodi the day before yesterday! Suppose there had been no other way, and that this was a sure way—if only you escaped the cannon! (*She shudders and covers her eyes for a moment with her hands.*) Would you have been afraid?

LADY: Oh, horribly afraid, agonizingly afraid. (*She presses her hands on her heart.*) It hurts only to imagine it.

NAPOLEON (*inflexibly*): Would you have come for the despatches?

LADY (*overcome by the imagined horror*): Don't ask me. I must have come.

NAPOLEON: Why?

LADY: Because I must. Because there would have been no other way.

NAPOLEON (*with conviction*): Because you would have wanted my letter enough to bear your fear. (*He rises suddenly, and deliberately poses for an oration.*) There is only one universal passion: fear. Of all the thousand qualities a man may have, the only one you will find as certainly in the youngest drummer boy in my army as in me, is fear. It is fear that makes men fight: it is indifference that makes them run away: fear is the mainspring of war. Fear! I know fear well, better than you, better than any woman. I once saw a regiment of good Swiss soldiers massacred by a mob in Paris because I was afraid to interfere: I felt myself a coward to the tips of my toes as I looked on at it. Seven months ago I revenged my shame by pounding that mob to death with cannon balls. Well, what of that? Has fear ever held a man back from anything he really wanted—or a woman either? Never. Come with me; and I will show you twenty thousand cowards who will risk death every day for the price of a glass of brandy. And do you think there are no women in the army, braver than the men, though their lives are worth more? Psha! I think nothing of your fear or your bravery. If you had had to come across to me at Lodi, you would not have been afraid: once on the bridge, every other feeling would have gone down before the necessity—the *necessity*—for making your way to my side and getting what you wanted.

And now, suppose you had done all this! Suppose you had come safely out with that letter in your hand, knowing that when the hour came, your fear had tightened, not your heart, but your grip of your own purpose! that it had ceased to be fear, and had become strength, penetration, vigilance, iron resolution! How would you answer then if you were asked whether you were a coward?

LADY (*rising*): Ah, you are a hero, a real hero.

NAPOLEON: Pooh! there's no such thing as a real hero. (*He strolls about the room, making light of her enthusiasm, but by no means displeased with himself for having evoked it.*)

LADY: Ah yes, there is. There is a difference between what you call my bravery and yours. You wanted to win the battle of Lodi for yourself and not for anyone else, didn't you?

NAPOLEON: Of course. (*Suddenly recollecting himself*) Stop: no. (*He pulls himself piously together, and says, like a man conducting a religious service*) I am only the servant of the French republic, following humbly in the footsteps of the heroes of classical antiquity. I win battles for humanity: for my country, not for myself.

LADY (*disappointed*): Oh, then you are only a womanish hero after all. (*She sits down again, all her enthusiasm gone.*)

NAPOLEON (*greatly astonished*): Womanish!

LADY (*listlessly*): Yes, like me. (*With deep melancholy*) Do you think that if I wanted those despatches only for myself, I dare venture into a battle for them? No: if that were all, I should not have the courage to ask to see you at your hotel, even. My courage is mere slavishness: it is of use to me for my own purposes. It is only through love, through pity, through the instinct to save and protect someone else, that I can do the things that terrify me.

NAPOLEON (*contemptuously*): Pshaw! (*He turns slightingly away from her.*)

LADY: Aha! now you see that I'm not really brave. (*Relapsing into petulant listlessness*) But what right have you to despise me if you only win your battles for others? for your country! through patriotism! That is what I call womanish: it is so like a Frenchman!

NAPOLEON (*furiously*): I am no Frenchman.

LADY (*innocently*): I thought you said you won the battle of Lodi for your country, General Bu—shall I pronounce it in Italian or French?

NAPOLEON: You are presuming on my patience, madam. I was born a French subject, but not in France.

LADY (*affecting a marked access of interest in him*): You were not born a subject at all, I think.

NAPOLEON (*greatly pleased*): Eh? Eh? You think not.

LADY: I am sure of it.

NAPOLEON: Well, well, perhaps not. (*The self-complacency of his assent catches his own ear. He stops short, reddening. Then, composing himself into a solemn attitude, modeled on the heroes of classical antiquity, he takes a high moral tone.*) But we must not live for ourselves alone, little one. Never forget that we should always think of others, and work for others, and lead and govern them for their own good. Self-sacrifice is the foundation of all true nobility of character.

LADY (*again relaxing her attitude with a sigh*): Ah, it is easy to see that you have never tried it, General.

NAPOLEON (*indignantly, forgetting all about Brutus and Scipio*): What do you mean by that speech, madam?

LADY: Haven't you noticed that people always exaggerate the value of the things they haven't got? The poor think they need nothing but riches to be quite happy and good. Everybody worships truth, purity, unselfishness, for the same reason: because they have no experience of them. Oh, if they only knew!

NAPOLEON (*with angry derision*): If they only knew! Pray, do you know?

LADY: Yes. I had the misfortune to be born good. (*Glancing up at him for a moment*) And it is a misfortune, I can tell you, General. I really am truthful and unselfish and all the rest of it; and it's nothing but cowardice; want of character; want of being really, strongly, positively oneself.

NAPOLEON: Ha? (*turning to her quickly with a flash of strong interest.*)

LADY (*earnestly, with rising enthusiasm*): What is the secret of your power? Only that you believe in yourself. You can fight and conquer for yourself and for nobody else. You are not afraid of your own destiny. You teach us what we all might be if we had the will and courage; and that (*suddenly sinking on her knees before him*) is why we all begin to worship you. (*She kisses his hands.*)

NAPOLEON (*embarrassed*): Tut! tut! Pray rise, madam.

LADY: Do not refuse my homage: it is your right. You will be Emperor of France—

NAPOLEON (*hurriedly*): Take care. Treason!

LADY (*insisting*): Yes, Emperor of France; then of Europe; perhaps of the world. I am only the first subject to swear allegiance. (*Again kissing his hand*) My Emperor!

NAPOLEON (*overcome, raising her*): Pray! pray! No, no: this is folly. Come: be calm, be calm. (*Petting her*) There! there! my girl.

LADY (*struggling with happy tears*): Yes, I know it is an impertinence in me to tell you what you must know far better than I do. But you are not angry with me, are you?

NAPOLEON: Angry! No, no: not a bit, not a bit. Come: you are a very clever and sensible and interesting woman. (*He pats her on the cheek.*) Shall we be friends?

LADY (*enraptured*): Your friend! You will let me be your friend! Oh! (*She offers him both her hands with a radiant smile.*) You see: I show my confidence in you.

This incautious echo of the lieutenant undoes her. Napoleon starts: his eyes flash: he utters a yell of rage.

NAPOLEON: What!!!

LADY: What's the matter?

NAPOLEON: Show your confidence in me! So that I may show my confidence in you in return by letting you give me the slip with the despatches, eh? Ah, Delilah, Delilah, you have been trying your tricks on me; and I have been as gross a gull as my jackass of a lieutenant. (*Menacingly*) Come: the despatches. Quick: I am not to be trifled with now.

LADY (*flying round the couch*): General—

NAPOLEON: Quick, I tell you. (*He passes swiftly up the middle of the room and intercepts her as she makes for the vineyard.*)

LADY (*at bay, confronting him and giving way to her temper*): You dare address me in that tone.

NAPOLEON: Dare!

LADY: Yes, dare. Who are you that you should presume to speak of me in that coarse way? Oh, the vile, vulgar Corsican adventurer comes out in you very easily.

NAPOLEON (*beside himself*): You she devil! (*Savagely*) Once more, and only once, will you give me those papers or shall I tear them from you?—by force!

LADY: Tear them from me: by force!

As he glares at her like a tiger about to spring, she crosses her arms on her breast in the attitude of a martyr. The gesture and pose instantly awaken his theatrical instinct: he forgets his rage in the desire to show her that in acting, too, she has met her match. He keeps her a moment in suspense; then suddenly clears up his countenance; puts his hands behind him with provoking coolness; looks at her up and down a couple of times; takes a pinch of snuff; wipes his fingers carefully and puts up his handkerchief, her heroic pose becoming more and more ridiculous all the time.

NAPOLEON (*at last*): Well?

LADY (*disconcerted, but with her arms still crossed devotedly*): Well: what are you going to do?

NAPOLEON: Spoil your attitude.

LADY: You brute! (*Abandoning the attitude, she comes to the end of the couch, where she turns with her back to it, leaning against it and facing him with her hands behind her.*)

NAPOLEON: Ah, that's better. Now listen to me. I like you. What's more, I value your respect.

LADY: You value what you have not got, then.

NAPOLEON: I shall have it presently. Now attend to me. Suppose I were to allow myself to be abashed by the respect due to your sex, your beauty, your heroism and all the rest of it! Suppose I, with nothing but such sentimental stuff to stand between these muscles of mine and those papers which you have about you, and which I want and mean to have! suppose I, with the prize within my grasp, were to falter and sneak away with my hands empty; or, what would be worse, cover up my weakness by playing the magnanimous hero and sparing you the violence I dared not use! Would you not despise me from the depths of your woman's soul? Would any woman be such a fool? Well, Bonaparte can rise to the situation and act like a woman when it is necessary. Do you understand?

The lady, without speaking, stands upright, and takes a packet of papers from her bosom. For a moment she has an intense impulse to dash them in his face. But her good breeding cuts her off from any vulgar method of relief. She hands them to him politely, only averting her head. The moment he takes them, she hurries across to the other side of the room, sits down, and covers her face with her hands.

NAPOLEON (*gloating over the papers*): Aha! That's right. That's right. (*Before he opens them, he looks at her and says*) Excuse me. (*He sees that she is hiding her face.*) Very angry with me, eh? (*He unties the packet, the seal of which is already broken, and puts it on the table to examine its contents.*)

LADY (*quietly, taking down her hands and showing that she is not crying, but only thinking*): No. You were right. But I am sorry for you.

NAPOLEON (*pausing in the act of taking the uppermost paper from the packet*): Sorry for me! Why?

LADY: I am going to see you lose your honor.

NAPOLEON: Hm! Nothing worse than that? (*He takes up the paper.*)

LADY: And your happiness.

NAPOLEON: Happiness! Happiness is the most tedious thing in the world to me. Should I be what I am if I cared for happiness? Anything else?

LADY: Nothing.

NAPOLEON: Good.

LADY: Except that you will cut a very foolish figure in the eyes of France.

NAPOLEON (*quickly*): What? (*The hand unfolding the paper involuntarily stops. The lady looks at him enigmatically in tranquil silence. He throws the letter down and breaks out into a torrent of scolding.*) What do you mean? Eh? Are you at your tricks again? Do you think I don't know what these papers contain? I'll tell you. First, my information as to Beaulieu's retreat. There are only two things he can do—leather-brained idiot that he is!—shut himself up in Mantua or violate the neutrality of Venice by taking Peschiera. You are one of old Leatherbrain's spies: he has discovered that he has been betrayed, and has sent you to intercept the information at all hazards. As if that could save him from me, the old fool! The other papers are only my private letters from Paris, of which you know nothing.

LADY (*prompt and businesslike*): General: let us make a fair division. Take the information your spies have sent you about the Austrian army; and give me the Paris correspondence. That will content me.

NAPOLEON (*his breath taken away by the coolness of the proposal*): A fair di— (*He gasps.*) It seems to me, madam, that you have come to regard my letters as your own property, of which I am trying to rob you.

LADY (*earnestly*): No: on my honor I ask for no letter of yours: not a word that has been written by you or to you. That packet contains a stolen letter: a letter written by a woman to a man: a man not her husband: a letter that means disgrace, infamy—

NAPOLEON: A love letter?

LADY (*bitter-sweetly*): What else but a love letter could stir up so much hate?

NAPOLEON: Why is it sent to me? To put the husband in my power, eh?

LADY: No, no: it can be of no use to you: I swear that it will cost you nothing to give it to me. It has been sent to you out of sheer malice: solely to injure the woman who wrote it.

NAPOLEON: Then why not send it to her husband instead of to me?

LADY (*completely taken aback*): Oh! (*Sinking back into the chair*) I—I don't know. (*She breaks down.*)

NAPOLEON: Aha! I thought so: a little romance to get the papers back. Per Bacco [By Bacchus], I can't help admiring you. I wish I could lie like that. It would save me a great deal of trouble.

LADY (*wringing her hands*): Oh, how *I* wish I really had told you some lie! You would have believed me then. The truth is the one thing nobody will believe.

NAPOLEON (*with coarse familiarity, treating her as if she were a vivandière*): Capital! Capital! (*He puts his hands behind him on the table and lifts himself on to it, sitting with his arms akimbo and his legs wide apart.*) Come: I am a true Corsican in my love for stories. But I could tell them better than you if I set my mind to it. Next time you are asked why a letter compromising a wife should not be sent to her husband, answer simply that the husband wouldn't read it. Do you suppose, you goose, that a man wants to be compelled by public opinion to make a scene, to fight a duel, to break up his household, to injure his career by a scandal, when he can avoid it all by taking care not to know?

LADY (*revolted*): Suppose that packet contained a letter about your own wife?

NAPOLEON (*offended, coming off the table*): You are impertinent, madam.

LADY (*humbly*): I beg your pardon. Cæsar's wife is above suspicion.[2]

NAPOLEON (*with a deliberate assumption of superiority*): You have committed an indiscretion. I pardon you. In future, do not permit yourself to introduce real persons in your romances.

LADY (*politely ignoring a speech which is to her only a breach of good manners*): General: there really is a woman's letter there. (*Pointing to the packet*) Give it to me.

NAPOLEON (*with brute conciseness*): Why?

LADY: She is an old friend: we were at school together. She has written to me imploring me to prevent the letter falling into your hands.

NAPOLEON: Why has it been sent to me?

LADY: Because it compromises the director Barras.

NAPOLEON (*frowning and evidently startled*): Barras! (*Haughtily*) Take care, madam. The director Barras is my attached personal friend.

LADY (*nodding placidly*): Yes. You became friends through your wife.

NAPOLEON: Again! Have I not forbidden you to speak of my wife? (*She keeps looking curiously at him, taking no account of the rebuke. More and more irritated, he drops his haughty manner, of which he is himself somewhat impatient, and says suspiciously, lowering his voice*) Who is this woman with whom you sympathize so deeply?

LADY: Oh, General! How could I tell you that?

NAPOLEON (*ill humoredly, beginning to walk about again in angry perplexity*): Ay, ay: stand by one another. You are all the same, you women.

LADY (*indignantly*): We are not all the same, any more than you are. Do you think that if *I* loved another man, I should pretend to go on loving my husband, or be afraid to tell him or all the world? But this woman is not made that way. She governs men by cheating them; and they like it, and let her govern them. (*She turns her back to him in disdain.*)

---

[2] In 61 B.C. when Caesar's second wife, Pompeia, was suspected of adultery, he at once divorced her—because his wife should be above suspicion.

NAPOLEON (*not attending to her*): Barras? Barras? (*Very threateningly, his face darkening*) Take care. Take care: do you hear? You may go too far.

LADY (*innocently turning her face to him*): What's the matter?

NAPOLEON: What are you hinting at? Who is this woman?

LADY (*meeting his angry searching gaze with tranquil indifference as she sits looking up at him*): A vain, silly, extravagant creature, with a very able and ambitious husband who knows her through and through: knows that she has lied to him about her age, her income, her social position, about everything that silly women lie about: knows that she is incapable of fidelity to any principle or any person; and yet cannot help loving her—cannot help his man's instinct to make use of her for his own advancement with Barras.

NAPOLEON (*in a stealthy, coldly furious whisper*): This is your revenge, you she-cat, for having had to give me the letters.

LADY: Nonsense! Or do you mean that *you* are that sort of man?

NAPOLEON (*exasperated, clasps his hands behind him, his fingers twitching, and says, as he walks irritably away from her to the fireplace*): This woman will drive me out of my senses. (*To her*) Begone.

LADY (*seated immovably*): Not without that letter.

NAPOLEON: Begone, I tell you. (*Walking from the fireplace to the vineyard and back to the table*) You shall have no letter. I don't like you. You're a detestable woman, and as ugly as Satan. I don't choose to be pestered by strange women. Be off. (*He turns his back on her. In quiet amusement, she leans her cheek on her hand and laughs at him. He turns again, angrily mocking her.*) Ha! ha! ha! What are you laughing at?

LADY: At you, General. I have often seen persons of your sex getting into a pet and behaving like children; but I never saw a really great man do it before.

NAPOLEON (*brutally, flinging the words in her face*): Psha! Flattery! Flattery! Coarse, impudent flattery!

LADY (*springing up with a bright flush in her cheeks*): Oh, you are too bad. Keep your letters. Read the story of your own dishonor in them; and much good may they do. Goodbye. (*She goes indignantly towards the inner door.*)

NAPOLEON: My own—! Stop. Come back. Come back, I order you. (*She proudly disregards his savagely peremptory tone and continues on her way to the door. He rushes at her, seizes her by the arm, and drags her back.*) Now, what do you mean? Explain. Explain. I tell you, or— (*threatening her. She looks at him with unflinching defiance.*) Rrrr! you obstinate devil, you. (*Throwing her arm away*) Why can't you answer a civil question?

LADY (*deeply offended by his violence*): Why do you ask me? You have the explanation.

NAPOLEON: Where?

LADY (*pointing to the letters on the table*): There. You have only to read it.

He snatches the packet up; hesitates; looks at her suspiciously; and throws it down again.

NAPOLEON: You seem to have forgotten your solicitude for the honor of your old friend.

LADY: I do not think she runs any risk now. She does not quite understand her husband.

NAPOLEON: I am to read the letter then? (*He stretches out his hand as if to take up the packet again, with his eye on her.*)

LADY: I do not see how you can very well avoid doing so now. (*He instantly withdraws his hand.*) Oh, don't be afraid. You will find many interesting things in it.

NAPOLEON: For instance?

LADY: For instance, a duel with Barras, a domestic scene, a broken household, a public scandal, a checked career, all sorts of things.

NAPOLEON: Hm! (*He looks at her; takes up the packet and looks at it, pursing his lips and balancing it in his hand; looks at her again; passes the packet into his left hand and puts it behind his back, raising his right to scratch the back of his head as he turns and goes up to the edge of the vineyard, where he stands for a moment looking out into the vines, deep in thought. The Lady watches him in silence, somewhat slightingly. Suddenly he turns and comes back again, full of force and decision.*) I grant your request, madam. Your courage and resolution deserve to succeed. Take the letters for which you have fought so well; and remember henceforth that you found the vile vulgar Corsican adventurer as generous to the vanquished after the battle as he was resolute in the face of the enemy before it. (*He offers her the packet.*)

LADY (*without taking it, looking hard at him*): What are you at now, I wonder? (*He dashes the packet furiously to the floor.*) Aha! I've spoilt *that* attitude. I think. (*She makes him a pretty mocking curtsey.*)

NAPOLEON (*snatching it up again*): Will you take the letters and begone (*advancing and thrusting them upon her*)?

LADY (*escaping round the table*): No: I don't want your letters.

NAPOLEON: Ten minutes ago, nothing else would satisfy you.

LADY (*keeping the table carefully between them*): Ten minutes ago you had not insulted me beyond all bearing.

NAPOLEON: I— (*swallowing his spleen*) I apologize.

LADY (*coolly*): Thanks. (*With forced politeness he offers her the packet across the table. She retreats a step out of its reach and says*) But don't you want to know whether the Austrians are at Mantua or Peschiera?

NAPOLEON: I have already told you that I can conquer my enemies without the aid of spies, madam.

LADY: And the letter? don't you want to read that?

NAPOLEON: You have said that it is not addressed to me. I am not in the habit of reading other people's letters. (*He again offers the packet.*)

LADY: In that case there can be no objection to your keeping it. All I wanted was to prevent your reading it. (*Cheerfully*) Good afternoon, General. (*She turns coolly towards the inner door.*)

NAPOLEON (*angrily flinging the packet on the couch*): Heaven grant me patience! (*He goes determinedly to the door and places himself before it.*) Have you any sense of personal danger? Or are you one of those women who like to be beaten black and blue?

LADY: Thank you, General: I have no doubt the sensation is very voluptuous; but I had rather not. I simply want to go home: that's all. I was wicked enough to steal your despatches; but you have got them back; and you have forgiven me, because (*delicately reproducing his rhetorical cadence*) you are as generous to the vanquished after the battle as you are resolute in the face of the enemy before it. Won't you say goodbye to me? (*She offers her hand sweetly.*)

NAPOLEON (*repulsing the advance with a gesture of concentrated rage, and opening the door to call fiercely*): Giuseppe! (*Louder*) Giuseppe! (*He bangs the door to and comes to the middle of the room. The lady goes a little way into the vineyard to avoid him.*)

GIUSEPPE (*appearing at the door*): Excellency?

NAPOLEON: Where is that fool?

GIUSEPPE: He has had a good dinner, according to your instructions, excellency, and is now doing me the honor to gamble with me to pass the time.

NAPOLEON: Send him here. Bring him here. Come with him. (*Giuseppe, with unruffled readiness, hurries off. Napoleon turns curtly to the lady, saying*) I must trouble you to remain some moments longer, madam. (*He comes to the couch.*)

She comes from the vineyard along the opposite side of the room to the sideboard and posts herself there, leaning against it, watching him. He takes the packet from the couch and deliberately buttons it carefully into his breast pocket, looking at her meanwhile with an expression which suggests that she will soon find out the meaning of his proceedings, and will not like it. Nothing more is said until the lieutenant arrives followed by Giuseppe, who stands modestly in attendance at the table. The Lieutenant, without cap, sword, or gloves and much improved in temper and spirit by his meal, chooses the lady's side of the room and waits, much at his ease, for Napoleon to begin.

NAPOLEON: Lieutenant.

LIEUTENANT (*encouragingly*): General.

NAPOLEON: I cannot persuade this lady to give me much information; but there can be no doubt that the man who tricked you out of your charge was, as she admitted to you, her brother.

LIEUTENANT (*triumphantly*): What did I tell you, General! What did I tell you!

NAPOLEON: You must find that man. Your honor is at stake; and the fate of the campaign, the destiny of France, of Europe, of humanity, perhaps, may depend on the information those despatches contain.

LIEUTENANT: Yes, I suppose they really are rather serious (*as if this hardly occurred to him before*).

NAPOLEON (*energetically*): They are so serious, sir, that if you do not recover them, you will be degraded in the presence of your regiment.

LIEUTENANT: Whew! The regiment won't like that, I can tell you.

NAPOLEON: Personally I am sorry for you. I would willingly hush up the affair if it were possible. But I shall be called to account for not acting on the despatches. I shall have to prove to all the world that I never received them, no matter what the consequences may be to you. I am sorry; but you see that I cannot help myself.

LIEUTENANT (*goodnaturedly*): Oh, don't take it to heart, General: it's really very good of you. Never mind what happens to me: I shall scrape through somehow; and we'll beat the Austrians for you, despatches or no despatches. I hope you won't insist on my starting off on a wild goose chase after the fellow now. I haven't a notion where to look for him.

GIUSEPPE (*deferentially*): You forget, Lieutenant: he has your horse.

LIEUTENANT (*starting*): I forgot that. (*Resolutely*) I'll go after him, General: I'll find that horse if it's alive anywhere in Italy. And I shan't forget the despatches: never fear. Giuseppe: go and saddle one of those mangy old posthorses of yours while I get my cap and sword and things. Quick march. Off with you (*bustling him*).

GIUSEPPE: Instantly, Lieutenant, instantly. (*He disappears in the vineyard, where the light is now reddening with the sunset.*)

LIEUTENANT (*looking about him on his way to the inner door*): By the way, General, did I give you my sword or did I not? Oh, I remember now. (*Fretfully*) It's all that nonsense about putting a man under arrest: one never knows where to find—(*he talks himself out of the room*).

LADY (*still at the sideboard*): What does all this mean, General?

NAPOLEON: He will not find your brother.

LADY: Of course not. There's no such person.

NAPOLEON: The despatches will be irrecoverably lost.

LADY: Nonsense! They are inside your coat.

NAPOLEON: You will find it hard, I think, to prove that wild statement. (*The lady starts. He adds, with clinching emphasis*) Those papers are lost.

LADY (*anxiously, advancing to the corner of the table*): And that unfortunate young man's career will be sacrificed?

NAPOLEON: His career! The fellow is not worth the gun-powder it would cost to have him shot. (*He turns contemptuously and goes to the hearth, where he stands with his back to her.*)

LADY (*wistfully*): You are very hard. Men and women are nothing to you but things to be used, even if they are broken in the use.

NAPOLEON (*turning on her*): Which of us has broken this fellow? I or you? Who tricked him out of the despatches? Did you think of his career then?

LADY (*conscience-stricken*): Oh, I never thought of that. It was wicked of me; but I couldn't help it, could I? How else could I have got the papers? (*Supplicating*) General: you will save him from disgrace.

NAPOLEON (*laughing sourly*): Save him yourself, since you are so clever: it was you who ruined him. (*With savage intensity*) I hate a bad soldier.

He goes out determinedly through the vineyard. She follows him a few steps with an appealing gesture, but is interrupted by the return of the Lieutenant, gloved and capped, with his sword on, ready for the road. He is crossing to the outer door when she intercepts him.

LADY: Lieutenant.

LIEUTENANT (*importantly*): You mustn't delay me, you know. Duty, madam, duty.

LADY (*imploringly*): Oh, sir, what are you going to do to my poor brother?

LIEUTENANT: Are you very fond of him?

LADY: I should die if anything happened to him. You must spare him. (*The Lieutenant shakes his head gloomily.*) Yes, yes: you must: you shall: he is not fit to die. Listen to me. If I tell you where to find him—if I undertake to place him in your hands a prisoner, to be delivered up by you to General Bonaparte—will you promise me on your honor as an officer and a gentleman not to fight with him or treat him unkindly in any way?

LIEUTENANT: But suppose he attacks me. He has my pistols.

LADY: He is too great a coward.

LIEUTENANT: I don't feel so sure about that. He's capable of anything.

LADY: If he attacks you or resists you in any way, I release you from your promise.

LIEUTENANT: My promise! I didn't mean to promise. Look here: you're as bad as he is: you've taken an advantage of me through the better side of my nature. What about my horse?

LADY: It is part of the bargain that you are to have your horse and pistols back.

LIEUTENANT: Honor bright?

LADY: Honor bright. (*She offers her hand.*)

LIEUTENANT (*taking it and holding it*): All right: I'll be as gentle as a lamb with him. His sister's a very pretty woman. (*He attempts to kiss her.*)

LADY (*slipping away from him*): Oh, Lieutenant! You forget: your career is at stake—the destiny of Europe—of humanity.

LIEUTENANT: Oh, bother the destiny of humanity! (*Making for her*) Only a kiss.

LADY (*retreating round the table*): Not until you have regained your honor as an officer. Remember: you have not captured my brother yet.

LIEUTENANT (*seductively*): You'll tell me where he is, won't you?

LADY: I have only to send him a certain signal; and he will be here in a quarter of an hour.

LIEUTENANT: He's not far off, then.

LADY: No: quite close. Wait here for him: when he gets my message he will come here at once and surrender himself to you. You understand?

LIEUTENANT (*intellectually overtaxed*): Well, it's a little complicated; but I daresay it will be all right.

LADY: And now, whilst you're waiting, don't you think you had better make terms with the General?

LIEUTENANT: Oh, look here: this is getting frightfully complicated. What terms?

LADY: Make him promise that if you catch my brother he will consider that you have cleared your character as a soldier. He will promise anything you ask on that condition.

LIEUTENANT: That's not a bad idea. Thank you: I think I'll try it.

LADY: Do. And mind, above all things, don't let him see how clever you are.

LIEUTENANT: I understand. He'd be jealous.

LADY: Don't tell him anything except that you are resolved to capture my brother or perish in the attempt. He won't believe you. Then you will produce my brother—

LIEUTENANT (*interrupting as he masters the plot*): And have the laugh at him! I say: what a jolly clever woman you are! (*Shouting*) Giuseppe!

LADY: Sh! Not a word to Giuseppe about me. (*She puts her finger on her lips. He does the same. They look at one another warningly.*

Then, with a ravishing smile, she changes the gesture into wafting him a kiss, and runs out through the inner door. Electrified, he bursts into a volley of chuckles.)

Giuseppe comes back by the outer door.

GIUSEPPE: The horse is ready, Lieutenant.

LIEUTENANT: I'm not going just yet. Go and find the General and tell him I want to speak to him.

GIUSEPPE (*shaking his head*): That will never do, Lieutenant.

LIEUTENANT: Why not?

GIUSEPPE: In this wicked world a general may send for a lieutenant; but a lieutenant must not send for a general.

LIEUTENANT: Oh, you think he wouldn't like it. Well, perhaps you're right: one has to be awfully particular about that sort of thing now we're a republic.

Napoleon reappears, advancing from the vineyard, buttoning the breast of his coat, pale and full of gnawing thoughts.

GIUSEPPE (*unconscious of Napoleon's approach*): Quite true, Lieutenant, quite true. You are all like innkeepers now in France: you have to be polite to everybody.

NAPOLEON (*putting his hand on Giuseppe's shoulder*): And that destroys the whole value of politeness, eh?

LIEUTENANT: The very man I wanted! See here, General; suppose I catch that fellow for you!

NAPOLEON (*with ironical gravity*): You will not catch him, my friend.

LIEUTENANT: Aha! you think so; but you'll see. Just wait. Only, if I do catch him and hand him over to you, will you cry quits? Will you drop all this about degrading me in the presence of my regiment? Not that *I* mind, you know; but still no regiment likes to have all the other regiments laughing at it.

NAPOLEON (*a cold ray of humor striking pallidly across his gloom*): What shall we do with this officer, Giuseppe? Everything he says is wrong.

GIUSEPPE (*promptly*): Make him a general, excellency; and then everything he says will be right.

LIEUTENANT (*crowing*): Haw-aw! (*He throws himself ecstatically on the couch to enjoy the joke.*)

NAPOLEON (*laughing and pinching Giuseppe's ear*): You are thrown away in this inn, Giuseppe. (*He sits down and places Giuseppe before him like a schoolmaster with a pupil.*) Shall I take you away with me and make a man of you?

GIUSEPPE (*shaking his head rapidly and repeatedly*): No no no no no no no. All my life long people have wanted to make a man of me. When I was a boy, our good priest wanted to make a man of me by teaching me to read and write. Then the organist at Melegnano wanted to make a man of me by teaching me to read music. The recruiting sergeant would have made a man of me if I had been a few inches taller. But it always meant making me work; and I am too lazy for that, thank Heaven! So I taught myself to cook and became an innkeeper; and now I keep servants to do the work and have nothing to do myself except talk, which suits me perfectly.

NAPOLEON (*looking at him thoughtfully*): You are satisfied?

GIUSEPPE (*with cheerful conviction*): Quite, excellency.

NAPOLEON: And you have no devouring devil inside you who must be fed with action and victory: gorged with them night and day: who makes you pay, with the sweat of your brain and body, weeks of Herculean toil for ten minutes of enjoyment: who is at once your slave and your tyrant, your genius and your doom: who brings you a crown in one hand and the oar of a galley slave in the other: who shows you all the kingdoms of the earth and offers to make you their master on condition that you become their servant! Have you nothing of that in you?

GIUSEPPE: Nothing of it! Oh, I assure you, excellency, my devouring devil is far worse than that. He offers me no crowns and kingdoms: he expects to get everything for nothing: sausages! omelettes! grapes! cheese! polenta! wine! three times a day, excellency: nothing less will content him.

LIEUTENANT: Come: drop it, Giuseppe: you're making me feel hungry again.

Giuseppe, with an apologetic shrug, retires from the conversation.

NAPOLEON (*turning to the Lieutenant with sardonic politeness*): I hope *I* have not been making you feel ambitious.

LIEUTENANT: Not at all: I don't fly so high. Besides, I'm better as I am: men like me are wanted in the army just now. The fact is, the Revolution was all very well for civilians; but it won't work in the army. You know what soldiers are, General: they *will* have men of family for their officers. A subaltern must be a gentleman, because he's so much in contact with the men. But a general, or even a colonel, may be any sort of riff-raff if he understands his job well enough. A lieutenant is a gentleman: all the rest is chance. Why, who do you suppose won the battle of Lodi? I'll tell you. My horse did.

NAPOLEON (*rising*): Your folly is carrying you too far, sir. Take care.

LIEUTENANT: Not a bit of it. You remember all that red-hot cannonade across the river: the Austrians blazing away at you to keep you from crossing, and you blazing away at them to keep them from setting the bridge on fire? Did you notice where I was then?

NAPOLEON: I am sorry. I am afraid I was rather occupied at the moment.

GIUSEPPE (*with eager admiration*): They say you jumped off your horse and worked the big guns with your own hands, General.

LIEUTENANT: That was a mistake: an officer should never let himself down to the level of his men. (*Napoleon looks at him dangerously, and begins to walk tigerishly to and fro.*) But you might have been firing away at the Austrians still if we cavalry fellows hadn't found the ford and got across and turned old Beaulieu's flank for you. You know you didn't dare give the order to charge the bridge until you saw us on the other side. Consequently, I say that whoever found that ford won the battle of Lodi. Well, who found it? I was the first man to cross; and I know. It was my horse that found it. (*With conviction, as he rises from the couch*) That horse is the true conqueror of the Austrians.

NAPOLEON (*passionately*): You idiot: I'll have you shot for losing those despatches: I'll have you blown from the mouth of a cannon: nothing less could make any impression on you. (*Baying at him*) Do you hear? Do you understand?

A French officer enters unobserved, carrying his sheathed sabre in his hand.

LIEUTENANT (*unabashed*): If I don't capture him, General. Remember the if.

NAPOLEON: *If*!! Ass: there is no such man.

THE OFFICER (*suddenly stepping between them and speaking in the unmistakable voice of the Strange Lady*) Lieutenant: I am your prisoner. (*She offers him her sabre.*)

Napoleon gazes at her for a moment thunderstruck; then seizes her by the wrist and drags her roughly to him, looking closely and fiercely at her to satisfy himself as to her identity: for it now begins to darken rapidly into night, the red glow over the vineyard giving way to clear starlight.

NAPOLEON: Pah! (*He flings her hand away with an exclamation of disgust and turns his back on them with his hand in his breast, his brow lowering and his toes twitching.*)

LIEUTENANT (*triumphantly, taking the sabre*): No such man! eh, General? (*To the Lady*) I say: where's my horse?

LADY: Safe at Borghetto, waiting for you, Lieutenant.

NAPOLEON (*turning on them*): Where are the despatches?

LADY: You would never guess. They are in the most unlikely place in the world. Did you meet my sister here, any of you?

LIEUTENANT: Yes. Very nice woman. She's wonderfully like you; but of course she's better-looking.

LADY (*mysteriously*): Well, do you know that she is a witch?

GIUSEPPE (*in terror, crossing himself*): Oh, no, no, no. It is not safe to jest about such things. I cannot have it in my house, excellency.

LIEUTENANT: Yes, drop it. You're my prisoner, you know. Of course I don't believe in any such rubbish; but still it's not a proper subject for joking.

LADY: But this is very serious. My sister has bewitched the General. (*Giuseppe and the lieutenant recoil from Napoleon.*) General: open your coat: you will find the despatches in the breast of it. (*She puts her hand quickly on his breast.*) Yes: there they are: I can feel them. Eh? (*She looks up into his face half coaxingly, half mockingly.*) Will you allow me, General? (*She takes a button as if to unbutton his coat, and pauses for permission.*)

NAPOLEON (*inscrutably*): If you dare.

LADY: Thank you. (*She opens his coat and takes out the despatches.*) There! (*To Giuseppe, showing him the despatches*) See!

GIUSEPPE (*flying to the outer door*): No, in heaven's name! They're bewitched.

LADY (*turning to the lieutenant*): Here, Lieutenant: you are not afraid of them.

LIEUTENANT (*retreating*): Keep off. (*Seizing the hilt of the sabre*) Keep off, I tell you.

LADY (*to Napoleon*): They belong to you, General. Take them.

GIUSEPPE: Don't touch them, excellency. Have nothing to do with them.

LIEUTENANT: Be careful, General: be careful.

GIUSEPPE: Burn them. And burn the witch too.

LADY (*to Napoleon*): Shall I burn them?

NAPOLEON (*thoughtfully*): Yes, burn them. Giuseppe: go and fetch a light.

GIUSEPPE (*trembling and stammering*): Do you mean go alone? in the dark! with a witch in the house?

NAPOLEON: Psha! You're a poltroon. (*To the lieutenant*) Oblige me by going, Lieutenant.

LIEUTENANT (*remonstrating*): Oh, I say, General! No, look here, you know: nobody can say I'm a coward after Lodi. But to ask me to go into the dark by myself without a candle after such an awful conversation is a little too much. How would you like to do it yourself?

NAPOLEON (*irritably*): You refuse to obey my order?

LIEUTENANT (*resolutely*): Yes I do. It's not reasonable. But I'll tell you what I'll do. If Giuseppe goes, I'll go with him and protect him.

NAPOLEON (*to Giuseppe*): There! will that satisfy you? Be off, both of you.

GIUSEPPE (*humbly, his lips trembling*): W-willingly, your excellency. (*He goes reluctantly towards the inner door.*) Heaven protect me! (*To the lieutenant*) After you, Lieutenant.

LIEUTENANT: You'd better go first: I don't know the way.

GIUSEPPE: You can't miss it. Besides (*imploringly, laying his hand on his sleeve*) I am only a poor innkeeper: you are a man of family.

LIEUTENANT: There's something in that. Here: you needn't be in such a fright. Take my arm. (*Giuseppe does so.*) That's the way. (*They go out, arm in arm.*)

It is now starry night. The lady throws the packet on the table and seats herself at her ease on the couch, enjoying the sensation of freedom from petticoats.

LADY: Well, General: I've beaten you.

NAPOLEON (*walking about*): You are guilty of indelicacy: of unwomanliness. Is that costume proper?

LADY: It seems to me much the same as yours.

NAPOLEON: Psha! I blush for you.

LADY (*naïvely*): Yes: soldiers blush so easily. (*He growls and turns away. She looks mischievously at him, balancing the despatches in her hand.*) Wouldn't you like to read these before they're burnt, General? You must be dying with curiosity. Take a peep. (*She throws the packet on the table and turns her face away from it.*) I won't look.

NAPOLEON: I have no curiosity whatever, madam. But since you are evidently burning to read them, I give you leave to do so.

LADY: Oh, I've read them already.

NAPOLEON (*starting*): What!

LADY: I read them the first thing after I rode away on that poor lieutenant's horse. So you see I know what's in them; and you don't.

NAPOLEON: Excuse me: I read them when I was out there in the vineyard ten minutes ago.

LADY: Oh! (*Jumping up*) Oh, General: I've not beaten you after all. I do admire you so. (*He laughs and pats her cheek.*) This time, really and truly without shamming, I do you homage (*kissing his hand*).

NAPOLEON (*quickly withdrawing it*): Brr! Don't do that. No more witchcraft.

LADY: I want to say something to you; only you would misunderstand it.

NAPOLEON: Need that stop you?

LADY: Well, it is this. I adore a man who is not afraid to be mean and selfish.

NAPOLEON (*indignantly*): I am neither mean nor selfish.

LADY: Oh, you don't appreciate yourself. Besides, I don't really mean meanness and selfishness.

NAPOLEON: Thank you. I thought perhaps you did.

LADY: Well, of course I do. But what I mean is a certain strong simplicity about you.

NAPOLEON: That's better.

LADY: You didn't want to read the letters; but you were curious about what was in them. So you went into the garden and read them when no one was looking, and then came back and pretended you hadn't. That's the meanest thing I ever knew any man do; but it exactly fulfilled your purpose; and so you weren't a bit afraid or ashamed to do it.

NAPOLEON (*abruptly*): Where did you pick up all these vulgar scruples? this (*with contemptuous emphasis*) conscience of yours? I took you for a lady: an aristocrat. Was your grandfather a shopkeeper, pray?

LADY: No: he was an Englishman.

NAPOLEON: That accounts for it. The English are a nation of shopkeepers. Now I understand why you've beaten me.

LADY: Oh, I haven't beaten you. And I'm not English.

NAPOLEON: Yes you are: English to the backbone. Listen to me: I will explain the English to you.

LADY (*eagerly*): Do. (*With a lively air of anticipating an intellectual treat, she sits down on the couch and composes herself to listen to him. Secure of his audience, he at once nerves himself for a performance. He considers a little before he begins, so as to fix her attention by a moment of suspense. His style is at first modeled on Talma's in Corneille's* Cinna [3]; *but it is somewhat lost in the darkness, and Talma presently gives way to Napoleon, the voice coming through the gloom with startling intensity.*)

NAPOLEON: There are three sorts of people in the world: the low people, the middle people, and the high people. The low people and the high people are alike in one thing: they have no scruples, no morality. The low are beneath morality, the high above it. I am not afraid of either of them; for the low are unscrupulous without knowledge, so that they make an idol of me; whilst the high are unscrupulous without purpose, so that they go down before my will. Look you: I shall go over all the mobs and all the courts of Europe as a plough goes over a field. It is the middle people who are dangerous: they have both knowledge and purpose. But they, too, have their weak point. They are full of scruples: chained hand and foot by their morality and respectability.

LADY: Then you will beat the English; for all shopkeepers are middle people.

NAPOLEON: No, because the English are a race apart. No Englishman is too low to have scruples: no Englishman is high enough to be free from their tyranny. But every Englishman is born with a certain miraculous power that makes him master of the world. When he wants a thing, he never tells himself that he wants it. He waits patiently until there comes into his mind, no one knows how, a burning conviction that it is his moral and religious duty to conquer those who possess the thing he wants. Then he becomes irresistible. Like the aristocrat, he does what pleases him and grabs what he

---

[3] Considered the greatest tragic actor of his time and fervently admired by Napoleon, François Joseph Talma took the part of Augustus Caesar in *Cinna* (1640) by Pierre Corneille, which deals with a conspiracy against the life of the Emperor.

covets: like the shopkeeper, he pursues his purpose with the industry and steadfastness that come from strong religious conviction and deep sense of moral responsibility. He is never at a loss for an effective moral attitude. As the great champion of freedom and national independence, he conquers and annexes half the world, and calls it Colonization. When he wants a new market for his adulterated Manchester [4] goods, he sends a missionary to teach the natives the Gospel of Peace. The natives kill the missionary: he flies to arms in defence of Christianity; fights for it; conquers for it; and takes the market as a reward from heaven. In defence of his island shores, he puts a chaplain on board his ship; nails a flag with a cross on it to his top-gallant mast; and sails to the ends of the earth, sinking, burning, and destroying all who dispute the empire of the seas with him. He boasts that a slave is free the moment his foot touches British soil; and he sells the children of his poor at six years of age to work under the lash in his factories for sixteen hours a day. He makes two revolutions, and then declares war on our one in the name of law and order. There is nothing so bad or so good that you will not find Englishmen doing it; but you will never find an Englishman in the wrong. He does everything on principle. He fights you on patriotic principles; he robs you on business principles; he enslaves you on imperial principles; he bullies you on manly principles; he supports his king on loyal principles and cuts off his king's head [5] on republican principles. His watchword is always Duty; and he never forgets that the nation which lets its duty get on the opposite side to its interest is lost. He—

LADY: W-w-w-w-w-wh! Do stop a moment. I want to know how you make me out to be English at this rate.

NAPOLEON (*dropping his rhetorical style*): It's plain enough. You wanted some letters that belonged to me. You have spent the morning in stealing them: yes, stealing them, by highway robbery. And you have spent the afternoon in putting me in the wrong about them: in assuming that it was *I* who wanted to steal your letters: in explaining that it all came about through my meanness and selfishness, and your goodness, your devotion, your self-sacrifice. That's English.

LADY: Nonsense! I am sure I am not a bit English. The English are a very stupid people.

NAPOLEON: Yes, too stupid sometimes to know when they're beaten. But I grant that your brains are not English. You see, though your grandfather was an Englishman, your grandmother was—what? A Frenchwoman?

---

[4] City in the English Midlands known for its textiles and other manufactured products.
[5] I.e. the head of Charles I, in 1649.

LADY: Oh no. An Irishwoman.

NAPOLEON (*quickly*): Irish! (*Thoughtfully*) Yes: I forgot the Irish. An English army led by an Irish general: that might be a match for a French army led by an Italian general.[6] (*He pauses, and adds, half jestingly, half moodily*) At all events, *you* have beaten me; and what beats a man first will beat him last. (*He goes meditatively into the moonlit vineyard and looks up.*)

She steals out after him. She ventures to rest her hand on his shoulder, overcome by the beauty of the night and emboldened by its obscurity.

LADY (*softly*): What are you looking at?

NAPOLEON (*pointing up*): My star.

LADY: You believe in that?

NAPOLEON: I do.

They look at it for a moment, she leaning a little on his shoulder.

LADY: Do you know that the English say that a man's star is not complete without a woman's garter?

NAPOLEON (*scandalized: abruptly shaking her off and coming back into the room*): Pah! The hypocrites! If the French said that, how they would hold up their hands in pious horror! (*He goes to the inner door and holds it open, shouting*) Hallo! Giuseppe! Where's that light, man? (*He comes between the table and the sideboard, and moves the second chair to the table, beside his own.*) We have still to burn the letter. (*He takes up the packet.*)

Giuseppe comes back, pale and still trembling, carrying in one hand a branched candlestick with a couple of candles alight, and a broad snuffers tray in the other.

GIUSEPPE (*piteously, as he places the light on the table*): Excellency: what were you looking up at just now? Out there! (*He points across his shoulder to the vineyard, but is afraid to look round.*)

NAPOLEON (*unfolding the packet*): What is that to you?

GIUSEPPE: Because the witch is gone: vanished; and no one saw her go out.

LADY (*coming behind him from the vineyard*): We were watching her riding up to the moon on your broomstick, Giuseppe. You will never see her again.

GIUSEPPE: Gesu Maria! (*He crosses himself and hurries out.*)

NAPOLEON (*throwing down the letters in a heap on the table*): Now! (*He sits down at the table in the chair which he has just placed.*)

LADY: Yes; but you know you have THE letter in your pocket. (*He smiles, takes a letter from his pocket, and tosses it on top of the heap. She holds it up and looks at him, saying*) About Cæsar's wife.

NAPOLEON: Cæsar's wife is above suspicion. Burn it.

---

[6] The Duke of Wellington, who was born in Dublin, was more than a match for Napoleon at Waterloo (1815).

LADY (*taking up the snuffers and holding the letter to the candle flame with it*): I wonder would Cæsar's wife be above suspicion if she saw us here together!

NAPOLEON (*echoing her, with his elbows on the table and his cheeks on his hands, looking at the letter*): I wonder!

The Strange Lady puts the letter down alight on the snuffers tray and sits down beside Napoleon, in the same attitude, elbows on table, cheeks on hands, watching it burn. When it is burnt, they simultaneously turn their eyes and look at one another. The curtain steals down and hides them.

Suggestions

1. The introductory paragraphs speak of plays as though they were written to be read, for most people meet them in this form, and the printed text of *The Man of Destiny* is a reading version. The Italian children and the sentinel with the painted moustache, for instance, are not really part of the action of the play. Shaw added them in the published text as a sprightly way of making the reader visualize the scene. He knew that the practised reader of plays acts them out in the theatre of his imagination, and that the playwright must appeal not only to the ears of the audience with stirring dialogue, but also to their eyes, by inventing bodily action for the performers and surrounding them with interesting objects. A striking visual effect climaxes *The Man of Destiny:* the darkening of the stage and the appearance of the stars provide a symbolic accompaniment to the projection of Napoleon's future—his *destiny*—which proves to be the ultimate theme. Other skilful stage-effects should be carefully noted.

2. That *The Man of Destiny* is the work of a playwright of genius is shown by the way it develops its thesis in dramatic terms. Napoleon was able to conquer Europe, Shaw suggests, because, like the "high people" and "low people" whom he describes, he was unhampered by scruples or morality; and, like the "middle people," he possessed both knowledge and purpose. (The play offers only a joking explanation of Napoleon's future downfall, the joke's essence being that an Irish playwright made it for an English audience. Perhaps Shaw feared to overburden his comedy with serious meaning.) Napoleon's essence, then, is the topic, made to live for us through Napoleon's dynamic relations with the other three characters: with the Lieutenant, through simple contrast; with the other two, through a near-identity—except that from the world of war and politics both of them are excluded, one by sex, the other by choice. Trace these relations in detail: does Giuseppe admire Napoleon as much as Napoleon admires him? Does the Lady not succeed in frustrating the trouble-maker? Analyze the Lieutenant's account of the battle: is it an example of characterization giving way to a thesis? Show how the business concerning the witch restores Giuseppe and the Lieutenant to their proper subordinate positions.

3. Trace the conflicts in *The Man of Destiny:* at what point is the major one introduced? Show how the tone of the play is established at its outset by minor conflicts. Do you find that the interest declines when Napoleon begins his explanation of the English character?

4. Decide whether the Lady is morally superior to Napoleon, considering the action surrounding his line, "If you dare," at the crucial point of their contest. She at first calls him selfish and mean (small-minded, ignoble—not "vicious"), then speaks of his "strong simplicity." Analyze these judgments: is the audience supposed to approve when Napoleon, as the Lady wishes, ignores his wife's infidelity?

5. The Lady's presence in the scene of the campaign and her success in swindling the Lieutenant have been attacked as improbable. Evaluate this judgment. Is the question an important one, considering the success of the play in establishing its meaning?

6. Shaw writes in his Preface that he does not care whether the people in his audiences laugh; "I want to see how many of them, laughing or grave, are in the melting mood." Write an essay evaluating *The Man of Destiny* by this criterion.

7. Write an essay contrasting Shaw's idea of history with that of † "History."

THE SHORT POEM

"What is a poet?" asks Sir William Temple, and offers an answer in the essay beginning on page 494 of this book. His theory of poetry resembles most of the other well-known ones in one vital respect at least: poems, he suggests, concern situations that move human beings to strong feelings, and this concern outweighs the thoughts or ideas, in the abstract sense, that a poem may advance. De Quincey's † "Literature of Knowledge and Literature of Power" likewise asserts that poetic power operates through "human passions, desires, and genial emotions," and reading poems affects our minds in a definite and desirable way: it "rescues them from torpor." Ruskin defines poetry as "the suggestion by the imagination of noble grounds for the noble emotions," grounds that are established by the concrete details of the poem. The details are not present for realism's sake alone: they "are employed so as to bring out an affecting result" († "The Great Style").

Ruskin, to be sure, is defining one kind of poem, which includes *The Iliad* and others written in what he calls The Great Style. But poetry as a defining term is not restricted to nobility, for just as its language is but a specialization of ordinary speech (similes and metaphors, for instance, occur in daily talk and not solely in poetry), so its situations may be anything of human concern, and its methods of treating them appear to be innumerable. Hence a group of poems may be arranged in a variety of ways: by their kinds of experience (falling in love, fighting a war, losing a friend); by their dates of composition; by the emotions that figure in them. In this book, in order to stress the absence of an absolute distinction between poetry and prose, the poems are arranged as the essays in Part 2 are. The first four are called depictions of character, an arrangement that their subjects dictate. The last group is called Indirections, because of their way of treating their subjects. And so with those between.

What, then, is the *relative* difference between poetry and prose? First, though ordinary speech gives poetry its language, the words are chosen and arranged with more attention to their sound than is normal in prose. Second, as Temple and the others knew, situations conducive to emotion, commonly as these occur in prose, are indispensable to a poem. Whether or not a poem must elicit emotion from its readers, which is a moot question, the poetic substance is a speaker's strong feelings about something.

Poems are thus rhythmical utterances having an emotional subject-matter, the rhythm often—though not always—signalized by metre and rhyme. And as the emotional part of their meaning is to some extent conveyed by their sound, it is advisable to discover how they sound by reading them aloud. It is equally advisable to know what each of their words means. Generally poems consist of words in common use or, at worst, those in a small dictionary; but they may include a few others that need special comment. In this section of the book the explanatory notes are identified only by line-numbers. The music of a line of poetry ought not to be interrupted by even a number designating a footnote.

MY LAST DUCHESS

ROBERT BROWNING — *From* DRAMATIC LYRICS, *1842.*

FERRARA

That's my last Duchess painted on the wall,
Looking as if she were alive. I call
That piece a wonder, now: Frà Pandolf's hands
Worked busily a day, and there she stands.
5 Will't please you sit and look at her? I said
"Frà Pandolf" by design, for never read
Strangers like you that pictured countenance,
The depth and passion of its earnest glance,
But to myself they turned (since none puts by
10 The curtain I have drawn for you, but I)
And seemed as they would ask me, if they durst,
How such a glance came there; so, not the first
Are you to turn and ask thus. Sir, 'twas not
Her husband's presence only, called that spot
15 Of joy into the Duchess' cheek: perhaps
Frà Pandolf chanced to say, "Her mantle laps
Over my lady's wrist too much," or "Paint
Must never hope to reproduce the faint
Half-flush that dies along her throat": such stuff
20 Was courtesy, she thought, and cause enough
For calling up that spot of joy. She had
A heart—how shall I say?—too soon made glad,
Too easily impressed; she liked whate'er
She looked on, and her looks went everywhere.
25 Sir, 'twas all one! My favor at her breast,
The dropping of the daylight in the West,
The bough of cherries some officious fool
Broke in the orchard for her, the white mule
She rode with round the terrace—all and each
30 Would draw from her alike the approving speech,
Or blush, at least. She thanked men—good! but thanked
Somehow—I know not how—as if she ranked
My gift of a nine-hundred-years-old name
With anybody's gift. Who'd stoop to blame
35 This sort of trifling? Even had you skill
In speech—which I have not—to make your will
Quite clear to such an one, and say, "Just this
Or that in you disgusts me; here you miss,
Or there exceed the mark"—and if she let

40 Herself be lessoned so, nor plainly set
   Her wits to yours, forsooth, and made excuse,
   —E'en then would be some stooping; and I choose
   Never to stoop. Oh sir, she smiled, no doubt,
   Whene'er I passed her; but who passed without
45 Much the same smile? This grew; I gave commands;
   Then all smiles stopped together. There she stands
   As if alive. Will't please you rise? We'll meet
   The company below, then. I repeat,
   The Count your master's known munificence
50 Is ample warrant that no just pretense
   Of mine for dowry will be disallowed;
   Though his fair daughter's self, as I avowed
   At starting, is my object. Nay, we'll go
   Together down, sir! Notice Neptune, though,
55 Taming a sea-horse, thought a rarity,
   Which Claus of Innsbruck cast in bronze for me!

ULYSSES

ALFRED, LORD TENNYSON ⸻⟩ *From* POEMS, *vol. ii, 1842.*

It little profits that an idle king,
By this still hearth, among these barren crags,
Matched with an agèd wife, I mete and dole
Unequal laws unto a savage race,
5 That hoard, and sleep, and feed, and know not me.
I cannot rest from travel: I will drink
Life to the lees: all times I have enjoyed
Greatly, have suffered greatly, both with those
That loved me, and alone; on shore, and when
10 Through scudding drifts the rainy Hyades
 Vexed the dim sea: I am become a name;
For always roaming with a hungry heart
Much have I seen and known: cities of men,
And manners, climates, councils, governments,
15 Myself not least, but honored of them all;
And drunk delight of battle with my peers,
Far on the ringing plains of windy Troy.
I am a part of all that I have met;
Yet all experience is an arch wherethrough

19 arch: rainbow.

20 Gleams that untraveled world, whose margin fades
   Forever and forever when I move.
   How dull it is to pause, to make an end,
   To rust unburnished, not to shine in use!
   As though to breathe were life. Life piled on life
25 Were all too little, and of one to me
   Little remains: but every hour is saved
   From that eternal silence, something more,
   A bringer of new things; and vile it were
   For some three suns to store and hoard myself,
30 And this gray spirit yearning in desire
   To follow knowledge like a sinking star,
   Beyond the utmost bound of human thought.
      This is my son, mine own Telemachus,
   To whom I leave the sceptre and the isle—
35 Well-loved of me, discerning to fulfil
   This labor, by slow prudence to make mild
   A rugged people, and through soft degrees
   Subdue them to the useful and the good.
   Most blameless is he, centered in the sphere
40 Of common duties, decent not to fail
   In offices of tenderness, and pay
   Meet adoration to my household gods,
   When I am gone. He works his work, I mine.
      There lies the port; the vessel puffs her sail:
45 There gloom the dark broad seas. My mariners,
   Souls that have toiled, and wrought, and thought with me—
   That ever with a frolic welcome took
   The thunder and the sunshine, and opposed
   Free hearts, free foreheads—you and I are old;
50 Old age hath yet his honor and his toil;
   Death closes all: but something ere the end,
   Some work of noble note, may yet be done,
   Not unbecoming men that strove with gods.
   The lights begin to twinkle from the rocks:
55 The long day wanes: the slow moon climbs: the deep
   Moans round with many voices. Come, my friends,
   'Tis not too late to seek a newer world.
   Push off, and sitting well in order smite
   The sounding furrows; for my purpose holds
60 To sail beyond the sunset, and the baths
   Of all the western stars, until I die.
   It may be that the gulfs will wash us down:
   It may be we shall touch the Happy Isles,
   And see the great Achilles, whom we knew.

---

34 isle: Ithaca, off the western coast of Greece.
63 Happy Isles: one of the Greek ideas of Paradise.

65 Though much is taken, much abides; and though
We are not now that strength which in old days
Moved earth and heaven; that which we are, we are;
One equal temper of heroic hearts,
Made weak by time and fate, but strong in will
70 To strive, to seek, to find, and not to yield.

THE LOVE SONG OF J. ALFRED PRUFROCK

T. S. ELIOT ⟶

From COLLECTED POEMS *1905–1935 by T. S. Eliot.* © *1936 by Harcourt, Brace and Company, Inc. Reprinted with their permission and that of Faber & Faber Ltd.*

S'io credesse che mia risposta fosse
A persona che mai tornasse al mondo,
Questa fiamma staria senza piu scosse.
Ma perciocche giammai di questo fondo
Non torno vivo alcun, s'i'odo il vero,
Senza tema d'infamia ti rispondo.

[If I thought I were answering someone who would ever return to the world, this flame would shake no more, but since no one ever did return alive from this depth (if what I hear is true), I answer you without fear of infamy.   Dante, *Inferno* 27, 61–6.]

Let us go then, you and I,
When the evening is spread out against the sky
Like a patient etherized upon a table;
Let us go, through certain half-deserted streets,
5 The muttering retreats
Of restless nights in one-night cheap hotels
And sawdust restaurants with oyster-shells:
Streets that follow like a tedious argument
Of insidious intent
10 To lead you to an overwhelming question. . . .
Oh, do not ask, "What is it?"
Let us go and make our visit.

In the room the women come and go
Talking of Michelangelo.

15 The yellow fog that rubs its back upon the window-panes,
   The yellow smoke that rubs its muzzle on the window-panes,
   Licked its tongue into the corners of the evening,
   Lingered upon the pools that stand in drains,
   Let fall upon its back the soot that falls from chimneys,
20 Slipped by the terrace, made a sudden leap,
   And seeing that it was a soft October night,
   Curled once about the house, and fell asleep.

   And indeed there will be time
   For the yellow smoke that slides along the street,
25 Rubbing its back upon the window-panes;
   There will be time, there will be time
   To prepare a face to meet the faces that you meet;
   There will be time to murder and create,
   And time for all the works and days of hands
30 That lift and drop a question on your plate;
   Time for you and time for me,
   And time yet for a hundred indecisions,
   And for a hundred visions and revisions,
   Before the taking of a toast and tea.

35 In the room the women come and go
   Talking of Michelangelo.

   And indeed there will be time
   To wonder, "Do I dare?" and, "Do I dare?"
   Time to turn back and descend the stair,
40 With a bald spot in the middle of my hair—
   (They will say: "How his hair is growing thin!")
   My morning coat, my collar mounting firmly to the chin,
   My necktie rich and modest, but asserted by a simple pin—
   (They will say: "But how his arms and legs are thin!")
45 Do I dare
   Disturb the universe?
   In a minute there is time
   For decisions and revisions which a minute will reverse.

   For I have known them all already, known them all:
50 Have known the evenings, mornings, afternoons,
   I have measured out my life with coffee spoons;
   I know the voices dying with a dying fall
   Beneath the music from a farther room.
       So how should I presume?

55 And I have known the eyes already, known them all—
   The eyes that fix you in a formulated phrase,
   And when I am formulated, sprawling on a pin,

When I am pinned and wriggling on the wall,
Then how should I begin
60 To spit out all the butt-ends of my days and ways?
    And how should I presume?

And I have known the arms already, known them all—
Arms that are braceleted and white and bare
(But in the lamplight, downed with light brown hair!)
65 Is it perfume from a dress
That makes me so digress?
Arms that lie along a table, or wrap about a shawl.
    And should I then presume?
    And how should I begin?

            .   .   .   .   .

70 Shall I say, I have gone at dusk through narrow streets
And watched the smoke that rises from the pipes
Of lonely men in shirt-sleeves, leaning out of windows? . . .

I should have been a pair of ragged claws
Scuttling across the floors of silent seas.

            .   .   .   .   .

75 And the afternoon, the evening, sleeps so peacefully!
Smoothed by long fingers,
Asleep . . . tired . . . or it malingers,
Stretched on the floor, here beside you and me.
Should I, after tea and cakes and ices,
80 Have the strength to force the moment to its crisis?
But though I have wept and fasted, wept and prayed,
Though I have seen my head (grown slightly bald) brought in upon a platter,
I am no prophet—and here's no great matter;
I have seen the moment of my greatness flicker,
85 And I have seen the eternal Footman hold my coat, and snicker,
And in short, I was afraid.

And would it have been worth it, after all,
After the cups, the marmalade, the tea,
Among the porcelain, among some talk of you and me,
90 Would it have been worth while,
To have bitten off the matter with a smile,
To have squeezed the universe into a ball
To roll it toward some overwhelming question,
To say: "I am Lazarus, come from the dead,
Come back to tell you all, I shall tell you all"—
If one, settling a pillow by her head,
    Should say: "That is not what I meant at all.
    That is not it, at all."

[82] head: like John the Baptist's in *Gospel of St. Matthew* 14, 11.

And would it have been worth it, after all,
100 Would it have been worth while,
After the sunsets and the dooryards and the sprinkled streets,
After the novels, after the teacups, after the skirts that trail along the floor—
And this, and so much more?—
It is impossible to say just what I mean!
105 But as if a magic lantern threw the nerves in patterns on a screen:
Would it have been worth while
If one, settling a pillow or throwing off a shawl,
And turning toward the window, should say:
    "That is not it at all,
110   That is not what I meant, at all."

    .   .   .   .   .

No! I am not Prince Hamlet, nor was meant to be;
Am an attendant lord, one that will do
To swell a progress, start a scene or two,
Advise the prince; no doubt, an easy tool,
115 Deferential, glad to be of use,
Politic, cautious, and meticulous;
Full of high sentence, but a bit obtuse;
At times, indeed, almost ridiculous—
Almost, at times, the Fool.

120 I grow old. . . . I grow old. . . .
I shall wear the bottoms of my trousers rolled.

Shall I part my hair behind? Do I dare to eat a peach?
I shall wear white flannel trousers, and walk upon the beach.
I have heard the mermaids singing, each to each.

125 I do not think that they will sing to me.

I have seen them riding seaward on the waves
Combing the white hair of the waves blown back
When the wind blows the water white and black.

We have lingered in the chambers of the sea
130 By sea-girls wreathed with seaweed red and brown
Till human voices wake us, and we drown.

[113] progress: procession. [117] sentence: pompous maxims, like those of Polonius in Shakespeare's *Hamlet.*

GERONTION

(1920)

> *Thou hast nor youth nor age,*
> *But as it were an after-dinner sleep,*
> *Dreaming of both. . . .*
> [Shakespeare, *Measure for Measure* III. 1]

Here I am, an old man in a dry month,
Being read to by a boy, waiting for rain.
I was neither at the hot gates
Nor fought in the warm rain
5 Nor knee deep in the salt marsh, heaving a cutlass,
Bitten by flies, fought.
My house is a decayed house,
And the jew squats on the window sill, the owner,
Spawned in some estaminet of Antwerp,
10 Blistered in Brussels, patched and peeled in London.
The goat coughs at night in the field overhead;
Rocks, moss, stone-crop, iron, merds.
The woman keeps the kitchen, makes tea,
Sneezes at evening, poking the peevish gutter.
15   I an old man,
A dull head among windy spaces.

Signs are taken for wonders. "We would see a sign!"
The word within a word, unable to speak a word,
Swaddled with darkness. In the juvescence of the year
20 Came Christ the tiger

In depraved May, dogwood and chestnut, flowering judas,
To be eaten, to be divided, to be drunk
Among whispers; by Mr. Silvero
With caressing hands, at Limoges
25 Who walked all night in the next room;
By Hakagawa, bowing among the Titians;
By Madame de Tornquist, in the dark room
Shifting the candles; Fräulein von Kulp
Who turned in the hall, one hand on the door.
30   Vacant shuttles
Weave the wind. I have no ghosts,
An old man in a draughty house
Under a windy knob.

---

³ hot gates: Thermopylae, where in 480 B. c. a band of Greeks withstood the army of Persia.
⁹ estaminet: cheap bar. ¹² merds: excrement. ¹⁷ sign: i.e. as certain scribes and Pharisees asked to do
in *Gospel of St. Matthew* 12, 38. ¹⁹ juvescence: youth, early part—i.e. after the Last Supper and the
Resurrection had established Christianity.

After such knowledge, what forgiveness? Think now
35 History has many cunning passages, contrived corridors
And issues, deceives with whispering ambitions,
Guides us by vanities. Think now
She gives when our attention is distracted
And what she gives, gives with such supple confusions
40 That the giving famishes the craving. Gives too late
What's not believed in, or if still believed,
In memory only, reconsidered passion. Gives too soon
Into weak hands, what's thought can be dispensed with
Till the refusal propagates a fear. Think
45 Neither fear nor courage saves us. Unnatural vices
Are fathered by our heroism. Virtues
Are forced upon us by our impudent crimes.
These tears are shaken from the wrath-bearing tree.

The tiger springs in the new year. Us he devours. Think at last
50 We have not reached conclusion, when I
Stiffen in a rented house. Think at last
I have not made this show purposelessly
And it is not by any concitation
Of the backward devils.
55 I would meet you upon this honestly.
I that was near your heart was removed therefrom
To lose beauty in terror, terror in inquisition.
I have lost my passion: why should I need to keep it
Since what is kept must be adulterated?
60 I have lost my sight, smell, hearing, taste and touch:
How should I use it for your closer contact?

These with a thousand small deliberations
Protract the profit of their chilled delirium,
Excite the membrane, when the sense has cooled,
65 With pungent sauces, multiply variety
In a wilderness of mirrors. What will the spider do,
Suspend its operations, will the weevil
Delay? De Bailhache, Fresca, Mrs. Cammel, whirled
Beyond the circuit of the shuddering Bear
70 In fractured atoms. Gull against the wind, in the windy straits
Of Belle Isle, or running on the Horn,
White feathers in the snow, the Gulf claims,
And an old man driven by the Trades
To a sleepy corner.

75   Tenants of the house,
        Thoughts of a dry brain in a dry season.

53 concitation: stirring up.

Suggestions

1. † "The Curve of Subjectivity" makes a detailed comparison of "Ulysses" and "Gerontion." After studying it, summarize its distinction between an "objective" character (Ulysses) and a "subjective" one (Gerontion, the "little old man"). Several similarities between "My Last Duchess" and "The Love Song of J. Alfred Prufrock" make possible a corresponding comparison of them. Each implies that its main character has been shaped by the world in which he lives: the Duke of Ferrara by the Italian Renaissance, which reached the height of its power and wealth in the early 16th century; Prufrock by the leisurely metropolitan society of our era, which has rendered him incapable of resolute action. Each poem partly defines its "hero" through references to art: the Duke occupies a commanding position with respect to Pandolf and Claus; Prufrock shrinks from the women's chitchat about Michelangelo, and his habit of expressing himself through literary allusions suggests his lack of self-confidence. The outstanding likeness, however, is that each character is established through his attitude toward women: the Duke is masterful, Prufrock is paralyzed by timidity. His "overwhelming question," whether a proposal of marriage or a less decent one, will never be asked; the words "Love Song" are wholly ironical. Whereas Ulysses and Gerontion act or fail to act in the sphere of war and adventure, the Duke and Prufrock are defined in the sphere of sexual relations.

2. Discuss the following comments fully:

The Duchess is destroyed because the Duke wishes her to be a work of art rather than a human being.

The tone of lines 30, 45, and 56 of "Ulysses" is inappropriate to the speaker's character.

The change of tense at line 87 shows the point at which Prufrock gives up hope of action; from here on he merely rationalizes his failure.

"Gerontion" suggests that modern life is ugly ("decayed house"), lacking in purpose (the inmates of the rooming-house), lacking in real experiences ("being read to"), yearning for a faith, and unwilling to face death and its meaning.

3. Establish the *dramatic situation* of each poem by answering such questions as these: On what occasion are the words supposed to be uttered? To whom, if anyone? Is the speaker standing, sitting, walking, or what? Where and when? In short, explain what the audience would see if the poem were produced on a stage as a play.

4. "The Curve of Subjectivity" implies that the period in which "Ulysses" was written was an objective one. Perhaps so, but the publication of it and "My Last Duchess" in the same year suggests that these poets were decidedly interested in subjective states. It was they who developed the *dramatic monologue* and *dramatic soliloquy*. (*Dramatic* because the words are supposed to proceed not from the poet but from a

character; *monologue* or *soliloquy* because restricted to him. "Ulysses" is one of these, "My Last Duchess" the other. Which is which? This is easy once the dramatic situations are grasped.) These poets knew that everyone tends to "prepare a face to meet the faces that he meets," as Prufrock puts it, and the dramatic method shows the character's inner reality. He presents himself subjectively. Show what is revealed of Ulysses and the Duke that could not be known to a detached observer. What danger of obscurity results from this method?

5. The *metre* of both "Ulysses" and "My Last Duchess" is the ten-syllable *iambic* line, though the first adheres closely to the pattern, while the second is more conversational. This difference reinforces the implied attitude toward each character: unalloyed respect for Ulysses versus the ironic treatment of the Duke, who is self-righteous and revoltingly callous. Both poems, however, are strikingly formal compared with Eliot's, for the metrical freedom of "My Last Duchess" is offset by its *rhymes*. "Prufrock" rhymes irregularly, and its metre, like that of "Gerontion," might be called ten-syllable iambic which continually breaks down in confusion. How do these formal characteristics harmonize with the minds of the characters they help to create?

6. Decide whether the dictum presented in † "The Great Style," that details should bring out an affecting result, applies to each of the four poems. Comment particularly on the following objects: the figurine of Neptune taming a sea-horse; the lights twinkling from the rocks; the novels, teacups, and skirts; the tiger, spider, weevil, and gull.

7. Lines 35–43 of "My Last Duchess," 57–61 of "Ulysses," 111–119 of "Prufrock," and 66–71 of "Gerontion" are perhaps the most emotional passages in each. Identify the emotions, indicating the tone of voice in which you would read each one aloud, and point out other important emotions in the poems.

8. Explain: *officious, munificence, dowry* ("My Last Duchess"); *Hyades, Troy, Achilles* ("Ulysses"); *Michelangelo, Footman, Lazarus, Fool* ("Prufrock"); *stonecrop, Titians, Bear, Belle Isle* ("Gerontion").

9. † "The Curve of Subjectivity" considers the theme of "Gerontion" to be "exhausted subjectivity." Is this also the theme of "Prufrock"? Show that it applies more nearly to "Ulysses" than it does to "My Last Duchess."

10. Clearly an "objective" character may nevertheless be a great egotist. Decide which poem has the most egotistical hero.

11. Write an essay showing which phrases in lines 65–70 of "Ulysses" can be applied to the hero of each of the other poems.

LONDON

WILLIAM BLAKE --- *From* SONGS OF EXPERIENCE, *1794.*

I wander through each chartered street
Near where the chartered Thames does flow
And mark in every face I meet
Marks of weakness, marks of woe.

5 In every cry of every man,
In every infant's cry of fear,
In every voice, in every ban,
The mind-forged manacles I hear.

How the chimney-sweeper's cry
10 Every blackening church appalls,
And the hapless soldier's sigh
Runs in blood down palace walls.

But most, through midnight streets I hear
How the youthful harlot's curse
15 Blasts the newborn infant's tear
And blights with plagues the marriage-hearse.

COMPOSED UPON WESTMINSTER BRIDGE

WILLIAM WORDSWORTH --- *From* POEMS IN TWO VOLUMES, *1807.*

Earth has not anything to show more fair:
Dull would he be of soul who could pass by
A sight so touching in its majesty:
This city now doth like a garment wear
5 The beauty of the morning; silent, bare,
Ships, towers, domes, theatres, and temples lie
Open unto the fields, and to the sky;
All bright and glittering in the smokeless air.

662

Never did sun more beautifully steep
10 In his first splendor, valley, rock, or hill;
Ne'er saw I, never felt, a calm so deep!
The river glideth at his own sweet will:
Dear God! the very houses seem asleep,
And all that mighty heart is lying still!

DOVER BEACH

MATTHEW ARNOLD ---⟨ *From* NEW POEMS, *1867*.

The sea is calm tonight,
The tide is full, the moon lies fair
Upon the Straits; on the French coast, the light
Gleams and is gone; the cliffs of England stand,
5 Glimmering and vast, out in the tranquil bay.
Come to the window, sweet is the night air!
Only, from the long line of spray
Where the sea meets the moon-blanched land,
Listen! you hear the grating roar
10 Of pebbles which the waves draw back, and fling,
At their return, up the high strand,
Begin, and cease, and then again begin,
With tremulous cadence slow, and bring
The eternal note of sadness in.

15 Sophocles long ago
Heard it on the Ægean, and it brought
Into his mind the turbid ebb and flow
Of human misery; we
Find also in the sound a thought,
20 Hearing it by this distant northern sea.

The Sea of Faith
Was once, too, at the full, and round earth's shore
Lay like the folds of a bright girdle furled;
But now I only hear
25 Its melancholy, long, withdrawing roar,
Retreating to the breath
Of the night-wind down the vast edges drear
And naked shingles of the world.

---

¹⁸ misery: supposedly an allusion to Ode II in *Antigone,* one of the seven surviving tragedies of the Greek playwright Sophocles (496–406 B. C.). ²¹ Faith: religious belief; for its decline in the 19th century, see † "The Curve of Subjectivity."

Ah, love, let us be true
30 To one another! for the world, which seems
To lie before us like a land of dreams,
So various, so beautiful, so new,
Hath really neither joy, nor love, nor light,
Nor certitude, nor peace, nor help for pain;
35 And we are here as on a darkling plain
Swept with confused alarms of struggle and flight,
Where ignorant armies clash by night.

ANTIQUE HARVESTERS

JOHN CROWE RANSOM ⸱⸱⸱⸱

Reprinted from SELECTED POEMS *by John Crowe Ransom, by permission of Alfred A. Knopf, Inc.* © *1924, 1927, 1945 by Alfred A. Knopf, Inc.*

SCENE: *Of the Mississippi the bank sinister, and of the Ohio the bank sinister*

Tawny are the leaves turned but they still hold,
And it is harvest; what shall this land produce?
A meager hill of kernels, a runnel of juice;
Declension looks from our land, it is old.
5 Therefore let us assemble, dry, grey, spare,
And mild as yellow air.

"I hear the croak of a raven's funeral wing."
The young men would be joying in the song
Of passionate birds; their memories are not long.
10 What is it thus rehearsed in sable? "Nothing."
Trust not but the old endure, and shall be bolder
Than the scornful beholder.

We pluck the spindling ears and gather the corn.
One spot has special yield? "On this spot stood
15 Heroes and drenched it with their only blood."
And talk meets talk, as echoes from the horn
Of the hunter—echoes are the old men's arts,
Ample are the chambers of their hearts.

Here come the hunters, keepers of a rite;
20 The horn, the hounds, the lank mares coursing by

SCENE: *Kentucky and the states south of it.*

Straddled with archetypes of chivalry;
And the fox, lovely ritualist, in flight
Offering his unearthly ghost to quarry;
And the fields, themselves to harry.

25 Resume, harvesters. The treasure is full bronze
Which you will garner for the Lady, and the moon
Could tinge it no yellower than does this noon;
But the grey will quench it shortly—the fields, men, stones.
Pluck fast, dreamers; prove as you amble slowly
30 Not less than men, not wholly.

Bare the arm, dainty youths, bend the knees
Under bronze burdens. And by an autumn tone
As by a grey, as by a green, you will have known
Your famous Lady's image; for so have these;
35 And if one say that easily will your hands
More prosper in other lands,

Angry as wasp-music be your cry then:
"Forsake the Proud Lady, of the heart of fire,
The look of snow, to the praise of a dwindled choir,
40 Song of degenerate specters that were men?
The sons of the fathers shall keep her, worthy of
What these have done in love."

True, it is said of our Lady, she ageth.
But see, if you peep shrewdly, she hath not stooped;
45 Take no thought of her servitors that have drooped,
For we are nothing; and if one talk of death—
Why, the ribs of the earth subsist frail as a breath
If but God wearieth.

Suggestions

1. Poems of places, like the prose descriptions to which they correspond, are not mere photography. A literary work must have at least one kind of interest—human interest; and in a poem on a place it centers in the people associated with the place and in the speaker's emotions about it and them. This is obviously true of the first and last poems in this group: Blake views London as a place of human weakness and woe, and Ransom celebrates the affection binding the southern farmers (*antique* because engaged in a continuing, traditional activity) to the countryside. The statement may not seem to apply to the other two, for Wordsworth admires London at a time when its people are invisible, and the seascape in "Dover Beach" is described from a point too remote for

the inclusion of human beings. Yet "Composed upon Westminster Bridge" implies an attitude toward the normal, workaday London that is identical with Blake's, albeit presented obliquely instead of directly. Only at sunrise is the city fair and majestic, for only then is the ugliness of its smoky air and its people's bustling activity disguised by a garment of beauty. In "Dover Beach" the speaker's interest passes from the scene itself to the two kinds of human experience that it symbolizes. The visual images, which are *calm, fair, glimmering,* correspond to the innocent's anticipations of the mature world (lines 30–31); and the auditory images—*grating, tremulous, turbid*—reveal the world's true nature (lines 33ff).

2. "London" is a poem of outrage over the exploitation of the weak many by the powerful few; hence the expression *mind-forged manacles. Chartered* has at least two meanings—roughly *mapped out* and *monopolized*—one literally descriptive, the other emotive. Find other examples of this verbal strategy: e.g. *cry (street-cries)* and *blackening.* The emotive meaning of *blackening* shows that the misery of London is not confined to its poor, for the churches, disgraced by the suffering that they condone, are incapable of performing their function for the members of any class. Point out other examples of how the misery of the weak affects the powerful.

3. "Composed upon Westminster Bridge" is a perfect example of an *Italian* or *Petrarchan sonnet,* of which the chief structural characteristic is the contrast between *octave* and *sestet.* Can it be said that the octave of this sonnet is "objective," the sestet relatively "subjective"?

4. "Dover Beach" concludes with a simile, probably inspired by the description of the Battle of Epipolae in *The Peloponnesian War* (VII, 43–44) by Thucydides (c. 460–c. 400 B.C.). As an analogy for modern life it is supposed to reflect the publication of Darwin's *Origin of Species* eight years earlier. Discuss this supposition with the help of † "Evolution." As a forcible climax for the poem, how do the lines compare with the conclusions of "London" and "Westminster Bridge"?

5. The specified scene of "Antique Harvesters," along with the references to cornfields, a battle-ground, and fox-hunting, shows that *the Lady* (line 26) means The South. This way of speaking is relatively obscure, but the obscurity is offset by the added meaning, particularly of an emotional sort. E.g. such a use of *Lady* has religious associations, as in "Our Lady." Discuss fully, comparing the personification with that in † "To Autumn."

6. Three of these poems have interesting textual histories. The last paragraph of "Dover Beach" was written first and later united with the other lines. Are the two parts perfectly congruent? Like two of the other poems, "Dover Beach" also underwent revision after it was first printed. Decide whether or not the following changes are improvements:

"London": *chartered* was originally *dirty* in both lines, and the last stanza was

> But most the midnight harlot's curse
> From dismal street I hear,
> Weaves around the marriage hearse
> And blasts the newborn infant's tear.

(Does the stronger climax justify reversing the logical order of marriage and infant?)

"Dover Beach": the earlier version of lines 8–10 was

> Where the ebb meets the moon-blanched sand,
> Listen! you hear the grating roar
> Of pebbles which the waves suck back, and fling. . . .

"Antique Harvesters": the last stanza was added between 1927 and 1945.

7. With which of the essays in Part 2, pages 65–86, can the poems on London be most usefully compared? Base your comparison on the attitudes of the speakers toward the metropolis, and on the management of descriptive detail.

8. Technically, i.e. as to metre and rhyme, "Dover Beach" resembles † "The Love Song of J. Alfred Prufrock" and † "Gerontion." Are the irregularities of "Dover Beach" equally justified by being suited to the subject-matter?

9. Explain: *marriage-hearse* ("London"); *Aegean, northern sea, shingles* ("Dover Beach"); *Declension, sable, archetypes* ("Antique Harvesters").

10. Write an essay comparing "Antique Harvesters" with † "The Village." Note especially the contrasting attitudes of Ransom and Thoreau toward their native regions.

ODE TO A NIGHTINGALE

JOHN KEATS —⋖{ *First published in* ANNALS OF THE FINE ARTS, *July, 1819.*

> My heart aches, and a drowsy numbness pains
>   My sense, as though of hemlock I had drunk,
> Or emptied some dull opiate to the drains
>   One minute past, and Lethe-wards had sunk:
> 5 'Tis not through envy of thy happy lot,
>   But being too happy in thine happiness—

³ drains: dregs. ⁴ Lethe-wards: to oblivion.

That thou, light-winged dryad of the trees,
In some melodious plot
Of beechen green, and shadows numberless,
10 Singest of summer in full-throated ease.

O for a draught of vintage! that hath been
Cooled a long age in the deep-delvèd earth,
Tasting of Flora and the country green,
Dance, and Provençal song, and sunburnt mirth!
15 O for a beaker full of the warm South,
Full of the true, the blushful Hippocrene,
With beaded bubbles winking at the brim,
And purple-stainèd mouth;
That I might drink, and leave the world unseen,
20 And with thee fade away into the forest dim:

Fade far away, dissolve, and quite forget
What thou among the leaves hast never known,
The weariness, the fever, and the fret
Here, where men sit and hear each other groan;
25 Where palsy shakes a few, sad, last gray hairs,
Where youth grows pale, and specter-thin, and dies;
Where but to think is to be full of sorrow
And leaden-eyed despairs,
Where beauty cannot keep her lustrous eyes,
30 Or new love pine at them beyond tomorrow.

Away! away! for I will fly to thee,
Not charioted by Bacchus and his pards,
But on the viewless wings of poesy,
Though the dull brain perplexes and retards:
35 Already with thee! tender is the night,
And haply the Queen-Moon is on her throne,
Clustered around by all her starry fays;
But here there is no light,
Save what from heaven is with the breezes blown
40 Through verdurous glooms and winding mossy ways.

I cannot see what flowers are at my feet,
Nor what soft incense hangs upon the boughs,
But, in embalmèd darkness, guess each sweet
Wherewith the seasonable month endows
45 The grass, the thicket, and the fruit-tree wild;
White hawthorn and the pastoral eglantine;
Fast-fading violets covered up in leaves;
And mid-May's eldest child,
The coming musk-rose, full of dewy wine,
50   The murmurous haunt of flies on summer eves.

---

³³ pards: leopards.
⁶⁴ clown: peasant. ⁶⁷ corn: wheat—see *The Book of Ruth* 2, 2–3.

Darkling I listen; and, for many a time
I have been half in love with easeful death,
Called him soft names in many a mused rhyme,
To take into the air my quiet breath;
55 Now more than ever seems it rich to die,
To cease upon the midnight with no pain,
While thou art pouring forth thy soul abroad
In such an ecstasy!
Still wouldst thou sing, and I have ears in vain—
60 To thy high requiem become a sod.

Thou wast not born for death, immortal bird!
No hungry generations tread thee down;
The voice I hear this passing night was heard
In ancient days by emperor and clown:
65 Perhaps the self-same song that found a path
Through the sad heart of Ruth, when, sick for home,
She stood in tears amid the alien corn:
The same that oft-times hath
Charmed magic casements, opening on the foam
70 Of perilous seas, in faery lands forlorn.

Forlorn! the very word is like a bell
To toll me back from thee to my sole self!
Adieu! the fancy cannot cheat so well
As she is famed to do, deceiving elf.
75 Adieu! adieu! thy plaintive anthem fades
Past the near meadows, over the still stream,
Up the hill-side; and now 'tis buried deep
In the next valley-glades:
Was it a vision, or a waking dream?
80 Fled is that music.—Do I wake or sleep?

TO AUTUMN

From LAMIA, ISABELLA, THE EVE OF ST. AGNES, AND OTHER POEMS, *1820*.

Season of mists and mellow fruitfulness,
Close bosom friend of the maturing sun:
Conspiring with him how to load and bless
With fruit the vines that round the thatch-eves run;
5 To bend with apples the mossed cottage-trees
And fill all fruit with ripeness to the core;

To swell the gourd and plump the hazel shells
With a sweet kernel; to set budding more,
And still more, later flowers for the bees
10 Until they think warm days will never cease,
For Summer has o'er-brimmed their clammy cells.

Who hath not seen thee oft amid thy store?
Sometimes whoever seeks abroad may find
Thee sitting careless on a granary floor,
15 Thy hair soft-lifted by the winnowing wind;
Or on a half-reaped furrow sound asleep,
Drowsed with the fume of poppies, while thy hook
Spares the next swath and all its twinèd flowers:
And sometimes like a gleaner thou dost keep
20 Steady thy laden head across a brook;
Or by a cider-press, with patient look,
Thou watchest the last oozings hours by hours.

Where are the songs of Spring? Ay, where are they?
Think not of them, thou hast thy music too—
25 While barrèd clouds bloom the soft-dying day
And touch the stubble-plains with rosy hue;
Then in a wailful choir the small gnats mourn
Among the river sallows, borne aloft
Or sinking as the light wind lives or dies;
And full-grown lambs loud bleat from hilly bourn;
31 Hedge-crickets sing: and now with treble soft
The red-breast whistles from a garden-croft;
And gathering swallows twitter in the skies.

TEARS, IDLE TEARS

ALFRED, LORD TENNYSON ⸺⸏ *From* THE PRINCESS, *1847.*

Tears, idle tears, I know not what they mean,
Tears from the depth of some divine despair
Rise in the heart and gather to the eyes,
In looking on the happy autumn-fields,
5 And thinking of the days that are no more.

Fresh as the first beam glittering on a sail
That brings our friends up from the underworld,
Sad as the last which reddens over one
That sinks with all we love below the verge;
10 So sad, so fresh, the days that are no more.

Ah, sad and strange as in dark summer dawns
The earliest pipe of half-awakened birds
To dying ears, when unto dying eyes
The casement slowly grows a glimmering square;
15 So sad, so strange, the days that are no more.

Dear as remembered kisses after death,
And sweet as those by hopeless fancy feigned
On lips that are for others; deep as love,
Deep as first love, and wild with all regret;
20 O Death in Life, the days that are no more!

WINTER REMEMBERED

JOHN CROWE RANSOM

Reprinted from SELECTED POEMS *by John Crowe Ransom, by permission of Alfred A. Knopf, Inc.* © *1924, 1927, 1945 by Alfred A. Knopf, Inc.*

Two evils, monstrous either one apart,
Possessed me, and were long and loath at going:
A cry of Absence, Absence, in the heart,
And in the wood the furious winter blowing.

5 Think not, when fire was bright upon my bricks,
And past the tight boards hardly a wind could enter,
I glowed like them, the simple burning sticks,
Far from my cause, my proper heat and center.

Better to walk forth in the murderous air
10 And wash my wound in the snows; that would be healing;
Because my heart would throb less painful there,
Being caked with cold, and past the smart of feeling.

And where I went, the hugest winter blast
Would have this body bowed, these eyeballs streaming,
15 And though I think this heart's blood froze not fast,
It ran too small to spare one drop for dreaming.

Dear love, these fingers that had known your touch,
And tied our separate forces first together,
Were ten poor idiot fingers not worth much,
20 Ten frozen parsnips hanging in the weather.

Suggestions

1. "To Autumn" is less obviously a poem about an experience than "Ode to a Nightingale" is, yet it corresponds to it and shows that the same poet may, in different moods, express almost opposite emotions in response to similar experiences. All four poems in this group are *mutability* poems: their theme is change, or loss, conceived of as one of the deepest facts of human experience. The "Ode" begins by naming the emotions of the speaker as he imagines that the nightingale's song symbolizes a realm of unchanging beauty (lines 61–70), the reverse of the actual world of sorrow, illness, and death (lines 21–30) in which he himself is imprisoned. Despite his temporary success in uniting himself to the immutable, in the end the dying away of the song returns him to reality and to the emotions that he experienced at the beginning. The experience of the "Autumn" speaker is also saturated with the facts of change: change of the seasons (stanza I describes a farm at the very end of summer, II concerns autumn in its full maturity, and III glances back at the vanished beauty of spring); of the day (the mists of stanza I suggest early morning, the activities of II are those of midday, and in III the day is dying); and in human life (because of the series *soft-dying . . . wailful . . . mourn . . . sinking* in III). Yet in this poem the human experience is absorbed into the cosmic cycle that gives the year its maturity, the sunset its beauty, and so on, so that in place of the anguish expressed by the speaker in the "Ode," the tone of "To Autumn" is one of joy in the season's mellow fruitfulness and reconciliation with the process that of course includes the human being.

2. Your dictionary gives several synonyms for the adjective *idle*. Which is closest to the meaning of *"idle* tears"? Is any of them wholly irrelevant? To what extent may lines 4–5 have been influenced by Tennyson's reading of Keats? *The days that are no more* may obviously be *sad,* but what is the force of calling them *fresh, strange,* and *wild*? After explaining the paradox *Death in Life,* line 20, decide whether the implied question of line 1 is answered as the poem develops.

3. To a greater extent than "Tears, Idle Tears," "Winter Remembered" is a poem about love. Has the second lover been more successful than the first? (Consider Ransom's title in relation to the last stanza. Does this title recall any passage in "Tears, Idle Tears"?) "Winter Remembered" is notable for its *tactile images.* Analyze these (the cold-hot contrast) ; then estimate the effectiveness of the poem as a compliment to a loved person. If *parsnips* is an unusual word for a poem, particularly at the climax, is its inclusion justified by its expressiveness of the lover's emotions?

4. In line 21 of the "Ode," *Fade* is echoed from the previous line. This kind of transition suggests that the speaker is in what state of mind? (Compare † "Dream Children.") What similar transitions can you point out later in the "Ode"? Distinguish the three means by which the speaker considers uniting himself with the nightingale. What is the objection to each one? Discuss lines 73–74 as a comment on the foregoing stanza.

5. Keats's imagery is mainly visual, yet the suggestion of pregnancy in the opening lines of "To Autumn" is extended by the sense of heaviness in the images that follow. Analyze the metaphors and images of the poem, distinguishing the visual effects from other kinds, such as auditory and tactile. Show how the personification of autumn in line 2 receives detailed development in the next stanza.

6. Write an essay on the importance of reverie as a human activity, showing that the structure of the "Ode" and of "Tears, Idle Tears" is like that of reverie to a greater extent than those of the other two poems are.

7. Explain: *hemlock, dryad, Flora, Provençal, Hippocrene, charioted by Bacchus, viewless, fays, requiem, forlorn* ("Ode to a Nightingale"); *gleaner, stubble-plains, sallows, bourn, garden-croft* ("To Autumn").

SIR PATRICK SPENS

ANONYMOUS —⋙ First published in RELIQUES OF ANCIENT ENGLISH POETRY, 1765.

The king sits in Dumferling toune,
Drinking the blude-reid wine:
"O whar will I get guid sailor,
To sail this schip of mine?"

5 Up and spak an eldern knicht,
Sat at the kings richt kne:
"Sir Patrick Spens is the best sailor,
That sails upon the se."

The king has written a braid letter,
10 And signed it wi his hand,
And sent it to Sir Patrick Spens,
Was walking on the sand.

¹ Dumferling: Dumferline, in southeast Scotland. ⁵ eldern: elderly. ⁶ richt: right. ⁹ braid: broad, on large paper.

The first line that Sir Patrick red,
A loud lauch lauchèd he;
15 The next line that Sir Patrick red,
The teir blinded his ee.

"O wha is this has don this deid,
This ill deid don to me,
To send me out this time o' the yeir,
20   To sail upon the se!

"Mak hast, mak haste, my mirry men all,
Our guid schip sails the morne."
"O say na sae, my master deir,
For I feir a deadlie storme.

25 "Late, late yestreen I saw the new moone,
Wi the auld moone in hir arme,
And I feir, I feir, my deir master,
That we will cum to harme."

O our Scots nobles wer richt laith
30   To weet their cork-heild schoone;
Bot lang owre a' the play wer playd,
Their hats they swam aboone.

O lang, lang may their ladies sit,
Wi thair fans into their hand,
35 Or eir they se Sir Patrick Spens
Cum sailing to the land.

O lang, lang may the ladies stand,
Wi thair gold kems in their hair,
Waiting for thar ain deir lords,
40   For they'll se thame na mair.

Haf owre, haf owre to Aberdour,
It's fiftie fadom deip,
And thair lies guid Sir Patrick Spens,
Wi the Scots lords at his feit.

---

14 lauch: laugh. 17 wha: who. 23 sae: so. 25 yestreen: last evening. 29 laith: unwilling. 30 schoone: shoes. 31 owre a': before all. 32 aboone: above. 35 Or eir: Before ever. 38 kems: combs. 40 mair: more. 41 Haf owre: halfway back.

THE TWA CORBIES

ANONYMOUS — *First published in* THE MINSTRELSEY OF THE SCOTTISH BORDER, *1803*

As I was walking all alane,
I heard twa corbies making a mane—
The tane unto the t'other say,
"Where sall we gang and dine today?"

5 "In behint yon auld fail dyke,
I wot there lies a new-slain knight;
And naebody kens that he lies there,
But his hawk, his hound, and lady fair.

"His hound is to the hunting gane,
10 His hawk to fetch the wild-fowl hame,
His lady's ta'en another mate,
So we may mak our dinner sweet.

"Ye'll sit on his white hause-bane,
And I'll pick out his bonny blue een;
15 Wi ae lock o' his gowden hair
We'll theek our nest when it grows bare.

"Mony a one for him makes mane,
But nane sall ken where he is gane;
O'er his white banes when they are bare,
20 The wind sall blaw for evermair."

CORBIES: crows. 1 alane: alone. 2 mane: moan, i.e. conversing. 3 tane: one. 4 gang: go. 5 auld fail dyke: old turf wall. 13 hause-bane: neck-bone. 14 een: eyes. 15 ae: one; gowden: golden. 16 theek: thatch.

675

BROWN'S DESCENT

ROBERT FROST

From COMPLETE POEMS OF ROBERT FROST.
© *1930, 1949 by Henry Holt & Co.,
Inc. By permission of the publishers.*

or, *The Willy-nilly Slide*

Brown lived at such a lofty farm
 That everyone for miles could see
His lantern when he did his chores
 In winter after half-past three.

5 And many must have seen him make
 His wild descent from there one night,
'Cross lots, 'cross walls, 'cross everything,
 Describing rings of lantern light.

Between the house and barn the gale
10 Got him by something he had on
And blew him out on the icy crust
 That cased the world, and he was gone!

Walls were all buried, trees were few:
 He saw no stay unless he stove
15 A hole in somewhere with his heel.
 But though repeatedly he strove

And stamped and said things to himself,
 And sometimes something seemed to yield,
He gained no foothold, but pursued
20 His journey down from field to field.

Sometimes he came with arms outspread
 Like wings revolving in the scene
Upon his longer axis, and
 With no small dignity of mien.

25 Faster or slower as he chanced,
 Sitting or standing as he chose,
According as he feared to risk
 His neck, or thought to spare his clothes,

He never let the lantern drop.
30 And some exclaimed who saw afar
The figure he described with it,
 "I wonder what those signals are

676

"Brown makes at such an hour of night!
  He's celebrating something strange.
35 I wonder if he's sold his farm,
  Or been made Master of the Grange."

He reeled, he lurched, he bobbed, he checked;
  He fell and made the lantern rattle
(But saved the light from going out).
40   So half-way down he fought the battle

Incredulous of his own bad luck.
  And then becoming reconciled
To everything, he gave it up
  And came down like a coasting child.

45 "Well—I—be—" that was all he said,
  As standing in the river road,
He looked back up the slippery slope
  (Two miles it was) to his abode.

Sometimes as an authority
50   On motor-cars, I'm asked if I
Should say our stock was petered out,
  And this is my sincere reply:

Yankees are what they always were.
  Don't think Brown ever gave up hope
55 Of getting home again because
  He couldn't climb that slippery slope;

Or even thought of standing there
  Until the January thaw
Should take the polish off the crust.
60   He bowed with grace to natural law,

And then went round it on his feet,
  After the manner of our stock;
Not much concerned for those to whom,
  At that particular time o'clock,

65 It must have looked as if the course
  He steered was really straight away
From that which he was headed for—
  Not much concerned for them, I say,

But now he snapped his eyes three times;
70   Then shook his lantern, saying, "Ile's
'Bout out!" and took the long way home
  By road, a matter of several miles.

70 Ile: Oil.

MR. FLOOD'S PARTY

**EDWIN
ARLINGTON ROBINSON** ---⚓ *From* COLLECTED POEMS. *Reprinted by
permission of The Macmillan Com-
pany.*

Old Eben Flood, climbing alone one night
Over the hill between the town below
And the forsaken upland hermitage
That held as much as he should ever know
5 On earth again of home, paused warily.
The road was his with not a native near;
And Eben, having leisure, said aloud,
For no man else in Tilbury Town to hear:

"Well, Mr. Flood, we have the harvest moon
10 Again, and we may not have many more;
The bird is on the wing, the poet says,
And you and I have said it here before.
Drink to the bird." He raised up to the light
The jug that he had gone so far to fill,
15 And answered huskily: "Well, Mr. Flood,
Since you propose it, I believe I will."

Alone, as if enduring to the end
A valiant armor of scarred hopes outworn,
He stood there in the middle of the road
20 Like Roland's ghost winding a silent horn.
Below him, in the town among the trees,
Where friends of other days had honored him,
A phantom salutation of the dead
Rang thinly till old Eben's eyes were dim.

25 Then, as a mother lays her sleeping child
Down tenderly, fearing it may awake,
He set the jug down slowly at his feet
With trembling care, knowing that most things break;
And only when assured that on firm earth
30 It stood, as the uncertain lives of men
Assuredly did not, he paced away,
And with his hand extended paused again:

"Well, Mr. Flood, we have not met like this
In a long time; and many a change has come
35 To both of us, I fear, since last it was

---

* Tilbury: an imagined New England town. ¹¹ poet: Edward Fitzgerald, in *The Rubáiyát of Omar
Khayyám*, line 28. ²⁰ Roland: Charlemagne's knight who in *The Song of Roland* thus tries vainly
to summon help when ambushed at Roncesvalles in 778.

We had a drop together. Welcome home!"
Convivially returning with himself,
Again he raised the jug up to the light;
And with an acquiescent quaver said:
40 "Well, Mr. Flood, if you insist, I might.

"Only a very little, Mr. Flood—
For auld lang syne. No more, sir; that will do."
So, for the time, apparently it did,
And Eben evidently thought so too;
45 For soon amid the silver loneliness
Of night he lifted up his voice and sang,
Secure, with only two moons listening,
Until the whole harmonious landscape rang—

"For auld lang syne." The weary throat gave out,
50 The last word wavered; and the song being done,
He raised again the jug regretfully
And shook his head, and was again alone.
There was not much that was ahead of him,
And there was nothing in the town below—
55 Where strangers would have shut the many doors
That many friends had opened long ago.

Suggestions

1. The difference between poems we have called Experiences and poems of events is a narrow one, determined only by the degree of detachment in the speaker's point of view. *Point of view* is here meant technically, as in the comments on short stories, for "Sir Patrick Spens" and these other three poems are obviously stories in verse. Their total meanings depend upon their telling, and many readers, though they easily grasp the incidents, will overlook the speakers' feelings about the stories unless they pay attention to the points of view.

2. Identify the metre and rhyme of "Spens"; they make up what is called the *ballad-stanza*. Scan the other three poems and decide which ones are written in modifications of this form. Characteristically, ballads are impersonal in their method of telling; they suggest the attitude of a whole group toward the narrated events. Can it be said that "Mr. Flood's Party" is the least ballad-like of the four poems in both form and point of view?

3. In "Spens" the speaker's feelings are implied in the contrast of the nobles and the sailors: the poem plays off the folly of the king and the absurdity of the nobles, with their dressy shoes, against the expertness and dutifulness of Spens. (How are the ladies involved in this contrast?

Consider their properties and the change of *sit,* line 33, to *stand,* line 37.)
Yet the lack of comment suggests that the speaker is resigned to such contrasts and the catastrophes they bring about. In "The Twa Corbies"
there is an absence of contrast between the cruelty of nature (the crows
and the wind) and the knight's "retainers," so to speak. Is this speaker
as much resigned to the harsh facts of life as the speaker in "Spens" is?

4. Frost's humorous tone begins to establish itself in his very title, by
the contrast between the formal word *Descent* and the homely, offhand
subtitle. (Compare the formality of lines 22–24 and the simile in line 44.)
The humor is extended by the irony of lines 49–51; irony at whose expense? Summarize the qualities that are said to be characteristic of
Yankees; then decide whether the humorous tone is suitable to so serious
a thesis.

5. "Mr. Flood's Party" is also humorous in part, beginning with its
title, and its humor arises both from its events and from a simile (lines
25–26). Show that the humor helps to balance a potentially sentimental
situation by writing a comparison of the poem and † "Snapshot of a
Dog." What passages are most important for the *motivation* of Mr.
Flood? Analyze the figures of speech in stanza III. Can *hopes* be successfully likened to *armor?*

6. Explain: *hermitage, acquiescent, auld lang syne* ("Mr. Flood's
Party").

7. Write an essay comparing "Brown's Descent" and "Mr. Flood's
Party." Which poem has the more detached observer? Are there symbolic
overtones in Brown's fall and Flood's climb?

8. Write an essay showing that all four poems may be called mutability
poems, like those in the previous group. Make precise distinctions among
the various treatments of the theme.

SONNETS

WILLIAM SHAKESPEARE ⟩ *From* SHAKESPEARE'S SONNETS, *1609.*

55

Not marble nor the gilded monuments
Of princes shall outlive this powerful rhyme;
But you shall shine more bright in these contents
Than unswept stone, besmeared with sluttish time.
5 When wasteful war shall statues overturn,

And broils root out the work of masonry,
Nor Mars his sword nor war's quick fire shall burn
The living record of your memory.
'Gainst death and all-oblivious enmity
10 Shall you pace forth; your praise shall still find room
Even in the eyes of all posterity
That wear this world out to the ending doom.
 So till the Judgment, that yourself arise,
 You live in this, and dwell in lovers' eyes.

64

When I have seen by Time's fell hand defaced
The rich proud cost of outworn buried age;
When sometime-lofty towers I see down razed,
And brass eternal slave to mortal rage;
5 When I have seen the hungry ocean gain
Advantage on the kingdom of the shore,
And the firm soil win of the watery main,
Increasing store with loss, and loss with store;
When I have seen such interchange of state,
10 Or state itself confounded, to decay;
Ruin hath taught me thus to ruminate,
That Time will come and take my love away.
 This thought is as a death, which cannot choose
 But weep to have that which it fears to lose.

73

That time of year thou mayst in me behold
When yellow leaves, or none, or few, do hang
Upon those boughs which shake against the cold,
Bare ruined choirs, where late the sweet birds sang.
5 In me thou seest the twilight of such day
As after sunset fadeth in the west,
Which by and by black night doth take away,
Death's second self, that seals up all in rest:
In me thou seest the glowing of such fire
10 That on the ashes of his youth doth lie,

SONNET 55. ¹³ that: when. SONNET 64. ¹⁰ State: high rank. SONNET 73. ⁴ choirs: choir-stalls. ⁷ by and by: immediately.

As the death-bed whereon it must expire,
Consumed with that which it was nourished by.
This thou perceivest, which makes thy love more strong
To love that well which thou must leave ere long.

DEATH

EMILY DICKINSON ⟶

From POEMS BY EMILY DICKINSON, *ed. by Martha Dickinson Bianchi. Reprinted by permission of Little, Brown and Co.*

Because I could not stop for Death,
He kindly stopped for me;
The carriage held but just ourselves
And immortality.

5 We slowly drove, he knew no haste,
And I had put away
My labor, and my leisure too,
For his civility.

We passed the school where children played,
10 At wrestling in a ring;
We passed the fields of gazing grain,
We passed the setting sun.

We paused before a house that seemed
A swelling of the ground;
15 The roof was scarcely visible,
The cornice but a mound.

Since then 'tis centuries; but each
Feels shorter than the day
I first surmised the horses' heads
20 Were toward eternity.

12 consumed with: put out by.

THE SECOND COMING

WILLIAM BUTLER YEATS *From* COLLECTED POEMS. *Reprinted by permission of The Macmillan Company, Mrs. Yeats, and The Macmillan Company of Canada.*

Turning and turning in the widening gyre
The falcon cannot hear the falconer;
Things fall apart; the centre cannot hold;
Mere anarchy is loosed upon the world,
5 The blood-dimmed tide is loosed, and everywhere
The ceremony of innocence is drowned;
The best lack all conviction, while the worst
Are full of passionate intensity.

Surely some revelation is at hand;
10 Surely the Second Coming is at hand.
The Second Coming! Hardly are those words out
When a vast image out of *Spiritus Mundi*
Troubles my sight: somewhere in sands of the desert
A shape with lion body and the head of a man,
15 A gaze blank and pitiless as the sun,
Is moving its slow thighs, while all about it
Reel shadows of the indignant desert birds.
The darkness drops again; but now I know
That twenty centuries of stony sleep
20 Were vexed to nightmare by a rocking cradle,
And what rough beast, its hour come round at last,
Slouches towards Bethlehem to be born?

SAILING TO BYZANTIUM

I

That is no country for old men. The young
In one another's arms, birds in the trees,

THE SECOND COMING. ¹ gyre: Yeats said "ghire." ¹² *Spiritus Mundi:* World Spirit, the race's memory.
SAILING TO BYZANTIUM. ¹ That: The physical world, as described in the next sentence.
683

—Those dying generations—at their song,
The salmon-falls, the mackerel-crowded seas,
5 Fish, flesh, or fowl, commend all summer long
Whatever is begotten, born, and dies.
Caught in that sensual music all neglect
Monuments of unaging intellect.

II

An aged man is but a paltry thing,
10 A tattered coat upon a stick, unless
Soul clap its hands and sing, and louder sing
For every tatter in its mortal dress,
Nor is there singing school but studying
Monuments of its own magnificence;
15 And therefore I have sailed the seas and come
To the holy city of Byzantium.

III

O sages standing in God's holy fire
As in the gold mosaic of a wall,
Come from the holy fire, perne in a gyre,
20 And be the singing-masters of my soul.
Consume my heart away; sick with desire
And fastened to a dying animal
It knows not what it is; and gather me
Into the artifice of eternity.

IV

25 Once out of nature I shall never take
My bodily form from any natural thing,
But such a form as Grecian goldsmiths make
Of hammered gold and gold enameling
To keep a drowsy Emperor awake;
30 Or set upon a golden bough to sing
To lords and ladies of Byzantium
Of what is past, or passing, or to come.

Suggestions

1. The past-present-future process, the most significant one in human experience, forces itself on our attention by our knowledge that we are part of "Whatever is begotten, born, and dies" and that our civilization participates in the historical process of rising, maturing, and falling. Both kinds of death meet in the sonnets of Shakespeare, which sometimes

---

[17] sages: Byzantium, or Constantinople, is famous for its mosaic depictions of religious leaders. [19] perne in a gyre: whirl, come alive to me. [27] form: "I have read somewhere [perhaps in the letter of Liudprand, Bishop of Cremona, to the Emperor Otto I in 968] that in the Emperor's palace at Byzantium was a tree made of gold and silver, and artificial birds that sang."—*Yeats's note.*

seem to have explored every possible variety of emotion about them. Sonnets 55, 64, and 73 express wholly different responses: the first hyperbolically celebrates poetry's exemption from the process, the speaker of the next mourns the involvement of the loved one in it, and the last pathetically argues that if the speaker were not involved in it, he could not be strongly loved. Yet not even Shakespeare exhausted the topic of death. Emily Dickinson's fantasy—the poem seems to dramatize that common reverie in which one wonders how it feels to be dead—expresses a mood of pure acceptance, or reconciliation with death. The two poems by Yeats also accept the processes of mortality, but are more enigmatic, because of Yeats's highly personal beliefs about history and about individual old age. "The Second Coming" proceeds from the disorders of the European world at the end of World War I. Believing that every civilization passes away after about two thousand years, Yeats interpreted this "anarchy" as signaling the close of Christian civilization. He knew that such transitions are violent, but regarded them as inevitable. Born in 1865 and nearly fifty before reaching the height of his poetic powers, Yeats was both more than normally resentful of growing old and more aware of the possibilities of one's later years. Byzantium, his holy city, though founded on the historical Constantinople (now Istanbul, in Turkey), is a creation of the mind and imagination, comparable to the ideal realm of changeless beauty suggested to Keats by the nightingale.

2. Shakespeare's sonnets are in form *English sonnets* (or *Shakespearean*). Compare them with Wordsworth's † "Westminster Bridge," noting the identities and differences of the two forms. The difference of rhyme supports a structural difference: Sonnet 73, for instance, consists of three metaphors followed by a comment—a pattern that all strictly organized English sonnets exhibit. To what extent do 55 and 64 conform to the strict pattern?

3. Consider line 11 of Sonnet 64 as a possible title for all three sonnets—and for all *mutability* poems (see page 672).

4. Characterize Death as personified by Emily Dickinson. The third stanza of "Death" is said to symbolize the three stages of life. Discuss fully, deciding whether the word *gazing* can be justified. In one version of the poem an additional stanza follows the third:

> Or rather, he passed us;
> The dews grew quivering and chill,
> For only gossamer my gown,
> My tippet only tulle.

Do you think it is rightly omitted? Show how the details of the next stanza strengthen the tone of acceptance. With special attention to the last stanza, write an essay comparing the tone of "Death" with your own feelings about the subject.

5. Explain: *sluttish, all-oblivious* (Sonnet 55); *fell, interchange of state, ruminate* (Sonnet 64); *falconer* ("The Second Coming"); *sensual, artifice of eternity* ("Sailing to Byzantium").

6. The first paragraph of "The Second Coming" has been quoted approvingly in editorials lamenting the rise of dictators and demagogues in the modern world. Do you think it reflects the history of our times fairly? Write an essay on the subject.

7. Evaluate the image in lines 14–17. Does it justify the adjective *vast?* Show how the reference to Bethlehem reflects a cyclical view of history. Considering the words *stony sleep* and *nightmare,* is the speaker's attitude toward the Christian epoch consistently set forth?

8. Compare lines 2–3 of "Sailing to Byzantium" with † "Ode to a Nightingale," lines 61–62. Does Yeats's stanza iv seem a direct reply to the "Ode"? Write an essay on the possibility that, just as its speaker reaches the nightingale "on the viewless wings of poesy," so Yeats's poetry is the fulfilment longed for in "Sailing to Byzantium." Show how the metaphor of music, line 7, is developed in the remainder of the poem.

MAN

GEORGE HERBERT ⫯ *From* THE TEMPLE, *1633.*

My God, I heard this day
That none doth build a stately habitation
But he that means to dwell therein.
What house more stately hath there been,
5 Or can be, than is man, to whose creation
All things are in decay?

For man is everything,
And more: he is a tree, yet bears more fruit;
A beast, yet is, or should be more:
10   Reason and speech we only bring;
Parrots may thank us, if they are not mute,
They go upon the score.

Man is all symmetry,
Full of proportions, one limb to another,
15   And all to all the world besides;
Each part may call the farthest, brother,
For head with foot hath private amity,
And both with moons and tides.

---

⁷ everything: i.e. according to the Hermetic philosophers, who considered him a microcosm corresponding in every part to the macrocosm, the universe (cf. 22). ¹⁰ only: alone. ¹² score: i.e. are indebted to us.

Nothing hath got so far
20 But man hath caught and kept it as his prey;
His eyes dismount the highest star;
He is in little all the sphere;
Herbs gladly cure our flesh, because that they
Find their acquaintance there.

25   For us the winds do blow;
The earth doth rest, heaven move, and fountains flow;
Nothing we see but means our good,
As our delight or as our treasure.
The whole is either our cupboard of food,
30   Or cabinet of pleasure.

The stars have us to bed;
Night draws the curtain, which the sun withdraws;
Music and light attend our head;
All things unto our flesh are kind
35 In their descent and being, to our mind
In their ascent and cause.

Each thing is full of duty:
Waters united are our navigation;
Distinguishèd, our habitation;
40   Below, our drink; above, our meat;
Both are our cleanliness. Hath one such beauty?
Then how are all things neat!
More servants wait on man
Than he'll take notice of; in every path
45   He treads down that which doth befriend him
When sickness makes him pale and wan.
O mighty love! Man is one world and hath
Another to attend him.

Since then, my God, thou hast
50 So brave a palace built, O dwell in it,
That it may dwell with thee at last!
Till then afford us so much wit
That as the world serves us we may serve thee,
And both thy servants be.

[21] dismount: bring near. [39] distinguished: set apart [, they permit]. [45] that: medicinal herbs.
[52] wit: knowledge and insight.

THE DEFINITION OF LOVE

ANDREW MARVELL —◦❦ *From* MISCELLANEOUS POEMS, *1681.*

My Love is of a birth as rare
As 'tis, for object, strange and high:
It was begotten by Despair
Upon Impossibility.

5 Magnanimous Despair alone
Could show me so divine a thing,
Where feeble Hope could ne'er have flown
But vainly flapped its tinsel wing.

And yet I quickly might arrive
10 Where my extended soul is fixed,
But Fate does iron wedges drive
And always crowds itself betwixt.

For Fate with jealous eye does see
Two perfect loves; nor lets them close:
15 Their union would her ruin be,
And her tyrannic power depose.

And therefore her decrees of steel
Us as the distant poles have placed
(Though Love's whole world on us doth wheel),
20 Not by themselves to be embraced.

Unless the giddy heaven fall,
And earth some new convulsion tear;
And, us to join, the world should all
Be cramped into a planisphere.

25 As lines, so loves oblique may well
Themselves in every angle greet:
But ours, so truly parallel,
Though infinite, can never meet.

Therefore the love which us doth bind,
30 But Fate so enviously debars,
Is the conjunction of the mind,
And opposition of the stars.

² for: in its. ¹⁴ close: unite. ²⁴ planisphere: flat representation of the earth, the poles joined. ²⁵ loves oblique: i.e. imperfect ones. ³² stars: in astrology, two stars in *conjunction* unite their influences, oppose them when in *opposition.*

TO THE MAN-OF-WAR BIRD

WALT WHITMAN ⸺⸰❧ *From* LEAVES OF GRASS, *1876.*

Thou who hast slept all night upon the storm,
Waking renewed on thy prodigious pinions
(Burst the wild storm? above it thou ascendedest,
And rested on the sky, thy slave that cradled thee),
5 Now a blue point, far, far in heaven floating,
As to the light emerging here on deck I watch thee
(Myself a speck, a point on the world's floating vast).

Far, far at sea,
After the night's fierce drifts have strewn the shore with wrecks,
10 With reappearing day as now so happy and serene,
The rosy and elastic dawn, the flashing sun,
The limpid spread of air cerulean,
Thou also reappearest.

Thou born to match the gale (thou art all wings),
15 To cope with heaven and earth and sea and hurricane,
Thou ship of air that never furlest thy sails,
Days, even weeks untired and onward, through spaces, realms gyrating,
At dusk that lookest on Senegal, at morn America,
That sportest amid the lightning-flash and thunder-cloud,
20 In them, in thy experiences, hadst thou my soul,
What joys! what joys were thine!

ARS POETICA

ARCHIBALD MACLEISH ⸺⸰❧ *From* COLLECTED POEMS OF ARCHIBALD MACLEISH. *Reprinted by permission of Houghton Mifflin Company.*

A poem should be palpable and mute
As a globed fruit,

Dumb
As old medallions to the thumb,

689

5 Silent as the sleeve-worn stone
Of casement ledges where the moss has grown—

A poem should be wordless
As the flight of birds.

❀

A poem should be motionless in time
10 As the moon climbs,

Leaving, as the moon releases
Twig by twig the night-entangled trees,

Leaving, as the moon behind the winter leaves,
Memory by memory the mind—

15 A poem should be motionless in time
As the moon climbs.

❀

A poem should be equal to:
Not true.

For all the history of grief
20 An empty doorway and a maple leaf.

For love
The leaning grasses and two lights above the sea—

A poem should not mean
But be.

Suggestions

1. A poem, which as we know dramatizes the response of a speaker to a situation, may seem remote from the intellectual art of definition. Yet sometimes it is the mind's encounter with the precise nature of a class of objects that arouses emotion, and poets have found these experiences as available as any others. Although the chief concern of Herbert's "Man" is to celebrate our divine potentialities, the definition is an inclusive one, not overlooking man's beastly side nor his liability to such evils as illness. "The Definition of Love" establishes, playfully and sadly at once, the quality of a lover's emotion when his love seems hopeless. "To the Man-of-War Bird" defines both human and subhuman experience by calling to mind their limitations: man, bound to the earth, can share the bird's encounters with nature only in imagination—yet the bird lacks the purely human capacity for ecstatic response. And "Ars Poetica" advances a definition of poetry through a series of loving similes.

2. Taking "O mighty love!" (line 47) as a summary of the emotion in "Man," summarize the reasons given for man's obligation to serve God. Point out examples of quiet humor (e.g. lines 11–12) in the poem, and of Herbert's meditative music (e.g. lines 25–26). The stanza beginning with line 43 was a favorite of Thoreau's; after reading his essay † "The Village" show why.

3. Explain that "The Definition of Love" defines only one kind of love, a kind in which the lover is peculiarly liable to self-pity. Do you think Marvell's speaker is guilty of this or any other sentimentality? Work out the mathematical-scientific metaphors and show their relevance to your answer. Would a lady to whom this poem was addressed be pleased by it?

4. Samuel Johnson wrote of such poets as Herbert and Marvell that "if their conceits were far-fetched, they were often worth the carriage." Explaining the sense in which he uses *conceits,* evaluate this judgment.

5. Describe the dramatic situation of "To the Man-of-War Bird" (lines 6–7). Which of the bird's experiences is the man able to share in reality? Show what the word *soul* means in line 20, and read the poem aloud, noticing how the sound of its lines helps to express its emotion.

6. Since "Ars Poetica" (literally "the poetic art") borrows the title generally given to Horace's *Epistle to the Pisos* (c. 15 B.C.), it may be taken as a rejection of Horace's didactic tendency—as seen especially in the passage beginning "Of writing well, be sure, the secret lies In wisdom, therefore study to be wise." MacLeish's similes express joy in poems that are not communications but creations, objects to be contemplated. Does this definition of poetry, whether acceptable or not, justify the paradoxes of the series *mute-silent-wordless* and of the last two lines? Explain *motionless* (lines 9 and 15) by references to the similes of the moon and *equal to* (line 17) by the metaphors following. Judged by its own definition, is "Ars Poetica" a poem?

7. Write an essay contrasting the human condition as presented in "Man" with its presentation in the poems of the first three groups, all of which were written in the past two centuries.

8. Write an essay contrasting love as it may be defined in Shakespeare's Sonnets 55, 64, and 73 with Marvell's "Definition."

9. Write an essay comparing the symbolic meanings of the man-of-war bird, the nightingale, and the two corbies.

10. Name the poem you prefer of all those studied so far, explain your preference, and decide whether it supports MacLeish's definition.

THE LOVER SHOWETH HOW HE IS FORSAKEN OF SUCH AS HE SOMETIME ENJOYED

SIR THOMAS WYATT   *First published in* SONGS AND SONNETS (*i.e.* TOTTLE'S MISCELLANY), *1557.*

They flee from me that sometime did me seek,
With naked foot stalking within my chamber.
Once have I seen them gentle, tame, and meek,
That now are wild, and do not once remember
5 That sometime they have put themselves in danger
To take bread at my hand; and now they range,
Busily seeking in continual change.

Thankèd be fortune it hath been otherwise,
Twenty times better; but once especïal,
10 In thin array, after a pleasant guise,
When her loose gown did from her shoulders fall,
And she me caught in her arms long and small,
And therewithal so sweetly did me kiss
And softly said, "Dear heart, how like you this?"

15 It was no dream, for I lay broad awaking.
But all is turned now, through my gentleness,
Into a bitter fashion of forsaking;
And I have leave to go, of her goodness,
And she also to use newfangleness.
20 But since that I unkindly so am served,
How like you this? what hath she now deserved?

SOMETIME: formerly.

FEAR NO MORE THE HEAT O' THE SUN

WILLIAM SHAKESPEARE — *From* CYMBELINE, *c.1610, first pub-*
lished in 1623.

Fear no more the heat o' the sun,
Nor the furious winter's rages;
Thou thy worldly task hast done,
Home art gone, and ta'en thy wages.
5 Golden lads and girls all must,
As chimney-sweepers, come to dust.

Fear no more the frown o' the great;
Thou art past the tyrant's stroke;
Care no more to clothe and eat;
10 To thee the reed is as the oak.
The sceptre, learning, physic, must
All follow this, and come to dust.

Fear no more the lightning-flash,
Nor the all-dreaded thunder-stone;
15 Fear not slander, censure rash;
Thou hast finished joy and moan.
All lovers young, all lovers must
Consign to thee, and come to dust.

No exorciser harm thee!
20 Nor no witchcraft charm thee!
Ghost unlaid forbear thee!
Nothing ill come near thee!
Quiet consummation have;
And renownèd be thy grave!

[11] physic: medical knowledge. [14] thunder-stone: thunderbolt. [18] consign: i.e. follow your example.
[19] exorciser: one who drives ghosts away.

ELEGIAC STANZAS

WILLIAM WORDSWORTH ---⟫   *From* POEMS IN TWO VOLUMES, *1807.*

SUGGESTED BY A PICTURE OF PEELE CASTLE IN A
STORM, PAINTED BY SIR GEORGE BEAUMONT

I was thy neighbor once, thou rugged pile!
Four summer weeks I dwelt in sight of thee:
I saw thee every day, and all the while
Thy form was sleeping on a glassy sea.

5 So pure the sky, so quiet was the air;
So like, so very like, was day to day!
Whene'er I looked, thy image still was there;
It trembled, but it never passed away.

How perfect was the calm! it seemed no sleep;
10 No mood which season takes away or brings:
I could have fancied that the mighty deep
Was even the gentlest of all gentle things.

Ah! then, if mine had been the painter's hand,
To express what then I saw, and add the gleam,
15 The light that never was on sea or land,
The consecration and the poet's dream,

I would have planted thee, thou hoary pile,
Amid a world how different from this!
Beside a sea that could not cease to smile;
20 On tranquil land, beneath a sky of bliss.

Thou shouldst have seemed a treasure-house divine
Of peaceful years, a chronicle of heaven;
Of all the sunbeams that did ever shine
The very sweetest had to thee been given.

25 A picture had it been of lasting ease,
Elysian quiet, without toil or strife;
No motion but the moving tide, a breeze,
Or merely silent nature's breathing life.

694

Such, in the fond illusion of my heart,
30 Such picture would I at that time have made:
And seen the soul of truth in every part;
A steadfast peace that might not be betrayed.

So once it would have been—'tis so no more;
I have submitted to a new control:
35 A power is gone, which nothing can restore;
A deep distress hath humanized my soul.

Not for a moment could I now behold
A smiling sea, and be what I have been:
The feeling of my loss will ne'er be old;
40 This, which I know, I speak with mind serene.

Then, Beaumont, friend! who would have been the friend,
If he had lived, of him whom I deplore,
This work of thine I blame not, but commend;
This sea in anger, and that dismal shore.

45 Oh, 'tis a passionate work!—yet wise and well;
Well chosen is the spirit that is here;
That hulk which labors in the deadly swell,
This rueful sky, this pageantry of fear!

And this huge castle, standing here sublime,
50 I love to see the look with which it braves,
Cased in the unfeeling armor of old time
The lightning, the fierce wind, and trampling waves.

Farewell, farewell, the heart that lives alone,
Housed in a dream, at distance from the kind!
55 Such happiness, wherever it be known,
Is to be pitied; for 'tis surely blind.

But welcome fortitude, and patient cheer,
And frequent sights of what is to be borne!
Such sights, or worse, as are before me here.—
60 Not without hope we suffer and we mourn.

54 the kind: humanity.

NEXT, PLEASE

PHILIP LARKIN ⸺

From THE LESS DECEIVED *by Philip Larkin, 1955. By permission of the Marvell Press; Hessle Yorkshire, England.*

Always too eager for the future, we
Pick up bad habits of expectancy.
Something is always approaching; every day
Till then we say,

5 Watching from a bluff the tiny, clear,
Sparkling armada of promises draw near.
How slow they are! And how much time they waste,
Refusing to make haste!

Yet still they leave us holding wretched stalks
10 Of disappointment, for, though nothing balks
Each big approach, leaning with brasswork prinked,
Each rope distinct,

Flagged, and the figurehead with golden tits
Arching our way, it never anchors; it's
15 No sooner present than it turns to past.
Right to the last

We think each one will heave to and unload
All good into our lives, all we are owed
For waiting so devoutly and so long.
20 But we are wrong:

Only one ship is seeking us, a black-
Sailed unfamiliar, towing at her back
A huge and birdless silence. In her wake
No waters breed or break.

Suggestions

1. Comparison, as we saw in Part 2, pages 207–208, is a fundamental action of the mind. It permeates all literature—all art, indeed—and a poem without comparisons would be hard to find. In the four poems of this group, though, particular comparisons, extended throughout, make up the fundamental situations with which the speakers are concerned. The complaint of Wyatt's lover turns upon the word *sometime;* bitterly

echoing the question "How like you this?" he compares the lady's present behavior with her past. Shakespeare's song consists of an extended contrast between the peace of the grave and the evils of life. "Elegiac Stanzas" contrasts a real picture of a stormy scene with an idealized, imaginary one, making each a symbol for a variety of human experience. "Next, Please" is in theme a contrast between what we expect and what we receive; in expression it is an elaborately developed analogy. Subordinate likenesses and contrasts support the central comparison in each of the four poems.

2. Analyze "The Lover Showeth How He Is Forsaken" as a generalization followed by a particular example. How would you formulate its theme? Do you condemn the speaker for self-pity, or is this tendency offset by twists of humor? (Notice the sarcasms in the third stanza.) Beginning with *stalking*, line 2, and continuing through the next sentence, to what are the ladies compared? What does this analogy suggest about the lover's attitude toward them?

3. The form of "The Lover Showeth How He Is Forsaken" is known as *rhyme royal*, because James I of Scotland wrote a poem called *The King's Quair* in it. List its characteristics, relating them if you can to the speaker's tone.

4. *Golden* in line 5 of "Fear No More the Heat o' the Sun" means, among other things, *fortunate*. In this sense it is part of what comparison? What other meanings do you find in it? Point out the most striking examples of the two kinds of evil that the dead person has escaped. Describe the change of metre and rhyme which gives stanza IV a tone of finality.

5. Explain: *newfangleness* ("The Lover Showeth How He Is Forsaken"); *censure, consummation* ("Fear No More"); *Elegiac, consecration, Elysian, deplore, passionate* ("Elegiac Stanzas"); *armada* ("Next, Please").

6. Compare the figurative uses of *armor* in *Elegiac Stanzas*, line 51, and † "Mr. Flood's Party," line 18. Show which stanzas make up the three parts of "Elegiac Stanzas": I. the picture that the speaker would have painted on an earlier occasion; II. the change in him; III. his attitude toward Beaumont's painting. Compare line 15 to line 54; then evaluate the last two stanzas as a climax. Has the moral already been clearly implied by the contrasting symbols?

7. Discuss the meaning of the title "Next, Please." How is its rather flippant tone supported by similar expressions within the poem? E.g. what do we mean when we say "Till then"? Show how this tone helps to offset the solemnity of the subject. Compare Larkin's symbol for death with Emily Dickinson's personification of it in † "Death."

8. Write an essay comparing the attitudes toward adversity in "Fear No More the Heat o' the Sun" and "Elegiac Stanzas."

9. Write an essay on your "habits of expectancy" ("Next, Please," line 2).

A VALEDICTION FORBIDDING MOURNING

JOHN DONNE   *From* SONGS AND SONNETS, *1633*.

As virtuous men pass mildly away,
And whisper to their souls to go,
Whilst some of their sad friends do say,
"The breath goes now," and some say, "No";

5 So let us melt and make no noise,
No tear-floods nor sigh-tempests move;
'Twere profanation of our joys
To tell the laity our love.

Moving of the earth brings harms and fears;
10 Men reckon what it did and meant;
But trepidation of the spheres,
Though greater far, is innocent.

Dull sublunary lovers' love
(Whose soul is sense) cannot admit
15 Absence, because it doth remove
Those things which elemented it.

But we, by a love so much refined
That ourselves know not what it is,
Inter-assurèd of the mind,
20 Care less eyes, lips, and hands to miss.

Our two souls, therefore, which are one,
Though I must go, endure not yet
A breach but an expansion,
Like gold to airy thinness beat.

25 If they be two, they are two so
As stiff twin compasses are two;
Thy soul, the fixed foot, makes no show
To move, but doth if the other do.

---

¹¹ trepidation: Ptolemaic astronomers supposed that the heavenly bodies revolved on invisible crystal spheres, whose trembling caused only harmless changes in the date of the equinox. ¹⁶ elemented: composed. ²⁶ compasses: drawing compass.

And though it in the centre sit,
30 Yet, when the other far doth roam,
It leans and hearkens after it,
And grows erect as that comes home.

Such wilt thou be to me, who must
Like the other foot obliquely run:
35 Thy firmness draws my circle just
And makes me end where I begun.

TO HIS COY MISTRESS

ANDREW MARVELL ─◦◦{ *From* MISCELLANEOUS POEMS, *1681.*

Had we but world enough, and time,
This coyness, Lady, were no crime.
We would sit down and think which way
To walk and pass our long love's day.
5 Thou by the Indian Ganges' side
Shouldst rubies find; I by the tide
Of Humber would complain. I would
Love you ten years before the Flood,
And you should, if you please, refuse
10 Till the conversion of the Jews.
My vegetable love should grow
Vaster than empires and more slow;
An hundred years should go to praise
Thine eyes and on thy forehead gaze,
15 Two hundred to adore each breast,
But thirty thousand to the rest;
An age at least to every part,
And the last age should show your heart.
For, Lady, you deserve this state,
20 Nor would I love at lower rate.

But at my back I always hear
Time's wingèd chariot hurrying near;
And yonder all before us lie
Deserts of vast eternity.
25 Thy beauty shall no more be found,
Nor, in thy marble vault, shall sound
My echoing song; then worms shall try
That long-preserved virginity,

MISTRESS: sweetheart—not paramour. ¹¹ vegetable: plant-like, inhuman. ¹⁹ state: honor. ²⁰ rate: cost.

And your quaint honor turn to dust,
30 And into ashes all my lust:
The grave's a fine and private place,
But none, I think, do there embrace.

Now therefore, while the youthful hue
Sits on thy skin like morning dew,
35 And while thy willing soul transpires
At every pore with instant fires,
Now let us sport us while we may,
And now, like amorous birds of prey,
Rather at once our time devour
40 Than languish in his slow-chapped power.
Let us roll all our strength and all
Our sweetness up into one ball,
And tear our pleasures with rough strife
Thorough the iron gates of life;
45 Thus, though we cannot make our sun
Stand still, yet we will make him run.

ON HIS BLINDNESS

JOHN MILTON   *From* POEMS, ETC. UPON SEVERAL OCCA-SIONS, *1673.*

When I consider how my light is spent
Ere half my days in this dark world and wide,
And that one talent which is death to hide
Lodged with me useless, though my soul more bent
5 To serve therewith my Maker, and present
My true account, lest he returning chide,
"Doth God exact day-labor, light denied?"
I fondly ask. But Patience, to prevent
That murmur, soon replies, "God doth not need
10 Either man's work or his own gifts. Who best
Bear his mild yoke, they serve him best. His state
Is kingly: thousands at his bidding speed,
And post o'er land and ocean without rest;
They also serve who only stand and wait."

TO HIS COY MISTRESS. 36 instant: eager. 40 slow-chapped: slow jawed, slowly devouring. 44 Thorough: through. 46 stand still: as Jehovah did at Gibeon (*Joshua* 10,12) and as Zeus did to prolong his night with Amphitryon's wife, Alcmene.   ON HIS BLINDNESS. 1 spent: Milton feared he could no longer write after his eyes began to fail when he was in his thirties. 3 death: as in Jesus' parable, *Gospel of St. Matthew* 25, 30. 8 fondly: foolishly. 11 yoke: "My yoke is easy"—*ibid.* 11, 30. 12 thousands: i.e. of angels.

DO NOT GO GENTLE INTO THAT GOOD NIGHT

DYLAN THOMAS

Do not go gentle into that good night,
Old age should burn and rave at close of day;
Rage, rage against the dying of the light.

Though wise men at their end know dark is right,
5 Because their words had forked no lightning they
Do not go gentle into that good night.

Good men, the last wave by, crying how bright
Their frail deeds might have danced in a green bay,
Rage, rage against the dying of the light.

10 Wild men who caught and sang the sun in flight,
And learn, too late, they grieved it on its way,
Do not go gentle into that good night.

Grave men, near death, who see with blinding sight
Blind eyes could blaze like meteors and be gay,
15 Rage, rage against the dying of the light.

And you, my father, there on the sad height,
Curse, bless, me now with your fierce tears, I pray.
Do not go gentle into that good night.
Rage, rage against the dying of the light.

Suggestions

1. Since the essence of drama is conflict, poems that take the form of arguments are particularly dramatic and interesting. Donne's "Valediction" urges the lady not to mourn his absence, on the grounds that, as their love is holy and spiritual, physical separation cannot harm it. The speaker argues by analogy with the peaceful dying of the virtuous, and by the famous similes of the sheet of gold and the drawing compass. Marvell's lover argues for love's immediate consummation by a sort of conditional contrary-to-fact syllogism, its conclusion introduced formally by *Now therefore*. The moral of "On His Blindness" is the need for

patience in the face of adversity, but instead of advancing this thought baldly in the form of a preachment, Milton dramatizes it as a dispute between his sense of grievance and Patience personified. The argument of "Do Not Go Gentle" is just the reverse: the speaker presents his emotion in a plea for resistance, not resignation. Which of the arguments would most nearly convince the implied hearer?

2. Point out the sarcasms in stanza ii of "A Valediction Forbidding Mourning," and show how the metaphors in lines 7–8 establish the lover's serious feelings. Stanza iii introduces the poem's basic contrast; trace its development in the following stanzas. Summarize the paradox of the lovers' souls, showing how each of its two parts is confirmed by a separate simile. Write a contrast of "Valediction" and † "Winter Remembered," discussing a possible influence of the first on the second.

3. "To His Coy Mistress" also develops its argument through a combination of light sarcasms and serious reasoning. Point out examples of both in its first two paragraphs: e.g. how many relevant meanings do you find in *quaint* (line 29)? Contrast the emotions implied in the second and third paragraphs. When the poem was first printed, line 34 ended with the word *glew*. A modern editor, deciding that the *g* had been accidentally repeated from *morning*, printed *lew*, an old word meaning *warmth*. Which of the three possibilities do you think should be used? The last two lines are said to mean: "Only gods can arrest the passage of time, but it is better to be human, for we can make time speed up." Discuss.

4. Compare the form of "On His Blindness" to that of † "Composed upon Westminster Bridge." What slight difference of structure is there? Show how "On His Blindness" dramatizes two opposed emotions, describing the tone of voice in which you would read line 7 aloud.

5. "Do Not Go Gentle into That Good Night" is the kind of poem called a *villanelle*. List its formal characteristics—not overlooking the repeated lines, which are requirements of this form. Evaluate the metaphors in the poem as expressions of the speaker's emotion, and compare those centering on the words *light, dark, lightning,* and *sun* with similar figures in the three preceding poems.

6. Explain: *sublunary, sense, Inter-assurèd, breach, obliquely* ("A Valediction"); *Ganges, Humber, transpires* ("To His Coy Mistress"); *state, post* ("On His Blindness").

7. Write an essay contrasting "A Valediction" and "To His Coy Mistress," stressing the speakers' attitudes toward mutability; or compare one of these poems to any of the other mutability poems that resemble it enough to make a comparison possible.

8. Write an essay contrasting the emotions presented in "On His Blindness" and "Do Not Go Gentle." Is the difference related to changing beliefs between 1673 and 1952?

A DESCRIPTION OF THE MORNING

JONATHAN SWIFT ---◄{ *First published in* THE TATLER, *30 April, 1709.*

Now hardly here and there an hackney-coach
Appearing, showed the ruddy morn's approach.
Now Betty from her master's bed had flown,
And softly stole to discompose her own;
5 The slip-shod 'prentice from his master's door
Had pared the dirt, and sprinkled round the floor.
Now Moll had whirled her mop with dexterous airs,
Prepared to scrub the entry and the stairs.
The youth with broomy stumps began to trace
10 The kennel-edge, where wheels had worn the place.
The small-coal man was heard with cadence deep,
Till drowned in shriller notes of chimney-sweep:
Duns at his lordship's gate began to meet;
And brickdust Moll had screamed through half the street.
15 The turnkey now his flock returning sees,
Duly let out a-nights to steal for fees:
The watchful bailiffs take their silent stands,
And schoolboys lag with satchels in their hands.

ELEGY

THOMAS GRAY ---◄{ *First published in 1751.*

WRITTEN IN A COUNTRY CHURCHYARD

The curfew tolls the knell of parting day,
The lowing herd wind slowly o'er the lea,
The plowman homeward plods his weary way,
And leaves the world to darkness and to me.

A DESCRIPTION OF THE MORNING. ³ Betty: any maid. ¹⁰ kennel-edge: rim of the gutter. ¹⁶ fees: money with which to pay the jailer for better food and other luxuries. ¹⁷ bailiffs: officers posted to prevent debtors from decamping.

5 Now fades the glimmering landscape on the sight,
    And all the air a solemn stillness holds,
Save where the beetle wheels his droning flight,
    And drowsy tinklings lull the distant folds;

Save that, from yonder ivy-mantled tower,
10   The moping owl does to the moon complain
Of such as, wandering near her secret bower,
    Molest her ancient solitary reign.

Beneath those rugged elms, that yew-tree's shade,
    Where heaves the turf in many a moldering heap,
15 Each in his narrow cell for ever laid,
    The rude forefathers of the hamlet sleep.

The breezy call of incense-breathing morn,
    The swallow twittering from the straw-built shed,
The cock's shrill clarion, or the echoing horn,
20   No more shall rouse them from their lowly bed.

For them no more the blazing hearth shall burn
    Or busy housewife ply her evening care:
No children run to lisp their sire's return
    Or climb his knees the envied kiss to share.

25 Oft did the harvest to their sickle yield,
    Their furrow oft the stubborn glebe has broke;
How jocund did they drive their team afield:
    How bowed the woods beneath their sturdy stroke!

Let not ambition mock their useful toil,
30   Their homely joys, and destiny obscure;
Nor grandeur hear with a disdainful smile
    The short and simple annals of the poor.

The boast of heraldry, the pomp of power,
    And all that beauty, all that wealth e'er gave
35 Awaits alike the inevitable hour.
    The paths of glory lead but to the grave.

Nor you, ye proud, impute to these the fault,
    If memory o'er their tomb no trophies raise,
Where through the long-drawn aisle and fretted vault
40   The pealing anthem swells the note of praise.

Can storied urn or animated bust
    Back to its mansion call the fleeting breath?
Can honor's voice provoke the silent dust
    Or flattery soothe the dull cold ear of death?

---

¹⁹ horn: hunting horn. ³⁹ fretted vault: carved church-ceiling. ⁴¹ storied urn: funerary urn with inscription; animated: lifelike. ⁴³ provoke: recall to life.

45 Perhaps in this neglected spot is laid
    Some heart once pregnant with celestial fire;
    Hands that the rod of empire might have swayed,
    Or waked to ecstasy the living lyre.

    But knowledge to their eyes her ample page
50   Rich with the spoils of time did ne'er unroll;
    Chill penury repressed their noble rage
    And froze the genial current of the soul.

    Full many a gem of purest ray serene
    The dark, unfathomed caves of ocean bear:
55 Full many a flower is born to blush unseen
    And waste its sweetness on the desert air.

    Some village Hampden, that with dauntless breast
    The little tyrant of his fields withstood;
    Some mute inglorious Milton here may rest,
60   Some Cromwell guiltless of his country's blood.

    The applause of listening senates to command,
    The threats of pain and ruin to despise,
    To scatter plenty o'er a smiling land
    And read their history in a nation's eyes

65 Their lot forbade: nor circumscribed alone
    Their growing virtues, but their crimes confined;
    Forbade to wade through slaughter to a throne
    And shut the gates of mercy on mankind,

    The struggling pangs of conscious truth to hide,
70   To quench the blushes of ingenuous shame,
    Or heap the shrine of luxury and pride
    With incense kindled at the Muse's flame.

    Far from the madding crowd's ignoble strife,
    Their sober wishes never learned to stray;
75 Along the cool, sequestered vale of life
    They kept the noiseless tenor of their way.

    Yet even these bones from insult to protect,
    Some frail memorial still erected nigh,
    With uncouth rhymes and shapeless sculpture decked,
80   Implores the passing tribute of a sigh.

    Their name, their years, spelt by the unlettered Muse,
    The place of fame and elegy supply;
    And many a holy text around she strews,
    That teach the rustic moralist to die.

[51] rage: creative fervor. [57] Hampden: John Hampden (1594–1643) opposed the tyranny of Charles I. [71] heap: i.e. write fulsome poems and dedications to rich patrons. [83] text: Bible verse.

85 For who, to dumb forgetfulness a prey,
This pleasing, anxious being e'er resigned,
Left the warm precincts of the cheerful day,
Nor cast one longing, lingering look behind?

On some fond breast the parting soul relies;
90 Some pious drops the closing eye requires;
Even from the tomb the voice of nature cries;
Even in our ashes live their wonted fires.

For thee who, mindful of the unhonored dead,
Dost in these lines their artless tale relate;
95 If chance, by lonely contemplation led,
Some kindred spirit shall inquire thy fate,

Haply some hoary-headed swain may say,
"Oft have we seen him at the peep of dawn
Brushing with hasty steps the dews away
100 To meet the sun upon the upland lawn.

"There at the foot of yonder nodding beech
That wreathes its old fantastic roots so high,
His listless length at noontide would he stretch
And pore upon the brook that babbles by.

105 "Hard by yon wood, now smiling as in scorn,
Muttering his wayward fancies he would rove;
Now drooping, woeful wan, like one forlorn,
Or crazed with care, or crossed in hopeless love.

"One morn I missed him on the customed hill,
110 Along the heath, and near his favorite tree;
Another came; nor yet beside the rill,
Nor up the lawn, nor at the wood was he;

"The next, with dirges due in sad array
Slow through the church-way path we saw him borne.
115 Approach and read (for thou canst read) the lay
Graved on the stone beneath yon agèd thorn."

THE EPITAPH

Here rests his head upon the lap of earth
A youth to fortune and to fame unknown.
Fair science frowned not on his humble birth,
120 *And melancholy marked him for her own.*

---

[86] being: life. [93] thee: the speaker, imagining his own fate. [95] If chance: if it happens that. [97] swain: countryman. [115] lay: i.e. the three stanzas following. [119] science: learning, from which his lowly origin did not cut him off.

Large was his bounty and his soul sincere;
Heaven did a recompense as largely send:
He gave to misery all he had, a tear,
He gained from heaven ('twas all he wished) a friend.

125 *No farther seek his merits to disclose*
Or draw his frailties from their dread abode
(There they alike in trembling hope repose),
The bosom of his Father and his God.

SUNDAY: OUTSKIRTS OF KNOXVILLE, TENN.

JAMES AGEE *Reprinted by permission of the James Agee Trust.*

There, in the earliest and chary spring, the dogwood flowers.

Unharnessed in the friendly sunday air
By the red brambles, on the river bluffs,
Clerks and their choices pair.

5 Thrive by, not near, washed all away by shrub and juniper,
The ford v eight, racing the chevrolet.

They cannot trouble her:

Her breasts, helped open from the afforded lace,
Lie like a peaceful lake;
10 And on his mouth she breaks her gentleness:

Oh, wave them awake!

They are not of the birds. Such innocence
Brings us to break us only.
Theirs are not happy words.
15 We that are human cannot hope.
Our tenderest joys oblige us most.
No chain so cuts the bone; and sweetest silk most shrewdly strangles.

How this must end, that now please love were ended,
In kitchens, bedfights, silences, women's-pages,
20 Sickness of heart before goldlettered doors,

Stale flesh, hard collars, agony in antiseptic corridors,
Spankings, remonstrances, fishing trips, orange juice,
Policies, incapacities, a chevrolet,
Scorn of their children, kind contempt exchanged,
25 Shouted corrections of missed syllables,
Hot water bags, gallstones, falls down stairs,
Old fashioned christmases, suspicions of theft,
Arrangements with morticians taken care of by sons in law,
Small rooms beneath the gables of brick bungalows,
30 The tumbler smashed, the glance between daughter and husband,
The empty body in the lonely bed
And, in the empty concrete porch, blown ash
Grandchildren wandering the betraying sun

Now, on the winsome crumbling shelves of the horror
35 God show, God blind these children.

AS I WALKED OUT ONE EVENING

W. H. AUDEN

Reprinted from THE COLLECTED POETRY OF W. H. AUDEN *by permission of Random House, Inc. and Faber and Faber Limited.* © *1940 by W. H. Auden.*

As I walked out one evening,
  Walking down Bristol Street,
The crowds upon the pavement
  Were fields of harvest wheat.

5 And down by the brimming river
  I heard a lover sing
Under an arch of the railway:
  "Love has no ending.

I'll love you, dear, I'll love you
10   Till China and Africa meet
And the river jumps over the mountain
  And the salmon sing in the street.

I'll love you till the ocean
  Is folded and hung up to dry
15 And the seven stars go squawking
  Like geese about the sky.

The years shall run like rabbits
  For in my arms I hold
The Flower of the Ages
20 And the first love of the world."

But all the clocks in the city
  Began to whirr and chime:
"O let not Time deceive you,
  You cannot conquer Time.

25 In the burrows of the Nightmare
  Where Justice naked is,
Time watches from the shadow
  And coughs when you would kiss.

In headaches and in worry
30 Vaguely life leaks away,
And Time will have his fancy
  Tomorrow or today.

Into many a green valley
  Drifts the appalling snow;
35 Time breaks the threaded dances
  And the diver's brilliant bow.

O plunge your hands in water,
  Plunge them in up to the wrist;
Stare, stare in the basin
40 And wonder what you've missed.

The glacier knocks in the cupboard,
  The desert sighs in the bed,
And the crack in the teacup opens
  A lane to the land of the dead.

45 Where the beggars raffle the banknotes
  And the Giant is enchanting to Jack,
And the Lily-white Boy is a Roarer
  And Jill goes down on her back.

O look, look in the mirror,
50 O look in your distress;
Life remains a blessing
  Although you cannot bless.

O stand, stand at the window
  As the tears scald and start;
55 You shall love your crooked neighbor
  With your crooked heart."

It was late, late in the evening,
The lovers they were gone;
The clocks had ceased their chiming
6o   And the deep river ran on.

Suggestions

1. Literary works known in this book as composites are distinguished by their presentation of characters who are representative rather than individual. Often these make up a picture that seems typical of a class or an age; yet, as always, it is a picture so painted as to reflect the attitude of an individual speaker. Thus in Swift's "Description of the Morning," each character not only brings to mind a class of Londoner but also contributes to an impression of idleness and corruption. The poet who eulogizes rustic life in Gray's "Elegy" is less an individual poet than a representative of the mute, inglorious Miltons with whom he identifies himself. The two modern poems are alike in several ways: they treat their pairs of lovers as typical of all lovers and suggest that lovers (and by extension humanity itself) are deserving mainly of pity.

2. Measure the details of "A Description of the Morning" by Ruskin's dictum in † "The Great Style" that every detail in a poem should have an affecting result. Which ones seem least disgraceful to the characters? Distinguish the visual images from the auditory ones. Does the poem end with a satisfactory climax?

3. Gray's "Elegy" is also concerned with the two classes of mankind, the "haves" and "have-nots." Its attitude toward the first is introduced at line 29. Compare the attitudes toward each implied in the two poems. Does line 73 of the "Elegy" apply to the "Description"? Identify the basic contrast in the "Elegy" by describing in detail the burial-places of the proud and the humble. After explaining the allusions to Milton and Cromwell, lines 59–60, decide whether the gem and the flower in the previous stanza are to be pitied or envied. Identify the subjects of the verbs in lines 6 and 35.

4. By comparing lines 16 and 36 show that the poem is not only about two classes of people but about humanity as well. Discuss the attitude of the hoary-headed swain toward the speaker. Compare the title of the "Elegy" with that of † "Elegiac Stanzas."

5. Line 4 of "Sunday: Outskirts of Knoxville, Tenn." shows that it too is primarily about a particular social class. (Point out the supporting details in lines 18–33.) Why is its meaning not limited to this class? Show that the contrast of the human and non-human worlds (line 12) corresponds to that in † "Ode to a Nightingale," † "The Twa Corbies," and other poems you have read. Can the apparent contradiction in line 35 be reconciled by assuming that the speaker wishes the lovers both to understand experience fully (cf. line 11) and to be spared such knowledge?

6. "As I Walked Out One Evening" implies a similar view of human life by distorting the usual lovers' endearments into grotesque images, and by introducing other nightmarish figures into the speaker's reverie. Compare the effectiveness of this method with the relatively straightforward lines 12–17 of the previous poem. Are the two identical in their attitudes toward life?

7. Explain: *hackney-coach, discompose, 'prentice* ("A Description of the Morning"); *lea, folds, straw-built shed, glebe, jocund, long-drawn aisle, celestial, penury, genial, circumscribed, ingenuous, tenor, forlorn* ("Elegy"); *chary, shrewdly, goldlettered doors, antiseptic corridors, winsome* ("Sunday").

8. Compare the personified abstractions in "As I Walked Out One Evening" with those in the "Elegy."

9. Write an essay on some of the impressions of eighteenth-century England that you have derived from "A Description of the Morning," Gray's "Elegy," other poems in this book, and † "The World of the Whigs."

DEATH, BE NOT PROUD

JOHN DONNE ---≼{ *From* DIVINE POEMS, *1633.*

Death, be not proud, though some have callèd thee
Mighty and dreadful, for thou art not so;
For those whom thou thinkest thou dost overthrow
Die not, poor Death; nor yet canst thou kill me.
5 From rest and sleep, which but thy picture be,
Much pleasure, then from thee much more must flow,
And soonest our best men with thee do go—
Rest of their bones and souls' delivery.
Thou art slave to fate, chance, kings, and desperate men,
10 And dost with poison, war, and sickness dwell;
And poppy or charms can make us sleep as well
And better than thy stroke. Why swellest thou then?
One short sleep past, we wake eternally,
And Death shall be no more: Death, thou shalt die!

A SHORT SONG OF CONGRATULATION

SAMUEL JOHNSON ---≫{ *First published in* BRITISH SYNONYMY, *1794.*

Long-expected one and twenty,
   Lingering year, at last is flown;
Pomp and pleasure, pride and plenty,
   Great Sir John, are all your own.

5 Loosened from the minor's tether,
   Free to mortgage or to sell,
Wild as wind and light as feather,
   Bid the slaves of thrift farewell.

Call the Bettys, Kates, and Jennys
10   Every name that laughs at care;
Lavish of your grandsire's guineas,
   Show the spirit of an heir.

All that prey on vice and folly
   Joy to see their quarry fly;
15 Here the gamester light and jolly,
   There the lender grave and sly.

Wealth, Sir John, was made to wander:
   Let it wander as it will;
See the jockey, see the pander,
20   Bid them come, and take their fill.

When the bonny blade carouses,
   Pockets full, and spirits high,
What are acres? What are houses?
   Only dirt, or wet or dry.

25 If the guardian or the mother
   Tell the woes of wilful waste,
Scorn their counsel and their pother.
   You can hang or drown at last.

[24] or . . . or: either . . . or.

SOLILOQUY OF THE SPANISH CLOISTER

ROBERT BROWNING —◦§{ *From* DRAMATIC LYRICS, *1842.*

Gr-r-r—there go, my heart's abhorrence!
Water your damned flower-pots, do!
If hate killed men, Brother Lawrence,
God's blood, would not mine kill you!
5 What? your myrtle-bush wants trimming?
Oh, that rose has prior claims—
Needs its leaden vase filled brimming?
Hell dry you up with its flames!

At the meal we sit together;
10   *Salve tibi!* I must hear
Wise talk of the kind of weather,
Sort of season, time of year:
Not a plenteous cork-crop: scarcely
Dare we hope oak-galls, I doubt:
15 *What's the Latin name for "parsley"?*
What's the Greek name for Swine's Snout?

Whew! We'll have our platter burnished,
Laid with care on our own shelf!
With a fire-new spoon we're furnished,
20   And a goblet for ourself,
Rinsed like something sacrificial
Ere 'tis fit to touch our chaps—
Marked with L. for our initial!
(He-he! There his lily snaps!)

25 *Saint,* forsooth! While brown Dolores
Squats outside the Convent bank
With Sanchicha, telling stories,
Steeping tresses in the tank,
Blue-black, lustrous, thick like horsehairs,
30   —Can't I see his dead eye glow,
Bright as 'twere a Barbary corsair's?
(That is, if he'd let it show!)

When he finishes refection,
Knife and fork he never lays
35 Cross-wise, to my recollection,

As do I, in Jesu's praise.
I the Trinity illustrate,
Drinking watered orange-pulp—
In three sips the Arian frustrate;
40   While he drains his at one gulp!

Oh, those melons! If he's able
We're to have a feast; so nice!
One goes to the Abbot's table,
All of us get each a slice.
45 How go on your flowers? None double?
Not one fruit-sort can you spy?
Strange!—And I, too, at such trouble,
Keep them close-nipped on the sly!

There's a great text in Galatians,
50   Once you trip on it, entails
Twenty-nine distinct damnations,
One sure, if another fails;
If I trip him just a-dying,
Sure of heaven as sure can be,
55 Spin him round and send him flying
Off to hell, a Manichee?

Or, my scrofulous French novel
On grey paper with blunt type!
Simply glance at it, you grovel
60   Hand and foot in Belial's gripe;
If I double down its pages
At the woeful sixteenth print,
When he gathers his greengages,
Ope a sieve and slip it in't?

65 Or, there's Satan!—One might venture
Pledge one's soul to him, yet leave
Such a flaw in the indenture
As he'd miss, till, past retrieve,
Blasted lay that rose-acacia
70   We're so proud of. *Hy, Zy, Hine* . . .
'St! There's Vespers! *Plena gratiâ,*
Ave, Virgo! Gr-r-r—you swine!

49 Galatians: *Letter to the Galatians* 3,10 or 5, 19–21. 55 Manichee: i.e. it would be a mortal heresy to believe that evil is as strong as good. 70 *Hy* . . .: sound of the vesper-bell (?). 71 *Plena* . . .: "Hail, Virgin, full of grace," a prayer used especially in the evening.

TERENCE, THIS IS STUPID STUFF

A. E. HOUSMAN

From A SHROPSHIRE LAD *by A. E. Housman. By permission of Henry Holt & Co., Inc. and The Society of Authors as literary representatives of the Trustees of the Estate of the late A. E. Housman, and Messrs. Jonathan Cape, Ltd., publishers of A. E. Housman's* COLLECTED POEMS.

"Terence, this is stupid stuff:
You eat your victuals fast enough;
There can't be much amiss, 'tis clear,
To see the rate you drink your beer.
5 But oh, good Lord, the verse you make,
It gives a chap the belly-ache.
The cow, the old cow, she is dead;
It sleeps well, the hornèd head:
We poor lads, 'tis our turn now
10 To hear such tunes as killed the cow.
Pretty friendship 'tis to rhyme
Your friends to death before their time
Moping melancholy mad:
Come, pipe a tune to dance to, lad."

15 Why, if 'tis dancing you would be,
There's brisker pipes than poetry.
Say, for what were hop-yards meant,
Or why was Burton built on Trent?
Oh, many a peer of England brews
20 Livelier liquor than the Muse,
And malt does more than Milton can
To justify God's ways to man.
Ale, man, ale's the stuff to drink
For fellows whom it hurts to think:
25 Look into the pewter pot
To see the world as the world's not.
And faith, 'tis pleasant till 'tis past:
The mischief is that 'twill not last.
Oh, I have been to Ludlow fair
30 And left my necktie God knows where,
And carried half-way home, or near,
Pints and quarts of Ludlow beer:

---

[1] this: the poetry of Terence, who defends it from 15 on. [18] Burton: Staffordshire city known for its breweries. [19] many a peer: i.e. brewers who have secured titles through their wealth. [20] man: see *Paradise Lost* I 26. [29] Ludlow: in Shropshire, the setting of many of Housman's poems.

Then the world seemed none so bad
And I myself a sterling lad;
35 And down in lovely muck I've lain,
Happy till I woke again.
Then I saw the morning sky:
Heigho, the tale was all a lie;
The world, it was the old world yet,
40 I was I, my things were wet,
And nothing now remained to do
But begin the game anew.

Therefore, since the world has still
Much good, but much less good than ill,
45 And while the sun and moon endure
Luck's a chance, but trouble's sure,
I'd face it as a wise man would,
And train for ill and not for good.
'Tis true, the stuff I bring for sale
50 Is not so brisk a brew as ale:
Out of a stem that scored the hand
I wrung it in a weary land.
But take it: if the smack is sour,
The better for the embittered hour;
55 It should do good to heart and head
When your soul is in my soul's stead;
And I will friend you, if I may,
In the dark and cloudy day.

There was a king reigned in the East:
60 There, when kings will sit to feast,
They get their fill before they think
With poisoned meat and poisoned drink.
He gathered all that springs to birth
From the many-venomed earth;
65 First a little, thence to more,
He sampled all her killing store;
And easy, smiling, seasoned sound,
Sat the king when healths went round.
They put arsenic in his meat
70 And stared aghast to watch him eat;
They poured strychnine in his cup
And shook to see him drink it up:
They shook, they stared as white's their shirt:
Them it was their poison hurt.
75 —I tell the tale that I heard told.
Mithridates, he died old.

⁷⁶ old: and so well immunized that to avoid captivity he had to order a slave to stab him. He ruled Pontus c. 115–63 B. C.

THE NEED OF BEING VERSED IN COUNTRY THINGS

ROBERT FROST ⟶ *From* COMPLETE POEMS OF ROBERT FROST. © *1930, 1949 by Henry Holt & Co., Inc. By permission of the publishers.*

The house had gone to bring again
To the midnight sky a sunset glow.
Now the chimney was all of the house that stood,
Like a pistil after the petals go.

5 The barn opposed across the way,
That would have joined the house in flame
Had it been the will of the wind, was left
To bear forsaken the place's name.

No more it opened with all one end
10 For teams that came by the stony road
To drum on the floor with scurrying hoofs
And brush the mow with the summer load.

The birds that came to it through the air
At broken windows flew out and in,
15 Their murmur more like the sigh we sigh
From too much dwelling on what has been.

Yet for them the lilac renewed its leaf,
And the aged elm, though touched with fire;
And the dry pump flung up an awkward arm;
20 And the fence post carried a strand of wire.

For them there was really nothing sad.
But though they rejoiced in the nest they kept,
One had to be versed in country things
Not to believe the phoebes wept.

Suggestions

1. When the meaning is presented indirectly, a work is certain to be ironical and will probably have a surprise ending. The climax of Donne's sonnet on immortality is very famous; its intensely dramatic structure, made possible by the oblique rendering of its meaning, should be contrasted with the more direct statement in St. Paul's *First Letter to the*

Corinthians 15, 55: "O death, where is thy sting? O grave, where is thy victory?" Johnson's "Short Song" begins innocently by referring to Sir John's twenty-first year, which sounds congratulatory enough; but its concealed weapon emerges in its third line. The last word of "Soliloquy of the Spanish Cloister," repeated from line 16, invites us to decide which of the friars it describes more accurately. In "Terence, This Is Stupid Stuff" the reader may be mystified about the connection between the king's antidotes and a defense of "sour" poetry—until the broad hint in the last line. And not before the last line of "The Need of Being Versed in Country Things" does it become clear that the speaker's topic is the sentimental attitude toward nature—whereupon the title takes on broader meanings than the same words have in the last stanza.

2. Identify all the reasons given in "Death, Be Not Proud" for denying that death is mighty and dreadful. Which of them are serious? Show how in rhyme-scheme and structure this poem resembles both kinds of sonnet that you have already identified.

3. List all those "that prey on vice and folly" who are named in "A Short Song of Congratulation." The metre of this poem is known as *trochaic;* discuss its fitness to the substance and theme. Decide whether or not the poem is ironical all the way through and whether or not it ought to be.

4. After reviewing the Suggestions for † "My Last Duchess," define the *dramatic situation* in "Soliloquy of the Spanish Cloister." Characterize the two friars; then show why the emotion expressed in line 3 suggests that the speaker is being presented ironically. Point out the most ingenious rhymes in the poem, deciding whether, as in line 23, they have exacted too many concessions. Evaluate lines 71–72 as a climax.

5. Show how Terence replies to his critic's taunt in lines 3–4. Punctuate lines 7–8. Decide whether Terence's recommendation of "the pewter pot" is serious or ironical. Discuss the fitness of the metre and tone, comparing them with those of "A Short Song." Identify the speaker's attitude toward Mithridates.

6. Describe the scene in "The Need of Being Versed in Country Things." Identify the emotion expressed in lines 15–16 and the speaker's attitude toward that emotion, relating it to the basic contrast. Show that the poem ends with an ironic reversal.

7. Explain: *guineas, pander* ("A Short Song"); *Barbary corsair's, Arian, Manichee, Belial's gripe, indenture* ("Soliloquy of the Spanish Cloister"); *pistil, brush the mow* ("The Need of Being Versed in Country Things").

8. Write essays on one or more of the following:
   I. The treatment of death by Donne, Shakespeare, Emily Dickinson, and Larkin.
   II. London life as presented by Johnson and other writers.

III. The peculiarities of dramatic monologues and soliloquies as poetic structures.

IV. Theories of life and poetry in Housman and MacLeish.

V. "The Need of Being Versed in Country Things," "To the Man-of-War Bird," and "To Autumn."

VI. The fitness of irony to poetic expression.

LEAVING THE REST UNSAID

ROBERT GRAVES

Finis, apparent on an earlier page,
With fallen obelisk for colophon,
Must this be here repeated?

Death has been ruefully announced
5 And to die once is death enough,
Be sure, for any lifetime.

Must the book end, as you would end it,
With testamentary appendices
And graveyard indices?

10 But no, I will not lay me down
To let your tearful music mar
The decent mystery of my progress.

So now, my solemn ones, leaving the rest unsaid,
Rising in air as on a gander's wing
15 At a careless comma,

Index

721